Criminal Violence, Criminal Justice

Charles E. Silberman

CRIMINAL VIOLENCE, CRIMINAL JUSTICE

VINTAGE BOOKS
A Division of Random House
New York

For Arlene
Who paid the price
Proverbs 31:28

VINTAGE BOOKS EDITION, January 1980

Copyright © 1978 by Charles E. Silberman

All rights reserved under International and Pan-American Copyright Conventions. Published in the United States by Random House, Inc., New York, and in Canada by Random House of Canada Limited, Toronto. Originally published by Random House, Inc., in November 1978.

Library of Congress Cataloging in Publication Data

Silberman, Charles E.   1925–
  Criminal violence, criminal justice.

  Bibliography: p.
  Includes index.
  1. Crime and criminals—United States. 2. Criminal Justice —Administration of—United States. 3. Violence—United States. I. Title.
[HV6789.S55 1980]   364′.973   79–2318
ISBN 0–394–74147–1

Manufactured in the United States of America

Grateful acknowledgment is made to the following for permission to reprint previously published material:

Aldine Publishing Co., a Division of Walter de Gruyter, Inc.: Excerpts from *Deep Down in the Jungle* by Roger D. Abrahams, 1970.

Columbia University Press: Excerpt from *Crime in the Community* by Frank Tannenbaum, 1938.

by Robert Lejeune and Nicholas Alex, reprinted from *Urban Life and Culture*, Vol. 2, No. 3, Oct. 1973. Reprinted by permission of the Publisher, Sage Publications, Inc. (Beverly Hills/London).

The Washington Post: Excerpt from July 7, 1976, Column by William Raspberry, entitled "Victimism."

Foreword

The only way to get through the newspaper each day, Russell Baker once wrote, is to ask, "Is this crisis really worth understanding?" Most of the time the answer is no; in the rush of daily journalism, it is difficult to distinguish the important from the merely urgent.

I have tried to make that distinction. Few social problems are more important—or more enduring—than that of criminal violence. Except for race, with which American criminal violence has always been intertwined, it is hard to think of a problem that evokes such intense and often ugly emotions or that is surrounded by so much misinformation and misunderstanding. As I discovered over and over again during my research, most of what is believed about crime and about the criminal justice system is false or irrelevant.

My goal is not simply to correct errors and clear up misunderstandings; it is to change the way Americans think about criminals and crime and about the operation of our system of criminal justice. This, in turn, means changing the way Americans think about race, ethnicity, poverty, and social class; about the police, juvenile and adult courts, and prisons and jails; and about such questions as justice, punishment, and deterrence. It would be feckless to expect everyone to agree with me; my hope is that all will find my meaning clear, and that those who disagree will feel obliged to come to terms with what I have to say.

My use of the first person singular is deliberate; few publishing conventions are sillier, or more misleading, than the one whereby writers substitute "we" or "this writer" for the pronoun "I." As Joan Didion points out, writing is "the act of saying *I*, of imposing oneself upon other people, of saying *listen to me, see it my way, change your mind.*" Given that fact, readers are entitled to know who is speaking to them, and from what perspective; for objectivity is impossible. A writer must select what to write about, and that process of selection necessarily involves judgments about what does and does not matter. To seek total objectivity is to condemn oneself to Sisyphus' fate.

But if objectivity is beyond reach, honesty and fairness are not. To attain them, writers must be conscious of their own biases, and they must be as ruthless in puncturing their own pieties and preconceptions as they are in stripping away the cant of others. For me, it has also meant trying to avoid the trap into which all too many contemporary liberals have fallen in discussing crime and violence: that of becoming, as George Orwell wrote of Jonathan Swift, "one of those people who are driven into a sort of perverse Toryism by the follies of the progressive party of the moment." In that effort, I have been helped by the discovery that the follies of the right are at least as great as those of the left.

To say that this book is my personal statement is not to imply that I worked alone or unaided. My debts are many and profound. I could not have written this book without the generous support of the Ford Foundation. By creating and funding (and renewing and renewing) The Study of Law and Justice, the Foundation made it possible for me to devote more than six years to research and writing, with the help of an able and dedicated research and administrative staff; for this I am deeply grateful. I am even more grateful to Mitchell Sviridoff, Vice President, National Affairs Division, and McGeorge Bundy, President of the Ford Foundation, for their unfailing encouragement, understanding, and moral support; for their tolerance of missed deadlines and their willingness to renew my grant more times than I (and I suspect they) care to remember; and most of all, for giving me complete freedom and autonomy to follow my scholarly and journalistic instincts wherever they took me. Nor is that all: Mr. Sviridoff was always available for advice and counsel; he provided assistance and extended friendship in countless ways. I owe appreciation as well to Sanford M. Jaffe, Officer in Charge, and R. Harcourt Dodds, Program Officer, Government and Law, for their continuing assistance and support, and to Helen Kecskemety and Arlene Feder of the Foundation's Division of National Affairs, for solving innumerable problems that would have loomed large without their sympathetic help.

I have also had the privilege of working with an Advisory Commission chaired by Judge Shirley M. Hufstedler of the U.S. Court of Appeals and composed of other distinguished jurists, legal scholars and practitioners, sociologists, and experts on the police, courts, prisons, and corrections. The Commission convened as a formal body for two-day meetings with me and my research staff at several points during the study; Commission members also read and commented on various drafts of the book. By appointing a Commission with powers of advice but not consent, the Ford Foundation gave me the best of both worlds; I received all the benefits of the Commission members' wisdom and expertise, without any of the inhibitions and restraints inherent in writing a committee report. I am profoundly indebted to Judge Hufstedler and the Commission members: the Honorable Barbara Babcock, Assistant Attorney General, Civil Division, and former Professor of Law, Stanford Law School; Paul Bator, Professor of Law and former Associate Dean, Harvard Law School; The Honorable George Crockett, Chief Judge, Recorder's Court, Detroit, Michigan; Alan Dershowitz, Professor of Law, Harvard Law School; Lolis Elie, Esquire, New Orleans; The Honorable Wilfred Feinberg, U.S. Court of Appeals; Richard Green, Esquire, Washington, D.C., former Deputy Director, Federal Judicial Center; the late Harry Kalven, Jr., Professor of Law, University of Chicago Law School; Reverend Dr. Pauli Murray, Virginia Theological Seminary, former Professor of Law, Brandeis University; Patrick V. Murphy, President, The Police Foundation, Washington, D.C., and former Police Commissioner, New York City, Detroit, Washington, D.C., and Syracuse, New York; William G. Nagel, Executive Vice President, The American Foundation, Inc., and Director, the American Foundation Institute of Corrections; Lee Rainwater, Professor of Sociology, Harvard University; The Honorable Cruz Reynoso, Associate Justice, California Court of Appeals and former Professor of Law, University of New Mexico Law School; Dr. Jonathan Rubinstein, Project Director, The Policy Sciences Center, Inc., New York City; Herman Schwartz, Esquire, Chief Counsel—Revenue Sharing, U.S. Department of the Treasury, and former New York State Commissioner of Corrections; and Melvin M. Tumin, Professor of Sociology, Princeton University, and former Cochairman, Task Force on Crimes of Violence, National Commission on the Causes and Prevention of Violence. I shall always be grateful to them for their collective friendship, criticisms, advice, and support.

I am even more indebted to Commission members as

individuals. Despite a mind-boggling schedule and unending demands on her time and energy, Shirley Hufstedler was always available for counsel and help. She
prodded me when I needed prodding, encouraged me
when I needed encouragement, and offered invaluable
comments on every draft of every chapter. In addition,
Judge Hufstedler chaired every Advisory Commission
meeting with unerring grace and tact. Evoking the best
in everyone, she turned an assemblage of individuals
with diverse interests, backgrounds, personalities, and
points of view into a closely knit group that became
considerably more than the sum of its individual members. She gave unstintingly of her wisdom and insight
and, most important, of her friendship. This book owes
much to her and is far better because of her.

The book is better, too, because of Melvin Tumin's
sociological imagination, editorial judgment, and friendship; his detailed critique of the first half led me to re-
arrange some chapters and modify my polemical stance.
The book could not have taken its present shape without the friendship, counsel, and example of Herman
Schwartz, William Nagel, and Lolis Elie, who shared
their encyclopedic knowledge of courts, prisons, and
prisoners and their passionate hatred of injustice in all
its forms. Barbara Babcock and Cruz Reynoso provided important insights derived from their experience
representing black, white, and Hispanic defendants in
the East, West, and Southwest. Wilfred Feinberg, a
faithful critic and good friend, contributed far more
than his modesty permits him to acknowledge. I learned
much, too, from Jonathan Rubinstein, who generously
shared the fruits of his pioneering research on organized crime and political corruption, as well as his intimate knowledge of policing. My chapter on the police
gained clarity and focus when Patrick Murphy criticized an earlier draft from the unique perspective he

has acquired as police commissioner in four cities and
now as a national leader in the movement for experimentation and reform. Pauli Murray offered a unique
perspective of another kind, gained from her varied
career as community organizer, civil-rights activist,
feminist, poet, practicing lawyer, legal scholar, and
now Episcopal priest. Paul Bator and Alan Dershowitz forced me to confront questions I would have preferred to duck. George Crockett and Richard Green
shared their intimate knowledge of the judicial process.
Before his untimely death, Harry Kalven, Jr., graced
Advisory Commission meetings with his presence, as
well as through his wide-ranging knowledge of the law;
what made his scholarship so significant was that it
grew out of his qualities as a human being. Everyone
who worked with Harry was enriched by the experience and is the poorer for his absence.

Although not formally members of the Advisory
Commission, David and Ellen Silberman, members of
the District of Columbia Bar, attended all meetings and
served as de facto members as well as unpaid research
associates. Despite the grueling pressure of law school
and law review, clerkships, and law practice, they commented on every progress report to the Commission and
every draft of the book with wit, wisdom, and imagination, together with painstaking attention to detail. They
corrected errors of tone and substance, uncovered repetitions and contradictions, called my attention to innumerable articles from law reviews and other scholarly
journals, and conducted a running dialogue on a number of major issues discussed in the book. Their
thoughtfulness, erudition, and good judgment, as well
as their filial love and devotion, are evident on every
page.

I could not have written this book without the help
of my colleagues on The Study of Law and Justice. For

three and a half years, my wife, Arlene Silberman, put aside her own career as a writer to serve as Chief of Research, at great personal sacrifice. Her insistence on seeing live human beings behind labels such as juvenile delinquent, status offender, probation officer, guard, and judge; her ability to establish rapport with people individually and in groups, within institutions and without, and in positions of authority and subordination; and her insight into how institutions operate (as opposed to how they are supposed to operate) and how they affect the people (especially the young people) caught up in them helped shape the direction of the research and the tone and emphasis of the book. Her contribution is most direct in Chapters 4, 9, and 10. I am deeply indebted as well to Richard D. Van Wagenen, Esquire, a wise, resourceful, and indefatigable Research Associate. His analyses of the scholarly literature on the operation of the criminal justice system and on the relationship between drug addiction and crime added breadth and depth to the book; his field studies of the police, prosecutors' offices, public defender services and the private bar, plea bargaining, and the judicial process were even more valuable and formed the basis for Chapters 7 and 8. Given the range of help Mr. Van Wagenen and Mrs. Silberman provided, identifying each specific contribution would have made my prose awkward or unduly cluttered with footnotes. Since their research has been filtered through my consciousness and in some instances used for conclusions they did not reach or for arguments with which they may not agree, I have merged their voices with mine. In addition to this general expression of gratitude, therefore, I have acknowledged their assistance at the beginning of each chapter in which their research played a significant role.

None of us worked in a vacuum; what we accom-

plished was due, in good measure, to the fact that my
administrative assistant, Doris Preisick, smoothed so
many paths for us. She organized and coordinated Advisory Commission meetings and ran the office, which
meant, among other tasks, locating out-of-print publications, borrowing books and periodicals from libraries
throughout the metropolitan area, and ordering (and
keeping track of) subscriptions to countless journals,
Ms. Preisick also kept the books and husbanded our
funds with meticulous care, and prepared detailed quar-
terly financial reports to the Ford Foundation. In addition, she performed the prodigious task of simultaneously typing three progress reports and countless drafts
of the book with great accuracy and speed while cor-
recting my spelling, grammar, and syntax and calling
my attention to contradictions, repetitions, and obscure
or garbled passages. I was able to finish the book because Norma Wolbert, my present administrative assistant, learned with astonishing speed how to decipher my
partially typed, partially handwritten, and wholly il-
legible copy. She typed the final draft quickly and accurately, and assumed responsibility for a host of administrative chores with unfailing good humor and
aplomb.

To thank all who shared their time and knowledge
with me and with the members of the research staff
would require a chapter of its own; but there are some
whose contribution was too large to go unacknowl-
edged here. Professor Bruce Jackson of SUNY–Buffalo, an indefatigable correspondent and good friend as
well as an extraordinarily knowledgeable criminologist
and folklorist, deepened my understanding of criminals
and crime, as well as of black culture, through his detailed comments on earlier drafts. I am indebted, too, to
Jeff Silberman, an able sociologist and devoted son, and
to Professors Hylan Lewis of Brooklyn College, Ralph

Ellison of New York University, and Charles V. Hamilton of Columbia University, for their invaluable criticisms of an earlier draft of what is now Chapters 4 and 5; they rescued me from errors of tone, emphasis, and substance, and encouraged me in my attempt to understand and write about black culture.

I owe much also to New York City Deputy Mayor Herbert Sturz, former President and Director of the Vera Institute of Justice, and Brian E. Forst, Senior Research Analyst, the Institute of Law and Social Research (INSLAW), for giving me access to unpublished research that helped shape the argument of Chapter 8, on the criminal courts. At every stage of the research, my friend and cousin, Bernard D. Fischman, Esquire, made me the beneficiary of his enthusiasm, his encyclopedic knowledge of the law, and his passion for justice. Professor Franklin E. Zimring of the University of Chicago Law School was generous in sharing his fertile imagination as well as his detailed and wide-ranging knowledge of the operation of the criminal justice system. Ricky Silberman, a thoughtful philosopher and loving son, helped me focus on ultimate questions and clarified my thinking about justice and punishment. Joseph H. Lewis of the Police Foundation and Professor Gerald Caplan of George Washington University Law School forced me to rethink (and rewrite) what I had written about the police (Chapter 7). My views on prisons and prison reform (Chapter 10) were heavily influenced by Professor James B. Jacobs of Cornell and the late Professor Hans W. Mattick of the University of Illinois.

Thanks are due a number of others who shared their knowledge with me, answered questions, and in some instances gave me access to unpublished monographs, papers, and statistics: Albert W. Alschuler, Elijah Anderson, Hugo Adam Bedau, Sheridan Faber, Judge

Marvin E. Frankel, Floyd Feeney, Fred W. Goldman, Herbert G. Gutman, Stephanie W. Greenberg, Richard Korn, Mark H. Haller, Leon G. Hunt, Francis A. J. Ianni, Roger Lane, Sar A. Levitan, Irving F. Lukoff, Mark H. Moore, Raymond T. Nimmer, Lloyd E. Ohlin, Edward Preble, James O. Robison, Kenneth Polk, Dale K. Sechrest, Stephan Thernstrom, Jackson Toby, Andrew von Hirsch, James Vorenberg, David Ward, and Marvin E. Wolfgang.

I owe a debt of another kind to my editor, Rob Cowley. The book is shorter, subtler, and more forceful because of his sensitivity and tact, and his uncanny ability to detect what I was trying to say and help me say it with greater clarity and grace than I could muster on my own. I am grateful, too, to Lynn Strong of the Random House copy editing department for contributing her literary taste and sense of style, and to C. A. Wimpfheimer, Vice President and Managing Editor, for once again doing the impossible with good humor and forbearance.

No one has been more understanding and supportive than Steve Silberman. The only one of my sons still at home during the years I was chained to the typewriter, he endured paternal neglect without complaint. The eagerness with which he read, and the interest with which he commented on, every draft of every chapter, encouraged me at times of despair and helped give me the strength to continue. It is appropriate, too, to acknowledge profound indebtedness to my late parents, Cel L. and Seppy I. Silberman, who made it easy to obey the Fifth Commandment. According to the Talmud, "they whose deeds exceed their wisdom, their wisdom will endure." My parents' wisdom was great and enduring; their lives continue to provide an unerring guide to conduct.

This book is dedicated to my wife, Arlene Silberman,

and properly so. My debts to her transcend her contributions to the research, which have been acknowledged above. The dybbuk that possessed me these past six years took its toll on her; for that, I can only make amends in private. But in a world of transient, often fleeting "relationships," it is fitting to acknowledge the constancy of our mutual love and respect. In thirty years of sharing life together, there has been no time when I have not learned from my wife—lessons about fortitude and courage, about empathy and compassion, about how to live as a giving and caring human being.

I hope that this book will serve as partial repayment of my intellectual and moral debts.

New York City   C.E.S.
July 1978

Contents

I

Criminal Violence

1

Fear

Men come together in cities in order to live; they remain together in order to live the good life.

—ARISTOTLE

One of the bargains men make with one another in order to maintain their sanity is to share an illusion that they are safe even when the physical evidence in the world around them does not seem to warrant that conclusion.

—KAI T. ERIKSON, *Everything in Its Path*

"Every time I'm mugged, I feel like I'm that much less of a person."

—STATEMENT OF A MUGGING VICTIM

I

All over the United States, people worry about criminal violence. According to public opinion polls, two Americans in five—in large cities, one in two—are afraid to go out alone at night. Fear is more intense among black Americans than among whites, and among women than among men. The elderly are the most fearful of all; barricaded behind multiple locks, they often go hungry rather than risk the perils of a walk to the market and back.

These fears are grounded in a harsh reality: since

the early 1960s, the United States has been in the grip of a crime wave of epic proportions. According to the Federal Bureau of Investigation's *Uniform Crime Reports,* the chance of being the victim of a major violent crime such as murder, rape, robbery, or aggravated assault nearly tripled between 1960 and 1976; so did the probability of being the victim of a serious property crime, such as burglary, purse-snatching, or auto theft. The wave may have crested—crime rates have been relatively stable since the mid-1970s—but criminal violence remains extraordinarily high. If recent rates continue, at least three Americans in every hundred will be the victim of a violent crime this year, and one household in ten will be burglarized.

In some ways, the crime statistics understate the magnitude of the change that has occurred, for they say nothing about the nature of the crimes themselves. Murder, for example, used to be thought of mainly as a crime of passion—an outgrowth of quarrels between husbands and wives, lovers, neighbors, or other relatives and friends. In fact, most murders still involve victims and offenders who know one another, but since the early 1960s murder at the hand of a stranger has increased nearly twice as fast as murder by relatives, friends, and acquaintances. (Much of the latter increase involves killings growing out of rivalries between drug dealers and youth gangs.) In Chicago, for which detailed figures are available, the number of murders of the classic crime-of-passion variety rose 31 percent between 1965 and 1973; in that same period, murders by strangers—"stranger homicides," as criminologists call them—more than tripled.[1]

Rape has been changing in a similar direction. In 1967, people known to the victim—estranged husbands and lovers, other relatives and friends, and casual acquaintances—were responsible for nearly half the rapes that occurred. (Some studies put the proportion even higher.) In 1975, two-thirds of all rape victims were attacked by strangers, with such attacks accounting for virtually the entire 140 percent increase in the number of reported rapes since the mid-1960s.

On the other hand, robbery—taking money or property from another person by force or the threat of force —has always been a crime committed predominantly by strangers. The chances of being robbed have more than tripled since the early 1960s, a larger increase than that registered for any other major crime. Robbers are more violent than they used to be: nowadays, one robbery victim in three is injured, compared to the 1967 ratio of one in five. Although firm figures are hard to come by, it would appear that robbery killings have increased four- or fivefold since the early 1960s, accounting for perhaps half the growth in stranger homicides.[2]

The most disturbing aspect of the growth in "street crime" is the turn toward viciousness, as well as violence, on the part of many young criminals. A lawyer who was a public defender noted for her devotion to her clients' interests, as well as for her legal ability, speaks of "a terrifying generation of kids" that emerged during the late 1960s and early '70s. When she began practicing, she told me, adolescents and young men charged with robbery had, at worst, pushed or shoved a pedestrian or storekeeper to steal money or merchandise; members of the new generation kill, maim, and injure without reason or remorse.

It would be an exaggeration to call viciousness the rule, but it is far from exceptional. The day I began revising this chapter for publication, the mother of a good friend—a frail (and frail-looking) woman in her seventies—was thrown to the sidewalk in the course of a mugging; she sustained a fractured hip and collarbone and will have to use a cane or "walker" for the rest of her days. During an earlier stage of my research, an acquaintance who was moonlighting as a cabdriver was held up by two passengers. After they had taken all his money—my acquaintance put up no resistance—one of the robbers shot him through the right hand, shattering a bone, severing a nerve, and leaving him with life-long pain; several operations later, he still has difficulty using his hand with the agility needed in the craft on which his livelihood depends. (Fortunately, my own family has escaped violent crime until now; but my home was burglarized, as was my son and daughter-in-law's, while I was writing this book.)

For a long time, criminologists, among others, tried to pooh-pooh talk about a rise in street crime, pointing out that the *Uniform Crime Reports* provide only a crude measure of the number of crimes committed each year.* But the increase has been too large, and conforms too closely to people's day-to-day experience, to be dismissed as a statistical illusion. The fact is that criminal violence has become a universal, not just an American, phenomenon. Once crime-free nations, such as England, Sweden, West Germany, the Netherlands, and France, as well as more turbulent countries, such as Italy, are now plagued with an epidemic of murder, kidnapping, robbery, and other forms of crime and violence—some of it politically inspired, all of it criminal in intent and consequence. (Within the United States, crime has increased more rapidly in suburbs and small cities than in large cities.) Wherever one turns—in virtually every free nation except Japan— people are worried about "crime in the streets." As Sir Leon Radzinowicz, director of Cambridge University's Institute of Criminology, has written, "No national characteristic, no political regime, no system of law, police,

* For an analysis of the problems involved in measuring crime, see Appendix.

justice, punishment, treatment, or even terror has rendered a country exempt from crime."[3]

Nor does any national characteristic render a country immune to the corrosive effects of crime. Criminal violence is debasing the quality of life in American cities and suburbs. Quite apart from the physical injuries and financial losses incurred, fear of crime is destroying the network of relationships on which urban and suburban life depends. Anger over crime is debasing the quality of American politics as well: witness the fact that the preeminent issue in the 1977 mayoral election in New York City was the death penalty, something over which the mayor has no control whatsoever. The issue was injected by the winning candidate as a way of shedding his previous image as a liberal. (The friend whose mother was robbed and injured told me, only half jokingly, "A liberal is someone who has not yet been mugged.") What is at stake is not liberalism or conservatism as such, but the ability to think clearly about what can (and what cannot) be done to reduce criminal violence, and at what cost. In any society beset by violence, there is a danger that people's desire for safety and order may override every other consideration; the United States has avoided that mistake so far.

II

Why are people as afraid as they are? The answer cannot lie in the number of violent crimes alone; from an actuarial standpoint, street crime is a lot less dangerous than riding in an automobile, working around the house, going swimming, or any number of other activities in which Americans engage without apparent concern. The chances of being killed in an automobile accident are ten times greater than those of being murdered by a stranger, and the risk of death from a fall—slipping in the shower, say, or tumbling from a ladder—are three times as great.

Accidents also cause far more nonfatal injuries than do violent crimes. More than 5 million people were injured as a result of automobile accidents in 1973 and some 24 million people were hurt in accidents at home —about 4 million of them seriously enough to suffer a temporary or permanent disability. By contrast, fewer than 400,000 robbery victims were injured, and about 550,000 people were hurt in incidents of aggravated assault. Yet radio and television newscasts are not filled with accident reports, as they are with crime news; people do not sit around their living rooms trading stories about the latest home or auto accident, as they do about the latest crime; nor has any candidate for high office promised to wage war on accidents or restore safety to our highways and homes.

In fact, it is perfectly rational for Americans to be more concerned about street crime than about accidents, or, for that matter, about white-collar crime. Violence at the hand of a stranger is far more frightening than a comparable injury incurred in an automobile accident or fall; burglary evokes a sense of loss that transcends the dollar amount involved. The reasons have a great deal to do with the nature of fear and the factors that produce it. From a physiological standpoint, what we call fear is a series of complex changes in the endocrine system that alerts us to danger and makes it possible for us to respond effectively, whether we choose to attack or to flee. The first stage—the one we associate most closely with fear or tension—prepares the entire body for fight or flight: the heart rate and systolic blood pressure go up; blood flow through the brain and the skeletal muscles increases by as much as 100 percent; digestion is impaired; and so on. The second stage provides the capacity for rapid aggression or retreat; the third for a slower, more sustained response.

Thus fear serves as a kind of early warning system. The hormonal changes involved also make it possible for us to respond to danger at a higher level of efficiency, as anyone who has been in combat or has faced other emergencies knows from experience. When life or reputation or honor are at stake, we achieve feats of speed, strength, and endurance—not to mention imagination and intellectual clarity—that we never thought possible, and that in fact we cannot attain under ordinary circumstances.

But as most of us also know from experience, fear can be counterproductive as well. The same hormonal changes that alert us to danger and make it possible to perform herculean feats get in the way of normal behavior. If stress continues too long without being resolved, it leads to illness or pathological behavior. If the danger is so great that it overwhelms us, or so sudden that the early-warning system, i.e., the first stage of hormonal change, is by-passed, we may become literally paralyzed with fear. The vulgar metaphors of extreme fear accurately describe the physiological processes; loss of control over the bladder and sphincter are common phenomena.

What this means, as the sociologist Erving Goffman writes, is that people exhibit two basic modes of activity: "They go about their business grazing, gazing, mothering, digesting, building, resting, playing, placidly attending to easily managed matters at hand. Or, fully mobilized, a fury of intent, alarmed, they get ready to attack or to stalk or to flee."[4] We can do one or the other; we cannot do both at the same time—at any rate, not for very long.

How, then, do we guard against danger while going about our normal activities? "By a wonder of adaptation," as Goffman puts it, people have "a very pretty capacity for dissociated vigilance" which enables us to monitor the environment out of the corner of the eye while concentrating on the task at hand. Sights, sounds, smells, and a host of other subtle cues give us a continuous reading of the environment. When that reading conveys a hint of danger, we take an unconscious closer look and may return to our task with just a microsecond's confirmation that things are in order; if that second look suggests that something is awry, our full attention is mobilized immediately.*

For this process to work, we have to know what to fear; we have to learn to distinguish cues that signal real danger from those that can be ignored, at least temporarily, without incurring too much risk. If a warning system is too sensitive—if it produces full mobilization at the merest hint of a danger—people so "protected" would live in a constant state of frenzy and thus would be unable to do all the other things, besides defending themselves, that are essential for survival. Too little sensitivity would be equally fatal.

Human beings tend to equate strange with dangerous; the most common early-warning signal of approaching danger is the sight of a stranger. Hence armies post sentries; frightened people use watchdogs. In tightly knit urban communities, as Jane Jacobs has described in sensitive detail, people are always watching the street, and an extraordinary network of communication announces the presence of strangers as soon as they appear.[5] (In some German and Polish neighborhoods in Milwaukee, a stranger driving through

---

* Police develop this capacity to an unusual degree. Experienced officers can operate a patrol car, listen to the police radio, and carry on a conversation with a partner while they simultaneously monitor the streets, sidewalks, and alleys, picking up cues that are invisible to the civilian.

the streets is enough to trigger several calls to the police.)

Life in metropolitan areas thus involves a startling paradox: we fear strangers more than anything else, and yet we live our lives among strangers. Every time we take a walk, ride a subway or bus, shop in a supermarket or department store, enter an office building lobby or elevator, work in a factory or large office, or attend a ball game or the movies, we are surrounded by strangers. The potential for fear is as immense as it is unavoidable.

We cope with this paradox in a number of ways. The equation whereby strange means dangerous has an obverse, in which familiar means safe. The longer something is present in the environment without causing harm, the more favorably we regard it and the warmer our feelings are likely to be. People who live near a glue factory become oblivious to the smell; city dwellers come to love the noise, often finding it hard to sleep in the countryside because of the unaccustomed quiet. In psychological experiments, people who were shown nonsense syllables and Chinese ideograms for a second time judged them "good" as opposed to "bad" in comparison with other nonsense syllables and ideograms they were shown, later on, for the first time. The more often people were shown photographs of strangers, the warmer their feelings became toward them.

In cities, familiarity breeds a sense of security. People who know that they have to be on guard in a strange neighborhood, especially at night, feel more secure in their own neighborhood and come to believe that they have a moral right to count on its being safe. This tendency helps explain a phenomenon that has puzzled social scientists: the fact that people's assessment of the safety of the neighborhood in which they live seems to bear little relationship to the actual level of crime there. In one survey, 60 percent of those queried considered their own neighborhoods to be safer than the rest of the community in which they lived; only 14 percent thought their neighborhood was more dangerous. What was striking was that people felt this way no matter how much crime there was in their neighborhood: in Washington, D.C., precincts with crime rates well above the average for the city, only 20 percent of respondents thought the risks of being assaulted were greater in their neighborhood than in other parts of the city.[6]

This same phenomenon makes crime a terribly bewildering, as well as fear-evoking, event when it is experienced on one's own turf. "Casual conversations with urban citizens or regular reading of the newspapers in recent years would indicate that many, if not most, inner-city residents live with the fatalistic expectation that sooner or later they will be mugged," Robert Lejeune and Nicholas Alex write in their richly informative study of the experiences of mugging victims. "But closer examination reveals that most of these fear-laden accounts are not associated with a corresponding mental frame necessary to develop the appropriate precautionary behavior."[7]

To the contrary, the mugging victims studied by Lejeune and Alex had all assumed before they were mugged that however dangerous *other* neighborhoods might be, they were reasonably safe from attack in their own. "I never felt afraid," said one victim, a widowed secretary. "Well, I'm not willing to say that I wasn't afraid at all," she addded. "Everybody has a little bit of feeling of fear." What she meant, it turned out, was that she had always been afraid of the neighborhood in which her daughter lived. "Because I heard things of that neighborhood—and it wasn't safe. I heard of people being mugged. And there I didn't feel secure." Her own neighborhood was something else again. As she explained, "Here I wasn't afraid. . . . In my neighborhood there are police cars, there are people walking. How can anybody be afraid? . . . And on *my* block—I'm not going to be afraid on Post Avenue."

But city dwellers rarely stay cooped up in their own neighborhood; most adults have to venture elsewhere to go to work, to shop, to visit relatives and friends, or to use the cultural and entertainment facilities that make cities cities. When we enter any environment, whether familiar or strange, we automatically take a quick "reading" or "sounding" in order to decide whether to be on guard or not. If things are as they should be, if appearances are normal, we can be off guard; we can concentrate on the task at hand, confident of our ability to predict what will happen from the cues we pick up out of the corner of the eye. The result is the sense of safety that comes from feeling in control of one's own fate. For if we can predict danger in advance, we can avoid it—if only by retreating in time to some safer haven.

The process is extraordinarily fragile. We can predict danger only if the subtle cues on which we depend—for example, people's dress or attitude or demeanor—are accurate, which is to say, only if things are as they appear. Ultimately, the whole fabric of urban life is based on trust: trust that others will act predictably, in accordance with generally accepted rules of behavior, and that they will not take advantage of that trust. For life to go on in public places—in city streets, building lobbies, elevators, and hallways— people must put themselves in other people's hands.

Consider the elaborate etiquette pedestrians employ to avoid bumping into one another. The American pedestrian maintains a scanning or check-out range of about three or four sidewalk squares, assuming that people beyond this range—whether in front or behind —can be ignored. As other people enter the scanning range, they are glanced at briefly and then ignored if their distance, speed, and direction imply that neither party has to change course to avoid a collision. When people have been checked out in this manner, Goffman writes, they can be allowed to come quite close without evoking concern. Moreover, pedestrians ignore oncomers who are separated from them by other people; thus someone may walk in dense traffic and be completely unconcerned about people just a few feet away.[8]

While one person is checking out those who come into his range in this manner, others are checking him out in the same way; none of them is aware, except in the vaguest sense, that this is what they are doing. And the process can become much more complicated. If an initial body check indicates that the pedestrian and a stranger are on a collision course, or if the stranger's course is not clear, an individual may follow one of a number of procedures. "He can ostentatiously take or hold a course, waiting to do this until he can be sure that the other is checking him out," Goffman writes. "If he wants to be still more careful, he can engage in a 'checked-body-check'; after he has given a course indication, he can make sure the signal has been picked up by the other, either by meeting the other's eye (although not for engagement) or by noting the other's direction or vision, in either case establishing that his own course gesture has not likely been overlooked. In brief, he can check up on the other's eye check on him, the assumption being that the other can be relied on to act safely providing only that he has perceived the situation."

This process of unconscious mutual accommodation

is even more complex when traffic is heavy. If pedestrian A is walking behind pedestrian B, A not only accommodates to the movements B makes to avoid colliding with pedestrian C; he frequently will adjust his movement to what he *assumes* B is about to do to avoid C. And when these adjustments are not possible—for example, if a narrow path has been cut through heavy snow or around a construction site or other obstacle—one of several other adjustments comes into play automatically. As Goffman observes, "City streets, even in times that defame them, provide a setting where mutual trust is routinely displayed between strangers."

This kind of voluntary coordination usually works because, under ordinary circumstances, no one has much to gain from violating the rules. At the same time, the fact that coordination is required provides a standing invitation to gamesmanship, and adolescents often pick up the challenge. When gaining face is important, the psychological payoff from violating the rules—staring someone down, for example, or maintaining a course that requires the other person to step aside—may be large. Under the system of racial etiquette that prevailed in the South until fairly recently, blacks were required to step aside—into a muddy street, if need be—in order to let whites (*any* whites) go past with full possession of the sidewalk. Equally important, eye contact with whites was prohibited as another means of symbolizing white superiority and black inferiority; for a black man to eye a white woman was to invite a lynching.[9]

It is not surprising that some members of the present generation of black adolescents find delight in reversing the old conventions—for example, walking four or five abreast so that white pedestrians have to stand aside, or conversing in the street in a group so that a white driver backing his car out of his driveway has to wait until the youngsters choose to move. As accompaniments to these triumphs of reverse gamesmanship, there may be eye contact as well, in the form of a long, hate-filled glare.

Encounters of this sort are discomforting, for they show how fragile the social order really is—how dependent it is (and always has been) on acceptance of the rules by people who never have had much reason to accept them. "It has always been the case that the orderly life of a group contained many more points of weakness than its opponents ever exploited," Goffman writes, and a breakdown in what we consider civility or decorum exposes those weaknesses.

III

Crime does more than expose the weakness in social relationships; it undermines the social order itself, by destroying the assumptions on which it is based. The need to assume that familiar environments are safe is so great that until they have become victims themselves, many people rationalize that newspaper and television accounts of crime are greatly exaggerated. "This kind of thing happens on television, but not in real life," a college student exclaimed after she and a friend had been held up on the Ellipse, an area adjacent to the White House. (Although the two students were not injured, a migrant worker sitting on a nearby bench was shot in the face and blinded when he told the robbers—correctly—that he had no money.) "You just don't shoot someone in the back like in a Western movie," a young woman who had been shot and seriously injured in a D.C. robbery attempt told a Washington *Post* reporter.

Even when they admit that crime does occur, people comfort themselves with the assumption that it won't happen to them—in much the same way that we assume our own immortality, or our invulnerability to earthquake or flood.* It is only in retrospect, as Lejeune and Alex explain, that victims realize they should have been more aware of their own vulnerability. "Of course the conditions have been getting worse and worse," one of their respondents observed. "Uh, someone thinks that accidents happen to other people but they don't happen to me. Then when it did happen I was very upset because I didn't think it could happen to me."[11]

The need to feel safe is so powerful that people routinely misread cues that should signal danger. They may simply delay responding to a stranger, to give him a chance to explain or apologize; intuitive knowledge of this tendency on the part of pickpockets, assassins, and saboteurs makes it possible for them to carry out their mission.[12] People also may redefine a danger signal as a normal event—for example, by assuming that a mugger is merely panhandling or playing a practical joke. Consider these explanations by three of Lejeune and Alex's respondents:

> "I was walking down the street. Four young men approached me. I say, 'Oh, cut this fooling out.' And then they put their hands in my pocket."

> "When I got into the elevator I felt a hand, you know, and I thought the fellow was joking. But then I started feeling the pain. He was very strong. It was no joke."

* "In this respect, as in many others, the man of prehistoric age survives unchanged in our unconscious," Sigmund Freud wrote. "Thus, our unconscious does not believe in its own death; it behaves as if immortal. . . ." We really believe that "'Nothing can happen to me.' On the other hand, for strangers and for enemies, we do acknowledge death. . . ."[10]

Similarly, a victim may perceive a threatening stranger
as a friendly neighbor who forgot his keys:

> "I thought: it's one of my neighbors waving to me not
> to close the door. He must have forgotten his key. Just
> then somebody grabbed me in the back of the neck
> and held my head in both his arms."

Or the victim may interpret a robber's demand for
money as a request for a loan:

> "When we started getting off the elevator he turned
> around and he said: 'Give me ten dollars.' I thought
> he wanted to borrow ten dollars. He said, 'I don't
> want any trouble. Give me ten dollars.' And I looked
> him up and down, and I see he has a knife in his hand.
> So I didn't let myself get knifed. I gave him the ten
> dollars and he got off."[13]

People *need* to be able to make sense out of their
environment; otherwise, life would be intolerable. To
"live with fear," as victims call it—to be suspicious
of every sound and every person—converts the most
elementary and routine aspects of life into an exercise
in terror. It is to avoid such terror that people who have
not been victimized (and some who have) interpret
threatening gestures and events in terms that are more
understandable and comfortable.

Thus the emotional impact of being attacked by a
stranger transcends the incident itself; it reaches a
primordial layer of fear unlike anything evoked by an
equally damaging encounter with an automobile or
other inanimate object, or even by a crime that does
not involve a direct encounter with another person. A
criminal attack is disorienting as well, evoking traumatic reactions similar to those the sociologist Kai T.
Erikson found among the survivors of the Buffalo

Creek Flood.* Victims of criminal violence, like victims
of earthquake or flood, develop what Erikson describes
as "a sense of vulnerability, a feeling that one has lost
a certain natural immunity to misfortune, a growing
conviction, even, that the world is no longer a safe
place to be." Because they previously had underestimated the peril in which they lived, the survivors of
a disaster lose confidence in their ability to monitor
their environment; as a result, they live in constant fear
that something terrible will happen again.[14]

Crime victims are affected in much the same way;
the inability to tell friend from foe—the sense that
they no longer know how to monitor their environment—can turn the most ordinary encounter into a
nightmare. Until the attack in which he was blinded,
James Martin, a nineteen-year-old former handyman,
never worried about crime. In the Washington, D.C.,
ghetto where he lived, talk about crime was a constant,
but Martin recalls, "I never paid any attention . . . I
felt safe. I thought people would look at me and say,
'the dude ain't got nothing.' " He was wrong. The men
who held him up at a bus stop were enraged when
Martin told them he had only $6 on his person; they
knocked him down, beat his head against the sidewalk, then smashed a soda bottle on the curb and
rammed the jagged edge into his right eye, completely
destroying his vision. Although the robbers were convicted and imprisoned, Martin found that there was no
way he could continue to live in Washington. Afraid
to go out alone and equally afraid to stay home, he
could not sleep, either, for fear his assailants would

* On February 26, 1976, 132 million gallons of mud and
debris broke through a faulty mining company dam in Buffalo
Creek, West Virginia, killing 125 and leaving 4,000 of the
hollow's 5,000 residents homeless.

break out of prison and return to attack him again. He and his family moved back home to a small town in North Carolina, to live in a trailer on his mother-in-law's farm.[15]

This sense of vulnerability and fear seems to be a universal feeling, regardless of whether the person attacked is injured or not. Instead of familiar environments being automatically defined as safe, they now are perceived as uniformly dangerous because of the victim's inability to rely on the old cues. Asked whether being mugged had changed their outlook on life in any way, respondents in Lejeune and Alex's survey replied as follows:

> "I am just so much more frightened wherever I turn, and it seems as though the entire city has turned into an incredible jungle. . . . It's incredible that I think that way, that I feel that way; it's so unlike me."

> "Yes. It's made the city more of a jungle to me. Yes it has. And I haven't got too long to retire. And where I had really thought I would stay in the city, you believe it, I'll get out."

> "Well it has. I mean I don't feel free, like to do things. You feel you like to go to the movies or something. You don't feel you could do it. You always fear that there's somebody, uh, even if you go to the movies and you're safe—you're inside—coming out you'll always have that fear, of my God, somebody's passing or something."

The worst fear is felt in the area in which the person was attacked, particularly if it is his own neighborhood. "I've been living here for three and a half years, and I've never had any real fear of it," a mugging victim who decided to move out of her neighborhood told Lejeune and Alex. "It's like it's my home. I know the block. I recognize people. It's all very familiar to me. Now it's become very unfamiliar to me, very threatening, very, very much like a jungle. I trust nobody. You know, I'm constantly looking around me. . . . I will never walk on *that* block again."

The most disorienting aspect of all is the senselessness of the whole experience, which shatters victims' belief that cause and effect have some relationship. They no longer can view the world as a rational, hence predictable, place over which they have some control. "The thing that bothers me, and always will, is why they shot me," says Sally Ann Morris, a twenty-six-year old woman badly injured in a holdup attempt. "I didn't pose any threat to them; I was running away. . . ."[16] Tommy Lee Harris, a sixty-two-year-old man who was badly beaten by two young muggers after he had given them all his money, says in obvious bewilderment, "I don't know why it happened; I didn't know the men." After beating Harris to the ground, breaking four ribs, the muggers put him in the trunk of his own car, which they proceeded to drive away. Harris' life was saved when a policeman saw the muggers run through a red light and pursued them in his patrol car.[17]

The victim's bewilderment is compounded by the realization of how large a role coincidence had played. For the first week after the shooting, Ms. Morris blamed the friend who had been with her at the time.

"I thought why couldn't it have been him, he could have taken it better. Why me?" she recalls. "Isn't that just terrible to think like that? . . . And then I spent a long time thinking: if it had just taken longer to park, or if we had gone down another street. . . ."

The discovery that life is irrational and unpredictable makes victims feel completely impotent. This, in turn, exacerbates their fear: whether or not we feel in control of a situation directly affects the way we respond to it. Indeed, psychological experiments indicate that fear is substantially reduced if people merely *believe* they have some control over a stimulus, even if their response has no effect. One such experiment, described to the forty students who participated as a study of "reaction time," was conducted at the State University of New York at Stony Brook. The students were given a series of electric shocks lasting six seconds each, after which they were divided into two groups. One group was told that if they pulled a switch rapidly enough, they could reduce the shock they received from six to three seconds; the other group was told that they would receive three-second shocks no matter what they did. In fact, both groups received shocks of the same duration—three seconds. But the members of the first group, who believed that their actions could reduce the shock, showed far less stress as measured by galvanic skin reactions than did the members of the second group.[18]

Thus accidents are far less terrifying than crime because they do not create the sense of impotence evoked by crime. "You can't slip in the shower unless you're *in* the shower," the psychologist Martin E. P. Seligman points out, and "You can't get into an automobile smash-up unless you're riding in an automobile." One can take precautions, moreover, that extend the sense of control over one's environment and fate—using a skidproof rubber mat in the shower, checking a ladder to make sure it is steady, swimming in the ocean only if a lifeguard is on duty and the surf and undertow are not too strong, and keeping a careful eye out for other drivers and pedestrians.

In some of these situations, such as driving a car, people know in advance that they must be vigilant. And the automobile itself acts as a kind of armor or shield, protecting both driver and passenger from the invasion of self that interpersonal crime involves. Indeed, when riding in an automobile, people usually behave as if they were invisible to other drivers and passengers—which in a psychic sense they are—and as if the other drivers and passengers were invisible to them. It is only young children, who have not yet been socialized into highway etiquette, who make eye contact with people in other cars. The rest of us display what Goffman calls "civil inattention" to others when we drive or walk in public.

In violent crime, there is a direct intrusion on the self that produces anger and shame, in addition to fear. "My whole life has been invaded, violated—and not just by the act itself," says a forty-seven-year-old woman who was raped in her apartment. "It didn't happen just to me but to my husband and children." The rape totally shattered her sense of self, leaving her with a feeling of having been defiled, of being "stained and different," that, ten months later, her husband's love and understanding had not been able to overcome. "She says, 'You don't want anything to do with me because I am so dirty,'" the husband reports, and the wife wonders if she can ever put her life together again. "There have been times when I wish [the rapist] had killed me—it would have been kinder. . . . It was as though there were something lacking in dignity in still being alive." At times, to be sure, she feels a glimmer of hope: "I know that somehow we will work it out. . . ." But she adds: "I have changed and the world has changed. I don't see things the way I used to." In the best of moods, in fact, she is besieged by fear, afraid to go out alone and afraid to stay home, obsessed, as so many victims are, that the attacker will come back to seek revenge on her or on her two younger children.[19]

Although the sense of shame and defilement is most evident (and most understandable) in instances of rape, robbery and assault victims have similar, if less intense reactions. Our sense of self is bound up with our ability to control the personal space in which we live. As administrators of prisons and concentration camps well know, stripping people of their clothes serves to strip them of the normal defenses of their egos, leaving them far more compliant and docile. Victims of muggings, robberies, and assaults also experience a diminishment in their ego defenses. Male victims feel stripped of some portion of their masculinity as well; hence they often display a compulsive need to explain why it was impossible for them to resist or prevail. This need is strongest of all in men who have been the victims of homosexual rape.

Crimes such as homicide and rape deprive both victims and their relatives of the protective mantle of privacy, converting their intensely private agony and pain into public experiences. "It's impossible for somebody who hasn't been through it to understand the difference between a father dying of natural causes and being murdered," the married daughter of a murdered Bronx pharmacist told a New York *Post* reporter a year after the event. "If I had to name one thing that I hate [the murderer] for the most, it is that he made my father's death—which you should have to cope with privately— a very public thing."[20]

Burglary, too, evokes considerable fear, even though there is no confrontation with a stranger. For one thing, burglary victims are highly conscious of the fact that there might have been a confrontation had they come home earlier, hence they often are afraid to be home alone. Children whose homes have been burglarized sometimes need psychiatric help to cope with the fear. More important, forced entry into one's home is an invasion of the self, for our homes are part of the personal space in which we live. We express our individuality in the way we furnish and decorate, and in the artifacts we collect; we may view some of our possessions in a casual manner, but others are invested with layers of meaning that bear no relationship to their monetary value. I can still feel the rage that overcame me when I discovered that the person who had burglarized my home had taken a set of cuff-links and studs worn by my father on his wedding day. The fact that they were covered by insurance was irrelevant; their value lay in their power to evoke my father's physical presence seventeen years after his death. I remember, too, the enormous relief my wife and I felt when we discovered that the burglar had been interrupted before he had a chance to take the candlesticks my mother had used to usher in the Sabbath every week of her life.

Because our homes are psychological extensions of our selves, burglary victims often describe their pain in terms strikingly similar to those used by victims of rape—and in a symbolic sense burglary victims *have* been violated. The saying that one's home is a sanctuary is no mere epigram; it expresses a profound psychological truth. One of the oldest and most sacred principles of Anglo-Saxon law held that no matter how humble a person's cottage might be, not even the King could enter without his consent. The principle is recognized, after a fashion, by totalitarian regimes. The dramatic symbol of totalitarianism is the harsh knock on the door in the middle of the night; as Goffman points out, the fact that even storm troopers knock implies their acknowledgment of the territorial rights of the residents. It is not too much to conclude that crime threatens the social order in much the same way as does totalitarianism.

In the United States, because of the abnormally low
base from which the crime wave of the 1960s and early
'70s began, the upsurge in criminal violence has been
even more traumatic than otherwise might have been
the case. Americans who came of age during the 1930s,
'40s, and '50s had their general outlook and expectations shaped by an atypical, perhaps unique, period of
American history. During their formative years, crime
rates were stable or declining, and the level of domestic
violence was unusually low. Never having experienced
the crime and violence that had characterized American life for a century or more, this generation of
Americans—the generation from which most governmental and other opinion leaders are drawn—came to
take a low level of crime for granted.

For people over the age of thirty-five, therefore, the
upsurge in crime that began in the early 1960s appeared to be a radical departure from the norm, a
departure that shattered their expectations of what
urban and suburban life was like. The trauma was
exacerbated by the growing sense that the whole world
was getting out of joint, for the explosive increase in
crime was accompanied by a number of other disorienting social changes—for example, a general decline in civility, in deference to authority, and in religious and patriotic observance. But this is getting ahead
of the story.

2

As American as Jesse James

O I see flashing that this America is only you and me,
Its power, weapons, testimony are you and me,
Its crimes, lies, thefts, defections, are you and me . . .

—WALT WHITMAN, 1865

Be not afraid of any man,
No matter what his size;
When danger threatens, call on me
And I will equalize.

—INSCRIPTION ON THE NINETEENTH-
CENTURY WINCHESTER RIFLE

"I seen my opportunities and I took 'em."

—GEORGE WASHINGTON PLUNKETT
OF TAMMANY HALL, C. 1900

I

"Men murdered themselves into this democracy,"
D. H. Lawrence wrote more than a half-century ago,
in an essay on James Fenimore Cooper's *Leather-Stocking Tales*. An exaggeration, perhaps; but crime,
violence, and lawlessness have been recurrent themes
throughout American history. The continent was con-
quered by the musket, as well as by the ax and the
plow. In the speech that first brought him to public
attention, delivered in Springfield, Illinois, in January,

1838, Abraham Lincoln argued that internal violence was the nation's major domestic problem and decried "the increasing disregard for law that pervades the country." Little has changed since then; as the National Commission on the Causes and Prevention of Violence wrote in its 1969 report, "Violence has been far more intrinsic to our past than we should like to think."

The fact that violence has been one of the most durable aspects of the American experience offers no comfort to victims of crime, or to those who live in fear of being attacked. Nor is there consolation in knowing that the country was more dangerous in the past than it is now. But we cannot understand our current crime problem, let alone find remedies for it, without understanding the ways in which crime and violence are rooted in American life.[1]

Since the colonies were first settled, each generation of Americans has felt itself threatened by the specter of rising crime and violence. In 1767, Benjamin Franklin, in his capacity as agent for Pennsylvania, petitioned the British Parliament to stop solving *its* crime problem by shipping convicted felons to the American colonies. Transported felons were corrupting the morals of the poor, Franklin complained, and terrorizing the rest of the population with the many burglaries, robberies, and murders they committed.

Crime continued to be a problem after the Republic was established, and Americans continued to attribute the problem to the current crop of immigrants, who were thought to be more given to crime than their predecessors. "Immigrants to the city are found at the bar of our criminal tribunals, in our bridewell, our penitentiary, and our state prison," the Managers of the Society for the Prevention of Pauperism in the City of New York reported in 1819. "And we lament to say that they are too often led by want, by vice, and by habit to form a phalanx of plunder and depredation, rendering our city more liable to the increase of crimes, and our houses of correction more crowded with convicts and felons."

Twenty years later, things seemed to have deteriorated further. "One of the evidences of the degeneracy of our morals and of the inefficiency of our police is to be seen in the frequent instances of murder by stabbing," Philip Hone, a former mayor of New York, wrote in his diary for December 2, 1839. Fear of crime was a tradition in every other city as well. In 1844, a Philadelphian wrote that people were arming themselves because experience taught them not to expect protection from the law. And just before the Civil War a U.S. Senate committee investigating crime in Washington, D.C., reported that "Riot and bloodshed are of daily occurrence, innocent and unoffending persons are shot, stabbed, and otherwise shamefully maltreated, and not infrequently the offender is not even arrested."

The law was even less effective in the South and West than it was in the East. In a single fifteen-month period in the 1850s, a total of forty-four murders were recorded in Los Angeles, then a town of only 8,000 inhabitants—about forty or fifty times as high as the city's current murder rate. The term "hoodlum" originated in San Francisco, to describe sadistic juveniles and young men who preyed on that city's Chinese population during the 1860s, robbing, raping, and torturing almost at will. In a typical exploit during the summer of 1868, a gang of hoodlums dragged a Chinese fisherman under a wharf, where they robbed him, beat him with a club, branded him in a dozen places with hot irons, then slit his ears and tongue.

During the first half of the nineteenth century, *all* cities were dangerous—those of Europe as well as the United States. In the second half, London, Paris, and

other European cities were bringing crime and disorder
under control, while American cities were not—or so
it appeared to contemporary observers. New Yorkers
are "even more dangerous" than Londoners, the
American reformer Charles Loring Brace wrote in
1872, in *The Dangerous Classes of New York*. "They
rifle a bank, where English thieves pick pockets; they
murder, where European proletaires cudgel or fight
with fists; in a riot they begin what seems about to be
the sacking of a city, where English rioters would
merely batter policemen or smash lamps." The same
year, *Wood's Illustrated Handbook* warned visitors to
New York not to walk around the city at night except
in the busiest streets and urged them to take particular
pains to avoid Central Park after sundown.

In the meantime, Chicago was already cementing its
reputation as the nation's crime capital. In the 1860s,
the Chicago *Tribune* gave the nickname "Thieves'
Corner" to the intersection of Randolph and Dearborn
streets. In the twenty years after the Civil War, the
murder rate quadrupled, far outstripping the growth in
population, and muggings were commonplace; in 1893,
one Chicago resident in eleven was arrested for one
crime or another.

Outside the cities, violence was very much on the
increase. The family blood feud, virtually unknown
before the Civil War, exploded into public view,
kindled by hatreds generated during the war and
refueled by political and economic conflicts. The
Hatfield-McCoy feud was only one of a number of
bloody Appalachian Mountain vendettas; equally
deadly feuds were fought in Texas, Arizona, and New
Mexico.

The second half of the nineteenth century was also
the time when that indigenous American institution, the

vigilante movement, flourished. Vigilantism was a response to the absence of law and order on the frontier.[2] An Indiana vigilante group argued that "the people of this country are the real sovereigns, and whenever the laws, made by those to whom they have delegated their authority, are found inadequate to their protection, it is the right of the people to take the protection of their property into their own hands, and deal with these villains according to their just desserts [*sic*]. . . ." Vigilantism was initiated by frontiersmen who were inadequately protected by the law, but it gained support, and often leadership, from members of the American political, intellectual, and business elite. Governors, senators, judges, ministers, and even two presidents—Andrew Jackson and Theodore Roosevelt —were vigilantes or vigilante supporters.

Vigilantes found it hard to distinguish between taking the law into their hands when it could not function and taking the law into their hands when it did not function as they wanted it to. In the twentieth century, therefore, vigilante movements turned their attention away from horse thieves, cattle rustlers, counterfeiters, and assorted criminals and outlaws, and toward those whose only crime was to join a trade union or to belong to a different racial, ethnic, religious, or political group. Vigilante violence has had a strong conservative bias.[3]

Vigilantism was one of the foundations on which the racial caste system was erected. Slavery began in violence, with the uprooting of Africans from their homes and their transportation first to the African coast, then to the New World; current estimates are that one-third of the Africans died en route to the ports of embarkation, and another third during the infamous "Middle Passage" to the United States.

Slavery was maintained by violence; and when slavery ended, violence was used to keep blacks "in their place." In the late nineteenth century, after federal troops were withdrawn from the South, the white leadership made vigilante violence against blacks an integral part of the system of white supremacy they were erecting. Between 1882 and 1903, no fewer than 1,985 blacks were killed by Southern lynch mobs. And violence against blacks was not limited to mob action; individual acts of violence and terror became an accepted part of the caste system.

During this same period, a new kind of criminal emerged in the small towns and rural areas of the Midwest and South: the outlaw turned social hero. These "social bandits" included such people as Wild Bill Hickok; Billy the Kid, who sprang to fame during the Lincoln County war, one of the more spectacular of the New Mexico family feuds; and Jesse and Frank James, former Confederate guerrillas turned bank robbers and killers.[4] The James brothers' criminal career is particularly instructive. During its fifteen-year existence, their gang held up at least eleven banks, seven railroad trains, three stagecoaches, and one county fair, for a total take estimated at a little under $250,000; during the course of these robberies, sixteen people were killed. This record of banditry made Jesse and Frank James popular heroes among Midwesterners who had been sympathetic to the Confederate cause, and they were lionized by the Midwestern press. When the James gang held up the Kansas City Fair in 1872, a Kansas City newspaper hailed the robbery as "so diabolically daring and so utterly in contempt of fear that we are bound to admire it and revere its perpetrators." Two days later, the paper compared the James brothers to the Knights of King Arthur's Round Table:

It was as though three bandits had come to us from storied Odenwald, with the halo of medieval chivalry upon their garments, and shown us how the things were done that poets sing of. Nowhere else in the United States or in the civilized world, probably, could this thing have been done.

To be sure, vicarious identification with outlaws seems to be a characteristic of modern societies. Robin Hood is a figure of English folklore, and American Western TV programs are popular the world over. Even so, the "evangelism of violence," as one critic calls it, has always held a peculiar fascination for Americans. "It seems quite possible that the place of Jesse James, Billy the Kid, and Wild Bill Hickok is as secure in the pantheon of American folk heroes as that of Bat Masterson and Wyatt Earp," the criminologists Gresham Sykes and Thomas Drabek have written. "We seem to remember our sheriffs and our outlaws with equal pleasure." One reason is that often it was hard to tell the difference between them; some of the most famous gunfighters worked both sides of the law, spending part of their careers as outlaws and part as lawmen, depending on which side offered the better opportunity.*

Back in the cities, meanwhile, disrespect for law helped usher in the age of the "Robber Barons." Cornelius Vanderbilt expressed the outlook of other busi-

---

* We continue to romanticize the bandits of the post–Civil War era. Hollywood has made no fewer than twenty-one movies about Billy the Kid: in one version, the hero was played by Paul Newman, and in another, by Kris Kristofferson, although in real life Billy was described as "a slight, short, buck-toothed, narrow-shouldered youth" who "looks like a cretin." Gary Cooper played Wild Bill Hickok; and in the best of the various movies made about the James brothers, Jesse was played by Tyrone Power and Frank by Henry Fonda.

nessmen in replying to criticism of the way he had amassed his $90 million fortune. "What do I care about the law," he scoffed. "Hain't I got the power?" In a rapidly expanding, urbanizing, industrializing America, the only law to which the Robber Barons gave obeisance was "the law of the survival of the fittest."

The intelligence, imagination, and daring that characterized the Robber Barons carried over to a new breed of professional thieves who emerged at about the same time. Forgers, embezzlers, confidence men, burglars, and robbers captured the popular imagination in the East, much as the "social bandits" did in the South and West. "The ways of making a livelihood by crime are many, and the number of men and women who live by their wits in all large cities reaches into the thousands," Inspector Thomas Byrnes, Chief of Detectives of the New York City Police Department, wrote in 1886 in his often admiring volume *Professional Criminals of America:*

> Some of the criminals are really very clever in their own peculiar line, and are constantly turning their thieving qualities to the utmost pecuniary account. Robbery is now classed as a profession, and in the place of the awkward and hang-dog looking thief we have today the thoughtful and intelligent rogue. There seems to be a strange fascination about crime that draws men of brains, and with their eyes wide open, into its meshes.[5]

The most successful, hence most admired of this new breed of professional thief, were the safe-crackers, who specialized in robbing bank safes. "It requires rare qualities in a criminal to become an expert bank-safe robber," Byrnes observed. "The professional bank burgler must have patience, intelligence, mechanical knowledge, industry, determination, fertility of resources, and courage—all in high degree." The rewards were commensurate; the booming industrial economy, with its heavy demand for capital, meant that banks kept large sums of currency and negotiable government securities in their vaults. In terms of the scale of their operations and the amount of money taken, the big-city professional thieves made folk bandits such as the James brothers look like adolescent street muggers.

• On April 6, 1869, "Big Frank" McCoy and his fellow safe-crackers stole $1 million in cash and government securities from the Catholic Beneficial Fund Bank of Philadelphia.

• Two months later, Jimmy "Old Man" Hope, Ned Lyons, and others took $1.2 million from New York City's Ocean National Bank, and in November of that year unknown safe-crackers took $500,000 from the Boylston Bank in Boston.

• On January 25, 1876, Eddie Goodie—"one of the smartest thieves in America, a man of wonderful audacity and resources," in Inspector Byrnes' description—led a gang that took $720,000 from the safe of the Northampton National Bank in Northampton, Massachusetts.

Although the professional thieves of this era did not belong to any "syndicate" or national organization, they did form a loose fraternity of sorts, moving about from place to place in the United States and Canada, and to some extent England and the Continent, according to the season and the opportunities. Their specialized criminal argot, much of it still in use, contributed to that sense of shared identity.

More important, the new professional thieves came from similar ethnic backgrounds; most were born in England or in the United States of English (or occasionally German or Irish) descent and had grown up in respectable working-class or middle-class homes. Ordinary street criminals, by contrast, generally were drawn from the poverty-stricken ethnic groups that formed the bulk of late nineteenth-century immigration. G. W. Walling, Byrnes' superior as Superintendent of the New York City Police Department, observed that "All the sneaks, hypocrites and higher grade of criminals, when questioned upon the subject, almost invariably lay claims to be adherents of the Republican Party; while, on the other hand, criminals of the lower order—those who rob by violence and brute force—lay claim in no uncertain terms to being practical and energetic exponents of true Democratic principles."

Whether Democrats or Republicans, the number of "criminals of the lower order" increased steadily after the turn of the century, as the corrosive impact of urban life destroyed the informal social controls under which the new immigrants, mostly from peasant backgrounds, previously lived.

II

The level of crime has always been high in the United States; the trend has fluctuated. From the turn of the century until the early 1930s, the trend was unmistakably upward. Judging by the homicide rate, the only crime for which reasonably accurate long-term statistics are available, the first three decades of the twentieth century saw an explosive increase in violent crime. The rate of death by murder, which ran only slightly above 1 per 100,000 population in 1900, shot up to 5 per 100,000 in 1910, and 7 per 100,000 in 1920. Cleveland, whose population in 1920 was one-tenth the size of London's, had six times as many murders and seventeen times as many robberies; Chicago, with one-third of London's population, had twelve times as many murders and twenty-two times as many robberies. And that was *before* the Roaring Twenties;

by 1933, the rate of death by murder had climbed to 9.7 per 100,000.*[6]

These were years of rampant violence in all its forms. The United States has the bloodiest labor history of any industrial nation, and the late nineteenth and early twentieth centuries constitute the bloodiest portion of that history. In Colorado, to pick one of a number of examples, a "Thirty Years' War" of strikes and violence reached a climax in 1913-14, when coal miners struck against the Colorado Fuel and Iron Company. During the first five weeks of the strike, there were thirty-eight armed skirmishes between strikers and the company's private army; eighteen people were killed. In April, 1914, there was a fifteen-hour battle between strikers and militiamen. The battle ended when the militiamen set fire to the strikers' tent city near Ludlow, Colorado; two mothers and eleven children suffocated to death in what came to be known as the "Black Hole of Ludlow."[7]

The close of World War I touched off a new wave of violence. The insatiable demand for labor during the war years broke the social and economic fetters that had kept black Americans bound to the rural South almost as effectively as they had been during slavery. When the war was over, many blacks were unwilling to return to their old subordinate status, and many whites were determined to return them to it. The ingredients for racial violence were present, and

* Some of this increase undoubtedly was due to more careful reporting of the cause of death, as well as to a less casual attitude toward murder. (In nineteenth-century Philadelphia, the historian Roger Lane has written, coroners had a financial incentive to record the cause of death as an accident rather than as a homicide.) But other factors served to dampen the increase in the murder rate; by 1933, a good many assault victims who would have died in 1900 were being saved by improved medical techniques and faster transportation to hospitals.

in the "Red Summer" of 1919, as James Weldon Johnson called it, there were approximately twenty-five
racial conflicts. Some were expanded lynchings; others,
brief clashes that were quickly dissipated. Seven incidents involved race riots of major proportions:
in Washington, D.C.; Chicago; Knoxville; Omaha;
Charleston, South Carolina; Longview, Texas; and
Phillips County, Arkansas. The Phillips County bloodshed grew out of white farmers' determination to destroy a newly created union of black sharecroppers; by
the time it ended, five whites and at least fifty to sixty
blacks had been killed.[8]

Criminal violence associated with organized crime
gave the 1920s their special flavor and made cities
such as Chicago notorious throughout the world. Before then, gambling and vice syndicates, the main-
stays of organized crime, were relatively free from
violence—at least by latter-day standards. January 17,
1920, the day the Volstead Act went into effect, represents the great watershed in the history of organized
crime in the United States. Prohibiting the manufacture
and sale of alcoholic beverages opened up the vast,
and extraordinarily profitable, illegal industry of bootlegging, which was racked with violence from the start.
Hijacking someone else's liquor was the fastest and
most profitable method of entering the new industry;
those who got a start that way were quick to create
their own armies, often formed by hiring off-duty (and
sometimes on-duty) policemen to protect them against
other would-be bootleggers. (In 1926, one Chicago
bootlegging "firm" alone had 400 policemen on its
payroll.) Established underworld leaders remained on
the sidelines, in part because they were content with
their existing illegal enterprises, and in good measure
because they were reluctant to use murder as a routine
business technique. And murder *was* routine: in his

classic 1929 study of organized crime in Chicago, John Landesco required four and a half pages just to catalog the principal casualties in the various Chicago "beer wars."[9]

Thus a new generation of Americans, born in this century, took over the leadership of organized crime. By the early or middle 1920s, the top bootleggers were men in their twenties—predominantly Italian- and Jewish-Americans, in contrast to the Irish-Americans who had dominated the earlier gambling and vice syndicates—and utterly ruthless, as well as enormously ambitious. The new leaders used their ruthlessness, along with their bootlegging profits, to move into gambling and labor racketeering and to invest in restaurants, night clubs, politics, and a host of other enterprises. They were not prepared to retire when Prohibition ended; with their capital, organizational ability, and nationwide contracts, they broadened their investments and continued to maintain a disproportionate amount of power within the American underworld.

Even so, the end of Prohibition marked another watershed in the history of American crime and violence. For a quarter of a century, the United States, perhaps for the first time in its history, enjoyed a period in which crime rates were either stable or declining and in which fear of crime was relatively low. The death rate from homicide dropped by 50 percent between 1933 and the early '40s; despite the FBI's highly publicized gun battles with John Dillinger and other criminals, the rate of other serious crimes (rape, robbery, assault, and burglary) declined by one-third. Crime rebounded somewhat from its artificial wartime low after the Japanese surrender. Nonetheless, the crime rate remained well below the levels of the 1920s and early '30s until the current crime wave got under way in the early 1960s.[10]

Several factors account for this unusual period of domestic tranquillity. Despite the proverty and mass unemployment of the 1930s—in good measure *because* of poverty and mass unemployment—Americans felt that they were all in the same boat; the severity of the Great Depression helped create a sense of community. Passage of the Wagner Act, recognizing trade unions' right to collective bargaining, ended the nation's long history of labor violence. Other New Deal social reforms, combined with Franklin D. Roosevelt's eloquence, made previously excluded racial and ethnic groups feel as though they had been incorporated into American society. And World War II forged an even greater sense of national unity and purpose.

Demographic changes also contributed to the low level of criminal violence. Mass immigration from eastern and southern Europe was cut off in the early 1920s, and the Depression temporarily halted the movement of blacks from the rural South to the urban North. As a result, the old cities of the East and Midwest enjoyed a respite from their traditional (and traditionally traumatic) task of helping newcomers adjust to city life. Between 1940 and 1950, moreover, the population aged fourteen to twenty-four—the group from which most criminals are drawn—actually declined in size as a result of the sharp decline in the birth rate during the 1920s and '30s. During the war years, most young men were in the armed forces; when they returned to civilian life, they were eager to get on with their careers or their studies.

The result was a profound change in Americans' expectations about crime and violence. When one looks at the whole history of violence in the United States, the historian Richard Hofstadter suggests, what is striking is less the record of violence itself than Americans' "extraordinary ability, in the face of that record, to persuade themselves that they are among the best-behaved and best-regulated of peoples." This general tendency to shrug off unpleasant memories turned into a real historical amnesia after World War II. Because domestic tranquillity appeared to be the norm, Americans who came of age during the 1940s and '50s were unaware of how violent and crime-ridden the United States had always been. Although they continued to romanticize violence in detective stories and Westerns, an entire generation became accustomed to peace in their daily lives.

To most Americans, therefore, the upsurge in criminal violence that began around 1960 appeared to be an aberration from the norm rather than a return to it. The increase can be explained, in part, by a new and extraordinary demographic change that occurred between 1960 and 1975; the population aged fourteen to twenty-four grew 63 percent, more than six times the increase in all other age groups combined. In 1960, fourteen- to twenty-four-year-olds accounted for 69 percent of all arrests for serious crimes, although they comprised only 15.1 percent of the population. Without any change in young people's propensity for crime, the increase in their numbers alone would have brought about a 40 to 50 percent increase in criminal violence between 1960 and 1975. In fact, the number of serious crimes increased more than 200 percent. The change in the age distribution of the population thus accounts for only 25 percent of the increase; the rest is due to the greater frequency with which members of every age group, but particularly the young, commit serious crimes.

One reason for this increased propensity toward crime is what might be termed "demographic overload": the growth in the fourteen- to twenty-four-year-old group was so enormous, relative to the growth of

the adult population, that the conventional means of
social control broke down. In each generation, adults
must grapple with the problem of inducting the young
into the norms and values of adult society; as Norman
Ryder, a Princeton University demographer, puts it,
"Society at large is faced perennially with an invasion
of barbarians." The task of "civilizing" those "barbarians" may be welcomed (as it is in the typical com-
mencement address) as a chance for society to renew
itself with youthful idealism, to reinvigorate its tired
ideas and institutions and bring them into line with
changing conditions. But the task is fraught with peril
as well—both for the youthful invaders and for the
society that must absorb them.[11]

The peril is particularly great when those who are
supposed to be doing the socializing are unsure of their
role—a familiar and poignant by-product of migration. When parents live on unfamiliar cultural terrain,
the conflict between the generations becomes anything
but benign; the process of acculturation breaks down,
and children find themselves adrift in a cultural no
man's land. This is why the crime rate has always
been particularly high among the first generation to
be born in this country. The Wickersham Commission wrote in 1931, in terms that apply to contemporary
migrants from Latin America, China, and the rural
South, that immigrant parents "do not understand the
American community, and are consequently at a disadvantage in dealing with their own children, who at
least *think* they understand it, and know they know
more about it than their parents."

> The ordinary relationship between child and parents is
> reversed, with the child developing a sense of superi-
> ority to the parent and an unwillingness to take any
> guidance from people so obviously out of tune with
> their surroundings.[12]

Social controls have been weakened, too, by the older generation's growing uncertainty about its own values. "The prime fact about modernity," Walter Lippman wrote nearly fifty years ago in *A Preface to Morals,* "is that it not merely denies the central ideas of our forefathers but dissolves the disposition to believe in them." The rise of science and the triumph of modern technology shattered the traditional molds in which, for several millennia, people had lived out their lives, thus undermining the institutional and intellectual bases of their faith. "The dissolution of the ancestral order," in Lippman's phrase, has been going on ever since, "and much of our current controversy is between those who hope to stay the dissolution and those who would like to hasten it." The rate of change has accelerated since the end of World War II, and the dissolution of tradition now feeds on itself. It is not simply that ordinary people increasingly question the legitimacy of rules and customs they once considered sacred, or that previously oppressed minorities refuse to remain in their "place," but that those who make or administer the rules have lost faith in their own legitimacy.

This is the background against which the demographic explosion of the 1960s took place. One way of looking at the magnitude of the task of socialization is to compare the size of the invading army of fourteen- to twenty-four-year-olds with that of the adult population. The years from fourteen to twenty-four are particularly important because it is during adolescence and youth that rebellion commonly occurs. Except among some segments of the lower class, where parents often lose control of their youngsters at an earlier age, children tend to be sufficiently influenced by their parents during the first twelve or thirteen years of life so that rebellion is an individual, rather than societal, concern. And rebellion tends to end in the early or mid-twenties, when young people settle down to jobs and careers and marriage and parenthood.

For a long time, the invading army was small enough to be contained without undue strain; from 1890 to 1960, the population aged fourteen to twenty-four increased slowly—in all but two decades, more slowly than the population aged twenty-five to sixty-four, which provides the time, energy, and resources needed to induct the young into American society. Thus the ratio of young to old either declined (as it did in five decades) or held steady.

Despite this demographic stability (and notwithstanding the relatively flat trend of crime in general), juvenile delinquency increased dramatically during the 1950s as the effects of large-scale migration and urbanization began to be felt once again. Even so, no one was prepared for the demographic dislocation that was to follow. Between 1960 and 1970, the number of fourteen- to twenty-four-year-olds grew more than 50 percent; in absolute terms, the increase came to 13.8 million people, a larger increase in that age group than had occurred during the preceding seventy years combined. As a result, the ratio of youths to adults shot up by 39 percent—the first time the ratio had increased in seventy years.

Already attenuated by social and cultural changes, the traditional channels for the transmission of culture from one generation to another broke down from demographic overload. Hence the young increasingly turned to one another for guidance; the youth culture emerged as a major socializing force, taking over a large part of the burden traditionally carried by parents, teachers, clergymen, and other adults. That culture had been in the making for several decades. The disappearance of the family as a unit of production, together with the growth of near-universal high school education and the increase in college attendance, radically altered the institutional settings in which young people live their lives. Instead of being part of multi-age, multi-generational family and work groups, the young now spend almost all their time in segregated settings, having contact only with members of their own age group and adults in positions of formal authority.

Increasingly, therefore, adolescents and youths derive their values, tastes, and life styles from their peer group rather than from their elders.* The inward-looking character of the youth culture draws added strength from the increased affluence of most of its members. Just three or four decades ago, young people's labor was needed to help support the family; it was taken for granted that adolescents would turn their earnings over to their parents. Now many families have enough income to permit their children to spend some of it on their own tastes, and when teen-agers do work, the tacit assumption seems to be that

* One important by-product has been a rapid growth in the use of heroin and other drugs. Initiation into heroin use is a phenomenon of youth: two users in three begin using the drug between the ages of fifteen and twenty-one, with the great concentration occurring at age eighteen. Initiation is a peer group phenomenon as well. Despite the popular image of the evil pusher corrupting innocent children, the great majority of heroin users begin using the drug because a friend—usually someone who has only recently discovered the euphoria a heroin "rush" can provide—offers it to them. "Like marijuana, alcohol, cigarettes, slang, clothing fads, and popular music," Leon Hunt and Carl Chambers write in their authoritative study of the epidemiology of heroin use, use of the drug "spreads within groups of closely associated youths by a process of peer emulation and influence."[13] Heroin use has contributed to the growth in street crime, but to a far lesser degree than is generally assumed. (For an analysis of the complex relations between heroin use, law enforcement, and criminal activity, see Chapter 6.)

they will spend their earnings on themselves. This change in the economic relationship between the generations is symbolized by the different payroll practices of the Civilian Conservation Corps of the 1930s and the Job Corps of the 1960s and '70s. The CCC deducted a small allowance for the young people it employed, automatically sending the bulk of the money home to the parents; the Job Corps, by contrast, turns the paychecks over to its enrollees, sending an allotment home only on their request.

The result is that the young now control a substantial portion of the nation's discretionary income, a fact that gives the youth culture a power it otherwise would not have. Young people now "can back up their tastes with money," the sociologist James S. Coleman writes. "They can buy the records they like and the clothes they like, can go to the movies they like, can pay for underground newspapers if they like. Their inward-lookingness need not be confined to finding their popular heroes among youth, or to conformity with norms laid down to their peers; it can be expressed also by the power of their dollars."[14]

The size of young people's discretionary spending has led businessmen to direct much of their sales effort at the youth market; this, in turn, has increased young people's "need" for more and more discretionary income. Indeed, "keeping up with the Joneses" sometimes seems to be a characteristic of the young even more than of the old; certainly, peer pressures are far more intense among adolescents than among any other age group, and a teenager's status often depends on the ability to buy the "right" records and wear the "right" clothes. The adolescent need for money, combined with the weakening of adult social controls, has provided a lethal crimogenic force.

The pressure appears to be easing now. After a 10 percent increase in numbers during the first half of the decade, the fourteen- to twenty-four-year-old population will grow a scant 1.5 percent in this half-decade and then will decline by 6.6 percent over the next five years. The crime rate seems to have stabilized, and criminologists have begun to express cautious optimism about the outlook for the 1980s.*

Optimism may be premature. Among the groups most heavily involved in street crime, the demographic trends are less favorable than they are in the population as a whole. Although the birth rate has been declining in every segment of American society, it nonetheless is considerably higher among the poor than the non-poor; as a result the age distribution of the poverty population lags behind that of the rest of the population by a decade or more. In 1976, only 24.1 percent of American males were below the age of fourteen. Among the population officially classified as poor, on the other hand, 39.7 percent were under fourteen years of age; and among poor black males, no fewer than 48.3 percent were in that age group. (The proportions were even higher among poor Puerto Ricans and Mexican-Americans.) In short, although the total number of fourteen- to twenty-four-year-olds is declining, the number of *poor* fourteen- to twenty-four-year-olds will continue to grow, and grow rapidly, for at least another decade. And the most rapid growth of all will occur in urban slums and ghettos, where criminal violence has always been concentrated.

---

* The number of fourteen- to twenty-four-year-olds will turn up again in the 1980s. Although the birth *rate*—the number of children per couple—has been declining, the absolute number of births is increasing because of the huge crop of people—the teenagers of the 1960s—who are entering the child-rearing stage.

III

American crime is an outgrowth of the greatest
strengths and virtues of American society—its openness, its ethos of equality, its heterogeneity—as well as
its greatest vices, such as the long heritage of racial
hatred and oppression. Consider the emphasis on
equality, which Tocqueville thought to be the most distinctive part of the American character. There is "a
manly and lawful passion for equality that incites men
to wish to be all powerful and honored," Tocqueville
wrote in *Democracy in America.* "This passion tends
to elevate the humble to the rank of the great; but there
exists also in the human heart a depraved taste for
equality which impels the weak to attempt to lower
the powerful to their own level. . . ."

Depraved or not, the American emphasis on equality has often led the powerless to try to lower the
powerful to their level when barriers of race, ethnicity,
or class prevented them from achieving equality in any
other way. Since the time of Cain and Abel, violence
has been an effective leveler; nowhere was it more
clearly recognized as such than in the American West,
where the Colt six-shooter was lovingly referred to as
"the great equalizer." God created men, frontier Americans liked to say, but "Colonel Colt made them
equal."[15]

Colonel Colt and his numerous successors still make
people equal—or, more precisely, help the powerless
feel equal. Guns play a powerful symbolic role in
American life: it was no accident that the Black
Panthers made their entrance on the national scene by
carrying unloaded rifles into a session of the California
legislature. More than a century earlier, Frederick
Douglass had suggested that "The practice of carrying

guns would be a good one for the colored people to adopt, as it would give them a sense of their own manhood." The terminology of manhood in American culture is interwoven with firearm expressions: the coward is gun-shy, the forthright man is a straight shooter, and the methodical person makes every shot count. While the impulsive person shoots from the hip and the impatient goes off half-cocked, the prudent man keeps his powder dry. And all of them take a shot of whiskey.

The long encounter with the frontier has contributed to both the openness and the lawlessness of American society. "The whole history of the American frontier is a narrative of taking what was there to be taken," the historian Joe Frantz has written. "The timid never gathered the riches, the polite nearly never. The men who first carved the wilderness into land claims and town lots were men who moved in the face of danger, gathering as they progressed. *The emphasis naturally came to be placed on gathering and not on procedures.*" [emphasis added][16]

The frontier also played a powerful role in loosening the hold of tradition and custom. "Here on the edge of the forest, where civilized man was brought face to face again with nature and taught mainly to rely on himself," James Russell Lowell wrote, "mere manhood became a fact of prime importance." Forced to rely on themselves, Americans, even those who lived in the effete East, came to define manhood as freedom from restrictions of law and custom. "We should be men first, and subjects afterward," Henry David Thoreau declared, adding that he knew of no reason why a citizen should "ever for a moment, or in the least degree, resign his conscience to the legislator," or indeed to anyone else. Only a relative handful of Americans ever had any direct contact with the frontier. But the frontier ethos has had a profound effect on American consciousness, and the metaphors of the West retain their curious hold on the American imagination.

One consequence has been a general failure to relate means to ends. The problem is not unique to the United States; all societies prescribe certain goals as desirable and regulate the means that can be used, permitting some and forbidding others. Aberrant behavior arises because ends and means are not all of a piece; societies differ in the degree to which the norms covering conduct are integrated with the goals that are most highly valued. In the United States, the premium placed on winning—on success—encourages people to violate rules that get in the way, and to feel justified in doing so. As a minister-turned-con man once explained, "I tried truth first, but it didn't work."[17] Or, in Vince Lombardi's immortal formulation, "Winning is not the main thing; it is the only thing."

A society that believes winning is the only thing is likely to overlook a great deal if the victory is large enough. Certainly, the men who brought us Watergate believed that a prize as large as the presidency could justify almost any tactic. Consider this exchange between Senator Herman Talmadge and former Attorney General John Mitchell during the Ervin Committee hearings:

Q: Am I to understand from your response that you placed the expediency of the next election above your responsibilities as an intimate to advise the President of the peril that surrounded him? Here was the deputy campaign director involved, all around him were people involved in crime, perjury, accessory after the fact, and you deliberately refused to tell him that. Would you state that the expediency of the election was more important than that?

A: Senator, I think you have put it exactly correct. In my mind, the re-election of Richard Nixon, compared with what was available on the other side, was so much more important that I put it in just that context.

And the Nixon administration, as we have been learning to our sorrow, was not unique in its disregard for law and established procedure. What distinguished the Nixon presidency from the Kennedy and Johnson presidencies, it would seem, was less the existence of governmental lawlessness than its extent and the arrogance with which it was conducted. Unlike Lyndon Johnson and John F. Kennedy, Richard Nixon failed to understand the importance of appearing to maintain the sanctity of governmental rules while evading or thwarting them.

In business, too, success has often been its own justification. Richard W. Sears, the founder of Sears, Roebuck, started out as a railroad telegraph operator who sold watches on the side. Sears bought watches at $2 apiece, attached $20 price tags to them, and mailed them to fictitious addresses around the country. When the packages were returned as undeliverable, Sears would wait to open them until his fellow employees were around; he would then unload the watches on his colleagues at a bargain price of $10.[18] As Thorstein Veblen observed of the Robber Barons, "It is not easy in any given case—indeed it is at times impossible until the courts have spoken—to say whether it is an instance of praiseworthy salesmanship or a penitentiary offense." (If the success is large enough, or the venture sufficiently bold or clever, Americans have even been willing to overlook a penitentiary offense.)

Historically, moreover, minority-group members have often found it difficult to understand some of the fine distinctions between "crime" and "business" that members of the majority culture like to draw. "Everybody calls me a racketeer," Al Capone said during the

1920s. "I call myself a businessman." Capone went on
to explain, "I make my money by supplying a public
demand. If I break the law, my customers, who number
hundreds of the best people in Chicago, are as guilty
as I am. The only difference between us is that I sell
and they buy." That was not the only difference; Capone's customers did not generally eliminate business
rivals by murder. But Capone thought his customers
were hypocritical in calling him a racketeer. "When
I sell liquor, it's bootlegging," he complained; "when
my patrons serve it on a silver tray on Lake Shore
Drive, it's hospitality."

Capone aside, it is far more difficult to transmit and
maintain norms of behavior in a heterogeneous and
rapidly changing society than in a homogeneous
and stable one. Unlike England, Sweden, Denmark, and
Holland, with their monolithic cultures and centuries
of uninterrupted development, the United States has
been ethnically, racially, and religiously diverse from
the start.* Indeed, the nature of the ethnic mix has
changed almost continuously, each generation bringing
new groups of immigrants with cultural traditions and
norms of behavior different from those that had developed among the original immigrants of predominantly white Anglo-Saxon stock. Some immigrant
groups—for example, the Irish, Sicilians, and southern
Italians—which had suffered long periods of oppression and foreign occupation in their native lands found
adjustment particularly difficult, for they brought with
them a deep-rooted distrust of law and government
and a tradition of settling disputes within the community. And black and Hispanic Americans, who ex-

* England and Canada have been discovering in recent years
that the absorption of culturally diverse groups can be a slow
and painful process for both the immigrants and the receiving
society.

perienced lawlessness on the part of the white majority
in this country, have had good reason to view the legal
system with jaundiced eyes.

IV

For all these reasons, criminal behavior is endemic in
every sector of American society, not merely in the
decaying slums and ghettos of central cities. Just how
widespread crime is can be gauged by asking what
proportion of the population is arrested for a criminal
offense at one time or another. In 1967, the President's
Crime Commission estimated that if arrest rates remained at their 1965 levels, a boy born in that year
had a 62 percent probability of being arrested for some
non-traffic criminal offense over the course of his
normal life expectancy. (The comparable figure for
women was 13 percent.) More recent calculations by
Alfred Blumstein of Carnegie Mellon University put
the probabilties at 60 percent for males and 16 percent for females.[19]

These are staggering proportions. In part, they are a
tribute to the long reach of the American criminal law.
Many juvenile arrests are for truancy, "incorrigibility,"
running away from home, violating a curfew, and other
conduct that would not be criminal if committed by an
adult. Many adult arrests are for trivial offenses, such
as possession of small amounts of marijuana, public
drunkenness, or disturbing the peace. But the figures
also reflect the degree to which shoplifting, vandalism,
"joy-riding," burglary, and other delinquent and criminal acts are part of the process of growing up in the
United States. In the most elaborate study of delinquent behavior ever conducted in the United States,
Marvin Wolfgang, Robert Figlio, and Thorsten Sellin
of the University of Pennsylvania analyzed the delin-

quent records of an entire birth cohort, consisting of
every boy born in 1945 who lived in Philadelphia between his tenth and eighteenth birthdays—some 9,945
youngsters in all. No fewer than 35 percent of the boys
had at least one official contact with the police for a
non-traffic offense before they turned eighteen. By age
twenty-six, fully 43 percent of the cohort had been arrested either as a juvenile or as an adult, and Wolfgang thinks it likely that the proportion will reach 50
percent by age thirty-five.[20]

The number of people with delinquent and/or criminal arrest records is almost as high in nonmetropolitan
areas as it is in Philadelphia or other big cities. Since
the mid-1960s, Kenneth Polk and several colleagues at
the University of Oregon have been studying the delinquent and criminal records of a cohort about three
or four years older than the Philadelphia group: every
male (1,227 youngsters in all) who was a high school
sophomore in 1964 in Marion County, Oregon (1970
population, 151,309). In this rural and small-town area
with an all-white and almost wholly native-born population, no fewer than 25 percent of the boys had an
official record with the county juvenile department by
age eighteen—a considerably larger proportion than
Polk had expected to find. By age twenty-three, fully
40 percent of the cohort had been arrested as a juvenile and/or adult offender—almost as high a proportion as the Philadelphia cohort had reached at the
same age.[21]

If an arrest record is not the norm in American life,
clearly it is not an exception. Nearly all of us, moreover, break the criminal law without getting caught. In
both the United States and Europe, criminologists have
made numerous studies of "hidden," or undetected,
crime in which they ask people with and without arrest
records to record any crimes they may have committed.

Although the results vary somewhat from study to study and are subject to a sizable margin of error, two major conclusions emerge.

• An overwhelming majority of people have committed at least one crime without detection, and a substantial proportion have broken the law more than once.

• Criminal and delinquent behavior is distributed much more evenly among social classes than is indicated by police and court statistics.[22]

Much of the criminal and delinquent behavior might be considered innocuous—taking ashtrays or towels from a hotel room, or the petty shoplifting of gum or candy bars most youngsters indulge in at least once. And when undetected criminals or delinquents are compared with incarcerated offenders, significant differences appear. Members of the latter group generally admit to a wider variety of offenses, many of which are more serious than those admitted by the hidden offenders; in particular, adjudicated delinquents and criminals commit more violent crimes than do their respectable counterparts, and they break the law a lot more frequently.

But a considerable proportion of the undetected offenses committed by members of the middle class are of a more serious, or at least more problematic, sort. People who look like one's next-door neighbor—people who could well *be* one's next-door neighbor—engage in a wide variety of petty thefts whose cumulative total exceeds the sums lost through street crime. Thievery from hotels and motels is a common practice; industry security experts estimate that one guest in three takes some piece of hotel property on departure—sheets, bedspreads, lamps, silverware, and even television sets, as well as the more familiar ashtray and towel. "Believe me, I've paid for those things," a salesman who collects sheets and towels explains. "The places I've stayed at haven't lost anything because they jack their prices up so." "There's nothing wrong with taking little things from hotels," a suburban housewife remarks. "I think they expect you to take at least a towel." She and her husband have taken a good deal more—for example, a bedspread embroidered with a large "R" which they lifted from a Ramada Inn. "When I saw it in the motel room, I just knew I had to have it," the woman says, adding, "Anyway, if you have something marked with their crest, it's good publicity for them. After all, I show off these things to my friends."[23]

Stealing from employers is even more prevalent. According to estimates by the U.S. Department of Commerce, what retailers euphemistically call "inventory shrinkage" came to $5.3 billion in 1974. Shoplifting accounts for only 20 to 25 percent of that missing inventory; while some of the remaining "shrinkage" undoubtedly was due to honest mistakes in record-keeping, the great bulk was the result of employee theft of merchandise and fraudulent manipulation of inventory records.* And retailers were not the only ones victimized by employee theft; the Commerce Department estimated wholesalers' 1974 inventory losses at $2.1 billion and manufacturers' losses at $2.8 billion.

Then there are such widespread (and widely accepted) offenses as padding expense accounts and underreporting income or overstating expenses on income tax returns. Some measure of the prevalence of tax fraud was provided in 1964, when the federal govern-

---

* Over a period of two or three years, a ring of fourteen employees of a Dallas department store chain stole about $500,-000 worth of merchandise, including women's shoes and dresses, men's pants, jeans, suits, shirts, and socks, and cameras, radios, and TV sets. The private investigator who obtained confessions from the fourteen found seven other groups of employees stealing from the chain's warehouse and other stores.[24]

ment first required banks and corporations to report all interest and dividend payments to individuals; the amount of interest and/or dividends reported on individual tax returns jumped 45 percent, and taxes on this kind of income increased by 28 percent.[25] *The Wall Street Journal* has reported an interesting index of the number of people who seemingly commit securities fraud. When a Salt Lake City grand jury announced indictments of fifteen people for securities law violations but withheld their names pending arrests, nine persons surrendered to the U.S. Attorney. Only one of the nine had been among those indicted.

For all the theft it endures, American business is more sinner than sinned against; crimes committed by business firms cause damage on a massive scale—to the nation's health and well-being, in addition to its pocketbook. To obtain Food and Drug Administration approval to market MER/29, a drug designed to lower cholesterol levels in the blood, executives of Richardson-Merrell, a large pharmaceutical manufacturer, suppressed and falsified the results of laboratory tests indicating that the drug had dangerous side effects. (The results of some laboratory tests, e.g., one in which all female rats on a high dosage died within six weeks, were never reported to the FDA; in the case of other laboratory tests, wholly fictitious results were reported.) In the two years the drug was on the market, it was used by about 400,000 people. Some 500 of them are known to have developed cataracts, and some developed other symptoms as well—for example, skin rashes, scaling, and loss of hair. Although Richardson-Merrell's top management was not implicated in the fraud, the California Court of Appeals found that "responsible corporate officials, at least up to the level of vice-president, had knowledge of the true test results of MER/29 when used in animals, and that some, or all, joined in a policy of nondisclosure of this information to the Food and Drug Administration and the medical profession."[26]

Some entire industries appear riddled with fraud: among them, the operation of private nursing homes; door-to-door selling of encyclopedias and other products; large segments of the home improvement and land sales industries; the retailing of furniture and home appliances in slum and ghetto neighborhoods; and grain exporting, in which criminal fraud appears to have been a corporate way of life. Take the case of the Bunge Corporation, the third largest grain exporter in the world (annual sales, about $2 billion), which pleaded no contest to two federal counts of conspiracy involving systematic thefts of grain from its customers over a ten-year period. Company employees manipulated the scales at the company's grain elevator in New Orleans to record more grain being put aboard ships than was actually loaded. To account for the extra grain accumulated in that manner, the company created false records for "phantom" railroad cars, trucks, and barges of grain; other records were falsified to make it appear that the stolen grain, which was sold to other customers, had actually been purchased. The conspiracy involved Bunge officials in New Orleans, Galveston, and Kansas City, as well as in the main office in New York.

One side effect of the Watergate investigations has been a proliferation of evidence about the prevalence of certain other forms of corporate crime. Following the trail of the money raised by the White House and the Nixon campaign organization, the Special Prosecutor, the Securities and Exchange Commission, and private litigants uncovered a deeply entrenched pattern of illegal and criminal corporate contributions to candidates of both political parties. Between 1960 and 1972, Claude C. Wild, Jr., Gulf Oil's chief Washington lobbyist, distributed about $4.1 million of corporate funds, almost always in cash, to scores of public officials including Lyndon Johnson, Hubert Humphrey, Senators Jackson and Bentsen, Richard Nixon, Gerald Ford, and former Senate Republican leader Hugh Scott. The practice was known to a number of Gulf's top executives, some of whom also allegedly participated in the illegal contributions of corporate funds. Money for the slush fund was routed through a now-defunct Bahamian subsidiary. And Gulf was hardly unique: according to testimony before the SEC, many of its payments were made to stay on an "equal keel" with competitors who were doing the same thing.[27]

The Watergate trail also turned up evidence that defense contractors, such as Northrop and Lockheed, and other large corporations with foreign sales, such as Exxon and Gulf Oil, had a longstanding habit of paying bribes to foreign government officials, generals, and businessmen. As with the illegal campaign contributions in the United States, the corporations covered up payment of the bribes by a variety of accounting manipulations.

In one instance, a Lockheed subsidiary tried to take business away from another Lockheed subsidiary by offering Indonesian officials twice as large a bribe. "It's tough enough doing business nowadays without someone in your own house making the job more difficult," an executive of the second subsidiary complained in an angry memo to executives in corporate headquarters. The subsidiary suffered a second blow when the Indonesian officials asked to be paid directly instead of having the payoff routed through an intermediary. Its executives asked the Lockheed vice president in charge of international sales to decide how big a bribe they should pay, and how to pay it. They pointed out in a memo that if payments were direct, "some of the hazards that we might be exposed to are (1) . . . we have no legal means of charging off these commissions. Thus, they might not be considered allowable deductions by the Internal Revenue Service. (2) If such payments should some day become public knowledge, the repercussions could be damaging to Lockheed's name and reputation."[28]

The growth of the consumer movement and the increasing concern over the environment have persuaded Americans to take a far more serious view of industrial pollution, which has been a crime since the turn of the century. Air pollution appears to be a significant factor in the growing incidence of respiratory diseases, such as emphysema, lung cancer, and some forms of skin cancer. As Ralph Nader has written, " 'Smogging' a city or town has taken on the proportions of a massive crime wave, yet federal and state statistical compilations of crime pay attention to muggers and ignore 'smoggers.' "[29]

We tend to ignore "smoggers" and other white-collar criminals because they do not fit our preconceptions about the kinds of people who break the law; the common denominator in so-called white-collar crimes is that they are committed by people not generally thought of as criminals. "Sure, but you use the word 'stealing,' " a senior partner of J. P. Morgan protested to members of a Congressional committee investigating the thefts committed by Richard Whitney, president of the New York Stock Exchange and brother of another Morgan partner. "It never occurred to me that Richard Whitney was a thief. What occurred to me was that he had gotten into a terrible jam, and had made improper and unlawful use of securities; that his brother was proposing to try to make good his default."[30] But Whitney *was* a thief, who stole securities from Stock Exchange trust funds under his control; he was convicted in 1938 and sent to prison for his crime. (When his theft was uncovered, he tried to head off indictment by making restitution to the trust fund, borrowing over a million dollars from his brother, who in turn borrowed most of it from the partner who protested Whitney's innocence to Congress.)

Well-bred people steal far larger sums than those lost through street crime. In the extraordinary Equity Funding fraud, the losses to creditors and stockholders have been estimated at $500 million—roughly 70 percent as much as was lost through all the robberies and burglaries reported to the FBI in 1973, the year in which the fraud was uncovered. For eight years, with the cooperation of their outside auditors, the company's executives manipulated their computers and rigged their books so as to make their company's stock a favorite among the nation's most sophisticated financial executives. Among other things, the Equity Funding executives manufactured some $2 billion of bogus life insurance policies which they sold to other insurance companies for the equivalent of the first year's premium; they filed death claims against the phony policies; they recorded other nonexistent or fraudulently inflated assets on the corporation's balance sheet; and they failed to record loans on the debit side. "I met some of these guys at the 1972 annual meeting," a stockholder said of the firm's top executives, "and they looked fine to me—clean-shaven, clean shirts, nicely dressed. They certainly didn't *look* like crooks."[31]

Spiro Agnew didn't look like a crook, either. Neither did John Mitchell, H. R. Haldeman, John Ehrlichman, or Charles Colson, or Marvin Mandel, the Maryland governor convicted of fraud, or the late Otto Kerner, former Illinois governor and federal judge who was found guilty of corruption. There is no way to measure the direct costs of corruption with any precision, but as a high Justice Department official observed with mor-

dant wit, "when we finally stop payoffs to public officials at all levels in this country we will have found the
cure to inflation."

The indirect costs of corruption are incalculable.
"Simply put, official corruption breeds disrespect for
the law," the National Advisory Commission on Criminal Justice Standards and Goals observed in its 1973
report. "Public corruption makes an especially sinister
contribution to criminality by providing an excuse and
rationalization for its existence among those who commit crime." All the more so in our day, when the aura
of corruption has enveloped the White House itself. "As
long as official corruption exists," the Standards and
Goals Commission concluded, "the war against crime
will be perceived by many as a war of the powerful
against the powerless; 'law and order' will be just a
hypocritical rallying cry, and 'equal justice under law'
will be an empty phrase."[32]

If street crime threatens the social fabric of American life, governmental crime destroys the political fabric by undermining the trust and belief in the legitimacy
of government on which our entire political system is
based. "Our government is the potent, the omnipresent
teacher," Justice Louis D. Brandeis wrote. "For good
or ill, it teaches the whole people by its example."

> Crime is contagious. If the government becomes a law-
> breaker, it breeds contempt for laws; it invites every
> man to become a law unto himself; it invites an-
> archy. . . .

An armed robber, now forcibly retired, puts it more
simply: "Instead of taking money with a pistol, they
just take it with a pen."

3

Robbers, Hustlers, and Other Dudes

Now, most good hustling dudes, especially with robbery experience, they never go out to hurt people. The main thing is getting what you're going after and getting away. Occasionally somebody say, "I ain't giving up nothing." But you can change his tune easy. You ain't got to kill him. Smack him with the gun or shoot him in the foot or kneecap, he give it right up.

—JOHN ALLEN, *Assault with a Deadly Weapon:
The Autobiography of a Street Criminal*, 1977

"I didn't know him; why should I feel sorry about what happened to him?"

—STATEMENT OF A TEENAGE MURDERER,
ABOUT HIS VICTIM

If you don't want the name, don't play the game.

—UNDERWORLD MAXIM

I

Most Americans break the criminal law; only a small minority are criminals. As one shifts the focus from crime in general to violent crime in particular, the number of offenders declines and their distinctiveness increases. The great majority of people with an arrest record have been arrested only once or twice, or at most, three times; they account for a negligible amount of criminal violence. There are important differences between these occasional offenders and a much smaller group of chronic offenders who account for the bulk of street crime—differences involving the nature of the offenses committed and their frequency, as well as the offenders' backgrounds and life style.

Street criminals tend to be young and poor, with a large proportion coming from minority-group backgrounds. In 1976, the latest year for which detailed statistics were available when this book went to press, nearly 75 percent of those arrested for the seven serious crimes included in the FBI's Crime Index were under twenty-five years of age, and more than 40 percent were seventeen or younger.* One-third of those arrested were black, and Puerto Ricans and Mexican-Americans made up a significant proportion of arrestees classified as white.

Street criminals are also predominantly male: in 1976, women comprised only 7 percent of those arrested for burglary. The only major crime that women commit in large numbers is larceny-theft—shoplifting, pickpocketing, passing forged checks, stealing items from parked cars, and other forms of theft that involve neither breaking and entering nor the use or threat of force; 82 percent of the women arrested for Index crimes in 1976 fell into this category. There has been a lot of talk about increased participation by women in serious crime, but larceny-theft accounted for 87 percent of the increase in female arrests between 1967 and

* To measure serious crime in the United States, the FBI collects particularly detailed statistics on seven so-called "Index crimes." Four are classified as crimes of violence (murder, aggravated assault, robbery, and rape) and three (burglary, larceny-theft, and auto theft) are considered property crimes. (For a discussion of the problems involved in using arrest statistics, see Appendix.)

1976. If I talk only about men in the discussion of street crime and criminals that follows, it is because street crime is so predominantly a male activity.

Marvin Wolfgang's study of the Philadelphia birth cohort throws a good bit of light on the differences between chronic offenders and the much larger group of people who break the law from time to time. To repeat the statistic I used in the last chapter, 35 percent of the 10,000 boys in the cohort had accumulated an arrest record before their eighteenth birthday. But 46 percent of these delinquents committed only a single offense; they accounted for only 16 percent of the total number of offenses committed, and a much smaller proportion of serious crimes. Indeed, three out of four one-time offenders were arrested for a juvenile "status offense" such as truancy or running away from home; only ten of the 1,613 one-time offenders were arrested for robbery. In general, the one-time offenders resembled the nondelinquents in family background, social class, and school performance.

The 1,862 multiple offenders present a different picture. Although they comprised 54 percent of the delinquent group (and 19 percent of the total cohort), they committed 8,601 offenses, or 84 percent of the total, and accounted for 95 percent of the robberies and 90 percent of the serious crimes included in the FBI's Crime Index. Two-thirds of the multiple offenders came from lower-class backgrounds, and 51 percent were black; as a group, they had lower IQs and poorer grades in school than the one-time offenders, and a much larger proportion came from broken homes.

The differences are even sharper if we divide the multiple offenders into two groups: hard-core delinquents, with five or more arrests; and those with two to four arrests. The latter group, some 1,235 in all, committed a total of 3,296 offenses, or an average of 2.7

each. The 627 chronic offenders committed 5,305 delinquent acts, or an average of 8.5 each. Comprising 18 percent of the delinquent group, they were responsible for 52 percent of all offenses and 83 percent of all the Index crimes. Drawn predominantly (77 percent) from the lower class, the chronic offenders typically began their delinquent careers at a much earlier age than the one-time offenders or occasional recidivists. Only 9 percent graduated from high school, compared to 24 percent of the occasional recidivists, 58 percent of the one-time offenders, and 74 percent of the non-delinquents.[1]

This dichotomy between a relatively small number of chronic criminals and a far larger number of occasional offenders appears to be characteristic of adults as well as juveniles. The FBI's computerized Criminal History file contains data on some 208,000 offenders arrested in the years 1970 through 1974; the group as a whole had accumulated a total of 830,992 arrests over the course of their careers as adult criminals. (Since juveniles' arrest histories are supposed to be kept confidential, they are not included in the FBI's files.) Thirty-five percent had been arrested only once; they accounted for fewer than 9 percent of total arrests. About the same proportion had been arrested four times or more; averaging 8.2 arrests each, these hardcore criminals accounted for nearly 75 percent of all the arrests.*

For all the differences between occasional and chronic offenders, the latter do not constitute a homogeneous group. "Real criminals" differ from one another in the backgrounds from which they come, the kinds of crimes they commit, their competence as criminals, and their commitment to crime as an occupation and as a way of life. Since robbery (taking money or

---

* Calculations by the author from data presented in *Crime in the United States 1974*, pp. 47–48.

property from someone through force or the threat of force) is the street crime *par excellence,* and since it is not a crime that occasional offenders commit with any frequency, taking a close look at the sorts of people who rob is a good way of getting a handle on the different kinds of criminals and criminal behavior—the subject of this chapter.

Although not every chronic offender is a robber, almost every robber is a chronic offender. Four-fifths of the adults in the FBI's Criminal History file who were arrested for robbery between 1970 and 1974 were repeat offenders; they averaged five prior arrests each. Nearly 85 percent of the people arrested for robbery in Philadelphia between 1960 and 1966 were repeat offenders; a group of career robbers studied by the criminologist Julian Roebuck averaged more than eighteen arrests each. Analyses of arrest data in other parts of the country have yielded comparable results.[2]

Only a small minority of robbers—perhaps 5 to 10 percent—can be considered professional criminals, i.e., people who earn their living from crime, who take pride in their expertise and in their criminal identity, and who plan their crimes with care so as to yield the largest possible "score." The majority—perhaps as many as three out of four overall, and all the muggers and strong-armed robbers—are what the criminologist John Conklin, author of a study of robbery in Boston, calls "opportunist robbers." The members of this group are impulsive, highly disorganized lower-class adolescents and young adults who rarely plan their crimes; instead, they select targets such as disabled or older people because of their availability and vulnerability, rather than the size of the score. A third group of semiprofessionals, mostly in their late teens or early twenties, falls somewhere in between. They do some planning, but not much; their targets are likely to be gas stations, liquor stores, and other small retail establishments that stay open late at night, rather than the supermarkets and business payroll offices preferred by professional robbers.[3]

These are not hard-and-fast categories, but they are useful in distinguishing the different kinds of robbers and other chronic offenders. Certainly, there is a big difference between ordinary street criminals, who tend to be teenagers or young adults and who come almost exclusively from the lower class, and professional robbers, who usually are somewhat older—in their twenties or early thirties—and drawn from a broader social spectrum. In Boston, Conklin found that professional robbers tended to be whites from solid working-class, and occasionally middle-class, backgrounds, whereas opportunist robbers were predominantly black and lower-class. In crime, as in other professions, blacks tend to be concentrated in the lower rungs of the occupational ladder.

Professional criminals follow variegated routes into crime. Some never know any other calling. "People constantly saying, 'Why don't you do better? Why don't you do this or why don't you do that?'" John Allen, a former professional robber in Washington, D.C., remarks in his taped autobiography. "I don't know how to do this; I don't know how to do that. This is all I know. I know how to stick somebody up better than anything. I know how to take a small amount of narcotics and eventually work it way up and make me some money. Fencing property or credit cards. I know how to do all that. . . . No one ever taught me anything else."[4] (Having been paralyzed in a shoot-out, Allen is now retired from crime.)

Professionals like Allen grow up in high-crime neighborhoods where successful criminals are folk heroes; they serve an apprenticeship as juvenile delinquents, trying very hard to impress their elders with their ability and commitment. If they display sufficient promise, professional criminals or members of organized crime may give them odd jobs to do—for example, stealing cars or "boosting" (shoplifting) merchandise to specifications—until they become professionals themselves.

For other professionals—those from middle-class or solid working-class backgrounds—becoming a criminal is more a matter of deliberate choice. "I bet you wonder why a bright clean-cut kid like me from a good family turned to crime," a young professional thief remarked to the criminologist-folklorist Bruce Jackson. "I like the life," he explained, by which he meant, as Jackson writes, "the romantic business of spending big, carrying an automatic pistol in a special shoulder holster, moving in two worlds at once."[5]

Some professionals begin their careers in the straight world; they turn to crime because they cannot support their taste for gambling, travel, or women on a legitimate salary. Armed robbers known as "the Bobbsey Twins," whom Bruce Jackson credits with 200 armed robberies in an eighteen-month period, turned professional when the two partners realized that they would have to "do something in order to live in the manner to which we'd become accustomed." Before that decision, they had merely moonlighted at crimes such as auto theft, check forging, strong-arm robbery, and embezzlement to supplement their legitimate incomes. When one of the Twins lost his job, the two men decided that to get as much money as they wanted as quickly as they wanted it, they would have to work at crime full time. Crime "is just like any other business," they told Jackson. ". . . there's setbacks in crime and there's deficits, just like you run a business and there's a chance that you might burn down or you might go bankrupt or your employee might have embezzled everything you

got without insurance to cover it, and it's the same way
with crime. Of course, the penalty for going bankrupt
in crime is much stiffer, but at the same time your material gain is much more than it is in a regular business." Having decided to turn professional, the two men
chose robbery as the fastest way to make money.[6]

Whatever their reasons for "turning out" (becoming
a criminal), professional criminals become committed
to crime as both an occupation and a life style. The
professional criminal "works at crime as a business,"
the linguist-criminologist David Maurer has written;
"he makes his living at it; he is recognized and accepted
by other professionals in his class as a professional; he
knows and uses the argot or semi-secret language of the
profession. . . ." The professional tends to be contemptuous of amateur crooks, as well as of "suckers"
(victims) and of society in general.[7]

Professionals may "pack the racket in" (retire) because the going gets too hot, because they can no longer
endure prison life (it is the rare criminal, professional
or amateur, who avoids prison altogether), because
they can no longer do the physical work that is involved, or because their hands have lost their skill or
their nerves the capacity to withstand the tensions of
professional crime. But "packing it in" does not necessarily mean reforming. Some professionals turn to less
arduous, or less dangerous, criminal occupations, such
as the numbers or other illegal gambling operations.
Others tend to remain criminals at heart, occasionally
moonlighting at crime while they hold down a legitimate job.

Since most professional robbers are better educated
than street criminals and come from stabler family
backgrounds, they generally plan their crimes with some
degree of thought and care. The ten-man gang that
pulled off the famous Brink's robbery in Boston in 1950

spent nearly two years planning the crime. Before the robbery was carried out, each of the ten had become familiar with Brink's premises and had carefully studied the firm's schedules and shipments. The group practiced their approach and getaway in several trial runs and on several occasions abandoned plans to carry out the robbery when conditions were not favorable.

The Brink's robbery was unusual both in the degree of planning and the size of the score—$1,218,000 in cash and $1,557,000 in money orders—but it represents the ideal to which professional robbers aspire. Most professionals follow at least some of the same procedures: picking a target where there is some assurance of finding a large sum of cash; "casing the joint" beforehand; assigning roles (most professionals work in groups of two to four) and establishing a precise and detailed timetable; making a practice run; and planning the getaway. "Casing" the target means determining where the cash is kept and whether it is locked in a safe (and if so, who can open the safe or when the safe is opened by a timing device); studying the flow of customers and the movement of employees; and so on. And preparing the getaway means selecting a target that makes it possible to leave the scene rapidly, without getting stuck in traffic or dead-end streets—and without having to go through a red light, which might attract the attention of an otherwise uninterested traffic cop or patrol car.[8]

Street robbers, muggers, and purse-snatchers seem incapable of that kind of forethought or planning; in their illuminating study of robbers and robbery in northern California, Floyd Feeney and Adrianne Weir describe in rich detail the erratic, impulsive behavior that most robbers display.[9] More than 40 percent of the juvenile robbers whom they interviewed, and 25 percent of the adult offenders, had not even *intended* to rob anyone when they went out. "It was just a sudden thing," one juvenile said. "I didn't really mean to do it. I didn't plan or nothing; it just happened. Just like that. Because he offered it to me." What "just happened" was that the victim bumped into the robber on the street, whereupon the latter assaulted him and beat him up. Fearing for his life and assuming that robbery was the motive for the unexpected attack, the victim "offered" the robber the $4 he was carrying.

A jostle, stare, mildly derogatory remark, or any number of other stimuli that seem utterly trivial to the middle-class eye and ear may trigger an explosive reaction on the street corners and in the bars and "take-out" restaurants where slum and ghetto youths spend much of their time.[10] Hence unpremeditated robbery in retaliation for some real or imagined slight is fairly common, as Feeney and Weir found.

ITEM: Waiting for a bus, a juvenile decides he does not want to break the $5 bill he is carrying and asks a bystander to give him a quarter for the fare. When the man refuses, the juvenile decides to "jump" him, threatening the victim with a knife and taking $10 from him. "He was acting real bad—talking all kinds of stuff," the robber explains.

ITEM: An adult offender tries to pick up a young woman; when she rejects his advances, he robs her instead—"because I felt she was disrespecting me kind of. I did it because I seen fear in her so I knew if I took this, she might start acting right. . . ."

ITEM: Two teenagers visit a neighborhood gas station to ask for a job; when they continue to hang around the gas station after the proprietor has told them no work is available, he orders them to leave. In anger, one boy pushes the owner while the other grabs money from the cash register.

Robbery also can be a means of relieving the boredom that hangs heavy over urban slums. "Just something to do, I guess," was one juvenile's explanation for robbing. "Just to cause some trouble," another commented. "Well, we just wanted to try that, you know. Goof around, you know, have some fun—jack up somebody. . . . We thought we were really big and stuff like that." Since robbery often is a group activity, participation may demonstrate a youngster's manhood to his doubting friends. "People got to prove things to people," one juvenile robber said. "My partner didn't think I could do it." Another youngster, who had $265 in his pocket when he committed a robbery, went along on the crime because his friend accused him of being scared when he initially demurred:

> "I think the reason why I did it is 'cause he said, 'Come on, man, let's go pull a robbery,' I said, 'No man.' He said, 'You scared.' I said, 'Man, I ain't scared.' 'Show me you're not scared.' That's why I did it . . . prove to him I'm not scared."

Lower-class youths turn to robbery to prove things to themselves, as well as to others. "You say, 'Wow, here I am,'" a twenty-two-year-old California robber explains. "'I'm nothing but a youngster at heart, a child at heart, and here I be playing the part of a bad guy.'" And "playing the part of a bad guy" is a highly effective antidote to the feelings of inadequacy and inferiority experienced by so many slum and ghetto dwellers. "I get a kick out of it, really," another California robber says. "Watch people's faces when they see you. They scared." As another robber puts it, "I just like the feeling of the dude, you know . . . like if I had a .38 right now, I can make you do just about anything I wanted you to do, see, and you couldn't do nothing about it. And like just about all my life, people had been doing that to me, see . . . but now I like to get that feeling where I can make you do anything I want you to do."

Robbers' sense of potency is further enhanced when they acquire money as a result of their exploits. "Having money makes you feel good inside," a fifteen-year-old robber observes; "it makes you feel older." Having money is the only way one can gain respect, young criminals in every part of the country told me; as one of them put it, "The buck is what makes you an American citizen." The buck also makes it possible for robbers to throw a party, take their girl friends out on the town, inject heroin or snort cocaine, buy fancy clothes, or do or buy whatever it is that defines them to their friends as "doing all right."*

Although 75 percent of the adult robbers interviewed by Feeney and Weir, and 45 percent of the juveniles, gave money as their primary motive, most robbers do little or no advance planning. They may go out looking for an easy mark, or they may simply rob on impulse if they see a vulnerable target. Often the impulse strikes them after a heavy bout of drinking, as was the case with the seventeen-year-old whom John Conklin describes as the prototypical opportunist robber:

> One night, George and two friends stole a car. While driving around the city, one suggested that they get a little extra spending money. The driver stopped the

* Most heroin users use heroin the way social drinkers use alcohol: on weekends, at parties, or at other occasional events that call for relaxation or celebration. Some "chippers," as they are called, use heroin more frequently, or in heavier doses, than others, just as social drinkers differ in how much and how frequently they drink. About one heroin user in ten is an addict, i.e., someone who uses heroin every day—about the same as the ratio of alcoholics to the drinking population.[11]

car next to an elderly woman who was alone on the street. George got out and grabbed the lady's purse, then ran back to the car and the group drove away.

George asserts that he used no force against the woman, since he had no desire to harm her. Neither he nor any of his accomplices had a weapon with them.

The victim summoned the police to the scene. She claimed that she had been knocked to the ground and kicked, after having her handbag stolen. The police pursued the offenders and caught them in the stolen car about one mile from the scene of the crime. They were charged with unarmed robbery.

Neither George nor his friends had any particular need for the stolen money. None was using drugs at the time. He thinks they might have used the money for clothes or for throwing a party, but said the $17 they got would not have lasted very long.

Most street robbers are a bit more purposeful than George, but purposefulness is not synonymous with planning. When he and his friends were younger, John Allen recalls, "we never did no real skillful planning or taking down notes when we were checking out a place we wanted to rob. Not like I learned to do later on when I'd watch how many times a police routine check went by. It was just like we see a place, and if it was easy for us to get in by like climbing the drainpipe or going through a window, then we'd decide to do just that. And most of the time is *was* very easy." It is this peculiar combination of purposefulness and impulsiveness that makes street robbers so dangerous.

II

Unlike any of the other offenses in the FBI's Crime Index, robbery is both a property crime and a crime of violence. For professional robbers, violence tends to be instrumental—a means to an end—rather than a form of self-expression, as it often seems to be for impulsive street robbers. "Robbing is an art, and the whole art of robbing is fear, and the main reason for robbing is to get what you came after—the money—and get away," John Allen explains. "You don't go there to hurt people."[12]

Indeed, professional robbers take pride in their ability to avoid violence through "front"—their skill in handling people. Unless they can persuade victims to cooperate immediately—split-second timing is essential in large-scale robberies—and not to call the police or pursue them, robbers run a high risk of getting caught. Hence successful robbers convey self-confidence and a commanding presence. "If you instill the fear the moment that the robbery started to take place," Allen says, "then you got more than half the battle won." A Midwestern professional told me, "The whole thing depends on the first impression you give. If you're afraid yourself, they'll know it right away," in which case the victims may balk. Victims "can tell by the sound of your voice, by what you say and how you go about things, whether or not you mean business," a Canadian robber observes.

Lest victims doubt that they do mean business, professional robbers almost always carry guns. Victims are much more likely to cooperate when a gun is pointed at them than they are if the robbers are unarmed, or armed only with knives or some other weapon. For that reason, as well as because of the symbolism associated with guns, robbers feel more in command when they carry a gun. "You're a pretty big man standing there with your gun," one robber explains. "Makes you feel oh—kinda important—big, somebody people don't mess with."

Professional robbers also tend to avoid small businesses where the owner may be present, no matter how
large the potential score. People are far more likely to
resist if their own money, rather than an impersonal
corporate employer's, is involved, and professional robbers prefer not to shoot anyone if they don't have to.
The noise may attract attention, and if caught, a robber
is more likely to be convicted, and more likely to draw
a long prison term, when someone has been injured.

To avoid unnecessary resistance, professionals will
not stop to rob customers and employees who happen to
be present. Such encounters are too personal, and they
also delay the getaway, thereby increasing the risk out
of all proportion to the possible take; "never grift
(steal) on the way out" is a sacred maxim among professional thieves of every sort. "I learned that rule the
hard way," a professional thief says. "When I was
twenty-one, I leaned across the counter of a grocery
store and pulled a roll of bills out of this cigar box he
had shoved down between two piles of empty sacks. I
was really proud of myself and everything was cool.
. . . But the bastard sees me taking an Old Nick [a
candy bar]. . . . yelling and beefing he chases me
down the street into a corner of four cops."[13]

That same professionalism means having no inhibitions about using force if circumstances require it. "You
can't afford to be squeamish or anything," an old-timer
says. "If they haven't got sense enough to do what you
want 'em to, you can't just stand there blah-blahing at
'em." "I don't indulge in it, you know, for the pleasure
of the thing," another professional explains. "But on a
day-to-day level it just happens that it's a tool of my
trade and I use it—like an engineer uses a slide-rule,
or a bus-driver the handbrake, or a dentist the drill.
Only when necessary, and only when it can't be
avoided."[14]

There are times when professional robbers use force unnecessarily because they have misread a victim's intentions; part of a robber's expertise in managing people involves the capacity to interpret body language and other nonverbal communication correctly. This requires considerable skill, since the terror that victims feel may produce bizarre behavior. Equally important, a robber needs the ability to stay cool when something unexpected happens. "Every robbery—no matter how much you've rehearsed it—you've got things come up you didn't look forward to or into," one of the Bobbsey Twins told Bruce Jackson. "And you've got to be, I guess you'd call it cool enough to play these things by ear and handle them as you go." When a robber loses his cool, he may misread an innocent act—with disastrous consequences.

Professional criminals are contemptuous, therefore, of street robbers—"on again, off again, hooligans-mulligans," as one thief calls them—who use violence in an impulsive rather than disciplined manner and who are responsible for much of the increase in violent crime. Indeed, older professionals view young criminals as both crazy and dangerous because they are "not under control." "I myself walk light when I'm in the ghetto," a professional robber from Chicago remarks. "I know the value of life has no weight.* These younger criminals, they're sick. They have no motive for what they're doing."

It would be more accurate to say that younger criminals' motivation is expressive rather than instrumental; for reasons I will explore in detail in the next two chapters, violence can be its own reward, as well as a means

* The man is not engaging in hyperbole. In just a five-year period (1965 to 1970) in Chicago, robbery killings by offenders aged fifteen to twenty-four increased 718 percent. (Robbery killings by all other age groups went up 67 percent.)

to some other end. "That was a couple of years ago, but I remember it real good, because it made me feel like high," a fourteen-year-old mugger says, recalling the first time he used a knife on an elderly victim who tried to resist. When he was ten, the boy left home to move in with his girl friend, leaving his parents a note with the girl's telephone number; his parents never called. His career as a robber began when his girl friend's mother did not receive her welfare check and, as a result, there was nothing to eat. Now the youngster robs as much to re-create that "high" as to acquire money. "You feel big, like you can do anything," he explains. "You know what I mean, really big. And it don't go away, how you feel, not like you had a lot to drink."[15]

Violence offers more than just an occasional high; it provides a sense of being "somebody" to adolescents and young men who feel that they are nobody, whose experience of poverty and discrimination conveys a sense of rejection, even ostracism, by the larger society. Guns, in particular, continue to be "the great equalizer." "Having a gun made me feel like a judge. I held the power to take a life or not to take a life," a black ex-offender recalls. "When I had a gun, I thought I was Jesse James." Another ex-convict says, "If you feel like you're nothing, a gun can make you feel like a king." "It's like playing God, knowing you have the power of life and death at your fingertip," still another reformed criminal says. "The fear it instills in groups of people gives immense satisfaction to the user, accustomed as he is to being held in low esteem by legitimate people. It allows you the rare position of being in total control of a situation. . . ."[16]

These attitudes are old; the ease with which adolescents and young men can obtain guns is new. To be sure, people concerned about criminal violence have been announcing the arrival of a new era in weaponry

for more than half a century.* But after all the skepticism in the world has been brought to bear on the question, one conclusion is inescapable: in sheer number,
as well as in quality and sophistication, the weapons
now in the hands of youth gangs and criminally bent individuals far surpass anything the United States has
seen before. As a result, there is a fundamental qualitative difference between individual and gang violence
of today and that of the 1920s—or even that of the
1950s, the era glamorized in the Broadway musical and
film *West Side Story*.[17]

On any measure, there has been an extraordinary and
explosive increase in possession of guns by young
street criminals since the early 1960s. Manufacturing
and importing guns has become one of the great American growth industries: sales of handguns quadrupled
between 1962 and 1968, and sales of long guns (rifles
and shotguns) doubled. According to estimates made
by members of the staff of the 1969 Violence Commission (the National Commission on the Causes and Prevention of Violence), 10 million new handguns were
sold in the United States in the ten years ending in
1968; almost as many were sold in the next *five* years.
A large number of new guns find their way into the
hands of impulsive, disorganized young street criminals.
Although public discussion has focused on the so-
called "Saturday night special" (a cheap, short-barreled
.22 revolver), most of the guns confiscated by the
police when they make arrests are expensive, high-
quality weapons—handguns, such as the Colt and
Smith & Wesson .38, and sawed-off shotguns and automatic rifles.[18]

* "In the last two years, when the two gangs realized the
impotency of using bare knuckles and ragged stones, each
turned to firearms," a Chicago reporter wrote in 1919, in a
newspaper story reporting the killing of a fifteen-year old gang
member by members of a rival gang.

This explosive increase in the number of guns has transformed the technology, and thereby the character, of street crime. It is a commonplace to describe technology as neutral—to argue that what matters is not the instruments of technology themselves, but the ends to which people put them. But purpose does not exist in a vacuum; human beings do not choose from an infinite array of alternatives. A new technology creates new alternatives and erases old ones, thereby altering the choices that are available.[19] Supply creates its own demand, so to speak. In this instance, the more guns there are, the more they are used—and the more guns that are used, the greater the need people, especially gang members and other adolescents and young men living in high-crime neighborhoods, feel to carry them. Since guns are far more lethal than other weapons—the mortality rate in firearm assaults is five times the rate in attacks with a knife—both the number of robbery killings and the total number of homicides have gone up sharply.*

In short, street criminals are more lethally armed, and they appear to be a good bit readier to use violence of any sort. Killing without apparent reason or remorse is not new; the phenomenon appears in every period of rampant criminal violence. But the crime statistics, as well as the reports of victims, policemen, social workers, and others who have contact with violent youth, make it clear that random, senseless violence is more widespread now than at any time in the recent past, and that younger and younger boys are involved. "Sonny, you're too young for this," a middle-aged guard in a

---

* Technology has changed in another way as well. The old-style gang rumble on foot, with chains and crowbars the major weapons, has given way to the motorized foray, in which gang members drive through a rival gang's turf, firing rifles, shotguns, and other weapons.

Midwestern supermarket gently told a thirteen-year-old robber; by way of reply, the youngster shot him to death. Another teenage robber who was asked how he felt about having killed a storekeeper—his usual procedure had been to pistol-whip his victims into submission—responded, "Just one more storekeeper dead."

Sometimes, in fact, murder seems to be just a form of recreation.

ITEM (from the Miami *Herald,* October 23, 1973):

A twelve-year-old, a 13-year-old, and a boy in tattered cutoff corduroy pants who says he can't remember how old he is, were arrested by Miami police Monday and charged with the weekend murder of a derelict who police said was doused with lighter fluid and set afire as he slept.

"The boys said it was kind of a spontaneous thing," a Miami police spokesman said Monday. "They had four cans of lighter fluid they bought and stole at a local supermarket.

"They set fire to a cat first and then it ballooned. They saw the men sleeping behind the building, and suggested setting them on fire," the spokesman said. "And the next thing they were doing it."

Charles Scales, 38, his clothes totally burned off him, police said, died Sunday at Jackson Memorial Hospital. . . . Acting on Scales' description—before he died, he identified his attackers to police as neighborhood youths —homicide detectives rounded up the youths one by one Monday and charged them with first degree murder and two counts each of assault with intent to commit murder. . . . [The children had set fire to two other derelicts who had been able to douse the flames.]

Police Monday said all three youngsters have long records of petty larceny, burglary, narcotics possession, robbery, and vandalism. One, police said, was brought before juvenile authorities last month charged with setting fire to a dog. . . .

All three youngsters admitted their involvement to a probation officer, explaining that they had set fire to the three derelicts as a prank; they simply wanted to see the men's reactions when they woke up and found themselves on fire.

This absence of "affect," as psychiatrists call it, is the most frightening aspect of all. In the past, juveniles who exploded in violence tended to feel considerable guilt or remorse afterwards; the new criminals have been so brutalized in their own upbringing that they seem incapable of viewing their victims as fellow human beings, or of realizing that they have killed another person. "They seem to have no ability to distinguish between someone being shot in a movie and shooting someone themselves," a youth worker told a New York State Assembly subcommittee. "To them, everything is one big movie."

Increasingly, psychiatric reports on juveniles arrested for murder are filled with phrases such as "shows no feeling," "shows no remorse," "no discernible emotional reaction," and "demonstrates no relationship."

ITEM: From the transcript of a psychologist's interview of a fourteen-year-old who had murdered a woman by setting her on fire, in order to collect a $500 "commission":

Q. Did you have a good night's sleep?

A. Yeah.

Q. . . . In the morning, what happened then? How did you feel? What was your mood? Did you feel upset at all, after you had poured gasoline on the woman and she burned to a crisp?

A. No. She didn't burn to a crisp.

Q. She didn't burn to a crisp?

A. No. She lived for a week before she died. It was just like on every other day. . . .

Q. Did you ever cry afterwards?

A. No. To tell you the truth, I had no feeling after I did it.

Q. No feelings at all?

A. No, I forget all about it until they caught me.

The result seems to be a turn toward viciousness and sadism, as well as violence. Rather than wear masks or otherwise disguise themselves, some robbers prefer to kill or mutilate their victims in order to prevent being identified. "You know that glass I was drinking out of," a St. Louis, Missouri, robber told his friends, by way of explaining why he had blood on his pants. "I broke it and stabbed her eyes out. One thing about it she won't be looking at no pictures," i.e., at mug shots.[20] In a New York City robbery of a toy store, five youths handcuffed the owner while they emptied his cash register and then calmly shot him to death.

Other robbers kill or seriously injure their victims because that is the easiest way to control them.

ITEM (from the Washington *Post,* January 24, 1976):

Three teenagers, aged 13 to 16, were charged with murder yesterday in the fatal beating of Gladys Hinckley Werlick, 85, a matron of Washington society who fell victim January 13 to a gang allegedly on a rampage of purse-snatching and robbery near DuPont

Circle. The 85-year-old woman was mugged across the street from the house in which she had lived for seventy years. One of the assailants knocked her down with a karate chop in the knee, while another hit her over the head with a soda bottle; she died without regaining consciousness after being in a coma for five days with a fractured skull.

Revenge may also be a motive. Two fourteen-year-old boys, having been reported to the principal by a schoolmate whom they had been shaking down for money, enticed the youngster to the roof of his tenement and then threw him over the edge. (The boy's life was saved when he landed on a metal screen wedged between his building and the one adjoining it.)

The new breed of robber may also explode with fatal anger if his target of opportunity has too little money or, as sometimes happens, none at all. "I told him I didn't have any money," an impoverished itinerant worker from Florida (p. 16) recalled a day after he had been held up while sitting on a park bench in the Ellipse, behind the White House. "He took a step back and put two hands on the trigger. I told him I didn't have anything. He just went ahead and shot." The bullet entered at the bridge of the victim's nose and lodged behind his right eye, blinding him.

Street robbers may kill, too, if an impoverished victim is reluctant to hand over what he does have.

ITEM (from the New York *Times,* November 17, 1974):

A 35-year-old father of five young children was shot and killed yesterday while walking near his home in Cambria Heights, Queens, by two youths after he refused to give them 25 cents and his leather jacket, the police said.

The victim, Henry Heyward . . . was stopped by two youths in their 20's in a car near the intersection of 218th Street and 118th Avenue—not far from his home—at 12:30 a.m.

The men in the car asked him for 25 cents. He told them he had no money. Then they demanded his leather jacket with a rabbit fur collar. When he refused to hand over his coat, he was shot in the left shoulder. . . .

Mr. Heyward managed to walk to his house, where he told his sister-in-law, Grace Taylor, who also lives there, "I've been shot." He then collapsed. . . . Miss Taylor said that her brother-in-law was unemployed and did not have any money with him when he was killed.

"Such a cheap thing to kill a man for," she said.

III

For all the increase in violence, most crimes do not involve overt use of force. There are more than seven times as many burglaries as robberies each year, and twice as many larceny-thefts as burglaries. Given most robbers' impulsiveness and their tendency to select targets because of their availability and vulnerability, it should not be surprising to discover that robbery is far from being the only crime they commit. If robbers have any single characteristic in common, Andre Normandeau concluded after studying the prior records of all robbers arrested in Philadelphia between 1960 and 1966, it is that they are not particular about the kinds of crimes they commit. Only 10 percent of the robbers with an arrest record had specialized in robbery alone, although nearly 44 percent had at least one prior robbery arrest. Nearly twice as many had been arrested for burglary and other forms of theft. In short, robbers appear to be generalists rather than specialists—thieves who commit whatever crime seems opportune.[21]

This is particularly so in the case of juveniles, whose crimes follow such a random pattern that knowing how many offenses a youngster has committed and what kind provides no help in predicting his next offense.[22] The random pattern of juvenile crime reflects the nature of adolescence, which in American society tends to be a period of personal exploration and growth —a "psycho-social moratorium," as Erik Erikson terms it, involving a "search for something to be true to." Since they have not yet learned who they are, let alone decided what they want to be, most delinquents display neither the commitment to crime as a way of life nor the calculated rejection of the "straight" world that are the mark of the professional criminal. There are exceptions, of course; some juveniles are as devoted to crime and as contemptuous of conventional values as are their elders. But most delinquents live in what the sociologist David Matza calls a state of "drift," in which they have not yet committed themselves either to crime or to conformity.

Some delinquents turn to crime as a means of supplementing their families' meager incomes; parents for whom every day is a struggle to survive may make a point of not asking the source of the money their child contributes. More frequently, crime is a source of pocket money—the lower-class youngster's substitute for the middle-class adolescent's allowance. And without an allowance, from whatever source, adolescents cannot afford the clothes, records, and other expenditures that are required for acceptance by their peers. As I pointed out in the last chapter, membership in contemporary adolescent culture requires a high level of consumption.

All these factors may draw adolescents into crime. Indeed, some delinquents draw a sharp distinction between their "hustle" (the crimes designed to produce income) and what they do for, and as part of membership in, their gang. "Hustling activities tackle the problem of scarce money resources," Barry Krisberg, a sociologist who worked with Philadelphia gang members, has written; "gang activities focus on quite another scarce commodity in ghetto areas: social recognition and status." "You want respect. You want respect from this group right here," one of Krisberg's informants says. "Like, when you say you walking down the street, you know? You don't mess with me. Cause you know what'll happen. See, that's what all this gang warfare is all really about. . . . See, like, say 29th Street—they got respect. They got respect."[23]

Given these diverse motives, along with adolescents' impulsiveness and susceptibility to peer pressures, it is not surprising that juvenile crime tends to be both an individual and group activity, or that the activity takes such variegated forms. For delinquents, it may be a matter of indifference whether they hold someone up, "boost" (shoplift) merchandise from a store, grab money from a cash register, steal a camera or tape deck from a parked car (or steal the car itself), attack rivals who have impugned the honor of the group or one of its members, vandalize a school or other public facility, break into a warehouse to steal whatever might be available, take copper wire or plumbing from an abandoned building, break windows, set fires, "hustle" by acting as a prostitute for male homosexuals or by extorting money from homosexuals, "jack-roll" drunks, peddle narcotics, and so on. Which offense they commit may depend on where they are, whom they are with, how they feel, and what opportunities seem to be immediately available.

This same indifference and lack of commitment, however, means that even chronic delinquents may desist from crime as they mature. The approach of adulthood creates new alternatives for delinquents and makes existing legitimate alternatives seem more attractive. "Work, marriage, and other conventional adult statuses may be considered stupid or 'square,'" David Matza writes, "but they are obviously not kid stuff. To that extent they invite affiliation. . . ."

In the majority of cases, pairs of delinquents discover one after the other that they had shared misunderstandings. They had not really been committed to delinquency—it was fun and each thought that others demanded it, but *they* had never really believed in it.[24]

The most compelling reason for going straight is that young men fall in love and want to marry and have children; marriage and the family are the most effective correctional institutions we have. For married men, prison is a far more effective deterrent than it is for single men. And, prison aside, a stable marriage and family life are incompatible with a career in crime. "Most thieves are cross-roaders—they travel around so they can't have a family," Harry King, a professional "box man" (safe-cracker), explained to the criminologist William Chambliss. There are exceptions, of course, "but the average guy, you see, we don't associate with square-john broads. I mean there's too much explaining to do to a square-john broad."

More to the point, a criminal life style that once seemed attractive to the teenager or young adult begins to be seen in a much colder and more realistic light, with the glamour and excitement stripped away. "I remember sometimes hearing stories about good bars and pneumatic women, being told how we could go to these places and drink the good booze and groove on the groovy music and ball the pneumatic ladies," Bruce Jackson writes.

But behind the pretense lies an ugly reality. "Sometimes I went with some people when they were on the streets and found the attractions depressingly grubby," Jackson continues. "It *is* a grubby existence, as a rule. And after you sit there and drink with the other characters [criminals] and talk about the other people you know who have disappeared or are locked up or on the run or dead or perhaps even making it somewhere, there isn't much else to talk about, so everybody gets high on booze or pills or on grass and watches a pro football game someplace there is a color TV, or balls someone and *then* watches the pro football game on the color TV, or if there is no game and nothing else to talk about and you don't feel like balling anymore you drink or smoke or pill yourself insensate or even unconscious." In the underworld, Jackson found, people spend an extraordinary amount of time sleeping, sex tends to be completely lacking in affect, and the "kicks" never satisfy anyone for very long.[25]

When crime is viewed in this light, a legitimate job and conventional life style appear far more attractive than they seemed during adolescence. As delinquents begin to settle down, they make the startling discovery that honest work pays better than crime. To adolescents, crime appears to be easy, well-paying work; the reality is that few people have the talent to earn a good living from it.

A substantial minority of delinquents do *not* go straight. Some discover that they really *are* committed to crime, and they decide to fulfill their avocation; depending on their ability, they become what I have called professional or semiprofessional criminals.

Others, whose personalities may be too disorganized to commit themselves to anything, continue in a state of drift. These "disorganized criminals," as the criminologist John Irwin calls them, "pursue a chaotic, purposeless life, filled with unskilled, careless, and variegated criminal activity" as well as occasional stints at casual, unskilled labor.[26]

Understandably enough, disorganized criminals lack the skills to specialize in any crime, and their need for money forces them to utilize whatever opportunity is available; they remain "jack-of-all-trades offenders." "Well, you know, some time I thought about the big time," one of Julian Roebuck's informants told him. "You got to work hard at one kind of game for that. I had to have quick bread, though, all my life. I had to get what I could get. You know, any way I could get it. I grew up in the bottom with the small hustlers. The Cadillac boys didn't have nothing to do with us." He did apply for a steady job with a "numbers man" he knew on a number of occasions, but was turned down each time. "He say, 'Man, what you talking about? You just don't have the class for the numbers.'"

> "I say, 'Well, I can learn.' He say, 'Hell, man, you been arrested for every petty crime in the book. You been locked up too much. All the cops know you too good. You got jail fever.' He say I should put the life down and get me a lunch pail [a legitimate job]. I guess he was right. Here I am in the joint again. I just couldn't settle down to no one type of hustle. Some small scores and many busts is the story of my life. I'm a jack-of-all-trades and no master of none."[27]

Some criminals do become masters of a particular criminal trade. Successful robbers require talent at organization and planning, as well as the capacity to persuade victims to cooperate. Big-time burglars need considerable electrical and, increasingly, electronic

know-how in order to circumvent or thwart burglar-
alarm systems, and if they are "box men" as well, they
need mechanical expertise and knowledge of explosives
in order to open safes. Pickpockets, check forgers, confidence men, and grifters need "grift (or larceny)
sense" to spot an easy and profitable mark, and wit
and "front" to relieve the mark of his money.

Given these skills, professionals understandably prefer to commit their crime of choice when opportunity
permits, and they tend to view their specialty as superior to all others. Career robbers take pride in the
open, direct way they go about their stealing, in contrast to the furtiveness and stealth of burglars, shoplifters, pickpockets, confidence men and other "light"
thieves. "I didn't *talk* him out of it—I *took* it off him,"
a robber proudly told the criminologist Ned Polksy
about one of his scores. "I never thought about writing
checks or stealing," another robber told Werner Einstadter, "somehow, I don't know—this will sound
funny, but it just never seemed honest. . . . I just
couldn't steal anything. You know—behind someone's
back."[28]

Light thieves, on the other hand, view robbers (and
sometimes burglars) as unskilled "heavies" who use
brute force instead of intelligence and wit. "Robbery,
at best, was a desperate measure, attractive only to men
who had no significant talent for anything else," one
of the figures in Malcolm Braly's prison novel, *On The
Yard,* muses to himself. "This is the highest form of
character that you can have," a Texas thief observes,
"to be able to use intellectual means rather than physical violence to obtain money."

Burglars and safe-crackers prefer their line of work
because its anonymity reduces the chances of being
caught for any given crime. "Burglary in the long run
is safer," an old-time thief says. "You'll get away with

a hundred burglaries where you'll get away with five stick-ups"; and indeed the proportion of crimes solved is a good bit lower for burglary than for robbery. As a "box man" explains, "There is more of a chance of identifying a man who sticks up the place. They just go down and get so many mugs, take them out there and chances are he'll be identified among those pictures. But a safe man, he comes in the middle of the night and leaves in the middle of the night, nobody sees him."[29] Understandably enough, these preferences tend to reflect differences in personality and cultural backgrounds. Robbers tend to be verbally as well as physically aggressive and self-confident, while burglars are more likely to be retiring and withdrawn.

Although these likes and dislikes help shape criminal careers, it is the rare criminal who can allow himself to indulge his preferences completely. Just as few lawyers can afford to take only the cases that excite them, few criminals can afford to limit themselves to just one kind of crime. "You know, it's a hard thing to steal for a living," a thief remarks. "When you're stealing for a living that means you're out every day. And you're not going to run into gravy every day of the week."

Thus, to support themselves, career criminals are alert to potentially profitable scores outside their own specialty—all the more so since some criminal skills are easily transferable from one kind of offense to another. "Over and over, when we asked professional criminals what they did," Leroy Gould and a team of criminologists who studied professional crime for the 1967 Crime Commission reported, "they would answer, 'I hustle.' "

To "hustle" in this sense is "to be persistently on the lookout for an opportunity to make an illegal buck." For run-of-the-mill criminals, in particular, it means "moving around the bars and being seen; it means finding out what's up."

It means "connecting" in the morning with other individuals who have a burglary set up for the evening, calling a man to see if he wants to buy ten stolen alpaca sweaters at five bucks each, scouting the streets for a "mark" who can be "paddy hustled," and maybe all these things in a single day. Tomorrow it means more of the same. It means being versatile: passing checks, rolling a drunk, driving for a stick-up, boosting a car, "hitting" a store window. It is a planless kind of existence—but with a purpose—to make as much money as can be found, no holds barred. "You can't pass up money; it just isn't right." We heard this phrase or one like it many times. Professional criminals, we were assured, rarely pass up a good "touch."[30]

There are a handful of criminals who are above this seamy life—but only a handful, and seemingly only in the largest cities. Gould and his colleagues discovered that in Chicago and New York, but not Atlanta or San Francisco, some highly skilled professional thieves earn $100,000 a year or more. In both cities, too, groups of thieves with ties to organized crime have the ability to pull off hijacking jobs and warehouse thefts involving hundreds of thousands of dollars each. These thieves are so successful and so well organized that they do not have to hustle; they delegate the responsibility for finding appropriate targets to group members who constitute a criminal "new business" department. And, as happens with succesful entrepreneurs in any field, profitable business opportunities are brought to them with some frequency.

Apart from this tiny elite, criminals must hustle if they are to prosper or even survive. Successful criminals may be able to go days or weeks (in rare cases, months) between scores, and thus may be able to turn down opportunities that seem too risky or that they simply find distasteful. But they are not likely to remain criminals for very long—and certainly not successful criminals—if they are not always on the lookout for opportunities in a variety of criminal fields.

Indeed, success itself seems to require versatility; to specialize too narrowly is to miss too many profitable opportunities. Gould and his colleagues cite as a typical professional criminal an armed robber who has also been involved in safe-cracking, passing checks, and a variety of con games and other "scams," as well as acting as an armed guard (for a $150 fee) for burglar teams. John Allen thinks of himself as an armed robber, too, but he also worked as a heroin dealer and as a pimp. The professional burglars studied by Neil Shover had been involved in armed robbery, strong-arm robbery, hijacking, shoplifting, auto theft, picking pockets, passing bad checks, and dealing in stolen merchandise. The most successful burglars, Shover found, had committed a wider variety of crimes than their less competent colleagues.[31]

The changing economics of theft requires diversification. In the past, a professional "box man" might have been able to stick to opening safes because business firms and banks kept large sums of money on hand. In today's economy, transactions are completed through transfers of credit rather than of cash; since there are banks with night depositories on almost every corner, most firms deposit their cash receipts at the end of each day rather than keep them in a safe. (During their busy season, retail stores may make deposits several times a day.) Individuals, too, keep less cash in their wallets and hidden away at home than they

used to, except for crooked doctors, lawyers, and other
self-employed people who may hide unreported cash
income in a wall safe in their bedroom or den. (Self-
employed professionals and businessmen comprise
about two-thirds of all those prosecuted for income tax
fraud.)

One consequence is that virtually every burglar and
safe-cracker, not to mention every pickpocket, purse-
snatcher, and robber, now is in the check and credit
card business, too. In the past, most burglars did not
even think of looking for checks, and those who did
usually would sell them to other criminals who had
mastered the art of forgery. (Forgers were thought to
be a breed apart.) But the growing use of personal,
business, and payroll checks has sharply lowered the
technical barriers to forgery, making it much easier
to pass stolen checks. And the exponential increase in
the number of credit cards and the uses to which they
can be put has opened criminal possibilities that an
earlier generation could not have imagined, let alone
taken advantage of. Although street criminals generally
sell the checks and credit cards they acquire, seasoned
professional and semiprofessional criminals are more
likely to pass the checks and cards themselves. (An
interesting side effect has been to stimulate an active
traffic in stolen driver's licenses, Social Security cards,
and other identification papers that make it easier to
pass stolen credit cards and checks.)

A variety of factors have transformed bank robbery
from a crime committed almost entirely by professionals to one committed mainly by amateurs. Because
bank robbery is now a federal crime, professionals
have largely abandoned the field; with the FBI investigating most bank robberies and U.S. attorneys handling the prosecuting, the risk of being caught, convicted, and imprisoned is too high for thoughtful profes-

sionals to bear.* (The FBI reports that it makes an arrest in 80 percent of the cases over which it has jurisdiction; 85 precent of the defendants brought to federal court for bank robbery are convicted, with 90 percent of them drawing a prison term averaging more than ten years.) [32]

Opportunist robbers have more than filled the vacuum left by professionals; the number of bank robberies shot up 74 percent in 1972–76 alone. The reason is simple: changes in the location of banks, as well as in their architecture, have substantially reduced the amount of planning needed to pull off a bank robbery. It is much easier to scoop up the money from tellers' drawers in a modern bank, with its low, open counters, than it was in the banks of a generation ago, where tellers stood behind metal cages. And the getaway is a lot faster and easier in suburban drive-in banks, located in shopping centers or near parkways, than it was (or is) in downtown locations, where a robber may be stalled in traffic.

The growth of consumer spending on portable durable goods has made residential burglary something of a growth industry. Before World War II, only the well-to-do had items in their homes worth stealing; today, even poor people's homes may contain black-and-white or color television sets, stereo equipment, tape recorders and portable radios, cameras and projectors, electric razors, ten-speed bicycles, and so on. With clothing an important status symbol among the young, especially among young males, small clothing stores as well as homes have become attractive targets.

* The federal government has jurisdiction over the robbery of any bank whose deposits are insured by the Federal Deposit Insurance Corporation; only a handful of small country banks are *not* insured by the FDIC. (Savings and loan association deposits are insured by another federal agency.)

And thefts of cameras, tape decks, and other merchandise from parked cars have increased steadily.

The extraordinary increase in the number of automobiles on the road has converted auto theft from a juvenile prank into one of the largest and most lucrative criminal industries. In most major cities, criminals who operate behind the façade of a used-car lot or body shop engage independent groups of thieves to steal cars for them on demand, specifying the make and model and year of the car or cars they want. Cars may be stolen for resale, or so that they can be stripped for specific parts that have been ordered by "legitimate" body shops and service stations whose owners want to increase their profit margins. "The phone never stops ringing," says a New York City dealer. ". . . I'm on call from at least fifty legit collision shops who know I can supply them with parts for their repair jobs; they never ask no questions, they just want the part supplied. And I am one great supplier."[33]

The more an individual is immersed in crime, the more criminal opportunities are likely to come his way. Just as construction workers, longshoremen, and other casual laborers "shape up" at a hiring hall, dock, or other site, so street criminals and semiprofessionals hang around particular bars, taverns, cafeterias, take-out food stores, pool halls, bowling alleys, gambling joints, after-hours clubs, luncheonettes, or street corners, waiting for something to turn up—whether it be a job from a professional criminal or a chance to hustle a noncriminal mark who also patronizes the establishment. Professional criminals know where to look if they need someone to drive a getaway car or steal it in the first place, to act as "point man" (lookout) for a burglary or robbery, to boost merchandise or steal a car on order, to peddle narcotics or make a buy, or to kill or injure someone against whom they have a

grudge. "It only costs half a yard [$50] to get some-
body's legs broken," one of William West's Toronto
informants told him. "Lay you up for five months. I
know guys around the pool hall who'll do that." (In
Philadelphia, Barry Krisberg found, the price was only
$10.)

Professional criminals are likely to have their own
hangouts. "The bars along 48th and 49th from 6th
to 8th Avenues are to me what the golf and country
clubs are to the execs," a Brooklyn-born professional
thief told James Inciardi. "That's where we do *our*
business, where we meet key people, and where we
relax. Whenever you get in town you know where you
need to go and each of us has our favorites. They are
the only places on earth where I feel free to talk to
my own kind." "This joint's really too rich for a steady
diet," a thief in another city remarks about an expensive after-hours club that is patronized by swinging
"square johns," "night people" (entertainers, musi-
cians, night club owners and managers), police and
politicians on the take, call girls, and "businessmen,"
i.e., organized crime executives, as well as professional
thieves. "But it's a swell place to be if you want to go
first class. . . . In here, you can find out what's going
on all over town—who's scoring, who ain't. Who's
busted and who's about to get busted. And you get a
line on different kinds of jobs."[34]

To succeed in crime, in short, or merely to obtain
steady employment, a criminal has to "make connections." An "old boy" network is as important to a
criminal as it is to a diplomat, banker, or lawyer. Neighborhood ties forged during adolescent play a role in
creating such networks, as does membership in a juvenile gang; for some ethnic groups, kinship relationships
are critically important.

For large number of criminals, prison is where the

most important connections of all are made; prison plays much the same role in creating "old boy" networks for criminals that prep school or college does for diplomats and businessmen. Although offenders may pick up technical skills while serving time, such learning is far less important than the contacts that facilitate criminal activity when they are released.

IV

Prison is the criminal's alma mater because, sooner or later, almost everyone who persists in crime gets caught. "Of course we got busted. We were at it four years to the month," one of the Bobbsey Twins told Bruce Jackson, with evident pride in the length of time they had gone without a conviction. They avoided prison for so long, the other partner explained, because they took such great pains to avoid injuring anyone, especially policemen, and to avoid putting the police department in an embarrassing position—for example, by holding up a government official or prominent citizen. "As long as it's a straight holdup and nobody gets hurt and nobody's feathers are ruffled, they don't bug you about it," i.e., the police do not go all out to catch you for any particular crime. They don't have to: "They know that you're not going to quit and that they'll get you eventually."[35]

The belief that "they'll get you eventually" is not unique to the Bobbsey Twins; it is firmly embedded in the folk wisdom of criminal subcultures. "If you want to play, you have to pay," criminals in every part of the United States told me. Older criminals seem to prefer the maxim "If you can't do the time, don't do the crime." One professional expressed the same idea in a jauntier and more upbeat manner: "Everyone has to take a vacation now and then," he told me. "I take mine at government expense."

This is not to suggest that criminals look forward to doing time, only that they take it for granted as part of their way of life. "I didn't fear punishment because I knew I could handle it," John Allen remarks. Being able to handle punishment is essential in his world, because "anybody with anything on the ball knows that regardless of what you're doing, eventually you're going" to jail.

For the career criminal, doing time is simply an unavoidable cost of doing business. "I don't like it. But it was one of the necessary things about the life I had chosen," Harry King responded when William Chambliss asked him whether he had minded spending time in prison. "Do you like to come here and teach this class?" (He was addressing Chambliss' criminology seminar at the time.) "I bet if these students had their wishes they'd be somewhere else, maybe out stealing, instead of sitting in this dumpy room," he continued. "But they do it because it gets them something else they want. The same with me. If I had to go to prison from time to time, well, that was the price you pay. On the other hand, I could buy new Cadillacs and $200 suits when I had found a fat mark. How often do you do that, doctor?"[36]

To assert that almost everyone gets caught is to run counter to the conventional wisdom among criminologists, which holds that only incompetent offenders are arrested and convicted, and that prison inmates thus are not representative of the criminal population as a whole. Since most crimes are unsolved, the reasoning goes, there must be a great many highly skilled criminals who operate with impunity. Superficially, at least, the crime statistics seem to support this view. In 1976, according to the *Uniform Crime Report,* police departments "cleared" by arrest 27 percent of the robberies reported to them, 17 percent of the burglaries, and 19 percent of the larceny-thefts. Since Census Bureau surveys of crime victims indicate that only about half of all robberies, less than half of all burglaries, and about one-fourth of all larcenies are reported to the police, the actual clearance rates are much lower.

But clearance rates relate arrests to the number of *crimes,* not the number of criminals. Since career criminals generally commit considerably more than one crime a year, clearance rates obviously understate the proportion of criminals who are arrested each year. And since clearance rates are annual figures, while criminal careers span a number of years, the figures tell us almost nothing about the proportion of criminals who are arrested over the course of their careers. Some offenders may be so inept that they are caught and convicted every time they break the law, but such people are in a distinct minority. As one of the Bobbsey Twins says, "there are crimes that are pulled and got away with, but one man might have pulled twenty armed robberies before he's caught, so they got him on one and there's nineteen unsolved. *Statistics-wise it looks like everybody's getting away, but actually they're not.*" [emphasis added]

The Bobbsey Twins were more successful than most criminals, even most professionals; Edward Bunker, a prison inmate-turned-novelist, writes that by thief underworld standards success is measured by "how long the run of victories rather than the eventual fall, which is considered inevitable." A group of Utah offenders with whom I talked may be more typical of professional criminals as a group. One man had committed ten burglaries before his first arrest; another had been selling marijuana in bulk for nine months before he was caught with 300 pounds in his possession; a woman thief had been stealing for a year and a half before she was caught; and so it went. The most successful (and most hardened) criminal in the group had committed twenty-four burglaries and robberies before his first arrest, which he managed to beat on the grounds of entrapment. This man was contemptuous of the Salt Lake City police—"they're so bad they have to entrap in order to catch you"—and of most prosecutors as well—"I'm usually smarter than they are." But he also believes, as do his colleagues, that "in the end, everyone gets caught." "I don't care how good you are; you'll end up in the slammer sooner or later," he insists. "The law of averages is against you." Indeed it is. Although a robber has less than a 20 percent chance of being arrested on any one offense, the criminologist Daniel Glaser has calculated, he has a 90 percent chance of being arrested at least once if he commits ten robberies, and the odds go up to 99 percent by the twenty-first offense.[37]

Indeed, none of the criminals I interviewed knew, or had ever heard of, anyone who had been a criminal for any length of time without having been imprisoned. The same was true of the robbers studied by John Conklin in Boston, Werner Einstadter in California, and Floyd Feeney and Adrianne Weir in Oakland; the Illinois burglars studied by Neil Shover; the check forgers studied by Edwin Lemert in California and elsewhere; the young Toronto thieves studied by William West; and the robbers, safe-crackers, burglers, boosters, and thieves from various parts of Canada studied by Peter Letkemann. (Clearance rates are about the same in Canada as they are in the United States; hence criminal experience can be presumed to be comparable.)

Every criminal to whom Leroy Gould and his colleagues spoke in their study of professional crime for
the Crime Commission had done at least some time in
prison or jail, and the thieves, robbers, and assorted
criminals whose lives Bruce Jackson describes in such
vivid detail have all spent time in prison. On the basis
of analysis of the American and Canadian crimino-
logical literature, together with his own field experiences, William West estimates that professional criminals spend a quarter to a third of their careers in jail
or prison, while run-of-the-mill criminals (opportun-
ists and semiprofessionals) are incarcerated two-thirds
to three-quarters of the time.*[38]

It is possible that some criminals do manage to elude
detection altogether; the fact that police, along with
criminals who *have* been caught, do not know any
criminals who have *not* been caught does not, by itself,
constitute proof that such people do not exist. "If there
were such," a safe-cracker told Peter Letkemann, "I

---

* The belief that able criminals are able to remain outside
the clutches of the law gained such strength because, for a long
time, American criminologists took at face value what professional criminals had to say about the efficacy of "the fix," i.e.,
the ability to avoid arrest or to get charges dropped through
bribery and/or personal or political influence. The classic statement of this faith in the fix is contained in E. H. Sutherland's
seminal volume *The Professional Thief,* which shaped criminologists' thinking for at least thirty years after its publication
in 1937. "If a thief is to make a profession of stealing, it is
necessary that he keep out of the penitentiary," Chic Conwell,
Sutherland's protagonist, declares. "There is no one who cannot be influenced if you go at it right and have sufficient backing, financially and politically." But criminologists who took
Conwell's statement at face value ignored the fact, which Sutherland himself dutifully noted in his introduction, that Conwell
served three terms in federal and state penitentiaries, as well as
several shorter terms in local jails. Thus the man who served as
the prototype of the professional criminal's ability to stay *out*
of prison through his use of the fix in reality spent about one-
third of his criminal career *in* prison.

wouldn't know about them because if they never got caught, how would you know? But any of the ones I ever knew, they all done time at one time or another."

It is easy to understand why almost everyone gets caught; as the journalist-novelist Jimmy Breslin has written, quoting an underworld figure he calls "the Great Fats Thomas," "Ninety percent of the people in crime don't belong in it because they're no good at it." The most obvious manifestation of incompetence is the failure to plan, or even to think about, ways of avoiding capture. Over half the robbers interviewed by Feeney and Weir said they had given no thought at all to getting caught; half of the remainder had concluded that there would be no problem and thus had made no contingency plans.

The failure to plan or think about escape often leads to blunders that would be comic if the crimes in question were not so serious.

ITEM: A pair of armed bank robbers park in front of a bank, jump out of the car and dash to the doors, only to find that they are locked; they had chosen a bank holiday for their robbery.

ITEM: A robber who had planned the holdup of a tavern told his accomplices to herd the tavern's customers into the basement. Not having cased the tavern, he did not know that the basement had a back door through which the customers were able to flee and call the police. Thus the robbers, who netted only $175 (they had expected to find between $4,000 and $8,000 in the register), were still sitting in their stalled getaway car, trying to get it started, when the police arrived.[39]

Being unable to start the getaway car is a fairly common reason for robbers being caught; Feeney and Weir report a number of such cases. Getaway cars lead to capture in other ways. In one instance, a pair of robbers borrowed their getaway car from a friend without knowing the car was stolen. They were stopped by the police after their third robbery of the evening; when they couldn't produce the car's registration papers, they were arrested on suspicion of having stolen the car, and only later on were connected with the robberies. In four instances that Feeney and Weir encountered, robbers used their victims' cars for their getaways and were arrested several hours later, when the police had descriptions of the stolen cars.

Robbers can be careless in other ways. In a case I observed in a New York City court, two men were accused of holding up a commuter bus with a pistol and a sawed-off shotgun. After relieving the driver and passengers of their money, watches, jewelry, and other valuables, they order to driver to stop at a specified parkway exit, ran to a blue Pontiac parked near the exit, and drove away. But the robbers had not covered or changed the license plate; several passengers were able to read part of the license number as the men drove away. Three months later, one of the robbers was caught sitting in the Pontiac; he was carrying a watch that had been reported stolen in the robbery, as well as a .25 automatic handgun resembling the one used to hold up the passengers. A palm print on the newspaper in which the shotgun had been wrapped tied him to the robbery more directly; he had tossed the newspaper aside when he brandished the gun. (He had also fired the shotgun accidentally during the robbery, impairing his own hearing for a time.)

This list of blunders is almost endless: dropping merchandise while shoplifting; making noise during a burglary; driving over the speed limit during the getaway; leaving the keys to the getaway car on the counter of a store during a robbery; using one's own name to endorse and cash a stolen money order; holding up people who know one's identity without bothering to use a disguise. In one instance, a robber held up the front desk of a hotel where he had been employed as a desk clerk; in another, a robber held up the bank in which he had been depositing the proceeds from other bank robberies.

Frequently, robbers are arrested when they hang around the site of a robbery or return to it at a later time. "We just didn't figure the police would come around the corner into Jiffy's looking for the dudes that did it," John Allen says, recalling an instance in which three friends were arrested in their hangout near a drugstore they had held up. John McDonald describes three incidents of the same sort.

ITEM: Two robbers hold up a man outside a tavern, then go inside to have a leisurely drink; the victim calls the police, who find the men inside the tavern, where they are easily identified.

ITEM: A pair of robbers who fled the scene of robbery after stabbing and seriously injuring their victim return thirty minutes later to look for their victim's pocketbook, which had been dropped during the struggle.

ITEM: A young man brings a pair of slacks to a laundry to be cleaned, and returns ten minutes later to demand the contents of the cash register at gunpoint. A month later, another young man returns with the claim check for the trousers; the clerk, seeing that the robber is sitting in his parked car outside, waiting for his friend, calls the police, who arrive in time to make the arrest.

Even professional criminals make careless mistakes; on one occasion, James Earl Ray was caught when he drove the wrong way down a one-way street. The tension criminals feel before or during a crime may account for some of the blunders. "All the time you are stealing I don't think you ever relax," one of Shover's burglars explains. "At night, whenever we'd go out," Bruce Jackson's Sam reports, "before we made the first one, I'm scared, I'm scared to death. But after I get in there and make the first one, all my fear leaves and I get maybe too careless. Then I think I'm invincible, and I'd walk up in broad daylight if I wanted to do something."

To reduce their tension and control their fear, many criminals drink or use drugs before going out on a job. "People underestimate the importance of alcohol," a professional burglar told me. "I never went out on even the simplest burglary without a drink under my belt. Make that a few drinks," he added by way of correction. But whereas liquor and drugs fortify the nerves, they also muddy the judgment, leading to carelessness during the theft or getaway—speeding, for example, or going through a red light, or (frequently) getting into an auto accident. "It's amazing I didn't kill someone, I was so liquored up most of the time," another criminal told me.

Because the tension is so great, especially in the early stages of a criminal career, criminals adopt a bravado they do not really feel, forcing all thoughts of capture out of their minds. Unless they suppress their fears, they will be too tense to caper. "Don't ask me about my doubts. That will only hang me up," a street mugger tells his biographer. "If I'm gonna survive—a motherfuckin' outlaw, man!—I have to be cool."[40]

Like people in other dangerous occupations, such as soldiers, racing car drivers, and professional boxers, criminals try to allay their fears through recourse to superstitious rituals and rites—carrying a rabbit's foot or other talisman, wearing the same shirt on every caper or eating the same meal beforehand, and so on. Like soldiers, too, criminals steel their will through a belief in fate. If fate is on your side, nothing can go wrong; if fate is against you, you haven't got a chance.[41]

Belief in fate serves another function: it relieves the criminal of personal responsibility for what happens to him or his victims. Fate also relieves the criminal of any need to feel guilty that he did not plan more carefully or exercise greater caution during the crime. If it is just a matter of bad luck, then it is nobody's fault that things went wrong; success was not in the cards.

By the same token, a few successes may be enough to persuade criminals that fate is with them, and that they really *are* invincible. "The first time I did it, see, I was just going along with E and C," one of William West's informants recalled.

"They said, 'Hey, you want to come? We gonna pull a score.' I went and I was scared out of my mind—paranoid. Then we got it down to a routine. We'd case the place, set it up, leave our tools hidden and meet at a place, then just hit it, and split. *Afterwards, it was just like going to work. Nothing to it, no sweat.*" [emphasis added]

This sense that "there's nothing to it" encourages criminals to continue. "Anyone who does two banks and he succeeds going all through and he has no police suspicion on him," a Canadian bank robber remarks, "he becomes overconfident, you know. You say, 'Well, now I'm a master criminal and I know how to do it. They didn't catch me, they're not aware that I'm working on it, and everything goes smoothly—it will

work forever like that.' " "Yeah, we thought we'd go
on indefinitely and not get caught," a California robber
says. "I think this is everybody's feeling—that they'll
never get caught."[42]

Given the multiple rationalizations with which criminals (like the rest of us) live, the fact that others have
been caught tends to be dismissed as evidence that they
didn't know what they were doing. "When someone
else was arrested," a reformed burglar told me, "I just
told myself I wouldn't make that kind of stupid mistake. And I didn't; I made my own kind of stupid mistake." But as the novelist Malcolm Braly, who served
a number of prison terms before going straight, has
written, "The police can afford dozens of mistakes;
[criminals] get only one."[43]

Professional criminals often feel the need to test
themselves by pulling off particularly difficult scores.
If nothing else, they are men who are fulfilled, rather
than alienated, by their work. "There are few enough
places in the world today where a man can find real
frontiers and sure enough adventure, where he can
gamble his wits and freedom against a powerful and
implacable authority," one professional says of the
appeal of crime; "few enough ways to lift himself above
the banality of a commuter culture or to relieve himself of the burden of pretending to be honest."[44] Given
this point of view, it is not surprising that professionals
sometimes are so carried away by the challenge of
crime that they take too many risks or fail to take the
necessary precautions.

It is the rare criminal, in any case, who quits while
he is ahead; as Chic Conwell, the thief in E. H. Sutherland's *The Professional Thief,* remarks, "the thief refuses to think seriously about his ultimate end. There
is no serious discussion or consideration of the future."
Thieves' conversation, to be sure, is filled with talk

about the big score that will enable them to retire; but as Conwell says, "this ambition to get the big one and retire is very vague."[45]

The talk is vague because most criminals know that they will blow whatever score they make in short order. "A thousand-dollar rip-off means you can relax a while, right?" the writer James Willwerth asks the mugger he calls Jones. "Oh, no!" Jones replies. "I go through it in three or four days. I buy clothes, I go out, I get high. I get shoes, or a knit, or slacks—I get a lot of things I don't need."

> "You just live while the money's there; that's the rule of the street. . . . When I've got money, I don't sleep for three or four days—you're just *buying* something all the time. If you've got the money that easy and that fast, it doesn't have any value."

Most professional criminals behave the same way. "I never really went into the things I wanted to get into," John Allen reflects. "I just kept spending everything as soon as I got it"—on clothes, cars, gambling, and partying. "The average box man doesn't save any money," Harry King told Bill Chambliss. "I had a partner that anytime we'd make a score, he'd fly to Reno and three days later he's broke. We're all suckers for somethin', I guess." Criminals are always broke after a big score, Bruce Jackson's Sam explains, because they feel the need to "high play."

For criminals, too, as for the rest of us, success creates a desire for more and more income. To satisfy their rising expectations, criminals go for bigger and bigger scores (or more and more frequent capers), defying the law of averages until they are caught. It takes extraordinary good fortune for a frequent criminal *not* to be caught. The Bobbsey Twins had an unusually long "run" without a conviction; the run was ended because of a mistake on the part of the FBI. Assuming, incorrectly, that the Twins were responsible for a bank robbery (they had stayed away from bank robbery precisely because it was a federal crime), the FBI began an intensive search for them, distributing photographs and descriptions to police departments around the country. A rookie policeman who had read the flier that morning recognized the license plate as the men were driving through Kansas City and made the arrest after calling for reinforcements. If the Twins had not built up so many "negative credits" in California, Jackson guesses, the FBI might not have pursued them quite so avidly.

If a bad break does not lead to a criminal's capture, chances are that an informer will. Although professional criminals pay lip service to "The Code" (Never squeal), few observe it in practice. On the contrary, criminals take it for granted that their friends and accomplices will inform on them if arrested; as the saying goes, the first one to tell his story gets the lightest sentence.

Professionals also know that there is a steady flow of information from the underworld to the police. And yet this knowledge does not inhibit them from celebrating a good score; as one safe-cracker puts it, "What's the point of scoring if nobody knows about it?" The need to talk involves more than just braggadocio; being known to other criminals is essential if one is to find (or be offered) work, and criminals also rely on their peers for information about which particular fence needs a particular kind of merchandise, which part of the city is "hot" for a particular crime, and so on.

To get information, detectives (and patrolmen, to a lesser degree) usually frequent the same restaurants, bars, bowling alleys, and other hangouts that professional criminals patronize. Being known to one's criminal peers thus means, almost by definition, that a criminal will be known to the police as well, a fact that troubles criminals less than one might think. The professional criminal does not mind the police knowing that he is responsible for a particular caper, Peter Letkemann argues, so long as they do not have the evidence needed to convict. (Police are known to "set up" a criminal when they lack the evidence, but that's another matter.) On some level, Letkemann suggests, the professional criminal *wants* the police to know about his scores because he is eager for them to think well of his craftsmanship. Other than his fellow criminals, the police are the only ones capable of evaluating, and consequently admiring, his professional talent.[46]

Arrest is almost inevitable, therefore, even if conviction is not. And arrest, in turn, unleashes a chain of events that makes further arrests more likely. It is the rare criminal who puts money aside to pay the costs associated with arrest; "if they had any money," Sam explains, "they wouldn't be out stealing, they'd be partying. It's as simple as that." Thus an arrest places a criminal in a severe financial bind. He needs substantial amounts of money in order to put up bail and hire a lawyer; and since most criminal lawyers insist on being paid in advance, he has to borrow from a "juice man," whose exorbitant interest rates may double or triple the amount that has to be repaid.*

With his debt increasing day by day, a criminal has no alternative but to commit additional crimes. Be-

---

* Street criminals usually have no choice but to use a court-appointed lawyer or a public defender. Although public defenders frequently are more competent than private lawyers, most criminals prefer to hire their own lawyer if they possibly can; believing as they do that "you only get what you pay for," they are convinced that a lawyer paid by the defendant will always outperform one paid by the government.

cause of his desperation, he must violate the underworld dictum never to steal when you have to—a dictum based on the knowledge that, under the pressure of necessity, professional criminals will take risks they would eschew under ordinary circumstances. The result is to increase the probabilities of being caught again.

Impulsive street criminals are caught far more frequently than are professionals. Some do not bother taking any precautions at all; seeing themselves as born losers, they take it for granted that things will go bad for them no matter what they do. "Man, it don't matter how good things are goin' for me," one of John Irwin's informants told him. "You know, I may have a nice little job and everything running along smooth and I'll fuck it up, I'll fuck it up somehow. I always do. . . . I've been fucking it up for so long that it's always going to be like that."[47]

Criminals who feel this way often seem to arrange their own capture. After talking to many of them, and reading an even larger number of case histories, I found it hard to avoid concluding that many criminals arrange their own capture. It is equally hard to avoid concluding that they do so because, on some level, they feel they are "bad" and should be punished, or because they want someone to stop them from doing the terrible things they keep doing. One youngster I met in California had held up a gas station in his own neighborhood without wearing a mask or disguising himself in any way; a few hours later, he stopped by in his car to get a tankful of gas, at which time he was arrested. Another offender had broken into a penny arcade that fronted on a busy thoroughfare; after taking what money he could find, he proceeded to play the pinball machines until the police arrived. A third youngster, nineteen or twenty years old, whom I visited in jail, had been arrested a month or two before he was due to go off parole, for stealing the tires off a car parked in front of its owner's home. Lest anyone not know that he was there, he dropped his steel wrench on the pavement a few times, making a loud clanging noise; when the owner came outside to see what was happening, the young offender pulled a gun on him, thereby converting a possible misdemeanor into a certain felony charge, and then walked away. The police arrested him several blocks from the scene, still walking.

Older ex-offenders who have gone straight and who seem to be "making it" on the outside often do the same sort of thing just as everything seems to be falling into place for them. In one instance I encountered, an ex-offender hired by a government agency had been rising steadily within the lower ranks of the organization; a few days after being promoted to a job with a good salary and considerable responsibility, he was arrested for stealing fifty-nine cents' worth of chicken bones in a supermarket.

What happens in such cases, it would seem, is that the ex-offenders' lives and personalities have been organized around failure for so long that they become terrified, almost paralyzed, by the prospect of success. "I've been locked up all my life anyway," a character in *No Beast So Fierce,* Edward Bunker's novel about criminal life, declares. "The food's okay in the pen and I can play handball. I've got more fuckin' troubles when I'm out than when I'm in."[48] Bunker knew what he was writing about; until recently, his life imitated his art. He was paroled in April 1972 after W. W. Norton had accepted his novel and *Harper's* magazine had used an article of his as its lead story. Two months later, Bunker was arrested when he and a friend tried to hold up a bank while narcotics agents were tailing them. "I don't know why I was out robbing banks," he wrote a reporter-friend. "Conditioned reflexes, maybe?" Sentenced to five years in federal prison, Bunker was paroled again in December 1976. Since then, he has worked on the movie version of his first novel, starring Dustin Hoffman, and has published a second novel; a third novel is in the works.

4

Poverty and Crime

"I really think there's a lot of similarity between the people who live out in the middle-class neighborhoods and the people I know. . . . Everybody wants to have their own joint, own their own home, and have two cars. It's just that we are going about it in a different way. I think keeping up with the Joneses is important everywhere."

—JOHN ALLEN, ARMED ROBBER

". . . vice and crime constitute a 'normal' response to a situation where the cultural emphasis upon pecuniary success has been absorbed, but where there is little access to conventional and legitimate means for becoming successful. . . . In this setting, a cardinal American virtue, 'ambition,' produces a cardinal American vice, 'deviant behavior.'"

—ROBERT K. MERTON, SOCIOLOGIST

"Sounds like you've got to have a master's degree in math to understand all that."
"Nope. You just gotta be poor to understand."

—CONVERSATION BETWEEN A WASHINGTON *Post* REPORTER AND A "NUMBERS" OPERATOR

I

Why are violent criminals drawn so heavily from the ranks of the poor? The answer lies not in the genes, but in the nature of the lives poor people lead and of the communities in which they reside. The close association of violent crime with urban lower-class life is a direct result of the opportunities that are *not* available. Psychological factors may help explain why some individuals turn to street crime and others do not. But the question posed in this chapter is not why particular individuals choose a life of crime and violence; it is why the people who make that choice are concentrated more heavily in the lower class than in the middle or working class.

Children growing up in urban slums and ghettos face a different set of choices than do youngsters growing up in middle-class neighborhoods, and they have a radically different sense of what life offers. By the time children are six or eight years old, their view of the world has been shaped by their surroundings and by their parents' as well as their own experiences. Children of the upper class and upper-middle class develop what the psychiatrist Robert Coles calls a sense of "entitlement." "Wealth does not corrupt nor does it ennoble," Coles writes. "But wealth does govern the minds of privileged children, gives them a peculiar kind of identity which they never lose, whether they grow up to be stockbrokers or communards." That identity grows out of the wide range of choices with which privileged children live—choices about toys and games, food and clothing, vacations and careers. Their identity grows out of their sense of competence as well, for they (and, to a lesser degree, ordinary middle-class children) live in a world in which their parents and, by reflection, they themselves exercise authority, in which they influence and often control their environment. They are, in a phrase, the masters of their fate; their world, as an eleven-year-old boy told Coles, is one in which "If you really work for the rewards, you'll get them." This view is confirmed in school. "Those who want something badly enough get it," the boy's fourth-grade teacher wrote on the blackboard, "provided they are willing to wait and work."[1]

To the "children of poverty," those who want something badly enough usually do *not* get it, no matter how hard they work or how long they wait. Nothing about their own lives or the lives of their parents (or relatives or friends) suggests that "If you really work for the rewards, you'll get them." Quite the contrary: poor children grow up in a world in which people work hard and long, for painfully meager rewards. It is a world, too, in which parents and relatives are at the mercy of forces they cannot control—a world in which illness, an accident, a recession, an employer's business reverses, or a foreman's whim can mean the loss of a job and a long period of unemployment, and in which a bureaucrat's arbitrary ruling can mean denial or loss of welfare benefits and, thereby, of food, clothing, fuel, or shelter.

Understandably, poor children come to see themselves as the servants, not the masters, of their fate. When I was doing research on secondary education in the late 1960s, I attended a number of high school graduations. In schools with a predominantly middle-class population, the valedictorians typically spoke of how they and their classmates would affect and change American society. In schools with a lower-class student body, the student speakers sounded a different theme. In one such school, the valedictorian read a long Edgar Guest–type poem that began, "Sometimes you win, and sometimes you lose; here's luck." The poem continued in the same vein, with the refrain "Here's luck" repeated at the end of each stanza. For lower-class adolescents, this is an all too accurate assessment of the world they inhabit.

It is hard to be poor; it is harder to be poor in the

United States than in most other countries, for American culture has always placed a heavy premium on "success." ("Winning is not the main thing; it is the only thing.") It is not the success ethic alone that causes problems, the sociologist Robert K. Merton observes, but the fact that the emphasis on success is coupled with an equally heavy emphasis on ambition, on maintaining lofty goals whatever one's station in life. "Americans are admonished 'not to be a quitter,' " Merton writes, "for in the dictionary of American culture, as in the lexicon of youth, 'there is no such word as "fail." ' "2

Crime and violence are more frequent among the poor than among members of the middle class, Merton argues, because American culture imbues everyone with the importance of ambition and success without providing everyone with the opportunity to achieve success through conventional means. And the cultural emphasis on success is greater now than it used to be: Every day of the week, in the films they see, the television programs they watch, and the public schools they attend, poor people are bombarded with messages about success—vivid images of the life style of the middle class. Television, in particular, drives home the idea that one is not a full-fledged American unless one can afford the goods and services portrayed in the commercials and in the programs themselves. To poor people, the TV screen provides a daily reminder, if any is needed, of the contrast between their own poverty and the affluence enjoyed by the rest of society.

It should not be surprising that many poor people choose the routes to success that seem open to them. To youngsters growing up in lower-class neighborhoods, crime is available as an occupational choice, much as law, medicine, or business management is for adolescents raised in Palo Alto or Scarsdale—except that lower-class youngsters often know a good deal more about the criminal occupations available to them than middle-class youngsters do about their options. In my conversations with young offenders, I was struck by the depth of their knowledge about robbery, burglary, "fencing," the sale and use of hard and soft drugs, prostitution and pimping, the "numbers" business, loan-sharking, and other crimes and rackets. In a great many cities, I was impressed, too, by their detailed knowledge of which fences, numbers operators, and other criminals were paying off which police officers, as well as by their cynicism about governmental corruption in general.

Thus the fabric and texture of life in urban slums and ghettos provide an environment in which opportunities for criminal activity are manifold, and in which the rewards for engaging in crime appear to be high—higher than the penalties for crime, and higher than the rewards for avoiding it. "It seems to me that the kind of neighborhood you come up in may make all the difference in which way you go and where you end up," John Allen suggests. In his neighborhood, most people earned their living from illegitimate activity. "Hustling was their thing: number running, bootlegging, selling narcotics, selling stolen goods, prostitution," he continues. "There's so many things that go on—it's a whole system that operates inside itself."

"Say I was to take you by it. You want some junk, then I would take you to the dude that handles drugs. You want some clothes, I could take you somewhere that handles that. You want some liquor, I could take you someplace other than a liquor store. Of course, it's all outside the law."[3]

It is not simply a matter of opportunity; role models are important as well. "When I think about who's got the power in my neighborhood," John Allen says, "I mostly think about people who've got to the top in strictly illegal ways." As a child, his hero was a successful numbers operator: "he was about the biggest because everybody respected him, he always had plenty of money, he always dressed nice, and everybody always done what he wanted them to do. I dug the respect that he gave and that he got. . . ." "The ones you see are the ones who interest you," an ex-offender says, recalling his childhood. "If it had been doctors and lawyers who drove up and parked in front of the bars in their catylacks, I'd be a doctor today. But it wasn't; it was the men who were into things, the pimps, the hustlers and the numbers guys."[4]

In some lower-class neighborhoods, youngsters learn to become criminals almost as a matter of course. "Education for crime must be looked upon as habituation to a way of life," the late Frank Tannenbaum wrote in 1938, in his neglected classic, *Crime and the Community*. "As such, it partakes of the nature of all education. It is a gradual adaptation to, and a gradual absorption of, certain elements in the environment." Since it would be hard to improve upon Tannenbaum's description, I shall quote from it at length.

The development of a criminal career has "elements of curiosity, wonder, knowledge, adventure," Tannenbaum wrote. "Like all true education, it has its beginnings in play, it starts in more or less random movements, and builds up toward techniques, insights, judgments, attitudes." Like all true education, it also uses whatever is available in the environment, including "such humble things as junk heaps, alley ways, abandoned houses, pushcarts, railroad tracks, coal cars." Children begin with things that can be easily picked up and carried away, and easily used or sold.

Education for crime is a social process as well—

"part of the adventure of living in a certain way in a certain environment," Tannenbaum continued. "But both the environment and the way of using it must already be there." If his career is to develop, the young criminal must have encouragement, support, and instruction from his friends and elders, particularly from what Tannenbaum calls "the intermediary," i.e., the fence. Even if he is nothing more than a junk dealer or peddler, the fence will "purchase bottles, copper wire, lead pipes, bicycles, and trinkets. He will not only pay cash which can be used to continue the play life of the growing children, for movies, candies, sweets, harmonicas, baseball bats, gloves, and other paraphernalia, but if he is a friendly and enterprising fence he will throw out suggestions, indicate where things can be found, will even supply the tools with which to rip and tear down lead pipes or other marketable materials. And the young gang will accept the suggestions and carry out the enterprise as a part of a game, each act providing a new experience, new knowledge, new ways of seeing the world, new interests."

Other factors are needed, too. There must be a cynical attitude toward the police and toward property belonging to business firms and government agencies. There must be older criminals who use adolescents as messengers or lookouts, and to whom the youngsters look for approval. And there must be a conflict between delinquent youngsters and older, more settled people who are their victims, and who call for police protection. "All these elements are part of the atmosphere, of the environment" within which education for crime proceeds.[5]

The "slow, persistent habituation of an individual to a criminal way of life" occurs frequently and naturally in lower-class neighborhoods because so many criminal opportunities are available: numbers operations, book-

making, and other illegal gambling enterprises; selling
heroin, cocaine, marijuana, "uppers," "downers," and
other drugs; loan-sharking; male and female prostitution; pimping; bootlegging and after-hours sales of alcoholic beverages; and hustling and theft in all their
manifold forms.

Theft is in the very air that lower-class youngsters
breathe. It is visible not just because of its frequency,
but because crimes such as burglary, boosting, "clout-
ing" (taking merchandise from a delivery truck while
the driver is occupied), and stealing from parked cars
are not isolated acts by isolated individuals. On the
contrary, the individual act of theft is just the beginning
of an elaborate process whereby "stolen merchandise is
acquired, converted, redistributed and reintegrated into
the legitimate property stream."[6] This "stolen property
system," as the criminologists Marilyn Walsh and Duncan Chappell call it, is an integral part of the economy
of urban lower-class neighborhoods. "About 95 percent
of the people around here will buy hot goods," one of
William West's Toronto informants told him. "It's a
bargain, they're not going to turn it down."

Reluctance to turn down a bargain is not unique to
the lower class. Many middle-class people knowingly
buy stolen merchandise, and some respectable merchants increase their profits by selling stolen goods unbeknownst to their customers. It is not just coincidence
that a particularly good bargain is referred to col-
loquially as a "steal." "Everybody's looking for a bargain," the professional fence whom the criminologist
Carl Klockars calls Vincent Swaggi observed. "If the
price is right and a man can use the merchandise, he's
gonna buy. No question about it."

Swaggi had reason to know; he was speaking from
the vantage point of more than twenty-five years' ex-

perience as a fence, selling to judges, prosecutors, policemen (high officials as well as patrolmen), independent businessmen, and buyers for department stores and retailing chains, in addition to ordinary consumers. He did a booming retail business in merchandise acquired through manufacturers' close-outs and other legitimate channels; his reputation as a fence cast an aura of "bargain" over his entire inventory. "See, most people figure all of the stuff in my store is hot, which you know it ain't," Swaggi told Klockars. "But if they figure it's hot you can't keep 'em away from it. . . . People figurin' they're gonna get something for nothing. You think I'm gonna tell 'em it ain't hot? Not on your life."[7]

For lower-class people, buying stolen merchandise is more than just a matter of picking up a bargain or accommodating the larceny that confidence men, as well as fences, tell us is in almost everyone's heart. Buying from a "peddler" at the back door may be the only way impoverished parents can afford to serve meat to their families, and patronizing a "bargain store" the only way they can afford shoes for their children's growing feet or name-brand sneakers so that teenagers do not lose face among their friends. For many poor people, too, buying stolen property is a way of buying into the American Dream, of being able to afford those consumption items—Stacy Adams shoes, Johnny Walker Black Label Scotch, a stereo or color television set, a motorcycle or ten-speed bike, a sporty-looking car—that the mass media tell them are the mark of a "successful" American. Because they lack the job titles and other devices that shore up middle-class people's sense of self, members of the lower class feel an even greater need than members of the middle class to define themselves through consumption.

Buying stolen property also provides a way of get-

ting back at "them."* Many people on Clay Street had
had problems resulting in what they called 'getting
screwed,'" Joseph T. Howell writes about the lower-
class, mainly Southern white neighborhood in Washington, D.C., in which he lived for a year as a participant-
observer. "For this reason, few people thought twice
about 'getting back.'"

> For instance, hot merchandise was plentiful on Clay
> Street. At Christmas, June and Sam gave Sammy a
> five-speed chopper bike, listing at seventy-five dollars
> but for which they paid a "friend" thirty dollars. Les
> gave Phyllis a twenty-one inch color TV in exchange
> for a new high-powered automatic rifle, both of which
> were hot. Les said about half of everything in their
> house was stolen. . . . Although few disclosed how
> they came upon the hot merchandise, they would us-
> ually take pride in getting an especially good deal.
> Having this merchandise was in no way considered
> dishonest.[8]

Far from being considered dishonest, patronizing the
stolen property system is a way of evening the score, of
getting one's fair share in an unfair world. From a
lower-class perspective, buying a name-brand item at
50 percent or more below list price is a means of cor-
recting a social imbalance, of redressing the maldis-
tribution of income from which they suffer. Their sense
of the rightness of the enterprise is enhanced by their
conviction—often right, sometimes wrong—that local
merchants and local outlets of national chains sell
shoddy merchandise at premium prices. Since "hot"
merchandise often is stolen from "downtown" retailers
as well as from factories, warehouses, trucking firms,
and middle-class residences, the stolen property system

---

* Frequent use of the pronoun "them" reflects both the way
poor people see the rest of society and their conception of how
the rest of society sees them.

(like the progressive income tax) is a means of redistributing income from rich to poor. It may also serve to expand the overall consumer market and hence total production and employment; without the large "discounts" the stolen property system provides, Leroy Gould and his colleagues speculate, poor people might not be able to buy certain kinds of merchandise at all.[9]

At the same time, poor people's readiness to buy stolen merchandise contributes significantly to their own poverty. Thieves do not limit their scores to middle-class targets; juveniles, addicts, and other impulsive and semiprofessional thieves tend to prey on their own communities, where apprehension is less likely. The result is a vicious circle: normally law-abiding people who have been victimized by burglary or some other form of theft feel justified in buying hot merchandise to recoup their losses as cheaply as possible; but their patronage, in turn, makes it easier for thieves and fences to dispose of their wares and encourages further theft.

Thus, the stolen property system develops its own dynamic, with supply and demand feeding on one another. Because lower-class people feel aggrieved, and because they are persuaded that American society is little more than one gigantic "hustle," there is no more opprobrium attached to selling stolen merchandise than to buying it. "That's the only way to make a living up here," a deliveryman who supplemented his salary by selling merchandise he stole from his own truck told Joseph Howell. "You earn half and you steal half." The man learned his illegal trade through on-the-job training given him by a more experienced driver. "You work hard, don't you?" the older man had pointed out. "Why not take out your cut?" Why not, indeed, when the cops are known—or, what amounts to the same thing, are believed—to be taking *their* cut from the

local fences, as well as from numbers runners and
bankers, bootleggers, after-hours clubs, gambling
joints, prostitutes, pimps, and heroin dealers.

Corruption aside, lower-class people's readiness to
support the stolen property system is upheld by the benign view the rest of society takes toward fencing.
Judges, prosecutors, police, and the public at large
share a myopic legal tradition that focuses on individual acts of theft rather than on the stolen property system as a whole. One consequence is that judges rarely
give prison sentences to fences, preferring to reserve
the harsh penalty of incarceration for people they deem
dangerous. Prosecutors and police administrators, in
turn, are reluctant to proceed against fences. Building
a strong case against a fence requires the investment of
a great deal of prosecutorial and/or police time and effort, and the investment appears to be a poor allocation
of resources when the end result is likely to be no more
than probation or a fine for the convicted fence. From
a police perspective, therefore, it often makes more
sense to offer a fence protection in exchange for information. But from the perspective of people living in
lower-class neighborhoods, the fact that fences go free,
while burglars go to prison, serves to reinforce their
cynicism about the law and law enforcement.

Be that as it may, fencing is a relatively low-risk
criminal "industry" with great ease of entry. Some
thieves act as their own fences, peddling their stolen
wares themselves; most prefer to sell to a professional
fence, who may retail the merchandise himself or sell to
other "retailers."[10] Although thieves receive less money
from a fence than they might earn if they sold direct to
the consumer, they are relieved of the burden of carrying a retail "inventory" which constitutes incriminating
evidence that can be used to tie them to their crime.
The sooner a thief disposes of his loot, the better he

likes it—a fact that fences take into account in deciding what price to offer.

For residents of lower-class neighborhoods, stolen merchandise is likely to be available wherever they turn: in beauty parlors, barbershops, restaurants and bars, newsstands, after-hours clubs, gambling joints, appliance stores and repair shops, jewelry stores, pawnshops, liquor stores, junkyards, dry-cleaning stores, auto-repair and body shops, auto accessory stores, used-car lots, lumberyards, and retail clothing stores, as well as from cabdrivers, truckdrivers, delivery and "route" men, and so on.

Some of these outlets are primarily sellers of stolen merchandise, with the legitimate business serving only or mainly as a front. Most are more or less legitimate businesses whose owners supplement their incomes by selling stolen merchandise on the side. Such firms may be quite prosperous; or they may be small, often marginal, enterprises for whom the trade in stolen merchandise means the difference between losing money and making a small profit. Moonlighting as a fence may also mean the difference between earning a decent living and just scraping by for bartenders, waiters, beauticians, and other employees.*

For safety's sake, professional thieves prefer to deal with the same fence or fences on a regular basis; a fence is far more likely to "finger" an unknown or occasional thief than one on whom he depends for his inventory. When thieves know beforehand what their take will be, they may negotiate a price in advance; or they may simply know what the market price is for

* Marilyn Walsh has analyzed the occupations of a group of 110 fences in a northeastern city. Seventy owned their own business; 11 worked for others; and 14 ran a fencing operation as an adjunct to some other illegal enterprise, such as loan-sharking or the numbers. Most of the remainder were burglars who did their own fencing.[11]

stolen merchandise of a particular sort and plan their scores accordingly. For their part, professional fences may have their own thieves whom they employ on a regular basis, or to whom they turn when they need merchandise of a particular variety.

II

Theft is only one of a great many criminal occupations available to residents of lower-class communities. For those eager to "make it" in American society, organized crime often seems to offer a faster and more effective route to success than either street crime or a legitimate job. The most visibly successful people in poor neighborhoods are members of organized crime. Organized crime does not merely provide success models for lower-class youngsters to emulate; it is a major employer as well, and it is the principal—for many lower-class and minority-group people, the only —source of credit.

Organized crime also plays a central role in creating and maintaining an environment in which street crime flourishes. To understand why, we need to know something about how organized crime operates. That knowledge has been hindered in recent years by a heated, at times acrimonious, and often downright silly debate about the Mafia: whether or not the Mafia really exists; whether it is called the Mafia or La Cosa Nostra; whether it is limited to Italian-Americans or includes members of other ethnic groups; whether or not there is a national syndicate, or "crime confederation," that controls organized crime throughout the United States; and whether or not that syndicate is controlled, in turn, by the Mafia. The argument is too complex to unravel here; in any case, it is tangential to the problem that concerns us: the relationship between organized crime and street crime.[12]

Neither side in the debate questions the *existence* of organized crime or the seriousness of the problems it poses. Indeed, scholars on the anti-Mafia side of the debate argue that preoccupation with the Mafia obscures the degree to which organized crime is indigenous to American society. Whether or not there is a Mafia, in other words, and whether or not the syndicate (if it exists) is directed by the Mafia (if it exists), there can be no question but that *organized crime* exists. Organized crime is deeply embedded in state and local politics; it flourishes with the sufferance, and at times the cooperation, of large numbers of respectable people; and it exerts a corrosive impact on the quality of American life in general and life in lower-class communities in particular.*[13]

Organized crime differs from street crime in a number of important respects. The most obvious is the scale and complexity of organization. Members of organized crime are organization men, in contrast to the loners who commit conventional robberies or burglaries. Even the most successful professional thieves lack anything resembling an organization; although they usually work in groups, the groups come together for a specific score or group of scores and then disband. Organized crime networks, on the other hand, are corporate enterprises designed to last indefinitely. As with corporations, there are occasional (in some periods, frequent) battles for control, but the organization usually survives several changes in top management. (In some of its manifestations, organized crime

* The discussion of organized crime relies in part on research by Richard D. Van Wagenen. I am indebted, too, to Dr. Jonathan Rubinstein and Professor Mark Haller for frequent advice and counsel, as well as for access to unpublished papers.

also resembles business cartels and trade associations, and, at times, governmental regulatory agencies.) The complexity and duration of its organization, in turn, enables organized crime to operate—as it does, for example, in the international traffic in heroin and weapons—on an economic and geographic scale far beyond that of professional crime.

These differences in organization and scale grow out of a fundamental difference in function. Even at its most professional, ordinary crime is predatory and parasitic; robbers, burglars, shoplifters, check forgers, and other thieves do their best to avoid further contact with their victims once their crime has been consummated. Organized crime, to the contrary, has customers rather than victims; it is in the business of supplying goods and services—narcotics, gambling, credit, prostitution, protection against business competitors or trade unions—that people willingly (often eagerly) buy despite their illegality. Indeed, organized crime is organized precisely because of its need to develop congenial, long-term relationships with customers and suppliers, both of whom are co-conspirators, so to speak, in breaking the law.

This distinction between organized and professional crime is not absolute. Professional criminals sometimes supply goods and services, as in the domestic traffic in guns and the retail sale of narcotics, and organized crime networks engage in parasitic crimes such as hijacking and extortion. The line between providing services, such as loan-sharking or "protection," and pure extortion can be very thin; organized crime uses violence freely to persuade potential "customers" to purchase the services being offered or to pay for those already consumed, as well as to get rid of unwanted competitors. In short, the term "organized crime" covers a broad spectrum of activities. At one end, organized crime is almost indistinguishable from "heavy" professional crime. At the other end, it may be indistinguishable from ordinary business—for example, liquor wholesaling and distribution, the operation of hotels and gambling casinos in Nevada and the Caribbean, the distribution of meat, the "fixing" of labor disputes, ownership and operation of "singles" and homosexual bars, and speculation in land.

Many middle-class people live out their lives oblivious to the existence of organized crime; others feign ignorance. Business and professional people who patronize gambling casinos do not think of themselves as doing business with organized crime.* Neither do the millions of respectable people who use bookmakers to gamble on horse races or on football, baseball, or basketball games. (With big bettors, transactions usually are handled over the phone, so that the bookmaker remains a shadowy, even invisible presence.) Meatpackers who pay racketeers to ensure that their meat will be sold in large supermarket chains think of themselves as smart or aggressive businessmen; so do corporate executives who use organized crime to avoid strikes or arrange a "sweetheart contract" with a crooked trade union. And people who snort cocaine think of themselves as part of the avant-garde, not as customers of organized crime.

Members of the lower class cannot feign this kind of ignorance or innocence; they come into contact with organized crime and the subeconomy it operates almost everywhere they turn. For one thing, the popularity of

---

* They may be disabused of their pretense if they roll up gambling losses they cannot cover, or if they need to borrow to keep their business afloat after legal sources of credit have been closed to them.

gambling on the numbers (or policy, as it is also called)
makes it a highly visible presence, as well as a major
economic and financial force, in the old cities of the
East and Midwest, and, to a lesser degree, of the South.
Although playing the numbers is not limited to the
black and Hispanic poor (in New York City, more than
half the numbers players are non-Hispanic whites), the
proportion of people who place bets is considerably
higher in poor black and Hispanic neighborhoods than
in white middle-class areas.* In their study of organized
crime in Bedford-Stuyvesant, a Brooklyn neighborhood of about 280,000 people, 95 percent black, Harold Lasswell and Jeremiah McKenna found that the
numbers business was the largest single private employer in the area. (Although Bedford-Stuyvesant has
a large and thriving black, predominantly West Indian,
middle class and a stable working-class population, the
bulk of its residents are lower-class; with 3.4 percent of
New York City's population, Bedford-Stuyvesant receives only 1.2 percent of total city income.) In 1970,
there were five identifiable policy banks with a "handle" (total amount bet) of some $37 million.[14]

Contrary to popular impression, most of the money
bet in Bedford-Stuyvesant stays there. Of the $37 mil-
lion handle, Lasswell and McKenna estimate, $18.5
million was returned to winning bettors. The five banks
laid out another $14.8 million in salaries and commis-
sions for the 1,345 "runners" or "collectors" they employed, all of whom lived in the neighborhood, and the
76 "controllers," most of whom lived either in Bedford-Stuyvesant or in contiguous neighborhoods. That

---

* A survey taken by the federal Commission on the Review
of the National Policy Toward Gambling indicated that about
4.3 million adults placed a numbers bet in 1974, and that some
10.4 million people have bet on the numbers at some time in
their lives.

left the "bankers" a net profit of about 10 percent of the total handle.*

Poor people generally see nothing wrong with playing the numbers, and nothing invidious about working for a numbers operation.† Few jobs—certainly few jobs available to residents of impoverished neighborhoods—pay as well, and numbers runners are viewed with fondness and respect. In Bedford-Stuyvesant, the numbers runner usually is "a person of obvious affluence who is visible in the community throughout the day," Lasswell and McKenna report. "To the community residents he is a symbol of 'upward mobility'. . . ."

---

* Some runners are merely local residents who collect the bets from others in their house, in return for a free "dollar play" each day; other runners cover an entire city block, collecting several thousand bets a day. *Controllers* also vary in the scale of their business, employing anywhere from four or five runners to as many as twenty-five or thirty. Controllers have a franchise, so to speak, to operate the numbers business in a particular neighborhood; in most cities, they are expected to pay off the police to avoid arrests of their runners, whose activities are blatantly visible, and to cover legal fees and bail whenever a runner does have to "take a fall." *Bankers* handle the bookkeeping for the controllers in their employ, both as a service and as a means of assuring honesty on the part of runners and controllers; they also provide a hedging operation, "laying off" bets for a controller who has a dangerously heavy play on a particular number.

† The fact that the numbers are illegal merely encourages cynicism about the double standard the larger society employs. Poor people know that churches and synagogues finance themselves by running bingo games and "Las Vegas nights," that states add to their revenues by running lotteries, and that rich people fly to Las Vegas or follow the horses to Florida. Legislation outlawing the numbers is seen—correctly—as evidence of class discrimination as well as of middle-class hypocrisy. (Creation of New York City's Off-Track Betting Corporation made class bias even more blatant: betting on horses, the form of gambling preferred by the middle and working class, was legalized, while the numbers—the type of gambling preferred by the lower class—remained illegal.)

He is a good deal more than that. "Numbers in Harlem has built churches, fed preachers, poor people have put a dime on a number and fed their kids," a resident told a member of a survey team headed by the anthropologist Francis A. J. Ianni. ". . . most of the numbers runners in Harlem are people that send the kids to camp, do a lot of good things in the community. They are respectable people. . . ." Or, as the young protagonist of a novel about growing up in Harlem puts it, "A number runner is something like Santa Claus, and any day you hit the number is Christmas."[15]

Santa Claus or not, numbers runners are important community resources, for the numbers is not just a game of chance. Since there are rarely receipts, people deal with a numbers runner whom they like and trust —either someone who makes the rounds of the neighborhood each day, imparting information as he collects the bets, or a collector who operates out of a small grocery store, barbershop, beauty parlor, newsstand, pool hall, or bowling alley that serves as a neighborhood hangout. (Runners, in turn, accept bets mainly from people they know; someone who moves to a new neighborhood must be introduced to the runner by a friend.) When placing a bet in an established numbers station, the bettor has a chance to chat with the proprietor and whoever else may be hanging around. These relationships are solidified every time someone wins, for it is customary to give the runner a 10 percent tip and, in some neighborhoods, to hold an open house so that friends and neighbors can join in the celebration.

This friendly social atmosphere contributes, in turn, to the important economic and financial functions that the numbers fulfill. Betting on the numbers is a form of savings; lower-class blacks often refer to their bets as "investments," as do working-class football pool bettors in Great Britain. As the sociologist Ivan Light points out, the numbers plays much the same role for lower-class people that savings and commercial bank Christmas Club accounts do for members of the lower middle class: converting small change into lump sums of a substantial amount. The dimes, quarters, and half-dollars bet on the numbers aren't really missed, and in any case would be frittered away on inconsequentials, the argument goes, whereas when one does ultimately win, the payoff is large enough to be really useful. And it *is* small amounts that are usually bet; the average bet in Bedford-Stuyvesant in 1970 was 37.5 cents.[16]

Middle-class people often look askance at poor people's penchant for gambling, but it makes more sense for poor people to play the numbers than for middle-class people to bet on the horses. With the numbers, luck really does have the power to change one's life; a winning number pays 550 or 600 to 1—a far higher payoff than one can get from any other form of gambling. By way of contrast, the average winning bet on a horse race pays about 7 to 1, and the daily double pays about 50 to 1; a winning number on a roulette wheel returns only 64 to 1. Although the odds of winning are only 1 in 1,000, a $1 "hit" on the numbers brings in $550 to $600—enough to pay off a lot of bills, or buy a new color television set or a second-hand car. And a $10 hit means $5,500 or $6,000—enough to send a child to college or to make a down payment on a house outside the ghetto. The fact that luck is random, unlikely, and fickle in no way alters its appeal, Bruce Jackson writes, for "there is nothing else on the horizon of a comparable power. What difference —what *real* difference—will a ten percent weekly wage increase make, or a ten percent drop in the rent?"[17]

In any event, the cash flow generated by numbers betting provides the basis for most of the credit extended in lower-class neighborhoods. Many grocery stores and other small retail shops use the profit from collecting numbers bets to extend credit to their impoverished customers. This makes it possible for small businessmen to compete with supermarkets and chainstore outlets; the credit that small stores extend also makes it possible for parents to feed and clothe their children when, as is often the case, they are short of cash.

While they are making their rounds, moreover, numbers runners often pass the hat for people who are down on their luck; through the intervention of the runner, the people who regularly deal with him are pulled together into a loose mutual assistance society. Equally important, controllers and the more successful runners customarily lend money, either without interest or at a nominal rate, to good customers who are temporarily short of funds because their pocketbook has been snatched, their home broken into, their welfare check stolen, or any of the other financial disasters to which poor people are prone. The loss of a $20 bill, which some readers of this book might simply shrug off (if they notice it at all), may mean no food for a week for a family that lives from day to day, with no savings to fall back upon.

In minority-group communities, too, numbers bankers and other members of the middle and upper echelons of organized crime traditionally have been the major source of venture capital and long-term loans for aspiring businessmen and professionals. William Foote Whyte points out, in his classic study of an Italian-American neighborhood in Boston in the 1930s, that since Yankee bankers had no interest in lending to young Italian-American entrepreneurs, especially if they planned to compete with established businesses, ambitious young men routinely turned to racketeers for help. "The support of racket capital has helped a number of able men to rise to positions otherwise unattainable."[18]

The same has been true in black communities, although on a considerably smaller scale. "It would be interesting to find out how many businesses in Harlem survived because some numbers man loaned the money knowing the fellow who borrowed was reliable and that he would pay it back," New York City Deputy Mayor Basil Paterson speculates. Indeed, one reason blacks are so badly underrepresented in business is that organized crime funding has not been available to black businessmen in anything like the amounts that Irish, Italian, and Jewish-American entrepreneurs have been able to tap.*

In minority-group communities, numbers operators and other racketeers have been major philanthropists as well, contributing to churches, hospitals, ethnic defense groups, and other community institutions. "I feel as though I am sending Santa Claus to jail," a federal judge said as he sentenced a Reading, Pennsylvania, slot-machine distributor. "Although this man dealt in gambling devices, it appears that he is a religious man having no bad habits and is an unmeasurably charitable man." And when the leading numbers operator in Reading came into federal court in the early 1960s, to

---

* Historically, blacks have been pushed out of one occupation after another when it became attractive to whites; organized crime is no exception. In the 1930s and '40s, Jewish and Italian organized-crime syndicates, looking for new "investment" opportunities to replace bootlegging, took over control of the numbers business in black and Hispanic neighborhoods. Until the last few years, when blacks began trying to gain control of the numbers and the even more profitable heroin trade, blacks who prospered in organized crime—for example, "Bumpy" Johnson, the folk hero who was the model for the "Shaft" movies—generally did so by serving as middlemen for white syndicates.[19]

be sentenced for income-tax evasion, he brought character references from Protestant, Catholic, and Jewish clergymen, in addition to those from officials of two hospitals and a home for the aged.

Racketeer-philanthropists do not always limit themselves to status-enhancing public causes. "These gangsters are the finest fellows you want to meet," one of William Foote Whyte's Boston informants told him. "They'll do a lot for you, Bill. You go up to them and say, 'I haven't eaten for four days, and I haven't got a place to sleep,' and they'll give you something. Now you go up to a businessman, one of the respected members of the community, and ask him. He throws you right out of the office."[20]

Small wonder that many members of lower-class communities identify with organized crime rather (or more) than with the police or other agencies of law enforcement. "Those who participate in organized crime are rewarded with power, wealth, well-being, skill, loyalty and respect," Lasswell and McKenna write. "Legitimate society can't match such rewards," and indeed offers very little to those who avoid criminal activity. There are risks in crime, to be sure, as well as rewards. But as a street-wise Los Angeles youngster observes, "Any kind of way a cat's gonna make it, be a risk, always a risk."

One of the risks that appears to be justified by the potential rewards is to try to get a foothold in the drug business. Although use of heroin is much more widely diffused throughout the United States than is generally realized, the heroin trade is most visible in lower-class neighborhoods of big cities, where bags of heroin are sold, by brand name, on certain well-known street corners. According to Mark Moore of Harvard, who has made the most careful study of the "heroin industry" in New York City, retail sales came to $470 million a year in the early 1970s.*[21]

The size of the heroin market makes for easy entry at the bottom rung. In New York in the early 1970s, Moore estimates, there were 18,000 "jugglers" (heroin users who act as small retailers in order to finance their own habits) and 6,000 "street dealers" (larger-scale retailers who may or may not be users themselves). Jugglers average about $1,000 a year in cash earnings, over and above the heroin they consumed; street dealers earned $15,000 a year—more than most unskilled youths can earn from legitimate employment. The big money is made at the importing and distributing end, which is controlled by organized crime. According to Moore, the twenty-five importers, who rarely see the drug, averaged net profits of $200,000 a year each; the twenty-five "kilo connections" (the major distributors) netted $500,000 a year each. Street dealers are not likely to become kilo connections, but they may aspire to positions in the two levels of distribution between them and the kilo connections. Moore estimates that there were some 125 "connections" (large whole-

---

* As Moore points out, his estimates are subject to a wide margin of error. No one really knows how many heroin users there are, how much heroin they consume, or the prices they pay; each figure is at best an educated guess, over which experts often disagree sharply. Moore's estimates of retail sales are based on the assumption that there were 100,000 heroin users in New York in the early 1970s; most informed estimates put the figure at somewhere between 70,000 and 150,000, implying a lower limit of $329 million and an upper limit of $705 million in retail sales. Different estimates of the amount of heroin each user consumes would change those figures, as would different estimates of retail price. Since methadone has replaced heroin as the drug of choice for some users in the last few years, both the size and organization of the market probably are different now than they were in the early 1970s.[22]

salers) who netted $160,000 and about 750 "weight
dealers" (the jobbers from whom street dealers acquire
their heroin) who netted $75,000 a year, on average.

For a youngster growing up in a lower-class neighborhood, therefore, organized crime may seem the like-
liest route to success. To get started on that road, he
needs to bring himself to the attention of those in
charge; but as is the case with elite clubs, etiquette
requires that one wait for an invitation to join. "You
know who is connected and who is involved but you
can't go to them and say 'Hey, man, I want to be one
of you!' " one of Ianni's informants in Paterson, N.J.,
explained. "This is the way it happens. If he has been
watching me and likes what he sees and he wants to
give me a little play, he might tell me one day to go see
Joe. He won't ever turn around and commit himself the
first time. You just take it for granted that you don't approach these guys at that level. . . ."[23]

One way to be invited is to make the right friends
while you are growing up, just as ambitious members
of the middle class do. "For every friend you have, you
have that much more chance to get in on deals, to make
it in crime," a Harlem informant says. "Otherwise you
are outside looking in—you are nobody. . . . *You got
to prove yourself or have somebody vouch for you.*"
[emphasis added]

The desire to "prove yourself" is an important stimulus to street crime of all sorts. In neighborhoods where
organized crime is active, its members study teenagers'
street "reps" and behavior as carefully as a professional
baseball scout analyzes a sandlot player's ability to hit
curve balls or hold a base runner close to the bag.
"These kids in the neighborhood all want to do things
and after a while you learn what they can do and what
they can't do," the controller of a Brooklyn numbers

operation explains. "They are all different. Some of them would do anything you asked them because they are tough kids but smart and they are looking for a way to get ahead. Some of the others you can trust with little things, but as soon as they get a couple of hundred bucks in their hands they go crazy and they start stealing from you. The worst ones though are the kids who are on dope and will rob you blind if they get a chance. I watch all these kids and I know their families. I know their fathers, their uncles, and their cousins and I can tell you who has good blood and whose has got bad blood, and who you can trust and who you can't."[24]

The youngsters know they are being watched, and that they will be carefully graded on the skill, courage, trustworthiness, and judgment they display as robbers, burglars, boosters, hustlers, fighters, messengers, lookouts, coffee-fetchers, or what have you. In some neighborhoods, even murder can be a way of proving one's *bona fides* (and perhaps earning a little money on the side) for a youngster hopeful of becoming a hijacker, bodyguard, or "hit man" for the mob.

ITEM (from the New York *Times,* December 16, 1977):

"A Manhattan gang, whose members worked just a decade ago as teen-age errand boys for major narcotics traffickers, has now emerged as a new and violent force of its own in organized crime in New York, according to confidential police and Federal agency intelligence reports.

"The group, which calls itself the Purple Gang, after the band of criminals that terrorized Detroit during the Prohibition era, has been identified by law enforcement agencies as being involved in the following criminal activities:

• "The murder—and in many cases dismembering—of 17 individuals with criminal backgrounds, including at least two police informers.

• "The large-scale distribution of narcotics in the South Bronx and Harlem.

• " 'Muscle' jobs for two organized crime family's extortion networks.

• "International gun-running, including alleged ties to Latin-American terrorists.

"Citing a December 1976 report by the Drug Enforcement Administration that speaks of the Purple Gang's 'enormous capacity for violence' and 'lack of respect for other members of organized crime,' the police say the group may attempt to become this region's sixth organized-crime family. That effort, the police say, could result in a mob war. The enforcement administration's report asserts that one generation of criminals influenced and perpetuated a new, more violent generation: 'The younger group, impressed by the antics, violence and wealth of the older traffickers began to emulate them and after a while became . . . uncontrollable.' "[25]

The Purple Gang, with thirty members and eighty "associates," is an outgrowth of a youth gang on Pleasant Avenue, an Italian-American organized-crime enclave in East Harlem. The gang members, many of them related to the area's established organized-crime figures, started out as deliverymen and "spotters" for major narcotics dealers. When the Pleasant Avenue drug boss and two other high-ranking officials were convicted in 1973, the gang members moved rapidly to fill the vacancies themselves. Although membership is restricted to young Italian-Americans who were raised on Pleasant Avenue between 110th and 117th streets, the gang serves as the link between the five old-line

Italian-American organized-crime families and the black groups who now control the street sale of heroin and other drugs.

It is unusual for adolescent gangs to stay together when their members grow up, if only because so many of their members end up in prison; it is even rarer for them to challenge existing organized-crime networks. But youth gangs do make a significant contribution to street crime, and not just as the means by which young criminals prove themselves to their elders. For one thing, youngsters learn criminal techniques from older or more experienced friends. More important, there is a synergistic quality to juvenile gangs and informal groupings that enables youngsters to do things in groups that they would not (or could not) do on their own. "Countless mothers have protested that their 'Johnny' was a good boy until he fell in with a certain bunch," the sociologist Albert Cohen points out—but the mothers of each of Johnny's companions say the same thing about *their* sons. Although some of the mothers may be naïve and others self-serving, there are times when they are all correct; none of the boys would have turned to crime if it had not been for the chemistry of the group.[26]

Organized crime's biggest impact is indirect. Its omnipresence and prosperity undermine the credibility of those who preach compliance with the law; to be "a poor working slob," in the old Chicago argot, hardly compares with the glamour that surrounds successful racketeers. The fact that the rest of society looks down on organized-crime figures as criminals serves to solidify the community's sense of ethnic solidarity and intensify its sense of being victimized by a hypocritical, as well as corrupt, society. Why pick on a numbers runner, bootlegger, or fence, the reasoning goes, when the *real* criminals—bribe-taking police, corrupt government officials, slumlords who fail to maintain their buildings, merchants who "rip off" the poor, congressmen who keep their mistresses on their Congressional payroll, corporate executives who offer bribes, a vice president of the United States who takes bribes, and a president who cheats on his income tax—all seem to go scot free?

The double standard that lower-class people see applied produces a deep-rooted cynicism about government, business, and, indeed, American society as a whole. "They talk about me being on the legitimate," Al Capone once remarked to a woman reporter. "Why, lady, nobody's on the legit. You know that and so do they. . . . Nobody's really on the legit, when it comes down to cases." Capone's comment reflects a world view that permeates the lower class; as Frank Tannenbaum wrote, "The sense that the world about one is all crooked must be taken as the root of the problem."

III

Most criminals do not succeed; they earn a poor living through crime, and they spend much of their career locked up in jail or prison. Moreover, much of the violence of lower-class life has little or nothing to do with earning money or impressing potential employers in organized crime. Assaults, murders, rapes, and even some robberies and burglaries, frequently are a by-product of disputes between spouses or lovers, arguments that develop during a barroom discussion or street-corner crap game, gang warfare over "turf" or gang members' "rep," or any number of other more or less routine happenings.

Like theft, violence is part of the fabric and texture of life in lower-class neighborhoods—so much so that some scholars argue that poor people belong to a separate and fairly autonomous "culture of poverty," with norms and values different from those of the larger society. In this view, criminal violence is part of a distinctive lower-class life style, and that life style, in turn, is the product of a distinctive lower-class culture that is passed along from generation to generation. The real deviants in lower-class communities are not criminals, the sociologist Walter B. Miller argues, but the people who seek success through legal means; criminals are simply conforming to the norms of their own culture. "The cultural system which exerts the most direct influence on behavior is that of the lower class community itself," Miller writes, "a long-established, distinctively patterned tradition with an integrity of its own. . . ." Crime represents "a positive effort to achieve what is valued within that tradition, and to conform to its explicit and implicit norms."[27]

Those who hold this view argue that poverty and criminal violence reinforce one another, and that members of the lower class are unable to penetrate the cultural barrier separating them from the rest of American society. The culture of poverty "tends to perpetuate itself from generation to generation because of its effect on children," according to the late Oscar Lewis, an anthropologist who helped popularize the concept. "By the time children are six or seven, they have usually absorbed the basic values and attitudes of their subculture. . . ."

The political scientist Edward Banfield takes a harsher, more disparaging view, implying that lower-class culture is less a matter of enculturation than of individual or group choice. According to Banfield, the lower class "consists of people who would live in squalor even if their incomes were doubled or tripled." In his view, "the lower class individual lives in the slum and sees no reason to complain. He does not care how dirty or dilapidated his housing is either inside or out, nor does he mind the inadequacy of such public facilities as schools, parks, and libraries; indeed, where such things exist he destroys them by acts of vandalism. Factors that make the slum repellent to others actually please him. . . ."

> In the slum one can beat one's children, lie drunk in the gutter, or go to jail without attracting any special notice; these are the things that most of the neighbors themselves have done and that they consider quite normal.[28]

These are one-dimensional views—in Banfield's instance, a caricature—of a complex and multidimensional reality. Poor people's behavior is influenced by lower-class norms, to be sure; but they are also profoundly affected by norms and values stemming from their ethnic background, religion, and race, as well as from their region and from their membership in American society as a whole. This is equally true of members of the middle and working classes; we all live in several cultures at once. Which set of values is most influential depends on the circumstances in which we find ourselves.*

---

* When Americans are abroad, others see them as Americans, not as Southerners or Northerners, blacks or whites, or "ethnics" or "natives." Equally important, Americans' sense of their own identity changes when they are abroad. American Jews who settle in Israel are confounded when they hear themselves described as "Anglo-Saxons," and black Americans who spend time in Africa often gain a dramatically new sense of themselves as Americans rather than as blacks. "It's ridiculous," one black American in Africa told Harold Isaacs of M.I.T., "but I had never before realized how much of my life had nothing to do with the race problem at all. I mean just the way you do everything you do, what you mean when you say something, and how you understand what the other fellow means."

One need not postulate an autonomous "culture of poverty" to understand why the incidence of violence is higher among the lower than among the middle class. Poor people accept the norms and values of American society. If they do not always act in accordance with those norms, if they follow a life style that includes a good deal of criminal violence, it is mainly because the circumstances of their lives make it difficult or impossible for them to do otherwise. As the sociologist Hylan Lewis puts it, the poor are "frustrated victims of middle class values."[29]

Every human being needs a sense of being a person of value and worth, of being "a somebody" who is recognized as a full and valid member of society. But in a society that rewards success and penalizes failure— a society in which we determine other people's identity by asking what they "do" rather than what they are— to be poor is to live with continual self-doubt. The poor may be invisible to the rest of us, but we are not invisible to them; their television sets thrust them inside our homes every day of the week. For members of the lower class, consequently, life is a desperate struggle to maintain a sense of self in a world that offers little to nourish, and much to destroy, it. As the sociologist Lee Rainwater writes, "The identity problems of lower-class persons make the soul-searching of middle-class adolescents and adults seem like a kind of conspicuous consumption of psychic riches."

Poor people's struggle for identity is desperate because of the degree to which our sense of self depends on the "success" we enjoy. "I had never realized how

---

But back in the United States, where what one does and what others mean by what they say tend to be taken for granted, the part of life that *does* revolve around the race question again comes to the fore.

much of my identity was built on academic achievement until I ran into trouble that first semester," a third-year law school student told me. "I was shattered—almost disoriented—until I discovered I wasn't the only one— that everybody was having trouble." But poor people lack the consolation that comes from being part of the majority; to be poor in an affluent society is to feel alone and inadequate.

The sense of self is shaped, too, by the way other people act toward us, and by the attitudes about us that they convey through words and, even more, through tone of voice, posture, and facial expression. No matter what psychic armor we wear, none of us is immune to the messages we receive from others about our own worth. And the primary message lower-class people receive about themselves is that they have no worth—and they are irrelevant or expendable, if indeed they exist at all. The message is exacerbated if the lower-class person belongs to a despised minority group.[30] Hence the poignancy of this poem by an eighteen-year-old black boy I know:

> Who am I, and why am I hear
> And why does my heart hold so much fear . . .
> Who am I, and where do I stand,
> Will I ever have a chance to become a man.
> Will I ever have a chance to see the day,
> When my children can run and play.
> Please, tell me who do you think I am,
> Or dose it matter, you just dont give a goddam.

Because their sense of self is so precarious, poor people invest considerable energy in a search for excitement, or "kicks," which is to say, for activities that can tell them they *do* exist and they *do* matter. This search for "action," to use a more inclusive term, may involve individual or gang fighting; sexual conquests;

ritualized exchanges of insults; competitive recitations of poems, songs, and jokes, and other forms of verbal repartee; vandalism; gambling for heavy stakes; use of alcohol and drugs; or one or another variety of criminal activity.

The search for action is not unique to the lower class; it runs through every segment of American society. Americans who can afford to travel may look for action in the casinos of Las Vegas, the Caribbean, or the Riviera. If they have a different temperament, they may scale the smooth and perpendicular cliffs of Yosemite, climb the mountains of Maine or the High Sierras, ride the rapids downstream in Colorado or Idaho, hunt big game in Africa, practice the "sport" of parachute jumping from a chartered plane, or take an LSD "trip." With still a different temperament, the search for action may take vicarious forms: attending the Indianapolis Speedway or other auto races, or watching Evel Knievel in one of his daredevil feats. The purpose is the same: the heightened awareness and sense of self and the testing or demonstration of character that people gain from confrontation with danger, whether physical (as in rock climbing, mountain climbing, parachute jumping, or riding the rapids), psychic (as in using hallucinogens), or financial (as in casino gambling).[31]

What is distinctive about the lower-class preoccupation with action is simply the arena in which the search takes place. Poor people have fewer resources than do members of the middle or upper class and a far greater need to heighten their sense of self. Hence they look for action wherever it can be found—and, as we have seen, opportunities for crime are plentiful. "Burglary is an elemental act and the emotions it generates are profound," Malcolm Braly has written, describing his own career. "It's a treasure hunt as well as The Lady and the Tiger, a complete and separate experience outside whatever ordinary life you may be pretending to live. It's another way to reach the *now*." When he stood on the rooftops of his hometown, preparing to break into a store, Braly recalls, "the town lost its capacity to change or diminish me. Here I came to power. This I, here on this dangerous height, hugging himself with excitement, was not the same adolescent who walked these streets in the daylight."[32]

John Allen felt much the same way about robbery. He tried pimping for a while, but it did not provide the same satisfaction. "What I really missed was the excitement of sticking up and the planning and the getting away with it—whether it come out to a car chase or just a plain old-fashioned foot race outrunning the police—knowing all the little alleys and shortcuts to go through," he says. Even now, paralyzed in his wheelchair, he sometimes dreams of resuming his career: "I still like the notoriety, the excitement, the danger—that's cool."[33]

Being "cool" is important to lower-class males, for it is synonymous with courage. Action, in whatever form, provides a chance to demonstrate their ability to face a challenge and overcome it, and hence to offset the impotence they normally feel. At the very least, the excitement that action generates provides evidence to the individual that he is alive, and that significant others know that he exists.[34]

Action of an illegal or riotous sort also allows a lower-class adolescent or adult to defy the rules "they" make and the morality "they" try to impose on him—another way of gaining some sense of being in control, rather than of being controlled. ("They may make the rules, but they can't force me to abide by them.") Consequently, it is its very pointlessness, from a middle-class perspective, that is the real purpose of much juvenile and young-adult vandalism and crime.[35]

It has long been thus. "We liked anything that had a thrill in it and it didn't make any difference what it was," a Chicago delinquent of the 1920s told the criminologists Clifford Shaw and Henry McKay. "Shooting 'craps,' playing coppers and robbers, making raids on news stands, bumming from school, junking, snatching pocketbooks and playing games in the prairie. I always liked anything that gave me a kick and was always looking for thrills. . . . I always wanted to be in the midst of any excitement, whether it was stealing, breaking windows, breaking in school houses and tearing up the furniture, or playing a ball game."[36]

As this account suggests, the lower-class pursuit of action and toughness also involves a seeming indifference to the future consequences of one's behavior—at times, it would appear, an indifference to the future itself. Edward Banfield sees this apparent indifference as an inability to defer gratification and regards it as the critical characteristic of lower-class life: "The lower-class forms of all problems are at bottom a single problem," he writes, "the existence of an outlook and style of life which is radically present-oriented and which therefore attaches no value to work, sacrifice, self-improvement, or service to family, friends, or community."[37]

But orientation to the present is a realistic adjustment to a world that seems to have no future, a world in which it takes all the strength one can muster to get through each day. "Well, I made it through today," a beleaguered and, in some ways, heroic black mother once told me. "Now I'll wait and see if I can make it through tomorrow."

For such people, the choice is not between immediate and deferred gratification; it is between immediate gratification and no gratification at all. To defer is to risk—in some situations, almost to guarantee—forgoing the gratification altogether. What appears to the outside observer as an orientation to the present, the anthropologist Elliot Liebow writes, "is, to the man experiencing it, as much a future orientation as that of his middle-class counterpart." The difference lies not in the orientations, but in the futures to which they are oriented. For the lower-class man, in particular, Liebow adds, "It is a future in which everything is uncertain except the ultimate destruction of his hopes and the eventual realization of his fears. The most he can look forward to is that these things do not come too soon." Thus, when a lower-class man "squanders a week's pay in two days, it is not because, like an animal or a child, he is 'present-time oriented,' unaware or unconcerned with his future. He does so precisely because he is aware of the future and the hopelessness of it all."[38]

Members of the lower class live for the moment, too, because they have no emotional surplus to sustain them *beyond* the moment. It is hard enough to defer gratification of hunger or other physical needs; it is even harder to postpone support for an already fragile sense of self. Lower-class males must constantly reaffirm and prove the credentials on which their identities are based. "You got to maintain who you are at all times. You do it for the people watching," John Allen remarks. "I remember one time in Lorton [a prison outside Washington] the psychiatrist asked me, 'Do you sometimes grow weary portraying the image of a tough guy?' And I say, 'Yeah, I really do.' Because you can't ever let your guard down."

Men like Allen cannot let their guard down for an instant, because "the people watching"—their peers— will reassess their status on the spot. Since status is in such hopelessly short supply, life appears to be a zero-sum game, in which one man's loss is another's gain. Hence lower-class adolescents and men lack the devices that middle-class people rely on to sustain their status. Bruce Jackson points out that a member of the middle class can call himself a filmmaker even though he hasn't made a film in five years, or a scholar even though he has done no research since his doctoral dissertation.* "But the pimp who drove a shiny pimp-mobile yesterday is nobody if he turns up in a VW today."

To understand almost any aspect of lower-class life, in fact, it is useful to keep in mind Everett Hughes' dictum that "concealment and ego-protection are of the essence of social intercourse." In the case of lower-class males, concealment is necessary in order to protect the ego; men have to conceal their weaknesses from themselves, as well as from others. Hence the importance of street-corner society, with its male camaraderie and the expressive life style it fosters. It is on the street corner, as Eliott Liebow writes, that men can be men—"provided they do not look too closely at one another's credentials. . . ."

> The street corner is, among other things, a sanctuary for those who can no longer endure the experience or prospect of failure. There . . . failures are rationalized into phantom successes and weaknesses magically transformed into strengths.

* Members of the middle class have other sustaining devices as well. A large part of what is called "personnel management" is devoted to inventing tangible and intangible tokens of status: a key to the executive toilet; a coffee cup with the corporate seal; a title (calling clerks "executives" or "managers," salespeople "sales executives" or "account executives," and janitors "custodial engineers"); or an expense account, so that employees can live beyond their means at lunch and thus identify with their employers.

What all this means is that the distinctive features of lower-class life have their origins in the fact that American culture goals transcend class lines, while the means of achieving them do not. Members of the lower class are profoundly influenced by the universal values of American society; parents, in particular, want the same things for their children that middle-class parents want for theirs. "When I was a kid, before I really got into the stickup thing, my family kind of had other hopes for me and sometimes so did I," John Allen recalls. His grandmother "wanted me to be a doctor, because I was good with my hands. And my mother, she wanted me to be a lawyer." But none of them had any real conception of what becoming a lawyer or a doctor entailed; and, in any case, school, from the beginning, was an alien place that served only to reinforce Allen's sense that legitimate opportunities were closed to him. As Hylan Lewis warns, "it is important not to confuse basic life chances and actual behavior with basic cultural values and preferences."

Instead of abandoning middle-class values altogether, the sociologist Hyman Rodman suggests, members of the lower class "stretch" those values to accommodate deviations that their life circumstances seem to require.*[39] I know one impoverished mother who struggled with all her might to instill middle-class norms in her children. But she also felt it necessary to teach them how to forge a weapon by breaking the

---

* "Value stretch" is not a uniquely lower-class phenomenon. There is virtually no societal norm or value that is always followed by every person; for every value there is a fall-back position—a secondary set of rules to govern behavior after the first rule has been violated. When people retreat to this secondary set of rules or values, they do not necessarily abandon or reject the primary set but stretch them instead. A familiar example of middle-class value stretch is the motto "That's business" to explain unethical or illegal conduct.

bottom off a bottle, so that they could defend themselves against the violence that was, in the literal sense, a fact of daily life in their neighborhood.

Thus lower-class life involves an almost unbearable tension between the ideal and the reality—between the desired adherence to the norms of the larger society and the insistent demands of life on the streets. The behavior of the lower-class male is "his way of trying to achieve many of the goals and values of the larger society, or failing to do this, of concealing his failure from others and from himself as best he can," Elliot Liebow writes. "If in the course of concealing his failure, or of concealing his fear of even trying, he pretends . . . that he did not want these things in the first place and claims that he had all along been responding to a different set of rules and prizes, we do not do him or ourselves any good by accepting this claim at face value."[40]

But neither do we do anyone any good by discounting the claim altogether. Lower-class life is a response to the strains imposed by the American emphasis on success, but it is not only that. As Lee Rainwater observes, members of the lower class "are not simply passive targets of the destructive forces which act upon them." Lack of opportunity profoundly affects and limits the choices that individuals and groups can make, but it does not prevent them from *making* choices, from creating a way of life that is more than just a reaction against middle-class values. In his foreword to John Allen's memoir, Hylan Lewis points out that Allen's "choices, his style, his fate appear to have been not so much imposed upon him by the world around him as chosen by him as a central reaction to that world." Indeed, Allen has a clear sense of who and what he is: "I always thought of myself as a hustler. I come from a hustling family."[41] In deciding to become a hustler, Allen was not merely choosing a different route to success from those of his contemporaries who became policemen, businessmen, and dentists; in the last analysis, he was selecting a different end, as well as a different set of means.

5

"Beware the Day They Change Their Minds": Race, Culture, and Crime

> White man goes to college,
> Nigger to the field;
> White man learns to read and write;
> Poor Nigger learns to steal . . .
>
> —BLACK AMERICAN FOLK SONG

> I can hear you say, "What a horrible, irresponsible bastard!" And you're right. I leap to agree with you. . . . But to whom can I be responsible, and why should I be, when you refuse to see me? And wait until I reveal how truly irresponsible I am.
>
> —RALPH ELLISON, *Invisible Man*

> Looks like what drives me crazy
> Don't have no effect on you—
> But I'm gonna keep on at it
> Till it drives you crazy, too.
>
> —LANGSTON HUGHES, "Evil"

I

In the end, there is no escaping the question of race and crime. To say this is to risk, almost to guarantee, giving offense; it is impossible to talk honestly about the role of race in American life without offending and angering both whites and blacks—and Hispanic browns and native American reds as well. The truth is too terrible, on all sides; and we are all too accustomed to the soothing euphemisms and inflammatory rhetoric with which the subject is cloaked.

But race and racism continue to shape American life, as they have for three and a half centuries. At its core, the urban problem is a problem of race; so is the welfare problem, the migrant and farm labor problem, the school busing problem—and, to a degree that few have been willing to acknowledge openly, the crime problem. The uncomfortable fact is that black offenders account for a disproportionate number of the crimes that evoke the most fear. Whites of good will have shied away from acknowledging this fact for fear of hurting black sensibilities, and both they and blacks have avoided talking about the problem lest they provide ammunition to bigots.

To the extent to which they do talk about black crime, liberals of both races generally attribute it to the wrenching poverty in which so many black Americans live. In 1976, blacks comprised 11.5 percent of the American population, but 31.1 percent of those officially classified as poor.* Since most street criminals are drawn from the ranks of the poor, it would be surprising if blacks did not turn to theft more often than do whites. In fact, the rate of property crime is just about what one would expect from the poverty statistics; in 1976, blacks comprised 31 percent of the people

* Each year, the U.S. Bureau of the Census estimates the cash income needed to provide a minimally decent standard of living for unattached individuals and for families of various sizes; all those with incomes below this level are classified as poor. In 1976, the poverty threshold for a non-farm family of four people was $5,815.

arrested for the three property crimes (burglary, larceny-theft, and auto theft) in the FBI's Crime Index.

It is violent crime, however, that evokes the most fear—and blacks commit more violent crimes than one would expect from the income statistics alone. As we have seen, robbery is the prototypical street crime, involving both violence (or the threat of violence) and theft. Injury is frequent—one robbery victim in three is injured nowadays—and robbery always has been a crime committed predominantly by strangers. It is also preeminently a black offense: in 1976, 59 percent of those arrested for robbery were black, and black offenders account for nearly three-quarters of the increase in robbery arrests since 1960. Black offenders are disproportionately involved in other violent crimes as well; in 1976, more than half those arrested for murder, nearly half those arrested for rape, and two-fifths of those arrested for aggravated assault were black.*

It is essential that we understand why black offenders are responsible for so much violent crime. The explanation does not lie in the genes; as Mark Twain once observed, "there is no distinctly native American criminal class except Congress," which has few black members. Black crime is rooted in the nature of the black experience in this country—an experience that differs from that of other ethnic groups. To be poor and black is different from being poor and Puerto Rican, or poor and Chicano, or poor and a member of any other ethnic group.

* It is quite possible, even probable, that because of race prejudice police are more likely to arrest blacks than whites for minor offenses such as drunkenness, shoplifting, or disturbing the peace. It is highly unlikely, however, that discriminatory behavior on the part of police can account for much of the disparity between black and white arrest rates for homicide and robbery. (For a more detailed discussion, see Appendix.)

Not the least of these differences involves ethnically distinctive patterns of crime. New York City, with its large numbers of poor black and Hispanic residents, provides an interesting case in point. The two minority groups are roughly comparable in size: blacks comprise a little more than 20 percent of the city's population; Hispanics (mostly Puerto Ricans, but with a growing number of immigrants from Cuba, the Dominican Republic, Colombia, Ecuador, and other Latin-American countries), between 15 and 20 percent. (Since no one knows how many illegal immigrants from Latin America there are in New York, the exact size of the city's Hispanic population is a matter of considerable dispute; some estimates run as high as 30 percent.)

As a group, New York's Puerto Ricans are poorer than its blacks. The median family income among Puerto Ricans is 20 percent below the black median, and the proportion of families officially classified as poor is half again as high. Puerto Rican New Yorkers have less education than blacks, and a larger proportion hold menial jobs.[1] To the degree to which it exists as a distinctive entity, lower-class culture encompasses Puerto Ricans and other Hispanics, as well as blacks; the anthropologist Oscar Lewis coined the term "culture of poverty" to describe the lower-class Mexican and Puerto Rican families he had studied.

If violence were a simple function of poverty and social class, therefore, one would expect as much violent crime among Puerto Rican and other Hispanic residents of New York as among black residents. In fact, the rates are strikingly different. According to an analysis of police statistics by David Burnham of *The New York Times,* 63 percent of the people arrested for violent crimes in the period 1970–72 were black, and only 15.3 percent were Hispanic.* Relative to population, blacks were arrested for a violent crime more than three times as often as were Hispanics, and for robbery nearly four and one half times as often. Although the disparities vary from crime to crime, they remain consistently large:

Crime	% Black	% Hispanic	Disparity Between Black and Hispanic Crime, Relative to Population
Homicide	59	25	1.8 to 1
Robbery	69	12	4.4 to 1
Felonious assault	56	14	3 to 1
Forcible rape	58.5	16.6	2.7 to 1

The same picture emerges from a profile of the New York State prison population. Of a random sample of felons sentenced to state prison in 1973, two-thirds of them for a violent crime, 58.3 percent were black and 15.3 percent Puerto Rican; relative to population, three times as many blacks are incarcerated.[2]

There are similar, and equally striking, differences between the criminal activity of blacks and of Mexican-Americans, the second-largest minority group in the country. In 1976, according to Census Bureau estimates, there were 6,590,000 people of Mexican origin

* Most of the usual objections to the use of arrest statistics as an index of criminal activity disappear when we compare black and Hispanic arrest rates, since members of both groups are the objects of prejudice and discrimination. It would be hard to convince a Puerto Rican New Yorker that the police treat Puerto Ricans more deferentially than they treat blacks. It would be even harder to persuade Mexican-Americans in the Southwest that they receive preferential treatment from the police; as a bitter joke among Chicanos in southern Texas has it, members of the feared and hated Texas Rangers all have Mexican blood—"on their boots."

in the United States, nearly 85 percent of them living
in the five Southwestern states of Arizona, California,
Colorado, New Mexico, and Texas; the Census estimate almost certainly is on the low side.* As a group,
Mexican-Americans are only marginally better off
than black Americans; nationwide, 28.6 percent of the
former were living below the official poverty threshold
in 1975, compared to 31.1 percent of the latter.

In Texas, Mexican-Americans (18.4 percent of the
population) are about as poor as blacks (12.5 percent
of the population); yet 40 percent of the felons committed to state prison in 1973 were black, and 14.2
percent were Chicano. Relative to population, four
times as many blacks as Chicanos were committed to
prison for a felony. In San Antonio, a south Texas

---

* There is uncertainty, and heated controversy, over just how
many Mexican-Americans and other Hispanic Americans there
are in the United States; it is only in the last several years, in
response to pressure from Mexican-American organizations,
that the Census Bureau and other federal agencies began to
view Hispanic Americans as ethnic groups worth studying with
care. Illegal immigration makes it difficult to get a precise
count of the number of Mexican-Americans. The enumeration
problem has been compounded by the fact that there is no
single term to describe Americans of Mexican ancestry that is
acceptable to all segments of that community—no term that
does not evoke pride in some and anger in others. The divisions
are partly (but not wholly) generational: younger people tend
to prefer "Chicano," which older people often consider de-
meaning. There are regional differences as well. In New Mexico and Colorado, and to a lesser degree in Arizona, many
Hispanic Americans dislike "Mexican-American" almost as
much as "Chicano"; they consider themselves descendants of
the Conquistadors and call themselves "Hispanic," "Hispanos,"
or "Spanish-American"—a practice that those who call themselves Chicanos consider an affectation at best, evidence of
self-hatred at worst. (To confuse the matter still more, some
people prefer "Mexican" or "Mexicano.") Because there is no
universally accepted term, I will alternate among Mexican-
American, Chicano, and Hispanic, where possible using the
term that is most appropriate for the particular subgroup being
described.

city that is 52.1 percent Mexican-American and 7.6 percent black, blacks account for 44 percent of the robbery convictions, Mexican-Americans for 40 percent; blacks account for 20 percent and Chicanos for 62 percent of the burglary convictions. Relative to population, blacks are convicted 7.5 times as often as Chicanos for robbery, and more than twice as often for burglary.

More detailed information is available for San Diego, a large city that is 7.6 percent black and 12.7 percent Mexican-American. (San Diego was one of the few cities whose police departments willingly supplied arrest data broken down by ethnicity, as well as by race. The FBI does not ask for such data, and most departments pretended that they do not collect it—hence I had to supplement arrest statistics with data on prison admissions.) Below are the arrest rates for the years 1971 to 1973; the last column shows the disparity between black and Chicano arrest rates, relative to population.

SAN DIEGO ARRESTS, 1971–73

Offense	% Black	% Mexican-American	Disparity, Relative to Population
Homicide	46.9	11.6	7 to 1
Forcible rape	39.9	14.3	4.6 to 1
Robbery	53.4	11.4	7.8 to 1
Felonious assault	38.5	15.0	4.2 to 1
Burglary	29.2	13.8	3.5 to 1
Theft (grand and petty)	18.6	12.1	2.6 to 1

The same pattern shows up in statewide data on first admissions to the California Youth Authority, to which offenders under the age of twenty-one are committed for incarceration. The table below shows the proportions of Mexican-Americans and blacks committed to the Youth Authority for various crimes in the fiscal year 1973–74; as in the San Diego table, the last column shows the ratio of black to Mexican-American offenses, relative to population.

Offense	% Black	% Mexican-American	Disparity, Relative to Population
Homicide	55.3	18.4	4.9 to 1
Sex offenses	39	32	2 to 1
Robbery	49.9	12.3	6.6 to 1
Assault	35.4	30.1	1.9 to 1
Burglary	35.9	14.4	4.1 to 1
Auto theft	21.4	20.4	1.7 to 1
Narcotics	11.6	23.7	.8 to 1

Much the same picture obtains for commitments to the Department of Corrections, which receives offenders twenty-one years of age and older; relative to population, three times as many black felons as Mexican-Americans were committed to the Department in 1973.

The pattern cuts across states as well as age groups.

• In Arizona, the number of blacks in prison at the end of 1973 was five times as large, relative to population, as the number of Mexican-Americans.

• Relative to population, 3.4 times as many blacks as Chicanos were in the Utah state prison for the first time in 1972, and more than five times as many were in prison for the second time.

• In Colorado, in 1972, nearly five times as many blacks as Mexican-Americans were committed to prison for robbery; for burglary, the disparity was 1.25 to 1.

• In New Mexico, in 1973, the number of black prison inmates was nearly three times as large as the number of Mexican-American inmates, relative to population.

The pattern has also been stable over time; analysis of data assembled by the 1931 Wickersham Commission suggests that there were large disparities between black and Mexican-American arrest and conviction rates for violent crimes in the 1920s as well.[3]

II

A propensity to violence was not part of the cultural baggage black Americans carried with them from Africa; the homicide rate in black Africa is about the same as in western Europe, and well below the rate in either white or black America. Indeed, the black American homicide rate is three to five times the black African rate. Violence is something black Americans learned in this country.[4]

They had many teachers; violence has been an intrinsic part of the black American experience from the start. Every other immigrant group came here voluntarily, often illegally; Africans came in chains, having been uprooted from their homes and transported across the sea, at a ghastly cost in human life. (Two Africans in three died en route.) Moreover, slavery was maintained by violence; so was the racial caste system that was erected after Emancipation and that still endures, in diminished form, in parts of the rural South.

For most of their history in this country, in fact, blacks were victims, not initiators, of violence. In the Old South, violence against blacks was omnipresent—sanctioned both by custom and by law. Whites were free to use any methods, up to and including murder, to control "their Negroes." As Raymond Fosdick learned when he studied American police methods shortly before the country's entry into World War I, Southern police departments had three classes of homicide. "If a nigger kills a white man, that's murder," one official

told Fosdick. "If a white man kills a nigger, that's justi-
fiable homicide. If a nigger kills another nigger, that's
one less nigger." A quarter of a century later, Gunnar
Myrdal found little change: "Any white man can strike
or beat a Negro, steal or destroy his property, cheat him
in a transaction and even take his life without fear of
legal reprisal."[5]

There was little blacks could do to protect themselves. To strike back at whites, or merely to display
anger or insufficient deference, was not just to risk one's
own neck, but to place the whole community in danger.
It was equally dangerous, or at best pointless, to appeal
to the law; two lines from an old blues song describe
the "justice" blacks received in court:

> White folks and nigger in great Co't house
> Like Cat down Celler wit' no-hole mouse.

Or, as Nate Shaw, the extraordinary black farmer and
farm-union organizer, whose life story has been recorded by Theodore Rosengarten, remarked, "Nigger
had anything a white man wanted, the white man took
it. . . ." It was, Shaw observed, "a time of brutish acts,
brutish acts."[6]

Life has been brutish for other minority groups. During the nineteenth century, Irish immigrants were objects of scorn and derision, as well as intense discrimination; a generation weaned on "Polish jokes" may be
surprised to learn that "Irish jokes" were a staple of
American humor until the 1930s or '40s. Prejudice
against Jews, Italians, and Poles became intense in the
late nineteenth century and reached a peak in the
1920s, when nativist sentiment led Congress to cut immigration from southern and eastern Europe to a
trickle; for those in their fifties, or older, the prejudice
of those days remains a vivid memory.

And the treatment accorded Chinese, Japanese, Mexican, and native Americans makes the discrimination suffered by European immigrant groups seem like a royal reception. Hysteria over "the yellow peril" waxed and waned (but mainly waxed) for a century; it was not until after World War II that prejudice against Chinese- and Japanese-Americans began to lose some of its sting. The record of perfidy and violence in white people's dealings with native Americans remains a national disgrace; so is the exploitation, brutality, and outright chicanery with which Mexican-Americans have been treated. Both groups continue to suffer from prejudice and discrimination, mingled with indifference.[7]

If I emphasize the violence and oppression visited upon black people, therefore, it is not to gloss over the discrimination from which other minority groups have suffered. It is to argue that other groups' scars notwithstanding, the black experience has been different—in kind, not just degree—from that of any other American group. It is to argue, too, that we cannot understand the contemporary crime problem, let alone do anything about it, without understanding that difference and the ways in which it contributes to criminal violence.

Some distinguished scholars claim the reverse. In their view, poverty, crime, family breakdown, welfare dependency—all the problems we associate with race —are simply manifestations of the difficulty every rural group has had adjusting to city life. Like the European peasants who flocked to American cities in the nineteenth and early twentieth centuries, these scholars argue, black city dwellers today come from backward rural areas. These black migrants—the "last of the immigrants"—turn to crime and other forms of deviance because they are not yet "acculturated" into American society; they have not yet acquired the education, attitudes, values, and skills needed to hold decent jobs or

to function effectively in contemporary urban, industrial life. Because black migration is of such recent
origin, the argument continues, the problems that always
have been associated with migration and urbanization
have not had time to run their course, as they inevitably
will. Patience is required. Just as European ethnics
ultimately "made it" into the mainstream of American
life, so too will blacks—given enough time.[8]

It would be hard to imagine a more profound misreading of American history. Rural black migrants to
metropolitan areas face all the problems of acculturation that other rural migrants have faced, but they carry
two additional burdens: their color and their heritage
of slavery. Prejudice against black people is more virulent and intractable than is prejudice against Orientals,
Chicanos, Native Americans, Catholics, or Jews. Negative symbolism about blackness is built into our language: "black" connotes death, mourning, evil, corruption, and sin, while "white" implies purity, goodness,
and rebirth. The white lie is the permissible misstate-
ment; the black lie, the inexcusable falsehood. The
black sheep is the one who goes astray; and when he
does, he receives a black mark on his record. And so
it goes; the symbolism began long before Englishmen
encountered Africans. As early as the fourteenth century, according to *The Oxford English Dictionary,*
black meant "soiled, dirty, foul"; by the fifteenth century, it meant "malignant" and "sinister" as well.[9]

This deep-rooted distaste for blackness helped make
it possible for white men to turn Africans into slaves
without any qualms; once they had done so, prejudice
and slavery served to reinforce one another in an unending spiral. The distinguishing characteristic of slavery in the United States, Alexis de Tocqueville wrote,
was the fact that "the abstract and transient fact of
slavery is fatally united with the physical and perma-

nent fact of color. The tradition of slavery dishonors the race, and the peculiarity of the race perpetuates the tradition of slavery."

The result of this vicious circle was that racism took on a life of its own; in Tocqueville's words, "slavery recedes, but the prejudice to which it has given birth is immovable." Indeed, Tocqueville found that race prejudice was stronger in states that had abolished slavery than in those which retained the institution; "and nowhere is it so intolerant as in those states where servitude has never been known." There seemed to be no escape. "To induce whites to abandon the opinion they have conceived of the moral and intellectual inferiority of their former slaves, the Negroes must change," Tocqueville concluded; "but as long as this opinion persists, they cannot change."

Intractable white prejudice and discrimination condemned the great majority of black Americans to poverty and isolation for more than a century after Tocqueville wrote. Until the racial barriers began to come down after World War II, black city dwellers were confined to "Negro jobs," which is to say, to the lowest-paying and most menial jobs around. It made no difference whether blacks were born in the North or South, or whether they came from urban or rural backgrounds; nor did it matter whether they were first-, second-, or third-generation city dwellers. No matter how much education they had, no matter what their background or how "acculturated" they were, blacks, with rare exceptions, were locked into the lower class.

This was not the experience of European ethnic groups. The United States has always had a lower class; but, except for blacks, its composition has changed from generation to generation, as one immigrant group has taken the place of another, earlier group whose members were moving up the social and economic ladder. Some European ethnic groups have moved into the middle class more easily and rapidly than others; but for all of them membership in the lower class was temporary.

To be sure, descendants of earlier immigrant groups have always believed that *their* poor were different— that whatever the situation may have been in the past, they were bedeviled by a new breed of immigrants who preferred a dissolute life of crime and poverty to the austere discipline of respectability. "Of those who come to it very few, either by their own efforts or through outside agency, ever leave it," a group of scholars wrote about Hell's Kitchen, an Irish- and German-American slum in New York, shortly before World War I. "It is as though decades of lawlessness and neglect have formed an atmospheric monster. . . ." For the most part, the children and grandchildren of those who lived in Hell's Kitchen in 1912 are now members of the middle class; some of them undoubtedly express anger over the new breed of slum dweller who prefers welfare, heroin, and crime to work and sobriety.[10]

For members of European immigrant groups, upward mobility has been the norm, as the historian Stephan Thernstrom of Harvard has demonstrated in *The Other Bostonians,* a landmark study of social and economic mobility in that city over the course of the last century.*[11] Even over periods as short as a decade,

---

* Thernstrom is one of a new group of historians, able to use painstaking statistical analysis and computer technology to serve the ends of historical research. In this study, Thernstrom pieced together the life histories of some 7,965 representative Bostonians, using published and unpublished data from the decennial Census of Population, the Massachusetts Bureau of Statistics of Labor, city and state vital statistics, municipal archives, and numerous other sources. By coding the information for computer analysis, he was able to trace changes in occupations, income, savings, home ownership, education, and other indices of social status over the course of each individ-

substantial numbers of unskilled laborers—on average, more than one in three—moved to jobs on a higher occupational level; and over the longer interval between men's first and last jobs, the proportion moving up was roughly one in two. Much of this movement, to be sure, was mobility *within* the blue-collar world, from low-status, badly paying casual labor to higher-status, more regular and better-paying jobs. But roughly one unskilled laborer in four managed to move into white-collar occupations.

Mobility was far greater *between* generations. Sixty percent of the children whose fathers were unskilled or semiskilled laborers moved into skilled or white-collar jobs—a staggering proportion, given the widespread view that poverty tends to perpetuate itself from generation to generation. This is not to deny that there were pockets of poverty, instances in which poverty was transmitted from father to son. The point is, they were precisely that—pockets. And Boston seems to be typical of the United States; for nearly a century, upward mobility has been more common than perpetuation of poverty.[12]

With one exception: black Bostonians remained mired in poverty from 1860 until 1940. The contrast between the black and Irish experience makes it clear that it was white prejudice and discrimination, not black people's unfamiliarity with urban life or lack of preparation for industrial jobs, that was responsible. To isolate the effects of unfamiliarity with urban and in-

---

ual's lifetime, and from generation to generation as well. The result is the most comprehensive measurement of mobility ever made in an American city. (Because the popular image of Boston has been that of a stagnant, caste-ridden city with a large and immobile Irish and Italian lower class and an entrenched and self-perpetuating WASP upper class, Thernstrom's findings are particularly important.)

dustrial life, Thernstrom compared the occupational
distribution of first-generation Irish and black Bostonians and of their second- and third-generation off-
spring. In 1860, Irish residents ranked below blacks
in Boston's occupational hierarchy; by 1890, 32 percent
of second-generation Irish workers, but only 17 percent of second-generation black workers, held white-
collar jobs.[13]

Even more striking, third-generation black Bostonians, who "should have been an economic elite if
familiarity with the culture indeed made a great difference," were hardly better off than first-generation migrants from the rural South. In 1890, 83 percent of the
third-generation blacks were still manual workers, most
of them in jobs characteristically held by new black
migrants—laborer, servant, waiter, janitor, or porter.
For another half-century, black workers continued to
be barred from all but the most menial jobs. In 1940,
53 percent of the black males employed in Boston held
jobs as unskilled laborers, servants, janitors, and porters; only 11 percent held white-collar jobs.

Blacks did not stay in servile jobs because of any
inability to adjust to the demands of urban or industrial
life. Much has been made of the alleged weakness of
the black family; both black and white scholars have argued that the high rate of family breakdown among
black city dwellers handicapped black males in the
struggle for economic success. But in late nineteenth-
century Boston, black family life was a good bit *more*
stable than was family life among European, and especially Irish, immigrants. In 1880, both husband and
wife were present in 82 percent of black households;
only 16 percent were headed by a female. Among the
Irish of south Boston, the comparable figure was 27
percent. Nor was Boston atypical in this regard. As the
historian Herbert Gutman of New York's City College

has demonstrated in his monumental study of the black family, the much discussed and debated deterioration of the black family is a recent phenomenon. In slavery and freedom, in cities as well as in the rural South, black family life showed remarkable strength and stability. From the middle of the eighteenth century until the fourth decade of the twentieth, the majority of black children lived with both parents, and most adults lived together in long-lasting marriages.[14]

That discrimination, not their own lack of qualifications, kept blacks at the bottom is evident from the fact that blacks were hired for unskilled jobs in manufacturing and transportation, but were almost totally excluded from semiskilled jobs in those same industries. Semiskilled jobs paid a lot more than unskilled "Negro jobs," but they did not require any higher level of education, discipline, or skill. As Thernstrom writes, "It is hard to believe that it was anything but their race that prevented Negroes from entering [these jobs] in large numbers."

From time to time, blacks did fill, and sometimes even dominated, skilled and semiskilled occupations—as railroad locomotive firemen, brakemen, switchmen, and mechanics; carpenters, bricklayers, painters, and masons; barbers; waiters and caterers; and a host of other jobs. But blacks were forced out of these occupations with monotonous regularity—not because they filled them badly, but because white workers wanted the jobs instead. With each wave of immigration from Europe, black workers were displaced by whites.* And

---

* A major theme of Booker T. Washington's famous speech at the opening of the Cotton States and International Exposition in Atlanta in 1895 was his appeal to white employers to "cast down your bucket where you are"—to continue to employ "those people who have, without strikes or labor wars, tilled your fields, cleared your forests, builded your railroads and

when jobs were scarce enough, native whites were only too happy to take over Negro jobs, in the process redefining them into white jobs. The growth of trade unions solidified the process; for many whites, the opportunity to monopolize desirable jobs for members of their own race was a major attraction of union membership.

• In 1865, blacks dominated the construction industry in the South, filling 80 percent of the skilled jobs. By 1890, only 25 percent of the carpenters and painters were black; by 1930, the black proportion was down to 17 percent. And blacks were completely excluded from the new, and growing, occupations of electrician and plumber.

• Until the turn of the century, the job of locomotive fireman was considered too dirty for a white man to fill. Technological change, combined with an end to the expansion of railroad employment, made the occupation attractive to whites. During the early 1930s, members of the all-white Brotherhood of Locomotive Firemen and Engineers used physical intimidation and even murder—there were twenty-one documented shootings, some of them fatal—to drive the few remaining black firemen and brakemen out of their jobs.[15]

The explosive growth of Jim Crow legislation during the 1890s and early 1900s played an equally large role in blocking upward mobility for blacks on anything but a piecemeal scale. In the post-Civil War era, Southern whites were far from united on the virtues

---

cities, and brought forward treasures from the bowels of the earth. . . ." If they would use black workers, instead of replacing them with European immigrants, Washington promised his white listeners, "you and your families will be surrounded by the most faithful, law-abiding, and unresentful people that the world has ever seen. . . . we shall stand by you with a devotion that no foreigner can approach. . . ."

of or necessity for segregation; on the contrary, the caste system was a relatively late mutation.[16] Until the 1890s, blacks voted in large numbers, and white Southern conservatives and radicals competed for their vote. Given the franchise and the protection of the law for the first time, blacks showed a remarkable zeal for self-improvement, believing, as noted by the publisher of the monthly literary magazine *Anglo-African,* that "No one thing is beyond the aim of the colored man in this country." Thus the motto of the Class of 1886 at Tuskegee Institute was "There Is Always Room at the Top."

By the end of the nineteenth century, it had become apparent that there was room only at the bottom. In the South, blacks were rapidly and totally disfranchised; in Louisiana, the number of registered black voters plummeted from 130,334 in 1896 to a mere 1,342 in 1904. Disfranchisement was accompanied by an intensive campaign of race hatred and anti-black violence and harassment, as well as by the adoption of Jim Crow legislation affecting every aspect of life. (In some states, black court witnesses were even required to take their oaths on separate Jim Crow Bibles.) The rest of the country quickly followed the Southern lead, barring blacks from previously integrated theaters, churches, restaurants, YMCAs, and the like. The process was completed when Woodrow Wilson was elected president on a platform pledging the "New Freedom" and guaranteeing "fair and just treatment" for all. A white Southerner by outlook as well as birth, Wilson was shocked to discover that white and black federal employees used the same lunchrooms and toilets and ordered the latter to use separate facilities. Wilson also dismissed all but two of the black officials who had been appointed by his predecessor, William Howard Taft.

And so it went, until the desperate shortage of labor during World War II left employers no alternative but to hire and train black employees. The speed and ease with which blacks took over semiskilled factory jobs made it all the more evident that it had been discrimination, not any lack of qualifications, that had kept them out of those jobs before the war broke out. As Thernstrom concludes, the barriers to black advancement have been external, not internal—"the result not of peculiarities in black culture but of peculiarities in white culture."

For all the poverty, prejudice, and discrimination from which Mexican-Americans have suffered, their lot has not been as hard as that of black Americans. Animosity against Mexican-Americans is not as deeply rooted in the consciousness of Americans of European descent as is prejudice against blacks. Blacks were excluded from white society, no matter what their accomplishments. But Anglos tended to distinguish between "high-type" and run-of-the-mill Mexican-Americans, accepting (and even marrying) the former, while discriminating against the latter.[17] Perhaps the critical difference between the black and Mexican-American experiences is that Mexicans were not captured, transported thousands of miles, and forced into slavery. On the contrary, large numbers of Mexicans continue to cross the border into the United States; oppressed and impoverished as they are, they still are better off doing stooped labor in the fields of Texas, Florida, California, and other states than they would be in Mexico, where there often is no work at all. Others, particularly those who prefer to be called Hispanos or Spanish-Americans, settled the Southwest long before the Anglos arrived. In New Mexico, in particular, many Hispanic American families live on land their families have worked for two or even three centuries—land that had belonged to their ancestors before the Anglo conquerors took title by force or fraud.

Whether migrant workers or old settlers, whether rich or poor, Mexican-Americans share a common language and religion, as well as a common cultural heritage. It would be hard to exaggerate the succor that possession of their own language provides. Robert Coles points out that Spanish offers "a constant reminder that one is not hopelessly Anglo, that one has one's own words, one's way of putting things and regarding the world, and, not least, one's privacy and independence." Their profound Catholicism, which makes God and Church an intimate part of daily life, also protects them against destructive blows to their sense of self. "Chicano children grow up to regard themselves as members of a particular community of people, a community under the surveillance of Almighty God," Coles writes. Language and religion reinforce one another; since the Spanish language is a treasure handed down by God, being Mexican is a privilege—"a separate way of being alive," as Coles puts it. The result is that even the poorest Chicanos display a sense of self that confuses (and often angers) Anglos.[18]

Puerto Ricans, too, have escaped the stigmatizing experience of slavery. Equally important, most Puerto Ricans arrived in the mainland during the late 1940s, '50s, and '60s, when the United States was passing laws forbidding discrimination on the basis of race, religion, or national origin. In 1910, there were only 1,500 Puerto Ricans living in the mainland, and in 1940, only 70,000; in 1950, there were still only a little more than 300,000. The number nearly quintupled in the next twenty years; by 1976, 1,753,000 people of Puerto Rican origin were living in the mainland. Puerto Ricans have encountered prejudice, of course; but the experi-

ence is too recent to have insinuated itself into the
Puerto Rican consciousness the way racism has affected
black life and thought.

III

When one reflects on the history of black people in this
country, what is remarkable is not how much, but how
little black violence there has always been. Certainly,
it would be hard to imagine an environment better calculated to evoke violence than the one in which black
Americans have lived. As the late Abraham Joshua
Heschel once wrote, "There is a form of oppression
which is more painful and more scathing than physical
injury or economic privation. It is public humiliation."

Black Americans have been given—and, to a degree
most white Americans fail to understand, continue to
be given—humiliation, insult, and embarrassment as a
daily diet, without regard to individual merit. Under
the Southern caste system, not only were most blacks
confined to humble and servile jobs; they were expected
to *be* humble and servile. On this, Southern whites were
insistent; for it, they were willing to pay a heavy price.
Black workers came to be paid as much for their ser-
vility and adeptness at flattering their employer as for
their ability or performance. The one sure way for
blacks, especially black men, to place themselves in
jeopardy was to show signs of ambition—to be "up-
pity," to seek to rise above their "place." And if by
chance black men and women did succeed in securing
an education or bettering themselves economically,
they were well-advised to conceal the fact and to continue to "play the fool" before middle- and upper-class
whites.

The caste system is disappearing rapidly; white
Americans are learning to avoid overtly racist remarks

and behavior. But the racial attitudes the caste system engendered are a good bit more durable—in the North as well as the South. In matters of race, Northern whites always have been more Southern than they realized or acknowledged. It was less than fifteen years ago that the white housekeeper inspecting my wife's hospital room bestowed a gracious compliment on the black porter who had washed the floor. "The floor looks beautiful," she told him. "You're a good boy, Jimmy." Jimmy was forty-eight years old.

Whites continue to patronize blacks and, in the process, to deny their existence as full human beings. "Why, she hears everything we say!" a well-to-do acquaintance told me recently, with genuine astonishment in his voice. He was referring to the black housekeeper he and his wife had employed for the last ten years; the night before, the newly militant woman had commented on something her employer had said at dinner while she was removing the dishes. Until then, the couple had always talked to one another, and to their guests, as if she were not present.

This white assumption of black invisibility cuts to the marrow, for it denies black people's existence as full human beings. In time, it makes them wonder if they really do exist—if they really are full human beings. It also makes them angry. "It's when you feel like this, that out of resentment, you begin to bump people back. And let me confess, you feel that way most of the time," Ralph Ellison's protagonist remarks in the opening scene of *Invisible Man*, one of the great American novels. "You ache with the need to convince yourself that you do exist in the real world, that you're part of all the sound and anguish, and you strike out with your fists, you curse and you swear to make them recognize you. And, alas, it's seldom successful."[19]

The frustration that invisibility generates has been a

central theme of black literature from the start, each
writer using his own metaphor. To James Baldwin, it
is a sense of being nameless and faceless; to W. E. B.
DuBois, it was a feeling of never being heard. "It is as
though one, looking out from a dark cave in a side of
an impending mountain, sees the world and speaks to
it; speaks courteously and persuasively, showing them
how these entombed souls are kindred in their natural
movements, expression and development; and how their
loosening from prison would be a matter not simply of
courtesy, sympathy and help to them, but aid to all the
world." DuBois wrote. "One talks on evenly and logi-
cally in this way but notices that the passing throng
does not even turn its head, or if it does, glances curi-
ously and walks on."

> It gradually penetrates the minds of the prisoners that
> the people passing do not hear; that some thick sheet
> of invisible but horribly tangible plate glass is between
> them and the world. They get excited; they talk
> louder; they gesticulate. Some of the passing world
> stop in curiosity; these gesticulations seem to be point-
> less; they laugh and pass on. . . . Then the people
> within may become hysterical. They may scream and
> hurl themselves against the barriers, hardly realizing
> in their bewilderment that they are screaming in a
> vacuum unheard and that their antics may actually
> seem funny to those outside looking in.[20]

Over the last fifteen years, white Americans have
discovered how deep is the store of anger and hatred
that three and a half centuries of humiliation have built
up in black Americans, and how quickly that anger can
explode into violence. The potential for violence always
has been present. "To be a Negro in this country and
to be relatively conscious," James Baldwin has written,
"is to be in a rage almost all the time." Black Ameri-

cans had to invent ways of channeling their anger and controlling their hate; they had to create nonsuicidal forms of courage. Had they not done so, the United States would have gone up in smoke long ago. What has happened in the last fifteen years, in good measure, is that the cultural devices that kept black violence under control have broken down, and that new cultural controls have not yet emerged. To comprehend the reasons for the high level of black violence now, we need to understand what those controls were, how they worked, and why they have lost their effectiveness.

To do so—to arrive at the necessary understanding —we need to take a detour through black life and culture. That black Americans have a culture at all is something that had escaped white attention until quite recently. What was truly surprising about the extraordinary white reaction to *Roots,* a black friend commented to me, was that it was all such a surprise—that white Americans were so amazed to discover that black Americans have roots, indeed whole family trees, of their own. Yet the popular reaction was inevitable, given the scholarly view that has prevailed. "It is not possible for Negroes to view themselves as other ethnic groups viewed themselves," Nathan Glazer and Daniel P. Moynihan wrote in *Beyond the Melting Pot,* "because—and this is the key to much in the Negro world —the Negro is only an American, and nothing else. He has no values and culture to guard and protect."[21]

Glazer and Moynihan were reflecting the dominant —and incorrect—scholarly view. Black Americans are Americans, to be sure; no less than the members of any other ethnic group, they are heirs to all of American culture—to all of Western civilization. But they are not *only* Americans; blacks have fused American culture with the civilization they brought with them from Africa to create their own culture as well—their own music and dance, their own vocabulary and rhythm of speech, their own values and folklore, their own religious denominations, their own ethos and life style.

They have done so, moreover, out of the sight and hearing of white people. Until recently, their own survival required blacks to hide their thoughts and feelings; in the words of a black folk song popular for generations,

> Got one mind for white folks to see,
> Another for what I know is me;
> He don't know, he don't know my mind.

Indeed, black people derived a certain wry amusement from the total ignorance about black life and thought on the part of whites who boasted that they "knew their Negro." "Negroes have always met this remark with a certain faint, knowing smile," Robert R. Moton, the second president of Tuskegee Institute, wrote in 1929. "Their common experience has taught them that as a matter of fact there are vast reaches of Negro life and thought of which white people know nothing whatever, even after long contact with them, sometimes on the most intimate terms."[22]

There is considerable risk and not a little arrogance in any white writer's attempt to describe black life and culture. The difficulty any outsider has in penetrating another culture is magnified, in this instance, by white Americans' deep-rooted tendency to view black Americans through the distorted lenses of their own stereotypes. White foes have regarded blacks as objects; white friends have seen them as victims. Neither group has been willing to discard its own stereotypes and see black people as full human beings.* But the manifold

---

* For a writer, understanding black culture is complicated still more by the fact that its characteristic expressions have been oral, rather than literary; I have had to immerse myself in

truths of black life are no more barred to a white writer than the truths of white life—or of life in general—are barred to a black writer. If I have learned anything from Ralph Ellison's and Albert Murray's novels and essays, it is, in Ellison's phrase, "the basic unity of human experience," and the writer's capacity (and obligation) to express that unity, along with the rich diversity of life and thought in which it is concealed.

The effort must be made, in any case; for too long, serious students of race, both white and black, have concentrated exclusively on the nature of white oppression and the toll it has exacted in the lives of black people. But as Ralph Ellison has pointed out over and over again, a people "is more than the sum of its brutalization." This is not to deny the ruggedness of black life, "nor the hardship, the poverty, the sordidness, the filth," Ellison remarked in 1967, in the course of an attack on some recent portraits of life in Harlem. "But there is something else in Harlem, something subjective, willful, and complexly and compellingly human. It is that 'something else' which makes for our strength, which makes for our endurance and our promise." To understand that "something else" does not mean ignor-

---

black humor, folklore, music, dance, and speech, as well as in novels, short stories, and plays. I have approached the task with trepidation, therefore, but also (I would like to think) in good faith. I have tried to learn from those, especially Albert Murray and Charles Keil, who criticized the shortcomings of my earlier attempt in *Crisis in Black and White,* and from friends—Lolis Elie, Ralph Ellison, Herbert Gutman, Charles V. Hamilton, Bruce Jackson, Hylan Lewis, Dr. Pauli Murray, Lee Rainwater, Melvin Tumin—who have given generously of their time to instruct me and to correct my errors. (My task would have been easier had Lawrence Levine's monumental study *Black Culture and Black Consciousness* been published before, rather than after, I had finished the first three drafts of this chapter.[23])

ing the suffering. "I get damn tired of critics writing of me as though I don't know how hard it is to be a Negro American," Ellison added. "My point is that it isn't *only* hard, that there are many, many good things about it."[24]

A lesser people might not have survived at all. The black achievement has been not only to survive, but to do so with style—with grace and wit, irony and irreverence, and an exuberant vitality that demonstrates an extraordinary capacity to affirm, even celebrate, life under the most life-destroying conditions. Black humor, black music, and black folklore all reveal this ability to give life significance; in the language of black folklore, they are all means of "making a way out of no-way."

"Making a way out of no-way" is not an exclusively black American attribute; every group that has survived oppression has done so through a kind of spiritual or cultural alchemy. What distinguishes the black American way is its playfulness and expressiveness, its sense of the comic possibilities contained within tragedy. "He remembered once the melancholy-comic notes of a 'Blues' rising out of a Harlem basement before dawn," the poet-novelist Claude McKay wrote a half-century ago in one of his novels. "He was going to catch an early train and all that trip he was sweetly, deliciously happy humming the refrain and imagining what the interior of the little dark den he heard it in was like. 'Blues' . . . melancholy-comic. That was the key to himself and his race. . . ."

> No wonder the whites, after five centuries of contact, could not understand his race. . . . No wonder they hated them, when out of their melancholy environment the blacks could create mad, contagious music and high laughter.[25]

Thus the blues, used in the broadest sense to include the whole genre of jazz, spirituals, gospel and "soul music," and other forms of black folk music and dance, are not simply an art form, although certainly they are that. The blues are the quintessential expression of the black American approach to life: "an impulse to keep the painful details and episodes of a brutal experience alive in one's aching consciousness, to finger its jagged grain, and to transcend it, not by the consolation of philosophy but by squeezing from it a near-tragic, near-comic lyricism," as Ralph Ellison defines it. "As a form, the blues is an autobiographical chronicle of personal catastrophe expressed lyrically."[26]

The bitter-sweet, tragic-comic character of the blues —the insistence on keeping the pain alive even while transcending it—reflects the dual life that black Americans have had to live, and the dual consciousness they have had to maintain. Forced to wear a mask of sweet docility, they became marvelously adept at forging that mask into a weapon that could be turned against the unsuspecting oppressor. "Our life is a war and I have been a traitor all my born days, a spy in the enemy's camp," the protagonist's grandfather, until then considered "the meekest of men," tells the children and grandchildren assembled around his deathbed in an early scene in *Invisible Man.* "Live with your head in the lion's mouth," he continues. "I want you to overcome 'em with yeses, undermine 'em with grins, agree 'em to death and destruction, let 'em swoller you till they vomit or bust wide open."

Indeed, black Americans have always taken pride in the fact that while whites boast that they "know their Negroes," in reality it is the Negro who knows—and manipulates—his whites. If done adroitly enough, "playing the fool" could make the white man appear

the fool, persuading him to accept shoddy workman-
ship and malingering—for poor blacks, the only forms
of sabotage available—or otherwise to accede to black
desires. "The Negro uses his intimate knowledge of
the white man to further his own advancement," Robert
Moton wrote, from long experience as Booker T. Washington's disciple and successor.

> Much of what is regarded as racially characteristic of
> the Negro is nothing more than his artful accommo-
> dation of his manners and methods to what he knows
> to be the weakness and foibles of his white neighbors.
> Knowing what is expected of him, and knowing too
> what he himself wants, the Negro craftily uses his
> knowledge to anticipate opposition and to eliminate
> friction in securing his desires.

Or as Dr. Bledsoe, the crafty Negro college president
in *Invisible Man,* whom Ellison may have modeled
after Dr. Moton, exclaims to the naïve young protagonist, "My God, boy! You're black and living in the
South—did you forget how to lie? . . . Why, the
dumbest black bastard in the cotton patch knows that
the only way to please a white man is to tell him a lie!"

He had to "play the nigger" to get where he is, Bledsoe goes on to explain, but now he has power; although
white people support the college, he controls it—and
unbeknownst to the white donors, he controls them
as well.

> "I's big and black and I say 'Yes, suh' as loudly as any
> burr-head when it's convenient, but I'm still the king
> down here. I don't care how it appears otherwise.
> Power doesn't have to show off. . . . You let the
> white folk worry about pride and dignity—you learn
> where you are and get yourself power, influence, con-
> tacts with powerful and influential people—then stay
> in the dark and use it."

The overwhelming majority of black Americans have had to stay in the dark without power and influence, and without contact with powerful and influential people. Hence they have had to find their own sources of dignity and pride—their own ways of investing their lives with meaning and significance, and their own outlets for their anger. One way has been through an elaborate fantasy life of heroism and triumph, a life in which the poor and oppressed triumph over the rich and powerful. Nowhere is this fantasy life revealed or celebrated more clearly than in black folklore and narrative poetry—"primary devices," as the folklorist-ethnographer Roger D. Abrahams of the University of Texas observes, "by which the Negro self-image has been formulated, transmitted, and maintained."[27]

Because they are so familiar to white Americans, and so misunderstood by them, the "Uncle Remus" stories provide a useful starting point. Uncle Remus himself —"the venerable old darkey" with the "beaming countenance"—was the brainchild of Joel Chandler Harris, a white Southern journalist, but the stories he tells are the product of the black imagination, with only modest distortions in the retelling. The setting is always the same: the little white boy, son of "Miss Sally" and "Mars John," comes into the old Negro's cabin back of the "big house"; Uncle Remus' face "breaks up into little eddies of smiles," and he takes the admiring child on his lap, caresses him, and tells him innocent-sounding stories about Brer Rabbit and other members of the animal kingdom. The relationship appears to be one of unadulterated love and tenderness between white and black.

Appearances are deceptive; "if one looks more closely," Bernard Wolfe writes in a now-classic essay, "within the magnanimous caress is an incredibly malevolent blow."[28] In the first and best-known collection of Uncle Remus stories, Brer Rabbit bests the Fox nineteen times in twenty encounters, using guile and wit rather than brute force. Brer Rabbit also triumphs over the Wolf, the Bear and, on one occasion, the entire animal kindom. In all, there are twenty-eight victories of the Weak over the Strong; ultimately, all the predators die violent deaths at the hands of their ostensible prey. "Admittedly, folk symbols are seldom systematic, clean-cut, or specific," Wolfe writes; "they are cultural shadows thrown by the unconscious, and the unconscious is not governed by the sharp-edged neatness of the filing cabinet." But it hard to avoid the conclusion that Brer Rabbit is "a symbol—about as sharp as Southern sanctions would allow—of the Negro slave's festering hatred of the white man."

The stories involve far more than just a generalized expression of hatred; they offer a direct and sharply focused attack on white Southern racial etiquette in general, and the taboos about food and sex in particular. "The South, with its 'sanctions of fear and force,' forbids Negroes to eat at the same table with whites," Wolfe comments. "But Brer Rabbit, through an act of murder, *forces* Brer Fox and all his associates to share their food with him."

> The South enjoins the Negro, under penalty of death, from coming near the white man's women—although the white man has free access to the Negro's women. But Brer Rabbit flauntingly demonstrates his sexual superiority over all the other animals and, as the undisputed victor in the sexual competition, gets his choice of *all* the women.

The real contest is over power and prestige, rather than food and sex; the latter are sought less for the immediate gratification they provide than for their symbolic value. From Brer Rabbit's perspective, life is an unending battle for power and prestige—a battle in which rules and codes are simply devices by which the powerful try to rig the outcome in their own favor. "The South is the most etiquette-ridden region of the country," Wolfe writes; "and the Rabbit sees all forms of etiquette as hypocritical and absurd. Creatures meet, address each other with unctuous politeness, inquire after each other's families, pass the time of day with oily cliches— and all the while they are plotting to humiliate, rob, and assassinate each other."

In short, the animal tales (the Brer Rabbit stories are part of a much larger genre) provided a biting parody of white society, as well as an outlet for black fantasies about the day when the weak would triumph over the strong. As the historian Lawrence Levine explains, the animals in the stories were replicas of whites as blacks saw them—people who "mouthed lofty platitudes and professed belief in noble ideals but spent much of their time manipulating, oppressing, enslaving one another." In these stories, moreover, it was not only the weak who functioned as tricksters; the strong were just as deceitful and indirect. The ultimate lesson was that the weak must always be on guard to avoid being victimized even more than they already are.[29]

And animal stories represent only a small part of the rich store of black folklore. During the eighteenth and nineteenth centuries, contemporary folklorists believe, stories about a slave named John were even more prevalent, although generally unknown to whites. Like Brer Rabbit, John is a "trickster"—one who, despite his apparent weakness and impotence, gains control of his world through verbal agility and guile. In the "John tales," the hostility is both more guarded and more overt: John gets the better of "Old Marster," and usually makes him appear ridiculous, by turning the white man's stereotypes of blacks (e.g., their laziness, stupidity, superstition, and thievery) against him.[30]

IV

The central task of any culture is to make life significant for its members. In some ways, Emancipation made the task more difficult, and certainly more complex. Under slavery, the barriers had been absolute; with freedom, they became more permeable but also more unpredictable. Blacks began to move up into the larger society only to be thrown back, increasing their anger and frustration. With freedom, too, it became harder for blacks to reconcile their situation with the rhetoric of American democracy. "One can understand slavery," Tocqueville had predicted, "but how allow several millions of citizens to exist under a load of eternal infamy and hereditary wretchedness?"

Blacks had to develop new outlets for their anger and frustration—new mechanisms for controlling the violence to which they were being provoked—as well as new ways of nurturing a sense of self-worth in a world designed to persuade them of their worthlessness. Brer Rabbit and John tales continued to be told, but their cathartic role was taken over in good measure by the development of the blues and by the creation of a vast store of narrative poetry, or "toasts." For lower-class black males, in particular, toasts played a central role from the late nineteenth century until quite recently.*

To understand the role of toasts, we need to start with the fact that they form part of an oral rather than

---

* I am indebted to Professor Bruce Jackson for his help in guiding me through the world of the toasts.

literary tradition. Oral cultures differ from literary cultures in a number of ways. The rhetoric is different: since stories, poems, and legends are passed down from one generation to another without recourse to the printed page, alliteration, repetition and rhyme, and other devices to aid memory play a central role. Any one toast or story is likely to have had a number of authors, for different audiences changed parts they did not like or thought could be improved. Folk audiences "are intolerant of what bores them and tend to discard boring things quickly and to reject boring performers immediately," Bruce Jackson writes. "The process of oral narrative is such that any active participant can change parts he doesn't like or understand or redesign parts not meaningful to his immediate audience."[31] As a result, folk poetry does not contain private meanings or private constructions; if it is to survive, it must be easily and immediately understood by its audience.

In an oral culture, moreover, words have power—to comfort, wound, sexually arouse, destroy, exorcise, and so on. This is true in all societies; witness the importance everywhere attached to names. But in an oral culture, words have power far beyond that which they have in a literary world. And among a people denied access to any other form of power, words have been especially prized as a surrogate for power; verbal contests account for a large proportion of the conversation among adolescent boys and young men, and also, to a considerable degree, among women. "Proverbs, turn of phrases, jokes, almost any manner of discourse is used," Roger Abrahams writes, "not for purposes of discursive communication but as weapons in verbal battle."[32]

Almost any gathering may turn into a "sounding" (or "joning") session—a verbal performance or contest, involving an escalating exchange of tall stories, boasts, jokes, or insults. (The adolescent version, "playing the dozens," involves a highly ritualized exchange of obscene, rhymed insults directed at the contestants' mothers or other female relatives.) Since conversation is entertainment and contest, as well as communication, how one speaks may be as important as what one says; a given word may have multiple and even opposite meanings according to the tone, gestures, and style of discourse. "The Black man has been lied to so often that he has had to learn to 'play past' words very quickly in order to arrive at the truth of a situation," the anthropologists Christina and Richard Milner write. And the truth resides in body language as much as, or more than, in words themselves. When lower-class black men gather at parties, in bars, or on street corners, they refer to the conversation as "talking shit"—as the Milners write, "a linguistic recognition that words are worthless excrement" compared to the messages exchanged through real, i.e., nonverbal, communication.[33]

Verbal contests play an important role in a number of cultures besides that of black street-corner society, for they provide an alternative to actual fighting—a way of dissipating enmity without bloodshed. In the case of black youth, who had to learn to substitute verbal for physical aggression against whites, "playing the dozens" serves to develop verbal proficiency and speed. Equally important, as Lawrence Levine observes, verbal duels provide training in self-discipline. The participant who responds to the escalating insults through physical violence is considered the loser—someone who is unable to "take it." And for blacks in the South, being able to exercise self-control under extreme provocation was essential to survival.[34]

Toasting sessions, on the other hand, are more entertainment than contest, although competitive elements may enter as participants respond to a toast with another version or a different style of presentation. On the surface, toasts are told as a way of passing the time, of entertaining one's friends, and, at the same time, of demonstrating one's own ability at recitation. But as Bruce Jackson writes, there are many ways of passing time—many ways of evoking laughter or displaying verbal skill. How men choose to pass the time tells us a lot about who and what they are, about what they value and what they fear, and how they relate to one another and to the larger society—all the more so, as Jackson says, because "Toasts, like much folk literature, deal with problems of human relations . . . in a special, highly filtered and exaggerated way."[35]

As in the Brer Rabbit and John tales, the toasts deal with the struggle for power and the perquisites that go with it. The heroes gain power or control either through verbal ability and guile, through brute strength, or, in rare cases, through some of both—but always with a flagrant rejection of rules and contempt for authority. Indeed, the heroes flaunt their defiance of any kind of order and revel in their amorality.

But the heroes of the toast world are admired less for their defiance than for their style. What a man *is* is more important than what he *does;* in this essentially aristocratic approach to life, a man's measure lies not in his achievement but in his character, and character is revealed by the style and grace with which he lives his life and with which he endures defeat. For the heroes of the toasts, after all, as for their lower-class black male audience, defeat seems inevitable and victory, if it does come, turns out to be either short-lived or Pyrrhic. In a line that captures the spirit of the toasts, a character in Lonne Elder III's play *Ceremonies in*

Dark Old Men exclaims, "Think of all the life you had before they buried you!" A joke popular among black Americans reflects the same outlook:

> A brother died and went to heaven. He was appropriately outfitted with white robe, halo, and wings. The wings fascinated him; he fluttered them, stretched them, and began tentatively to fly. As he gained experience he tried long swooping glides, he flew high, he flew low, he flew backward, he flew upside down, and finally he made dive-bombing attacks on the peaceful citizenry below. Swoosh—within inches of the golden streets. Down over their heads he came, scaring the hell out of cherubim and seraphim. Finally his antics were too much for the management to bear and he was grounded, his wings removed and locked up. As he sat forlornly on the curb a black brother came up.
>
> "Now ain't you a bitch—the way you were performing and carrying on. I told you you were going to lose your wings. If you'd listened to me you'd still have them. No, you had to perform—and now here you sit grounded with no wings!"
>
> The miscreant looked up. "But I was a flying son of a bitch while I had 'em, wasn't I!"*[36]

This is the world view of the toasts as well. Consider the "Signifying Monkey" toasts—one of the three most popular groups, the others being the "Stackolee" and "Shine" (or "Titanic") toasts.[37] Like Brer Rabbit, the Monkey is a trickster; through clever word play and guile ("signifying"), he persuades his archenemy, the Lion, to pick a fight with the Elephant in which the former is badly beaten. For the brawn he lacks, the Monkey substitutes a kind of verbal jujitsu, using the Lion's ego to bring about his undoing.

* Although the humor is characteristically black, the underlying theme is universal—a black retelling of the ancient Greek myth of Daedalus and Icarus.

Here is a text that Roger Abrahams recorded in Philadelphia.[38] The opening lines set the tone:

Deep down in the jungle, so they say,
There's a signifying motherfucker down the way.
There hadn't been no disturbing in the jungle for
    quite a bit,
For up jumped the monkey in the tree one day and
    laughed, "I guess I'll start some shit."

Without any apparent provocation, the signifying begins, and the Monkey persuades the Lion to attack the Elephant.

Now the Lion come through the jungle one peaceful day,
When the signifying monkey stopped him and this is
    what he started to say:
He said, "Mr. Lion," he said, "a bad-assed motherfucker
    [elephant] down your way,"
He said, "Yeah, the way he talks about your folks is a
    certain shame.
I even heard him curse when he mentioned your grand-
    mother's name."
The lion's tail shot back like a forty-four
When he went down that jungle in all uproar.

The toast goes on to describe a battle of epic proportions in which the Lion is badly beaten (*"I'll be damned if I can see how the lion got away"*). When the fight is over, the Monkey, signifying again, taunts the Lion from the safety of his tree. But the Monkey gets so excited by his own gloating that he jumps up and down, loses his footing, and falls to the ground. Now he must use all his wit and guile to escape with his life—to get out of a danger of his own making. He succeeds by appealing first to the Lion's sympathy, and then to his pride:

The monkey looked up with a tear in his eyes.
He said, "Please, Mr. Lion, I apologize."

He said, "You lemme get my head out the sand,
Ass out the grass, I'll fight you like a natural
    man."
The lion jumped back and squared for a fight.
The motherfucking monkey jumped clear out of sight.

Thus, the Monkey wins, but his "victory" is laden
with irony: although he makes a fool out of the Lion,
he nonetheless must remain cooped up—segregated—
in his tree if he wants to stay alive. In some versions of
the toast, in fact, the Monkey resumes his signifying,
loses his footing again, and this time his life as well.
(*"Lion said, 'Ain't gonna be no apologizing. I'ma put
an end to his motherfucking signifying.'"*) The message seems clear enough: words are powerful, but ultimately inadequate, perhaps even self-destructive. In
the contemporary scene, at least, the man who has no
other weapon, who fights back *only* with words, may
be admired for his verbal ability, but not necessarily
for his manliness. Even so, the appeal of the Signifying Monkey toasts is easily understood: for people who
feel no sense of control over their own destinies—for
men whose situations prevent them from striking back
at the source of their anger—the toasts provide a form
of release and escape.

The escape is more direct in the "badman" toasts, of
which the most popular are those celebrating the exploits of a hero named Stackolee (or Stagolee—or, in
nineteenth-century ballads, Stacker Lee). If the trickster is nothing but words and guile, the badman is nothing but brute force. In Abrahams' admiring (and somewhat romanticized) description, the badman "is consciously and sincerely immoral. As a social entity he is
revolting against white men's laws. As a male he is re-

volting against woman's potential domination. As a poor man he is reacting against his perpetual poverty. . . ."

He is the "hard man," able to accept the challenge of the world because of his strength. Anything that threatens his domain threatens his ego and must be removed. Where guile and banter are the weapons of the trickster, arrogance and disdain serve the badman. . . . He is the epitome of virility, of manliness on display.

But manliness and virility are defined as random violence and joyless, indeed affectless sexuality. Stackolee is "a mean man, a purveyor of violence" who "does not hesitate to hurt, taunt, kill if someone offers him the slightest hint of challenge." In Jackson's appraisal, Stackolee is "the archetypal bully blindly striking out, articulating or discharging his rage on any passing object or person." His violence seems to be an end in itself, for it solves nothing and is aimed at nothing; the badman is all style—more precisely, perhaps, all pose and bluster. Like so many young criminals, the badman is more concerned with demonstrating his "badness" than with achieving any goal or accomplishing any purpose.

Here is the text of one of the versions Jackson has recorded. The opening scene sets a somber but low-key mood: frustrated and dissatisfied (his woman has left him and his cards are bad), Stackolee picks up stakes and moves on to the main setting of the toast, a town—or bar—known as the Bucket of Blood. But the mood changes rapidly: because the bartender expresses contempt for his name and reputation, Stackolee kills him. "Reputation on the streets is important," Jackson explains, "but in the toast the demand for recognition of what one's name means seems at times to go beyond

the merely important; the questions become critical and
ontological."

And I asked the bartender for something to eat,
he give me a dirty glass of water and a tough-assed
    piece of meat.
I said, "Bartender, bartender, don't you know who I am?"
He said, "Frankly, my man, I don't give a goddam."
I said, "My name is Stackolee." He said, "Oh, yes,
    I heard about you up this way,
but I feed you hungry motherfuckers each and every day."
'Bout this time the poor bartender had gone to rest—
I pumped six a my rockets [bullets] in his motherfucken
    chest.

Stackolee then insults the dead man's mother and ig-
nores her warning that another badman—Billy Lions
(or Benny Long), in some versions the dead bartender's brother—will take revenge. While waiting for the
challenger to appear, Stackolee demonstrates his sexual prowess.

A woman run out the back screamin' real loud, said,
    "I know my son ain't dead!"
I said, "You just check that hole in the ugly mother-
    fucker's head."
She say, "You may be bad, your name may be Stack,
but you better not be here when Billy Lions get back."
So I walked around the room and I see this trick,
and we went upstairs and we started real soon.
Now me and this broad we started to tussle
and I drove twelve inches a dick through her ass before
    she could move a muscle.
We went downstairs where we were before,
we fucked on the table and all over the floor.

The stage is set for the great confrontation as Billy
Lions enters. To show his own virility and to demonstrate that he, too, is a badman, Billy taunts Stack and

shoots a bystander (in some versions, he kills several onlookers). But all to no avail; Billy, too, is killed.

'Bout that time you could hear the drop of a pin—
that bad motherfucker Billy Lions had just walked in.
He walked behind the counter, he seen the bartender dead,
he say, "Who put this hole in this ugly motherfucker's
    head."
Say, "Who can this man's murderer be?"
One motherfucker say, "You better speak soft, his name
    is Stackolee."
He say, "Stack, I'm gonna give you a chance to run
    before I draw my gun."
Bitch jumped up and said, "Billy, please."
He shot that whore through both her knees.
A pimp eased up and turned out the lights
and I had him dead in both my sights.
When the lights came back on poor Billy had gone
    to rest,
I had pumped nine a my rockets in his motherfucken
    chest.

The toast ends with a confrontation—usually flippant—with the judge.

The next day about half-past ten
I was standin' before the judge and twelve other good
    men.
They say, "What can this man's charges be?"
One sonofabitch say, "Murder in the first degree."
Another say, "What can this man's penalty be?"
One say, "Hang him," another say, "Give him gas."
A snaggle-tooth bitch jumped up and say, "Run that
    twister through his jivin' ass!"
My woman jumped up and said, "Let him go free,
'cause there ain't nobody in the world can fuck like
    Stackolee."[39]

The profanity and obscenity of the toasts are of a piece with their intent; together with the manner in which they are recited, they establish the performer as the same kind of strong man as Stackolee himself. "The poems are created to excite the emotions, by their sound, by their diction, by their breath-taking, and by their subject matter," Abrahams observes. *The subject treated is freedom of the body through superhuman feats and [freedom] of the spirit through acts that are free of restrictive social mores (or in direct violation of them), especially in respect to crime and violence.* [emphasis added]

> The heroes of most of these stories are hard men, criminals, men capable of prodigious sexual feats, bad men, and very clever men (or animals) who have the amorality of the trickster.[40]

The amorality is deliberate; toasts, like so much black folklore, are built around inverted stereotypes. Because black Americans, and especially black men, have been imprisoned by white stereotypes of them—because they have found it so difficult, if not impossible, to escape those stereotypes—they have fought back, in part, by accepting the stereotypes and turning them upside down. Through the medium of folklore, black men have converted their supposed exaggerated sexuality, physical prowess, and animal-like (or child-like) inability to control their impulses from negative to positive attributes.

They have also turned white morality upside down. "If being Black means one is the 'bad guy' according to White majority culture," Christina and Richard Milner write, "the question becomes how one can turn 'badness' into 'goodness' without either 'acting White' or destroying oneself. That is the personal problem of every Black kid who grows up in America."

> Since being "good" by White standards has usually meant "knowing your place," "doing what you're

told," and being subservient, Black people have developed a counter-standard. The White man's definition of "goodness" is seen to be emasculating and
stultifying, which is bad for Blacks; the man who asserts his masculinity and refuses to bow before authority is therefore "good." Thus, a "bad nigger" is
one who is so "bad" he is "good"; he is admirable in
his defiance.[41]

The inversion is a mixed blessing; a really *bad* "bad
nigger"—in slave folklore, the docile fieldhand who
suddenly goes berserk—can pose a threat to blacks, as
well as to whites. "It seems that every community had
one or was afraid of having one," the psychiatrists William Grier and Price Cobbs write. The preoccupation
remains. "Today black boys are admonished not to be
a 'bad nigger,' " Grier and Cobbs continue. "No description need be offered; every black child knows what
is meant. They are angry and hostile. They strike fear
into everyone with their uncompromising rejection of
restraint or inhibition. They may seem at one moment
meek and compromised—and in the next a terrifying
killer."[42]

For all the danger he poses to his own community,
the badman serves an important function. "Got a tomb-
stone disposition and a graveyard mind, I'm a mean
motherfucker and I don't mind dying," The Great
MacDaddy, another badman, likes to exclaim. Because
he does not mind dying, the badman cannot be threatened by the system of white controls, or by the self-
controls that blacks have had to erect in order to survive; and because he cannot be threatened, the badman
prevents those controls from becoming total. In doing
so, he creates and maintains a measure of psychic freedom for all black men, for somewhere inside himself
every black American harbors a potential bad nigger.
The same can be said for members of every oppressed

and persecuted group; as the sociologist Hylan Lewis remarks, there is a little Stackolee in everyone who has had that experience. I recall the secret glee that many Jews the world over felt right after World War II, when Jewish terrorists in Palestine blew up a British installation or penetrated the British blockade to land a shipload of refugees. Even those who condemned acts of terror stood a little straighter because their coreligionists were fighting back. Many Irish-Americans have much the same schizophrenic reaction to the IRA's campaign of terror against British soldiers in Northern Ireland, applauding and condemning the acts at the same time.

This was the basis of the enormous impact on black consciousness exerted by the late Malcolm X. Until the last year or two of his life, when he was struggling to develop a more goal-oriented approach, Malcolm X deliberately cultivated a "bad nigger" image, and black Americans in every walk of life loved him for it. "That Malcolm ain't afraid to tell Mr. Charlie, the FBI or the cops or nobody where to get off," a New York cabdriver observed. "You don't see him pussyfootin' 'round the whites like he's scared of them." "Malcolm says things you or I would not say," a civil-rights leader remarked. "When he says those things, when he talks about the white man, even those of us who are repelled by his philosophy secretly cheer a little outside ourselves, because Malcolm X really does tell 'em, and we know he frightens the white man. We clap." It is also why Jack Johnson has been a black folk hero ever since he defeated "the Great White Hope," Jim Jeffries, on July 4, 1910. Johnson was not merely the heavyweight champion of the world; he was a "bad nigger" as well, reveling in his display of wealth and virility and defying white taboos about interracial sex. Visitors to his Chicago night club were greeted by a larger-than-life portrait of Johnson embracing his white wife, and he conspicuously paraded his entourage of white women.[43]

The badman's role in black folklore is analogous to the role of the madman in the modern novel and play: to force the audience to ask who is really mad and who is really sane—to qusetion whether sanity resides in conformity to an irrational world or in rebellion against it. In a world that refuses to see or hear them as individuals, black people often have felt that only madness (and certainly Stackolee is mad) can force white people to take note of them. "Don't nobody pay no attention to no nigger that's not crazy!" a character in *Ceremonies in Dark Old Men* remarks.

But the badman toasts also grow out of the nihilistic impulse that black Americans have always felt. In moments of despair, as Negro spirituals reflect, slaves turned to Sampson as well as—or instead of—to Moses: "If I had my way, I'd tear this building down," a popular spiritual declared. James Forman of the Student Nonviolent Coordinating Committee expressed the same sentiment in 1965: "if we can't sit at the table," he told an angry SNCC audience, "let's knock the fucking legs off." A quarter-century earlier, in one of the unpublished monographs he wrote for Gunnar Myrdal's study, Ralph Bunche spoke of "Negroes . . . who, fed up with frustration of their life here, see no hope and express an angry desire to 'shoot their way out of it.' "

I have on many occasions heard Negroes exclaim: "Just give us machine guns and we'll blow the lid off the whole damn business." Sterling Brown's "Ballad for Joe Meek" is no mere fantasy and the humble Negro turned "bad" is not confined to the pages of fiction, granted that he is the exception. The worm does turn and a cornered rat will fight.[44]

V

The great achievement of the toasts, as of the blues,
the dozens, and black folklore in general, has been to
deaden the pain felt by black Americans, especially
black men, and to transform their rage into a source of
entertainment and play. The process no longer works;
black adolescents and young men have begun to act out
the violence and aggression that, in the past, had been
contained and sublimated in fantasy and myth. It is
this shift from the mythic to the real—from toasting,
signifying, and playing the dozens to committing robbery, murder, rape, and assault—that underlies the
explosive increase in criminal violence on the part of
black offenders.

The explanation cannot lie in black culture alone.
Criminal violence has been increasing in Britain,
France, Italy, Sweden, West Germany—indeed, in
every part of the globe, as well as in every segment of
American society. Given the provocations black Americans have endured, there is no reason to expect them
to be unaffected by this universal trend. It is a good bit
harder to comprehend the kidnappings and murders
committed by the upper-middle-class members of the
Baader-Meinhof Gang and other West European ter-
rorist groups than the robberies and robbery killings
committed by impoverished black youth in this country.

At the same time, there are factors specific to the
black American community that help explain the
change. To begin with, we need to understand the fear
of whites in which, until recently, most black Americans lived. The fear was well-grounded; as we have
seen, whites kept blacks in their place through sheer
terror and brutality. But the Southern Negro's fear of
the white man went beyond the purely rational; it had

elements of an almost magical taboo that kept black people down even in the absence of overt repression. "In the main we are different from other folks," Richard Wright wrote in 1941, "in that, when an impulse moves us, when we are caught in the throes of inspiration, when we are moved to better our lot, we do not ask ourselves, 'Can we do it?' but 'Will they let us do it?' "

> Before we black folks can move, we must first look into the white man's mind to see what is there, to see what he is thinking.

Nate Shaw described the phonemenon with equal eloquence:

> Here's the rule of our colored people in this country, that I growed up in the knowledge of: they'll dote on a thing, they'll like it, still a heap stays shy of it. They knowed that their heads was liable to be cracked, if nothin' else, about belongin' to something that the white man didn't allow 'em to belong to. *All of 'em was willin' to it in their minds, but they was shy in their acts.* [emphasis added]

Blacks are no longer "shy in their acts." The poet Langston Hughes foresaw the change some thirty-five years ago, in a bitterly sardonic poem he wrote when the great tenor Roland Hayes was beaten by a white mob in Georgia:

> Negroes,
> Sweet and docile,
> Meek, humble, and kind:
> Beware the day
> They change their mind.

> Wind
> In the cotton fields,
> Gentle breeze:
> Beware the hour
> It uproots trees!

The change has come; blacks *have* changed their minds, and more than trees are being uprooted. After 350 years of fearing whites, black Amercians have discovered that the fear runs the other way, that whites are intimidated by their very presence; it would be hard to overestimate what an extraordinarily liberating force this discovery is. The taboo against expression of anti-white anger is breaking down, and 350 years of festering hatred has come spilling out.

The expression of anger is turning out to be cumulative rather than cathartic. Instead of being dissipated, the anger appears to be feeding on itself; the more anger is expressed, the more there is to be expressed. Understandably so, for "with rebellion," as Albert Camus wrote, "awareness is born." Until an individual rebels, Camus explained, he tends to accept indignities as inevitable—indignities far more terrible than the ones at which the rebel now balks.

> He accepted them patiently, though he may have protested inwardly. . . . But with the loss of patience—with impatience—a reaction begins which can extend to everything that he previously accepted, and which is almost always retroactive.

This retroactive rage has overwhelmed the devices for its containment. In black as in white America, what Walter Lippmann called the "dissolution of the ancestral order" has been proceeding at an accelerated pace. The lowering of racial barriers has dissolved some of the social glue that held black communities together. Because housing had been denied them elsewhere, for example, black lawyers, doctors, teachers, owners of businesses, skilled craftsmen, and others with stable, well-paying jobs were forced to live in the same neighborhoods as poor blacks. Although successful black people bitterly resented the fact that discrimination denied them a choice of where to live, their presence exerted a powerful stabilizing influence on black neighborhoods.[45]

The result was that black neighborhoods were communities, with all the informal norms and values that distinguish a community from a mere neighborhood. "God knows I tried to act out when I was an adolescent," a middle-aged black friend remembers, "but I didn't have a chance. Somebody always stopped me before I could get very far." Wherever he went in the medium-sized Midwestern city where he grew up, there were people who knew him—more to the point, people who knew his parents, grandparents, and aunts and uncles. They either took him in hand directly or got in touch with a member of his family; either way, the informal controls kept him in check.

The sense of community was enhanced by segregated education. Black children attended schools that were separate and grossly unequal; they used texts and materials that had been discarded by white schools, and were taught by underpaid teachers in run-down buildings that often lacked heat and light. But black children began the school day by singing "The Negro National Anthem," they studied black American history, and they celebrated the birth dates of black American heroes and heroines. As respected leaders of the black community, teachers and principals were part of the system of social control. The best of them also conveyed a clear set of expectations to their students, selecting those who had promise and giving them extra encouragement and help. "They thought I was going to be special," recalls Dr. Benjamin Mays, the eighty-three-year-old chairman of the Atlanta School Board, speaking of the adults of the community in which he grew up. "I thought I'd have to live up to their expectations." Dr. Mays tried to convey the same expectations to the students at Morehouse College in Atlanta, exhorting them every Tuesday morning, at compulsory chapel services, during his twenty-seven years as president of the school.[46]

To avoid any misunderstanding, let me emphasize that segregation was immoral and indefensible; the Jim Crow system had to be abolished for the sake of white as well as black Americans. But precisely because segregation was so patently and totally evil, it helped blacks maintain a sense of community. And the dismantling of legal segregation has swept away some of its unintended and unrecognized benefits. To be sure, most black students still attend segregated schools, but the schools are under white, rather than black, control. The school day no longer starts with the singing of "The Negro National Anthem," whose words—and even existence—are unknown to most contemporary black students. Far from being part of the system of social control, black schools have become arenas where youngsters act out the "bad nigger" myth.

The erosion of authority has been encouraged by a change in the nature of black communities themselves. Most black Americans, like most whites, still live in segregated neighborhoods. But the number of middle-income blacks has increased dramatically in recent years; so has the supply of housing available to them. As housing barriers have come down, both middle-class and stable working-class families have moved away, turning the old multi-class black neighborhoods into almost exclusively lower-class enclaves. As a result, the distinctive aspects of lower-class black culture have taken on a significance and power they never had before.

At the same time, black folklore was losing its power to exorcise black rage. For one thing, transistor radios, portable phonographs, and tape recorders have had a

stultifying effect on performance; street-corner performers of the toasts cannot match the appeal of B.B.
King, James Brown, or other folk heroes. But listening
to a recorded version of the blues or other black music—not to mention watching the omnipresent TV—is
passive behavior, in sharp contrast to the active role
that spectators to a toasting session used to play. One
consequence, Bruce Jackson reports, is that new toasts
no longer are being written; it is only in jail that the
tradition retains its strength.[47]

Equally important, black men have new and more
effective ways of deadening the pain; as narcotics,
toasts and the dozens cannot compete with heroin, cocaine, or the increasingly popular (and potent) combination of methadone and wine. Drugs not only kill the
pain, they provide a euphoric high as well. Nor can
toasts or the dozens provide as much (or as satisfying)
"action" as a mugging, robbery, or burglary, or as
much evidence of an individual's manhood. "Spectacle
is not good enough when one cannot hide the real
world," Jackson writes, "nor when the real world
offers more attractive options."

But toasts and the other elements of black folk culture continue to shape behavior; they provide the role
models that black adolescents and young men are
emulating, and the ambience within which those roles
are enacted. Large numbers of black males were given
their first opportunity to play the "bad nigger," in fact
as well as fantasy, during the riots of the mid- and late
1960s, and they enjoyed themselves to the hilt. In a
sense, the riots were the Stackolee and Signifying Monkey toasts writ large; for the participants, they were as
much entertainment as social protest. Or as one scholarly study puts it, the riots were "affective rather than
instrumental in character." Even sympathetic white observers were puzzled by the apparent pointlessness, and

at times self-destructiveness, of the rioting—the failure to relate the means being used to any coherent set of aims or goals. From the perspective of lower-class black culture, the means *were* the end.

Although the toast tradition itself is weakening, the "bad nigger" myth has grown in popularity and importance. In the only Brer Rabbit tale that Roger Abrahams collected from a younger man, the story had been turned around to suggest that "the old ways of Rabbit no longer work; only the assertion of power with devices like a gun will answer the problems of conflict."[48] And technological change—the invention of the "Saturday night special" and other inexpensive handguns—has made that peculiarly American metaphor of equality, the gun, available to virtually everyone in black urban neighborhoods. Young black males, in particular, have made it clear that they agree with Frederick Douglass' suggestion that "The practice of carrying guns would be a good one for the colored people to adopt, as it would give them a sense of their own manhood."

The association of manhood with violence has been strengthened by the popularity of *Shaft, Super Fly,* and a host of lesser-known "black films" that retell the Stackolee myth in modern dress. These films have had a profound impact on the consciousness of black adolescents and young men, in part because of the power of the medium itself, and in good measure because the films make it easier for young blacks to identify with movie heroes. The psychiatrist Roland Jefferson argues that black adolescents "are profoundly vulnerable to strong identification with Black characters on the movie screen. The identification is so intense that acting out, more often than not, is the end result."[49]

Black novelists and playwrights have drawn on toasts and other folklore in more inventive ways. Paul

Carter Harrison's musical play *The Great MacDaddy* takes its title from an old and popular badman toast; the characters in the play include Shine, Signifyin' Baby, and Stagolee. Joseph A. Walker's prizewinning *The River Niger* begins by subjecting Stackolee-type posturing to withering contempt. But the play concludes with an orgy of bloodshed in which the determinedly middle-class father kills as many white policemen as possible before being killed by them—evidence that the most conforming black man harbors a "bad nigger" within himself. At the performance I attended, the predominantly black audience came to its feet cheering as the curtain fell.

Thus Stackolee continues to cast a long shadow. "Like man, when black people get their shit together, they're going to be *bad*. They're going to be *bad!*" a Harlem resident remarks. Indeed, the current level of black violence can be partly understood as the internalization and acting out of the "bad nigger" myth. "I was growing up now, and people were going to expect things from me," Claude Brown writes of his childhood in Harlem. "I knew that I was going to have to get a gun sooner or later and that I was going to have to make my new rep and take my place along with the bad niggers of the community. . . ."

> The bad nigger thing really had me going. I remember Johnny saying that the only thing in life a bad nigger was scared of was living too long. This just meant that if you were going to be respected in Harlem, you had to be a bad nigger; and if you were going to be a bad nigger, you had to be ready to die. I wasn't ready to do any of that stuff. But I had to. I had to act crazy.[50]

It is not only young criminals who "act crazy." The Black Panthers deliberately and self-consciously chose to act as "bad niggers," as a way of emboldening, and therefore mobilizing, the mass of lower-class blacks. They first gained national attention by their massed entry into the California legislature, wearing paramilitary uniforms and carrying rifles, and they maintained attention through their exaggerated rhetoric about violence and revolution, i.e., through "signifying."

That the Panthers were drawing on the imagery of toasting can hardly be doubted; Bobby Seale gave his son the name Stagolee "because Stagolee was a bad nigger off the block who didn't take shit from nobody," and he dedicated his history of the Black Panther Party to "Huey P. Newton . . . the baddest motherfucker ever to set foot in history." But as so often happens in the toasts, the Panthers fell victim to their own signifying; because the FBI and local police departments were unfamiliar with the role of exaggeration and insult in black folk culture and unaware of the toast tradition of substituting rhetoric for action, they took the Panther threat to "off the pigs" literally, and "offed" the Panthers instead.*

The politicalization of the "bad nigger" myth has further weakened the constraints on black anger and violence. For more than a decade, militant black writers and political activists, cheered on by white fellow travelers, have portrayed murder, robbery, and rape as political acts, and murderers, robbers, and rapists as "political prisoners." "Rape was an insurrectionary act," the young Eldridge Cleaver wrote in one of the early essays collected in *Soul on Ice*—an essay that the white critic Maxwell Geismar hailed as demonstrating "the innocence of genius." "It delighted me

---

* The police and the FBI may have been more sophisticated about black culture than they appeared. Recently disclosed FBI files indicate that *agents provocateurs* were used to foment violence among members of rival black nationalist groups.

that I was defying and trampling upon the white man's law, upon his system of values, and I was defiling his women." But Cleaver was defiling black women as well. "To refine my technique and *modus operandi*," he explains, "I started out by practicing on black girls in the ghetto—in the black ghetto where dark and vicious deeds appear not as aberrations or deviations from the norm, but as part of the sufficiency of the Evil of the day. . . ."

Through his writing and, later on, his exile, Cleaver came to view his criminal career as a manifestation of pathology, and to believe that "The price of hating other human beings is loving oneself less." But while he was raping and robbing, Cleaver was, unknowingly, carrying out the message urged upon young blacks in the poetry of Imamu Baraka, then known as LeRoi Jones: "Come up, black dada nihilismus. Rape the white girls. Rape their fathers. Cut the mothers' throats."[51] Although Cleaver changed his view of crime, Baraka continued to glorify it. "You know how to get it," he wrote in his prose poem "Black People!", "you can't steal nothin from a white man, he's already stole it he owes you anything you want, even his life. All the stores will open if you will say the magic words. The magic words are: Up against the wall mother fucker this is a stick up!"

> . . . Run up and down Broad Street niggers, take the shit you want. Take their lives if need be, but get what you want what you need. . . . We must make our own World, man, our own world, and we can not do this unless the white man is dead. Let's get together and kill him, my man, let's get to gather the fruit of the sun, let's make a world we want black children to grow and learn in. . . .[52]

But a small number of violent black adolescents and young men have made a world in which black children cannot grow and learn—a world in which they cannot even live. In Chicago, whose homicide statistics have been analyzed more carefully than those of any other city, the number of fifteen- to twenty-four-year-old black males arrested for homicide more than tripled between 1965 and 1973; the number of fifteen- to twenty-four-year-old black male murder victims quadrupled. For blacks in that age group, the death rate from murder is twenty times the comparable white rate.[53]

To have expected any other outcome was to have ignored one of the lessons the toasts drove home—that oppression brutalizes as well as ennobles people. To look only at the toll that white oppression has extracted from black lives is to distort the nature of the black experience; but it is equally misleading to ignore the toll altogether. Black folklore did not make that mistake; an absence of pretense and illusion is one of its distinguishing characteristics. The badman toasts developed at the same time that legends about the James brothers and other "social bandits" became popular among whites. In the white bandit legends, Jesse James, Wild Bill Hickok, Billy the Kid, and other killers were portrayed as Robin Hoods. The black bandits, on the other hand, were never depicted as innocent or good. "Black legend did not portray good bad men or noble outlaws," Lawrence Levine points out. "The brutality of Negro bad men was allowed to speak for itself without extenuation." The bad men "preyed upon the weak as well as the strong, women as well as men. They killed not merely in self-defense but from sadistic need and sheer joy. . . ."

They were not given any socially redeeming characteristics simply because in them there was no hope of social redemption. Black singers, storytellers, and audiences might temporarily and vicariously live through the exploits of the bandit heroes, but they were not beguiled into looking to these asocial, self-centered, and futile figures for any permanent remedies.[54]

Thus white Americans are not the only ones concerned about black crime. Although whites account for a larger proportion of homicide victims now than they did in 1960, black people are still murdered eight times as often as whites, relative to population. The black victimization rate for rape is two and one half times the white rate and four times the rate for persons of Spanish origin. For robbery, the black victimization rate is nearly three times the white rate and twice the rate among Hispanic Americans; and blacks are victims of aggravated assault about half again as often as whites. It is only for crimes of theft that the white and Hispanic victimization rates equal or exceed the rates among black Americans.[55]

More to the point, black-on-black violence has changed character. In the past, it tended to be contained within the "nonrespectable" portion of the community; street-corner men may have attacked one another with some frequency, but they rarely preyed on "respectable" blacks. As a young woman in Harlem in the 1930s, Dr. Pauli Murray recalls, she and her friends used to sleep on the rooftops of their apartment houses on hot summer nights—something no sane man or woman would do today. (A distinguished lawyer, poet, feminist, and civil rights leader, Dr. Murray is now an Episcopal priest.) During the 1930s, too, young black people camped out at night in Morningside and Mount Morris parks, areas that now are off-limits to anyone but addicts and muggers during daylight, as well as at night. Still another index of the change in the character of black crime and criminals

is the fact that A. Philip Randolph, one of the great
civil-rights leaders of the last half-century, was forced
to move from his Harlem apartment several years ago
after he had been mugged repeatedly.

And Harlem is no exception. "This street here, it is
almost worse than Vietnam," a black Marine veteran
says about the Atlanta street on which he, his wife, and
two children live—a street on which there are few
families that do not own a gun. "On Friday night they
are all out on the streets trying to kill each other."[56]

The turn toward random violence and vicious brutality is evident everywhere—in shiny new public housing projects, no less than in run-down old tenements.
"I would like to say I'm black and I'm proud," says a
fifty-nine-year-old female resident of Tyler House, a
five-year-old Washington, D.C., apartment complex
that had been built for middle-income families and
then converted to low-income family occupancy, "but
I can't say that so easily because I'm not proud of what
black people are doing to each other in this building.
When we first moved in," she adds, "I would go down
the hall and wash off things that had been written on
the walls. Now I'm even afraid to go out into the halls."

> I'm like most of the other elderly people here. I'm
> afraid of my own people—not only in Tyler House,
> but everywhere I go. The men will come up to you
> and say, "How you doing, sister?" Then they'll snatch
> your pocketbook.[57]

More and more black people are talking openly and
candidly about the dimensions of the crime problem
and the need for black communities themselves to try
to bring it under control. The Woodlawn Organization
(TWO), a black community group on Chicago's South
Side, has put crime at the top of its agenda because, as
Joe Gardner, a TWO officer, explains, "the complaint

that it was not safe to walk the streets has dominated every community meeting we've had since 1971." Although TWO had been concerned about crime for some time, its public posture had been to emphasize poverty and racism as the real cause. That posture has changed, Gardner says, because "we couldn't tell a welfare mother who just got her check and was then bopped on the head that we were looking at the underlying causes."

Other black Americans are speaking out in similar terms. According to M. Carl Holman, the poet, teacher, and former Atlanta civil-rights leader who is now president of the National Urban Coalition, black Americans no longer are willing to be "tricked by the hardened criminal who beats up a seventy-eight-year-old woman and whom someone wants to regard as a political prisoner." He was making that point at a meeting, Dr. Holman recounts; as he got to the words, "We are no longer going to be tricked by—" he was interrupted by a young man who called out, "—by these jive brothers who are ripping off the community." And A. Reginald Eaves, Atlanta's Commissioner of Public Safety, was applauded when he told a 1976 National Urban League conference, "I am tired of some of the alibis we hear in our communities about the reasons we commit crimes."

To understand black crime, in short, is not to condone it. Understanding is essential; unless we comprehend the reasons why black adolescents and young men commit so many acts of criminal violence, we are not likely to find effective remedies. But to excuse violence because black offenders are the victims of poverty and discrimination is racism of the most virulent sort; it is to continue to treat black people as if they were children incapable of making moral decisions or of assuming responsibility for their own actions and choices.

"There is no surer expression of superiority than to treat people primarily as victims," the Washington *Post* columnist William Raspberry has written. "There is no more crippling an attitude than to think of yourself primarily as a victim." For "victimism," as Raspberry calls it, teaches black children "to see themselves not as intelligent beings with the capacity to shape their own destinies but as victims of a racism they can't do anything about. . . ."

> To attack victimism is not to deny that people get dumped on, horribly, illogically, repeatedly. Nor is it to suggest that victims of discrimination and disadvantage should be left to their own devices, with no proffer of assistance from the rest of society.

> The distinction is between being concerned about people and feeling pity for them. Concern can lead to joint undertakings, based on mutual respect, to undo the effects of victimization. Pity defines its object as weak, inferior, and ineffectual.[58]

But, if black history teaches any lesson, it is about strength, not weakness. Referring to that strength, and to the need to bring it to bear on the problem of black violence, Reverend Jesse Jackson, the Chicago-based civil-rights leader, has put the matter simply: "Nobody will save us from us—but us."

VI

The genie is out of the bottle; it will not be easy to get it back. With his usual prescience, Tocqueville foresaw the cause of our present dilemma. "If ever America undergoes great revolutions," he warned, ". . . they will owe their origin not to the equality, but to the inequality of condition" between black and white. The converse is equally true: if the United States is to secure the domestic tranquillity for which the Union was established, white Americans will have to give up some of the inequality we have, until now, enjoyed. The framers of the Constitution decreed that for purposes of representation, a black slave would count as only three-fifths of a man. Nearly two centuries later —110 years after Emancipation—per capita income of blacks is barely three-fifths that of whites. To be sure, contemporary census takers give blacks the same weight as whites. But Americans tend to judge a person's worth by the size of his income; in that sense, blacks still count as only three-fifths of a white.[59] We are not likely to secure any substantial and lasting reduction in black violence until that gap is closed—until black Americans become full, participating members of American society.

It has become fashionable to argue otherwise. Few scholars have had so profound an influence on contemporary thought about crime as James Q. Wilson of Harvard. Wilson derides the notion that there is any relationship between reductions in poverty and reductions in crime—at least, any relationship that intelligent citizens or policy-makers ought to be concerned about. During the 1960s, Wilson points out, the United States saw the longest period of uninterrupted prosperity in this century, and the federal government mounted what he calls "a great array of programs aimed at the young, the poor, and the deprived." Yet crime soared—to the highest levels since crime statistics have been collected.[60]

The lesson Wilson draws is that if our aim is to reduce street crime, we should forget about measures designed to eliminate its underlying causes. "I have yet to see a 'root cause' or to encounter a government program that has successfully attacked it," Wilson writes. More important, "the demand for causal solutions is,

whether intended or not, a way of deferring any action
and criticizing any policy. It is a cast of mind that inevitably detracts attention from those few things that
governments can do reasonably well and draws attention toward those many things it cannot do at all." In
Wilson's view, what government *can* do is reduce
crime by sending more convicted felons to jail; I will
examine the strengths and weaknesses of that argument
in the chapters that follow. What government cannot
do at all, according to Wilson, is turn lower-class criminals into law-abiding citizens through measures to reduce poverty and discrimination.*

But the experience of the 1960s does not prove the
irrelevance of social reform; it merely demonstrates the
complexity of the crime problem and the naïveté of
those who thought that every reduction in poverty or
discrimination would have a direct and immediate payoff in reduced street crime. The President's Crime Commission meant well, but it raised false expectations
when it promised, in its 1967 report, that "Warring on
poverty, inadequate housing, and unemployment is
warring on crime. A civil rights law is a law against
crime. Money for schools is money against crime."

In the long run, yes; the history of ethnic groups in
the United States demonstrates that upward mobility
is the most effective cure for criminal violence. In the
second half of the nineteenth century, most of the people responsible for street crime were Irish- and Ger-

---

* Wilson does not deny government's ability to eliminate
poverty as such; his thesis is that eliminating poverty would
have no noticeable effect on crime, because lower-class criminals prefer to retain their lower-class life style, of which crime
is an intrinsic part. "One could supply the lower class with more
money, of course," he writes, "but if a class exists because of
its values rather than its income, it is hard to see how . . .
increasing the latter would improve the former." Thus Wilson
is part of a long tradition of distinguishing between the "deserving" and the "undeserving" poor.

man-Americans; in the first half of the twentieth century, they were mostly Italian-, Jewish-, Polish-, and Greek-Americans. The James Q. Wilsons of both periods were certain that reducing poverty would have little effect on crime, since (in their view) the "new immigrants," unlike their predecessors, really preferred their dissolute and crime-ridden way of life.

But each of these groups moved out of crime as it moved into the middle class. The same will be true— the same *is* true—of black Americans; involvement in street crime drops sharply as blacks move into the middle class.[61] And as we have seen, it has been white discrimination, not blacks' attachment to their own culture, that prevented them from moving into the middle class until quite recently.*

The short run is something else again. The connection between poverty and criminal violence is far too complex to expect a drop in violence to follow automatically, and without delay, from every reduction in poverty. In periods as short as a decade, the relationship may run the other way; this is what happened during the 1960s. The "Great Society" programs, a strong civil-rights movement, and a booming economy combined to produce dramatic improvements in the condition of poor people in general, and blacks in particular. The crime rate skyrocketed—not because of perversity on the part of those who benefited, but because of in-

---

* Because upward mobility is so recent, blacks with incomes high enough to be called middle-class are far more likely to hold semiskilled factory or service jobs than whites in the same income bracket; similarly, middle-class blacks are far less likely than whites to hold managerial, professional, or other white-collar or skilled blue-collar jobs. For the same reason, blacks who are "making it" have been in the middle class for a much shorter period of time than have middle-class whites; hence middle-class values have had less time to affect behavior. It is not surprising, therefore, that arrest rates are higher among middle-class blacks than among middle-class whites.

creased anger and alienation on the part of those who
did not share in the gains.

They still are not sharing in the gains. As a group,
black Americans have not improved their position during the 1970s; they have barely held on to the gains
they made during the preceding decade. After dropping
28 percent between 1959 and 1969, the number of
blacks officially classified as poor has not changed; on
some measures, such as youth unemployment, poor
blacks are worse off now than they were a decade ago.

It will take more effort and commitment than the
Carter administration has displayed so far to bring
about changes of the magnitude that are required.
Three and a half centuries of racial oppression have left
a heritage that cannot be overcome in just a few years.
If black Americans were to improve their status at the
rate achieved during the 1960s, it would take two generations before they achieved economic parity with
whites.

We cannot afford to wait that long. If we are to reduce the level of criminal violence, we will have to pay
the price. It would be disingenuous to contend that an
end to racial inequality will guarantee domestic tranquillity. "That the problems of social reform present
dilemmas of their own, I do not pretend to deny," Professor Herbert Wechsler, a distinguished authority on
the criminal law, told a conference on crime control
some forty years ago. "I argue only that one can say for
social reform as a means to the end of improved crime
control what . . . cannot be said for drastic tightening
of the process of the criminal law—that even if the end
should not be achieved, the means is desirable for its
own sake."

II

Criminal Justice

6

"The Insufficiency of Human Institutions": An Introduction to the Criminal Justice System

> The mere existence of a problem is no proof of the existence of a solution.
>
> —YIDDISH PROVERB

> "The chief cause of problems is solutions."
>
> —ERIC SEVAREID

> "Such is the insufficiency of human institutions that we see melancholy effects resulting from establishments which in theory promise none but happy results."
>
> —GUSTAVE DE BEAUMONT AND
> ALEXIS DE TOCQUEVILLE

I

"What is your solution?" friends and acquaintances have asked me ever since I began working on this book. For years, an enigmatic smile sufficed. No more; anyone who has read this far is entitled to an answer.

In the long run, the answer is clear enough: the elimination of poverty, inequality, and racial discrimination as significant factors in American life. As we have seen, the high level of criminal violence among mem-

bers of the lower class stems from poor black and Hispanic youths' sense of impotence and exclusion, and
the desperation of their search to be "somebody"—to
believe that they are persons of substance and worth.
If criminal violence is to be reduced to a tolerable
level, those who now feel excluded must become full,
participating members of American society with a major stake in its preservation. How—or whether—this
can be brought about is too large and complex a question
to be answered here; it requires a research project of
its own. What can be said with certainty is that changes
of the necessary magnitude will require faster and more
sustained economic growth than we have experienced
in the 1970s, and greater effort and commitment than
any recent administration has displayed.

In the meantime, we must consider how the criminal
justice system can contribute to a moderation of criminal violence; when muggers may get us in the short run,
there is unintended force in Lord Keynes' frequently
quoted aphorism, "In the long run we are all dead." In
the chapters that follow, I will analyze the role of the
police, criminal and juvenile courts, and prisons and
other correctional institutions. My emphasis is on what
these institutions do and do not do, and on what they
may reasonably be expected to accomplish. In brief,
they can do more to reduce crime than liberal rhetoric
implies, but considerably less than conservatives suggest.

Since the turn of the century, liberals have underestimated the relevance of the criminal justice system
and have opposed the search for more effective law
enforcement as mere symptom alleviation—the equivalent of putting a Band-Aid on a cancerous sore. In
1901, Enrico Ferri, an Italian legal scholar who helped
develop criminology as an academic discipline, declared that "We have but to look around us in the reali-

ties of contemporaneous life to see that the criminal code is far from being a remedy against crime, that it remedies nothing." Ferri concluded that "punishment prevents the criminal for a while from repeating his criminal deed," but added, "it is evident that the punishment is not imposed until after the deed has been done. It is a remedy directed against effects, but it does not touch the causes, the roots, of the evil."

Instead of dealing with symptoms, Ferri argued, we should attack the disease itself: "That which has happened in medicine will happen in criminology." The discovery that malaria is transmitted by mosquitoes led not only to the development of new medicines to cure those already infected, but to the draining of swamps to prevent people from incurring the disease in the first place.

> The same problem confronts us in criminology. In the society of the future we shall undertake this work of social hygiene, and thereby we shall remove the epidemic forms of criminality. And nine-tenths of the crimes will disappear . . . because the gradual transformation of society will eliminate the swamps in which the miasma of crime may form and breed.[1]

Liberals have been addicted to medical metaphors ever since. In dissenting from the 1931 report of the Wickersham Commission (the National Commission on Law Observance and Enforcement), Henry W. Anderson, chairman of its Committee on the Causes of Crime, wrote that "Like eruptions on the human body" criminal acts "are symptoms of more fundamental conditions of personal or social deficiency or imbalance. . . ." If "the crime problem is to be solved," Anderson added, "the attack must be made at the sources of the trouble and the remedy must be found in the removal of the causes."[2]

It is not a question of either/or; attacking the underlying causes of a problem does not preclude an attempt to alleviate the symptoms. Even Band-Aids have their uses; no competent or compassionate doctor would leave a festering sore unbandaged or fail to treat some other painful symptom, especially if a cure was not immediately at hand. There is no inherent reason why attempts to cut crime through more effective law enforcement must come at the expense of efforts to cure the underlying disease. The reverse may be closer to the truth. Reluctance to invoke the criminal justice system as a means of reducing crime in the short run may create a backlash against the social and economic reforms that are needed for the long run.

But if liberals have been too preoccupied with underlying causes, conservatives have exaggerated the gains that can be wrung from tougher law enforcement. To read critics such as James Q. Wilson and Ernest van den Haag, one would think that the current level of criminal violence represented a fall from some prior state of grace. Implicitly if not explicitly, they write as though, once upon a time, before policemen's and judges' hands were tied by the Warren Court, criminals were easily and quickly apprehended, rapidly tried and convicted, and promptly sent to prison for an appropriate term.[3]

There never was such a time—not in the United States in this century and perhaps not anywhere since the time of Cain and Abel, when criminals were caught and punished by a Higher Judge. As the late Dean Roscoe Pound of Harvard Law School, one of the giants of American jurisprudence, told the American Bar Association in 1906, "Dissatisfaction with the administration of justice is as old as law."

Dissatisfaction was abnormally high when Pound spoke because urban crime and violence seemed to be increasing at an explosive rate. Conservatives of that era, as of our own, thought they knew why: courts were unduly concerned with the rights of the accused, hence criminals were not being punished the way they used to be. "It is not too much to say that the administration of the criminal law in this country is a disgrace to our civilization," President (and later Chief Justice) William Howard Taft declared in 1909, "and that the prevalence of crime and fraud, which here is greatly in excess of that in European countries, is due largely to the failure of the law to bring criminals to justice. . . . The trial of a criminal seems like a game of chance, with all the chances in favor of the criminal."[4]

The same charge has been voiced over and over again. In the 1920s, some of the most basic safeguards of criminal procedures did not exist; the police routinely held suspects incommunicado for long periods and extracted confessions through physical and psychological torture, often with the prosecutor's knowledge or participation. Yet police chiefs, prosecutors, and other law enforcement officials complained that their hands were being tied. "There has been too much mollycoddling of the criminal population," Edwin Sims, head of the new Chicago Crime Commission, declared in 1920. A few years later, when a state court excluded a defendant's confession because it had been obtained through use of the third degree, a Chicago police official announced that 95 percent of the department's work would be rendered useless if the decision were allowed to stand. "We are permitted to do less every day," the chief complained. "Pretty soon there won't be a police department."[5]

To conservatives, in short, we have always been losing "the war on crime," and the remedy has always been the same: to unleash the forces of law and order so that criminals can be quickly caught, convicted, and punished. Like Richard Nixon forty years later, Herbert Hoover campaigned for the presidency in 1928 on a law-and-order platform. "Every student of our law enforcement mechanism knows full well . . . that its procedures unduly favor the criminal . . . and that justice must be more swift and sure," he told the Associated Press a month after he took office. "In our desire to be merciful the pendulum has swung in favor of the prisoner and far away from protection of society."

II

It would be nice if the real world were as simple as the ideologues of both camps suggest. It is not; if the past teaches us anything, it is that there are no quick and easy solutions to the enduring problem of criminal violence—not through social reform, and not through "law and order." On the contrary, the search for panaceas has often made matters worse. For one thing, the institutions of the criminal justice system are inordinately complex; as I will elaborate in the chapters that follow, their actual operations bear little resemblance to the image that people, even criminal justice professionals, have of them. Hence attempts to change the police, courts, and prisons often backfire.

Except in the most general sense, moreover, we know remarkably little about the relationship between what the police, courts, and prisons do, on the one hand, and what criminals do on the other. We know that punishment deters crime, for example; but for reasons discussed below, we do not know whether *more* punishment, or different *kinds* of punishment, than we now administer will deter crime more effectively than the punishments now being administered. Similarly, the existence of the police undoubtedly leads to less crime than we would have in their absence. But there is no evidence that more policemen will produce less crime; and the police themselves simply do not know what else to do to bring about a reduction in criminal violence. Nor is there any persuasive evidence that correctional officials know how to rehabilitate criminal offenders.

In trying to increase the effectiveness of our law enforcement machinery, therefore, we would do well to keep in mind the ancient and fundamental principle of medical practice: *Primum non nocere*—"First, do no harm." For the most part, the history of national and local "wars on crime" is a record of impotence and failure—of unintended consequences being larger than, and often in the opposite direction from, those that were intended. Before turning to a general discussion of how the criminal justice system affects crime, with particular emphasis on the role of punishment and deterrence, I shall describe, in some detail, the most recent example of the way a thoughtless attack on crime can do more harm than good: the Nixon administration's widely advertised "war" on heroin addiction.

Just four years ago, Professor James Q. Wilson of Harvard, perhaps the most influential academic expert on anti-crime policy, was hailing the Nixon program as a model of successful law enforcement. Success was achieved, Wilson argued in the introduction to his book, *Thinking About Crime,* because Nixon and Company abandoned the futile attempt to eliminate the root causes of addiction and concentrated instead on measures designed to reduce heroin use, whatever its causes. To do so, the administration adopted a two-pronged course of action: a "massive law enforcement effort . . . to reduce the availability of heroin" and an equally massive effort to reduce the demand for heroin by dispensing methadone instead. "Methadone was not a cure for addiction, and of course neither was law enforcement," Wilson wrote. "Indeed, methadone had some problems of its own."

> But methadone had one powerful advantage: As a relatively benign addictive drug that suppresses withdrawal pains, it is a powerful inducement for many addicts to enter and remain in treatment programs, and is a pharmacological tool for stabilizing the addict while in treatment and in the community. . . . Meanwhile, law enforcement has made heroin much harder to find and, when found, much less potent (i.e., more heavily diluted) and much more expensive. The combined effect of these two strategies, coupled (as government programs often must be if they are to work) with some fortuitous changes in slum life styles, has been to accomplish a dramatic reduction in several cities in recruitment of new addicts and the death or imprisonment of many old ones. Were the American public in a mood for celebrating their accomplishments rather than despairing over their failings, the modest, not unmixed, but substantial gains won in coping with heroin might be one such accomplishment.[6]

Wilson was not alone in this judgment; others were congratulating themselves as well.* "We have turned the corner on drug abuse," Richard Nixon told a White House Conference on Treatment Alternatives to Street Crime in September, 1973. Robert L. DuPont, Director of the White House's Special Action Office for Drug Abuse Prevention, was a bit more modest, telling the conference only that "The number of people becoming addicted has dropped." But Dr. DuPont's optimism continued to grow; in a June, 1974, report to the President, he and his fellow members of the cabinet-level

---

* As a consultant to federal agencies concerned with law enforcement and heroin use, Wilson helped devise the policies he found so successful.

Strategy Council on Drug Abuse announced that "an alarming six-year trend of an increasing heroin addiction rate has been reversed during the past two years."

In fact, according to the government's own estimates, heroin use was spreading. "The epidemic is continuing. It had never ended," DuPont admitted to a March, 1976, press conference. "What we had was an interruption—a temporary downturn—during an 18-month period in 1972 and 1973. . . . The trend is now for a worsening situation in heroin abuse." His earlier optimism had been plain wrong, DuPont confessed. "I have learned my lesson that these trends can change very quickly. They are much more volatile than I thought in 1973."

One reason the trends are so volatile is that they are based on conjecture rather than hard data. Indeed, the "alarming trend" of increased addiction to which DuPont referred was the product of a politically induced change in the statistical procedures used by the Federal Bureau of Narcotics and Dangerous Drugs (BNDD) to estimate the number of addicts, not of any sudden jump in heroin use. According to a register kept by the BNDD, based on reports from local police departments, there had been 68,088 addicts in 1969. In 1970, the BNDD reported that the number of addicts had shot up to 315,000; in 1971, the total reached 559,000.

What happened, as discovered by Edward Jay Epstein, a political scientist-turned-investigative reporter, was that the BNDD applied a new formula to the old 1969 data. In the past, the Bureau had assumed that most addicts would come to the attention of hospitals or the police and that its register therefore included virtually the entire addict population. Between 1969 and 1970, only 760 new addicts were added to the register. But the BNDD decided that the old assumption had been incorrect, and the new register figure was never published. "It is impossible to actually know the number of addicts in the United States," a statistician explained. "The best we can do is make some assumptions." The new assumption was that only about one addict in five was known to the authorities; after some statistical refinements, the BNDD multiplied the 1969 register of 68,088 by 4.626 to yield a new "epidemic" total of 315,000 addicts in 1970. The next year, BNDD statisticians decided that the "correct" ratio of unknown to known addicts was 8.2 to 1; applying this multiple to the same 1969 number yielded a total of 559,000 addicts in 1971–72. Afterwards, John Ingersoll, who had been the BNDD director from 1968 to 1973, told Epstein that "there was no drastic increase" in the addict population in the 1970s; "it is just that we vastly underreported it until 1969 and then probably over-reported it."[7]

The same sort of flimflam produced the subsequent "decline" in the number of addicts. In 1969, the White House had encouraged the BNDD to reinterpret its statistics and come up with larger numbers of addicts to justify the administration's crusade against heroin. But 1972 was an election year. With the press (using BNDD statistics) reporting a huge increase in heroin addiction, Haldeman and Ehrlichman became concerned that the Nixon administration would be blamed for the increase and ordered the BNDD to stop releasing statistics. The White House then arbitrarily cut back the official estimate of the number of addicts to 150,000—and took credit for the reduction. From beginning to end, as Epstein has documented in great detail, the crusade against heroin was nothing but a cynical public relations device to create the illusion that the Nixon administration was cracking down on crime.

To be sure, the "war of the poppies," as Epstein

dubbed it, did affect drug use—but not in the ways that were intended or that Wilson has described. A major part of the Nixon strategy was an attempt to break "the French connection" and thereby cut off the supply of heroin to the streets of Washington and New York. In the 1960s, most of the heroin used in Eastern cities was thought to come from Turkey, by way of Beirut and Marseilles and occasionally Montreal. In fact, Turkey was not the largest producer of opium; according to CIA estimates, India, Afghanistan, Pakistan, Thailand, Laos, and Burma all produced considerably more illicit opium than did Turkey; and in 1969, after a thirteen-year prohibition, Iran resumed cultivation of poppies. But the administration wanted dramatic action. Since it was unlikely that India—the largest producer—would respond to pressure, and it was felt to be impolitic to try to restrain the Shah of Iran, Turkey became the target. Threatened with an end to American military and economic aid, the Turkish government, in the middle of 1971, agreed to ban future planting of the opium poppy, from which heroin is derived in a three-step process.*[8] For the next year or so, heroin was in short supply in New York, Washington, and other parts of the East; its price rose and its purity and strength dropped.

Within eighteen months, heroin was again in ample supply, with prices down and purity up. In their preoccupation with "the French connection," policy makers had ignored the fact that heroin use was as widespread and longstanding in the West and Southwest as it was in the East, with Mexico the principal source of

---

* Opium resin is extracted from the poppy plant about ten days after it blossoms; among other chemicals, the resin contains morphine and codeine. Heroin is produced by treating morphine with acetic acid. (Heroin is chemically similar to morphine, but is far more powerful as a pain reliever.)

supply. Once new routes and connections were established, mainly through Cuban and other Latin-American dealers, Mexico became a major supplier of heroin
to the East as well.* At the same time, a new cadre of
black dealers began importing heroin from the
"Golden Triangle" of Southeast Asia. "The basic fact
that eluded these great geniuses," Myles J. Ambrose,
U.S. Commissioner of Customs (and later Director of
the Office of Drug Abuse and Law Enforcement) during the Nixon administration, told Epstein, referring to
his White House colleagues, "was that it takes only ten
square miles of poppies to feed the entire heroin market, and they grow everywhere." The anti-drug cru-
saders also overlooked the fact that it takes the capacity of just two ten-ton trucks to bring an entire
year's supply of heroin into the United States. (In
1970, approximately 65 million cars and trucks,
306,000 planes, 157,000 ships, and roughly 250 million persons entered the United States; customs officials
estimate that there are 30,000 hiding places where
heroin can be secreted on just one ship of average size
arriving at the Port of New York.)[9]

By 1974, therefore, "Mexican brown"—stronger and
cheaper than Turkish white heroin—had taken over a
larger share of the American market. Not surprisingly,
Turkey resumed planting opium poppies in 1974, and
a "heroin war" developed as the old white importers
and distributors tried to recapture the markets they had
lost to Hispanic and black competitors. Prices held
steady or declined (and purity increased) as heroin
users could now have their pick of competing "brands,"

* One by-product of the growing number of Hispanic dealers
has been an enormous increase in the supply of cocaine, which
in some cities may be becoming the drug of choice among
users in their twenties. Whether because of the new supply
routes, or simply in response to growing demand, imports of
marijuana have also risen sharply.

and in Washington and New York heroin use appeared to turn up sharply again.[10] While all this was happening, heroin use was spreading: from large cities to small and medium-size ones (e.g., Cheyenne, Wyoming, and Jackson, Mississippi); from men to women (the number of female addicts is approaching the number of male addicts); and from blacks, who used to predominate, to whites, who now seem to use heroin as frequently as do blacks.*[11] (In the 1960s, the overwhelming majority of those who died from heroin overdoses were black or Hispanic. By the mid-'70s, whites comprised three deaths in four.)

The growth of methadone maintenance programs also affected the demand for heroin—again, in ways that were not intended. To understand why, one must start with the fact that heroin is far less addicting, in the physiological sense, than was once thought. Although all heroin addicts are heroin users, not all users are addicts. Leon Gibson Hunt, a mathematician and epidemiologist who has studied heroin use throughout the United States, has found that only about one heroin user in ten is a daily user—the functional definition of an addict. Thus the ratio of addicts to the total number of heroin users is about the same as the ratio of alcoholics to the drinking population.[12]

Most heroin users use heroin the way social drinkers

* When I completed this chapter in the late spring of 1978, heroin seemed to be in short supply again in the East; federal drug enforcement officials attributed the shortage to their effort to persuade the Mexican government to destroy the Mexican poppy crop by spraying it with chemicals from the air. But although its purity was somewhat lower than in the recent past, heroin continued to be in ample supply in the West; and there have been other times in the past when heroin was in short supply in the East, only to reappear again in ample quantities. Some experts I talked to thought the shortage was a by-product of changing patterns of drug use—in particular, mixing wine and pills, and "mainlining" (injecting) cocaine.

use alcohol: on weekends, at parties, or at other occasional events that call for relaxation or celebration.
Some "chippers," as occasional users are called, snort
or inject heroin more frequently, or in heavier doses,
than others, just as social drinkers differ in how much
and how frequently they drink. As Leon Hunt and Norman Zinberg write, "Contrary to conventional wisdom,
occasional heroin users hold jobs, live in stable families
in conventional communities, and manifest none of the
outward signs of social distress associated with the
'junkie' addict. . . . Drug use is important to [them],
but it is only one of a number of activities for them,
and it is relegated to leisure time."

Others, who use heroin under one set of circumstances, give it up easily when their circumstances
change, as the American experience in Vietnam demonstrates. Some 40 percent of the American soldiers
stationed in Vietnam in 1970–72 used heroin or opium;
between 14 and 20 percent were addicted. Faced with
the threat of being kept in the army, 93 percent of those
classified as addicts, and almost all the "chippers,"
were able to stop using heroin for the rest of their military service.* A follow-up study found that virtually
none of the ex-addicts had become readdicted in the
year after discharge, although many continued to use
heroin on an occasional basis. Dr. Lee Robins of the
Washington University (St. Louis) Medical School observed that "The ability of men formerly dependent on
narcotics to use them occasionally without readdiction
challenges the common view of narcotic addiction as a
chronic and intractable condition."[13]

* Vietnam provided something of a controlled experiment,
since the army administered daily urinalysis tests to enlisted
men. (Heroin rapidly breaks down into morphine in the body,
and morphine can generally be detected in the urine for twenty-
four hours after use; quinine, with which heroin is usually
mixed, is present for about a week.)

Moreover, most long-term heroin addicts are able to cut down their heroin intake when the cost of a daily habit gets too high for them to manage. The need arises fairly regularly in an addict's career, in part because the price of heroin fluctuates, but in good measure because daily users develop a tolerance for heroin and thus require ever larger doses in order to "turn on." Addicts measure the cost of a habit less by the monetary price as such than by the amount of time and effort—the amount of "hassle"—needed to achieve a desired "high." As the size of a habit increases, the effort needed to supply it intensifies, until the cost exceeds the benefit. Some users can regulate their habit entirely on their own, either abstaining completely or switching to another drug or combination of drugs. Most users require some external device—voluntarily entering a treatment program or, if that seems to be too much trouble, simply arranging to be arrested and jailed.[14]

Methadone has made it much easier for heroin addicts to regulate the size of their habits. Some heroin users switch to methadone from time to time in order to get their heroin intake down to manageable size; they buy their methadone on the black market, to which a large proportion of methadone is diverted, or they enter a methadone maintenance program. Others use methadone to reduce the amount of heroin needed each day; when taken with wine and pills (barbiturates or tranquilizers), methadone does not block the effects of the heroin. (In street lingo, the wine and pills "eat up the methadone.")

The principal rationale for the development of methadone treatment programs was that it would enable ex-addicts to live socially useful and productive lives, and thus cut the amount of street crime associated with heroin use. Neither goal has been achieved. For one thing, methadone does not stop addicts from

using heroin, as its early advocates claimed; in some
programs that have been studied, as many as three
people in four were found to be still using heroin, and
25 to 30 percent were using barbiturates and amphet-
amines.[15]

Moreover, methadone is far from being the "benign"
drug that Wilson described; in some cities, such as Detroit and New York, it has become the drug of choice
for a significant number of drug abusers. Some get their
high from methadone alone; injecting the drug provides
a euphoric high similar (if not equal) to a heroin high.
Most get their high by combining methadone with wine
or, when they can afford it, with wine, pills, and heroin
or cocaine; addicts drinking wine from a bottle dis-
creetly hidden in a paper bag are a familiar sight in the
streets where methadone treatment programs are located. By 1974, deaths from methadone overdoses ex-
ceeded the number of deaths from heroin. Since then,
the number of deaths from methadone overdoses has
dropped, as addicts have learned how to use the new
drug; instead of methadone, drug abusers now die from
cirrhosis of the liver, malnutrition, or other alcohol-
related deaths. Based on three years of field work with
drug abusers in New York, Edward Preble, an anthropologist who has been studying changing patterns of
drug abuse since the early 1960s, believes that the
death rate from alcoholism is considerably higher
among contemporary methadone abusers than was the
death rate from heroin durinng the 1960s.[16]

Not surprisingly, there is a flourishing black market
in methadone in the cities in which its use is popular.
To obtain methadone to sell on the black market, addicts may enter a number of programs under different
names; whether in several programs or just one, they
mask their continued use of heroin by buying "clean"
urine, for which there also is a flourishing black market.

For those who do not use heroin but want to obtain methadone, either for their own use or for resale, there is a black market for heroin-dirty urine as well. In fact, when urine tests were given unexpectedly in a large methadone maintenance program in Detroit, some 30 percent of the methadone patients were found to be methadone-free. Beating the system in these ways is part of the joy of being an addict.

There is no evidence that methadone treatment programs have contributed to a reduction in crime. To be sure, fervent advocates of methadone, such as Drs. Vincent Dole and Marie Nyswander, have offered data purporting to show reductions in criminal activity of as much as 94 percent. When looked at more closely, however, the claims evaporate. Dole and Nyswander selected their patients with great care, accepting only those who showed a strong determination to "kick" their heroin habit. Most, therefore, were over thirty, the age at which criminal activity normally shows a sharp decline; 80 percent had not been arrested in the year prior to their admission to the program. Thus the actual drop in criminal activity was a lot smaller than claimed —from 20 percent to 6 percent—and might well have occurred if the patients had received no treatment; they were getting too old to hustle. But even this decline is suspect. Dole and Nyswander did not distinguish between drug offenses (possession or sale), which account for the overwhelming majority of addict arrests, and arrests for robbery, burglary, shoplifting, or other predatory crimes. In measuring criminal activity, moreover, they relied heavily on reports from the people they had hired as program counselors; mostly ex-addicts themselves, the counselors had a strong incentive to demonstrate success.[17]

More carefully controlled studies provide a radically different picture. Long-term evaluation of the results of a Bedford-Stuyvesant methadone program, directed by Professors Irving Lukoff of Columbia and James Vorenberg of Harvard Law School, showed that changes in criminal behavior were closely tied to age. Among addicts thirty years of age or younger, an apparent decline in criminal activity was due entirely to a precipitous drop in arrests for forgery, prostitution, and drug offenses; arrests for robbery, burglary, and other street crimes actually *increased*. By freeing young addicts of the need to spend most of their time "chasing the bag," methadone apparently gave them more time and energy to commit predatory crimes. In April, 1974, the Drug Enforcement Agency's statistical division reported that compared with heroin addicts, "methadone addicts are equally prone to arrest, are more prone to commit property crimes or crimes of assault, and they are equally unemployed." (The report was suppressed.) Other studies have shown a decline in criminal activity while addicts are enrolled in a methadone program, but an increase after they leave it.[18]

It is not surprising that this should be so; most addict criminals began their delinquent careers well before they became addicts. Their criminal activity may increase after addiction, but as the National Commission on Marijuana and Drug Abuse reported, "criminal behavior is not a by-product of dependence but results, as does the drug dependence itself, from psychological and social deviance which predates dependence."

> This conclusion challenges the theory that drugs cause crime and stresses that drug dependence and criminality are two forms of social deviance, neither producing the other.

It would be fatuous to suggest that the growth in heroin use has contributed nothing to the increase in crime; but we simply do not know how large that contribution is, or what the processes are through which drug abuse contributes to crime. Given the dimensions, as well as the complexity, of the drug abuse problem, no approach, be it decriminalization, tougher law enforcement, or new modes of treatment, can be counted on to bring about a major reduction in drug abuse or crime in the foreseeable future.

III

If we are to have any hope of reducing criminal violence to some more tolerable level, we would be well advised to proceed cautiously, and with modest goals and expectations. We also need as clear an understanding as possible of how the institutions of the criminal justice system operate, which means dispelling the haze of misconceptions and misinformation with which they are surrounded. As Artemus Ward remarked, "It is better not to know so many things than to know so many things that ain't so."

We must shed our ideological blinders as well. Crime control is the quintessential political issue, for the administration of the criminal law poses fundamental questions about the relationship between the individual and the power of the state. All of us, therefore, liberals and conservatives alike, approach the subject with intense emotions and preconceptions.

No aspect of criminal justice evokes quite so much heat as that of the proper role of punishment. To be sure, crime and punishment have always been closely linked in the popular mind; most people take it for granted that those who break the criminal law should be punished. There is sharp disagreement, however, over how severely criminals should be punished: witness the impassioned debates over the death penalty and over the proper uses of incarceration.

There is equally sharp disagreement over *why* criminals should be punished. For centuries, deterrence was thought to be the principal goal; the best way to prevent murder, robbery, or burglary, it was argued, was to punish murderers, robbers, and burglars. But the notion of deterrence fell into disrepute in intellectual (although never in law enforcement) circles around the turn of the century, when criminologists, sociologists, and legal reformers began to argue that crime was a symptom of individual or social pathology, rather than a deliberate, rational choice on the part of the criminal. "The deceptive faith in the efficacy of the criminal law still lives in the public mind," Enrico Ferri declared in 1901, "because every normal man feels that the thought of imprisonment would stand in his way, if he contemplated tomorrow committing a theft, a rape, or a murder. . . . But even if the criminal code did not exist, he would not commit a crime, so long as his physical and social environment would not urge him in that direction." Punishing criminals, Ferri went on to argue, was analagous to locking the barn door after the horse had been stolen: "it is evident that the punishment is not imposed until after the deed is done."

American criminologists and penal reformers flocked to the standard Ferri erected. "There is not a shred of evidence that punishment—severe or mild, with good intentions or bad ones—has beneficial effects on the future lives of men punished," Frank Tannenbaum wrote in 1938, in the closing paragraphs of *Crime and the Community*. "If experience proves anything, it proves the opposite. It proves that evil, even when done in a good cause, has evil consequences." In Tannenbaum's view, the case for deterrence rested on the assumption that human behavior is the product of deliberate, rational choice—that people embark on a course of action after calculating the degree of pleasure and pain that that action may produce. "The assumption is false and is derived from a false reading of human nature," Tannenbaum concluded. "Punishment does not reform. It does not alter the criminal who is already formed, nor does it act as a deterrent upon others who are thrown in the way of crime by the subtle incidence of companionship, habit, appetite, judgment, and opportunity."[19]

According to Dr. Karl Menninger, criminal acts are "signals of distress, signals of failure" on the part of people who need psychiatric help, and the fact that we continue to punish rather than treat criminals is evidence of our own pathology. "The inescapable conclusion is that society secretly *wants* crime, *needs* crime, and gains definite satisfactions from the present mishandling of it!" Menninger writes.

> The crime and punishment ritual is a part of our lives. We need crimes to wonder at, to enjoy vicariously, to discuss and speculate about, and to publicly deplore. We need criminals to identify ourselves with, to envy secretly, and to punish stoutly. They do for us the forbidden, illegal things we *wish* to do and, like scapegoats of old, they bear the burdens of our displaced guilt and punishment. . . . [emphasis in original][20]

What Menninger proposes is an approach remarkably similar to the one Aldous Huxley satirized in *Brave New World*—a society in which the report that someone has committed a crime is met by the response "I didn't know he was ill."

Unfortunately, there is no evidence to support Menninger's faith in the efficacy of psychotherapy in turning criminals away from crime. No approach to rehabilitation seems to work. Whether offenders are given traditional one-to-one psychotherapy or newer methods of group therapy, they return to crime at about the same rate as those given no therapy at all. Nor are recidivism rates affected by education, vocational training, social work counseling, or any other approach that has yet been tried.[21]

Far from eliminating punishment, moreover, an emphasis on rehabilitation simply continues punishment under another name. Whether an offender is "treated" or not, forced deprivation of liberty constitutes a punitive act. Indeed, benevolent motives have often led to more rather than less severe punishment; seeing prisoners as sick tends to remove any constraints on the length of their confinement or the nature of the "treatment" they receive. Twenty years ago, Professor Herbert Wechsler of Columbia Law School warned of the danger that "coercive regimes we would not sanction in the name of punishment or of correction will be sanctified in the name of therapy. . . ."[22] What is wrong, I should emphasize, is not the attempt to rehabilitate offenders, but the phony pretense that we are not punishing them at the same time.

The issue has been blurred because the liberal case against deterrence has been little more than a rationalization erected after the fact. Contemporary criticisms of punishment and deterrence have their origins in the angry question Sir Thomas More flung at his fellow Englishmen four and a half centuries ago, when a hungry child's theft of a loaf of bread could lead to the death penalty: "What other thing do you do than make thieves and then punish them?" Critics of deterrence would like to see more emphasis on removing the poverty and discrimination that lead to crime.

Critics such as Judge David Bazelon are reacting, too, against the mode of thought to which lawyers, judges, and legal scholars characteristically adhere: a preoccupation with abstract rules and constructs, and a consequent lack of interest in the individuals and groups out of whose concrete and often grubby conflicts the rules arise. To use the metaphor developed by the legal philosopher John T. Noonan, Jr., of Berkeley in his 1972 Oliver Wendell Holmes Lectures at Harvard Law School, the masks that lawyers wear enable, even encourage, them to avert their gaze from human beings, with all the pain and suffering and greed and lust to which people are subject, and to focus instead on antiseptic rules and doctrines. It is one thing to talk about punishment and deterrence in the abstract; it is quite another to see the cruelty and barbarism to which criminal offenders are condemned in many American jails and prisons.*[23] In the discussion of punishment and deterrence that follows, I have tried to keep in mind that it is human beings, not "cases," that I am writing about.

With that stricture, let me try to clarify the role of punishment and deterrence. A major source of confusion is the fact that like the criminal law itself, punishment serves a number of ends, of which deterrence is only one. In addition to suppressing crime, punishment is designed to express society's moral condemnation of behavior it is unwilling to tolerate. As Great Britain's Lord Justice Denning has written, "It is a mistake to consider the objects of punishment as being deterrent or reformative or preventive, and nothing else. . . . The truth is that some crimes are so outrageous that society insists on adequate punishment, because the wrongdoer deserves it, irrespective of whether it is a deterrent or not."

It is this element of moral condemnation that distinguishes crime from behavior which is merely antisocial or illegal, and that distinguishes criminal from civil

* Liberals sometimes forget that the converse also holds—that crime victims are no less human than the impoverished offenders by whom they are victimized.

penalties. In his now-classic paper on "The Aims of the Criminal Law," Professor Henry M. Hart, Jr., pointed out that crime "is not simply anything which a legislature chooses to call a 'crime.' . . . It is conduct which, if duly shown to have been taking place, will incur a formal and solemn pronouncement of the moral condemnation of the community." The sense of being condemned gives a special quality to the punishments meted out for criminal behavior, making imprisonment appear to be a more severe punishment, say, than the same (or longer) period of time spent in the harsher environment of a prisoner-of-war camp.[24]

In the past, condemnation was carried out in public: offenders were placed in the stocks, or they were branded on the forehead or mutilated in some other, recognizable way, if they were not flogged, hanged, or stoned in the town square or park. The "dramatization of evil," as it has been called, drew people's attention to the moral code, thereby strengthening its hold and heightening the sense of communal solidarity.* The mass media fulfill a similar function in contemporary society; reports about crime have always made up a considerable portion of what we call "news." When people bear witness, so to speak, against a criminal or his offense, they develop a closer sense of solidarity; preoccupation with crime creates a climate in which individuals who do not know one another are drawn together by a common sense of morality.

This is why no society can be entirely free from crime. If people stopped committing the acts we now call criminal, the sociologist Emile Durkheim ex-

* Public punishments and executions provided an inexpensive form of mass entertainment as well. Modern sensibilities are shocked by descriptions of the carnival atmosphere that prevailed among the crowds that attended public hangings in London's Tyburn Fields in the seventeenth and eighteenth centuries;

plained, "Crime would not entirely disappear; it would only change its form, for the very cause which would thus dry up the sources of criminality would open up new ones. . . ."

> Imagine a society of saints, a perfect cloister of exemplary individuals. Crimes, properly so called, will there be unknown; but faults which appear venial to the layman will create there the same scandal that the ordinary offense does in ordinary consciousness. If, then, this society has the power to judge and punish, it will define these acts as criminal and will treat them as such.[25]

To some degree, therefore, the level of crime in any community is affected by the amount of deviant behavior it feels able to withstand. In a heterogenous society such as the United States, disagreement often has arisen over where the boundaries should be drawn. Specifically, Americans have disagreed over whether we should outlaw as criminal a variety of behaviors generally lumped together under the rubric "sin" or "vice": gambling; public drunkenness; prostitution; homosexual acts between consenting adults; possession, use, or sale of marijuana, heroin, or other drugs (and, in earlier periods, of alcoholic beverages). In most parts of the United States, these are all defined as crimes.

---

but the same atmosphere characterized lynchings of black Americans in the South until the 1930s, and hangings of criminals were major events in the Old West until the turn of the century. In 1896, the sheriff of Navajo County, Arizona, sent county residents an invitation to a hanging that read as follows: "You are hereby cordially invited to attend the hanging of one George Smiley, murderer. His soul will swing into eternity on December 8, 1896, at 2 P.M. sharp. Latest improved methods in the art of scientific strangulation will be employed, and everything possible will be done to make surroundings cheerful and the execution a success."

A substantial number of criminologists, lawyers, and reformers argue that some or all of these behaviors should be removed from the reach of the criminal law. Their argument is partly pragmatic—scarce law enforcement resources should be saved for serious crimes —and partly a matter of principle, i.e., that these behaviors are not the legitimate concern of government, but should be left to individual choice. In its landmark report on homosexuality and prostitution, the British Wolfenden Committee wrote that "It is not the duty of the law to concern itself with immorality as such. . . . It should confine itself to those activities which offend against public order and decency or expose the ordinary citizen to what is offensive and injurious."

The problem with this definition is that judgments about which activities "offend against public order and decency" and which do not are highly subjective.* They are also highly political. In a pluralistic society, different ethnic and religious groups often have different norms of behavior, especially with regard to gambling, sexuality, and the use of liquor and drugs; what one group regards as appropriate or acceptable, another may consider sinful. The latter may try to convert the former to its own definition of virtue, as nineteenth- and early twentieth-century Protestant Americans often did to Catholic immigrants.

---

* Another formulation that has become popular in recent years is no more helpful, i.e., that the activities in question should not be considered criminal because there is no "victim" in the usual sense. It is true that both parties consent to transactions such as prostitution, gambling, and the sale of heroin, but the same can be said of a number of other offenses not normally categorized as "victimless crimes," e.g., bribery of public officials, sale of stolen merchandise, and the illegal sale or possession of guns. With these offenses, the fact that the "victim" consents to the transaction does not mean that *no one* is harmed; the same may be said of prostitution, heroin sale and/or use, and a number of other victimless crimes.[26]

But when a social or political elite feels its power slipping away, it often turns to the law instead, defining gambling, drinking, abortion, or prostitution as criminal. The sociologist Joseph Gusfield argues that such efforts can be understood only if we recognize that the law serves important symbolic, as well as instrumental, ends. To the people concerned, the fact that the law is on the books overshadows the fact that it is not enforced; as Gusfield writes, passage of a law prohibiting drinking or gambling "settles the controversies between those who represent clashing cultures. The public support of one conception of morality at the expense of another enhances the prestige and self-esteem of the victors and degrades the culture of the losers."[27] Thus American laws against gambling, drinking, and other "vices" are rooted in the continuing struggle for social and political ascendancy among ethnic, religious, and racial groups.

IV

For all our heterogeneity, few people question the need to condemn murder, rape, robbery, burglary, or other street crimes; no society can tolerate such conduct and survive. Nor is there real disagreement over the appropriateness or necessity of punishing those who commit such crimes. "I think we all understand that the maintenance of public order must be backed up by a system of sanctions, deprivations—punishments, if you please," Judge David Bazelton writes, toward the end of an essay attacking the conventional emphasis on punishment and deterrence. "Neither law nor morality can sustain itself, from generation to generation, without the threat of some form of punishment."[28]

Where controversy arises is over the kinds and amount of punishment that should be administered and the goals we should try to achieve thereby. We punish criminals for a variety of sometimes conflicting ends. The first and most important is to establish and maintain a sense of fairness and balance in society; failure to punish criminal offenders would mean that those who comply with the law voluntarily would be penalized, while those who break the law would gain an unfair advantage.[29]

We punish criminals, in short, because justice, i.e., fairness, requires it; punishment is a way of restoring the equilibrium that is broken when someone commits a crime. Hence punishment must be guided by the notion of desert, a less emotionally charged designation than the more familiar concept of retribution. This means focusing on the past—on what the offender has already done—rather than on what he may do in the future. It also means linking the nature and severity of the punishment meted out to the nature and severity of the crime that has been committed; if justice requires that criminals be punished, the notion of desert requires that punishment be commensurate with the severity of the crime.[30]

But justice is not the only goal. Punishment is also designed to reduce crime—to deter people from breaking the law, or to prevent those who have already committed a crime from doing so again. Future crime may be prevented by executing criminals, by incapacitating them in prison, by maintaining some form of surveillance or supervision over them, or by rehabilitating them, i.e., changing them so that they no longer want (or need) to break the law.

The debate over deterrence has been misleading, on both sides, because the wrong issues have been addressed. What is at stake is not whether punishment deters crime (or, put another way, whether punishment affects behavior); of course it does. The relevant question is whether *more* punishment (or speedier, or more severe, or more certain punishment) would deter crime more effectively than the punishment now being administered. As I will elaborate in the chapters that follow, there is reason to doubt that it would, except, perhaps, in juvenile court, where the wrong youngsters tend to be punished.

Those opposed to harsher punishment have weakened their case by attacking the usefulness of deterrence itself. Yet even the most adamant admit that the threat of punishment deters at least *some* crime; to argue otherwise would be to insist that crime would not increase at all if the police and the courts were to disappear. Something of the sort happened in Denmark during World War II. In September, 1944, the occupying German army arrested the entire Danish police force, substituting an unarmed and improvised corps in its place. In Copenhagen, there was an almost immediate tenfold increase in robbery and burglary, and the number of robberies continued to grow until the end of the war. There was little increase, on the other hand, in crimes such as embezzlement and fraud, where the perpetrator was more like to be known to others, and where informal social controls thus continued to operate.[31]

In assessing the role of punishment, we need to distinguish between *individual* and *general* deterrence, a distinction critics often fail to make. Unless a deterrent is 100 percent effective, there will always be some people who are not deterred. The fact that they are not tells us only that, for them, the threat of punishment was ineffective; it tells us nothing about the number of people who *might* have committed a crime in the absence of the threat. In any case, punishing a few

violators makes the threat of punishment credible to
the many; the sight of but one or two police cars handing out tickets is enough to persuade most motorists to
slow down.* Failure to punish offenders, on the other
hand, may weaken the rest of the population's willingness to conform to the law. Johannes Andenaes, a
Norwegian criminologist and legal scholar who helped
revive the serious study of deterrence, points out that
"The unthinkable is not unthinkable any longer when
one sees one's comrades doing it. Why should one be
honest when others are not? The risk seems less real,
and, at the same time, moral inhibitions are broken
down."[32]

A desire to avoid punishment is not unique to the
middle class, or to law-abiding members of the lower
class. To be sure, some lower-class criminals seem to
arrange their own capture; as I suggested in Chapter
3, it is hard to avoid the conclusion that they *want* to
be punished.† For them, the threat of punishment may
encourage rather than deter crime. But most criminals,
even the disorganized lower-class youths who do not
plan their crimes, would rather avoid a prison term if
they could. Their lack of planning reflects their general
incompetence, an exaggerated (and often liquor- or

---

* Some critics have attacked deterrence as immoral, citing
Immanuel Kant's basic principle that man should always be
treated as an end in himself, not merely as a means to some
other end. This interpretation represents a misreading of Kant.
Kant's argument was not that we must never treat men as
means; it was that we should never treat them *only* (or merely)
as means, "but in every case as ends also." Those who quote
Kant to bolster their argument against deterrence ignore Kant's
argument that "the penal law is a categorical imperative," a
formulation that led Kant to conclude that *failure* to punish
someone guilty of a crime is itself a violation of the moral law.

† Gary Gilmore, the only convicted murderer to be executed
in recent years, was clearly in this category.

drug-heightened) faith in their own omnipotence, or a belief in "fate," rather than indifference to punishment. Indeed, one cannot spend time with criminals and ex-criminals, as I have done, without being impressed by the importance they attach to the threat—and reality—of punishment. In explaining why they went straight, most ex-offenders I talked to emphasized their desire to avoid a prison term (or to avoid another such term). As young offenders approach adulthood, they attach a heavier weight to the threat of punishment—in part because adults are more likely to be incarcerated than juveniles, and in part because a prison term appears more painful as they begin to think about, or take on, the responsibilities of a job, marriage, and parenthood.

This is not to suggest that juvenile or adult offenders are Benthamite creatures, carefully calculating and weighing the relative costs and benefits of every act before proceeding. The threat of punishment affects behavior on the unconscious as well as conscious level; in Freudian terms, guilt and punishment are what the superego is all about. Freud aside, the fear of punishment affects attitudes and behavior in a variety of ways. Fear of punishment is an attention-getting device, opening people's eyes to the immoral nature of an act they otherwise might consider harmless or acceptable. Some people avoid crime out of fear of being punished. Others refrain from criminal activity because they consider such activity wrong. One reason they consider it wrong is that those who commit crimes are punished. Hardly a day goes by for any of us, in fact, in which the opportunity to break the criminal law is not present. Sometimes we are well aware of the opportunity and accept or reject it on a conscious level. Most of the time, we do not think about what we do; we simply act —or so it seems to us. But how we act—which alterna-

tive we choose—is affected by the fear of punishment
and sense of guilt to which we have become conditioned.

V

The fact that punishment deters crime does not mean
that we can guarantee a reduction in criminal violence
simply by cranking up the amount of punishment meted
out to offenders. For one thing, we already are punishing a large proportion of those found guilty of serious
crimes—a far larger proportion than most law-and-
order advocates assume—and punishment appears to
be subject to the law of diminishing returns. If no one
is being punished, introducing even a modest penalty
is likely to have a significant impact on behavior. But
if a majority of offenders are being punished, many of
them severely, it is not at all certain that increasing
either the number who are punished or the severity of
their punishment will have any noticeable effect.[33]

On the contrary, recent research on deterrence suggests that increasing the *certainty* of punishment has
considerably more impact on crime than does increasing its *severity*.* This appears to be true regardless of
the level of punishment; in other words, whether penalties are moderate or severe, an increase in certainty will
reduce crime more than a comparable change in severity. But the relationship is not symmetrical. The less

* Punishment is uncertain because criminals are not arrested
after every offense, because many of those who are arrested
escape conviction, and because not everyone who is convicted
is sent to prison. Thus certainty of punishment may be increased
if the police solve more crimes, if prosecutors prosecute and
convict a higher proportion of those who are arrested, or if
judges give prison sentences to a higher proportion of those who
are convicted.

certain punishment is, the smaller the impact that comes from a change in severity; the threat of punishment is not likely to loom very large if potential offenders feel confident that they will not get caught.[34] And ours is a system in which certainty of punishment is low and severity high; for any one crime, although not for a criminal career, the chances of being caught are small. (As we saw in Chapter 3, getting away with so many crimes is what helps persuade criminals that they are omnipotent, but sooner or later they *do* get caught.) Catching more criminals, therefore, would reduce the crime rate; so would convicting more of those who are caught. But as I will elaborate in the next chapters, we do not know how to do either.

To decide whether a particular punishment is an effective deterrent, we need to ask, As compared to what? Whether or not the death penalty deters murder in some absolute sense is beside the point, for convicted murderers do not go unpunished. The relevant question is whether the death penalty would deter murder more effectively than does life imprisonment or imprisonment for some other long term. To be sure, scholars have written impressive-looking papers on the subject, filled with mathematical equations unintelligible to anyone save mathematicians and econometricians. Some purport to prove that the death penalty does deter murder more effectively than existing penalties; others, that it does not. The National Research Council's Panel on Research on Deterrent and Incapacitative Effects took a long and searching look at these papers. After analyzing each scholar's assumptions and methodology, the panel concluded that the results "provide no useful evidence" on which a conclusion can be drawn. Indeed, the panel pronounced itself "skeptical that the death penalty . . . can ever be

subjected to the kind of statistical analyses" needed to
draw conclusions with confidence.

> . . . the Panel considers that research on this topic
> is not likely to produce findings that will or should
> have much influence on policy makers.[35]

Thus the debate over the death penalty must be resolved on other grounds, as must disagreements over
the punishments to be meted out for other crimes.
The margin of error in research on deterrence is simply too large for it to be the basis on which important
decisions are made. Because of the small number of
cases (and perhaps because passions run so high), the
margin is particularly large for research on the death
penalty. Isaac Ehrlich's paper "proving" that capital
punishment deters murder more effectively than other
sanctions provides a case in point. Ehrlich's analysis
covers the period 1933–69; when his equations are
applied to data for 1933–61, they indicate that there
was no deterrent effect whatsoever connected with the
death penalty. By picking other terminal years, critics
have been able to use Ehrlich's equations to "prove"
that the death penalty actually encourages crime. Be
that as it may, Ehrlich's conclusion that each execution deters between one and eight murders rests entirely
on what happened during the eight years 1962–69. But
robbery, burglary, larceny-theft, and aggravated assault
—crimes *not* punishable by the death penalty anywhere
in the United States—increased even more dramatically
than murder during that period, for the reasons explored in the last five chapters. Since Ehrlich's data indicate that the death penalty did not deter homicide
during the preceding twenty-nine years, it is reasonable
to assume that the 1962–69 increase was due not to the
rapidly declining use of the death penalty, but to an in-

dependent set of factors causing a rapid increase in all kinds of criminal violence.*[36]

I am not proposing that the debate over the death penalty be stilled; I suggest only that we recognize that the case for and against it is based on moral and political, rather than empirical, considerations. Those who favor the death penalty do so on retributive grounds. In their view, murder is so heinous a crime that only the most extreme punishment we possess can uphold the moral code; as Ernest van den Haag puts it, justice requires that murderers be executed.[37]

Perhaps it does; but justice can be purchased at too high a price. According to rabbinic legend, Abraham remonstrated with God over His unquestionably just decision to destroy every inhabitant of Sodom and Gomorrah.

> If it is the world you seek,
>   there can be no strict justice;
> and if it is strict justice you seek,
>   there can be no world.
> Why do you grasp the rope by both ends,
> seeking both the world and strict justice?
> Let one of them go,
> for if you do not relent a little,
>   the world cannot endure.

The world may not be at stake, but our sense of decency is. It is not some bloodless abstraction called "society" or "the state" that carries out the death sen-

---

* Ehrlich's case is weakened still more by his failure to compare the deterrent effect of the death penalty with that of imprisonment, which was used far more frequently during the period he studied. The average prison term served by convicted murderers also declined during 1962-69. It is quite possible that the increase in the number of murders was caused by the shortening of prison terms, rather than by reduced use of capital punishment. But since neither Ehrlich nor anyone else has addressed the question, we do not know the answer.

tence; human beings have to kill other human beings. When he was warden of Sing Sing, Lewis Lawes invited prosecutors and judges to witness the executions they recommended or imposed; no one ever accepted.

Capital punishment is wrong, too, because it is human beings, with all the imperfections to which humans are subject, who make the decision to take a condemned man's life. "Though the justice of God may indeed ordain that some should die," Charles Black of Yale Law School has written, paraphrasing a passage in the Talmud, "the justice of man is altogether and always insufficient for saying whose these may be." We may reduce the margin for error by erecting more and better rules and procedural safeguards, but there is no way to eliminate human error altogether. As John T. Noonan, Jr., points out, "it is no accident that in those trials which have been celebrated in literature and in the history of our consciousness—the trial of Socrates, the trial of Thomas More, the trial of Jesus—the rules were followed and yet the human judgment has been that injustice was done. . . ."[38]

The death penalty aside, decisions about punishment ultimately are moral judgments, to which the literature on deterrence has little to contribute. We simply do not know enough to predict with confidence how much crime will be deterred by any given change in punishment, or even whether stepped-up punishment will have any effect at all. There are too many other factors affecting the crime rate, in both directions, and the statistical techniques for estimating the separate influence of each of them are too crude. If, say, we find that the crime rate is higher in states that impose mild punishments than in those that impose severe ones, this does not, by itself, prove that the stricter penalties are responsible for the lower rate of crime. The causal relationship could run the other way: states with a low crime rate may have a lower tolerance for crime, hence impose stricter penalties, than states with a great deal of crime.* Looking at the complexity of the process of deterrence and the crudity of the techniques for measuring it, the criminologist Jack Gibbs has written, "Only an incorrigible ideologue would regard such evidence as conclusive one way or another."[39] Unfortunately, most of the literature on deterrence seems to have been written by incorrigible ideologues.

We also know very little about the effects of incapacitation. To be sure, separating offenders from society is bound to have *some* impact on crime; while they are in prison, criminals are effectively prevented from committing any additional crimes, except against prison guards and inmates.† Incapacitation need not be permanent. As we have seen, crime is a young man's occupation; like professional athletes, criminals lose the necessary physical stamina and coordination, as well as nerve, at a relatively early age. Thus criminal activity drops off sharply when offenders reach their mid-twenties, and again in their mid-thirties. If hardened criminals spend their most productive years in prison, the chances are that they will commit fewer crimes over the course of their careers.

How large a reduction in crime might be produced by incarcerating more offenders, or by keeping them in prison longer, is another question. To answer it with

---

* The causality may also run in both directions. States with a great deal of crime may view crime in general, or certain kinds of offenses, more tolerantly than states with a low crime rate, hence respond with milder penalties. But the milder penalties, in turn, may contribute to a further increase in crime.

† The exception cannot merely be brushed aside; for reasons explored in Chapter 10, the crime rate is at least as high inside prisons as it is outside.

any confidence, we would need to know far more than
we do. Some criminologists, among them David Greenberg and Stephan van Dine, Simon Dinitz, and John
Conrad, have tried to show that even large increases
would produce only a modest decline in crime. Others,
notably Reuel and Shlomo Shinnar, have tried to show
that "substantial, but not extreme" increases in the
prison population would produce dramatic reductions
in crime, especially street crime. These different conclusions can be traced directly to different assumptions the
various scholars make about the frequency with which
those now being caught and convicted break the law,
the kinds of crimes they commit (e.g., are they specialists or generalists), and the way their criminal activity
changes as they age.[40]

There is another kind of uncertainty as well. The
Panel on Research on Deterrent and Incapacitative
Effects observed that we do not know "the extent to
which offenders' criminal activity persists in the community even after they are incapacitated." If the people
locked up were members of criminal gangs, there may
be no diminution in the crime rate; the gangs may simply continue to operate without their missing members.
More important in the long run, as the panel points
out, a reduction in criminal activity that comes from
incapacitation may be offset if new people are recruited
into the criminal labor market. This appears to happen
with organized crime; when operations are hampered
by incarceration of old members, crime syndicates apparently "open their books" and recruit new members.

Much the same process may occur with street crime,
though in a less systematic fashion. The case for deterrence, after all, rests on the assumption that behavior
is affected by incentives—that increasing the cost of
crime will reduce its supply. The other side of the coin

is that criminal activity must also be affected by the return. If the supply of criminals is reduced through incapacitation while the number of criminal opportunities remains the same, economic theory tells us that the return from crime should increase, thereby attracting new people into the criminal labor market. How many would be attracted would depend on whether the return from crime increased more or less than the cost.

Incapacitation may backfire, moreover, if people perceive punishment as unduly harsh. This is a subjective judgment, of course; what the Shinnars call a "substantial, but not extreme" increase in the New York State prison population (needed to bring about a major reduction in violent crime) turns out to be a growth from 9,000 inmates to 40,000 to 60,000. I would call a 350 to 550 percent increase quite extreme; others may not. When people feel that the criminal justice system is too harsh, they become reluctant to cooperate with the police or the courts—and as we shall see in the next two chapters, both institutions are heavily dependent on citizen cooperation to catch and convict criminals.

Equally important, draconian sentences tend not to be imposed at all. Juries may acquit guilty defendants if the jurors feel the sentence would be too harsh, or they may find defendants guilty of some lesser charge; and the longer the minimum sentence, the larger the proportion of offenders who demand a jury trial. Moreover, prosecutors and the police are likely to charge offenders with crimes that carry lesser penalties if they feel the crime that was committed carries too harsh a penalty; and parole boards are likely to release offenders at the first opportunity if they feel that sentences are too long. Discretion is so central to the institutions of the criminal justice system, and there are so many points where it can be (and usually is) exercised, that any change imposed from the outside is likely to be neutralized.

VI

If we are to reduce crime, we will have to recognize that more punishment is not the answer. The law is an educating institution, shaping behavior through its pedagogical or moral influence, as well as through fear. From the law, as Johannes Andenaes has put it, "there emanates a flow of propaganda" that reinforces people's willingness to conform to social norms. The criminal law, in particular, may strengthen moral inhibitions against crime and make law-abiding behavior a matter of habit. "The achievement of inhibition and habit is of greater value than mere deterrence," Andenaes has written, since habit keeps people law-abiding even in situations in which they need not fear detection or punishment. When this is the case, the law-abiding majority is likely to exert social pressure toward conformity on those who may not, themselves, accept the moral code.[41]

Behavior that emanates from respect for law is different from behavior that reflects a fear of punishment; to ignore the distinction is to confuse authority with coercion. To be sure, coercion may reinforce respect for law. But in the last analysis, respect for authority depends on acceptance of its legitimacy—on people's willingness to obey the law because it is the law. Acceptance of the legitimacy of law is a far more effective instrument of social control than is fear of punishment. Thus the moral-pedagogical role of the law is central to the functioning of any society.

Extended contact with American courts and prisons is not needed to discover that the criminal law educates badly. From the institutions of the criminal justice system, there emanates a flow of propaganda that destroys, rather than encourages, respect for the law and the values it seeks to protect.

The criminal courts are particularly culpable in this regard; more than a half-century ago, Chief Justice Charles Evans Hughes warned of the consequences:

> A petty tyrant in a police court, refusals of a fair hearing in minor civil courts, the impatient disregard of an immigrant's ignorance of our ways and language, will daily breed bolsheviks who are beyond the reach of your appeals. Here is work for lawyers. The Supreme Court of the United States and the court of appeals will take care of themselves. Look after the courts of the poor, who stand most in need of justice. The security of the Republic will be found in the treatment of the poor and the ignorant; in indifference to their misery and helplessness lies disaster.[42]

7

The Wisdom of Solomon, the Patience of Job: What the Police Do—and Don't Do

. . . one may well wonder how any group of men could perform the tasks required of policemen. The citizen expects police officers to have the wisdom of Solomon, the courage of David, the strength of Samson, the patience of Job, the leadership of Moses, the kindness of the Good Samaritan, the faith of Daniel, the tolerance of the Carpenter of Nazareth, and, finally, an intimate knowledge of every branch of the natural, biological, and social sciences. If he had all of these, he *might* be a good policeman.

—AUGUST VOLLMER, *The Police and Modern Society*, 1936

I recall a sergeant in Chicago whose assignment required that he handle complaints from large numbers of persons who were . . . mentally ill. He frequently met their concerns about imaginary forces that were threatening them by informing them he was assigning the invisible squad. His resources were unlimited and his callers were apparently very pleased, because they would often make repeated requests for the same kind of assistance. This sergeant may unwittingly have put his finger on what a good deal of policing is about.

—HERMAN GOLDSTEIN, *Policing a Free Society*, 1977

We set out to learn about police operations by posing the question: What happens after arrest? What happens after arrest, most often, is that the prosecutor drops the case.

—BRIAN FORST, JUDITH LUCIANOVIC,
AND SARAH J. COX, *What
Happens After Arrest?*, 1977

I

"What are all those cops doing, anyway?" someone asked, with a good deal of heat, at a meeting of a neighborhood association in my community. "Why can't they protect us, instead of just handing out parking tickets?" "You ought to know you can never find a cop when you need one," someone else replied, with heavy sarcasm. A rash of burglaries had prompted the formation of the neighborhood association, and forty or fifty people had come to the meeting to demand that the police do something—anything—to prevent future burglaries and to catch the offenders responsible for the ones that had occurred.

My neighbors' anger was understandable, if misdirected. As we have seen, our homes are extensions of ourselves; to be burglarized several times is to feel personally violated and exposed. Nor was it surprising that they blamed the police for the fact that the culprits were still at large; after all, Kojak always gets his man. So does Columbo; so did Sherlock Holmes, Hercule Poirot, Inspector Maigret, and the other fictional sleuths who have shaped our perception of police omnipotence.

Unfortunately, that perception is wide of the mark; there is an enormous gulf between the image and the reality of policing. After the public schools, the police are the best-known agency of government; they are also the least understood—by policemen themselves, as well as by the public. As a result, Americans have come to

This chapter is based, in part, on research and field observations by Richard D. Van Wagenen.

expect far more of the police than they can possibly deliver.

The uncomfortable fact is that the police simply do not know what to do to reduce crime; some offbeat officials are not even certain there is *anything* they can do to produce a significant and lasting reduction in criminal violence. As Robert diGrazia, the controversial department chief of Montgomery County, Maryland (and former police chief of Boston and St. Louis), told a group of his fellow chiefs, "We are not letting the public in on our era's dirty little secret," namely, "that there is little the police can do" about crime.[1] DiGrazia may have been exaggerating for rhetorical effect—but not by much. For reasons I will elaborate below, the traditional remedies simply will not work.

• Short of creating a police state, there is no reason to believe that putting more cops on the street would affect the amount of street crime. The fifty-eight American cities with populations of more than 250,000 average 3.4 police per 1,000 residents. But individual departments vary in size from 1.7 to 7.0 police per 1,000 people; there is no observable correlation between the number of police a community has and either the number of crimes that are committed or the proportion of those crimes that are solved. In a controlled experiment conducted in Kansas City, moreover, the Police Foundation found that doubling or tripling the visible police presence had no effect on the number of crimes committed, or on people's feelings of safety.

• New technology does not help, either. Since the mid-1960s, police departments have invested huge sums in computerized telecommunication systems designed to cut the period that elapses between the time a citizen calls the police to report a crime and the time a patrol car arrives at the scene. But cutting a police department's response time does little good when, as researchers recently discovered, crime victims wait twenty minutes before they call the police. By keeping police officers locked up inside their patrol cars, the emphasis on mobility and rapid response time has reduced person-to-person contact between the police and the people being policed, thereby hampering policemen's ability to prevent or solve crimes.

• Repealing the so-called "exclusionary rule" would not make the police any more effective in their "war" against crime.* Despite loud and frequent complaints, the police have not been handcuffed by the rulings of the Warren Court. Except for minor drug offenses, there is no evidence to suggest that policemen make fewer arrests, or that prosecutors secure fewer convictions, because of Supreme Court decisions safeguarding the rights of the accused; on the contrary, the evidence runs the other way.

The police have been reluctant to acknowledge their impotence in the face of rising crime. Understandably so: their jobs and salaries (or, in the case of some law enforcement officials, their empires) have been at stake. Equally important, police are well aware of the mixture of fascination, fear, and contempt in which they are held. Policing is a "tainted occupation," as the sociologist Egon Bittner writes, "and no amount of public relations work can entirely abolish the sense that there is something of the dragon in the dragon-slayer."[2] Hence police have felt the need to surround themselves

---

* Under the exclusionary rule, evidence that was obtained illegally cannot be used in court. In a series of controversial decisions during the 1960s, the Supreme Court broadened the scope of the exclusionary rule. In *Miranda* v. *Arizona,* for example, the Court ruled that policemen must inform a defendant of his right to counsel and his right to remain silent before questioning him; confessions are admissible in court only if counsel was present, or if the defendant has made an informed waiver of his right to counsel. (After the Court's ruling, Miranda was tried, and convicted, a second time.)

with an aura of professional invincibility, to encourage an image of themselves capturing criminals through a combination of hard work, bursts of intuition, and the use of arcane scientific methods—dusting for fingerprints, analyzing samples of blood, hair, and fingernail dirt, tracking footprints and tiremarks, and other forms of "criminalistics," as they are called in police jargon.

Unfortunately, the police have become prisoners of their own mystique. They have been avid readers of detective stories since modern policing began, and many are fervent fans of Kojak, Columbo, Baretta, and other heroes of the television screen. The police definition of their role—indeed, their whole sense of self—has been shaped by these fictional accounts of their exploits.*[3] We're all recruited, like little boys, to play cops and robbers," Joseph McNamara, chief of police in San Jose, California, told me.

But playing cops and robbers is only a small part—in some ways, the least important part—of what the police do. Like lawyers and judges, police are in the business of resolving conflicts—in particular, conflicts that threaten to breach the peace and disturb public order. We tend to be more aware of this responsibility when looting or a riot occurs, or during protest meetings, demonstrations, celebrations, and parades. But the responsibility is a continuing one, especially in downtown shopping and entertainment districts, in suburban shopping malls (which in some parts of the country are replacing the street corner as a favored hangout for adolescents and young men), and in lower-class and working-class residential neighborhoods, where a

---

* Lincoln Steffens, who began his journalistic career as a police reporter, was one of the first to notice this curious inversion. "Instead of detectives posing for and inspiring the writers of detective function," he discovered, "it was the authors who inspired the detectives."

great deal of socializing occurs outdoors. Much of what the police do is designed to make sure that the sidewalks, streets, arcades, and intersections in their sectors are open to public use, so that shoppers, restaurant- and theatergoers, or just ordinary pedestrians and shopkeepers are not harassed by prostitutes and pimps, or by street-corner toughs or boisterous adolescents.

The police are also charged with maintaining and restoring order in private and quasi-public places; the tensions of urban life are such that violence is just below the surface, especially in lower-class neighborhoods. Thus the police spend much of their time breaking up fights in bars, clubs, and athletic stadiums, and settling private disputes between husbands and wives, lovers, neighbors, landlords and tenants, and other strangers and friends.

The police are called upon to provide a wide variety of social services as well. They rush accident victims to the hospital; bring alcoholics indoors on a winter's night; break into a locked house or apartment to see whether an elderly occupant is alive or well; persuade a mentally ill person who has barricaded himself in his apartment to return to the hospital; administer emergency first-aid to a heart attack victim, or someone who has taken a drug overdose, while waiting for the ambulance to come. Police also get cats down from trees, chauffeur dignitaries around town, rescue the drowning, talk suicidal people out of killing themselves, direct traffic, and provide advice and help to the sick and elderly, as well as to otherwise healthy people who simply cannot cope with some pressing problem.

Because their self-image is bound up so closely with their crime-control mission, policemen tend to look down on every other activity as "not real police work." But there are common denominators to almost all the

situations I have described that make them uniquely
a police responsibility. To begin with, the police are
called because they are available—twenty-four hours
a day, seven days a week. (In Bittner's phrase, they
are the only ones in American society who make house
calls without prior appointments.)

More important, the police are called because of a
sense of urgency; what unites the various situations
with which police deal is the fact that someone thought
emergency help was needed to prevent injury, loss,
harm, disorder, or inconvenience. Bittner writes that
whether a police officer is preventing someone from
jumping off a bridge, rescuing people from a burning
building, dispersing a crowd that might hamper the
firemen, battering down a door to see if an elderly
person has died, settling a domestic dispute or barroom brawl, breaking up a robbery in progress, or
arresting a suspected burglar, the incident involves
*"something-that-ought-not-to-be-happening-now-and-
about-which-someone-had-better-do-something-now."*
[emphasis in original][4]

Most important of all, the police are called into urgent situations because they, and only they, are em-
powered to use force to set matters right. The critical
characteristic of police work, as Bittner points out, is
that policemen may not be opposed in the course of
carrying it out, and that they may use force if they are.
Much of the artistry of police work lies in the ability to
handle explosive situations *without* resorting to force.
But the fact that the police can use force is uppermost
in the minds of those who call on them for help; it also
directly affects the way other people behave.[5]

Thus keeping the peace, settling private disputes,
and helping sick and bewildered people are as much
"real police work" as arresting criminals or riding a
patrol car in an effort to prevent crime. And these

various roles are not in conflict. For all their macho image, the police are heavily—in some ways, almost totally—dependent on the people being policed. Because they rarely come upon a crime in progress, police depend on members of the public for knowledge that a crime has been committed; they are equally dependent on victims, witnesses, and other informants for knowledge of who the offender is and where he might be found. To exaggerate just a bit, the police can solve a crime if someone tells them who committed it; if no one tells them, they do not know what to do. (When policemen catch an offender on their own, it is more likely to be the result of chance, or the criminal's incompetence, than of their own investigative efforts.)

The closer a police officer's relationship is with the people on his beat, the more people he knows and the more those people trust him, the greater his chances of reducing crime. Police cannot solve a crime if they do not know it has been committed—and the majority of Americans do *not* report the crimes in which they are the victims.* Those who do report a crime usually do not do so immediately, thereby giving the offender (and perhaps potential witnesses) time to get away. "Most communities are underutilizing their police departments," San Jose's Chief McNamara argues. "Members of the public have a critical role to play in crime control," he adds; "they are far more likely to play that role if the cop is someone they know and like, instead of his being a brusque aloof stranger." But a cop is not likely to become someone people know and like by playing cops and robbers all the time. It is

* According to the National Crime Survey for 1975, only 26 percent of the property crimes committed against individuals, and 47 percent of the violent crimes, were reported to the police. (The great majority of victims of commercial burglary and robbery reported those crimes.)

when they play Florence Nightingale, to use Egon Bittner's metaphor—when they see themselves as being
in the business of providing a wide range of services
to the community—that police are able to nurture the
relationships they need.

In short, improving police-community relationships
is not a goal that can be achieved through a public relations campaign, nor is it a task to be delegated to
a specialized staff division; it is what policing is all
about. Yet, consciously or not, almost everything about
the way most police departments are organized and
run is designed to discourage close relationships with
the people being policed. The New York City Police
Department is generally considered a model of en-
lightened police-community relations; but until Commissioner Robert McGuire repealed the rule shortly
after taking office in January, 1978, the Department
had forbidden patrolmen from holding "unnecessary
conversations" with members of the general public.

More effective policing will not be possible without
a radical change in the way the police conceive of
their jobs, and an equally radical change in the way
police departments are organized and run. Before talking about improvements, however, we need a clearer
and more detailed picture of what police do—and don't
do.

II

Police departments have always assigned a high priority
to crime prevention. By maintaining a conspicuous
presence on the streets, they try to reduce the number
of opportunities criminals have for committing crimes;
by making the precise time of their appearance at any
location unpredictable, the police hope to make poten-

tial offenders believe that criminal opportunities are fewer and riskier than the number of police alone might imply. A police presence also serves to deter crime (or so the police hope) by increasing the odds that someone who does commit a crime will be caught immediately afterward. And high visibility serves an important public relations function as well, conveying an image of omnipresence and efficiency.

So-called preventive patrol—uniformed police officers cruising the streets in marked cars, in more or less random fashion—constitutes most police departments' principal approach to crime prevention. (Except in the crowded downtown shopping and entertainment districts of a few large cities, foot patrols have become something of a rarity; the trend has come under sharp questioning in recent years.) Nationwide, about 60 percent of law enforcement officers are assigned to preventive patrol, although the precise proportion varies with the size of a department and its degree of specialization.[6]

While they are on preventive patrol, police will be interrupted with some frequency and dispatched to the scene of a crime, a barroom brawl, or domestic dispute; they may be sent to take an injured person to the hospital, or to provide any of the other services described above. One of the distinguishing characteristics of police work is that patrolmen are expected to drop what they are doing in order to handle some other matter that requires attention. Other people do this as a matter of courtesy; to patrolmen, emergencies form the routine of the job.

Since departments differ in the emphasis they attach to prompt response to service calls, there is some variance in the amount of time police actually spend on preventive patrol. In Kansas City, Missouri, site of

the most elaborate study of preventive patrol ever
conducted (see pp. 290–92), observers found that police were available for preventive patrol about 60
percent of the time they were on duty, but that they
used about half that time for meals, personal errands,
and other nonofficial activities. Before the research
experiment was conducted, officials had scheduled
patrol tours on the assumption that patrolmen had
only 35 percent of their time free for preventive patrol.[7]
(The Kansas City department is fairly representative of
large-city departments.)

In theory, police officers are charged with preventing
all crime in their beat; in practice, they are more concerned with crimes that are "on" them than with crimes
that are outside their line of sight. Where a crime
occurs determines its importance; police draw a fundamental distinction between "inside" and "outside"
crimes. Outside is any location an officer might reasonably be expected to see while on patrol; an inside crime
is one the officer could not have observed, no matter
how alert he was. When a burglar breaks into a building through a rear door, or a robber holds up someone
in a rear alley, this constitutes an inside crime, despite
the fact that it may have occurred in a place legally
defined as public. When a burglar breaks in through a
front door or window, on the other hand, or a safe-
cracker opens a safe that is clearly visible through a
building's plate-glass front, this is an outside crime,
even though it occurs indoors. From a professional
standpoint, Jonathan Rubinstein reports, police may be
more interested in a petty theft than a murder or rape;
if the burglary was an outside crime, it is an affront
to their sense of self in a way that an inside murder or
rape is not.[8]

Thus officers recognize what police leaders tend to

ignore: that even in theory, a visible police presence cannot deter all crimes. In the nature of things, murder, rape, and assault tend to be inside crimes. Burglary, too, is likely to be an inside crime; even the most amateurish burglar will usually break in through the rear, rather than the front. And although most robberies are outside crimes, a significant minority occur in dark alleys, apartment house lobbies, elevators and stairwells, and other places outside an officer's limited line of sight. According to one informed estimate, no more than two crimes in five occur in locations where they can be observed by someone other than the victim.[9]

As a result, it is rare for police to come upon a crime in progress. According to calculations by Albert Reiss of Yale, who has studied patrol activity in a number of cities, less than 1 percent of the time spent on routine preventive patrol yields a criminal incident that is worthy of attention. The 1967 Crime Commission's Science and Technology Task Force estimated that a Los Angeles patrolman could expect to detect a burglary once every three months, and a robbery once every fourteen years. With these facts in mind, Police Foundation President Patrick Murphy, who has headed the New York City, Detroit, District of Columbia, and Syracuse police departments, calls preventive patrol "aimless." Its major purpose, Murphy writes, "seems to be to reassure the citizen that the police department, like the city zoo, exists."[10]

In an effort to make preventive patrol a little less aimless, patrol officers have developed their own ways of using the time at their disposal. The first is to get to know the territory; it is not until people become police that they discover how little they know about the geography of the city, or even the neighborhood, in

which they may have lived all their life—and how much
they need to know. "It don't matter whether or not
you've lived here since year one, you don't know the
city until you become a cop," an experienced officer
told a rookie he was breaking in. "Particularly you're
gonna have to learn your sector inside and out."

> You gotta know every street and alley, every build-
> ing and vacant lot. You gotta know where the people
> are on a Friday night. Believe me, your life might
> depend on it someday. You learn not to take chances
> on this job and you'll start by memorizing every fuck-
> ing driveway in this sector 'cause if you don't know
> where you are all the time, you're a lousy cop.[11]

Depending on the size, configuration, and physical
complexity of the district, it may take anywhere from
a few months to a year to "memorize every fucking
driveway." While an officer is learning his district, he
will explore every passageway accessible to his patrol
çar. In the one year he spent in a Western city, observing new officers on patrol, John Van Maanen of
M.I.T. writes, he drove "across parks, down railroad
easements, under bridges, along dirt roads, through
storage yards and parking lots, traversing hiking paths
in the city's foothills, weaving through the backroads
in the warehouse district, and so on. It would seem
that anywhere a patrol car can conceivably be driven,
pushed, or pulled will eventually be attempted by the
officer as he explores his sector."

One measure of how much—or how little—a police
department values close police-community relationships is the length of time policemen spend on a single
beat. In the old cities of the East and Midwest, where
police departments used to be (and in some cities, such
as Philadelphia, still are) adjuncts of the dominant
political machine, officers tend to be assigned to a single

sector for a number of years.* Familiarity breeds close knowledge of the district.

Because familiarity may also breed corruption, police departments, especially in the West, that pride themselves on their "professionalism" have gone to the other extreme. These departments follow a policy of "stranger policing," which Patrick Murphy calls "one of the most emotionally debilitating and intellectually puzzling theories about American policing" to have emerged. In San Jose, for example, under long-standing practice that McNamara is trying to change, officers choose their own assignments on the basis of seniority; they generally move on to a new beat every four months. San Diego follows much the same procedure. Frequent rotation may help to prevent corruption, but the cure is worse than the disease, for officers develop no sense of identification with their beats, hence no emotional stake in improving the quality of life there. The result, as Murphy writes, is that "a police department is not so much a public service as an occupation army."[12]

Whether he remains for several years or moves every few months, an officer needs more than geographic knowledge of his beat. Bit by bit, he learns to distinguish streets, intersections, bars, restaurants, and other buildings and spaces by the uses to which they are put and by the people who congregate in and around them. In part from his own experience, in part from advice from others and from comments overheard during roll call or in the locker room, he begins to know which are the "bad spots" and which the good ones. And for every place, he develops related notions

* Because police are so heavily dependent on knowledge of their own turf, such departments use transfer to a new district as a form of punishment; when transferred to a new district, a veteran feels like a rookie.

of time and people. These notions tell him which people and which behaviors are appropriate to each place, thereby enabling him to decide in an instant whether a person or activity is "normal" or "abnormal" in that particular place at that particular time.

Police officers use their notions of appropriateness as a guide to crime prevention; their principal tactic is the so-called "suspicion stop," in which they stop and question—or merely "eyeball"—someone who looks suspicious, i.e., whom they suspect may be contemplating a crime or may have committed one already.* Police rely on suspicion stops to catch criminals, as I will describe below, but they have a great deal of faith in their utility as a crime deterrent as well. "The frequent stopping and questioning of suspicious persons usually tends to reduce the crime rate in a given district," a police manual declares. "Word travels quickly by the criminal grapevine that a certain area is being well patrolled. Criminals rarely frequent areas where they are continually stopped for interrogation, and tend not to choose such districts for criminal activity."

ITEM (from notes of a night on patrol): L.'s only interest was in crime, and he wanted nothing more than to find one and catch a "bad guy." He would frequently stop the car to shine his light on a doorway, or get out and ask someone who he was and what he was doing there. "Somewhere right around here a crime is being committed," he said as we turned a corner in a ghetto neighborhood later that night, "and I sure wish I knew where it was." . . . At one corner we saw half a dozen black men standing in front of a busy liquor store, and L. got out to ask one of them for identification. The

* There are few constitutional restraints on police authority to stop and question an individual.[13]

man apparently resembled someone who was wanted. When the man had rather incoherently identified himself and produced some kind of card, L. walked up the block past a couple of bars and a pool hall. He opened each door and stood in the doorway for a few seconds, eyeballing everyone in each place while conversation stopped and everyone stared back at him. It was not a friendly visit, but apparently it wasn't an unusual one, either. L. was looking for people he recognized as "bad guys," and people resembling descriptions given in recent crime reports. But nothing of interest turned up.

ITEM: A call reported a purse-snatch. The offender, described as a black man in his thirties, wearing a red sweater, had run away. We headed for the scene; on the way, not far from it, we saw a young black in a red jersey walking down the street. F. stopped him, using the spotlight on his car, and asked for identification. The kid was cooperative; he was eighteen, very tall and thin, and said he had just come out of his house down the block. F. decided he was not the one we were looking for and explained that he had had a report of a purse-snatch in the area by someone wearing a red sweater. "Right on," the kid said, smiling, and we left. When we got to the scene, the victim, a white nurse aged thirty-five, told us she really had no idea how old the man who took her purse was: "He could have been sixteen." She was sure he wasn't really thin, though, and he didn't have stripes on his sweater. (The kid we had stopped had them on his jersey.) After some moments of doubt, F. felt confident that we had not let our man get away. The nurse had chased the purse-snatcher for several blocks; apart from the fact that he did not fit the description, our kid had been relaxed and cool.

Police resent the suggestion that they stop people unnecessarily or without proper cause. Each time they stop a motorist or pedestrian, they are putting their personal safety, even their lives, on the line; it is the rare officer who does not know, or know of, someone who was injured or killed in the course of what had appeared to be a routine stop. Car stops are particularly hazardous; in approaching a car they have flagged down, experienced police will always stand to the rear of the front door. In that position, they cannot be knocked off balance if the door is suddenly flung open as a weapon; and a driver intent on shooting them has to turn around to do so, giving the police a split-second advantage. Danger aside, suspicion stops often mean a time-consuming or energy-draining argument, or an occasion for a citizen complaint against the officer in question. From their perspective, therefore, police are aware of all the people they do not stop, and they find it hard to believe that an honest person would object to answering the questions they put.

In any case, most police do not just stop people at random; much of the artistry of police work lies in the personal radars police develop to tell them who is and who is not worth stopping. Criminals, after all, do not carry billboards announcing their occupation: they are likely to avoid face-to-face contact with the police wherever possible. And everything about an officer—his car, his uniform, his gun and holster, his very bearing—is designed to make him as visible as possible. Hence a good cop must develop a host of subtle and not-so-subtle techniques for deciding who should be questioned or watched, and when.[14]

Police look for both physical and behavioral clues. A jacket worn on a warm day, or a hat worn squarely on the head, may suggest a concealed weapon; so, too, may a bulge in a pocket. A late-model car that has just been repainted may arouse suspicion that the car was stolen. Police also look for scratch marks around the trunk or door lock, and they notice whether a license plate is as dirty or faded as the rest of the car; a plate that is too clean or shiny may have just been put on. (Because of the contour of the car body, Volkswagen "Beetle" license plates fade particularly rapidly.) They notice, too, how the car is driven—whether the driver seems unfamiliar with the way the car handles, or unduly cautious. And so it goes; there are a host of other subtle signals for which the police are alert and of which they may not even be conscious.

ITEM (from notes of a night on patrol): While we were aimlessly cruising down the main shopping street in our beat, C. noticed that a car's license plate was attached crookedly, as if it had been put on hurriedly by someone who was not used to attaching license plates—an indication that it might be a stolen car. We ran a check on the car while following it off the main street down a couple of side streets into a residential area; the dispatcher reported that it was not stolen, but that there were parking warrants on it for $39. By this time, it must have been clear to the car's driver that we were tailing him, so C. stopped him and reminded him of his parking warrants. He also ran the name on the driver's license through the radio check; the way the license plate was attached had made C. wonder if the driver was wanted for any felonies, although he never told the driver what had aroused his suspicion. The driver, a black man in his mid-twenties, was surprisingly cheerful. The driver's attitude surely was due to C.'s low-key, friendly manner; they chatted about various unrelated things while waiting for the radio check, which indicated that there was nothing outstanding except the "parkers." The man acknowledged the warrants and said he had arranged to pay them in installments; C. said he really wasn't interested in them anyway and let him go.

What makes a police officer's judgments difficult, and potentially dangerous, is that his entrance on the scene itself alters the situation. For that reason, a good officer closely studies the way people react to his presence—whether they show concern as he approaches, or change their behavior after they think he is out of sight. Body language can provide any number of clues. Someone whose body is facing the street but whose head is looking elsewhere is signaling concern to the officer; so is someone whose body is facing away from the police car or officer on foot patrol, but whose head is inclined sideways to sneak a glance at what the officer is doing. But failure to show concern also can be a clue. "Gandy was standing a little too casually there in the parking lot," the hero of Joseph Wambaugh's police novel, *The New Centurions,* explains to the rookies riding with him. "He was too cool and he gave me too much of an 'I got nothing to hide' look when I was driving by and eyeballing everybody that could possibly be the guy."[15] (Wambaugh's novels are based on his ten years' experience as a member of the Los Angeles Police Department.)

Since criminals may control their anxiety while a police car is approaching, officers learn to use their rear-view and side-view mirrors to see what people do when they think they are not being watched. And after passing a suspicious-looking individual or group, they may suddenly reverse their car to see whether an unexpected second appearance alters behavior.

Whether because of faith in the efficacy of the tactic or merely because they do not know what else to do, police officials often maintain informal quotas on the number of "ped" and car stops officers are expected to make. When officials are under pressure from the mayor to "do something about crime" or to solve a particularly heinous offense, they raise the quotas. The result is likely to be an increase in racial and ethnic tensions in general, and in hostility against the police in particular. When an officer stops someone for questioning, he is conveying suspicion—suspicion of who the person is, what he may have done, and what image he projects to others. The suspicion and tension are exacerbated when, as is so often the case, the officer is white and the individual stopped is black or Hispanic; it often is hard for minority-group members *not* to believe that they have been stopped because of their race or ethnicity.

The tension may be heightened if the officer calls the individuals being questioned by their first names— a common technique to establish his control of the situation—or if he fails to explain why he made the stop. Some officers believe that it is a mistake to explain themselves to the people they stop; in their view, the effort only invites disrespect. "Keith was always telling me to be forceful, to not back down and to never try and explain the law or what we are doing to a civilian," a newcomer told John Van Maanen of M.I.T., referring to the officer who had broken him in.

> I didn't know what he was talking about until I tried to tell some kid why we have laws about speeding. Well, the more I tried to tell him about traffic safety, the angrier he got. I was lucky just to get his John Hancock on the citation. When I came back to the patrol car, Keith explained to me just where I'd gone wrong. You really can't talk to those people out there, they just won't listen to reason.[16]

Not every officer views the world in this "us" vs. "them" manner. The best and most effective police develop extraordinary skill at blunting hostility and defusing tense situations. The political scientist William Ker Muir, Jr., describes the way one such officer handled a potentially explosive and dangerous suspicion stop. As Muir tells the story, a veteran officer whom he calls Frank Benjamin noticed a suspicious-looking car parked in front of a liquor store which had been robbed several times; a black man in his early twenties was slumped behind the steering wheel, apparently asleep, with a floppy hat pulled down over his eyes. Benjamin approached the car to determine why it was there and what the driver's intentions were. Was he casing the liquor store for a future robbery or burglary? Was he waiting for an accomplice? Was he there to receive drugs or stolen merchandise? Was he drunk or high on drugs? Or was the driver ill—the victim of a heart attack or stroke, or a drug overdose?[17]

Before questioning the driver to gauge his intentions, Muir points out, Benjamin had to make a judgment about the way his own entrance on the scene might affect the driver's behavior. Would the driver be startled into an angry or irrational reaction? Would he pull a gun? Would he drive away, in a huff, sufficiently drunk or stoned to endanger himself and others? Was the situation a come-on, to attract Benjamin to the car so that a hidden gang could "jump" him? (While pondering these possibilities, Benjamin also had to assess what might happen if he ignored the situation altogether: might an ill man die for lack of medical attention?)

What Benjamin did was to manage the situation so as to deflect any hostile intent the suspect might have had: he approached the car from the right side (to increase the distance between himself and the driver, and protect himself from having the door flung open on him) and tapped on the window; while the man was rousing himself, Benjamin took a pack of cigarettes out of his pocket; as the driver leaned over to open the door, Benjamin offered him a cigarette. After refusing the cigarette, the man identified himself, explained that he had pulled over to take a nap, and drove away. The man may well have been casing the joint, waiting for an accomplice, or sitting there with some other illegal or hostile intent. But Benjamin had focused the man's attention on a single non-threatening factor—the offer of a cigarette—rather than on the threat posed by the appearance of a policeman, with his gun and other symbols of authority. In the process, Benjamin avoided offending and angering the driver, thus reducing the likelihood of an aggressive or irrational response. At the same time, he had a way of gauging the driver's dangerousness: had the man responded angrily or aggressively to the offer of the cigarette, it would have been a tipoff that he was there for a criminal purpose.

The way police handle suspicion stops and other relationships with the public is affected by the ethos of their department, as well as by their own personalities, skill, outlook, and experience.[18] There is a world of difference between the cold, aloof, impersonal "professional" style cultivated by Los Angeles police, whether white, black, or brown, and the warmer, more personal and civil—and, from the standpoint of effectiveness, more professional—orientation of police in cities such as Oakland and New York.

ITEM (from report of a night on patrol in Los Angeles): Cruising in a high-crime black neighborhood, the sergeant and patrolman I was with stopped several groups of young men standing on the sidewalks

and frisked them without explanation. Remembering
how familiar the Oakland cops had been with the
"cast of characters" in their districts, I asked the men
I was riding with if they had made any of the stops
because they recognized people who might be connected with one crime or another. No, I was told, they
had not recognized anyone; in fact, they added, they
would not have remembered them if they had stopped
the same people yesterday! This was implausible as a
statement of fact, but highly revealing as a statement
of attitude.

The traditional response to rising crime—on the
part of the general public, as well as of the police—has
been to call for more cops on the street. Skepticism
over the usefulness of that remedy has been growing
since the early 1960s. In its 1967 report, the President's Crime Commission pointed to the fact that there
were strikingly large variations in the number of police,
relative to population, from one large city to another,
without any comparable differences in the crime rate.

More recently, the Police Foundation, with the cooperation of the Kansas City Police Department, conducted a controlled experiment to determine whether
gross changes in the number of police on preventive
patrol would affect either the crime rate or citizens'
feelings of safety. The experiment ran for twelve
months (October 1, 1972, to September 30, 1973) in
a fifteen-beat, thirty-two-square-mile commercial-resi-
dential area with a population of 148,385.

• In five so-called "proactive" sectors, the number
of patrol cars was doubled, with two cars assigned per
shift, instead of the previous one per shift.

• In five sectors designated as "reactive," preventive
patrol was abolished altogether. Patrol cars entered
these sectors only in response to calls for service; when
not answering a call, the cars either remained at the

boundaries of their sectors or engaged in preventive patrol in an adjacent proactive beat.

• In the five sectors used as controls, the assignment of officers and patrol cars was unchanged.*

Crime statistics were monitored closely; Police Chief Clarence Kelly agreed to the experiment on the understanding that he would stop it immediately if there was evidence of any alarming increase in crime in the reactive beats.† (Victim surveys were used as a check on the accuracy of the crime statistics reported to, and by, the police.) Arrest statistics were monitored closely, too; and surveys were taken to measure possible changes in the level of fear people felt, in their perceptions of the level of police activity, and in their attitudes toward the police.

The results have undercut the assumptions on which preventive patrol has been based; as Joseph McNamara put it in his preface to the summary report, the Kansas City Preventive Patrol Experiment showed that "routine preventive patrol in marked police cars has little value in preventing crime or making citizens feel safe." (McNamara was Chief of Police in Kansas City when the report was released.) Specifically, the experiment indicated that doubling or tripling the number of cars assigned to preventive patrol did not reduce the

* A computer was used to compare and match the beats according to crime rates and patterns, the number of service calls, and the incomes, racial and ethnic composition, and transiency of the population. This made it possible to divide the fifteen sectors into five groups, each containing three comparable sectors—one proactive, one reactive, and one control.

† The experiment did have to be stopped—not because of a crime wave, but because some officers, who were convinced that there *would* be a crime wave, disregarded orders and maintained their traditional level of preventive patrol in the reactive beats. After Chief Kelly took disciplinary action, the experiment was begun again and ran for a full twelve months; observers assigned to the area found no further evidence of sabotage.

number of crimes committed, and that crime did not
increase in the sectors in which preventive patrol was
virtually eliminated. (Some police presence continued
in the reactive sectors, since patrol cars continued to
respond to service calls.) These gross variations in the
level of preventive patrol had no effect on citizens' fear
of crime or on the degree of their satisfaction (or dissatisfaction) with the police. Nor was there any evidence that crime was displaced from the proactive
sectors to sectors outside the experimental area. "Given
the large amount of data collected and the extremely
diverse sources used," the authors of the otherwise
understated report write, "the evidence [to support
these conclusions] is overwhelming."[19]

III

Looking at the available evidence, it seems clear that
we need to lower our expectations of the police, at
least so far as crime prevention is concerned; there is
little they can do. But what about other aspects of
the police function? The police are also charged with
catching the people responsible for the crimes they are
unable to prevent; most of the mystery and romance
of policing surrounds the job of investigating crimes
and catching criminals.

Here, too, we expect more than the police can deliver. To be sure, almost everyone who persists in
crime is likely to be caught. The reason is not that
the police are so efficient, but (as we saw in Chapter
3) that most criminals are so incompetent; to repeat
the aphorism of Jimmy Breslin's friend, "Fats"
Thomas, "90 percent of the people in crime don't belong in it because they're no good at it." Criminals
tend to be misled by the fact that the odds of being
caught for any one crime are quite low. The longer

they go without an arrest, the more they come to believe in their own omnipotence; sooner or later, they are tripped up by bad luck, their own bungling, or a tip by an informant. "The police can afford dozens of mistakes," Malcolm Braly, the ex-convict–turned-novelist, was told after his last arrest; "you get only one."[20]

When one examines the ways in which the police actually catch "the perpetrator," as he is called in police lingo, three factors stand out:

(1) the heavily reactive nature of policing—specifically, the degree to which police depend on the people they police for knowledge of who the criminal is and where he can be found, as well as for knowledge that a crime has been committed;

(2) the haphazard nature of criminal investigation, and the larger role played by accident and chance, as well as by the offender's own bungling, in the apprehension of criminal suspects;

(3) the variety of ways in which traditional police organization and attitudes inhibit effective use of what information is available about criminals and crime.[21]

We have already seen that police rarely come upon a crime in progress; they depend almost completely on victims and witnesses for knowledge that a crime has been committed. Police departments have known this fact for some time—hence the widespread adoption of a simple, central number, such as 911, to make it easier for people to call the police.

What has not been known, or at least not acknowledged, is that the police are equally dependent on the people being policed for knowledge of who the offender may be and where he may be caught. More than anything else, what determines whether or not the police will catch the person responsible for any given crime is whether the victim, a witness, or some other informant can provide the information needed to identify and catch the offender. To exaggerate somewhat, as I wrote in the beginning of the chapter, the police are able to solve a crime if someone tells them who committed it; if no one tells them, it is unlikely that they will make an arrest.

Crime victims, especially the victims of violent crimes, are by far the most important source of information leading to criminals' arrest. The reason, quite simply, is that they often know the offender. In 1975, according to the National Crime Survey, 41 percent of assault victims and one-third of rape victims were attacked by someone with whom they were acquainted. (There is little difference in the frequency with which "stranger crimes" and "acquaintance crimes" are reported to the police.) The relationship may be a close one, involving husbands and wives, lovers, parents and children, or other relatives and close friends; or the assault or rape may involve sex rivals, neighbors, or casual acquaintances who have gotten into a barroom or other dispute.[22]

Either way, the victim usually can furnish a good description of the offender, and often the offender's name and address as well. As a result, the police are able to "solve" a high proportion of violent crimes. The measure of effectiveness that police departments traditionally have used is the proportion of crimes "cleared" by arrest.* In 1976, police departments as a whole cleared only 21 percent of all Index crimes,

---

* Police departments clear a crime when they are satisfied they know who the offender is and have taken him into custody. The fact that a crime has been cleared does not mean that the arrested offender has been convicted—only that the police have closed their books on the case. Arrested offenders often confess to other crimes they may or may not have committed, which permits the police to show a higher clearance rate.

but 79 percent of all murders, 63 percent of all aggravated assaults, and 52 percent of all reported rapes.

Homicide cases are solved more often than other crimes because so many murders are crimes of passion, growing out of some sort of conflict between relatives, friends, or acquaintances; in 1976, according to the *Uniform Crime Report,* two homicides in three involved a prior relationship between victim and offender. Because of the seriousness of the crime, people who know (or suspect) the offender's identity are more likely to be willing to talk to the police. Frequently, too, the murderer, overcome by remorse, either calls the police himself, waits near the scene of the crime to be arrested, or turns himself in later on. If the murderer does not confess, or a witness does not identify the offender immediately, the police usually proceed on the assumption that the crime was committed by a relative, lover, friend, or acquaintance; they question everyone they can find to determine a possible motive, and thereby the identity of the killer.

Their dependence on victim identification of the offender, or, in the case of homicide, on the existence of a prior relationship between the victim and the offender, puts the police at a serious disadvantage when dealing with violent crimes in which the victim and offender are unacquainted.*[23] Since crimes committed by strangers have grown far more rapidly than crimes committed by acquaintances, the police have

* It took the Los Angeles police several months to solve the Manson gang's bizarre slaying of Sharon Tate and her house guests because the investigators assigned to the case took it for granted that the murders had been crimes of passion or revenge, committed by someone who knew the actress or one of the other victims. This mind-set led the investigators to treat other Manson gang murders as independent cases, and to ignore much of the evidence that managed to survive the bungling of the police who first arrived on the scene.

been able to make proportionately fewer and fewer
arrests. The homicide clearance rate has fallen steadily, from 92.3 percent in 1960 to 79 percent in 1976;
in New York, which has a considerably better-than-
average police department but a far larger proportion
of stranger homicides than other cities, the police were
able to clear barely more than half the murders that
occurred in 1976.

Much the same picture obtains for other crimes.
Since the 1960s, the proportion of rapes committed by
strangers has increased sharply; so has the proportion
of crimes reported to the police. The clearance rate
has dropped precipitously, from 72.5 percent in 1960
to 52.3 percent in 1976. In that same period, the clearance rate for aggravated assault has dropped from
75.8 percent to 62.9 percent.

The clearance rates for robbery (27 percent), burglary (17 percent), and other property crimes always
have been low, because these crimes typically involve
offenders who are not known (and, in the case of
burglary and most thefts, not seen) by the victim.
When an arrest is made, it usually is because a victim or witness is able to identify the offender; because
the police were called rapidly enough to catch the
offender at or near the scene of the crime; or because
a victim, witness, or police officer spotted evidence—a
license plate number, a stolen check or credit card,
or, on rare occasions, a set of fingerprints—that clearly
linked a suspect to the crime. Roughly two-thirds of
the arrests in robberies, burglaries, and other major
property crimes occur in this manner.[24]

If a suspect cannot be identified in one of these ways,
the odds are high that the case will not be solved.
According to Peter Greenwood of the Rand Corporation, who has directed several major studies of the way
police departments investigate crimes, "It is a rare

event when a property crime is solved through the clever piecing together of a fragile chain of evidence." In an analysis of New York City robbery cases, Greenwood found that an arrest was made at or near the scene of the crime in nearly one robbery in ten. Of the remainder, the police made an arrest in 46 percent of the cases in which the victim could name a suspect, but only 2 percent of the cases in which they had no more than a description to go on. In analyzing Los Angeles police statistics, the 1967 Crime Commission found that only 12 percent of the cases without a named suspect were cleared; of those cases in which a suspect was named, 86 percent were cleared.

How is it that robbery or burglary victims are able to name the offender? The reason is that even these crimes occasionally involve victims and offenders who know one another. Robbery, in particular, may be an outgrowth of a drunken brawl or a sober but bitter fight between husband and wife, lovers, siblings, in-laws, or other relatives and friends. In such situations, theft can be a way of demonstrating victory, evening the score in defeat, or just expressing anger. Domestic disputes aside, a pimp who believes his prostitute is "holding out" on him may take money from her by force; a prostitute may lure a customer to a hotel room so that his wallet can be taken by her pimp or other accomplices; an argument over gambling losses and winnings may be resolved by one person pulling a knife or gun and taking the pot; addicts frequently steal from relatives and friends in order to buy drugs; and drug users and dealers rob one another with some frequency.

Because the police find it so much easier to make an arrest when a robbery victim knows the offender, such cases account for a grossly disproportionate number of the cases that come to court. Only 2 to 6 percent of the robberies in New York City involve a prior relationship between robber and victim; according to a sample of felony arrests analyzed by the Vera Institute of Justice, such cases account for 36 percent of the robbery arrests. In Washington, D.C., the Institute for Law and Social Research (INSLAW) has analyzed total arrests over a six-year period; only 7 percent of the robberies, but roughly 35 percent of the robbery arrests, were cases in which victim and offender were acquainted.[25]

The same disproportion exists in arrests for burglary and other forms of theft. In New York City, according to the Vera Institute analysis, 39 percent of the burglary and larceny arrests were of offenders who had some prior relationship with the victims, and the proportions seem to be even higher in Washington, D.C. Although victims do not see the offender, as is the case in robbery, they frequently have a good idea of who committed the crime. In one of the cases Peter Greenwood and his colleagues describe in the Rand Corporation study, *The Criminal Investigation Process,* a rooming house owner reported the theft of furniture and a TV set, naming as the suspect a tenant who had absconded without paying his rent. The police had no trouble locating the suspect, since he had left a forwarding address with the post office; they found the furniture and television set in his new apartment. In another instance, a store owner reported the theft of two guns, valued at more than $200, that had been kept under lock and key; he named as a suspect a man who had visited the store many times without buying anything, and who knew where the guns were kept. A police investigation determined that the suspect used a nearby gas station as a site for selling stolen merchandise. When the suspect offered to sell the guns to an undercover agent, he was arrested and the guns recovered.[26]

Because impulsive street criminals commit crimes in their own neighborhoods, some cases are solved when a witness is able to identify the offender. In one instance in Oakland, a sixteen-year-old street criminal robbed at least eight cabdrivers over a four-week period. In each instance, he would order a cab and take it to his destination; on arrival, he would place a knife against the cabdriver's throat, take his money, and then, before fleeing on foot, slice the driver's skin to prevent him from following. In the next-to-last robbery, the suspect took a cab to a neighborhood in which he had once lived; a thirteen-year-old boy recognized him and identified him by name to the police. In the twenty-four hours before the police were able to track down the suspect, he robbed and sliced another cabby.[27]

In robbery cases, witnesses and victims, particularly the latter, play a decisive role in catching criminals even when they do not know their identity. As part of the study of robbery in Oakland, directed by Floyd Feeney and Adrianne Weir, William Smith analyzed the ways in which suspects were caught in a representative sample of cases. Of seventy instances in which one or more people played a role in catching the suspect or suspects, the victim played the most significant role in thirty-five. In most of these cases, the victims did not know the offender, but their alertness and determination made it possible for the police to make the arrests. In one instance, in which a man was held up in the parking lot behind an all-night restaurant and ordered out of his car, the driver of another car told him that a police car was just around the corner; the victim approached the police car, and

the officers arrested the suspects as they were walking
away. In another instance, in which a man was held
up at a bus stop, the victim took a bus toward his
destination but got off a few blocks later, when he
spotted a police car; he accompanied the police back
to the scene of the holdup and pointed out the suspect,
who had not yet left the area.

In twelve of the Oakland cases, a witness played the
decisive role. In one case, a man about to enter a bar
became suspicious of four strangers who had entered
ahead of him; he called the police from a nearby phone
booth. They arrived in time to catch the four men as
they were leaving, having held up the bartender and
customers. In another instance, a witness saw an elderly
drunk being held up on the street; he flagged down a
police car a few blocks away and directed them to the
scene. Although the robber had fled on foot, he was
caught a few blocks away. In still other instances,
witnesses provided the police with descriptions of the
getaway cars, together with license numbers.[28]

Sometimes the victims pursued the individuals who
had robbed them, pointing out the suspects to the police, whom they had flagged down or called. In one
case, the victim returned to the neighborhood in which
he had been held up, looking for the perpetrator, whom
he spotted and kept in view, after calling the police.
In two others, the victims spotted the offenders by
chance and called the police.

In five instances, the offender's own bungling was
the primary factor leading to his arrest. One such case
involved an attempted holdup of a liquor store. As
the clerk was locking the front door at 3 A.M., a
masked robber came from behind and placed a gun in
his back; the clerk was so startled that he dropped
the keys on the sidewalk. While the robber was trying to find the keys, a passing motorist saw what was

happening and backed up, to get a closer look with his headlights; the robber fled and the police were called. Before the police had finished taking the report from the clerk and the witness, the suspect returned, peering around a corner; he was spotted by an unmarked police car that had come as a backup—a frequent procedure with incidents involving a gun. The suspect ran again, but was caught nearby, with the gun, mask, and a glove on his person.

IV

None of this means that the police are irrelevant or unimportant. How much information a victim or witness provides (and, as we shall see in the next chapter, whether it stands up in court) depends, in good measure, on the skill with which the officer elicits, and the care with which he records, the information. And whether on not an arrest follows identification of an offender, or a description of the suspect or of his car, depends on the officer's initiative and skill. While they are on patrol, police are expected to keep an eye out for pedestrians and cars that are on the "wanted" list. An able officer can pick up the most subtle visual clues while simultaneously driving, listening to the police radio (which means sorting out relevant information and calls intended for them from what, to a civilian or a rookie, sounds like an unending and unintelligible stream of talk and static), and carrying on a conversation with a partner. Offenders may be spotted by an officer with an alert eye—and lost if he is careless in his approach.

ITEM (from report of a night on patrol in a Midwestern city): After about an hour of driving around, with H. telling me how much he loved his job, answering radio calls, and pointing out points of interest, he suddenly interrupted himself in mid-sentence to say, "I do believe that man is wanted for burglary!" He was talking about someone coming down the street on my side of the car; I had not even seen the man, let alone made out what he looked like! We made a right turn into a side street; H. looked back and said the man, who had evidently seen us, was running. We turned right at the next corner, went two or three blocks, then right again to come up to the same street right behind him. He was walking in front of a gas station; H. pulled into the station, then back onto the sidewalk so the man was between the car and the street. The man stopped; H. asked if he had any identification with him —he said no—and then asked for his name and address. The subject gave a name—a false one, I later learned—and said he lived at the corner of such-and-such a street; he claimed not to know the exact address. H. politely asked him to get into the front of the car; as I slid over and opened the door to shift into the back seat, I heard running footsteps and a shout of "Halt!" I turned around in time to see the man disappear around the corner of the gas station. After a brief, fruitless pursuit—the suspect had jumped over a fence and disappeared in a huge lot filled with junked cars—H. returned to the car and radioed a call for a helicopter and additional patrol cars, indicating that the man probably was armed. (H. knew his real name; the man was the person wanted for burglary.) Within a few minutes, several cars had arrived and a helicopter was circling overhead, shining a searchlight down into the area; the search was unsuccessful, and we headed in the general direction the man had taken.

In the above instance, the officer's alertness enabled him to spot a suspect—and his subsequent carelessness enabled the man to get away. The officer was furious with himself, in fact, for not having taken his flashlight and walkie-talkie when he first got out of the car. With the flashlight, he might have been able to follow the man; and the walkie-talkie would have enabled him to put in a call for reinforcements without having to go back to the car and without losing the trail; those two minutes may have meant the difference between catching the suspect and his getting away. (When I left the city two days later, the suspect was still at large. "We'll get him yet," H. assured me; the police were keeping a close watch on the neighborhoods in which the suspect's mother and girl friend lived.)

Because criminals often use a stolen car for their getaway, police officers usually are given a list of stolen cars at the beginning of each shift, for which they are on the lookout while riding patrol. In cities with a central computer hookup, officers can call in the license number of a car that looks suspicious, to find out if it has been reported stolen. (The Oakland, California, department has equipped some patrol cars with a computer console, so that officers have direct access to the computer.)

Some arrests are made as a by-product of a more or less routine pedestrian or car stop; after they have stopped a car because the driver is speeding or has gone through a red light, police may recognize the driver, or a passenger, as someone wanted on a felony charge. In one of the Oakland cases described by William Smith, officers on routine preventive patrol saw a speeding car drive past with its lights out; they gave chase, and after trying to escape, the car finally pulled to the side. Recognizing one of the three occupants as someone wanted on a felony warrant and another as wanted on a narcotics charge, the officers began a methodical search of the three men and the car. They found one revolver under the driver's seat and another on the floor of the car; inspecting further, they found two cigar boxes containing $887 in bills and rolls of coins. As they were arresting the men, the police radio reported an armed robbery of a grocery store some fifteen blocks away from where they had first noticed the speeding car.

Sometimes an arrest is even more accidental. The police may stop a car because of a warrant for unpaid parking tickets and discover that the driver is wanted on a felony. One of the Oakland robbery arrests came about as a result of a routine suspicion stop. When the driver showed his driver's license, the alert officer noticed that the wallet contained a credit card issued under another name; a check revealed that the credit card had been stolen as part of an armed robbery. In an incident I witnessed, an officer stopped a car because a taillight was burned out. In what may well have been an illegal search, the officer found some guns he suspected were stolen; he held the driver on the traffic violation in order to give headquarters time to check out whether or not the guns were stolen. (They were.)

Police do not rely on suspicion stops and on information provided by victims and witnesses; they develop their own sources of information. The best officers cultivate relationships with the people in their beat—especially people whose occupation or location gives them an opportunity to know what goes on in the neighborhood. These noncriminal sources include bartenders, waiters and waitresses, and bar and restaurant owners; liquor store proprietors and sales clerks; newsstand dealers; barbers and beauticians; pawnbrokers; apartment house superintendents, doormen, and elevator operators; cabdrivers; hotel desk clerks and bellhops; neighborhood gossips, some of them elderly people who pass the time watching the street from their apartment window or from a chair or stoop in front of the house; and younger people who just happen to know "what's happening." Because of the nature of their work or life style, some of these people may have contact with criminals or criminal networks and thus come into information directly. Others, who simply see or know about the passing scene, may be able to supply useful information—but only if the police can ask the right question.

Some people supply information to the police for no reason other than their interest in effective law enforcement; such altruism is rare. Even the most law-abiding citizens rarely are disinterested in their transactions with the police. Some informants are simply "police buffs," whose reward consists of the reflected glory and vicarious excitement or glamour they derive from association with the police; most law-abiding informants want something more concrete. In return for information, businessmen often want protection when making a bank deposit, more frequent "passes" by the precinct's patrol cars, assurance of an immediate response whenever a call for help is placed, or cooperation in overlooking some minor infringement of the law, e.g., the firm's trucks parked illegally on the street, or customers' cars double-parked outside.

With some businessmen or employees, the quid pro quo may be larger. For many small businessmen or employees, as we have seen in Chapter 4, illicit activities mean the difference between breaking even and losing money, or between a bare subsistence wage and one that permits a modicum of comfort. Furnishing the police with information they pick up in the course of their work is the price they pay the police to overlook their illicit trade. In the case of pawnbrokers, bartenders, barbers, beauty shop operators, truckdrivers, and others, it may be occasional traffic in stolen mer-

chandise or providing a front for bookmakers or numbers operators. Cabbies and hotel desk clerks and bellhops may be eager to have the police ignore occasional
solicitation for prostitutes or illegal sale of liquor or
drugs. Businesses and occupations for which a license
is required are particularly vulnerable to police action,
hence are particularly eager to maintain friendly (and
avoid unfriendly) relations with the police.

But the need for "credit" with a friendly officer is
not limited to businessmen or people in licensed occupations; normally law-abiding people are eager to have
a friend on the force whom they can call upon for help
should they get into trouble.

ITEM (from notes of a day on patrol): We stopped at
a diner for coffee, and J. was approached by a high
school friend, now twenty-six and unemployed, who
wanted to get into the drug war on the side of the police. He knew about a dealer in the area who was getting five pounds of marijuana over the weekend, and
would the police like to bust him? J. knew the dealer
in question—apparently he was another high school
classmate—and answered, "So Larry's a pusher, is he?"
The informant knew of someone else who was expecting some close-to-pure heroin about a week later. J. and
his friend arranged to meet again and set up some pur-
chases of marijuana. Later on, J. told me that although
he was not interested in the marijuana sale as such, he
would use the transaction to test his informant's reliability. If it stood up, he would feel more confident in
going after the heroin dealer; the informant's reliability
also would bolster his case in court, should the warrant
come under attack. (J. took it for granted that his high
school buddy–informant was trying to build up some
credit with him, in case he got into trouble with the law
himself.)

Important as these sources are, the police derive more information from criminals themselves. The information comes in three distinct, if often overlapping, ways: confessions obtained from a suspect through suspicion stops and artful interrogation; information about other offenders obtained from a suspect or defendant who hopes to get more favorable treatment thereby; and information provided by informers—usually criminals themselves—with whom officers have more or less ongoing relationships.

The first two are particularly valuable means of catching the ordinary jack-of-all-trades offender. When a suspicion stop yields a suspect, the officer making the stop is likely to question him without observing all the niceties required by the Miranda decision. Sometimes the failure to inform suspects of their constitutional rights (to remain silent, to be represented by counsel) before questioning them is deliberate.

Much of the time the failure is not deliberate, or at least not conscious; officers ignore or forget about the "Miranda warning" because to stop and read it to a suspect would disrupt the informal atmosphere they try to maintain as a way of defusing the hostility that an arrest generates. In one evening of riding patrol in a high-crime neighborhood, I witnessed six arrests; it was not until I was back in my hotel room, reviewing my notes, that I realized that nothing resembling a Miranda warning had been given in any of the six arrests. One thing followed another so quickly that I—and perhaps the officers—forgot about Miranda. In any event, only one of the suspects—a drunk who admitted stabbing another man with whom he had been drinking—made a statement that might have haunted him in court. The officer did not record the confession, since he was certain that the drunk would repeat it at the station house when the detectives took over the questioning; his only interest was in determining whether there was cause to arrest the drunk for a crime, or merely to bring him to a detoxification center. (If challenged in court, the officer would simply have lied, testifying that he gave the Miranda warning before beginning his questioning; it would have been his word against that of the drunk.)

If an officer finds some cause for arresting a suspect or holding him for questioning, he brings the suspect to the station house. There, the questioning may be handled by the officer and some colleagues, by detectives (or investigators, as some departments now call them), or by a member of the juvenile division if the suspect is young enough. The distinction between legitimate and illegitimate interrogation techniques is ill-defined; reasonable people may disagree on precisely where it should be drawn. The courts have been drawn into the question only because police administrators have abdicated their responsibility to draw up and enforce their own rules and guidelines for police behavior.[29]

Be that as it may, persuading suspects to confess is an art form in its own right; experienced detectives vary their technique according to their assessment of the suspect's personality and background. Burglars tend to be "immature" and have "ego problems," one detective told me; they often can be bluffed into admitting crimes the police would not otherwise be able to pin on them. Rapists, he added, often can be "opened up" by a show of sympathy which puts the blame on the victim; thus investigators begin their questioning by saying, "A lot of women are really asking for it, leading men on," or something of the sort. Robbers, on the other hand, tend to be much tougher; they have enough self-confidence to confront their victims directly, and they often rely on their verbal ability to persuade their victims to hand over the money without resisting. Hence "robbers can't be conned," the investigator told me; "you have to lay all your evidence in front of them and let them see that you have them dead to rights before they'll tell you anything."

Besides confessing their own crimes, criminals are frequent sources of information about the misdeeds of others—accomplices, friends, slight acquaintances, and people known only by hearsay. As the saying goes, "The first one to tell his story gets the lightest sentence"; disorganized street criminals, in particular, are often eager to be the first one.

ITEM (from report of a night on patrol in Los Angeles): We arrested a man for possession of a marijuana cigarette, found in his woolen cap during a frisk. (Only the Los Angeles police treat possession of marijuana as a serious offense.) As the man was being led from his group of friends to the police car, he told a patrolman that one of his friends had a shoe box full of marijuana in his car; all the friends' cars were searched, with their consent, but nothing was found. As we were driving back to the station, the man repeatedly asked if there wasn't some way he could "get out of this thing." The cops told him that though they couldn't help him, they'd be glad to listen to anything he had to say; but they made no real effort to question him. After his bum steer about the shoe box of marijuana, they didn't think he knew anything of value.

If they are to be effective, policemen need more than the random information they obtain from the people they arrest; they require more regular, and more reliable, sources. Bartenders, cabbies, pawnbrokers, and other "respectable" types represent one kind of source; professional criminals represent another. In New York

police circles, "information" is a technical term meaning "a deliberate, sub rosa identification of a crime or
perpetrator by some individual who himself is involved or on the borderline of criminal activity."[30]

The relationship always is reciprocal, although the
quid pro quo given the criminal in exchange for information varies from officer to officer, and from criminal
to criminal. Frequently, information is given the police
in return for some past favor or favors—reducing a
charge to some lesser offense or dropping it altogether,
recommending probation, finding a job for a youthful
offender or suggesting that he be placed in a drug rehabilitation program.

. ITEM (from notes of a night on patrol): H. put in a
radio call to the man in the adjoining district; one of
his informants had overheard two kids, each with long
records, mention a burglary they had committed in a
tavern belonging to the father of a friend. They had
broken into the tavern with their friend's help, and
they were planning to do it again on Saturday night.
. The informant was a kid H. had once arrested on a
minor charge; since H. thought he was a good kid, he
had urged probation, and subsequently helped find a
job for the boy, who had supplied him with information ever since. H. considered him reliable and would
not give away his identity to the other patrolman, in
whose district the tavern was located.

ITEM: We stopped a well-known prostitute and, during a long and basically friendly conversation, asked
her about a boyfriend who reportedly was selling pills
from the hospital where he worked; would she arrange
for him to sell some drugs to an undercover policeman?
Too risky, she thought, but she would see if she could

find anything out. As we left, one of the patrolmen turned to me and said, "She owes me a year in the workhouse; I've busted her three times for prostitution, and she's only drawn eighteen days."

The police-informant relationship can be more complex. Many professional criminals are police buffs themselves; but for some turn of fate, they would have joined the force instead of turning to crime. Professional criminals may also cultivate relationships with police for their own ego needs. As I suggested in Chapter 3, pros are eager for the police to think well of their craftsmanship; other than their fellow criminals, the police are the only ones capable of evaluating, and therefore admiring, their talent.

Moreover, police and criminals often feel that they are the only ones who understand each other. Bruce Jackson speaks of "the symbiotic relationship between junkies and the cops that follow them," with neither having friends in the square world who understand their problems as well as their opponent does. Professional criminals need a reciprocal relationship with a police officer for another, more practical reason. Since they are almost always known to the police, career criminals are vulnerable to being "set up" any time the police are being pressed to make an arrest in a particular case; they need a patrol officer or detective who is sufficiently indebted to them, or dependent on them, to provide the necessary assistance.

Detectives, on the other hand, especially those who specialize in thefts of jewels, antiques, and works of art, need informants who can come through when the heat is on the police department. If they have a choice, most victims would rather recover their property than have the offenders arrested; when the victim is politically influential, the police may be under heavy pressure to recover stolen jewels or paintings, and informants can be invaluable as go-betweens. As Lincoln Steffens remarked, the detective's trade consists not in pursuing criminals, but in forming friendships with them.

Police relationships with the underworld have always been shrouded in secrecy, and their management always has been a source of concern to conscientious police administrators because of the enormous temptation to corruption that such relationships entail. Police officers often pay off their informants in liquor or drugs; to do so, they hold back some of the heroin or cocaine they seize when they make an arrest.

It is a small step from violating departmental regulations in that manner and holding back larger amounts of heroin to sell on one's own account. In the notorious "French connection" case, New York City narcotics detectives diverted 188 pounds of heroin and 31 pounds of cocaine to their own use, making the Narcotics Bureau's Special Investigating Unit (SIU) perhaps the largest heroin and cocaine dealer in the city. (Some students of law enforcement would assign that honor to the New York office of the old Federal Bureau of Narcotics.)[31]

Most law enforcement officials continue to believe in the value of criminal informants, relying on a variety of administrative devices to hold corruption to a minimum. "Of course it would be nice to have priests, nuns, and rabbis provide information, but they're not involved in crime," one official says. "The people who can tell you about crime are those involved in it. It's an unpleasant business." But because of the secrecy surrounding the use of criminal informants, no one—*no one*—knows whether the gains are worth the cost.

As a result of recent research, it has become clear that the gains that come from the sharp division between patrol officers and detectives are *not* worth their cost. Detectives are the glamour boys of the police world; in no aspect of policing is the gap between image and reality quite so wide. Patrol officers are assigned the grubby work; when a crime has been committed, they tend to the victim, secure the scene of the crime to protect evidence, and begin collecting information —until the detectives arrive to take over the job of investigating the crime and catching the offender.

Detectives always have been resented by patrol officers, who feel that they bear the brunt of the risk and do the bulk of the work, only to see the detectives gain the prestige and glory. These officers are fully justified in their resentment. Each of the recent studies of how the police catch criminals has revealed that patrol officers make the overwhelming majority of felony arrests, and that a large proportion of the arrests and clearances with which detectives are credited are the result of information contained in the report filed by the patrol officers called to the scene.

It is not surprising that most of these officers are reluctant to give detectives any more information than is absolutely necessary. Resentment aside, there is no incentive for them to do so; police departments reward patrol officers and detectives for making good arrests, not for providing good information. Further obstacles to the flow of information stem from the fact that, at least in large cities, the detective force usually is organized along specialized lines, according to the type of crime. This organization dates back to the time when criminals were believed to be specialists; it was believed that by concentrating on a single type of crime, detectives could gain far greater knowledge of criminals and their distinctive criminal styles (modus operandi, or M.O.s, in police parlance). The assumption is no longer true, if indeed it ever was; however much they may prefer a particular crime, even professional criminals are generalists rather than specialists; and the crime that evokes the most fear tends to be committed by impulsive amateurs. As often as not, therefore, the same person may have committed crimes being investigated by two or three separate detective teams, none of which shares information with the others.

What this means is that most of what is known about crime and criminals is contained in individual officers' heads, not in written records. If the personnel were to disappear, the information would disappear with them. Some departments have tried to deal with this problem by creating centralized units to collect, evaluate, and disseminate "intelligence." But detectives and patrol officers are reluctant to share their private store of information with anyone else; and they are not likely to do so until police departments revamp their reward system so that police have as large an incentive to provide information as they have to make an arrest.[32]

V

Although police derive their self-image from playing cops and robbers, their other functions are every bit as important and actually predate their role in crime control. Initially, the police were more concerned with maintaining order than with catching criminals, which was the responsibility of the individual citizen. Before police departments as we know them began to take shape in the second quarter of the nineteenth century, cities of any size drafted citizens to serve on the nightly watch. Their responsibility, as an old Boston ordinance put it, was to "walk the rounds in and about the streets, wharves, lanes, and principal inhabited parts, within each town, to prevent any danger by fire, and to see that good order is kept."[33]

Maintaining order remains a major police responsibility; the great majority of the calls patrol officers receive involve breaches of the peace or requests for help, rather than reports of crimes in the usual sense of the term.[34] In poor neighborhoods, in particular, police spend large amounts of time responding to "family (or domestic) disputes"—arguments and fights between relatives, lovers, friends, and acquaintances. These calls are the most dangerous kind of police work. In violent disputes among friends or lovers, one of the parties often acts in irrational and unpredictable ways. When an officer arrives, moreover, disputants, including the one who called for help, sometimes unite and turn on him as the common enemy.

In dealing with a domestic dispute, a tavern or street-corner brawl, an incipient riot, or any other disturbance, enforcing the law usually is not the police's main concern. Their job is to restore order—to "deal with the situation" and return it to some semblance of normality. Since they have almost unlimited discretion in how they handle breaches of the peace, police vary enormously in the techniques they use and the skill with which they use them. When he was commanding a precinct house, a retired New York City police official told me, he knew that if he sent one particular patrol car to the scene of a barroom brawl, the result would be at least one injured cop and two civilians in the hospital; if he sent a different team, they would manage to settle the brawl without any injuries, and without any arrests.

To be effective in situations of this sort, a patrol officer needs three sets of qualities not normally found in the same person: great subtlety and sophistication in understanding and dealing with people; unusual verbal facility; and the willingness and ability to use physical force—to fight with no holds barred, and to kill if nec-

essary.* Although the relative emphasis varies from
person to person, according to personality, background,
native ability, and training, every effective patrolman
calls on all three attributes in the situations he handles.

More than anything else, as we saw earlier, what
distinguishes the police from other agencies of government is the right to use force when opposed. The central
paradox of policing, the political scientist William Ker
Muir, Jr., writes, is that although the cop appears to
others as "the supreme practitioner of coercion," he is
its most frequent victim. The possibility that violence
may be used against him is never far from an officer's
mind.[35]

In approaching someone, therefore, the officer
instinctively appraises the other person's size and
strength, deciding whether he can "take him" if need
be; at the same time, he concentrates on the person's
hands, to see whether he reaches for a weapon. If he
has a choice, the officer moves to his left, in order to
keep his right hand free; he stands at the other person's
right, at a slight angle, to keep his gun away from the
suspect and to avoid a kick to the groin. He also stands
closer to people than is usual when persons are conversing; crowding people reduces their opportunity to
kick or punch him, and also underscores his power and
dominance over them.

In dozens of ways, in short, police use their bodies
to express their authority and to establish control over
the situation and the people in it. Good cops try to
avoid force if they can, but they must be prepared to
use it at any time. They disagree among themselves over
how much force should be used *when,* but not over
whether force should be used at all. To be an officer, as

* I rely heavily on the insights of William Ker Muir, Jr.,
Jonathan Rubinstein, and Egon Bittner in the discussion that
follows.

Muir puts it, is to struggle constantly with "the contradiction of achieving just ends with coercive means."

The artistry of policing lies in the ability to reduce violence to a minimum—the officer's violence, as well as the violence of others. To do so—to defuse volatile situations—police use a wide variety of techniques. In a domestic dispute or other fight, they will try to separate the combatants, "bullshitting" one or the other until he or she calms down and is willing to leave or stop fighting. When a husband and wife (or man and woman) are fighting, one officer may invite the male partner to step outside with him to have a smoke and to tell his side of the story; he then will try to persuade the man to go for a walk, alone or with him, depending on the situation. By the time he returns, the adrenalin will have died down in both partners, and it is much easier to get them to settle matters peacefully. But whether a disturbance involves a fight or some other breach of the peace, the trick is to preserve people's dignity while giving them an "out."

ITEM (from report of a night on patrol): At 7:50 P.M., we were signaled to stop by the driver of a city transit authority bus. The driver (white) told us that a passenger (black), seated in the rear, had been playing his tape recorder very loudly and had refused to lower it or turn it off despite the driver's repeated requests, and despite the fact that the bus had a sign prohibiting such noisemaking. We got on the bus and went to the back. The man in question, a big and tough-looking twenty-year-old, had turned off the machine before we came aboard. S. came on mild: "What's this all about?" he asked. "I can play this if I want to," the young man answered. When S. pointed to the sign, the man argued, not very convincingly, that it referred to radios and phonographs, not tape recorders. Besides, he added,

lots of people in the bus were smoking, and that was
forbidden, too. S. turned around and told everyone who
was smoking to put out their cigarettes; half a dozen
butts hit the floor. The driver came back to tell us again
that the passenger had refused his requests to turn the
thing off; S. gently suggested that the driver go back to
his seat and let him handle it. "Come on," S. told the
guy in a low tone, "be reasonable. You don't have to
play that thing just to make a point; you're embarrassing your girl friend over nothing." (She did look a
little embarrassed.) After some more fuming, the passenger agreed not to play the machine and not to
"mess" with the driver; "I'm not petty," he said. S. went
back to the driver and asked him not to talk to the
passenger again unless he started acting up. We got off
the bus and it went on its way. "Five or six years ago
I'd probably have arrested him," S. said; he was pleased
that he had been able to settle the situation without an
arrest, which would have meant a noisy argument at
best and quite possibly a fight. Basically, he explained,
he had appealed to the guy's pride—he was making a
fool of himself in front of his girl and all those passengers for nothing—and by keeping the driver away
and ordering smokers to put out their cigarettes, he had
made it possible for the man to back down without losing face.

"Bullshitting"—the police term for the ability to use
language as an instrument of persuasion—does not always suffice. When a domestic dispute is violent or
noisy and neither party will succumb to police blandish-
ments, one solution is to bring both parties to the station house under the threat of arrest. "They listen better
when they're in front of the desk," a veteran officer told
me with a smile. Understandably so: the jail cells are
visible from the desk in his station house. Bringing

combatants there under the threat of arrest forces them to stop fighting each other and to concentrate instead on how to get out of the police station. Most of the time, therefore, bringing them in is all that has to be done; the parties calm down and agree to settle their dispute amicably, and they are released without any charges being filed.

There are times, of course, when police *do* arrest someone. Usually, they regard the arrest as a way of restoring order—of "dealing with the situation"— rather than as a means of enforcing the law as such. The formal charge that is lodged may *justify* the arrest, but it rarely is the *reason* for the arrest. The real reason is to stop a fight; to get a dangerous person off the street or out of the house before he follows through on a threat of violence; to remove a drunk who is standing at a busy intersection, shouting obscenities at and otherwise harassing and frightening female motorists; to prevent a tavern or street-corner brawl from escalating into a riot; to get a drunk off the street before he freezes to death; or any number of equally urgent considerations. The police are expected to dissolve problems, not solve them, and arresting someone can be a useful tool in that process.

ITEM (from notes of a night on patrol): Another call came, to check out a woman with a gun. This was a potential crime in progress, and M. used his siren and lights as we went to the address. Four young black men were standing in the driveway and one of them came up to our car. "I was in a fight with this dude, see, and he went to get his mother, and she came back with this gun and started waving it around." The "dude" was his cousin, and the woman his aunt; she had left in her car just as we turned into the block. We went the way the complainant pointed, after learning that the woman

had a small revolver; we found her driving slowly down
the block behind the one we had come up. M. pulled
her over and went quickly to the car's front door, asking, "Where's the gun?" "In the purse," she said, and
got out of the car at M.'s request. He looked inside the
purse and found it, loaded with six .22 bullets. After
taking some more information from the woman, he
made a call for a wagon to pick her up.

Over dinner, M. explained that he had arrested the
woman just to get her off the street for the night; he
was afraid that if she were not locked up for a few
hours, she would return and renew her dispute with the
complainant. M. had no interest in seeing her convicted; he felt certain that her anger would have cooled
by morning, when she would be released on bail. (M.
had made certain that she would be able to post bail
before arresting her, and had explained the procedure
to her.)

Police arrest people, in short, not only when they
have probable cause to believe that the offender has
committed a crime, but also when an arrest appears to
be the best way to handle a situation that will not brook
delay. Given the here-and-now urgency of police work,
a certain lack of concern for the niceties of legal procedure is almost inevitable. If arresting one party to a
fight and sending the other one home will stop a fracas
he fears may turn into a large-scale brawl or small riot,
an officer could not care less which of the two combatants is at fault; his job is to restore order.* To the

* The officer's choice may not be entirely random. In the
great majority of cases, police do not come upon a disturbance
on their own; they are called to the scene by someone, often a
participant and usually someone with a partisan interest in the
outcome. As Bittner puts it, a certain "strategic assymetry" results. By calling in the police, the complainant has aligned himself with the forces of order, which means that the other party
is more likely to be viewed as the "troublemaker."

district attorney or defense counsel or judge, on the other hand, not to mention the defendant, it makes all the difference in the world whether the officer arrested the "right" individual or the "wrong" one. Much of the tension and misunderstanding between police and lawyers and judges stems from the latter group's failure to understand the degree to which police actions are rooted in exigencies of the moment, in which reflection not only is impossible but may be terribly dangerous as well—to the officer or to the parties involved.

A significant proportion of the calls police receive direct them to situations that, on the surface, appear to have little to do with law enforcement or maintaining the peace. But only on the surface: in the crucible of urban life, as I learned while riding patrol, the most trivial-seeming disputes—over a car parked in someone else's space or so as to block (or partially block) someone's driveway, over children throwing snowballs or bouncing a rubber ball on a neighbor's steps or on the roof of his car, over a record player that is too loud—can erupt into violence in an instant.

In poorer neighborhoods, service calls often mean providing assistance to the sick and elderly—persuading their landlord to provide heat or transporting them to a clinic or hospital—or aiding otherwise healthy people who are simply helpless in the face of some (to them, at least) pressing problem. In these neighborhoods, the police often are the major—at night and on weekends, the only—social service agency.

ITEM (from report of a night on patrol): My overwhelming impression this night was of the helplessness of the people who called for assistance and their tendency to rely on the police to resolve problems middle-class people usually handle themselves or for which they turn to other professionals. A girl had overdosed

on barbiturates; her family called the police, called an
ambulance, and then sat helplessly in the dark, watching TV, until we arrived. On another call, a pair of
neighbors wanted to invoke our authority to settle a
longstanding and pointless dispute over a car in a
driveway. Another woman called to give official notice
that she would be justified in taking revenge on someone
else in a dispute that had started out as a fight between
two little children in a playground. The night before,
M. told me, he had answered several family fight calls
where the couple wanted him to decide which television program they should watch!

But people sometimes fabricate an emergency, reporting a serious illness to save cab fare to the hospital,
or reporting a domestic dispute to get a partner out of
the way in order to have a night (or weekend) on the
town.

ITEM (from report of a night on patrol): We answered
a call from a young woman whose husband had spent
the afternoon drinking with her and her mother, and
who was now hopelessly drunk. Her husband was an
alcoholic, the woman said, and she wanted him taken to
Detox (the city's new forty-six-bed detoxification center for alcoholics). The patrolman explained to her
that because of its limited bed-space, Detox was reserved for alcoholics who had nowhere else to go; her
husband would have to stay with her or her mother. As
we drove off, the cop told me that he knew the woman
from previous calls; based on past experience, he was
certain that she had spent the afternoon deliberately
getting her husband drunk and had called the police to
take him off her hands, so that she could go out with
someone else.

ITEM: Another domestic dispute; the complainant was a woman who said her common-law husband had threatened to beat her up, in violation of an "order of protection" she had received from Family Court. We found a peaceful scene when we arrived; the man was watching TV and was clearly surprised at our appearance. J. felt he had no alternative but to take the man in; the woman had an "order of protection" from Family Court forbidding the man from "verbally abusing" or "harassing" as well as physically beating her. If he did not arrest the man, the woman threatened, she would file a charge against him for failure to enforce a court order, which would leave him open to disciplinary action. J. was certain that the woman's motive was to get her husband out of the way for the weekend: violating a court order of protection is not a bailable offense, even though it is only a "violation," with a maximum penalty of fifteen days in jail. Since this is Friday night, the man will have to sit in jail until arraignment Monday morning. From J.'s standpoint, yelling at your wife is normal behavior to begin with; to see a robber go free on bail an hour after he calls his lawyer, while an apparently peaceful husband is locked up for the weekend because of, at most, yelling at his wife, makes no sense at all.

It is easy to become cynical and removed. Patrol officers often develop a highly skewed picture of the people who live in their sector; as one officer told me, "I get to know all the assholes in this neighborhood." It sometimes seems to him and his colleagues that the neighborhoods they police are peopled by nothing but "assholes," that universal police term for those who make the officer's lot difficult. With the exception of a few local merchants, police buffs, and others who supply information, the people with whom police have routine contact comprise an unappetizing cast of characters.

Even when they come in contact with respectable people, it is those people's seamier side that police often encounter. When a thief is caught with the stolen money or merchandise in his possession, police often find that the middle-class victim had exaggerated the extent of his loss in order to file a larger claim with his insurance company. Almost everywhere they turn, in fact, police encounter dishonesty and corruption, some of it petty, some of it large. Like con men, they come to believe that there is larceny in just about everyone's heart.

ITEM (from notes of an interview with a Los Angeles investigator): W. told me the story of one of his early cases, in which a monsignor from a Pennsylvania parish had come to Los Angeles for a few days' vacation before going on to his main destination—Las Vegas. The monsignor checked into a downtown hotel, and leaving the door to his room unlocked, proceeded to pray at the foot of his bed. During his prayer, he fell asleep (I'm not making this up; that was the monsignor's story) and a thief entered the room, taking $2,000 in cash from his suitcase. By the time the monsignor woke up, discovered his loss, and reported it to the hotel, the thief had been caught in another room and the $2,000 found on him. The monsignor was infuriated because W. could not give the money back to him; it was needed for evidence, and since the thief claimed that the money was his, only the court could decide between the two conflicting claims. The monsignor kept badgering him, saying over and over again that his vacation had been ruined; W. was as sure as he could be that the money had come from the church's poor box, to be used for gambling in Las Vegas.

For their own safety and well-being, moreover, police must learn to be professional skeptics. When people talk to an officer, it usually is not just to air a complaint; they complain because they want him to *do* something. The desire to enlist the officer's aid can make normally honest people stretch the truth to its outer limits, and beyond. "Any officer may begin his career by accepting as truth whatever he is told, but his experiences quickly encourage caution," Jonathan Rubinstein writes. "Even after he has developed cues and techniques for assessing the validity of claims made upon him, he will be conned into exertions and dangers. Each time this happens, his suspicion of things he is told deepens and the circle of people he is likely to believe shrinks."[36]

It is hard for police to avoid a jaundiced view of life and of their work. "The whole job is a joke," a veteran cop told me. "You start out with delusions of grandeur —how you're gonna save the world. But you find out soon enough that nobody cares. The people in the suburbs don't care as long as you keep it confined to the city, and the judges don't care as long as their dockets are current. After a while, you stop caring yourself, and you just do your job a day at a time and try to stay out of trouble." And if they do continue to care, police feel the need to act as if they did not. "The only way you survive on this job is to grow calluses," one of John Van Maanen's informants told him. "You put on a shell the beginning of every shift and take it off when you get home. When I'm working, I'm as hard as stone 'cause I gotta be, it's my only defense."

In fact, the most effective police do *not* "grow calluses." Some of the Oakland patrol officers Muir portrays, and many with whom I have spent time, understand how lonely the poor and elderly can be. They

know how desperate such people can be "for some
mediation, some advice, some consolation, some encouragement, some help to put their lives in order,"
and how difficult it is for them to find anyone to provide
that help. These officers also comprehend the fundamental unity of human aspiration that underlies large
differences in norms and behavior. "You take the lowest crumb," one of Muir's informants says. "Basically
he doesn't want to be that way. He'd like to be better,
and basically he'd like to have things better."[37]

Cops with that kind of understanding bring out the
best in the people they police; they contribute significantly to the quality of life in the neighborhoods
they patrol. What Muir calls "tragic understanding"
should not be confused with sentimentality or softness;
no patrol officer who values his life or well-being can
underestimate the brutality of which people are capable. They recognize that in a given situation or under
a particular set of circumstances, even saints turn into
sinners; but the other side of that coin is the recognition that, under the right circumstances, potential sinners may turn into decent human beings.

Muir describes the way one such officer restored
order, and reduced juvenile vandalism and delinquency, in his sector. Before Bill Douglas, as Muir
calls him, arrived on the scene, a group of high school
truants were wreaking havoc with the whole neighborhood around the school, in the process driving their
luncheonette hangout out of business. Douglas was
able to deal effectively with the high school students because he did not see them as a different breed; he himself had been something of a cutup in high school. But
in reflecting on his own adolescence, Douglas realized
that he had almost ruined his life chances by failing
to think about the future; the temptations growing out
of being popular and good-looking had diverted him

from his high school studies, and he missed the chance to go to college. Looking around him, Douglas concluded that this tendency to miscalculate, to fail to think about the next step, was an almost universal weakness—in bullying police officers, no less than in impetuous and thoughtless teenagers.[38]

Douglas asked himself, therefore, what it was that led people, especially adolescents, to accept responsibility—to think about the consequences of their own actions. He concluded that they had to be frightened —frightened enough to be forced to think things through, to have to come to terms with the damage that might flow from their behavior. "Fear was a great teacher, an indispensable one," Douglas decided. "It conditioned the mind wonderfully to lessons about self-restraint and concern for the long-term." But Douglas did not stop at that point. His greatest insight was his realization that although "fear got people to pay attention," paying attention served no purpose unless there was "a worthwhile and accurate lesson to pay attention to"—which is to say, unless the fear could somehow be transmuted into self-control.

Hence Douglas tried to persuade the rowdy juveniles on his beat that they were responsible for *all* the consequences of their actions, not just the short-term "kicks" they might get. But he recognized that the process would have to take time—that if he were in too big a hurry, the youngsters' sober second thoughts could not develop. Since adolescence involves a testing of limits, he reasoned, one has to assume that adolescents will miscalculate where the limits are and when they will be enforced. If teenagers are to learn from their miscalculations, if they are to develop their own controls as a result of such learning, they need time and psychological space in which to readjust their calculations.

What Douglas proceeded to do, therefore, was keep

a notebook with him, in which he recorded the names, misdeeds, and statements of all the juveniles who came to his attention. "In each encounter with juveniles," Muir writes, "Douglas anticipated miscalculation on their part and made allowance for it, giving them psychological room to readjust their initial estimates of matters." When he walked into Caesar's, the luncheonette that was being destroyed, "he allowed for the probability that they would misjudge him. He also concentrated on purposefully using time to dispel any irrationality." "So the next few days I walk into Caesar's, and I get myself about fifty names," Douglas explained, "and I tell each one, 'You do not play the machines. You go to school, and if you don't, I'll run you in.' So the first time down goes their name in my book. The second time I catch them, I make a little check right beside their name, just as big as I can. And the third time, I tell them, 'They go to jail.' Well, I only locked up one. And I had no more trouble."

VI

Where does all this leave us? What, if anything, can police departments do to reduce criminal violence?

The answer, in part, is that the police must recognize their own limitations; they must change their conception of their role from that of a law enforcement agency, dedicated to catching robbers, to that of a public service agency, devoted to close relationships with, and assistance to, the people and communities being policed. "Assigning the police full responsibility for the maintenance of order, the prevention of crime and the apprehension of criminals constitutes far too great a burden on far too few," the authors of the Kansas City Preventive Patrol Experiment Report have written. "Primary responsibility rests with families, the community and its individual members. The police can only facilitate and assist members of the community in the maintenance of order, and no more."[39]

For the police, there is profound truth in the architectural principle that less is more. Had Bill Douglas seen himself as Kojak, had his measure of his own success been the number of "assholes" and "bad guys" he put behind bars, he would have arrested a great many truants and vandals. The result, in all probability, would have been something akin to a state of war between juveniles and the police. But instead of fighting criminals, Douglas educated them; he cultivated their capacity to control their destructive impulses, diverting their youthful energy to more productive channels. Hence Douglas restored order, in the process making it possible for the luncheonette owner to remain in business; he also changed the lives of a number of youngsters, turning them away from delinquent careers that might have led them, in turn, to adult crime. In the end, he prevented a good deal of crime—far more than his crime-fighting colleagues.

There are many police officers with Douglas' understanding and ability; there are considerably more who are capable of developing along similar lines if given encouragement and help. There are notable exceptions, of course—callous individuals, even whole departments, such as Houston's, where brutality seems to be the norm. But for the most part, to spend time with police officers is to be impressed with how thoughtful and articulate they are—and how much of their thoughtfulness is wasted by the way police departments tend to be organized and run.

Police administrators must recognize that their principal resource is the information and expertise their line officers possess. In the most basic sense of the term, police departments are information-processing organi-

zations; but they have never thought of themselves that
way. Almost everything about the way most departments are organized and run serves to inhibit the flow
of information and expertise—from the community to
the police, and from one officer to another. Thus departments use only a minute fraction of the knowledge
that is at their disposal.

The first thing that needs to be done is to remove
the obstacles to close police-community relationships.
These obstacles have developed over the last half-
century as the unintended consequences of the search
for a technological solution to the problems of policing.
Like most Americans, police reformers have had an
abiding faith in technological change. A generation ago,
they thought they had found the panacea: equipping
patrol cars (the technological "fix" in which the preceding generation had placed its faith) with the newly
invented two-radio communication system. "Murderers
have been caught at the scene of a crime before they
had a chance to dispose of their weapons. Burglars
have been caught while still piling up their loot in
homes," Detroit Police Chief Rutledge told the annual
convention of the International Association of Police
Chiefs in 1929. "Bewildered auto thieves have gasped
as the police cruiser roared alongside of them a few
moments after they had stolen a car."

> Speeding hit-run drivers have been caputred and re-
> turned to the spot where they had run down and left
> their hapless victim a few seconds before. Thugs have
> been captured while in the act of robbing their vic-
> tim. Racketeers and bad-check passers have been
> caught. Bank stick-up men have been in handcuffs
> within 60 seconds of the time they fled the bank.

The 1931 Wickersham Commission shared Chief
Rutledge's heady optimism. "With the advent of the

radio-equipped car a new era has come," the authors of the Commission's report on the police announced. "Districts of many square miles, which formerly were officially watched by only a few men who in the very nature of the case could not watch the area, are now covered by the roving patrol car, fast, efficient, stealthy, having a regular beat to patrol, just as liable to be within 60 feet as three miles of the crook plying his trade—the very enigma of this specialized fellow who is coming to realize now that a few moments may bring them down about him like a swarm of bees—this lightning swift 'angel of death.' "[40]

Police chiefs retain that faith in speed and mobility. Since the mid-1960s, in particular, departments have made large investments in communication centers designed to shorten the interval between the moment the switchboard receives a telephone request for service and the moment a dispatcher orders a car to the scene. Departments have spent considerable sums, too, developing techniques to enable dispatchers to sort calls according to their importance and to select the patrol car closest to the scene. All this has been done on the assumption that cutting response time would increase the number of arrests and reduce the number of crimes.

It has not worked out that way. "It looks as if we asked the wrong question," Gerald Caplan, former director of the National Institute of Law Enforcement and Criminal Justice, told the chiefs attending a Police Foundation seminar. "The question should not have been, 'How long does it take the police to respond?' but rather 'How long does it take the victim to report the crime?'" "Shaving seconds or even minutes off response time is not likely to increase the number of arrests unless victims call the police immediately after a crime has been committed. They do not; most victims call a spouse, parent, or friend first—someone who can provide sympathy and advice. It is only after they have recovered from the immediate trauma that they remember to call the police.

These delays dwarf any lag in police response time. A study of victim behavior and police response time in Kansas City found that, on average, assault victims did not report the crime to the police until an hour after it had occurred; the police car arrived about three minutes later. The police car arrived at the scene within three and one-half minutes of receiving a robbery report—but robbery victims delayed calling the police for twenty-three minutes, on average. Burglaries were not reported for more than an hour after they were discovered, which, in turn, may have been several hours after the crime had occurred; it took the police six minutes to respond to a burglary call. And so it went.[41]

The point is not that short response time is irrelevant; there are occasions when a minute or two means the difference between an offender being arrested at the scene and his getting away. But police departments' single-minded pursuit of shorter response time has come at an inordinately heavy cost: making many patrol officers strangers to their own sectors. To hold response time to a minimum, for example, dispatchers routinely call a patrol car from an adjoining sector if all the cars assigned to the district from which the call has come are busy. During active periods, it is not unusual for a patrol car to respond to more calls outside its own sector than inside. The San Diego police found that "the vast majority of calls" are handled by patrolmen who are *not* assigned to the sectors from which the calls originate. The high frequency of "crossover," as it is called, reduces patrol officers' attachment to the neighborhoods they patrol; many officers do not even know their sector's boundaries.[42]

The emphasis on mobility also keeps patrol officers

encapsulated in their cars, unable to get to know, or be known by, the people on their beat. "A police car travels down the street like a tank," former New York City Mayor Robert Wagner once complained. "It can't see you; it doesn't know you." The result is something of a vicious circle; the more time officers spend in their cars, the more vulnerable and exposed they feel when they are out of them, and the more reluctant they are to leave their metal cocoons. The gulf between police and policed has been widened still more by the practice of rotating patrol officers from one assignment to another with some frequency—as mentioned above, a managerial device designed to minimize opportunities for police corruption.

Police departments have confused efficiency with effectiveness, sacrificing the latter to achieve the former. "We took the beat man off his feet, gave him radio communications and assigned him to a car so that he could cover more territory," a former big-city police chief has written. "We transferred him frequently and made him responsible only for his detail, which might vary from day to day, and to his commander."

> Our departments became more efficient in themselves, but by changing the role of the beat patrolman, we eliminated the effective, personal relationship between the police officer and the people he served. We severed communication with our greatest anti-crime ally, the citizens themselves.

There is some sentiment in favor of a return to old-fashioned foot patrol, especially in high-crime neighborhoods of large cities. The Washington, D.C., police department, which abolished foot patrol in 1966, restored the practice on an experimental basis in 1975, to test the chief's belief that officers on foot patrol become a more integral part of the neighborhood than

cops in patrol cars. Because officers on foot patrol develop closer relationships with citizens than do officers
who spend their time riding patrol, the theory goes,
they are more likely to develop sources of information
that enable them to catch criminal offenders. What
evidence is available suggests tentatively, but not conclusively, that the theory may be correct.[43]

A more promising innovation is so-called "neighborhood" or "team" policing, a shorthand term for a variety of approaches which involve turning over responsibility for a particular neighborhood to a team of
patrol officers, detectives and other specialists, and supervisors, usually with the rank of lieutenant. One or
another variant of team policing has been tried in New
York City; Los Angeles; Detroit; Syracuse and Albany,
New York; Dayton, Ohio; St. Petersburg, Florida; and
Oxnard, California.[44]

The most significant and elaborate experiment was
conducted, with Police Foundation support, in Cincinnati, Ohio.[45] A city of 450,000, with a police force
of about 1,100, Cincinnati is divided into six police
districts, each commanded by a captain. The Cincinnati Community Sector Policing Project, or Comsec, as
it was known for short, began early in 1971, when Carl
Goodin became chief of police, and was expanded, with
Police Foundation support, in March of 1973. In five
of the districts, policing continued as it had before; the
Comsec experiment was confined to District 1, an area
that includes Cincinnati's downtown business and entertainment areas and Skid Row, some surrounding
high-density residential neighborhoods with predominantly black public housing projects, and several areas
filled with warehouses, wholesaling firms, and railroad
yards. The population of District 1 is about 61 percent
black, compared to a city-wide average of 30 percent;
the District holds 8 percent of Cincinnati's population

but accounts for 28 percent of its robberies and 19 percent of its burglaries.

During the Comsec experiment, which ended in 1975, District 1 was divided into six sectors, each with its own team headed by a lieutenant. Depending on the size of the sector and the amount and nature of crime, the teams contained anywhere from sixteen to sixty members: three or four sergeants, a few plainclothes "specialists," as detectives are called, and some "community service assistants" (paraprofessionals), in addition to the patrol officers. Each team was responsible for all police services in its sector, except for homicide investigation—the province of a city-wide bureau—and the handling of special events, such as crowd control at Riverside Stadium.*

With authority to deploy manpower according to their judgment of neighborhood needs (the lieutenant in charge of each team was, in effect, a neighborhood police chief), the teams broke away from the traditional pattern of assigning the same number of police to each of the three shifts. In the downtown business sector, relatively few men were assigned to patrol duty late at night and on weekends, when there is little "activity" in the area; the reverse pattern was followed in another sector which contained a heavy concentration of bars, massage parlors, night clubs, and the like.

There was flexibility, too, in the teams' approach to patrol. A rash of purse-snatching in a large open-air market was stopped when team members made a num-

---

* Cincinnati avoided the "crossover" problem that has undermined most other experiments in team policing. With Police Foundation assistance, the department added new communication equipment and adopted new dispatching techniques, including the "stacking" of non-urgent calls. As a result, it was able to reduce crossover to slightly under 10 percent; i.e., the Comsec team members were called out of their sectors less than 10 percent of the time.

ber of arrests after keeping the market area under surveillance from a nearby rooftop; when another team
instituted regular foot patrol in a public housing project that was inaccessible to patrol cars, a number of
arrests cut the burglary rate there, too. In general,
patrol officers were encouraged to stop their cars from
time to time and walk around their neighborhood. Foot
patrol was facilitated by equipping officers with mini-
aturized two-way radios attached to their shirt or
jacket; since they used these radios in their cars as well
as on foot, the officers could leave their cars easily,
without having to carry the usual bulky walkie-talkie
held in the hand or awkwardly clipped to the belt.*

The results were disappointing. "What can be safely
said about the Comsec experiment in Cincinnati," Alfred Schwartz and Sumner Clarren write in the summary report, "is that it leaves no reason to believe
neighborhood team policing carries the risk of inviting
crime or that it is worse than regular police practices
in other ways." Over the thirty-month period, police-
community relations changed "only a little," and except for burglary, which decreased, the experiment had
no visible impact on serious crime.

Profound lessons were taught nonetheless—by the experiment's failures, even more than by its successes. If
a department wants to change patrol officers' behavior,
it must change its informal incentive system, which in
turn means altering the ways in which the officers are
supervised. In this instance, Cincinnati sought to transform police-community relations in the experimental

* Greater flexibility in assignments, together with the informality and camaraderie that the teams engendered, provided
fringe benefits to the officers themselves. It was much easier for
officers to arrange to have a free weekend to attend a wedding
or other family function; in some teams, a sheet was posted in
the station house so that members could sign up for duty on
weekends when they knew they would be free.

district. Patrol officers were *told* that effective policing required closer relations with the public, and they were told to spend their time getting to know the individuals and groups in their sectors.

But the department's administrative routines conveyed a different message. As is the case in most departments, each Cincinnati patrol officer fills out a daily work sheet at the end of his tour, reporting on his activity. As is also true of most departments, "activity" is defined in traditional police terms: "parkers" and "movers," arrests, and suspicion stops. Time spent conversing with storekeepers and residents was not considered an important enough activity to be recorded. The message was underscored by the department's system of incentives and rewards.

ITEM (from report of a week on patrol in District 1): Several officers told me that there is an informal quota system for tickets and arrests: although there is no fixed numerical goal an officer has to meet, questions will be asked if his "output" drops significantly below what it was the month before, or if it is consistently lower than that recorded by other officers. Several of the arrests I observed were followed by discussions among the cops involved, over who should take credit for the arrest and who for the "assist," a lesser but nonetheless valuable point on the credit scale. On several occasions, the officers I was riding with discussed whether or not to pull over a motorist they had just seen violating some minor traffic regulation; the point of the discussion was to decide whether either officer needed the "mover" for that month's quota.

The continued emphasis on arrests and tickets as the activity to be encouraged and rewarded, and the fact that failure to meet the informal quotas was pen-

alized, meant that patrol officers spent the bulk of
their time on traditional forms of "activity." They
had neither the time nor the incentive to develop
closer bonds with the people who lived and worked in
their sector. Nor were they given any training to learn
new approaches. Thus the principal form of officer-
citizen encounter continued to be the kind most likely
to anger local residents. Citizens' anger over those encounters, in turn, combined with the fact that patrol
officers were given no help in understanding the behavior of the people in their sectors, reinforced the
police perception that most citizens, and particularly
most black citizens, are "assholes."

ITEM: We were sitting in the parking lot of a fast-food
place, killing time. L. noticed that a man had left the
motor running in his car when he went inside to buy
something. Leaving the key in the ignition when you
leave your car is an offense in Cincinnati; the law is
designed to reduce the number of auto thefts that result
from owners' carelessness. The department has an informal quota on these violations, and L. had not filled
his quota for the month, so he walked over and started
to write a ticket. The owner came running out to explain that he had left the engine on to keep the heater
going—his four-year-old son had stayed in the car—
and that he had kept his eye on the car while he was
inside. L. ignored him and continued writing the ticket;
when the man protested some more, L. took his black-
jack out of his hip pocket and slapped it against his
hand a few times, until the man subsided. Hardly a
step forward in police-community relations! (I met the
man two nights later at a community meeting; he was
still seething over the ticket and over L.'s implied
threat of force, which had been completely unnecessary.)

Another kind of failure demonstrated the need to anticipate how threatening change can be, and to take measures to reduce the threat. Just as physicists believe in the law of conservation of energy, bureaucrats seem to believe in what has been called the law of conservation of power; they act as if there were a finite amount of power to be exercised in any organization. In this instance, members of middle and top management in the Cincinnati department feared that delegating authority to a patrol officer, sergeant, or lieutenant meant taking an equivalent amount of authority away from them. They suspected that decentralization would mean the loss of their jobs, or at least of their status and authority; the chief did nothing to relieve their anxieties, nor to provide new roles for them to fill.*

The result, not surprisingly, was what the evaluators came to call a "snapback of control." Bit by bit, members of middle and upper management took back the authority they had delegated to the teams. When the experiment began, team leaders were given authority to assign their men to work in uniform or plainclothes, depending on their judgment of what was needed. Six months after the full-scale experiment began, the chief took that authority away from the team leaders and returned it to the captain.

Shortly after that, the team leaders' authority was undermined still more by a high-level decision to have

* This could have been done without creating make-work for the displaced executives. One of the conclusions the evaluators drew was that new centralized services are needed if operations are to be decentralized successfully. It had been hoped that the teams would develop their own alternatives to arrest. For some situations, at least, it became clear that central facilities were needed—for example, if alcoholics were to be sent to a detoxification center, instead of being brought to jail. For team leaders to concentrate on field operations, moreover, they needed central staff assistance with budgeting and information handling.

them rotate responsibility for the night shift on a district-wide basis. The team leaders had been working a day shift, delegating responsibility for the night shift to their sergeants. Under the new arrangement, each team leader had to run the entire district one night a week; during that night, he had to supervise sergeants from all the teams, instead of being responsible only for his own men. More to the point, sergeants on night duty now were responsible to their team leader only one night a week, when he was in charge of the entire district; the other nights of the week, the sergeants reported to whichever lieutenant was in charge. Apart from creating dual lines of authority and responsibility, the change was disillusioning to everyone, making clear the enormous gap between the stated goals of the experiment and what officials were willing to see happen. Patrol officers' morale rose sharply during the early months of the experiment, then dropped sharply as disenchantment set in.

A major lesson—that decentralization need not lead to corruption—was driven home by coincidence. Shortly after the Comsec experiment ended, Cincinnati did have a major police corruption scandal—but it was central headquarters that was implicated, not the Comsec teams. In December, 1975, Chief Goodin was indicted on thirty-two counts of bribery, extortion, perjury, "soliciting for compensation," tampering with evidence, and obstructing justice. Six members of the centralized vice squad were indicted along with Goodin, who was accused of using vice squad members to shake down prostitutes and other unsavory characters.* The

---

* Goodin was also accused of soliciting $20 a week from two police officers assigned to local radio stations to broadcast traffic information from police department helicopters; since the men received a fee from the radio stations over and above their police salaries, they split the extra income with the chief.

chief was convicted on two counts and sentenced to four months in jail, with a fine of $5,000.

Goodin's indictment and conviction provided the ultimate irony of the Comsec experiment, for it demonstrated the hollowness of the rationale police chiefs always give for centralization of authority—their need to guard against corruption on the part of line officers. As Schwartz and Clarren write in their summary report, "Team policing is based, in part, on faith in the integrity of the officer-on-the-street. At its foundation are the assumptions that officers can carry out a broader range of tasks, make decisions for themselves, and provide better services in the process if they are allowed the necessary independence." Nothing in the experiment cast doubt on those assumptions.

But the hypothesis that delegating more responsibility to patrol officers will increase their effectiveness is no more than that—a plausible, but as yet unproved, hypothesis. Serious research and experimentation on policing are barely fifteen years old; their main contribution has been to destroy the assumptions on which most police activity has been based—to demonstrate the extent of our ignorance about what the police can, and cannot, do to reduce crime and improve domestic tranquillity. What is needed is not more hardware, communications equipment, or personnel, but more research and experimentation. In the meantime, we—police officials, government leaders, citizens, all of us—would do well to abandon our quixotic faith that there is a police solution to the problem of criminal violence.

8

Perry Mason in Wonderland: What Happens in Criminal Court

"But I don't want to go among mad people," Alice remarked.

"Oh, you can't help that," said the Cat: "we're all mad here. I'm mad. You're mad."

"How do you know I'm mad?" said Alice.

"You must be," said the Cat, "or you wouldn't have come here. . . ."

—LEWIS CARROLL, *Alice's Adventures in Wonderland*

Perhaps the principal barrier to reform is that knowledge of the actual workings of the system of criminal justice is not widespread in the community or even in the legal profession. The public generally tends to have a Perry Mason image—clouded but not dispelled by personal contact with traffic courts. Law students read appellate opinions, which deal in the main with serious crimes that were handled through traditional procedures of trial and conviction. Lawyers generally, . . . are almost as ill-informed as members of the public.

—EDWARD L. BARRETT, JR., 1965

"What kind of system of justice is it . . . where the final judgment that society makes—the hearing in court—takes less than five minutes?"

—FRANK W. MILLER, 1969

I

Criminal courts are on trial, charged with failing to protect the American people against criminal violence. Some critics attribute the failure to a gross shortage of resources which forces prosecutors and judges to indulge in plea bargaining, offering serious criminals a mild penalty in return for a guilty plea. Others put the blame on the Warren Court's concern for the rights of the accused; in their view, the "exclusionary rule" and other procedural requirements force judges to acquit, and prosecutors to release, large numbers of patently guilty offenders. Still others believe the major flaw to be the arbitrary and capricious nature of criminal sentencing, which leads to wide disparities in the punishments meted out to offenders guilty of the same crime.

Whatever their emphasis, the critics agree that the courts fail to administer swift, certain, and equitable punishment, and that this failure has undermined our ability to reduce, or even control, criminal violence. "American crime rates are high because punishment rates are low," the psychoanalyst-turned-social critic Ernest van den Haag has written. "The greatest indictment of the criminal justice system in the United States is simply that it fails in providing equitable justice," the Twentieth Century Fund Task Force on Criminal Sentencing declared in its report. "Lacking credibility, it also fails in its essential purpose of protecting society by deterring criminal and violent actions. . . . By failing to administer either equitable or sure punishment,

This chapter is based, in part, on research by Richard D. Van Wagenen.

the sentencing system . . . undermines the entire criminal justice structure."[1]

The critics are wrong—wrong in the "facts" they cite, wrong in the way they interpret them, and wrong in the policy conclusions they draw, as well as in the remedies they propose.

- It is *not* true that the courts have been hamstrung by the exclusionary rule or other decisions of the Warren Court; except for drug cases, few convictions are lost because "tainted" evidence is excluded from court.

- It is *not* true that the courts are more lenient than they used to be; the available data indicate that a larger proportion of felons are incarcerated now than in the 1920s.

- It is *not* true that disparate sentencing practices undermine the deterrent power of the criminal law. Within any single court system, the overwhelming majority of sentences—on the order of 85 percent—can be predicted if one knows the nature of the offense and of the offender's prior record. (There *are* disparities from one court system to another, reflecting differences in attitudes and values from one community to another; for the most part, these disparities would be untouched by the sentencing reforms now under discussion.)

- It is *not* true that plea bargaining distorts the judicial process. Contrary to popular impression, plea bargaining is not a recent innovation, nor is it the product of heavy caseloads; it has been the dominant means of settling criminal cases for the last century.

- Most important of all, it is *not* true that the guilty escape punishment; when charges are dropped, it usually is because the victim refuses to press charges, or because the prosecutor lacks the evidence needed to sustain a conviction.

When one examines what actually happens, in short,

what is remarkable is not how badly, but how well, most criminal courts work. Inefficient and unjust as they appear to be, criminal courts generally do an effective job of separating the innocent from the guilty; most of those who should be punished are punished. (The same cannot be said of most juvenile courts, which have jurisdiction over youngsters under a specified age—eighteen in most states, sixteen or seventeen in others. The failures of the juvenile court form the subject of the next chapter.) Thus there is no reason to believe that any of the reforms now being proposed—repealing the exclusionary rule, mandating prison terms for dangerous criminals, forbidding plea bargaining, or reducing or eliminating judges' freedom to determine the sentences offenders receive—would bring about any noticeable reduction in criminal violence.

This is not to suggest that we live in the best of all possible worlds; far from it. It is to argue that what is wrong with the judicial process is less the results it produces than the means by which it produces them. As the old maxim has it, the appearance of justice is as important as justice itself. Most criminal courts *do* do justice; almost none of them *appears* to do justice. Instead, they convey an aura of injustice that undermines respect for the law and belief in its legitimacy.

This is no small failure. If Watergate taught anything, it is what the legal historian Willard Hurst calls the substantive importance of procedure—the recognition that means shape ends, that *how* people do things may be as important as *what* they do. All the more so in criminal court, for the criminal law is an instrument of education as well as of coercion, shaping behavior through its moral influence as well as through fear of punishment. When the law is educating effectively, people conform to it because they want to; law-abiding be-

havior becomes a matter of habit, of voluntary (if unconscious) choice, rather than a means of avoiding
punishment. In a large and complex society such as
ours, respect for law—the willingness to obey the law
because it is the law—is a more effective instrument
of social control than is fear of punishment.

Most criminal courts undermine respect for law—
not by their results, but by the shabby, haphazard way
in which they are run. Files are misplaced; jailed defendants are brought to court on the wrong day; victims
and witnesses are not notified of the date on which
they are to appear (and when they are notified, they
arrive in court to find that the case has been postponed); prosecutors and defense lawyers are badly prepared, hastily leafing through their files for the first
time as the case is being called; the whole atmosphere
makes it difficult for anyone—defendants, judges, prosecutors, defense attorneys, victims, and witnesses alike
—to avoid developing a protective veneer of cynicism
and boredom.

Indeed, it is impossible to spend time in criminal
court without being appalled by the churlishness of the
physical and social environment: the peeling paint and
scuffed linoleum floors, the noise and movement, the
general surliness and lack of decorum. In atmosphere
and tone—in the impoverishment of their commitment
to the people they "process"—the courts are strikingly
reminiscent of the other bureaucratic institutions with
which poor people have to deal, such as welfare departments, hospital emergency rooms and outpatient clinics,
and public housing authority offices. Officials who may
be models of civility, sensitivity, and concern in their
private lives display a public face of callousness and indifference; their behavior is a prime example of what
Thorstein Veblen called "trained incapacity."

My first visit to a criminal court, in fact, reminded me of nothing quite so much as a long evening spent in the emergency room of a large city hospital, trying to get medical care for an elderly relative who had been knocked down by an automobile. In the courtroom, defendants, witnesses, and complainants, along with their families, sat in hard-backed chairs, waiting with the same air of resignation that patients and their families had displayed in the hospital emergency room; waiting sometimes seems to be a principal occupation of the poor. Almost everything significant that happened in court took place at the bench, in mumbled conversations between the judge, prosecutor, and defense lawyer, well beyond the earshot of those involved; in the emergency room, too, decisions were made by doctors and nurses, out of the patient's hearing. In both places, decisions were transmitted brusquely, as orders, without any attempt to explain what was happening, or why. Those who were affected by the decisions, and those who were just waiting, seemed to take it for granted that nothing would be explained to them, and that doctors and nurses, or judges, prosecutors, defense attorneys, and clerks, would fail to say "please" or "thank you" or otherwise observe the most elementary rules of civilized human discourse.

If the criminal courts are to contribute to a reduction in crime, it will not be by stuffing more people into already overcrowded prisons and jails; it will be by encouraging respect for law. For that to happen, the courts will have to change; they will have to become models of fairness and due process—living demonstrations that justice is possible, that human beings can be treated with decency and concern. I will discuss some possible changes later in the chapter; but first I need to explain my thesis that most criminal courts protect the

public by acquitting the innocent and convicting and
punishing the guilty.

II

To read most critics of criminal sentencing policy, one
would think that incarceration was a rare, almost idiosyncratic, event—that most criminals escape punishment altogether, or, at most, receive a slap on the wrist.
Ernest van den Haag rails against "the fact that so small
a proportion of all crimes committed—about 1 percent
—ever lead to actual imprisonment of the offender in
the U.S." Other scholars liken the judicial process to a

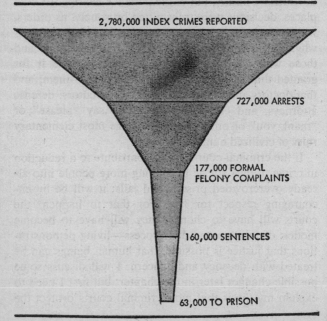

**FUNNELING EFFECT FROM REPORTED CRIMES
THROUGH PRISON SENTENCE**

2,780,000 INDEX CRIMES REPORTED

727,000 ARRESTS

177,000 FORMAL
FELONY COMPLAINTS

160,000 SENTENCES

63,000 TO PRISON

funnel, with large numbers of arrested offenders being poured into the courts at the top, and a mere handful exiting into prisons from the bottom.

The metaphor is misleading, and Van den Haag's statistics are plain wrong. Nationwide, at least one-third of the adults who are arrested on a felony charge, half or more of those who are formally charged with a crime, and about two-thirds of those who are convicted, serve time in jail or prison. Whether or not more people should be locked up is a question on which reasonable people may disagree. But it is one thing to attack judicial leniency if the "punishment rate," to use Van den Haag's term, is only 1 percent; it is quite another matter if the rate turns out to be 65 percent.

How did the impression arise that criminals typically escape punishment? The diagram above, developed by the Crime Commission's Science and Technology Task Force to illustrate the so-called "funneling effect," provides a useful starting point.*[2]

At first glance, the diagram seems to confirm the thesis that the courts permit the overwhelming majority of criminals to escape scot-free: some 2,780,000 Index crimes reported to the police in 1965 resulted in 63,000 offenders going to prison, a punishment rate of only 2.3 percent. If one begins with the number of arrests, rather than of reported crimes—a more appro-

* Because of the fragmentation of the criminal justice system, there are no national statistics tracing the flow of offenders as they move through the system; California is the only state that collects and publishes enough data to make such an analysis feasible. To develop its analysis of the operation of the criminal justice system nationwide, the Task Force first analyzed the flow of offenders through the California system in the period 1961–64 and then applied the resulting ratios to data from the *Uniform Crime Report* for 1965. The reanalysis that follows is based largely on statistics contained in the Task Force Report (pp. 57–61); I developed some additional detail through extrapolation, following the procedure used by the Task Force.

priate starting point if we are to assess the role of the courts, rather than of the police—punishment still seems to be a rare event. (The courts cannot be blamed for the fact that the police cleared only 26 percent of reported Index crimes through arrest.) Although 727,-000 arrests were made for an Index crime, only 177,000 people were formally charged with a felony; the statistics imply that only one felon in four was prosecuted, and one in twelve actually punished.

The statistics are grossly misleading. The fact that only one arrested suspect in four was prosecuted for a felony does not mean that the other three were turned loose. Some 260,000 arrestees were transferred to juvenile court—a mandatory procedure when the police arrest someone below the age at which the criminal courts have jurisdiction. Of the 467,000 adults who were arrested for an Index crime—the proper base from which to analyze the performance of the adult courts—charges were dropped against 128,000, or 27 percent.

That left 339,000 people—73 percent of the total—who were prosecuted for a crime. Charges were reduced to a misdemeanor in 162,000 cases, in exchange for a guilty plea; of the 177,000 who were charged with a felony, 130,000 pleaded guilty and another 30,000 were convicted after a bench or jury trial.* All told, therefore, 322,000 defendants were convicted on either a felony or misdemeanor charge—69 percent of all those who were arrested, and 95 percent of those who were prosecuted. (Whether more defendants should have

---

* In general, defendants convicted of a misdemeanor cannot be sentenced to more than one year in jail. Besides its longer sentence, a felony conviction carries more of a stigma and may involve the loss of certain rights—to vote, for example, or to receive a license for specified occupations. (A bench trial is a trial before a judge, without a jury; although the Constitution guarantees the right to a jury trial in criminal cases, defendants may waive that right and choose a bench trial instead.)

been prosecuted is a question I will consider below, when I examine why prosecutors release individuals whom the police have arrested.)

How many were punished? The answer depends on how one defines punishment. Critics of sentencing policy often write—and the Crime Commission's diagram of the funnel effect was drawn—as if a prison term were the only form of punishment convicted offenders receive. It is not; a considerably larger number of offenders are sentenced to jail than to prison. By and large, offenders are sent to prison only if their sentence exceeds one year; those receiving shorter sentences usually serve them in jail. Whether jail terms of less than one year constitute *sufficient* punishment is another question. But it is a strange and arbitrary view of sentencing to write as if jail did not constitute punishment at all.

In fact, a jail sentence constitutes far more severe punishment than comparable time in prison. Because they are thought of as temporary detention centers for people awaiting trial, jail cells generally are smaller and more crowded than prison cells, and they afford even less privacy.* According to a report prepared for the American Correctional Association, the majority of American jails "are not properly heated, ventilated nor lighted; they do not have the necessary facilities for the preparation and service of food; proper and adequate provision for bathing and laundering are missing; sanitary arrangements are, for the most part, primitive and in a bad state of repair . . . in general, complete idleness is the order of the day. Filth, vermin, homosexuality and degeneracy are rampant, and are the rule rather

* At the time of the 1970 National Jail Census, 52 percent of the inmates were awaiting trial and 5 percent were awaiting sentencing; the remaining 43 percent were serving post-conviction sentences.

than the exception." Richard Velde, the conservative administrator of the Law Enforcement Assistance Administration during the Ford presidency, described American jails as "without question, brutal, filthy cesspools of crime—institutions which serve to brutalize and embitter men to prevent them from returning to a useful role in society."[8]

With this perspective in mind, let me return to the question of how many of the adults who were arrested for an Index crime in 1965 were punished. As shown in the chart on page 348, 63,000 received prison terms; 103,000 offenders served time in jail, and another 21,000 initially sentenced to probation wound up in prison or jail as a result of having violated the terms of their probation. All told, 187,000 offenders were incarcerated—40 percent of all those who were arrested, 55 percent of those who were charged with a crime, and 58 percent of those who were convicted. (The fact that so many probationers ended up behind bars suggests that being sentenced to probation constitutes punishment, too.)

Those figures go back more than a decade; there is no evidence that the courts have become any more lenient. Carl Pope of the Criminal Justice Research Center in Albany, New York, has analyzed what happened to everyone arrested for a felony in two urban counties in California in the period 1969–71—some 17,649 adults in all. Charges were dropped against 27 percent, leaving 12,925 who were prosecuted. (Convictions were secured in 90 percent of the cases.) Some 1,141 convicted felons were sentenced to prison, and 5,042 offenders drew time in jail. All told, 35 percent of those who were arrested, 48 percent of those actually charged with a crime, and 53 percent of those convicted were sentenced to jail or prison. (Incarceration rates were higher for more serious crimes; for example, 46 percent of those arrested for burglary were sentenced to jail or prison.) And these figures understate the number who were incarcerated: some of those who were sentenced to probation spent time in jail awaiting trial, and others were locked up for violating the terms of their probation. If both groups were included, the incarceration rate would be around 40 percent.[4]

Incarceration rates are not significantly different in New York City, which has an annual felony caseload of about 100,000. The Vera Institute of Justice analyzed the records from arrest through disposition of a representative sample of 1,888 people arrested on felony charges in 1971. The dismissal rate was higher than in California, and the conviction rate (56 percent) somewhat lower; but, as in California, one convicted offender in two was sentenced to time in jail or prison.[5] Much the same picture obtains in Washington, D.C., where the Institute for Law and Social Research (INSLAW) has analyzed the outcome of some 100,000 street crime arrests (for serious misdemeanors as well as felonies) in the period 1969–74.[6]

For all the talk about the decline in punishment and the hobbling effect of the Warren Court, moreover, what data are available indicate that contemporary criminal courts prosecute, convict, and incarcerate a larger proportion of those arrested for a felony today than did the courts of the 1920s. Take two examples:

• Of the 12,543 people arrested for a felony in Chicago in 1926, only 2,449—19.5 percent—were convicted, three-quarters of them on a lesser charge than the one for which they were arrested; charges were dropped in about 70 percent of the cases. Jail or prison sentences, mostly the latter, were given to 1,892 offenders—15.1 percent of the number initially arrested.

• Some 4,514 people were arrested on felony charges in 1924 in Kansas City and St. Louis. Charges were dropped in 70 percent of the cases, and convictions obtained in 27 percent. The incarceration rate was 19 percent, divided almost equally between prison and jail sentences.[7]

By itself, the fact that proportionately more offenders are punished now than in the 1920s, or that fewer cases drop out of court, does not demonstrate that the courts are fulfilling their crime-control function in an adequate way. To assess the courts' performance, we need to know a lot more about the reasons for judges and prosecutors taking the actions they do. Why do prosecutors and judges dismiss all charges against one arrested felon in three? Why do prosecutors and judges permit another third to plead guilty to a misdemeanor, instead of being tried on the felony charges on which they were arrested? And why do judges sentence only about half of those who are convicted to time in jail or prison?

The most popular (and most enduring) explanation puts the blame on archaic procedures and excessive concern for the rights of defendants. "Our dangers do not lie in too little tenderness to the accused," Judge Learned Hand wrote in 1923. "Our procedure has been always haunted by the ghost of the innocent man convicted. It is an unreal dream. What we need to fear is the archaic formalism and watery sentiment that obstructs, delays, and defeats the prosecution of crime." More than a half-century later, President Gerald Ford echoed this sentiment. "For too long, law has centered its attention more on the rights of the criminal defendant than on the victim of crime," Ford told the Congress in 1975. "It is time for law to concern itself more with the rights of the people it exists to protect."

Arguments of this sort are rooted in ideological preferences rather than in empirical research. When the data are assembled and analyzed, it becomes clear that the pendulum has not swung too far. Only a handful of criminals go free or escape punishment because of exclusionary rules, search-and-seizure laws, collateral attacks or appeals, and other "technicalities" designed to protect defendants' rights. As part of their study of robbery in California, Floyd Feeney and Adrianne Weir analyzed what happened to a sample of 260 Oakland and Los Angeles robbery arrests. Not a single case was lost on "search-and-seizure" grounds; not a single case involved any serious legal issue involving interrogation; no evidence was excluded as a result of the Miranda rule, which requires policemen to inform suspects of their rights before questioning them; and not a single identification of a suspect was lost to the prosecution because of violation of the Supreme Court's rules governing identification of suspects in line-ups.[8]

Nor are the Oakland data atypical in any way. "Many believe that offenders escape punishment because of 'technicalities' induced by Supreme Court rulings or because of unwarranted leniency of judges," Brian Forst and his colleagues at the Institute for Law and Social Research have written. After analyzing what happened to everyone arrested for a street crime, and why, over a six-year period, the INSLAW researchers found both beliefs to be untrue, concluding that "the public needs to discard its myths and begin to ask 'Why?' "[9]

In New York City, the Vera Institute analyzed a sample of felony cases to determine why arrests did not stand up in court. The researchers found that exclusionary rules played no discernible role at all in the dismissal or reduction of charges in six of the seven offense categories—assault, rape, murder and attempted murder, robbery, burglary, and grand larceny—that were analyzed in depth.* And a Rand Corporation study of the prosecution of adult felony defendants in Los Angeles County, the largest prosecutor's office in the United States, found that only 3 percent of the burglary arrests were dismissed because of an illegal search and seizure, unlawful arrest, or other violation of defendants' rights; none of the burglary arrests were reduced to misdemeanors for those reasons.

The exclusionary rule seems unimportant in the Midwest as well. Of the 248 cases on the docket of the criminal court serving an Illinois county of 120,000 residents, 114 involved defendants who had made an oral or written admission to the police; yet only seven confessions were challenged, and only one challenge was sustained. (Two searches were also challenged, one of them successfully.)[10]

It is only in cases of so-called "victimless crimes" that any significant number of seemingly guilty offenders go free because tainted evidence—evidence acquired as a result of an illegal search, seizure, or arrest—is excluded from court; and even here, the number is considerably smaller than critics assume. In the Vera Institute sample, a number of gun possession cases *were*

---

* In addition to its "wide" sample of 1,888 cases selected to develop statistics on case mortality and disposition, the Vera researchers selected an additional probability sample of 369 cases that reached disposition in 1973. Researchers studied the files and interviewed the principal officials involved—policemen, prosecutors, defense attorneys, and judges—to determine the reasons for the decisions that were made in each of the cases in this "deep" sample. Because the cases in the deep sample were not weighted in the same way as those in the wide sample, the former is not a statistically valid subsample of the latter. From a substantive standpoint, however, the differences are so slight that the deep sample cases can be used with confidence to illustrate the reasons for the disposition patterns of the entire caseload. Moreover, a later sampling of 1976 court data indicated that the mix of cases and the way they were handled had not changed in the intervening years.

dismissed—but not because of search-and-seizure problems; the dismissals occurred because there was no evidence to connect the defendants with the guns (or, in one case, because there was no gun at all). Search-and-seizure problems did affect the outcome of some of the cases that remained, almost all of them involving defendants with minor records or none at all. Because the prosecutors themselves had doubts about the legality of the searches or arrests that uncovered the guns, they accepted guilty pleas to a misdemeanor count, preferring the certainty of a misdemeanor conviction to the possibility that the case would be dismissed altogether if it went to trial.[11]

Search-and-seizure problems play a larger role in drug cases, especially those where the defendant is charged with possession of a drug. Large numbers of drug arrests are made; in the Rand Corporation study of the prosecution of adult felons in Los Angeles, more than a third of the felony arrests were on drug charges, most of them for possession of marijuana, heroin, and other narcotics, and dangerous drugs ("uppers" and "downers"). The prosecutor rejected over 40 percent of the arrests, either through outright dismissal or reduction to a misdemeanor. In the case of arrests for possession of dangerous drugs, most of the rejections were due to insufficient evidence (32 percent) or trivial or insufficient quantity of contraband (40 percent). Search-and-seizure problems, illegal arrests, and other violations of defendants' rights accounted for only 17.5 percent of the overall rejections, and 25 percent of the outright dismissals.[12]

III

When charges against an arrested felon are dropped or reduced to a misdemeanor, it usually is not because

prosecutors and judges are unduly lenient, nor because
their heavy caseloads force them to give away the courthouse. Nor, as we have seen, is it because the exclusionary rule "punishes the constable by letting the
criminal go free." For the most part, prosecutors drop
felony charges or reduce them to a misdemeanor because they doubt the defendant's guilt, because they
lack the evidence needed to prove his guilt, or because
they feel the crime was not serious enough, or the defendant not sufficiently culpable, to warrant the stigma
and punishment that a felony conviction would bring.

To understand what happens in criminal court, then,
we need to look to the nature of the cases themselves
—particularly to the fact that so high a proportion of
them are felonies only in the technical sense of the
term. According to the authors of the Vera Institute
study of felony arrests, "at the root of much of the
crime brought to court is anger—simple or complicated
anger between two or more people who know each
other."[13] In New York City, they found, the victim and
offender had a prior relationship in nearly half the "victim crimes" that were brought to court.* The proportions ranged from a low of 21 percent in auto theft
cases to a high of 69 percent in assault and 83 percent
in rape arrests. But even with robbery and burglary,
which we think of as crimes committed exclusively by
strangers, victims and offenders were acquainted in 36
percent and 39 percent of the cases, respectively. And
as I pointed out in the last chapter, the INSLAW researchers found comparable proportions in their analysis of Washington, D.C. arrests.

By and large, prosecutors distinguish between "real

* In "victimless crimes," such as gambling and prostitution,
offenders have customers rather than victims. When arrests are
made, the complainant usually is the arresting officer.

crimes"—crimes committed by strangers—and "junk (or garbage) cases," i.e., those which grow out of a dispute between people who know one another. As the Vera Institute study makes clear, this dichotomy is central to any understanding of what happens in criminal court. Take robbery: the Vera researchers found that the defendant was convicted in 88 percent of the "stranger robbery" cases, but in only 37 percent of the robberies in which there was a prior relationship between victim and offender. In the stranger robberies, moreover, prosecutors and judges rarely accepted a plea to a misdemeanor; more than three-quarters of the convictions were on a felony charge, compared to only 14 percent of the prior relationship cases.

Sentences also were a lot tougher in the stranger cases: 65 percent of those arrested were incarcerated, half of them drawing "felony time," i.e., more than a year in prison. By contrast, only 21 percent of the prior-acquaintance robbers were incarcerated. The burglary cases show a similar pattern: nearly half the stranger burglars, but only 6 percent of the "acquaintance burglars," received a jail or prison sentence. In its analyses of the flow of cases through the Washington, D.C., courts, INSLAW found comparable differences in outcome between stranger and non-stranger crimes.

It would be hard to exaggerate the significance of this discovery. Until the Vera and INSLAW researchers analyzed the reasons why some arrests stand up in court and others do not, no one had realized how much of a criminal court's workload involves cases in which victims and offenders know one another; nor had anyone understood the degree to which this affects what happens to those cases. Prosecutors and judges view stranger crimes as more serious offenses than crimes involving a prior relationship between victim and offender; but they concentrate their resources on stranger crimes, too, because it is so much harder to get a conviction in prior relationship cases.

The reason, quite simply, is that when they know the offender, victims often refuse to press charges, to testify against the offender, or to cooperate with the prosecutor in other ways. No single factor has so large an impact on what happens to felons after they have been arrested: "complainant noncooperation" accounted for more than two-thirds of the dismissals of "victim felonies" in New York, and well over half in Washington, D.C.[14]

There are many reasons victims refuse to cooperate with the authorities. Sometimes they are afraid of retaliation on the part of the offender or his friends; occasionally, too, victims and witnesses lose interest after they have made several appearances in court only to have the case postponed. In larceny cases, victims often press charges as a way of forcing the offender to make restitution; once they have recovered the stolen money or property, they drop charges. (In one such case in the Vera sample, an employer-complainant actually rehired his employee-offender after restitution had been made.)

Frequently, victims decline to press charges or testify out of a reluctance to let authorities (or their families) learn about their own activities. An assault victim may have started the fight that led to the defendant's arrest; the victim of a robbery, burglary, or theft may be engaged in criminal activity, such as drug dealing, prostitution, fencing, or numbers running, that he would rather not be questioned about; and respectable robbery or theft victims may prefer that no one learn that they were in a prostitute's hotel room when their wallet was stolen. The same factors account for victim noncooperation in stranger felonies; to avoid involvement, victims frequently give a false name or address to the policeman taking the information.[15]

Most of the time, however, victims refuse to cooperate because they have become reconciled with the offender after one or the other has calmed down or sobered up. Prior-relationship assault cases usually involve domestic disputes that the police could not settle without an arrest, and prior-relationship robberies and burglaries often grow out of a dispute over money between husbands and wives, lovers or friends.

ITEM: "An auxiliary police officer watched a woman approach a man as he emerged from a liquor store. The officer thought he saw a knife flash in her hand, and the man seemed to hand her some money. She fled, and the officer went to the aid of the victim, taking him to the hospital for treatment.

"The officer saw the woman on the street a few days later and arrested her for first degree robbery on the victim's sworn complaint. It was presumably a 'high quality' arrest—identification of the perpetrator by an eye-witness, not from mugshots or a line-up, but in a crowd. Yet, shortly thereafter, this apparently airtight case was dismissed on the prosecutor's motion.

"What the victim had not explained to the police was that this defendant, an alcoholic, had been his girlfriend for the past five years; that they had been drinking together the night of the incident; that she had taken some money from him and got angry when he took it back; that she had flown into a fury when he then gave her a dollar outside the liquor store; and that she had slashed at him with a penknife in anger and run off. He had been sufficiently annoyed to have her charged with robbery, but as the judge who dismissed the case said, 'He wasn't really injured. Before it got into court they had kissed and made up.' The victim actually approached the defense attorney before the hearing and asked him to prevail upon the judge and the Assistant District Attorney (ADA) to dismiss the charges against his girlfriend." The ADA dropped charges reluctantly— not because he thought that prosecution was possible, but because he felt that the parties should be penalized for using the courts to settle a private dispute. "I wish they would do something about people using the courts to settle their personal quarrels," he said.[16]

But people *do* use the courts to settle their private disputes, or to "settle a score" with someone with whom they have been fighting. Even gun possession cases and other victimless crimes land in court because of a dispute or grudge between relatives or friends. In one of the cases in the Vera sample, a woman called the police to report that her husband had an unregistered gun. When the police searched the man and the apartment, they found nothing; they did find a loaded gun in the trunk of the couple's car—but the car was registered in the wife's name and was opened with her keys. The only evidence linking the gun to the husband was the wife's initial complaint; the case was dropped when she failed to appear in court to testify against him.

When they are not dismissed, prior relationship cases are likely to be knocked down to misdemeanors in exchange for a guilty plea. Even if the complainant promises to cooperate, the prosecutor usually prefers to get the case disposed of quickly, for fear that the complainant will change his mind later on. And unless the victim has been seriously injured, prosecutors and judges prefer to get their "garbage" cases out of the way, so that they can concentrate on the ones that really matter.

For the most part, the low priority attached to prior-relationship crimes is a realistic response to the nature of the offense and the frequency of reconciliation. But the downgrading may also reflect strong and unconscious bias of gender or race—a tendency to treat crimes lightly if they involve blacks assaulting other blacks, or husbands beating wives. In New York City, a dozen women have filed a class action suit against the police department and Family Court, accusing them, in effect, of encouraging wife-beating and other forms of male violence against women by treating such offenses lightly. One of the parties to the suit, whose ex-husband has beaten her several times and threatened to kill her, says that the first time she called the police for help, one of the officers who responded told her husband, "Maybe if I beat my wife she'd act right, too."[17]

Whether a crime involves strangers, relations, or friends, the weight that prosecutors and judges give to it reflects their evaluation of what the case is "worth." In effect, decisions about the worth of a case are deci--sions about the nature and amount of punishment the offender deserves—in particular, whether he needs to be incarcerated or not. "Good guys should get breaks, and bad guys shouldn't," a California prosecutor explains, meaning that charging and sentencing decisions are based in good measure on an evaluation of the offender's culpability and of his commitment to a criminal (or law-abiding) way of life."[18]

A gun possession case in the Vera sample provides a clear example of the way the "good guy–bad guy" dichotomy affects dispositions. The defendant was arrested when a policeman saw him walking along the street with what appeared to be a gun bulging out of his back pocket; the defendant claimed that he was a maintenance worker at Shea Stadium, that he had found the gun there, and that he was taking it to the station house up the block—the direction in which he was walking. The policeman made a felony arrest none-theless, explaining that the man "had no license. He hadn't gone through the right procedures to turn in a gun, and he had a record from way back." (The real reason may have been that the defendant had "flunked the attitude test.") Technically the policeman was cor-rect; there were no evidentiary problems and the prose-cution had a strong case. But after hearing his story at arraignment, the ADA and the judge felt that the de-fendant was telling the truth. Equally important, the defendant's prior arrests had been twenty years earlier; he had had no trouble with the law since then, and he had been working steadily at Shea Stadium for more than ten years. As a result, the prosecutor and judge agreed to dismiss the charge. "I'm very stringent on weapons charges," the judge explained, but "I couldn't see any criminal intent here." To the prosecutor, "it was a nothing case."

Decisions about the worth of a case also reflect judg-ments about the seriousness of the offense itself. In general, prior-relationship crimes are considered less serious than those involving strangers; but stranger crimes also may be ranked in ways that do not cor-respond to the letter of the law. In New York City, nighttime commercial burglaries are almost routinely reduced to misdemeanors; since stores, offices, and warehouses normally are not occupied at night, prose-cutors, judges, and even policemen view such offenses as nuisance crimes. Residential burglaries, on the other hand, are considered "real" crimes; they evoke consid-erable fear and anguish, and since a burglar can never be certain that no one is home, the possibility of vio-lence is always present.

Each prosecutor's office—indeed, each court—has its own set of informal and often not even articulated norms that shape the decisions individual prosecutors, defense attorneys, and judges make about the worth of the cases, they handle. Idiosyncratic factors enter, to be sure, but to a lesser degree than prosecutors and judges (or their critics) generally assume. Without realizing it, people who work together develop common understandings of how particular kinds of offenses and offenders should be handled—of what is fair in a particular case. Over time, these understandings take on a life of their own; new members are enculturated into the norms and values of the groups and come to accept them as their own, without quite realizing it. Thus there may be wide variations in charging and sentencing norms from one court and prosecutor's office to another; but within a single system, practice tends to be uniform.[19]

What appear to be departures from the norms—instances, say, in which "real criminals" get a "walk" or are permitted to plead guilty to a misdemeanor— usually turn out, on examination, to be cases the prosecutor was reluctant to take to trial. Sometimes the problem is the nature of the evidence itself. Robbery victims are not always able to identify the offender, even when he is caught with the victim's wallet in his possession; a prosecutor will prefer to accept a guilty plea to possession of stolen property or some other lesser offense, rather than risk acquittal on the robbery charge if the defendant should insist on going to trial. Frequently, too, a victim may identify the offender from mug shots but fail to recognize him in a line-up; sometimes a victim identifies the offender if he is caught shortly after the crime, but becomes uncertain about the identification a few weeks later. Identification problems are more frequent in muggings and strong-arm robberies than in armed robberies; the latter offense usually involves a face-to-face confrontation, whereas muggers and strong-arm robbers frequently approach their victims from the rear.[20]

Even when there are no evidentiary problems as such, prosecutors may accept a guilty plea to a misdemeanor or lesser felony because the victim or key witness lacks credibility. If the victim was drunk or "stoned" at the time the crime occurred, the defense attorney may be able to discredit his testimony; victims with long criminal records or records of drug addiction may also have their credibility undermined at the preliminary hearing or at a trial. In such cases, prosecutors are likely to prefer the certainty of conviction on a misdemeanor or lesser felony to the possibility of acquittal on the original felony charge.

The decision to prosecute is actually a series of decisions, the first of which involves a judgment as to whether or not to "book," or file charges against, someone who has been arrested. That judgment, in turn, involves a decision as to whether or not there is sufficient probability of guilt to justify subjecting the defendant to the cost and trauma of the judicial process, not to mention giving him the permanent stigma of an arrest record. Thus a prosecutor may drop charges if he believes that the elements of a crime were not present or that there is insufficient evidence to connect the accused with a crime that was committed. If the prosecutor agrees with the arresting officer on both counts, he may still disagree over the specific crime that was committed. A purse-snatching, for example, may be charged as robbery or larceny-theft, depending on the amount of force that was used; in other instances, what initially appeared to be a robbery may turn out to have been an assault.

If a prosecutor agrees that the accused probably did commit a crime, he may still reject the case if he feels

that prosecution would not be in the public interest—
because the crime was too trivial, because the defendant
has suffered or been punished enough, or because the
accused will provide information or help the prosecution by testifying voluntarily in another, more important case.* In some cities, prosecutors reject as
many as half of all felony arrests at the initial screening; in others, prosecutors file charges in almost every
case, shifting the screening function to a later stage.
Given this discretion, it is only a partial exaggeration
to suggest, as Mr. Justice Jackson wrote in 1940, that
"the prosecutor has more control over life, liberty, and
reputation than any other person in America."[21]

In deciding where to concentrate their scarce resources, prosecutors generally consider the defendant's
"convictability," in addition to the seriousness of his
offense. If the choice is between two cases, one a robbery, the other a larceny, in which the evidence of
guilt is about the same, prosecutors naturally concentrate on the robbery. But the choice usually is more
troublesome—say, between prosecuting a larceny case
in which the evidence of guilt is overwhelming and a
robbery case in which conviction is uncertain.

Most prosecutors will emphasize the former—in
part because they like to win and, more importantly,
because they do not like to lose. In general, prosecutors
care less about winning than about not losing; to lose
any significant number of cases weakens their sense of
self and undermines their credibility in the courtroom
and in the larger community. Most prosecutors believe
that they should not press charges unless they are convinced of the defendant's guilt. Thus the fact that a

---

* Prosecutors have also been known to drop charges because
a defendant had political or personal connections, or because
"the fix" was in; the practice was far more frequent in the past
than it is today.

prosecutor does proceed with a case is an announcement, in effect, that he has investigated the facts, weighed their merits, and found the defendant guilty. When a judge or jury acquits a defendant, they are not just reversing the prosecutor's adjudication but questioning his judgment; to the prosecutor, in fact, it feels as though his honesty and credibility, as well as his professional competence, are being challenged.[22]

Even when evidence of guilt is overwhelming and the case involves a "bad guy" who has committed a serious crime, prosecutors prefer to settle the case through a guilty plea to a lesser felony, so long as the lesser charge carries an appropriate sentence. The reason is that taking a case to trial always involves some risk of acquittal; what seems to be an airtight case may come apart, and one can never be sure of the impression witnesses or the defendant may make, or of the way a jury will react to them.

It is a rare prosecutor, therefore, who does not prefer the certainty of a negotiated plea to the uncertainty of a trial. Even the Watergate Special Prosecution Force, which had unusually able prosecutors and a call on virtually unlimited resources, settled the overwhelming majority of its cases through negotiated pleas. "In assessing the likelihood that the evidence will convince a jury of the defendant's guilt when presented under the conditions of a trial," the Force wrote in its report, "prosecutors recognize that their familiarity with all the facts of a case and their assessment of the credibility of witnesses cannot necessarily be transferred to a trial jury, where evidence is strictly limited by trial rules and cross-examination can leave unpredictable impressions."

One of the cases in the Vera sample helps explain why prosecutors avoid trials if they can: a seemingly guilty defendant was acquitted against all the odds.

Charged with first-degree sexual abuse and assault, the defendant had a record of five convictions, including a prison term for rape. The case went to trial only because the defendant rejected his lawyer's advice and refused the bargain offered by the prosecutor; he also insisted on taking the stand, despite his prior record. "My client had a long record, his story was unconvincing, he was crazy," his attorney recalled. "He would jump up and down in the court yelling that everyone was lying," as a result of which he had to be handcuffed to the rail in the courtroom. "But he was my client and insisted on his innocence, so we went to trial—handcuffs and all." Despite the fact that the complainant—a fifteen-year-old-girl—made an unusually credible witness, the man was acquitted. When asked about his prior record, he responded, "I pleaded guilty in the past—five times—because I committed those crimes. This time I didn't do anything and I didn't plead because I'm not guilty." The jury believed him, even though his own lawyer did not.

In any system in which guilt has to be proven, some offenders will go free, not because they are innocent, but because there is insufficient evidence to prove their guilt. The evidence may be insufficient because victims or witnesses refuse to cooperate; because they become hazy or confused about what happened, or unsure of their identification of the offender; because the circumstances of the crime or the nature of the victim's background makes a jury reluctant to convict the defendant; or for any of a number of other reasons. Although some conservatives would like to make conviction easier, not even the harshest critic of "legal technicalities" proposes that defendants be convicted *against* the weight of the evidence.

Not all the losses are inevitable; in some cases, greater effort, care, or imagination on the part of

policemen and prosecutors could prevent or overcome
the evidentiary weaknesses that lead to acquittal or dismissal of charges. The most frequent reason for dismissal of stranger robbery arrests is a failure in identification—often a failure to confirm at a later time an
identification that was made with confidence right after
the crime occurred. It is not surprising that this should
be so; identification of a suspect is subject to all the
frailties and vagaries of memory and perception. Quite
apart from the obvious ways in which clothing, hair
style, grooming, and lighting can alter someone's appearance, an individual may look different in different
environments. Perception also may be affected by the
viewer's emotional state—for example, by the trauma
of recalling a robbery or assault, or by the stress of
cross-examination. And memory of details—the offender's height and weight, the clothing he wore, the
words he spoke, his general demeanor—may evaporate
with time or be wiped out by stress or fear.

Given these possibilities, one might expect policemen and prosecutors to take particular care to preserve
an identification once it has been made. Generally they
do not—less because of carelessness or incompetence
than because the pressures of time and place turn their
attention elsewhere. The arresting officer's written report usually is the principal record—sometimes the
only record—prosecutors have of a positive field identification of a suspect. Occasionally, the patrolman's
own account will be supplemented by a statement from
the victim; as often as not, what the prosecutor gets
is simply the patrolman's handwritten and fragmentary
notes. If the victim's memory does not fail, and if
the victim continues to cooperate, and if the victim's
character or motives cannot be impeached, and if the
victim can stick to the identification under cross-

examination, the patrolman's report may be sufficient. But those ifs are not always present simultaneously.[23]

One way to preserve field identifications, Alan Carlson and Floyd Feeney suggest, would be for policemen to make a photographic record. The arresting officer would ask the witness or victim if he sees the person who committed the crime; if the answer is yes, the victim or witness would be asked to point to the offender, and the officer would take a picture of the scene. The patrolman would also record a statement by the victim or witness, explaining the basis of the identification. In addition to the obvious use to refresh the witness' memory later on, the photograph might be admissible as evidence that a positive identification had been made. Witnesses may also be less likely to feign loss of memory—a frequent tactic when people decide not to cooperate with the prosecutor through boredom or self-interest.

More felons would be convicted, too, if detectives did a better job of collecting evidence and presenting it to the prosecutor; in good measure, the courts are taking the blame for what the police fail to do. Although detectives contribute relatively little to the identification of offenders or to their arrest, as we have seen, careful investigation is needed to collect the additional evidence required to demonstrate guilt. But once an arrest has been made, policemen have little incentive to collect additional evidence or to "waste" time preparing the evidence for submission to the prosecutor; their job satisfaction comes from making arrests, and the traditional reward system reinforces this outlook.

The result, all too often, is that prosecutors do not receive the information they need to convert an arrest into a conviction. Sometimes necessary information is not collected; frequently, the information is collected, but it remains in the patrolman's or detective's head and is not transmitted to prosecutors in the detail and form they need. As part of the Rand Corporation study of the investigation process, Peter Greenwood and his colleagues compared the written reports given prosecutors in a sample of robbery cases in two California jurisdictions. To analyze the amount of information provided, the Rand researchers interviewed prosecutors, detectives, and police administrators. On the basis of the replies, they constructed a list of thirty-nine questions that a prosecutor might want answered to prosecute a robbery case in the most effective manner—questions about the offense itself (whether force was used, whether the victim was injured, whether a weapon was used and, if so, what kind), about the suspect (possible motive, possible defense, prior record), about the victim and/or witness (relationship with suspect, credibility, whether the victim or witness identified the suspect through mug shots or a line-up, and, if so, what procedures were followed, whether the victim had improper motives in reporting the crime), and about the arrest (how the suspect was located, how the arrest was made).

There were dramatic differences in the information prosecutors received from the two departments. One department gave 70 percent more information than the other; the qualitative differences were even greater. The first department gave the prosecutor typewritten reports in painstaking detail, with investigators' activities documented in chronological order; the second department provided handwritten reports that were hard to read and understand, and that generally contained only the major facts of the case, with little detail or documentation. The handwritten reports, for example, might simply note that the victim identified the offender from mug shots or at a police line-up; the typewritten reports would provide a detailed description of the procedures used in showing mug shots or conducting a line-up, the identity (including police number) of the people or pictures used, the verbatim instructions given the viewer, and the precise language used in making the identification—for example, "I am positive that Number 3 is the guy who robbed me," or "Number 4 looks like him but I can't be 100 percent sure." The extra detail helps prosecutors decide how to file the case; it also lends credence to an identification when it is made. Providing the victim's verbatim account of what the offender said also can be important in robbery prosecutions, as a means of establishing that there was a credible threat of force. (Without evidence of the use or threat of force, a prosecutor cannot prove that an offense was robbery rather than larceny.)

What is striking is how much information was *not* provided; indeed, the reports submitted by the better department contained only 45 percent of the information detectives and prosecutors agreed was important. Nor was the missing detail trivial; it was rare for either department to provide any information at all on prior relationships between victims and offender, on the credibility of victims and witnesses, or whether the victim had improper motives in reporting the crime— the factors that play the largest role in dismissals and reductions of charges.

Given the frequency and bitterness of police complaints about the courts' failure to convict and incarcerate arrested felons, it is hard to understand the lack of interest police chiefs show in monitoring or improving the quality of felony arrests. In analyzing Washington, D.C., arrest data for 1974, Brian Forst and his colleagues at INSLAW found that a mere 249 officers— fewer than 6 percent of the D.C. police force—made

half the felony arrests resulting in conviction. The statistic is not the result of the assignments policemen
draw; the "high-productivity" officers were distributed
remarkably evenly among the seven police districts into
which Washington is divided. Nor is Washington
unique in this regard; the same pattern appears to
exist in other cities.[24]

Even so, prosecutors bear much of the responsibility
for the gaps in the information they receive; it is rare
for them to give policemen guidance about the kind of
information they need and why they need it, and even
rarer to explain why charges have been reduced or dismissed. To be sure, prosecutors often *think* that they
have explained their actions to the police; in one study
of police-prosecutor relations, half the prosecutors who
were queried said they routinely told the police the
reasons why cases were disposed of through plea bargaining. Policemen saw things differently; only 19
percent said they were informed as a matter of routine,
and more than a third reported that they were "seldom"
or "never" given the reasons for prosecutorial dispositions.[25]

This difference in perception is not just a breakdown in communications; it is rooted in the different
worlds in which prosecutors and policemen live and
the different social classes from which they come. All
too often, prosecutors treat policemen with the unconscious patronization that middle-class professionals
tend to show to members of the working class. Most
policemen *feel* patronized, and their feeling is exacerbated when they see prosecutors socializing with defense attorneys.*

* The social distance is widened by the fact that most assistant prosecutors regard their job as a stepping stone, rather
than as a career; they become prosecutors to gain trial experience, before moving on to a better-paying position in politics or

Some of the cases that are lost through victim or witness noncooperation might be saved if policemen and prosecutors treated victims and witnesses with greater sensitivity and thoughtfulness. Victims are frustrated and angered when they have to repeat their story three, four, or even five times as their case is passed from one assistant district attorney to another. And witnesses understandably lose interest when they spend a whole day in court, waiting for the case to be called, only to find that the judge has rescheduled it to suit an attorney's convenience. Criminal courts are run for the convenience of judges and lawyers, not of victims, witnesses, or defendants.[26]

IV

The picture I have been drawing of criminal courts bears little resemblance to the popular image. Just as the Sherlock Holmes legend has shaped our image of the police, what might be called the Perry Mason myth dominates thinking about criminal courts. In the popular view, adults who have been arrested for a crime retain Perry Mason, or some equally able and telegenic, but mythic, defense lawyer, to defend them. In short order, but after the defense lawyer's staff of investigators have combed the country in search of evidence to support the defendant's alibi, his fate is determined by a jury trial in a dignified, attractive wood-paneled and marble-floored courtroom. Indeed, the focal point of the whole legal process—its very essence and reason for being—is the jury trial, de-

---

private practice. (Turnover is rapid; a survey by the National District Attorney's Association found that, on average, assistant prosecutors stayed in their jobs less than two years.) Being a policeman, on the other hand, is not a stepping stone to any other kind of work; it is an all-consuming career.

signed to determine the defendant's innocence or guilt.
The jury discovers the truth through trial by combat
between two equally armed (or, if the lawyer is Perry
Mason, unequally armed) lawyers who adhere to the
sportsmanlike rules of the game because of the careful attention of a wise and scrupulously objective judge.

This is not the system most defendants encounter.
Jury trials are rare events, occurring in only 5 to 10
percent of criminal cases in the United States. Perry
Masons are equally rare: if a defendant is represented
by counsel at all—many are not—the lawyer is likely
to be a member of the staff of the local public defender
service or an attorney assigned by the court. In either
situation, defendants do not choose their lawyers, and
they are likely to view the attorneys assigned to their
defense as agents of the prosecution. In the 90 to 95
percent of the cases that are not tried, guilt and innocence are determined by the prosecutor or judge in
negotiation with the defendant or his attorney.

Such is the hold of the Perry Mason myth that most
discussions of the way criminal courts operate sound
as though plea bargaining represented some recent fall
from grace. Even those who favor the practice usually
apologize for their position. They write as if universal
jury trials had been the norm until quite recently, and
they defend plea bargaining as an unfortunate departure
from the norm that is necessary if courts are to handle
the explosive increase in their caseloads.

If trials were the norm and plea bargaining simply a
device by which big-city courts dispose of their heavy
caseloads, one would expect to find relatively little
plea bargaining in smaller cities and rural areas, where
caseloads are light. But the overwhelming majority of
criminal cases are disposed of by negotiated pleas in
every part of the United States, rural as well as urban,
small cities as well as large. As I pointed out in the

last section, the Watergate Special Prosecution Task Force, which had virtually unlimited resources, settled most of its cases through negotiated pleas.

No one should be surprised that this is so. Plea bargaining is not a recent innovation; it was the subject of heated debate during the 1920s, when there was great public clamor over criminal violence. Most of the contemporary arguments against plea bargaining were made then, and most of the recent proposals for doing away with plea bargaining were tried and found wanting. Moreover, research by the political scientist Raymond Moley, who helped direct a number of state and local crime commissions during the 1920s, demonstrated that plea bargaining was not new then, either. On the contrary, Moley discovered that negotiated pleas had replaced jury trials as the principal means of settling criminal cases as early as the second third of the nineteenth century.[27] If plea bargaining is a fall from grace, the fall occurred over a century ago.

Clearly, plea bargaining stems from causes more deeply rooted in the judicial process than court congestion. To be sure, heavy backlogs and inadequate trial facilities may distort the plea bargaining process. To keep the assembly line moving, prosecutors sometimes recommend, and judges impose, more lenient sentences than they think desirable; this happens far less often than critics allege.[28] More important, jailed defendants who assert their innocence and who might be acquitted at trial sometimes are forced to choose between pleading guilty and gaining their freedom, and pleading not guilty and remaining in jail. There can be no excuse for plea bargaining under circumstances of that sort. But what is indefensible is not plea bargaining as such, but a bail system that makes defendants' liberty contingent on the financial resources at their disposal, and court congestion that keeps defendants rotting in jail for months on end, awaiting trial.

In any case, abolishing plea bargaining is more easily said than done. "The range of methods by which criminal charges can be disposed of is so great," Moley wrote, "that merely to shut off one practice will open up others." Philadelphia's experience provides a case in point. During his tenure as district attorney (1969–73), Arlen Specter gained national acclaim for having abolished plea bargaining. The reputation was undeserved; all that Specter did was shift its locus. Instead of bargaining over the charge to which defendants would plead guilty, prosecutors and defense lawyers under Specter's regime did their bargaining over whether or not defendants would waive their right to a jury trial and elect a bench trial instead. Since bench trials can be completed in a matter of minutes, they serve substantially the same purpose as guilty pleas; in some jurisdictions, a bench trial (or, in Los Angeles, a trial on the transcript of the preliminary hearing) is referred to as "a slow plea of guilty." To induce waivers, Specter's ADAs offered defendants the same kind of implied sentencing concessions they previously provided to induce a guilty plea; a further inducement came from the fact that bench trials were conducted by judges with reputations as soft sentencers, while the tough sentencers were assigned to jury trials. In short, plea bargaining was abolished in name only.*

The same kinds of adjustments were made in a suburban county in the Midwest, in which a new county

---

* The discrepancy between form and substance was even more profound. For all his strictures against the exercise of prosecutorial discretion, Specter placed great emphasis on early screening and diversion. ADAs were stationed in police stations, with a mandate to get the "junk" cases out of the system at the earliest point, through dismissal, reduction of charges, or diversion.

prosecutor, elected after a "law-and-order" anti-drug campaign, instituted a strict policy forbidding assistant prosecutors from plea bargaining over the charge in drug sale cases. The new policy did eliminate guilty pleas to a reduced charge, the principal form of disposition in the past. But it had little effect on plea bargaining itself; as in Philadelphia, the bargaining simply shifted to a new arena. Instead of seeking implicit sentence concessions through reduction in charges, defense attorneys began negotiating over the sentence itself, thereby drawing judges into the negotiating process in a more direct way. Prosecutors began making sentencing recommendations, which most judges tended to follow; defense attorneys would tell the judge what they expected the probation report to say about their client and ask him what sentence he would be likely to give. (If the lawyer guessed wrong and the probation report suggested a harsher sentence, many judges allowed defendants to withdraw their guilty pleas.)

The fact that prosecutors no longer could *reduce* the charge, moreover, did not prevent them from dropping charges altogether, either on their own motion or by failing to oppose a defense motion to suppress evidence or to dismiss charges. And prosecutors retained several other discretionary devices for including pleas: they could decide whether or not to charge a recidivist under the state's "habitual offenders" statute; they could drop other cases or charges pending against a defendant; and they could persuade the probation department to recommend a light sentence.[29]

Eliminating plea bargaining would be undesirable even if it were possible. Proponents of abolition assume that the question to be resolved in a criminal case is always simple and clear-cut: Is the defendant guilty or not guilty of committing the crime with which he is charged? If the answer is Not guilty, the defendant should be freed; if it is Guilty, he should receive the "proper" punishment for the offense. To convict a defendant of any lesser charge, in this view, or to sentence him to any lesser punishment, is a perversion of justice.

It is a curious notion of justice to tie it so completely to the prosecutor's uncontrolled discretionary decision about the crime with which an offender will be charged. Opponents of plea bargaining attribute an objectivity to the charging decision that most prosecutors would be loath to claim; as Professor Arnold Enker has written, the opponents of plea bargaining seem to assume that there is "an objective truth existing in a realm of objective historical fact" that can best be ascertained through a jury trial. But the "truth" of an offense usually is neither objective nor absolute; it is embodied in the way "the facts" are interpreted and in the significance attached to them, as much as in the facts themselves.

In the great majority of criminal cases, "the facts" are not in dispute. What is at issue—what needs to be adjudicated—is the significance that should be attached to the facts. Decisions about the seriousness of the offense and the degree of the offender's culpability involve complex and often highly subjective judgments about such factors as premeditation, intent, force, credibility, negligence, threat, recklessness, and harm. What is being adjudicated is not guilt or innocence, but the punishment the offender deserves.[30]

Take one of the cases in the Vera Institute's sample. The facts seemed clear enough: the gate to a factory was broken one night and $2,000 in cash and inventory was stolen; the nineteen-year-old defendant was arrested inside the factory at 1 A.M. and charged with burglary. Initially, the ADA treated it as a serious crime, offering to reduce charges only to a lesser felony, which might have carried a term in jail or prison; the defendant refused to plead guilty. His attorney argued that "it was not a real burglary," pointing out that there had been forty other young men wandering inside the factory a few minutes before the defendant's arrest; that the defendant had been the only one who had been caught; and that no money or stolen goods had been found on him. As a result, the ADA agreed to accept a plea to trespass—a misdemeanor—for which the defendant was sentenced to three years' probation. "He was found just wandering around, looking far from sinister," the judge explained, "and it wouldn't have been fair to punish the one who wasn't quick enough to get out when forty other men were equally guilty. . . . This was trespass, no more, and he had already been ten weeks in custody; any more time would have been damaging—and unjust."

When the facts *are* in dispute—when there is reasonable doubt that the defendant committed the crime with which he is charged—a jury trial is the most appropriate means of adjudication. Whether a defendant chooses to go to trial depends on his (and his attorney's) assessment of the risks that may be involved. Although the potential gain of complete acquittal is large, the price of defeat may be just as large. If the defendant is convicted of the highest charge against him, or if the judge is in the habit of imposing stiffer sentences on defendants who insist on a trial than on defendants who plead guilty to the same offense, conviction at trial may bring a long prison sentence. In deciding whether or not to go to trial, therefore, the defendant and defense lawyer weigh the strength of the evidence and the credibility of the witnesses who may be called, including the defendant himself. They also consider the sentence the defendant is likely to draw if he pleads guilty to a lesser charge; the stiffer the sentence, the smaller the risk attached to conviction at trial.

For that same reason, defendants may opt for trial in the opposite situation—one in which evidence of guilt is so overwhelming and the crime (or the offender's prior record) so serious that the defendant will draw "heavy time" whether he pleads guilty or not. In situations of this sort, defendants have little to lose and much to gain from a trial, since there always is *some* possibility of acquittal. In general, therefore, the more serious the offense, the larger the proportion of cases that are settled by trial.[31]

The fact that trials are infrequent does not mean that they are unimportant. Quite the contrary: in cases that involve the public interest to an unusual degree (for example, the trial of the principal conspirators in the Watergate affair), trials play a vital symbolic role as evidence that justice is being done. In good measure, trials of major crimes provide the contemporary equivalent of the medieval morality play.

More important, run-of-the-mill criminal trials exert a decisive influence over the far larger number of cases that are disposed of through plea bargaining or through the unilateral exercise of discretion by prosecutors. As we have seen, decisions by prosecutors and defense attorneys are shaped very heavily by their expectations of the way in which a jury might respond to the complainant, the defendant, the witnesses, the nature of the evidence, the seriousness of the offense, and the offender's culpability. Those expectations, in turn, are based on the experience prosecutors and defense lawyers have had in cases that have gone to trial. What this means, Harry Kalven, Jr., and Hans Zeisel wrote in their path-breaking study of the American jury, is that jury trials are only the tip of the iceberg. Juries do not merely determine the outcome of the cases they hear; their decisions profoundly influence the 90 to 95 percent of cases that are settled through informal means.[32]

Jury trials are vital for another reason. Prosecutors have virtually unlimited discretion, both in deciding whether or not to charge someone with a crime and in selecting the particular offense with which he will be charged. There are almost no legislative rules for prosecutors to follow, and the courts have been reluctant to set down any norms or to overrule prosecutors' decisions. The absence of effective limits on prosecutorial discretion creates the potential for corruption, as well as for abuse of power for personal or partisan political ends. The latter potential is exacerbated by the fact that the post of prosecutor always has been a stepping stone to the judiciary or to higher elective office.

The right to trial by a jury of one's peers is virtually the only protection defendants have against abuse of power by prosecutors. Juries are not infallible, to be sure; but the system works remarkably well. Seeing themselves as the representatives of the whole society, jurors tend to rise to the challenge (Kalven and Zeisel called this the "halo effect"). The result is that jury verdicts usually are more responsible, and more rational and thoughtful, than one would expect from the sum of its individual members.[33]

It is essential, therefore, that defendants be free to exercise their right to a jury trial. A number of legal scholars argue that plea bargaining denies defendants that freedom by penalizing them for exercising it. When defendants convicted at a jury trial receive a stiffer sentence than they would have drawn had they pleaded guilty, they are paying a price for having gone to trial; in effect, the state is punishing them for exercising their constitutional right.[34]

The penalty can be extraordinarily high. In one recent case, a man charged with forging an $88 check was offered a five-year term if he pleaded guilty, instead of the ten-year maximum the law allowed. The offer was coupled with a warning: if the defendant insisted on going to trial, the prosecutor would file a second indictment charging him with being a "habitual offender," an offense that carries a mandatory life sentence under Kentucky law.* The defendant turned down the offer and went to trial; he was convicted on both the original forgery and the added "habitual offender" counts and sentenced to life imprisonment. The U.S. Court of Appeals for the Sixth Circuit threw out the conviction, finding a "vindictive exercise of the prosecutor's discretion." In a 5–4 decision that left observers incredulous, the Supreme Court reversed the Court of Appeals' decision, holding that the defendant had not been deprived of his constitutional rights. The majority conceded that "To punish a person because he has done what the law plainly allows him to do is a due process violation of the most basic sort," but held that the stricture did not apply in this instance. "In the give-and-take of plea bargaining there is no element of punishment or retaliation so long as the accused is free to accept or reject the prosecution's offer," Mr. Justice Stewart wrote in his opinion for the majority.[35]

This is freedom at a heavy price. The Court's decision is bound to make future defendants hesitate long and hard before they turn down a plea bargain offered by a vindictive prosecutor. Yet banning plea bargaining altogether serves little purpose; as we have seen, attempts to eliminate discretion at one stage of the criminal process serve only to shift the discretion to

* The defendant was eligible, since he had two prior felony convictions; but the prosecutor had total discretion in deciding whether or not to invoke the "habitual offender" statute.

some other, usually less visible stage. A more effective solution would be to try to hold the "price" of going to trial to a reasonable level—to keep the difference between the sentences meted out after trial and after a guilty plea small enough so that choosing a trial remains a viable option.

My "solution" is conceptually untidy, acknowledging in practice what constitutional theory denies. The argument for it is wholly pragmatic; if a practice cannot be eliminated, more is to be gained from regulating than from forbidding it. There is ample precedent, in any case; the fact that there is a cost attached to exercising one's constitutional prerogative is not limited to the choice of a jury trial. The presumption of innocence, too, is a basic constitutional right. Yet everyone charged with a crime is punished. Unless they are indigent, the most innocent and falsely accused defendants must pay to hire an attorney; in most jurisdictions, they must put up bail in order to be released; if they cannot make bail, they may spend weeks or months in jail; and they bear the stigma of an arrest record, not to mention the trauma of arrest and accusation. Some of these costs can be eliminated by a sensitive and thoughtful government—for example, by providing for release on recognizance, instead of on bail, and by having the police issue summonses instead of making an arrest. Others—attorneys' fees and the stigma—are inherent in the criminal process. They can be minimized by more careful screening of arrests, and by expunging the arrest records of people found to be innocent; but they cannot be eliminated altogether.

v

I have been arguing a heretical and paradoxical thesis: that a seemingly irrational and unjust adult judicial process produces results that are surprisingly rational and just. Exceptions—too many of them—do occur; but for the most part, prosecutors and judges use their discretion to carry out the intent, if not the precise letter, of the law, i.e., to prosecute, convict, and punish "real criminals," while showing appropriate leniency to those whose crimes are not serious, or who seem to pose no real danger to the community.

What this means is that the courts are fulfilling their crime-control function remarkably well: they are punishing most of those who should be punished. They are doing so, moreover, in a far more equitable way than is generally thought; the sentences offenders receive tend to be proportionate to the seriousness of their offense, the nature of their prior record, and the degree of their culpability.

The lawyers, judges, and defendants—indeed, to almost anyone who has spent time in court—my thesis will seem to fly in the face of common sense. The one position on which liberals and conservatives agree is that the present system of sentencing is arbitrary and capricious—that it leads to large and indefensible disparities in the sentences given defendants guilty of the same crime. I shared that view during most of my research; I was a member of the Twentieth Century Fund Task Force on Criminal Sentencing and joined in its declaration that "the irrationally disparate sentences currently imposed" in American criminal courts "undermine the effectiveness of the entire criminal justice structure."[36]

Sentences are "irrationally disparate," the Task Force went on to argue, because of the virtually unfettered discretion judges enjoy—discretion that permits individual judges to sentence individual offenders according to their own values, their own predictions about the offender's future dangerousness, and their own likes, dislikes, prejudices, and whims. Because sentences are "capricious and arbitrary," the Task Force concluded, offenders cannot know in advance what punishment they will receive, or even whether they will be punished at all; the result is to reduce respect for law and to undermine its deterrent power, which requires certainty, more than severity, of punishment.

The Task Force was so outraged by the fact that a defendant's sentence may depend more on the personal philosophy, biases, and state of mind of the sentencing judge than on the specific offense that was committed that it took the existence of disparity as a given, without examining *how many* sentences really are capricious. Other scholars, including many for whom I have the greatest respect, have made the same mistake. "Some writers have quibbled about the definitiveness of the evidence showing disparity," Judge Marvin Frankel wrote in his influential volume on sentencing policy.

> It is among the least substantial of quibbles. The evidence is conclusive that judges of widely varying attitudes on sentences, administering statutes that confer huge measures of discretion, mete out widely divergent sentences where the divergences are explainable only by variations among the judges, not by material differences in the defendants or their crimes. *Even in our age of science and skepticism, the conclusion would seem to be among those still acceptable as self-evident.* [emphasis added][37]

The quibble is substantial; what appears self-evident turns out to be riddled with doubt. One reason is that critics of disparity in sentencing generally fail to distinguish between sentencing disparities that grow out of differences in philosophy or bias from one *judge* to another, and disparities that reflect different attitudes toward criminals and crime—different sentencing norms—from one *community* to another. The latter is by far the more important source of disparity in the sentences actually received by criminal offenders; yet it hardly would be touched by sentencing reform.*

Consider the striking difference in the way shoplifting cases are disposed of in Albuquerque, New Mexico, and Charlotte, North Carolina—two cities that have roughly the same population and the same rate of serious crime. In Albuquerque, 80 percent of those arrested for shoplifting are diverted from the criminal court; prosecution is deferred for a specified period of time—generally six months—with defendants being told that charges will be dismissed at the end of the period if no new charges are brought against them. In Charlotte, on the other hand, fewer than 5 percent of shoplifting arrestees are treated in this manner; the great majority are prosecuted, and those who are convicted receive close to the statutory maximum prison term for the offense.

These differences in sentencing policy reflect radically divergent views of the seriousness of the offense, the nature of the offenders, and the purposes of punishment. Charlotte judges and prosecutors see shoplifting as a serious crime that must be deterred by imposing harsh sentences on convicted offenders. Albuquerque judges, on the other hand, believe that, for the most part, shoplifters are not "real criminals," and that the trauma of being arrested usually is enough to deter them from future offenses; in their opinion, it would be wrong to stigmatize one-time offenders with

---

* In fairness to Judge Frankel, he is mainly (although not entirely) concerned with disparities within the federal system. It *is* possible to reduce the disparities in average sentences from one federal district court to another.

a criminal record.[38] Examples of this sort can be multiplied indefinitely.

One may be appalled at the harshness of the Charlotte judges, as I am, or troubled by the lenience of the Albuquerque court; but the disparity is an inevitable consequence of the fact that each state (and in many states, each community) has its own autonomous system of courts with jurisdiction over state and local crimes. That autonomy, in turn, means that sentences will reflect different state and local attitudes; the Charlotte sentences are consistent with those given by judges throughout North Carolina, which puts more people in prison, relative to population, than any other state in the union. Unless the various states were willing to cede jurisdiction over intrastate crime to the federal government, it is hard to imagine how this kind of sentencing disparity could be eliminated.*

By the same token, it is difficult to see how disparity, by itself, weakens the deterrent power of the law. Except for a handful of professionals who may travel from state to state, most criminals stay close to their own communities. Shoplifters in Charlotte, North Carolina, are not likely to know that their Albuquerque counterparts will have charges against them dismissed if they do not commit a new offense in six months. Nor would it matter if they did know; what affects their

---

* It might be possible to reduce disparities growing out of different sentencing norms from one court to another within the same state; whether that would be desirable is another question. In general, sentences tend to be harsher in rural areas than in cities, and harsher, too, in small cities than in large ones; the harsher sentences in smaller communities reflect their lower level of tolerance for deviant behavior. Since legislators from rural areas have a disproportionate influence in most state legislatures, adoption of uniform sentences throughout a state probably would mean imposing rural norms on big-city courts; such a change would not necessarily improve the quality of justice.

behavior is the way the Charlotte courts respond to
shoplifting. The same is true for robbers, burglars, and
most other offenders.

Critics of sentencing policy also fail to make the
critical distinction between disparities in the sentences
judges give and the sentences defendants receive. The
distinction is neither specious nor academic; it explains
an apparent paradox—that those who look at judges'
behavior find enormous disparity in sentencing, while
those who examine the sentences defendants receive
(and equally important, the sentences they actually
serve) find that sentences tend to be proportionate to
the seriousness of the offense and of the offender's prior
record.

The general impression of capriciousness is understandable. Every court has its hanging judges and its
soft touches; and every court has judges who are harder
to categorize—judges who are harsh with some kinds of
offenses or offenders and lenient with others. But the
same kind of discretion that enables individual judges
to act capriciously makes it possible for prosecutors
and defense attorneys to limit those judges' impact.
What happens, quite simply, is that in large court systems hanging judges impose far fewer sentences than
do judges who follow court norms. If a defendant
knows that a judge will impose the maximum sentence whether he pleads guilty or not, he has no reason
to plead guilty and every incentive to insist on going
to trial. There always is at least some chance that a
jury will acquit, not to mention the chance that the case
may be transferred to another, more lenient judge.
And prosecutors, and often chief judges or court administrators, usually cooperate with defense attorneys
in manipulating dockets so that cases will come before
a judge who will impose a sentence commensurate with
the plea that has been negotiated.[39]

The Detroit Recorder's Court, that city's principal trial court, provides a case in point. At the time a member of my research staff visited the court, one judge was notorious for the harsh sentences she imposed—"Some of her sentences make us shudder," a senior prosecutor confessed. Since defendants almost always receive the maximum sentence permitted by law whether they plead guilty or not, it was the rare felony defendant who entered a guilty plea in her court; in 1972, the judge received only sixty-three pleas in felony cases. (By comparison, a colleague, whom prosecutors and defense lawyers considered a "capable and conscientious quality judge," received 1,567 guilty pleas in the same period.) With almost every defendant demanding a jury trial, the judge always had a huge backlog of cases waiting to be tried. Periodically, therefore, cases were removed from her docket and assigned to other judges; this, in turn, gave lawyers a strong incentive to delay their cases—often with the prosecutor's cooperation—in the hope of getting a reprieve. All told, the tough sentencer disposed of only 152 cases in 1972, compared to 2,176 dispositions for the "quality judge" referred to above, and an average of 800 dispositions for the eleven other judges on the court.

In good measure, the amount of sentencing disparity in any court is a function of the caseload pressure under which judges operate; the greater pressure on judges to "move" cases rapidly, the less opportunity they have to indulge their personal preferences and biases. "We are slaves to the system," the trial judge to whom Willard Gaylin gives the pseudonym "Judge Garfield" declares. "While I have the appearance of great discretion, I don't have the reality of it. I work under the constant awareness of the burden of cases in this court which demand resolution."[40]

As it happens, I spent time in the court presided over by "Judge Garfield"; knowing his background and views, it was easy to recognize the man behind the pseudonym Gaylin used. The judge had forty-seven cases on his docket on a representative day in which I sat next to him on the bench; he had disposed of thirty-one of them by the time the day ended. Judges can "move" cases that rapidly, Garfield explained, only if they have "a realistic orientation as to what a case is worth," which is to say, only if they conform to the norms of the court.*

Because court norms almost never are articulated, let alone spelled out in formal guidelines, judges usually do not realize the degree to which their sentences are predictable. On the contrary, their own perception is that there are no norms at all—that they handle each sentence differently because no two cases and no two defendants are alike. Indeed, most judges take professional pride in their ability to tailor each sentence to the peculiar circumstances of each case.

Parole board members, who act as judges in deciding whether, and when, to release offenders from prison, have the same perception; their actions often are more important than the judge's original sentence in determining how much time an incarcerated offender will serve. For years, in fact, members of the U.S. Parole Commission insisted that their decisions were so individualized that it was impossible to explain how

---

* Judges in Garfield's court have a strong incentive to conform to court norms. The chief judge sends every judge a weekly "report card," listing the number of cases on each judge's calendar for the preceding week, the number of dispositions, and each judge's "batting average," i.e., the percentage of cases disposed of during the week. The message is abundantly clear: judges who want to be reappointed or promoted to a higher court had better dispose of cases quickly, in order to maintain a high batting average.

the decisions were reached. But when a team of scholars headed by the criminologists Don Gottfredson and Leslie Wilkins spent several years sitting in on parole hearings and analyzing the decisions that were taken, they found that Parole Commission members followed a simple and clear-cut set of norms. Specifically, their research demonstrated that 80 to 85 percent of the decisions could be predicted if one knew three sets of factors: the seriousness of the offense (whether or not the victim was injured, and how seriously, and how big a financial loss the victim suffered); the nature and seriousness of the offender's prior record; and the way he conducted himself in prison.* As a result, Gottfredson, Wilkins, et al. were able to develop a set of guidelines that the Parole Commission now follows.[42] (Since institutional behavior played a relatively minor role in parole decisions, the guidelines gear decisions to the first two factors.)

Since finishing the Parole Commission study, Wilkins and Gottfredson have turned their attention to judicial sentencing. In a detailed study of the factors affecting sentences in the criminal courts of Denver, Colorado, and the state of Vermont, supplemented by less detailed studies of the Newark, New Jersey, and Des Moines, Iowa, courts, they again documented the power of informal norms. Specifically, they discovered

---

* Gottfredson and Wilkins, along with the Parole Commission, refer to the "probability of recidivism" or "parole prognosis" rather than to the nature and seriousness of the offender's prior record; such judgments are based on the offender's so-called "Salient Factor Score." But eight of the eleven salient factors refer to the nature and seriousness of the offender's prior record; the other three involve information about his social stability, e.g., whether or not he has held a job for six months or more.[41] Since the Parole Commission is charged with protecting the public against crimes by offenders they release on parole, it is understandable why it casts its decisions in that form.

that 80 to 85 percent of the sentences could be predicted, given a small core of information about the
nature and seriousness of the offense and of the offender's prior record. Their report also clarifies a phenomenon that most discussions of sentencing policy
tend to blur: the fact that the sentencing decision actually involves two separate decisions. The first is
whether or not the offender should be incarcerated; it
is only after this "in or out" decision has been made
that judges determine the amount of time that should
be served.[43]

Wilkins and his colleagues found that the offender's
prior record played the largest role in sentencing decisions, except in particularly serious crimes; in general, judges are reluctant to send first offenders to
prison. The same finding emerges from the Vera Institute study of the New York City Criminal Courts: 84
percent of convicted defendants who had a prior criminal record as an adult were sent to prison, compared to
22 percent of those without a record.[44]

In deciding whether or not to incarcerate an offender
and for how long, judges also look to the nature of the
"real crime"—the harm or loss that the victim suffers
—as opposed to the offense with which the offender is
technically charged.[45] What appear to be disparities in
sentences reflect differences in the seriousness that
judges (and the general public) attach to specific
crimes. In big-city courts, for example, robbery often
involves an incident in which a hustler takes money
for heroin but fails to deliver (or delivers adulterated
merchandise); when the dealer refuses either to provide the heroin or return the customer's money, the
latter pulls a gun and forcibly recaptures his money,
and perhaps an additional sum as well. Few judges
treat that sort of armed robbery as seriously as one

in which a criminal takes money from a total stranger at gunpoint.

What the law calls "unarmed (or strong-arm) robbery" also encompasses a wide variety of crimes, ranging from a playground altercation in which one youth forcibly takes a basketball from its owner to a potentially violent criminal's mugging of an elderly woman. And so it goes with most offenses; judges treat stranger crimes far more seriously than crimes in which there is a prior relationship between victim and offender. Whether judges *should* take these sorts of extralegal factors into consideration is another question; the point here is that they do, and that these considerations explain much of what appears to be sentencing disparities.

When one puts together information about the nature and seriousness of the offense and of the offender's prior record, to repeat, the Wilkins study found that at least four sentences in five are the result of more or less routine application of court norms. On closer examination, moreover, more than half the remaining sentences were easily explained by some unusual fact or circumstance. Only 7 to 10 percent of the sentences involved real departure from court norms—instances in which the sentences did seem to reflect arbitrary or idiosyncratic judicial behavior. And the courts that were studied seem to be reasonably representative; the overall findings are consistent with those of the Vera Institute analysis of the New York City courts and a study of the Chicago, Detroit, and Baltimore criminal courts by the political scientists James Eisenstein and Herbert Jacob.[46]

It follows that most of the sentencing reforms now being proposed—mandatory minimum prison terms, "flat time" or "determinate" sentencing, "presumptive sentencing," sentencing councils, appellate review of

sentences—are aimed at the wrong problem. Some of
the remedies may be worse than the disease. In an
adaptation of David Fogel's so-called "justice model"
of sentencing, for example, the Illinois legislature has
set a fixed prison term for each offense. But offenders
serve those terms only if the judge chooses to send
them to prison; judges retain full discretion over the
"in or out" decision. The same is true in the revised
California criminal code, which, as Albert Alschuler
of the University of Colorado Law School points out,
"leaves the most important component of the sentencing decision—the choice between prison and probation—to the same lawless discretion as in the past.
The seemingly ludicrous result is that a judge may have
an unfettered choice between probation and a specified
prison term but no power to impose an intermediate
punishment." The statute abolished the old Adult Authority (or parole board) in the name of determinate
sentencing. But as Alschuler demonstrates in some detail, what the legislature took away from the Adult Authority it gave to the state's prosecutors, whose power
and discretion have been magnified by the new
statute.[47]

Indiana has taken a different approach: judges are
also required to sentence incarcerated offenders to a
determinate, rather than indeterminate, term in prison
—but they are free to select the term from the range
allowed by law. On average, the maximum terms permitted are four times as long as the minimums. In
some instances, the ranges are considerably longer; indeed, with offenders convicted of a third burglary
charge, judges are authorized to give a determinate
sentence of anywhere from one to seventeen years.
Clearly, terms such as "determinate sentencing" are
little more than buzz words that have no meaning apart
from the specific legislation in which they are embodied.

The most sophisticated approach to sentencing reform is the "presumptive sentencing" system advocated
by the Twentieth Century Fund Task Force on Criminal Sentencing. The Task Force proposal is designed
to substantially reduce judicial discretion in sentencing
without eliminating it altogether. Instead of the present
system, in which most judges are free to give an offender any sentence they choose, up to the maximum
set by law, legislatures would define a single "presumptive sentence" for every offense, the presumptive sentence being the one that would be imposed "on typical
first offenders who have committed the crime in the
typical fashion." The presumptive sentence would increase geometrically for offenders with a prior record;
for example, one previous felony conviction within the
preceding five years might increase the sentence by 50
percent, with the increment being 100 percent for two
prior convictions, 200 percent for three convictions,
and so on, up to the maximum for the current offense.

Judges would be expected to impose the presumptive
sentence unless the offender or the offense was not
"typical"; the legislature would define, in specific detail,
the aggravating or mitigating factors that could justify
such a departure from the presumptive sentence and
would set the percentage by which the sentence could
be lengthened or shortened. Judges could impose sentences outside this relatively narrow range only when
there was "truly extraordinary and unanticipated circumstances"; such sentences would have to be justified
in writing and would be subject to "a searching review
on appeal." (The legislature also would set absolute
minimum and maximum limits beyond which judges
could not stray.) Parole boards' power to release inmates before their full term had been served would be
sharply circumscribed, and limited to special circumstances defined by the legislature.[48]

The approach might very well increase, rather than reduce, "the arbitrary and capricious nature of criminal sentencing," to use the Task Force's phrase. The attempt to attach a single presumptive sentence to each offense and to specify in advance all the factors to be taken into account in fixing the actual sentence would substitute the capriciousness of the legislature for the capriciousness of individual judges. In order to attach a single sanction to each offense—to set in advance the sentence to be given to "typical first offenders who commit the crime in the typical fashion"—legislators would have to define every offense with a foreknowledge and precision that mortals cannot muster.[49]

Consider the definitions the Task Force offered to illustrate how a presumptive sentencing system might operate. In proposing a presumptive sentencing statute for armed robbery, the Task Force broke down the crime into six different offenses, with presumptive sentences ranging from six months' imprisonment to five years. Similarly, the Task Force specified five varieties of nighttime burglary, carrying presumptive sentences of six to twenty-four months; three kinds of aggravated assault, with sentences of six months, two years, and six years, respectively; five kinds of homicide (sentences ranging from one year's probation to ten years' imprisonment); three forms of rape (six months' to six years' imprisonment); and five varieties of larceny, the most severe carrying a twenty-four-month presumptive sentence, the least serious a probationary term of six months.[50]

For all the attempt at specificity, the definitions do not begin to convey the variety of situations one encounters as a matter of course in any large criminal court, or the nuances that prosecutors and judges take into account in making their charging and sentencing decisions. As we have seen, the presence or absence of a prior relationship between victim and offender has a major effect on dispositions; yet the question is not even raised in any of the proposed statutes, except for rape, where it is mentioned only in connection with rape in the third degree.

In each of the model statutes, moreover, arbitrary distinctions have major consequences on the sentence that would be given. Under the broad category of aggravated assault, a "premeditated assault in which the defendant was the initial aggressor and in which serious, permanent physical harm was intended for the victim and accomplished" would carry a presumptive sentence of six years in prison; but an assault in which the defendant did not "intend serious, permanent physical harm" would carry only a two-year prison term. Law is filled with fine distinctions; but one would have to be a metaphysician to believe that so stark a dichotomy could be applied in a mechanical way to the continuum of assaults with injury that come before any metropolitan criminal court. One prosecutor's "premeditation" can easily become another prosecutor's "intent"; with a three-to-one sentencing disparity turning on subjective definitions of an offender's state of mind, capriciousness is inevitable.

Minor technical distinctions can have an even larger impact on the sentences offenders receive. For example, armed robbery in the sixth degree—"the forcible taking of property from the person of another by the display of or threat to use a deadly weapon other than a loaded gun"—carries a presumptive sentence of six months in jail. But the identical offense carries a presumptive sentence of twenty-four months in prison if the prosecutor decides to charge the offender with first-degree larceny, the crime designated for "any person who with threats of force or violence but without actual resort to force or violence takes the property of another." The definitions are interchangeable; either one could be applied to a purse-snatch, or to holdup at knife point. In this proposal to eliminate disparity in sentencing, a four-to-one disparity turns on the prosecutor's discretionary decision.

As is true of proposals for mandatory minimum and flat-time sentencing, presumptive sentencing would not reduce the total amount of discretion exercised in the system; it would simply shift the discretion now exercised by judges and parole boards to prosecutors—who already exercise more discretionary power than anyone, with the possible exception of the police. Since the offense for which offenders were convicted would largely determine the sentence they received, prosecutors would become the sentencing authority through their control of the charging process.[51]

The result is likely to be a net increase in the amount of capriciousness and disparity in the sentences offenders serve. Under the present system, discretion is diffused among three more or less autonomous groups of officials: prosecutors, judges, and parole board members. Diffusion creates a certain untidiness that fastidious legal scholars find upsetting; but when people's lives and liberties are at stake, untidiness may be preferable to an antiseptically neat and conceptually clean sentencing system. In practice, diffusion of discretion provides a leavening effect: judicial discretion frequently provides a check on abuse of prosecutorial power; parole board discretion serves to limit abuse of judicial power; and discretion in all three agencies serves to temper the harshness that prosecutors, judges, and legislators feel compelled to show in making sentencing decisions.

Parole provides an interesting case in point. The horrors of the parole system—the capriciousness of decisions to release prisoners and to revoke their parole, the widespread refusal by parole board members to explain their actions, the anxiety and uncertainty that parole creates among prison inmates—have been amply documented.[52] And yet most of those who favor abolishing parole in principle are reluctant to press the argument too far; for the net effect of parole appears to be a significant reduction in the length of sentences actually served and, to a lesser degree, in sentencing disparities.[53] Parole permits prosecutors and judges to have the best of both worlds: to satisfy public opinion by recommending and imposing long sentences without requiring inmates to serve them. Long sentences seem to reinforce prosecutors' and judges' machismo; if defendants actually served those sentences, our prison population would be several times larger than it now is. But for all their rhetoric about releasing inmates when they show evidence of having been rehabilitated, most parole boards in fact release most offenders when they have served the usual term for their offense and prior record; in New York State, for example, the Parole Board releases seven inmates in ten at their first appearance before the Board.

The system may be irrational and untidy, but it works a lot less capriciously than would a tidier and more rational system. It works because it neatly offsets the irrationality that seems to be deeply engrained in the American approach to sentencing. "In a system that seems addicted to barking louder than it really wants to bite," Franklin Zimring writes, parole "can help protect us from harsh sentences while allowing the legislature and judiciary the posture of law and order."[54]

VI

Criminal courts are multipurpose institutions, charged with protecting society against criminals and with protecting the innocent individual against the coercive power of the state. Practitioners and scholars have tended to emphasize the conflict between these goals.[55]

That there is a certain tension between the desire to convict the guilty and protect the innocent, the greater the chances that we may acquit some guilty persons; the greater certainty we seek in convicting the guilty, the greater the probability that innocent people will be subjected to the burden of prosecution, and the greater the risk that some of them may be convicted. This tension is not unique to American courts; it is inherent in any system of justice, be it the inquisitorial approach characteristic of continental Europe or the adversarial approach of Anglo-American nations. Both systems of justice seek to convict the guilty, and both are concerned with protecting the innocent; they differ in the procedures used to achieve those goals and in the relative weight they give to each.[56]

Clearly, the weight given to due process in American criminal courts has not undermined their ability to convict and punish the guilty. "Real criminals" are not "getting away with it" in criminal court. As the authors of the Vera Institute study wrote, "Where crimes are serious, evidence is strong, and victims are willing to prosecute, felons with previous criminal histories ended up with relatively heavy sentences."[57] It is doubtful, therefore, that sending more criminals to jail or keeping them there longer would bring about a significant reduction in criminal violence.

The fact that the courts are so much better than most people think does not mean that they are as good as they should, or can, be. Appearances count, especially where justice is concerned. One of the fundamental "laws" of sociology holds that what people think is real is real in its consequences. The courts are the institutional embodiment of our society's commitment to the rule of law and to the idea (or ideal) of justice. It matters greatly that people perceive the courts as unjust, for this perception undermines respect for law and belief in its legitimacy.

It need not be; by and large, the criminals with whom I have spoken would like to believe in the legitimacy of the law and its institutions. As Jonathan Casper, a political scientist who has made a systematic study of defendants' attitudes, has written, "defendants find in the law a moral imperative they are willing to embrace," even though they violate it in their daily lives. How else explain the fact that the overwhelming majority of defendants return to court when they have been released on bail or recognizance, or that they turn to the police and the courts for help with problems they cannot solve themselves? Moreover, defendants and their families expect the law to be better than they are; somewhere in society, they are sure, there must be *someone* who is honest and fair, and they assume that that someone will be the judge.

They are disillusioned by the unfairness—apparent or real—that they experience in court. From a defendant's perspective, Casper writes, "outcomes do not seem to be determined by principles or careful consideration of persons, but by hustling, conning, manipulating, bargaining, luck, fortitude, waiting them out, and the like." Indeed, "the system has no real moral component in the eyes of the defendant." On the contrary, defense lawyers and judges, no less than prosecutors, policemen, and probation officers, seem to be operating on a moral level no different from the one on which criminals themselves operate.[58] This can only encourage criminal behavior; as I have argued several times, respect for law and belief in its legitimacy are more effective instruments of social control than is fear of punishment.

If we are serious about reducing criminal violence, we need more due process, not less; we have to recognize the powerful educating role of the courts, and the degree to which procedures shape attitudes. Simple courtesy would go a long way toward encouraging respect for law; but major procedural changes are needed as well. What is required, in good measure, is to make the appearance of justice conform to its substance. That, in turn, means making the invisible visible— spelling out the informal norms that guide the actions judges and prosecutors take, so that defendants, not to mention judges and prosecutors themselves, can see and understand what is happening.

The first step would be to take the mystery out of criminal sentencing—to turn informal sentencing norms into formal guidelines for structuring judicial discretion, as Gottfredson, Wilkins, et al. have done for the U.S. Parole Commission and, more recently, for several city and state court systems. If guidelines are to work, judges themselves must be involved in drawing them up and in reviewing them from time to time. To devise a set of guidelines, it is necessary to find out what the court norms are and the degree to which they are followed. That means analyzing the kind of information judges use (as opposed to the information they *think* they use) in making sentencing decisions, the kinds of decisions they make, and the reasons for those decisions.*

---

* Judges generally collect considerably more information than they actually use; much of the information is overlapping, and some of it is simply ignored. Instead of urging probation

When court norms have been laid bare, they can be converted into sentencing guidelines that judges would be expected to follow; the fact that judges participate in drawing up the guidelines, and that the guidelines are based on their own experience and judgment, greatly increases the likelihood that the guidelines would be used. Judges would retain discretion to depart from the norms when departure seems appropriate. But, depending on the specific approach taken, judges who depart from the guidelines would be required either to provide an explanation in writing or to confer with a "sentencing council" composed of their peers. (A third alternative would be to provide for appellate review of sentences falling outside the guidelines.)

One of the advantages of such an approach is that it focuses attention on the exceptions—in the typical court, between 5 and 15 percent of all sentences—rather than on the run-of-the-mill decisions. If judges were required to give a written explanation of every sentence, the odds are high that the explanations would be routine and *pro forma;* and if sentencing councils have to review every sentence, they are likely to do little more than ratify their colleagues' decisions. But if only the exceptions are reviewed or explained, there is a reasonable chance that the explanations and reviews will be made with some care and thought.

At the same time, requiring special treatment for exceptions to the guidelines is likely to reduce their number. If judges have to explain a disparate sentence or submit it to others for review, they are likely to take a harder, closer look before they leap; this self-consciousness should check the exercise of judicial biases

---

officers to collect large quantities of information for the "social history" and sentencing report, as is often the case, judges would be better advised to direct their probation officers to improve the quality of the information they actually use.

and whims. Requiring written opinions and/or peer review also provides a basis for periodic—say, semi-annual—review of the guidelines by judges sitting as an administrative body. And periodic review makes it possible to revise the guidelines from time to time as experience dictates.

Such an approach would greatly improve the quality of justice. Instead of seeming to act in an arbitrary and capricious manner, judges would be seen as officials following a rule of law. One consequence would be to remove much of the "smoke-filled room" aura that now surrounds plea bargaining. Negotiations would be more open, since defendants would be able to predict their sentences with reasonable accuracy. This, in turn, would make it harder for defense lawyers to "con" their clients. (A frequent ploy of lawyers who want to show clients that they are earning their fees is to pretend that the sentence the defendant receives—the sentence he would have received anyway—was extracted from the prosecutor and judge by the lawyer's skill, "pull," or bribery.)

If courts are to appear to do justice, prosecutors must also come out of the shadows and convert their informal norms into formal guidelines and procedures. The Detroit prosecutor's office provides a model of sorts, hence is worth describing in some detail. In the usual prosecutor's office, the appearance of arbitrariness, as well as a great deal of inefficiency, waste, and delay, is due to the fact that procedures are organized on the assumption that every case will go to trial. Given that assumption, informal processes such as plea bargaining appear to be departures from the rule of law, and lawyers have no incentive to reach a speedy resolution.

The Detroit prosecutor's office, by contrast, is organized around the recognition that most cases will *not* go to trial. This recognition makes it possible to decide, at an early stage, which cases can and should be settled informally and which involve questions of fact that should be brought before a judge or jury. District Attorney William Cahalan places considerable emphasis on "front loading," i.e., careful screening of cases before charges are filed. The screening unit has eight ADA's, 14 percent of the office's total manpower; the eight all have trial experience (ranging from three to twelve years at the time of our visit), and each one has a private office where he can review the cases that are brought in.* On the basis of their trial experience, the screening officers judge each case according to their assessment of the state's chances of winning it at trial. This means that not only do screening officers decide whether the acts described in the police report constitute a crime, and if so, what crime, but they make a series of other judgments as well. They assess the complainant's demeanor and credibility; they estimate how a jury is likely to respond to the defendant, the complainant, and the crime itself; and they consider the whole range of evidentiary problems that might be raised at or before trial.

Thus no case goes forward unless an ADA with trial experience has made a judgment that the chances of conviction justify the effort involved in proceeding. There is a good deal of uniformity in the way ADAs decide whether or not to charge someone with a crime and the way they select the specific offense with which the defendant will be charged. This uniformity is

---

* Many prosecutors assign their least experienced assistants to the screening unit; the result is that cases in which charges should be dropped or reduced move into the courtroom, to be disposed of informally at a later stage.

achieved through informal understandings and policies, which could just as easily be translated into formal rules and guidelines.

Initial screening is not the only point at which the Detroit prosecutor's office tries to give some coherence and rationality to informal, discretionary decisions. A pretrial conference is held in every felony case, shortly after the preliminary hearing. The conference has two purposes: to separate the minority of cases that should be tried from the majority that are likely to be settled through a negotiated plea; and to fix the parameters within which the plea bargaining will occur. Three assistant prosecutors handle all such conferences. The three have considerable trial experience (from six to twelve years at the time of our visit); their offices are adjoining, and they confer with one another with some frequency to ensure a reasonable degree of uniformity.

The pretrial conferences tend to be dignified, if informal, proceedings which include the defense attorney and, in a fair number of cases, the arresting policeman and the victim and/or defendant as well. The lawyers discuss the evidence and any other relevant information; the case is not forwarded to a judge until the pretrial conference has produced either a plea bargain or a decision to go to trial.* If the prosecutor and defense lawyer are unable to make a decision because of a question about the admissibility of evidence, for example, or about the defendant's mental condition or some other substantive problem, the case will be sent to the judge for a hearing on the question. If the case survives

---

* Judges adhere to the decision to go to trial in about 85 percent of the cases. In the remaining 15 percent, a new plea bargain is reached at the request of the judge or through the judge's direct participation. This 15 percent provides a kind of safety valve to correct the earlier decision, on the basis of information that may not have been available when the pretrial conference was held.

that hearing, it is returned to the pretrial conference unit for a decision as to whether to negotiate a plea or go to trial. Decisions are facilitated by the fact that the Detroit Recorder's Court uses the individual calendar system, which means that both parties know in advance which judge will preside if the case is tried, and which judge will do the sentencing if the defendant is convicted through a trial or plea.

The Detroit system produces roughly the same proportion of pleas as do other big-city courts but without the long delays that are endemic elsewhere. Because lawyers know that they cannot improve on the bargain offered in the pretrial conference by pretending to go to trial, the majority of cases are terminated in three months, with six months as the outside limit. This, in turn, avoids some of the distortions that the New York–Chicago approach can produce, such as guilty pleas by innocent or unconvictable defendants who are eager to get the ordeal over with. Because only three experienced assistants handle the plea bargaining, moreover, similar cases tend to be handled similarly, with explicit (but unwritten) policies laying out the maximum reduction in charge that will be permitted in serious cases. And because the victim and arresting officer frequently are present, the prosecutor is able to explain the reasons for negotiating a plea to a lesser charge and to hear their objections before the bargain has been completed. Prosecutorial decisions that otherwise might appear arbitrary become comprehensible; this, in turn, shores up the legitimacy of the system.

Nothing would contribute more to respect for law—and indirectly, thereby, to a reduction in crime—than to provide defendants with the "effective assistance of counsel" guaranteed them by the Constitution. As Judge David Bazelon of the U.S. Court of Appeals for the District of Columbia Circuit has argued so force-

fully, effective assistance of counsel is fundamental, for
without it defendants are not likely to be able to assert
any other rights they possess. ". . . if the right to counsel guaranteed by the Constitution is to serve its purpose," the Supreme Court has declared "defendants
cannot be left to the mercies of incompetent counsel."[59]

Most of the time they are; incompetence is more the
rule than the exception—if defendants are represented
by counsel at all. Many defendants are bludgeoned into
waiving their right to counsel altogether, under threat
of a harsh sentence if they refuse. Those who do have a
lawyer often have little more than "a warm body with a
legal pedigree," to use Judge Bazelon's phrase. Whether
public defender, court-appointed attorney, or counsel
retained by the defendant, defense lawyers frequently
are inexperienced, incompetent, unprepared, and uninterested in their clients' interests and needs. "The practice of criminal law is just a little above shoplifting in
this city," a Boston defense attorney told Professor
Albert Alschuler, author of a major study of criminal
defense.[60] The lawyer's summary could apply to much
—perhaps most—of the United States.

The economics of private practice tend to militate
against real concern for any but affluent clients. Few
run-of-the-mill offenders can afford to pay large fees,
and the fees paid court-appointed attorneys usually are
modest. Most lawyers in private practice try to offset
low fees through large volume; successful "wholesalers," as they are called, may handle five to ten cases a
day, for fees ranging anywhere from $50 per case to
$200, $300, or even $500 per case. The only way to
handle that kind of volume is to plead everyone guilty;
as one defense lawyer puts it, "A guilty plea is a quick
buck."[61]

A guilty plea may be in many clients' best interest, as

we have seen. But a lawyer can plea-bargain effectively only if he is prepared to go to trial when appropriate—and only if he has the necessary trial ability. Many defense lawyers with active practices have not tried a single case in years. Every urban bar has a rich lode of stories about these "professional writ-runners and pleaders," or members of the "cop-out bar," as they are often called. Alschuler tells a story about "Plead 'Em Guilty" Fenn, an alcoholic Philadelphia lawyer who allegedly has "represented" a client for as little as a bottle of whiskey. On one occasion, Alschuler reports, a client rejected Fenn's advice and refused to plead guilty to a rape charge. Terrified of trying the case himself, Fenn approached a young lawyer and asked him to handle the trial, telling him, "There's seven-fifty in it for you." The young lawyer won an acquittal and Fenn kept his bargain: he paid the lawyer, not the $750 he expected, but $7.50—half of Fenn's total retainer.

Most cop-out lawyers are not satisfied with such trivial fees; some make comfortable livings pleading defendants guilty, often without investigating the case or spending time interviewing the defendant. (Many defendants meet their attorneys for the first time when they come to court to plead guilty.) At a mere $50 a case, a lawyer averaging five pleas a day can earn well above $50,000 a year; some "wholesalers" handle considerably more than five pleas a day, at fees well above $50 each. Alschuler describes a Los Angeles lawyer who sometimes enters as many as twenty-five guilty pleas a day, at a standard fee of $200, and an Austin, Texas, solo practitioner who needs four secretaries to handle the referrals from all the Texas jails where he is "well connected," which is to say, where sheriffs, judges, and jailers "encourage" defendants to engage his services. As Alschuler dryly remarks, "because these attorneys almost invariably collect their fees in cash, they are sometimes remarkably conservative in reporting their incomes to the Internal Revenue Service."

Lawyers of this sort use all their advantages of position, style, and verbal skill to browbeat clients into pleading guilty. Since they usually receive a flat fee per case, payable in advance, rather than billing on an hourly basis, defense lawyers have a strong incentive to persuade clients to plead guilty whether they maintain their innocence or not. "It does not lie in a defendant's mouth to say that he is innocent," one lawyer told Alschuler. "The defense attorney must make that decision because it is his reputation that goes on the line." All too often, what goes on the line is the lawyer's reputation for moving cases with great speed: a Houston defense lawyer told of being in a trial judge's chambers when the judge was informed that a particularly notorious cop-out lawyer had been indicted for a felony. The judge turned to a prosecutor who was present and said, "God damn, why indict him? We need him if we're ever going to clear up this backlog!"

None of this is to deny that there are many lawyers of unquestioned integrity and ability, although even these lawyers concede that the pressure of their caseload sometimes influences their judgment. But these lawyers represent only a minority of the defendants with private counsel. Estimates of the size of the cop-out bar vary from 10 percent to well over half—and even those lawyers who set the figure as low as 10 percent agree that "pleaders" probably appear in a majority of the cases in which defendants are represented by private counsel.

Fortunately, public defender services have begun to take over much of the work that used to be handled by

wholesalers of the sort I have described, although the
proportion defended by such services varies widely from
city to city.* Unfortunately, many defender services
seem to feel as much of a responsibility to the court as
to the individual defendant; consciously or uncon-
sciously, they see themselves as production workers
whose job is to move cases along the assembly line as
rapidly as possible. In some cities, where judges hire
and fire public defenders, that *is* their job. (Court-
appointed attorneys, too, are often beholden to individual judges, who not only control their appointments
but can also hold up approval of the vouchers that have
to be signed if the lawyers are to be paid.)

It is not surprising that most defendants do not see
public defender service lawyers as their advocate. Jonathan Casper writes, "For the bulk of defendants—represented by Public Defenders—their attorney is at best
a middleman and at worst an enemy agent. Not only is
the process of criminal justice—with its bargaining,
politics, charades—an assembly line dedicated to turning over cases and based upon a production ethic, but
the defendant's own attorney is thought often to be himself a production worker on the line. He is not 'their'
representative, but in league with those who would determine the defendants' fates."[62] At one point or another, in fact, most of the men Casper interviewed
either referred to the public defender as the prosecutor
or the prosecutor as the public defender, a slip of the
tongue that demonstrated the near interchangeability
they saw between "their" lawyer and the prosecutor.

My own observations are similar to Casper's. The de-

---

* To simplify the discussion, I am including privately and
publicly financed legal aid societies under the generic term
"public defender services." From the defendant's standpoint,
the differences are insignificant.

fendants with whom I spoke tended to see their lawyers
as representing the legal system to them, rather than
representing them to the system. "He's not my lawyer,
he's the Legal Aid," New York City defendants often
respond when judges, before accepting a plea, go
through the ritual of asking the defendant whether the
individual standing alongside him is his attorney. Understandably so: when judges ask who the lawyer is in
the case at hand, Legal Aid lawyers typically answer,
"I'm standing up for this case," not "I'm representing
this client," let alone "I'm representing Mr. Jones."

Effective advocacy requires two things: that the lawyer represent the client rather than the case, and that
the lawyer succeed in persuading the client that this *is*
the situation. It takes a good deal of conscious effort to
do the latter, since defendants are naturally and inevitably suspicious of any service provided them by the
state. Suspiciousness or paranoia aside, some defendants have trouble understanding why anyone would
want to help *them,* let alone someone paid by the
same society that is prosecuting them. And many defendants feel that he who pays the piper inevitably calls
the tune; in their view, what you don't pay for, you
don't get.

Public defenders are coming to recognize, therefore,
that such seemingly trivial things as where their office
is located can have a large impact on their clients'
perception of the lawyer-client relationship. The offices
of the Contra Costa County (California) Public Defender Service are scattered through four or five small
houses near the court house; the overcrowding and inefficiency that results is more than offset by the pleasant, informal atmosphere the arrangement provides. By
contrast, lawyers who work for the New York Legal
Aid Society have office space in the courthouses them-

selves.* In a similar vein, the business cards given lawyers who work for the Massachusetts Public Defender
Service display the state seal in a prominent way: "How
can I get a client's confidence after I show him a card
like that?" one of the lawyers asked me.

The experience of the public defender services in
Washington, D.C., Seattle, and Contra Costa County,
California, demonstrates that it is possible to provide
a high quality of representation to indigent defendants.
Although budgetary limitations exert inevitable constraints, these defender services are independent of
judicial and political pressures. In Washington and
Seattle, in particular, staff lawyers operate in much
the same way as do members of large law firms. Indeed,
they have access to a range of client services that only
the largest and most prestigious law firms can command. These services include a staff of investigators to
visit the scene of the crime, interview witnesses, and
examine police reports; a large legal library, and time
to do research on legal issues connected with the case; a
staff of social workers or former probation officers to
recommend sentencing alternatives to the probation department and/or the judge; an appeals department; and
"senior partners" to consult on difficult questions of law
or strategy. Attorneys have much the same freedom and
flexibility that private lawyers have in arranging their
own schedules. A P.D.S. lawyer can organize his time
as he wishes—for example, reserving one day primarily
for picking up new cases, some days for preliminary

* Until 1971, the criminal division of the New York Legal
Aid Society was called the "Criminal Courts Branch," a term
that underscored its symbiotic relationship with the courts; to
try to change the Society's image when he was brought in as
director in 1971, Robert Kasanof changed the name to the
"Criminal Defense Division."

hearings and motions, other days for trials, others for research, client interviews, and so on.*

The professional autonomy public defenders enjoy in Washington, D.C., is made possible by the stringent limit the public defender service sets on its attorneys' caseloads. P.D.S. lawyers carry a load of only twenty active cases at one time—an unusually low limit that permits the lawyers to give a great deal of attention to each case, as well as enabling them to schedule their time with a good deal of flexibility. Unfortunately, this self-imposed caseload limit permits P.D.S. to represent only about 30 percent of the indigent defendants—half as many as the service is authorized to represent. By accepting a caseload about double that of the D.C. defenders, the Seattle Public Defender Service manages to provide high-quality representation to 75 percent of the indigent felony defendants, and most of the indigent misdemeanants.

In the last analysis, good representation depends on the quality of the lawyers themselves. Public defender services cannot attract or retain able lawyers unless their salaries are comparable to those offered by competing institutions.† Thus the District of Columbia and Seattle public defender services pay starting salaries equal to those paid to prosecutors, and close enough to

---

* This degree of professional freedom and responsibility is a major attraction in hiring able lawyers and in persuading them to stay; lawyer turnover is much lower than in most defender offices.

† It is not enough to hire lawyers who want to "help the poor"; people of this sort may be attracted to the poor in the abstract, but all too often they become indifferent to, or repelled by, the unromantic and frequently unattractive (or paranoid) individuals who make up "the poor" in the concrete. And lawyers whose primary goal is to "change the system" may be too willing to subordinate the grubby needs of their individual clients to larger, more romantic ideological goals.

those offered by the elite law firms, for them to be able to have long waiting lists of applicants.

To bring criminal defense in most large cities up to the standard that Seattle provides would require doubling or tripling the amount of money now being spent for the defense of the indigent. Increases of this magnitude are well within recent experience. It was not until 1963, after all, that the Supreme Court held that representation must be provided to all indigent defendants in felony cases; until the Court's decision in *Gideon* v. *Wainright,* representation had been mandated only in capital offenses. The right to free counsel was extended to indigent misdemeanor defendants in 1972, in the Court's decision in *Argersinger* v. *Hamlin.*[63] In jurisdictions that have tried to comply with the Supreme Court's rulings (many have not), expenditures for legal defense have increased at a geometric rate. New York City contracts with the Legal Aid Society to represent almost all indigent defendants; expenditures for this purpose rose from $1 million in 1967 to $4 million in 1971 and $10 million in 1974, two years after the Argersinger decision.

Even so, defense of the indigent in New York came to less than 9 percent of the cost of operating the criminal courts, and well under 7 percent of the cost of operating the entire criminal justice system. In Seattle, which provides a useful bench mark, the public defender service budget comes to about 18 percent of the total court budget, and 1.5 percent of the cost of the entire criminal justice system. Hence guaranteeing effective assistance of counsel to every defendant is well within our capability.

9

Juvenile Justice: "How Could It Happen When We Were So Sincere?"

". . . there's the King's Messenger. He's in prison now, being punished; and the trial doesn't even begin till next Wednesday: and of course the crime comes last of all."

"Suppose he never commits the crime?" said Alice.

"That would be all the better, wouldn't it?" the Queen said.

—LEWIS CARROLL, *Through the Looking-Glass*

. . . experience should teach us to be most on guard to protect liberty when the government's purposes are beneficent.

—MR. JUSTICE BRANDEIS, DISSENT IN *Olmstead v. United States*, 1928

I say that the blame for not developing more and better resources cannot be laid at the judges' door, because I know of their active concern. But looking at the record I am reminded of the Peanuts cartoon showing him sadly leaving the ballfield with the scoreboard showing "Visitors 99, Home Team 0." "Ugh," he says. "How could it happen when we were so sincere?"

—HON. WILLIAM SYLVESTER WHITE,
PRESIDING JUDGE, COOK COUNTY
(ILLINOIS) CIRCUIT COURT, JUVE-
NILE DIVISION

I

"The great hopes originally held for the juvenile court have not been fulfilled," the President's Crime Commission declared in its 1967 report. "It has not succeeded significantly in rehabilitating delinquent youth, in reducing or even stemming the tide of delinquency, or in bringing justice and compassion to the child offender. To say that juvenile courts have failed to achieve their goals is to say no more than what is true of criminal courts in the United States. But failure is most striking when hopes are highest.

Except for the common school, no public institution has had such high hopes attached to it. Since they were established around the turn of the century (the watershed usually is taken to be 1899, when Illinois established a separate court in Chicago), juvenile courts have been monuments to American optimism. In their rhetoric, if not their actual operation, the courts represent expressions of faith in judges' capacity to change human behavior and thereby turn wayward children into law-abiding citizens.

From the beginning, juvenile court judges have proclaimed their commitment to rehabilitation rather than punishment. "The problem for determination by the judge is not, Has this boy or girl committed a specific wrong," Judge Julian Mack wrote in 1909, "but What

This chapter is based on research by Arlene Silberman.

is he, How has he become what he is, and What had
best be done in his interest and in the interest of the
state to save him from a downward career." The court's
goal is "not so much to punish as to reform, not to de-
grade but to uplift, not to crush but to develop, not to
make him a criminal but a worthy citizen."[1]

For the first fifty years of its existence, the juvenile
court was generally thought to be a triumph of progressive reform. Roscoe Pound called it one of the great
social inventions of the century, and reformers such as
Julian Lathrop, Jane Addams, and Edith and Grace
Abbot considered creation of the court to be a major
breakthrough in public policy toward children and
crime. "There was almost a change in mores when the
juvenile court was established," Jane Addams, who
played a significant role in the founding of the Chicago
court, wrote in 1935. (For the first few years of its existence, the Chicago juvenile court was located across
the street from Miss Addams' Hull-House, and its first
probation officer was a Hull-House member who had
been doing the same work on an informal basis for several years.) Miss Addams' enthusiasm was shared by
law enforcement officials as well; one prosecutor predicted that the new Chicago juvenile court would
"prove the dawn of a new era in our criminal history."[2]

That enthusiasm has become muted, to say the least;
over the last two decades, the operation of the juvenile
court and, more recently, the underlying concept itself,
have come under increasingly harsh attack. Hardly a
month goes by without a newspaper story, magazine
article, or television documentary accusing the juvenile
courts of being soft on criminals and crime, of treating
hardened, vicious criminals as if they were naughty
children. "People have always accused kids of getting
away with murder," a *Time* cover story declared. "Now

that is all too literally true. . . . Especially in ghettoes of big cities, the violent youth is king of the streets. When he is caught, the courts usually spew him out again."[3]

This view is widely shared, especially by prosecutors and policemen, many of whom feel that the institution of the juvenile court has outlived its usefulness. "The law says a kid should be treated differently because he can be rehabilitated," a West Coast policeman told me, "but they weren't robbing, killing and raping when kiddie court was established. Kids are different now, but the law hasn't caught up with the change."

The critics have a point—but not for the reasons they think. When cases are "spewed out," as they often are, it usually is because victims and other complainants are unwilling to press charges; "complainant noncooperation" plays an even larger role in juvenile than in criminal courts. Juvenile court judges are more lenient than their counterparts in criminal court, but they administer vastly more punishment than is generally realized—more, certainly, than their talk about pursuing "the best interests of the child" would lead one to believe.

The problem is not that juvenile courts are too lenient, but that they are too lenient toward the wrong people. As we have seen, criminal courts do an effective job of separating the "garbage" cases from the "real crimes," so that resources can be concentrated on the latter. The opposite is true of juvenile courts. As I will explain further in this chapter, juvenile court judges are the prisoners of their own rhetoric. In their desire to "help" troubled youngsters, they spend the bulk of their time on juveniles charged with offenses such as "incorrigibility," "ungovernability," truancy, running away from home, and other behaviors that do not involve any direct threat to public safety. These "status offenses" (so-called because it is the offenders' status as minors that make the acts illegal) account for at least half, and perhaps as much as two-thirds, of juvenile court time. As a result, little time or energy is left to deal with those juveniles who commit serious crimes.

It is not only time that is allocated poorly. The distorted priorities that have juvenile court judges concentrating on "juvenile nuisances," rather than on juvenile delinquents and criminals, lead them to allocate punishments in the same irrational way. Nationwide, runaways and incorrigibles (juveniles whose offense is defiance of parental authority) are more likely than burglars to be incarcerated, and at least as likely to be locked up (often in adult jails) as robbers. For the most part, sentences bear little or no relation to the seriousness of the offense or to the offender's culpability. In "juvie" court, unlike criminal court, sentences really *are* arbitrary and capricious.

Indeed, most juvenile courts make criminal courts look like models of due process. In his majority opinion in the Supreme Court's landmark case *In re Gault,* in 1967, Mr. Justice Fortas referred to the "kangaroo court" atmosphere in which juveniles were tried. Not until the Gault's decision, in fact, did the Supreme Court hold that the constitutional guarantee of due process applied to juveniles as well as to adults. As a group, juvenile courts have been slow to follow the spirit, as well as the letter, of Gault; some have devised ingenious ways of evading the Supreme Court's strictures altogether. In most juvenile courts, it remains true, as Justice Fortas observed, that "the child receives the worst of both worlds: that he gets neither the protections accorded to adults nor the solicitous care and regenerative treatment postulated for children."[4]

Youngsters sent to juvenile detention centers and training schools are likely to be brutalized rather than rehabilitated. "There are things going on, methods of discipline being used in the state training schools of this country that would cause a warden of Alcatraz to lose his job if he used them on his prisoners," Austin Mac-Cormick, the dean of American correctional officials, warned the members of the National Council of Juvenile Court Judges in 1950.

Alcatraz is no more, but juvenile court judges are still "placing" youngsters in institutions that make adult prisons seem almost benign. Uncontradicted testimony in 1974, in the case of *Morales* v. *Turman,* provided a sordid catalog of the kinds of physical and psychological torture used by members of the staff at the six state juvenile institutions run by the Texas Youth Council. Instead of denying that these methods were used, the state agency defended them as necessary to control the "violent" youngsters under their supervision. Yet fewer than 10 percent of the TYC wards had committed a violent crime; more than 25 percent had been committed for "disobedience," a catch-all category for such offenses as running away from home, truancy, and being an "ungovernable child." After hearing the evidence, U.S. District Court Judge William Wayne Justice ruled that the disciplinary methods violated the Eighth Amendment's prohibition against cruel and unusual punishment, and ordered massive changes in Texas Youth Council policies and practices. He also ordered two training schools—the Mountain View and Gatesville School for Boys—closed as soon as possible. "If ever confinement in an institution constituted a form of cruel and unusual punishment," Judge Justice declared, "Gatesville and Mountain View fully meet the applicable criteria."[5]

II

How did this come to be? The answer, in part, is that public policy toward youth is inherently ambivalent, at times almost schizophrenic. Ambivalence is built into the very marrow of the juvenile court, which is expected both to nurture and protect the young against older members of society, and to protect society against the misbehaving young. When these goals come into conflict, as they often do, it is perfectly reasonable for judges, probation officers, and correctional officials to attach a higher priority to the protection of society than to securing the best interests of the child.

What is not reasonable is to pretend that no conflict exists. "The great enemy of the truth," John F. Kennedy once remarked, "is very often not the lie—deliberate, contrived, and dishonest—but the myth—persistent, persuasive, and unrealistic." In the case of the juvenile court, no myth has been more persistent and unrealistic, and none a greater barrier to understanding how the court actually works, than the myth which holds that juvenile courts are run "in the best interests of the child." Thus juveniles are not arrested, jailed, or charged with a crime; they are "taken into custody," "detained," and "referred" to juvenile court, where a "petition" may be filed "in their behalf." Instead of being tried, a "hearing" is held at which (rather than plead guilty) a youngster may make an "admission." Either way, juveniles are not convicted or sentenced; rather, the judge makes a "finding of delinquency," after which delinquents may be "placed" in a "training school" or other residential facility to "correct" their conduct and help them grow into law-abiding citizens.

Juvenile court judges have used a variety of metaphors to describe their role. Judge Ben Lindsay, the evangelical founder of the Denver Juvenile Court, described the ideal juvenile court judge as part educator, part artist, and part physician. But not part judge; as Lindsay explained, "a child's case is not a legal case." Judge Richard Tuthill, the first judge appointed under the Illinois Juvenile Court Act of 1899, saw himself in a paternal role. "I have always felt, and endeavored to act in each case," he said, "as I would were it my own son who was before me in the library at home, charged with some misconduct."

The most popular imagery has been medical and therapeutic. From the beginning, juvenile court judges have liked to think of themselves as wise and benevolent physicians who disgnose the nature of the illness displayed by the youngsters brought before them and prescribe the course of treatment best designed to bring about their patients' full rehabilitation and recovery. "Years ago I talked with an outstanding Juvenile Court judge in one of our western states and heard him explain what I think was the original purpose of the juvenile delinquency acts of the various states," Justice William O. Douglas, a man not usually given to sentimentality, wrote in 1975. " 'I, the judge,' he told me, 'and the bailiff and the other court attendants are like those on a hospital staff, dressed in white. We are doctors, nurses, orderlies. We are there not to administer a law in the normal meaning of criminal law. We are there to diagnose, investigate, counsel and advise. We are specialists in search of ways and means to correct conduct and help reorient wayward youngsters to a life cognizant of responsibilities to the community.' "[6]

The joker is contained in that last sentence, which makes it clear that the goal of the physician-judge is not healing—certainly not healing for its own sake—but social control, i.e., to "reorient wayward youngsters

to a life cognizant of responsibilities to the community."
If the judge does not administer the law "in the normal
meaning of the criminal law," it is nonetheless the law
that the judge administers. All the euphemisms in the
world cannot change the fact that "juvie court" is a
court. Like all courts, it has the "muscle" to administer
sanctions to those who violate the law; and juvenile
court judges, including (perhaps especially) those addicted to medical metaphors, like to flex those muscles.
Judge Harvey Baker of Boston, one of the most influential of the early juvenile court judges, compared himself to a doctor in a dispensary; there was no more
formality in his courtroom, he declared, than there was
in a "physician's examination room." Yet Judge Baker
insisted that children and parents appearing before
him stand the entire time, to drive home to them the fact
that the court was "a department of public authority
. . . having power to compel compliance."[7]

The juvenile court is a coercive and punitive, as well
as rehabilitative, institution. A half-century ago, Judge
Edward Waite argued that the critical distinction between a juvenile and a criminal court was the difference
between a court "avowedly concerned only with doing
something *for* a child because of what he *is* and needs,"
and one designed "to do something *to* a child because
of what he *has done*."[8] [emphasis in original] But there
is no way to do something *for* a child without doing
something *to* him (or her; as we shall see below, girls
are punished with surprising frequency) when that
"something" involves the loss of liberty and separation
from family and friends.

"Good intentions and a flexible vocabulary do not
alter this reality," Dean Francis Allen has written. Nor
do euphemisms change another reality: that when juveniles commit serious crimes, punishment is the goal,
not just the consequence, of judicial intervention. Yet

many juvenile court judges continue to deny that they do anything but "help" the youngsters who come before them. According to Judge Walter Whitlatch of the Cuyahoga County (Cleveland) Juvenile Court, a past president of the National Council of Juvenile Court Judges, his state's juvenile code "is neither criminal nor penal in nature; rather, it is an administrative police regulation of a corrective character." The underlying concept, Judge Whitlatch remarks, "is that a child who has violated the law is not a criminal, but rather he is to be taken in hand by the state as protector and ultimate guardian rather than as his enemy." Incarcerating youngsters in a state training school is not punishment or imprisonment, Whitlatch insists, but simply the exercise of a parental restraint by the ultimate parent, the State. In any case, Whitlatch argues, citing a frequently quoted formulation by an earlier commentator, " 'Juveniles have particular and peculiar rights and they require particular and peculiar treatment. The basic right of a juvenile is not to liberty but to custody.' "[9]

The consequences are profound. The euphemistic language and medical metaphors of "the juvenile court philosophy" persuade judges of their own benevolence, blinding them to the havoc they sometimes wreak in children's lives. "If you see a man approaching with the obvious intent of doing you good," Thoreau warned, "you should run for your life." But children usually are not in a position to run; and if they do, their running itself becomes a basis for further intervention by the court. There are exceptions, to be sure—courts in which concern for children's well-being is not merely semantic, in which the atmosphere is warm and humane and judges genuinely try to reconcile the interests of society and of the youngsters who are there. But, by and large, it is difficult to spend a day in juvenile court without finding example after example of what Francis

Allen calls "that arrogance and insensitivity to human values to which men who have no reason to doubt their own motives appear particularly susceptible."

ITEM: A sixteen-year-old black girl appears before the avuncular judge, for a decision as to whether she may be released from the state training school to which she had been committed for "incorrigibility" and for having run away from home a number of times. A representative of the training school urges Martha's release, commenting on how helpful and cooperative she has been. Martha's probation officer also recommends release, telling the judge that plans have been made for Martha to attend an "alternative school" half a day and work the other half; a job already has been found. The probation officer assures the judge that Martha and her mother have been working through the problems originally dividing them and that ongoing social work will help them complete the process. To underscore the family's stated desire to have the youngster back home, Martha's father has taken the day off from work to sit next to his wife in court.

Peering into the record, the judge responds, "Martha, I see that you are not interested in cosmetology any more; you told the court last time that you wanted to be a beautician." Furrowing his brow in puzzlement, he asks, "Aren't all girls interested in fixing their hair and looking pretty?" He tells the probation officer that if Martha returns to public school, she will no longer be able to study cosmetology. The probation officer explains again that under the proposed plan, Martha would be attending an alternative school, not the public high school, and that a job is waiting for her. "I still think you could do better," the judge tells Martha by way of response, adding that Martha is fortunate to be in a training school that offers a course in cosmetology. "Someday you will all thank me for this," he tells the weeping youngster and her parents as he announces his decision to return Martha to the training school.

The judge's action and his confidence in his own wisdom and benevolence are typical of juvenile court judges in every part of the United States; such confidence appears to be a major occupational hazard of being a juvenile court judge. And this particular judge enjoys an enviable reputation among his peers; he has served as president of the National Council of Juvenile Court Judges, and the walls of his office are lined with awards attesting to his "ceaseless devotion to both young and old" and other virtues.

Juvenile court judges are armed with extraordinary power as well. Their authority has its origins in the ancient common law doctrine of *parens patriae,* under which the Crown was the ultimate parent of every child, with both the right and the obligation to protect the property rights of orphans and other children. When the English legal system was transplanted to the United States, state courts took over the *parens patriae* role; in the early nineteenth century, the courts, with legislative approval, broadened the role to include the right to protect children—especially the children of impoverished immigrants—from parental neglect, bad companions, their own lack of diligence or virtue, or any other condition or trait that right-thinking people believed might doom the youngsters to a life of idleness, poverty, "depravity," or crime. Genuine concern over children's well-being often was intertwined with real distaste for the new immigrants' life style. Toward the end of the nineteenth century, as the number of delinquent or "predelinquent" youngsters increased, courts began hearing cases involving minors in separate courtrooms or on separate days. In the first two or three decades of this century, legislatures delegated the *parens patriae* role to separate juvenile courts, which became the dumping grounds, literally and symbolically, for a large portion of the unsolved problems of urban life.*[10]

Today, children may come under the jurisdiction of a juvenile court as a result of either their own, or their parents', misbehavior. Jurisdiction over minors on account of their parents' absence or misdeeds is almost breath-taking in its scope. In California, for example, anyone under the age of eighteen may be adjudicated "a dependent child of the court" if he or she "is in need of proper and effective parental care or control and has no parent or guardian, or has no parent or guardian willing to exercise or capable of exercising such care or control"; the definition of "proper and effective parental care or control" is left to the discretion of the judge. The language of most other juvenile codes is just as broad.[11]

Thus juvenile court judges are given almost a godlike role, with broad discretion to remove children from their homes—to place them temporarily in publicly or privately operated shelters or group or foster homes, or to "terminate" parental rights altogether. For some judges, and some probation officers, social workers, and welfare department caseworkers, "dependency" and "neglect" cases pose agonizing and momentous problems of choice. All too many approach questions of placement in a casual and indifferent, and often callous, manner, whether the question be to remove children from their homes and place them in foster care, or to

---

* More recently, some states have replaced juvenile courts with family courts—in effect, juvenile courts with added jurisdiction over marital disputes. Since the differences between juvenile and family courts are insignificant for the purposes of this chapter, I shall refer to all of them under the generic term "juvenile court."

remove children from long-term foster homes and return them to their families. Decisions reflect the interests of child-care and welfare institutions or the biases
or convenience of child-care and welfare workers,
rather than the best interests of the children themselves.[12]

Juvenile court jurisdictions over juvenile misbehavior is every bit as broad. Minors may be brought before the court for committing a criminal act; in draft-
ing juvenile legislation, most state legislatures have
simply incorporated their criminal codes in their en-
tirety, or with a few specified exceptions.* But juvenile
courts also have jurisdiction over a variety of offenses
that apply only to juveniles. The obverse of the special
protections afforded by the minors' *parens patriae* doctrine is a special set of obligations youngsters have by
virtue of their status as minors. They must obey the
orders of their parents; they must attend school and
obey the orders of their teachers; they must refrain
from drinking alcoholic beverages and, in some jurisdictions, from smoking cigarettes; they may not run
away from home; and they must avoid "incorrigibility,"
"immorality," "knowingly associating with vicious or
immoral persons," "idly roaming the streets at night,"
and a number of other broadly and vaguely defined
behaviors. In California, "Any person under the age of
18 years . . . who from any cause is in danger of

* In some states, the most serious crimes, such as murder
and rape, automatically come under the jurisdiction of the
criminal, rather than juvenile, court (or come under criminal
court jurisdiction if the offender is over a certain age); in other
states, the least serious crimes, such as traffic offenses, are not
included in juvenile court jurisdiction. And most states have a
provision whereby juvenile courts may waive their jurisdiction
over certain categories of minors under certain circumstances—
for example, any minor (or any second offender) accused of
murder or rape, or any minor fifteen years of age or older accused of a felony.

leading an idle, dissolute, lewd, or immoral life" may
be adjudged a ward of the court.

The label assigned to youngsters found guilty of a
status offense varies from state to state. In the majority,
minors who violate any provision of the juvenile code,
criminal or noncriminal, are adjudicated as "delinquents." Other states reserve the term "delinquent" for
minors found guilty of a criminal offense; a youngster
who commits a status offense may be referred to as a
Person in Need of Supervision, generally abbreviated
as PINS (or as a Minor, or Child, or Juvenile in Need
of Supervision, abbreviated as MINS, CHINS, or
JINS), or as a Wayward (or Unruly, Ungovernable,
Incorrigible, Miscreant, or Beyond-Control) Child. But,
until the last few years, these differences in terminology
were not accompanied by any differences in disposition;
in the great majority of states, status offenders faced the
same range of sanctions as youngsters found guilty of
criminal behavior, including commitment to maximum
security training schools and reformatories.[13]

It is not surprising, therefore, that the juvenile justice system delivers vastly more punishment than treatment. To be sure, any attempt to quantify the amount
of punishment is necessarily crude and arbitrary. For
children, time has a different dimension than it does for
adults: to a child, a day can seem as long as a week,
and a month may feel like a year. (This is a major
justification for giving juveniles significantly shorter
sentences than adults.) Thus the cold statistic that juveniles held in detention are kept for eleven days, on average, cannot begin to convey how much punishment
detention involves, especially if the time is spent in a
locked facility, as it usually is, or in an adult jail, as it
frequently is.

It is even harder to quantify the amount of treatment that is provided; merely knowing the number of

hours of counseling or psychotherapy a youngster is given tells little about the amount of help he receives—and it is difficult to know how much and what kinds of treatment juveniles receive. Indeed, the paucity (and often the inaccuracy) of data on what is done to and for children is a national scandal.* But since juvenile court practices often are justified as being "in the best interests of the child," we need to gain at least some rough idea of how much punishment and treatment are administered.

The most striking fact is the sheer quantity of punishment meted out by a system that boasts of having replaced punishment with rehabilitation. In 1974, some 460,000 youngsters spent time in detention centers, the juvenile counterpart to the adult jail; their average stay was a little under two weeks, but significant numbers of juveniles spent a month or even two in detention centers. Another 70,000 juveniles served terms, averaging nine months, in state training schools and other long-term correctional institutions.

To look only at juvenile institutions is to understate the number of youngsters who are incarcerated, for

---

* Twenty-two states keep no juvenile detention statistics at all; the Children's Defense Fund discovered that one state did not even keep records of the number of children referred to juvenile court, let alone what happened to them. (In that same state, the Fund found, the agency responsible for fish and game can provide the number and species of fish to be found in every body of water in every county.) What statistics are provided, moreover, are often of questionable accuracy. As part of a study of juvenile court operations, the National Assessment of Juvenile Corrections sent a detailed questionnaire to a random sample of judges, court administrators, and probation officers in some 600 courts. Fewer than half the courts provided adequate data on the age of young offenders and the offenses they committed, and an even smaller proportion provided information on the services offered juveniles. When information was provided, many internal inconsistencies were discovered that raised doubt about the reliability of the data.

juveniles frequently are locked up in adult jails, often in clear violation of state laws requiring minors to be kept in separate facilities. Judging by the Law Enforcement Assistance Administration's Jail Censuses and other studies of individual states, it would appear that at least 250,000 juveniles were jailed in 1974; Rosemary Sarri, co-director of the National Assessment of Juvenile Corrections, estimates that the number could be as high as 500,000.[14] Adding the figures together, at least 780,000 juveniles (and perhaps as many as 1,030,000) were incarcerated in 1974.*

"The placement of a child in detention or shelter is drastic action," a *Handbook for New Juvenile Court Judges,* published by the National Council of Juvenile Court Judges, declares. "A child should be detained only when a failure to do so would place the child or the community in danger." Clearly, the "dangerousness" standard is invoked with great frequency. To gauge how frequently, we need to compare the number of youngsters held in pretrial detention with the number who are formally charged with an offense. Some 70 percent of the youngsters who spent time in juvenile detention centers in 1974 were being held pending court action or transfer to another jurisdiction. The LEAA's Jail Census indicated that about the same proportion obtained for juveniles held in jail. Adding the adult jail and juvenile detention statistics together, it would appear that at least 500,000 juveniles, and

---

* These statistics measure the number of admissions to detention centers, training schools, and jails. Since some youngsters were detained or jailed more than once, and since some who were detained or jailed also served time in a training school, the number of individuals was smaller. How much smaller is unknown; the data do not make it possible to estimate how many separate individuals were incarcerated. But the same is true for all other statistics of the juvenile justice system.

perhaps as many as 680,000, were locked up in 1974 while awaiting court action or transfer to another jurisdiction.

Why were so many youngsters detained before trial? The answer does not lie in their dangerousness to society; only 77,500 juveniles were arrested in 1974 for one of the violent crimes in the FBI's Index. If every juvenile burglar had been detained as well, only 300,000 youngsters would have been locked up. In fact, most of those who are locked up before trial are set free afterwards: of the 500,000 to 680,000 juveniles held in pretrial detention in 1974, only 70,000 were subsequently sentenced to state training school, and another 75,000 to 150,000 were sentenced to terms in jail. In some states—Arizona is a striking example—fewer than 10 percent of the juveniles detained before trial are deemed sufficiently dangerous to be removed from the community after adjudication.[15]

Detention is used more to punish youngsters than to protect them, or society. The ease with which juveniles can be detained provides an enormous temptation to judges, policemen, and probation officers and parole agents to lock youngsters up for a few days, or longer, to "teach them a lesson"—to "put a little fear in them" as an incentive to "shape up."* In a national survey conducted by the National Assessment of Juvenile Corrections, 49 percent of the judges believed that "placing a youth in detention is a good way to show him that the court means business." (By contrast, only 28

---

* In fifteen states at this writing, a juvenile may be placed in detention on the decision of the policeman, probation officer, or parole agent alone, without any court order or hearing being required. In sixteen states, all that is required is a court order, issued in the judge's chamber without any hearing. Only eighteen states require a hearing—in half of them within forty-eight hours, in the remainder within four days, or with no time limit at all.

percent of those in charge of detention centers agreed
with the statement; apparently one cannot really dislike
those institutions unless one knows them well!) It is
commonplace, therefore, for youngsters to be held in
detention and then released, without any formal charges
placed against them.[16]

Detention is used just as frequently as a means of
asserting social control—of reinforcing the authority
of parents and school officials and enforcing conventional norms of sexual behavior. Reflecting the double
standard that applies in society at large, judges are more
concerned with what they consider premature or pro-
miscuous sexual activity on the part of girls—especially
white girls—than on the part of boys.[17] The result is
that girls (especially white girls) are substantially over-
represented in detention centers; although they account
for an insignificant proportion of serious crime, girls
make up one-third of the detention center population.
Fully 75 percent of the girls in detention, and 25 percent of the boys, are charged with "status offenses,"
such as truancy, running away from home, and "incorrigibility" or "ungovernability." All told, 40 percent of
the juveniles in detention centers, and 18 percent of
those in jail, are charged with one or another status
offense; no more than 10 percent are accused of robbery or other violent crimes.

There are occasions, of course, when juveniles who
have not committed a crime do need to be detained. It
is appropriate to hold a runaway of whatever sex until
the parents have been contacted or a reunion arranged;
and no one can reasonably object if the police pick up
a twelve-year-old girl or boy who is soliciting in Times
Square (or its equivalent in other cities), or a fourteen-
year-old who has passed out from too much alcohol or
drugs. There are times, too, when juveniles have to be
held somewhere to protect them against physically

assaultive parents, or parents who simply refuse to permit the child inside their home. Probation officers and detention center workers with whom I have spoken generally estimate the latter two categories at 10 to 15 percent of detention center populations, although some estimates run as high as 25 percent.

But there can be no excuse for holding status offenders or youngsters accused of minor offenses in adult jails, or in secure detention centers of the sort I saw almost everywhere I went. Yet extraordinary numbers of juvenile court judges, including some of the most sensitive and thoughtful, have persuaded themselves, as one such judge told me, that "detention does work therapeutically in most cases." "Too well," the judge added; "some kids will commit an offense just to get in" —a notion that brought stares of amazement, mixed with horror, from staff members of the detention center attached to the judge's court.

Juvenile Hall is secure, another judge told me, "but it's not such a terrible place"—by which she could only have meant that the walls were painted in pastel colors instead of institutional green; by any other standard, it *was* a terrible place, in which juveniles are locked in their cell-like rooms for an hour and a half twice a day, for "quiet hour," in addition to the nine hours at night during which they are in lockup. (Whatever signs I saw on the walls served only to reinforce the negative, punitive atmosphere—for example, "Treats are a privege [*sic*] don't ask for them," "No personal articles allowed in this section," "All arts and crafts projects go in drawers—not rooms," and so on.) And this center is far from being the worst; in the Pima County (Arizona) detention center, which serves Tucson and its environs, every youngster who enters is locked in isolation for twenty-four hours, to permit the child to "orient" himself to the facility.

There are exceptions; some detention center directors try hard to make their facilities as noninstitutional as possible. The Hennepin County (Minneapolis) detention center is physically designed to make locks and buzzers as unobtrusive as possible; the brightly colored walls are filled with graffiti, psychedelic paintings, and posters that give the place an ambience responsive to juveniles and their needs. One poster read, "Please be patient; we will help as soon as possible." That message of concern was reinforced by another: "The trouble with caring is . . . too few do"

Most judges (and many detention center directors) fail to realize how traumatic being forcibly separated from their parents is for all but the most crime-hardened youngsters. The trauma is accentuated several-fold by being locked up. The best facilities in the world cannot compensate for the pain of separation, a fact that a judge who boasts about the luxuries he has acquired for his lakeside detention center seems unable to comprehend. Thus the judge missed the real point of the story he told me to demonstrate that some children just can't be pleased, no matter what one does. According to his own account, he asked a boy in the detention center how he liked the horses—a point of particular pride to the judge.

"They're great," the boy replied.

"How do you like the lake?"

"It's great, too."

"I guess you like it here, then?"

"Nope."

"Why not?"

"My mom isn't here."

Other judges seem to believe that a euphemistic name turns a detention center into a home; the prize goes to a New Jersey facility called Cloud Nine. And most judges are simply oblivious to what goes on in detention.

ITEM: I had another insight into Judge ———— when he took me for a tour of what he obviously viewed as a very fine detention center. He was so damned jovial with the girls—the boys gave him the evil eye, and he never went near them to chat—that one would have imagined the kids were in a college dorm, voluntarily. And that was what troubled me the most. Judge ———— seemed to think that if you put enough ping-pong tables, pool tables, and posters in a detention center, it was just like home. His jocular manner with the girls was so out of keeping with their plight (and in some instances their obvious misery), it seemed to me that this well-intentioned man simply did not understand the implications of enforced confinement.

One girl, for example, to whom the others directed me when they learned I was from New York, was sitting in an almost catatonic trance, her body rigid and her face masked. For a long time, I could not get her to talk at all; when I finally broke through, her story almost put *me* in a trance. This fourteen- or fifteen-year-old child had run away from her home in a New York City suburb. Apparently, this was the first time the girl had ever been away from home, let alone confined in a detention center; she had been sitting there for *six days*—an eternity to a frightened child—without so much as a contact with a probation officer, let alone a conversation with a lawyer or a phone call to her parents. As a result, she had no sense whatsoever of when or how—or even whether—she would be able to return home.

In fairness to the judge, he did seem distressed when I called him over, and he took copious notes. The next

morning, he managed to get the child on a plane en
route home. The plans had been made all along, the
judge told me; there simply had been a breakdown in
communications. Maybe so—but the detention center
seems to be afflicted with such breakdowns. On the
same visit, I spoke with another girl, a more experienced runaway (most of the girls there seemed to be
runaways), who had been in the center for five days
and was still waiting for permission to call her mother;
the matron in charge claimed to be too busy with files
and paperwork to arrange for the call.

In some detention centers—for example, the Los
Angeles Central Juvenile Hall—the right to call one's
parents has been converted into a "privilege" that must
be bought with tokens or "points" earned through good
behavior. Almost everywhere, in fact, the therapeutic
technique known as "behavior modification" has been
distorted into an instrument of social control. When
youngsters enter the Jefferson County (Colorado)
Youth Center for the first time, they are placed on
"Zero Status," meaning they are confined to their rooms
for two days; the symbolism of the label is underscored
by their being allowed no personal possessions whatsoever—no books, no pictures of parents or sweet-
hearts, no hair curlers—nothing, in short, that might
suggest that they have an identity of their own or that
might shore up a sense of self that has been fractured
by arrest. (Half the detainees are runaways and "incorrigibles," described by a Youth Center official as
"spoiled suburban kids who just can't deal with their
feelings"; 97 percent of the status offenders processed
in one ten-month period came from broken homes.)

After completing Zero Status, youngsters automatically become a "Level I." As the regulations inform
them, "You may have two books in your room (three

comic books equals one book). Nothing else is permitted in your room (one magazine equals one book)."
If they reach Level II, they may have "two books and four room decorations," the latter being defined as "things like pictures, posters, paper flowers, waste baskets, etc.," but excluding anything "made of glass, pottery, wood, etc." Unfortunately, the regulations also explain, youngsters may only "apply for promotion to Level II on Wednesday (and possibly Sunday if time permits)."[18]

The Jefferson County youngsters can earn the "privilege" to keep some of their own belongings. Other detention centers are more austere. At the time I visited Spofford, New York City's fortress-like maximum-security detention center, boys were not permitted to keep any personal belongings in their rooms, not even photographs or clothing; each morning, each boy was doled out underwear, a shirt, and pants for the day. When I asked why—even the toughest maximum-security prisons permit inmates to keep *some* personal belongings in their cells—the director explained that a secure facility has to keep kids under scrutiny all the time; since surveillance is easier when youngsters are in the TV room or game room, they are not permitted to keep a radio in their room. Why permitting kids to keep their own clothing would interfere with security remained a mystery. Nor did the director explain why youngsters were permitted only four cigarettes a day during designated smoking periods—a real hardship, since most are chain smokers. I did hear an explanation from one of the counselors—an explanation that summed up the atmosphere of the whole place. The dialogue went like this:

New boy: "Why can't I carry my own cigarettes?"

Counselor: "Because you're only allowed four a day."

New boy: "Why only four?"

Counselor, with an air of having explained everything: "That's the way it's set up."

III

To sum up, the juvenile justice system metes out vastly more punishment than is generally acknowledged. It also provides far less "treatment" (or "help," to use a less invidious term) than its rhetoric suggests.

In assessing the amount of help that is offered, let me begin with youngsters who have been removed from their homes. It is possible to provide an extraordinary amount of assistance to youngsters in residential settings of the right sort; I have visited "group homes" that appeared to have transformed the lives of the youngsters living in them. At dinner in one such home in the Bronx, my first impression was of a comfortable middle-class family that routinely says grace before beginning to eat (and that eats with table manners that would have put my own children to shame when they were in their teens). The impression evaporated rapidly; as I talked to the ten teenage girls, I heard one heartbreaking life history after another. I also saw the degree to which they had absorbed their "housemother's" aspirations and values. All the girls took it for granted that they would finish high school; the older ones were already making plans for the next stage. Some were applying to college; others expected to enroll in technical training programs—one as a computer programmer, another as a laboratory technician.

Not until the evening wore on, however, did I fully appreciate the impact the group home was having on the girls' lives. Bit by bit, I became aware of the fact that none of them smoked; the absence of cigarettes was striking, since the youngsters in every other juvenile facility I had visited were chain smokers. When the girls were comfortable enough with my presence for me to ask questions, I commented on the fact that they were not smoking and asked if there were any particular reason. There was: the girls had become concerned about the health of Aunt Bea, as they called the housemother, because she, too, was a chain smoker. To put pressure on Aunt Bea to cut back on her smoking, the girls had decided to stop smoking themselves; none of them had touched a cigarette in several months, and their quiet campaign was having its desired effect.

It is even possible to turn a secure detention center into an effective therapeutic environment, as Sister Mary Paul, former director of social services for the Order of the Good Shepherd, did with Euphrasian Residence, a detention center for girls run by the order under contract with the New York Family Court. "We offered girls all the amenities; we even gave them their choice of three kinds of soap," Sister Mary Paul says, describing the benign but ineffectual institution she found when she took over her post in 1968. "But it was all so trivial, given the kinds of problems the girls faced."

One problem was the almost total unpredictability of the length of a girl's stay. Although a youngster typically arrived with a card promising that her case would be heard in court in three days, she quickly learned that this was simply one more hustle; within half an hour of her arrival, she met girls who had been detained as long as three months. Another problem was the arbitrariness with which judges decided the girls' fates; whether a girl was sent home or to a state training school depended, as often as not, on whether she appeared sullen or contrite. The girls' grapevine spread stories of judicial capriciousness as rapidly and effectively as it spread the story of indeterminate detention.

Before making any changes, Sister Mary Paul spent

months in the courts and probation offices, observing what went on and talking to everyone she could corner. The end result was a program that has become a model of what detention and probation can be, in New York City and anywhere else. The old detention center was converted into a Crisis Intervention Center in which girls normally stay no more than three weeks; Sister Mary Paul extracted a commitment from the Family Court that judges would reach their dispositional decision precisely on the target date. Together with a full, rich dossier on each child, the Sisters give each judge a detailed description of the sentencing options that are available and their own recommendation as to which one is the most desirable. The reports are so persuasive that, in the first four years, there was only one instance in which a judge ignored the Sisters' recommendation.

Euphrasian Residence demonstrates how judges can be helped to make wise and compassionate decisions; it also shows what wise and compassionate care can do for troubled adolescents in a short period, even in a locked facility. Sister Mary Paul and her staff understand that love is not enough. "We're not just kind to children," Sister Marie Elaine, the Residence director, explained to me (although kindness is endemic). "We try to convey to each girl the feeling that 'you *can* do it,' and that we'll teach you how. But we won't lie to them, we won't tell them something is right until it *is* right.

In addition to the psychological testing and social work interviews and counseling it provides, therefore, Euphrasian Residence has made its school an integral part of the program. (The school is staffed by two Board of Education teachers who volunteered for the assignment.) My wife and I stopped off at the school one day for a five-minute visit, more out of politeness than interest; we stayed three hours, and left only because I felt obliged to keep an appointment. When we arrived, the girls were taking a break from their normal school routine, to rest and to prepare for that evening's "Talent Night." Two girls rehearsed a hilarious improvised skit, consisting of a conversation between an exasperating child and her exasperated social worker. Apart from the humor itself, the skit was impressive for the self-awareness and self-mockery that it revealed. Then my wife, Sister Mary Paul, and I chatted with the girls.

It was an extraordinary experience: this was as bright, lively, verbal, and high-spirited a group of kids as we had seen in a long time. What made it extraordinary was in part the kind of self-awareness the two girls had displayed in practicing the skit, in part the agonizing life histories they described, and in good measure our own knowledge that if we had met these girls in almost any other setting—in school, in court, or in some other program—they would have appeared sullen, hostile, dull, apathetic, and completely inarticulate. The difference provided a striking measure of the terrible waste of human potential that our society countenances.*

Unfortunately, detention centers and group homes of this sort are the rare exception. They are more admired than imitated; officials have a way of copying the form (or sometimes just the label) without the substance. Group homes constitute a good example. Because delinquents generally come from disorganized, impoverished, often brutal homes, the reasoning goes, we are more likely to turn them away from crime and toward pro-

---

* Euphrasian Residence's distinctiveness has nothing to do with the fact that it houses girls rather than boys. Every juvenile correctional worker with whom I spoke who has dealt with both sexes told me that delinquent girls were harder to control than their male counterparts.

ductive, law-abiding lives by "placing" them in warm, affectionate, but firm and structured homelike settings than in traditional state training schools. At their best, group homes fulfill their promise, becoming what the psychologist Richard Korn calls "intentional families."

But I have visited group homes, many of them housing only seven youngsters, that are more rigid and repressive than the average training school. In some, the boys or girls in residence are not permitted to keep pictures or other belongings on their dresser tops, to hang posters on their bedroom walls, smoke in their rooms, or have friends visit. Furthermore, dinner is served, institution-style, at five in the afternoon; strapping adolescent boys are not permitted in the kitchen for a snack until breakfast the next morning—and are not permitted to have food in their rooms.*

The overwhelming majority of detained juveniles receive no help worthy of the name. Those who are kept in adult jails receive no services at all—unless being sodomized is classified as a service. Detention centers do provide schooling, as a rule, but not much else. What data are available indicate that only 1 percent of the youngsters in detention receive psychiatric treatment; 15 percent receive counseling from a social worker, and 9 percent from a probation officer. Yet detention center staff believe that eight youngsters in

* In one group home, proudly shown to me as an example of "community-based corrections," boys were not permitted out of the house without an adult for the first four months of their nine-month stay. The regulation made a certain amount of sense; boys had to be socialized into the group home, the director explained, before they could resist the lure of the surrounding streets. What made no sense was to call this "community-based corrections." I do not think I visited any community-based residential programs, moreover, in which the youngsters in residence came from the community in which the program was housed. As I came to realize, "community-based" is simply a "buzz word" for "urban."

ten have some emotional disturbance, half of them of a moderate to severe nature.[19] There is no information at all on *how much* counseling or therapy is provided those youngsters who get any at all; my own observations suggest that it is the rare youngster who sees a psychiatrist, social worker, probation officer, or "counselor" more than an hour a week. "Counseling," especially of a group nature, is more frequent and more extensive in training schools; it usually is aimed at improving inmates' adjustment to the institution, rather than at preparing them to function in the outside world.

Not much more help is given juveniles who escape incarceration. Because of the paucity of statistics, I have had to make rough estimates based on my own, and other students', observations, as well as on what fragmentary data do exist. To understand the basis of the estimates, it is necessary to understand something of how juvenile courts operate, and the ways in which they differ from criminal courts.

One difference involves the way the two courts decide who will, and who will not, be prosecuted, and for what offense—a process known as "intake" in juvenile court jargon. When juveniles are arrested for a crime or brought to court on the complaint of their parents or school authorities, they are interviewed by probation officers rather than by prosecutors These "intake officers," as the probation officers are called, have the major responsibility for deciding whether to file a petition—the juvenile equivalent of prosecution—or to drop or "adjust" the case, i.e., dispose of it through informal nonjudicial means.* In 1974, the latest year

---

* There is a growing tendency to create juvenile prosecutors' offices with power to review intake decisions; in most instances, review is *pro forma,* and the prosecutors do little more than ratify the intake officers' decisions. There also is some sentiment in favor of taking the screening function away from pro-

for which statistics were available when I put the book to press, petitions were filed in only 53 percent of the delinquency cases brought to juvenile court.[21]

Thus intake officers handle the screening function performed by prosecutors in the adult system.* The difference is not just organizational or semantic. Prosecutors' offices are staffed by lawyers who see themselves as law enforcement officials; "intake" departments are staffed by probation officers who see themselves as members of one of the "helping" professions. They have a different orientation as a result. "We don't give retribution for infractions," a Denver intake supervisor explains; "we give remedies for situations."[22]

In general, intake officers are less concerned with assessing guilt and "convictability" than with understanding the juvenile offender's "situation" and selecting the most appropriate "remedy." The intake process is not just a screening device to reduce the judge's caseload to manageable proportions; it is also a way to provide social services and impose social controls without invoking the formal court process. According to one judge, the intake process "is unique because it permits the court to screen its own [cases] not just on jurisdictional grounds, but, within some limits, upon social grounds as well. . . . It provides machinery

---

bation departments and assigning it to an independent agency, located in the executive rather than judicial branch of government.[20]

* Until recently (and in some courts, even now), probation officers also were responsible for investigating the facts of a case, developing and putting them together, and presenting them in court. Hence the probation officer, sometimes assisted by the judge, acted as de facto prosecutor at juvenile trials (or adjudication hearings, as they are called); there was no need for a prosecutor, the argument went, since the proceeding was "on behalf of" and not against the child.

for referral of cases to other agencies when appropriate and beneficial to the child. It gives the court an early opportunity to discover the attitudes of the child, the parents, the police, and any other referral sources."[23] It also gives the court an early opportunity to prejudge the case.

If intake officers decide not to file a petition, they generally have four options from which to choose: the case may be dismissed outright; the juvenile may be counseled and warned, and then released (CWR, in the lingo of some probation departments); the youngster—or the youngster and his family—may receive help from the probation department or be referred to another agency; or the juvenile may be placed on "informal probation."

Except in overloaded urban courts, dismissal is infrequent because it means the juvenile receives no "help" at all.* The most popular "adjustment" is to counsel, warn, and release the youngster. Some intake workers attach great importance to the procedure, and a few I have seen are able to establish rapport with juveniles with surprising ease. Without doubt, some youngsters are deeply impressed with the warning they receive; being "busted" is a frightening experience for any juvenile, especially first offenders, and some intake workers are skillful in using the crisis atmosphere to "reach" youngsters and deter them from further offenses. But given the tiny, noisy, and shabbily furnished cubicles in which most intake officers conduct their interviews, along with the brief time that is avail-

---

* When prosecutors play an active role in intake, the dismissal rate tends to rise sharply; if there is insufficient evidence to sustain a charge, or if the complainant is uncooperative, prosecutors generally drop charges altogether, whereas probation officers prefer to "adjust" the case in some other way.

able, it takes an extraordinary leap of faith to believe
that more than a handful of youngsters really benefit
from the "counseling" they receive.

If an intake worker feels that a juvenile's problem is
too serious to be handled through the CWR procedure,
he or she will choose one of two other options: referral
to another agency or program better able to handle the
problem, such as a mental health clinic, drug treatment
program, or family service agency; or placing the
youngster on informal probation. (Occasionally, an
intake worker will combine both options.) When a
youngster is placed on informal probation, the charge
is not dismissed; it is held in abeyance until the youngster finishes the probation period, which may be anywhere from two to six months, depending on the jurisdiction. If the juvenile fails to observe the terms of the
informal probation—attending school regularly, observing a curfew at home, avoiding bad companions, or
whatever—probation can be revoked and a petition
filed on the original complaint, along with any new
offenses that may have been committed.

On the other hand, when a youngster is referred (or
"diverted") to another program, charges usually are
dropped. The referral may be to another branch of the
probation department itself, or to some other governmental agency or private organization. The latter is
relatively infrequent.[24] Many intake officers do not
know what services are available in their communities;
those who are familiar with outside agencies often are
reluctant to use them because of honest, and often well-
founded, doubts about the quality of the services they
offer. "If I send a hostile, acting-out kid to the mental
health clinic for therapy or counseling," one intake supervisor told me, "the therapist usually calls me in a
couple of days to say, 'I can't work with the boy; he's

too aggressive.' I *know* the kid is aggressive," the supervisor added, almost exploding with anger himself; "that's why I sent him there in the first place!"

Most of the "help" juveniles receive comes from the probation department itself. When one looks at the services themselves, it becomes clear that they do not add up to very much. Even model programs turn out, on closer examination, to provide little more than a few hours of counseling by probation officers. Take the lavishly praised Sacramento County Diversion Program, cited as a national "exemplary project" by the Law Enforcement Assistance Administration. Evaluated in terms of "diversion" alone, the project has been a spectacular success: in its first two years of operation, it cut in half the number of status offenders who were kept in juvenile detention and reduced even more sharply the number of petitions that were filed, without any increase in criminal or illegal behavior. (There was, in fact, a small net reduction in the recidivism rate.) This result lends credence to the view that status offenders can be kept out of juvenile court without endangering society or the youngsters themselves.

But the Sacramento County Diversion Project purports to do far more than keep juveniles away from juvenile court; its sponsors describe it as an exemplary family counseling project as well. By using the techniques of "crisis intervention" and "family crisis counseling," Roger Baron and Floyd Feeney write, the project tries to get a status offender's entire family "to approach the situation not as a question of blame involving a child to be dealt with by some external agency, but rather as a situation involving the whole family and to which the whole family must seek to respond. The attempt is to loosen the family communication processes and to help the family achieve both

the desire and the capability of dealing with the problem." All this is achieved through "immediate, intensive
handling of cases."[25]

Immediate, yes—but not intensive. No family receives more than five counseling sessions, each lasting
one to two hours; the average is only 1.4 sessions per
family, or a grand total of two to three hours of counseling. It defies credulity (and strains the language) to
suggest that in just two to three hours even the most
skilled therapist can "loosen the family communication
processes and . . . help the family achieve both the
desire and the capability of dealing with the problem,"
when "the problem" involves parents so angry or dis-
traught that they have asked the court to remove their
defiant child from home, or adolescents so disturbed
or unhappy that they have run away from home. And
the counselors are not the most highly skilled imagin-
able. One with whom I spent time had had no training
or experience at all; a former guard in Juvenile Hall, he
had "qualified" for the counseling program by passing
a civil-service examination for probation officers.

My purpose is not to denigrate the Sacramento project, but to point out that if the services offered by a
nationally acclaimed program are so meager, it is unlikely that run-of-the-mill "diversion" programs are
any more substantial. Wherever I went, I asked to see
the best programs the city, county, or state had to offer;
the overwhelming majority were as devoid of substance
as the one in Sacramento.

Juveniles who go through the court process are no
better off. Traditionally, juvenile courts have had only
two dispositions available for youngsters adjudicated
as delinquents: placing them on probation, or incarcerating them in a training school, forestry camp, or
ranch. In recent years, a third alternative has emerged
—placement in a group home.

Probation is the most frequently used disposition; it is both a form of punishment—a restriction on a youngster's liberty and freedom of choice—and a means of delivering services to juveniles who need help. Most probation officers I have met prefer the helping role to "playing cop," but most lack the time (and many the expertise) to convert that preference into genuine assistance. In its study of a national sample of juvenile courts, the National Assessment of Juvenile Corrections found that, on the average, probation officers contacted their probationers one and a half times a month, with contacts lasting on average only thirty minutes. It is patently impossible to provide much help to a troubled youngster in forty-five minutes a month—especially when the forty-five minutes are largely devoted to checking up on how youngsters are getting along at home, whether they are attending school (or, if not, whether they are working or looking for a job), whether they are drinking or using drugs, and other forms of surveillance and control.[26]

IV

After seventy-five years of talk about substituting rehabilitation for punishment, it is difficult to find the rehabilitation, and all too easy to find the punishment.*

---

* On a purely quantitative basis—estimating the number of juvenile days of punishment and the number of days of treatment—it would appear that the juvenile justice system provides something on the order of 100 times as much punishment as it does treatment. The estimates are admittedly crude. To calculate the amount of punishment, I multiplied the number of juveniles who were incarcerated in detention centers, training schools, and jails in 1974 by the average length of stay in each. The amount of treatment had to be estimated indirectly, since there are no statistics on the number of juveniles who receive counseling, therapy, or any other social or psychological services in a given year, let alone the number of

One might be able to justify this imbalance if the punishment were directed against juveniles who commit violent crimes. But it is not: although such youngsters account for a significant proportion of the training school population, they represent only a small minority —no more than 10 percent—of those held in juvenile detention centers, and a slightly larger proportion of juveniles in adult jails. Most of the punishment meted out by juvenile courts is directed against youngsters who have committed petty crimes, such as vandalism, shoplifting, and other forms of theft, or offenses that would not be criminal if committed by adults.

The main judicial rationale for treating status offenders more seriously than delinquents is that this is the way to nip delinquency in the bud. "I think that the Status Offenses are among the most serious matters that come before our courts," Judge Lindsay Arthur of Minneapolis, a former president of the National Council of Juvenile Court Judges and a frequent spokesman for the organization, told a 1973 meeting of the National Council on Crime and Delinquency. "Status offenses are the tip of the iceberg, or maybe more appropriately the tip of the volcano. What we see on the surface: skipping some school, staying out late, dating boys that Father doesn't like, these look pretty small and pretty harmless," Arthur continued. *"But there usually is so much under the surface.* Status offenses are the beginning indication of some serious trouble. This is the place where we can help, where we can and

---

hours or days of treatment they receive. As a surrogate for the amount of treatment, I used the number of juveniles on formal and informal probation in 1974, multiplied by the average number of hours of supervision each probationer received —a procedure that almost certainly overstates the treatment provided.

should provide involuntary help if the family is not willing to get involved by itself. *This is the place where we can reduce the crime rates of the future. Because, if we can help a child to unravel incorrigibility, absenting, truancies, drinking, then I think maybe we can prevent children from getting in the future into conduct harmful to others.*" [emphasis added][27]

Arthur's argument in defense of current modes of dealing with status offenders reflects the traditional juvenile court philosophy that judges should respond to what children are and to what they need, rather than to what they have done. To Arthur, as to the majority of juvenile court judges for whom he speaks, what counts is not what the youngster has done but what the judge believes to be the *meaning* of what the youngster has done (or is alleged to have done; standards of proof are a good bit less rigorous for status offenses than for criminal offenses). To repeat Arthur's formulation, "there usually is so much under the surface." And it is what is *under* the surface—what the judge thinks the youngster *will* do, as opposed to what the youngster in fact has done—that forms the basis for judicial intervention.

The result is that in most states a "pretty small and pretty harmless" act, in Judge Arthur's phrase—running away from home, say, or drinking—can lead to a severe and perhaps harmful punishment, such as incarceration in a maximum-security institution. "If you want to get locked up, run away from home," a Minneapolis social worker told me about the city's juvenile court. "If you want to be returned home, commit a burglary." The social worker is not exaggerating by much; 83 percent of the juveniles charged with incorrigibility are held in detention in Minneapolis, compared to 51 percent of those charged with burglary.[28]

Nationwide, status offenders are far more likely to be
detained in secure facilities than are youngsters accused of burglary and other serious property crimes,
and every bit as likely (in some jurisdictions, more
likely) to be detained as youngsters accused of violent
crimes. Moreover, status offenders are less likely to be
released from detention than are youngsters accused of
a crime.[29]

This approach places singular faith in the accuracy
of judges' predictions, as well as in the efficacy of the
"treatments" they prescribe. Youngsters who *might*
cause harm to others in the future often are treated
more firmly than those who already *have* caused harm;
youngsters who are guilty of truancy (regardless of how
bad their school may be) or of refusing to obey parental orders (no matter how unreasonable the orders
or how abusive the parents) may be punished as
harshly as those convicted of robbery, murder, and rape
—for example, by incarcerating them in the same barbarous institutions.

There is no evidence to support judges' faith in their
own, or anyone else's, ability to predict future delinquent or criminal behavior. On the contrary, controlled
experiments such as the twenty-year-long (and, at the
time, much heralded) Cambridge-Somerville Youth
Study have demonstrated the unreliability of such predictions and how counter-productive they tend to be.
When the study began in 1937, its directors asked
teachers, social workers, clergymen, and policemen in
the cities of Cambridge and Somerville, Massachusetts,
for the names of boys they felt were "headed for trouble" and, for purposes of comparison, a group of "average" (or "good") boys. These predictions were then
carefully refined: after each boy had been given a medical examination and his parents and teachers had been

interviewed, a panel of three judges—two social workers and a psychiatrist—made their own expert predictions of the probability that the boy would get into trouble with the law.

Since the boys' delinquent and criminal records were followed until they reached age thirty, and since both the experimental and control groups included youngsters expected to have criminal and noncriminal records, the study provided a clear test of the accuracy of the original predictions. The judges did pretty well in predicting nondelinquency: 88 percent of those expected to be "good" boys had no arrest record by the time they were thirty. But the judges were grossly inaccurate in predicting delinquency: no fewer than 63 percent of the boys expected to be delinquent turned out to be "good" boys, i.e., had not been arrested for a major crime by age thirty. In short, the great majority of "predelinquents" did not become delinquents.* The error appears to be congenital; in a later experiment that tested a different and more elaborate method of predicting delinquency developed by Sheldon and Eleanor Glueck, the New York City Youth Board overpredicted delinquency by an even larger margin.[30]

* Since the hypothesis that was being tested was that without early and substantial intervention "predelinquents" would become hardened delinquents or criminals, it is theoretically possible that the huge overprediction of delinquency was a tribute to the effectiveness of the treatment methods that were used. In fact, it was not. Those predicted to be delinquent were divided equally between the experimental group, which received intensive social work, and the control group, which received none. Moreover, treatment began early—by age ten for 48 percent of the youngsters and by age thirteen for the remainder—and lasted a long time (for four years or more for two boys in three). Yet a larger proportion of the boys receiving treatment than of those in the control group were convicted of at least one major crime. Far from helping, the treatment seems to have had a boomerang effect.

Nor is there any evidence to support the belief that there is an almost inevitable progression from status offenses to serious crimes. Analysis of unpublished data from the Wolfgang cohort study, the largest and most comprehensive body of data on delinquency ever assembled, shows that youngsters whose first offense was a status offense were far less likely to commit another crime than were boys whose first offense was an Index crime. When status offenders did recidivate, they were far less likely to become chronic offenders than were the latter group, and they committed less serious, and fewer, crimes. Indeed, the one-time offenders—youngsters who did not develop into delinquents—were predominantly status offenders, whereas the chronic offenders—those with five or more offenses—typically committed an Index crime as their first offense.[31]

Why, then, do judges persist in treating status offenders more seriously than they treat delinquents?

One reason is a genuine desire to help. It can hardly be denied that many status offenders desperately need help—in overcoming alcohol and drug abuse, in dealing with the turbulence, confusion, and anxieties of adolescent sexuality, in coping with brutal or rejecting parents or with parents so overwhelmed by their own poverty and misery that they are unable to function. To spend time in juvenile courts around the country is to confront the enormous toll that poverty takes from the lives of parents and children.

To spend time in juvenile court is also to witness the massive failure of social welfare agencies and institutions, and, all too often, the callousness or indifference of those who work within them; the juvenile court is a dumping ground for those whom welfare agencies have served badly or are reluctant to serve at all. Understandably, some decent and thoughtful juvenile court judges use their jurisdiction over status offenses, as well as cases of dependency and neglect, as an opportunity to make good the failures—as a chance to knock heads together, to force social agencies to assume their responsibilities. "There is no basis for a finding of delinquency here," a judge told me after hearing arguments on a petition alleging truancy and incorrigibility on the part of an obviously troubled (and frightened) ten-year-old boy. "But the child needs help, and *someone* has to pull it all together." Left unstated was the conclusion evident to anyone in the courtroom: that neither the well-meaning but ineffectual probation officer nor the aggressively insensitive welfare caseworker was about to do that "pulling together." To make sure that the child was referred to a mental health clinic, that the probation officer put him in touch with a Big Brother able to teach him to read, and that the welfare caseworker pry loose enough welfare funds to enroll the boy in an appropriate summer camp program, the judge decided to postpone her finding until the summer, thereby enabling her to maintain jurisdiction until all the arrangements had been made.

Most of the time, judges use their coercive power over status offenders to force youngsters to receive help they otherwise might reject. "The reality is that a lot of kids don't want to go to school, or stay home, or receive treatment for their drug addiction or drinking problem," says the judge I have just described above. "Unless authority is used, the kids just won't receive the help they need; and anytime authority is required, you need a court."

When I began my research, I agreed with the judge; my bias was strongly in favor of intervention. It was only after I had sat in one courtroom after another—. only after I had seen the way judges "helped" children and the human wreckage produced by that help—that I gradually changed my mind. Undoubtedly, some

youngsters benefit from judicial intervention; without
coercion, their self-destructive tendencies might win
out. But far more youngsters are harmed than are
helped.

The real and often serious problems that status offenses present tend to be badly suited, if not totally immune, to resolution (or even amelioration) by the judicial process. Judges and courts are well equipped to
decide whether or not someone committed a particular
act and, if so, what punishment is appropriate. But as
Joseph Goldstein, Anna Freud, and Albert Solnit write,
the "law is incapable of managing, except in a very
gross sense, so delicate and complex a relationship as
that between parent and child."[32] Nor is the law no-
ticeably better able to manage the relationship between
child and school.

When judges do try to manage these relationships,
both they and the youngsters involved tend to get
trapped in a vicious circle from which neither can
escape. The first time a runaway girl appears in court
(and most runaways are girls), the judge is likely to
send her home with a warning that she remain there,
observe a curfew, go to school, and otherwise obey her
parents' orders, which often means no longer seeing her
boyfriend. But without some major change in the home
situation, or without unusually successful therapy or
social work counseling, the youngster is likely to "run"
again. (One study of a sample of runaways found that
three out of four had run away one, two, or three times
before.) The second time, the judge may keep the
youngster in detention for a day or two or three, then
send her home with a warning that the next offense will
bring a much firmer response.

By the third or fourth offense, the judge is trapped;
having put their authority on the line, even the kindest

and gentlest judges feel compelled to follow through on their threats. Since there seems to be no other way to compel the runaway—or truant, or ungovernable child —to obey court orders, and since the runaway is now guilty of the juvenile equivalent of contempt of court, a judge who began intervening in order to help a child ends up punishing the youngster by incarcerating her in a state training school—about the worst "cure" for sexual promiscuity one can imagine. The irony is compounded by the fact that if a girl continues to run away, the judge usually gives up and turns her loose. Judges who try to "cure" truancy end up in the same bind: to order a boy to attend the school that failed to teach him to read and that makes him feel (and, in all probability, has formally labeled him) stupid is almost to guarantee continued truancy.

Watching judges try to help status offenders in this manner, it becomes clear that their desire to help is closely bound up with a desire to assert social control —to reinforce the authority of parents and school officials, to establish the primacy of middle-class norms of behavior (especially sexual behavior), and to require lower-class youngsters to conform to such norms. As the Juvenile Justice Standards Commission wrote, juvenile court jurisdiction over status offenses provides "a kind of moral thumbscrew by which we seek to demand of our communities' children a greater and more exacting adherence to desired norms than we are willing to impose upon ourselves."

In dealing with ungovernable boys, judicial benevolence often is coupled with a strong undercurrent of hostility. For reasons rooted in American attitudes toward adolescents and adolescence, many juvenile court judges seem to find male runaways, truants, and "ungovernables" less attractive and more threatening

than delinquents, whom they view with a benign "boys
will be boys" attitude. "Give me a good clean burglar
anytime, over a messed-up status offender," the director of intake for a large juvenile court told me. "I
think some of the status offenders are some of our
really corrupting types mentally and emotionally," says
Lindsay Arthur, by way of explaining his strong opposition to legislation and appellate court decisions forbidding state corrections departments from putting status
offenders in the same institutions as delinquents. Instead of worrying that status offenders may be cor-
rupted or criminalized by contact with delinquents,
Judge Arthur argues, "Possibly the shoe should be put
on the other foot: we shouldn't have a nice little joy-
rider who took a car just to show off to some girl mixed
in with the *rather cynical and sometimes pessimistic
counter-culture types* that we often get in the Status
Offenses." [emphasis added] Only in the Alice in Wonderland world of the juvenile court—or the Nixon
White House—would cynicism, pessimism, or membership in the counter-culture be considered more serious than theft.

But juvenile court *is* an Alice in Wonderland world
—or more precisely, perhaps, a Catch-22 universe in
which, once entangled, it is difficult for juveniles to
escape the clutches of those determined to help them. If
the youngsters before them did not need help, judges
and probation officers reason, they would not have
been brought to court in the first place. Hence officials
get locked into the need to prove that something is
drastically wrong with the child or the family.

ITEM: A slight, fourteen-year-old boy is in court after
his third or fourth minor scrape with the law. The investigations probation officer urges the judge to "place"

the boy in a residential program while his parents receive intensive counseling. Placement is necessary, the P.O. tells the judge with a straight face, because Johnny is "caught in a cultural crossfire" between his immigrant parents; unable to cope with their radically different child-rearing expectations, he responds by doing the opposite of what they both expect. The home is so damaging, the P.O. argues, that Johnny should be kept in detention (an enormous and repressive maximum-security facility) until the placement has been made—a procedure that will take at least a month, and perhaps a good bit longer.

Fortunately for Johnny, he has an alert young attorney, who makes the following points in rapid order:

• The "cultural crossfire" in which Johnny allegedly is caught is between a Norwegian father and a Swedish mother; the P.O. neglected to mention the parents' nationalities, nor did the judge ask;

• Different parental expectations have not had any adverse effect on Johnny's four older brothers, none of whom have had trouble with the law or with school.

• Johnny's misbehavior did not begin until after a serious accident a year or so earlier. Tests had pointed to the likelihood of brain injury, but his frightened mother refused to authorize the arteriogram and other surgical procedures needed to complete the diagnosis, and instead removed him from the hospital;

• None of Johnny's offenses involved nasty or vicious behavior; a burglary charge to which the P.O. referred had involved his breaking into a summer cottage owned by his parents;

• The boy has already been held behind bars, in a maximum-security detention center, for seventeen days —fourteen more than the law permits.

Judge ——— clearly is reluctant to go against the

P.O.'s recommendation. "I have to believe that Probation has the kids' best interests at heart; they're social workers," he told me at lunch, and at one point in the proceedings he said rather sharply to the defense attorney, "I'm sure that Miss ———— wouldn't make this request if there weren't some reason." But the judge is troubled by the fact that Johnny has been kept in secure detention for so long, in clear violation of state law. After satisfying himself that the boy is appropriately remorseful—"This time I ain't gonna stay with the kids I was staying with," Johnny assures him—the judge decides to let him go home, orders the mother to take him to the hospital for the diagnostic tests, and sets a new hearing date in six weeks, at which time he will make a decision about placement.

The vagueness with which "ungovernability" statutes are drawn makes it easy for judges and probation officers to find a basis for intervention. To prove ungovernability (or "incorrigibility," or "beyond control," or whatever term the particular statute uses), one need only show that the juvenile disobeyed his parents on more than one occasion. The reasonableness of the child's—or the parents'—behavior is statutorily irrelevant; the law usually proscribes *any* behavior that violates a lawful parental command, and judges tend to assume that the child is in the wrong in any parent-child conflict. It is the rare adolescent who has not committed one or more of the offenses with which juveniles have been charged in ungovernability petitions—for example, refusing to bathe regularly, refusing to do household chores, being "selfish and self-centered," and banging a door in response to a parental command.[33] Hence juvenile court judges use ungovernability petitions to establish jurisdiction over youngsters who "need help," but against whom delinquency charges might not be sustained.* "You're much more hung up on due process than I am," one judge told me when I protested that the practice smacked of abuse of judicial power.

There are remarkably few limits on the discretion of juvenile court judges—far fewer, certainly, than there are on most criminal court judges. What limits do exist are of recent origin; it was not until the Gault decision in 1967 that juveniles gained the most elementary standards of due process, such as timely, written notification of the specific charges against them; the right to counsel; the right to question evidence and cross-examine witnesses; and the right to offer testimony in their own behalf. When the Supreme Court handed down its ruling, defendants were represented by counsel in no more than 5 to 10 percent of juvenile cases. In some cities, public defender services now provide first-rate representation to indigent juveniles. But in much of the country representation by counsel remains the exception rather than the rule.[84]

One by-product of the indifference to due process in juvenile court is that judges often read the defendant's "social history" before adjudication. The practice makes it impossible for the defendant to get a fair trial; state appellate courts generally have held that it is a clear denial of due process. (A juvenile has no way of knowing what information is in the social report, let alone of having a chance to correct, explain, or rebut it; and social histories typically contain hearsay evidence and other information that would not be admissible at a trial.) Yet in some jurisdictions, once an

---

* In delinquency cases, the state must prove that the defendant committed a specific act at a specific time. Under most state juvenile codes, moreover, allegations of delinquency must be proved "beyond a reasonable doubt," whereas ungovernability may be established by the less stringent test of "a preponderance of the evidence."

intake officer decides to file a petition, an intake or investigations P.O. routinely prepares the social report,
sometimes with dispositional recommendation as well,
and submits it to the judge.[35] In other jurisdictions
where the social report is not supposed to be submitted
to the judge until after adjudication, the judge may read
it on an informal basis or may be briefed orally on its
contents.

Fred Wiseman's *cinéma vérité* documentary of the
Memphis–Shelby County juvenile court provides a dramatic illustration of the way a judge's familiarity with a
defendant's social history can prevent the youngster
from getting a fair trial. In one of the cases filmed by
Wiseman, a fifteen-year-old boy was charged with
molesting a four-year-old girl for whom he had been
baby-sitting. The boy denied the charge; the only witness against him was the girl's mother, who was clearly
obsessed with her child's sexuality. ("I've never used
boys as sitters before," she told the judge, " 'cause I
have a little girl"; the boy testified that the mother told
him she was afraid to let the girl out of the house
" 'cause winos might jump her.") Whether the boy was
guilty or not seemed to be of no interest to the judge.
"He's capable of doing this," he commented to the defense attorney. "The psychiatric report shows he's disturbed." As indeed he was: his twin brother was seriously ill with Hodgkin's disease. "Regardless of
whether you did this," the judge told the boy, "we've
decided you need help, to straighten out your thinking."

The near-absence of any limits on judges' power to
"straighten out" juveniles' thinking, along with judges'
congenital certainty about the purity of their own motives, makes them particularly susceptible to what one
of the more sensitive of their members, Judge John
Farr Larson of Salt Lake City, calls "the tin god com-

plex." With their staffs of probation officers and other officials, many juvenile court judges have retinues reminiscent of the crowd that is said to have greeted Pope Urban IV with the chant *"Deus es, Deus es"* ("Thou art God, Thou art God"); the judges respond much as did the Pope, who is reported to have replied, "It is somewhat strong, but really very pleasant."[36]

The tin god complex is not unique to juvenile court; it is an occupational hazard of trial judges as a whole. But juvenile courts lack a number of important checks on abuse of power that are present in the adult system. Juvenile court proceedings usually are closed to all but the participants, with outsiders admitted only with the judge's permission. There are sound reasons for this tradition: a small, closed hearing permits a kind of informality and intimacy—a level of human contact between judge and juvenile—that is not possible in the conventional large courtroom; and publicity also can be damaging to children, destroying their privacy and exacerbating the labeling process that is inherent in coming to court. But the disadvantages of privacy may very well outweigh the advantages, for it removes a major check on abuse of judicial power.[37]

More significantly, most juveniles do not have the same right to appeal that adults have. The right to appeal is statutory, rather than constitutional, and some states have not granted the right to juveniles; in others, appeals are heard by trial judges, who are more likely than appellate court judges to uphold another trial court's ruling. In any case, few juvenile court statutes require courts to keep transcripts of juvenile proceedings, and without a transcript it is virtually impossible to file a successful appeal.[38]

Most important of all, juvenile court judges often exercise a kind of absolute reign that is not available to their criminal court counterparts. In many jurisdictions, there is only one juvenile court judge—frequently someone who has held the post for more years than most people can remember. This means that defendants or their lawyers cannot maneuver to bring a case before another judge, which is one of the most important checks on arbitrariness in large criminal courts. Even when the caseload is too big for one person to handle, the juvenile court judge often maintains control through the power to appoint acting judges, referees, or commissioners.

• In the Hennepin County (Minneapolis), Minnesota, Juvenile Court, not so fondly known to participants as "King Arthur's Court," Lindsay Arthur has been the only judge since 1960. The caseload exceeds 5,000 a year; instead of other judges being appointed, the solution, until now, has been for Judge Arthur to appoint five referees, who wear judicial robes and perform most judicial functions. So far as defendants and their parents are concerned, the referees *are* judges; but lacking tenure or even a contract—they serve at Arthur's pleasure—the referees, with one notable exception, are very much Lindsay Arthur's people. Arthur has opposed appointment of other judges because, as he puts it, the referee system guarantees "consistency," whereas another judge might lead to "confusion" or "divisiveness." "We may be consistently wrong," Arthur told my researcher, "but at least we are consistent."*

• The Boston Juvenile Court has only one judge, Francis Poitrast, who appoints attorneys—some of them lawyers who practice in juvenile court—as acting

---

* The consistency may be coming to an end; the Minnesota state legislature has abolished the referee system, effective July 1, 1978, and the governor will be appointing judges to take their place.

judges on a day-to-day basis, according to the caseload;
two or three of Judge Poitrast's appointees usually are
sitting each day. Poitrast also appoints the probation
officers, who serve at his pleasure—a fact that guarantees a Boston version of consistency. (The chief probation officer occupies an office across the hall from
Judge Poitrast's chambers.) Judge Poitrast has been
ruling Boston Juvenile Court since 1964; indeed, that
court has had only five judges in its seventy-year
history.

• As of 1974, the Los Angeles Juvenile Court had
only four judges, supplemented by twenty-two commissioners and one senior referee. Five years earlier, Los
Angeles had had only one juvenile court judge and
twenty-two commissioners, some of whom were probation officers.

It is not surprising that many juvenile court judges
run their courts as if they were medieval fiefdoms, or
that they feel free to make findings of fact and to order
dispositions on the basis of "truths" known only to
them.

ITEM: Judge ——— is given to highly original tru-
isms. Toward the close of one case, he pointed out to
me that Jimmy was "a fat kid," and that "fat kids have
inherent problems." To solve Jimmy's inherent problem, Judge ——— ordered him sent, not to Weight
Watchers, an endocrinologist, or a psychiatrist, but to
a state training school. But then the judge likes to
quote an 1883 Connecticut court opinion holding that
"The boy is not proceeded against as a criminal. Nor
is confinement in the State Reform School a punishment, nor in any proper sense imprisonment. It is in
the nature of parental restraint." Judge ——— exer-
cises that "parental restraint" with some frequency.

V

Far from reducing crime, the preoccupation with status offenses has encouraged criminal behavior in several ways. It has produced a heavy overload on the judicial process, leaving judges and probation officers too little time and too few resources to respond in appropriate ways to juveniles who commit criminal acts. And the frequency with which status offenders have been incarcerated—the fact that there has been little relationship between the seriousness of the offenses committed by juveniles and the severity of the punishment meted out to them—has created a caricature of justice that undermines respect for law. As the Joint Commission on Juvenile Justice Standards commented, "A system that allows the same sanctions for parental defiance as for armed robbery—often with only the barest glance at the reasonableness of parental conduct—can only be seen as inept and unfair."[39]

Some attempts are being made to reduce the unfairness—in particular, to cut back on incarceration of status offenders. The principal catalyst has been the federal Juvenile Justice and Delinquency Prevention Act of 1974, which enjoins states receiving funds provided by the act from placing status offenders in adult jails or existing juvenile training schools and detention centers. Compliance has been slow and spotty, but a few states, among them California, Massachusetts, and New York, have adopted new laws or administrative regulations that seem to be having the desired effect.[40] Nationwide, there appears to be a trend away from "placing" status offenders in state training schools and toward greater use of group and foster homes for both short-term detention and long-term placement. How much of an improvement these "alternatives to incarceration" will be over the institutions they replace remains to be seen. In good measure, the history of the juvenile justice system is one of broken promises and failed reforms; officials have shown an extraordinary talent at neutralizing external pressures for change by pouring old wine into new bottles—more precisely, pouring old wine into old bottles refurbished with new labels.

In any case, reforming the way juvenile courts respond to status offenders leaves unanswered the question of what judges should do to juveniles accused of serious crimes. For reasons I will explain below, some of the solutions being proposed—to lower the age at which juvenile court jurisdiction ends and to permit (or require) juvenile court judges to sentence juvenile offenders to long terms in training schools or prisons—are misguided; they are the legislative equivalent of throwing the baby out with the bath water. This is not to deny that juvenile courts sometimes blunder in their handling of young criminals or that misplaced leniency and archaic procedures encourage the development of criminal careers. It is impossible to spend time with young offenders, as I have done, without being impressed by the contempt in which some of them hold "juvie court" or the degree to which they feel themselves immune to real punishment. "When you're a kid, man, you don't have to worry," one young robber told me. "You don't have to do real time until you're an adult." But the number of such youngsters is smaller, and both the problem and the remedy are considerably more complex, than the attacks on "kiddie court" suggest.

It is easy to understand why juvenile courts have gained their reputation for leniency, notwithstanding the harshness with which status offenders have been treated. In large cities, courts convict only a small proportion of the youngsters charged with serious crimes, and they punish an even smaller proportion. Just how small a proportion is indicated by an analysis the New York State Office of Children's Services made of what happened to every juvenile arrested for a violent crime in New York City in the twelve months ending June 30, 1974. The researchers found records that enabled them to track 90 percent of the arrests—5,666 cases in all.* Some 3,032 cases—53.5 percent of the total—were "adjusted" at intake; charges were dismissed or withdrawn at a later stage in another 1,401 cases in which petitions were filed, and there were 143 acquittals. Convictions were obtained in only 521 cases—9 percent of the total and 20 percent of those actually charged with a crime. Forty percent of those convicted (but only 3.7 percent of those arrested and 8.5 percent of those actually charged with a crime) were punished by incarceration in a training school, prison, group home, or other institution.[41]

Why is the "dropout rate" so high? As in the adult system, the main reason juvenile courts fail to convict arrested offenders is that they lack the evidence needed to sustain the charges—and the main reason they lack the evidence is that victims, witnesses, and other complainants fail to cooperate with the prosecution. In its study of the New York City Family Court, the Office of Children's Services found that fully half the cases that were adjusted at intake, and nearly half those dismissed at a later stage, were dropped because the victim, complainant, or key witness did not show up or was unwill-

---

* The 5,666 arrests involved 4,847 separate individuals, some of whom were arrested more than once, and 3,639 separate crimes. (A significant proportion of juvenile crimes involve more than one offender; looking only at arrest statistics gives an inflated picture of the number of crimes.) The researchers were unable to locate any information about 656 arrests.

ing to proceed. Some of the complainants may have been afraid of reprisal from the offender or his friends; some were satisfied because the juvenile was appropriately remorseful or because restitution was made; and some undoubtedly lost interest because of long delays and frequent adjournment of cases. As in the adult system, too, victims refuse to cooperate because of their prior relationship with the offender; they may become reconciled with the offender or they may wish to conceal what was an unsavory, even criminal, relationship.

Unlike the adult system, policemen and other law enforcement officers made up a significant proportion of the noncooperative complainants. "Assault on a police officer" is an offense that usually is prosecuted with particular vigor; yet 47 percent of the juvenile arrests for that crime were adjusted at intake. Nearly 55 percent of the arrests for possession of a dangerous weapon were adjusted; as with assault on a peace officer, such arrests usually are made on police initiative. Robbery cases, too, were lost because law enforcement officers failed to press charges; one such case involved a public school guard who had to break down a bathroom door in order to stop a robbery in progress but who then declined to follow through.

In assessing the performance of juvenile courts, we need to distinguish between their failure to convict youngsters charged with serious crimes and their failure to give sufficiently tough sentences to those who are convicted. The *Time* cover story to which I referred in the beginning of the chapter illustrates the confusion that can be engendered when critics do not make that distinction or look closely enough at the reasons seemingly guilty offenders are turned loose. To document unwarranted leniency on the part of the New York City

Court, *Time* offered six case histories; the stories show instead how many cases are lost because victims or key witnesses do not testify.

• A twelve-year-old "chicken" (male prostitute) stabbed his "chicken hawk" (homosexual customer); after his wounds were stitched, the customer changed his mind and refused to testify. The prosecutor had no alternative but to drop the charge.

• Three boys aged twelve, thirteen, and fifteen were charged with sexually abusing a thirteen-year-old girl; the girl's mother refused to let her appear and testify. The *Time* story does not indicate whether the mother's action was due to concern over the trauma a court appearance would cause her daughter, fear of reprisal from the offenders, or mere indifference on her part. Whatever the reason, her action made prosecution impossible; here too, charges had to be dropped.

• A fourteen-year-old boy was charged with brandishing a loaded pistol in school; a police department ballistics expert was called as an expert witness to establish the fact that the pistol was operable—essential testimony if a felony charge was to be sustained. The policeman failed to appear twice in a row; the judge set a new date for the hearing, warning the prosecutor that he would have to dismiss the case for lack of prosecution if the witness did not appear at the next hearing, which the *Time* reporter did not attend.

• A fourteen-year-old charged with robbery and assault in the theft of bicycles from two younger children made an "admission," i.e., pleaded guilty to third-degree grand larceny—a lesser charge but a felony nonetheless. As I pointed out in the last chapter, larceny and robbery are almost interchangeable offenses, depending on the amount of force that is used; in this case, one of the victims claimed to have been struck and knocked down, but he was not injured. In any event, the reduction in charge would not have affected the sentencing options available to the judge. (*Time* did not report what sentence was given.)

• In an "intake part," a court which holds hearings to determine whether or not arrested juveniles should be held in detention until trial, a fourteen-year-old boy charged with possession of a loaded .38 revolver was released in his mother's custody; the formal hearing was set for three weeks later. "The kid is now free to buy another gun," *Time* bitingly commented. Perhaps so, but from the information presented in the *Time* account, it would appear that this was the boy's first offense and that he came from a stable family background; detaining him would not have been justified under the state's Family Court Act. (Since the *Time* writer did not attend the formal hearing, the outcome is unknown.) Nor can the boy's release be considered special treatment because of his age; charged with the same offense, an adult first offender with a stable family background would have been released in his own recognizance pending trial—unless the case had been "adjourned in contemplation of dismissal" at the arraignment itself.

• A fifteen-year-old, already detained on a narcotics charge, failed to appear for an intake hearing on a new charge of auto theft. A "chronic absconder," according to the probation officer, the youth had run away from the privately run shelter to which he had been sent on the first charge.

Of the six case histories *Time* offered, only the last involved what might be termed "undue leniency." Even here, one would need more information than *Time* provided to be certain that the court had erred in sending the boy to a nonsecure detention shelter; no one who has visited Spofford, the city's only secure detention center, would send any youngster there except as a last resort.* In the two cases in which charges were dropped, one may regret the fact that seemingly guilty defendants were turned loose; the experience may well have persuaded the youngsters that they were immune from punishment. But the solution cannot be to convict them without the evidence needed to sustain guilt; this is how all too many juvenile courts have operated for all too long. In any event, dismissing charges against a juvenile for failure to prosecute can hardly be called "leniency."

The juvenile court's reputation for leniency is partly to blame for the frequency with which charges are dropped against guilty offenders. Because of their contempt for "kiddie court," policemen often fail to follow through the way they would in criminal court; since nothing is going to happen to the juvenile anyway, they reason, why waste time going to court?† This attitude undoubtedly influences civilian complainants as well; if a policeman tells victims that "nothing will happen to the kid," they, too, may be reluctant to appear in court, especially if an appearance means taking time off from work. The result is a self-fulfilling prophecy: because policemen believe that "nothing will happen" in juvenile court, they (and the citizens they influence) fail to press charges; and because they fail to press charges, violent youngsters go free, thereby confirming the policemen's suspicions.

---

* While I was writing this chapter, the New York City Council's Committee on Public Safety formally recommended that Spofford be shut down and replaced by five smaller detention centers, one in each borough.

† Some of the cases in which policemen failed to press charges undoubtedly represented instances in which the arrest was unjustified. In others, the arrest itself may have been all the policeman had in mind; his goal may have been not prosecution, but to get the juvenile off the street in order to stop a fight or to "put a little fear into him" as a deterrent to future crimes.

The remarkable inefficiency with which juvenile courts are run also contributes to the high "dropout rate." As is true in most big cities, New York's court is plagued with too few judges and probation officers, inadequate mental health facilities, a paucity of secretaries, typists, and clerks, and archaic systems of record-keeping and administration. When I visited the Brooklyn branch, the mental health clinic attached to the court had only one typist; this false economy meant that judges had to wait six to eight weeks for the report of a psychiatric examination to be typed.

That was almost the least of the delays with which the court was, and is, plagued. Intake interviews frequently are not scheduled until a month or more after a juvenile has been arrested, and it sometimes takes as long as eight months after adjudication for the probation department to conduct its investigation and prepare a social history for the judge's use in sentencing. It is commonplace, too, for records to be misplaced or lost. And it is rare for judges to hear all the cases on their dockets on the day they are scheduled; having sat all day, waiting for their case to be called, victims, witnesses, complainants, and defendants learn at five o'clock that they must come back still another day. After a few such experiences previously cooperative complainants may simply refuse to appear again; others may find that their memory has faded.

Even when victims and witnesses do cooperate, their testimony may not be credible enough to prove the defendant's guilt—hence the prosecutor may drop charges or the judge may dismiss the case.* Other

* Delinquents generally receive a fair trial in the juvenile courts in New York City, Washington, D.C., Seattle, Denver, Bridgeport, Connecticut, and a handful of other jurisdictions where judges comply with the spirit, as well as the letter, of the Gault decision.

cases drop out because of a belief that the victim pre-
cipitated the offense, or because the offense seems to
be petty, or the offender insufficiently culpable, to
justify taking up court time. In the Office of Children's
Services study in New York, a large proportion of
the assault cases turned out, on closer examination, to
be little more than street or playground fights that had
gotten out of hand.

Many cases are dropped, however, because judges,
prosecutors, probation officers, and other officials share
a deep-seated conviction that invoking the full sanctions of the juvenile court may make youngsters more,
rather than less, delinquent. "It would probably be
better for all concerned if young delinquents were not
detected, apprehended, or institutionalized," the director of New York State's Division for Youth suggested some years ago. "Too many of them get worse
in our care." The 1973 Standards and Goals Commission reached the same conclusion and called for a 50
percent reduction in the number of criminal cases
disposed of by juvenile courts over the next ten years.
"There are a number of studies which suggest that many
children mature out of delinquent behavior," the Commission wrote. "If this is true, the question is whether
it is better to leave these persons alone or put them in
the formal juvenile justice system. Because there are
no satisfactory measures of the effectiveness of the
juvenile system, there is a substantial body of opinion
which favors 'leaving alone' all except those who have
had three or four contacts with the police."[42]

In practice, big-city courts tend to "leave alone"
youngsters who have had considerably more than three
or four contacts with the police. To begin with, police
departments rarely bring a youngster to court on his
first or second arrest; instead, the juvenile is likely to
be "counseled and released" by the arresting officer or

a member of the police department's juvenile division. The policemen I have met are generally sympathetic to juveniles; many had brushes with the law themselves when they were adolescents. Unless the crime is particularly serious or the victim insistent on prosecution (or unless the juvenile flunks "the attitude test"), most of the cops I know are willing to give young offenders a second or even third chance before referring them to juvenile court. Intake officers know that this is what policemen do; but with heavy caseloads to get through, they often treat the referral as if it were the youngster's first offense and "adjust" the case more or less automatically. The younger a juvenile is, the more likely his case will be adjusted at intake; in the New York study, twelve-year-olds had their cases adjusted a third to a half more often than did fifteen-year-olds.

Age is a mitigating factor throughout the entire criminal justice system: the younger adult offenders are, the less likely they, too, are to be convicted in criminal court and, if convicted, the less likely they are to be incarcerated. For example, twenty-year-olds are sent to prison about two and a half times as often as are nineteen-year-olds arrested for the same offense.[43] Thus a major reason New York Family Court appears so lenient is that its jurisdiction ends at a youngster's sixteenth birthday. In most states, juvenile court jurisdiction ends at age eighteen; since sixteen- and seventeen-year-olds account for more than half of all juvenile arrests for violent crimes and 45 percent of burglary arrests, that two-year difference in the age of jurisdiction has an extraordinary impact on the number of cases that come before a juvenile court and on the way those cases are handled. If the New York Family Court had jurisdiction over juveniles until age eighteen, a much smaller proportion of cases would drop out of court; a larger proportion of offenders would be con-

victed, and more of those who are convicted would be
incarcerated.

Indeed, looking only at juvenile court can provide a
misleading picture of what happens to juvenile offenders. For all its apparent leniency, New York has
the toughest juvenile sentencing policy of any state in
the union: it incarcerates comparatively few youngsters
in juvenile facilities, but it jails large numbers of
sixteen- and seventeen-year-olds. Relative to its total
juvenile population, the state's combined jail and detention rate in 1971 was half again as high as California's
and four to four and one-half times the rate in Illinois,
Ohio, and Pennsylvania.[44] Some of the difference undoubtedly reflected the higher rate of robbery by young
offenders in New York than elsewhere; most of it was
testimony to the freer use of punishment by the adult
system.

VI

If crime is to be brought under control, juveniles must
learn that there are limits to permissible behavior—
that acts such as robbery, rape, burglary, and assault
cannot, and should not, be tolerated by any society.
To explain why criminal violence is more frequent in
lower-class neighborhoods is not to excuse or condone
it; adolescents understand such a response for what
it is—a form of unconscious patronization that denies
them their dignity as full human beings. It is, as well,
a response that penalizes the majority of juveniles
who do conform to the law.

Initially, at least, juveniles *expect* some kind of
punishment when they are found guilty of behavior
that threatens the safety and security of others. If
"nothing happens" until the fourth or fifth offense (or,
in some instances, the ninth or tenth), young offenders

are persuaded that they have an implicit contract with the juvenile court permitting them to break the law. Therefore, when something *does* happen—when a severe sanction is imposed at an earlier point—delinquents feel that their contract has been violated unilaterally, and their sense of justice is outraged. "I was sent here on a bum rap," a youngster in a California training school told me, in tones of great moral indignation. What he meant, I discovered, was not that he was innocent of the robbery charge on which he had been convicted, but that "the judge sent me here on the third offense, instead of waiting until the fifth."

It is hard to imagine a system better designed to reinforce delinquent behavior. This does not mean that delinquents (or adult offenders) are utilitarian creatures, rationally planning their acts and weighing and calculating their relative benefits and costs. What it does mean, David Matza explains, is "that the will to crime is encouraged when the predictable counteracting efforts of official authority are not seen as so menacing and thwarting that the potential offender is immobilized."[45] Juveniles' expectation of punishment is reflected in the street-corner adage, "If you want to play, you gotta pay."

The price that has to be paid should be lower for juveniles, however, than it is for adults. Juveniles are less mature—less able to form moral judgments, less capable of controlling their impulses, less aware of the consequences of their acts. In a word, they are less responsible, hence less blameworthy, than are adults; their diminished responsibility means that they "deserve" a lesser punishment than does an adult who commits the same crime. By "lesser punishment" I mean more sparing use of incarceration; because juveniles are emotionally dependent on their parents in ways that adults are not, removal from the home tends to be a more severe punishment. I also mean significantly shorter terms, for time has a wholly different dimension for children than it does for adults.

The diminished responsibility of juveniles flows from another, equally important, consideration. The socialization of the young is an obligation of the whole society, not just of the parents involved; school attendance is compulsory, and courts have the power to take children away from parents who neglect or abuse them. Thus society bears a responsibility for youth crime that it does not have in the case of adults. To point out that most juvenile criminals are victims as well as offenders is not just an expression of liberal guilt. Their acts must be condemned; but society has an obligation to do more than merely punish them for their offenses.

In the last analysis, it is juveniles' malleability—their capacity for change—even more than their diminished responsibility that creates the need for a different, and more lenient, sentencing policy. Particularly in a society that segregates adolescents from adults, it takes time for youngsters to learn to conform their conduct to societal norms; adolescents who grow up in an environment that offers larger rewards for criminal than for noncriminal behavior need more time than most. Moreover, adolescents are more susceptible to peer pressure than are adults, and their peer groups are more likely to push them toward criminal activity. As youngsters mature, they take on more responsibilities—jobs, wives or husbands, children, installment loans, mortgages. As their stake in society increases, so do the pressures to conform to societal norms. Since the majority of juvenile offenders do in fact age out of crime, it makes sense to respond to juvenile crime with that possibility in mind.

If shorter sentences were all that were involved,

there would be no need for a separate juvenile court; criminal court judges could simply take a juvenile's age into account in setting the sentence. But more *is* involved. Juveniles' capacity for change means that less stigma should be attached to conviction and punishment of a juvenile than of an adult; a teenager's criminality should not hang over him like a cloud for the rest of his life. Although it would be naïve to suggest that the juvenile court has eliminated stigmatization, as its early advocates had hoped, the stigma nonetheless is milder and less enduring than that provided by the criminal courts.

More important, juveniles' capacity for change means that punishment ought to be accompanied by help. It has become fashionable of late to belittle (in some circles, almost to sneer at) the idea of rehabilitation. We may not know enough to help every troubled juvenile; we do not know so little that we ought to stop trying. If rehabilitation has largely failed (and it has), the remedy is not to abandon the effort with an air of sophisticated disillusionment; it is to try to understand why, and to intensify the search for approaches that offer some hope of working. This, after all, is what we would do if our own children were involved. Juveniles should not be incarcerated, or their liberty restricted in other ways, for the *purpose* of rehabilitation. But once the decision to punish a youngster has been made, there must be a serious attempt to provide whatever help he needs to become a productive member of society.

In the best juvenile courts, sentencing decisions are made with more care and more knowledge than in the best adult courts; judges make an honest effort to balance the need to punish with the obligation to provide offenders with the help that might make change possible. The best juvenile courts also operate on a human scale that is hard to capture in criminal court. The informality of the proceedings, the smaller size of the courtroom, the absence of a raised platform on which the judge sits—all encourage a person-to-person contact between judge and child that makes it easier for the defendant to see the judge as a full human being and not as an abstract and forbidding embodiment of The State. Juvenile offenders often cover up their fear with an air of bravado or defiance; the atmosphere of a good juvenile court also makes it easier for the judge to cut through the barriers the juvenile may have erected—to see the defendant as an adolescent (or child) with strengths and weaknesses, virtues and vices, rather than as a "case" or "file" to be moved along as rapidly as possible.

To be sure, some juveniles are so brutalized, so hardened in their criminality, that it may be quixotic to talk about their capacity to change; their crimes are too horrible to apply the concept of diminished responsibility. But their number is not large enough to abandon the institution of the juvenile court. In 1976, the police arrested nearly two million youngsters under the age of eighteen; but fewer than 75,000—3.8 percent of all juvenile arrests—were for the four violent crimes in the FBI Crime Index. Some of those crimes were brutal and vicious, causing serious injury or profound trauma to the victims; others were not. As we have seen, taking a basketball away from another youngster on a school playground may be called robbery, and a schoolyard fight may be counted as aggravated assault. Only a small fraction of juvenile arrests were for crimes so vicious that they required punishment more severe than those available to the juvenile court.*

* Since February 1, 1977, fourteen- and fifteen-year-old New Yorkers charged with committing a "designated felony" such as murder, armed robbery, aggravated assault, or rape have

The most sensible way to respond to criminal violence by juveniles is through waiver to criminal court. Instead of decreeing draconian punishments that could be applied indiscriminately, thereby destroying the distinctive qualities of juvenile court, youngsters whose crimes are so terrible that only criminal court sanctions will suffice ought to be tried in criminal court. Most juvenile courts have the right to waive jurisdiction in criminal cases and transfer the defendant to criminal court. Because the consequences are so profound (life imprisonment or the death penalty, in some instances, instead of a three-to-five-year maximum), waiver should not be a casual affair. Decisions ought to be made on a case-by-case basis, and there should be a presumption that juvenile court jurisdiction will be retained unless a number of conditions are met.*[46]

Use of waiver would make it possible to keep juvenile court jurisdiction until age eighteen while satisfying the public's desire to see hardened criminals punished. One can construct a plausible case for ending juvenile court jurisdiction at any age from sixteen on. But in recent years the eighteenth birthday has become the dividing line between innocence and responsibility; eighteen is the age at which suffrage begins, at which

---

been tried in a separate "designated felony part" of the Family Court; if convicted of a Class A felony, they must be committed to the State Department for Youth for five years, with a minimum of one year in a secure facility and a second year in an open residential setting. In the first eleven months, only 608 such petitions were filed.

* Under the standards proposed by the Juvenile Justice Standards Commission, waiver would be limited to sixteen- and seventeen-year olds who have committed offenses for which the maximum sentence for an adult would be death, life imprisonment, or imprisonment for a term of more than twenty years. To be eligible for waiver, juveniles also would have had to have been convicted at least once before of an offense involving "the infliction or threat of significant bodily injury."

the military draft (when it is operative) begins, and, in a good many states, at which someone may legally marry, and buy (and consume) liquor. All told, the eighteenth birthday seems to be the most plausible place to draw the line between juvenile and adult status.

Wherever the line is drawn, there will be large disparities in the sentences faced by youngsters whose age difference is as little as one day. The solution is not to treat all juveniles as adults, but to recognize that passing the magic birthday does not transform an adolescent into an adult. In actual practice, most juvenile and criminal court judges take age into consideration; adult criminal codes often permit (or mandate) separate institutions for those under twenty-one. Explicit recognition that the transition from childhood to adolescence to adulthood is gradual would make sentencing policy more rational and less disparate.

The critical defect of juvenile court is that it is a musclebound institution. To be more effective in dealing with youth crime, judges desperately need a broader range of sentencing options than they now have. In particular, they need an array of noncustodial punishments—ways of responding to delinquent or criminal behavior that make it clear that sanctions *are* being imposed, without incarcerating or otherwise damaging the youngsters in the process. As things now stand, judges generally face a Hobson's choice between dispositions that are either too lenient or too harsh. In big cities, in particular, it is rare for there to be anything in between probation and incarceration. The latter is harsh and may be damaging; the former hardly differs from dismissal.

Some judges use probation more freely than they would wish because they are reluctant to send any but the most hardened criminals to state training school. (The real purpose of probation, Charles Shireman suggests, is to make it possible for judges to appear to be "doing something about crime" without having to incarcerate anyone.) Other judges use incarceration freely for lack of another option. "I cry when I put a kid in jail, and I probably put more away than anybody," says Judge George Nicola of Middlesex County, New Jersey. Nicola acknowledges that "kids come out worse than when they go in," and he tells stories of youngsters who have been sodomized and otherwise sexually assaulted in the institutions in which he placed them. "But what the hell is left between freedom and that?" he asks. "I'm not a reformer of institutions. All I can do as a judge is use what they give you and be frustrated."[47]

Under present circumstances, therefore, juvenile courts tend to underreact or overreact. The latter is more frequent in smaller communities, such as Nicola's; in big cities, where youth crime is high but where judges have all they can do to get through each day's caseload, they are more likely to underreact. The result is to confirm delinquents' conviction that they can break the law with impunity.

Juvenile courts need not be so restricted. "I agree that prosecution must be vigorous. I only ask that punishment be neglected in favor of *control*," the psychiatrist Robert Coles, hardly a hard-liner, has written. "I have been tricked and fooled enough by sly, criminally bent youths to know the folly of meek, naive trust which is for the criminal involved but an invitation for his contempt or manipulative zeal. Many of our criminals need every bit of watching, every bit of emphatic authority over them and their inclinations that our society can muster," Coles continues. "Too often have psychiatrists been placed in the camp of those fatuous caricatures of the kindly whose recommendations for 'clemency' or 'understanding' become all too quickly invitations for more crime. . . . Crime in America today needs every bit of control we can arrange, control of our own passions and confusions as well as those of our criminals."[48]

Putting the emphasis on social control opens up a variety of sentencing options, making is possible to convert probation into a useful and effective sanction, as the probation department of the Salt Lake City Juvenile Court has done. (Although Salt Lake City is atypical in many respects, its approach to probation can be applied just as easily in larger, more ethnically and racially diverse cities.) "Field probation"—the branch concerned with supervising juveniles found guilty of some offense—has been decentralized into six Neighborhood Probation Centers, usually located in a big house that is furnished as if it were a home. Casually dressed young men and women who are called probation counselors (rather than probation officers) are able to meet their charges in an informal, homelike atmosphere, instead of seeing them across a desk in the ugly cubicles usually assigned to probation officers in the courthouse or a nearby government office building. The change is more than cosmetic. Counselors have been relieved of responsibility for investigating a case when a probationer is returned to court on another complaint; the intake department now handles all investigations.

Probation counselors continue to play the "cop" role if their charges violate the terms of their probation —by cutting school, for example, or by not attending a drug rehabilitation program or mental health clinic. The counselors are able to do this without destroying their relationship with the youngsters because of the way terms of probation are established and reviewed. When a juvenile is first placed on probation, the youngster, his family, the entire team of probation counselors attached to the neighborhood center, and the judge together develop a probation program. The program is then formulated as a contract, which all the parties—the child, the parents, the probation counselor, and the judge—sign in a formal ceremony.

Equally important, the terms of the probation contract are monitored periodically by the judge who signed it. Every two or three months, the judge conducts an informal hearing in the Neighborhood Probation Center, at which the probation counselors, the youngster in question, and the family go over the probationer's progress since the last hearing. Because the judge has traveled to the probation counselors' turf, they are less defensive than they would be if they had to appear in court; the same is true for the kids themselves. Sitting in a room furnished as if it were a den or living room, the judge, probation team, and probationer can review progress and problems in a relaxed, informal manner.

The probation contract, together with periodic judicial review of a probationer's progress, puts probation counselors in a different relationship with their probationers. Juveniles know that their counselor will be asked whether they are fulfilling the terms of the contract; they also know that while a little bending of the truth may be possible, outright lying to the judge is not. Hence counselors can say to a youngster, "Look, I might be willing to overlook what you're doing, but I signed the contract, too; when the judge asks me how you're doing, my job is on the line." This makes it a good bit easier for counselors to enforce the terms of probation without losing their probationers' respect or trust.

The hearing thus converts probation into an effective form of social control. If a youngster has been violating the terms of the contract in a serious way, the judge may warn him that if the next report is also unsatisfactory, he will be sent to the state training school—harsh treatment, perhaps, but at least the youngster knows in advance what the punishment will be if he continues to violate probation. If the next report is unsatisfactory, the judge often will order the youngster to the training school but stay the order for another month or two. The advantage of this approach, Judge John Farr Larson suggests, is not only that it gives the child a second chance, but that it makes it possible for the judge to respond in a positive way—canceling the order—if the youngster's behavior improves.

The hearing provides other opportunities for positive reinforcement. If a probationer has been living up to the terms of probation, the judge may modify the initial order or indicate what changes will be made at the next hearing if the good behavior continues.

ITEM (from notes of a Salt Lake City probation hearing): One boy, who had been living with his sister because of problems at home and in his neighborhood, was particularly eager to return to his mother, and he rebutted each of the judge's objections about transfer to a new school with information he had obtained himself in preparation for the hearing. It was a bravura performance: after a lengthy exchange of opinions and information, the judge was persuaded that having demonstrated perfect behavior for three months, the boy was entitled to test his ability to return to the old neighborhood. It is difficult to imagine anything remotely like this taking place if the hearing had been held in the courtroom itself.

At times, the judge may terminate probation altogether as a result of the hearing.

ITEM: One hearing, in which probation was terminated, was particularly moving. When the judge had signed the termination paper, the youth's mother, a poorly dressed, poorly educated woman, asked, "Judge Garff, may I please say something?" Since the question was rhetorical, she continued, "I just want to say how much I appreciate what you and all the probation counselors have done for my son. I felt so safe knowing you were here. When he needed firmness, you were firm—and when he needed a little understanding, or a little leeway, you gave him that. I just can't thank you all enough."

As the last anecdote suggests, probation counselors are able to provide help as well as control. In part, they simply play the traditional probation role of helping youngsters "slide" between the demands of their peer groups, on the one hand, and the demands of their parents, teachers, and the police, on the other; much of what a good probation officer does is to teach juveniles how to avoid "bugging" authorities, and to teach authorities to be more tolerant of juvenile behavior.[49]

Salt Lake City probation counselors do more than that. Having their offices in a house, rather than in a usual court building rabbit hutch, makes it possible for counselors to meet frequently as a collegial team to discuss mutual problems and to share insights, rather than (as is so often the case) to gossip about their charges. Their emphasis is less on turning their youngsters' head around than on changing the youngsters' home or school environments—for example, getting a child moved from one teacher (or one school) to another, persuading parents to use different methods of discipline—so that the kids can function more effectively and thus feel better about themselves. "We try to take the shrink out of counseling," Carlon Cooke, Director of Probation, explains.

The Salt Lake City approach does not exhaust all possibilities. The Massachusetts Department of Youth Services (DYS) is trying another promising-sounding approach to probation called "tracking." By assigning counselors to youngsters on a 1:1, or 1:2, or at most 1:4 basis, the "trackers" can make sure that the boy gets up on time, leaves home on time for school or work, stays at school or work for the requisite period of time, attends the assigned after-school or after-work counseling or tutoring or therapy program, and so on. Tracking thus supplies intensive supervision and control to youngsters who otherwise might need institutionalization; the hope is that, after a month or two, youngsters will be able to function successfully in a more conventional probation or parole situation. And tracking, even with a 1:1 or 1:2 ratio, costs less than institutionalization.

These methods of control can be supplemented with other sanctions such as requiring youngsters to make restitution by spending nights or weekends working in some form of community service or depriving them of their right to drive for a time—a severe sanction for adolescent boys in most parts of the country. And if these approaches do not work, it is possible to step up the level of punishment through use of "periodic detention," a technique New Zealand has been using with juvenile offenders since 1962.[50] Periodic detention provides a sanction more severe than probation but considerably milder than a term in a training school. As practiced in New Zealand, young offenders who have violated probation must report to a detention center on Friday evening; they work hard at some community service job on Saturday and return home around noon on Sunday. Failure to report means full-time incarceration; since the threat is carried out, it is rare for youngsters not to report.

The work that is done is real, not the make-work characteristic of most prisons and training schools; the youngsters work in nursing homes, shelters for unwed mothers, housing developments for the elderly, and so on. Performing some real community service is valuable for the juveniles. Many poor youngsters have never had the experience of being in a position to help someone else. They have always been on the receiving end, a debilitating and degrading experience; to become full adults, they need to learn how to give as well as to receive.

Periodic detention provides considerable flexibility; a judge can step up the punishment without having to go all the way from probation to training school. If weekend detention does not work, a youngster might be kept until Monday morning instead of being sent home Sunday afternoon. If that doesn't work, one or two nights a week might be added; and if *that* doesn't work, the youngster might be kept in detention every night, going to school (or to work) in the morning and returning to the detention center when school or work ended. Each increase involves a significant loss of liberty, but without the disruption of schooling, work, or family life that incarceration in a training school entails.

If a juvenile court is to provide help as well as control, it needs a wide variety of social services, in addition to punishments, at its disposal. Although judges and probation officers generally complain about the shortage of resources, most do not begin to use the resources that are available—often because they do not know that they exist. The best way to remedy this lack of knowledge and to improve the overall quality of juvenile sentencing is to turn the dispositional (or sentencing) hearing into a fully adversarial process. For this to happen, a strong public defender service is essential. (The majority of juvenile defendants are indigent.) The public defender services in Washington, D.C., Seattle, Minneapolis, and Contra Costa County, California, and the juvenile division of New York City's Legal Aid Society give daily evidence that defender services can provide representation of the highest quality.

To discharge their responsibility to their clients, public defender services need their own staffs of social workers and paraprofessionals, who often are able to uncover a wide variety of social services and sentencing options unknown to the probation department.

ITEM: In 1969, the Santa Clara County (California) public defender office, by way of an experiment, hired two social workers to help prepare presentence reports. In three months of field visits, the social workers came up with eighty-one programs that were unknown to the probation department or to the court; most of the programs had never before considered the possibility of accepting court referrals. As a result, the defender office lawyers were able to recommend probation with a treatment plan geared to the offender's specific needs; in contrast, the probation department tended to recommend a jail sentence followed by probation, but with no treatment during the probation period. (The defender's social workers and the P.O.s recommended the same sentence in only 18 percent of the cases.) Although the defender reports provided extensive background information on the defendant, the probation department reports contained little more than a description of the offense and a recitation of the defendant's prior record.

A staff of social workers, ex-probation officers, retired policemen, and ex-offenders is essential for a number of other reasons. Former policemen and rehabilitated offenders play a crucial role in investigating the facts of a case, often uncovering new information. Working with social workers or former probation officers, they make it possible for the defense lawyer to turn the dispositional hearing into more than just a ceremony to affirm the decision that already has been made. Ex-offenders are useful also because they know the neighborhoods from which juvenile (and adult) offenders come, and because they often are more skilled than anyone else in determining whether a youngster is genuinely remorseful or is simply skilled at "conning" adults.

Social workers or retired probation officers perform two additional functions. They subject the probation department's social history and sentencing recommendation to a professional critique. Social histories often lack vital information or contain errors or easily rebutted psychiatric judgments—as in the case of the boy caught in "the cultural crossfire" between his Norwegian father and Swedish mother—and sentencing recommendations often are made in a routine, *pro forma* way. When they know that their reports will be analyzed by people with equal professional knowledge, P.O.s tend to prepare their reports with far greater thought and care.

With services of this sort available, lawyers tend to define their role in a broader and more appropriate manner. As Judge Kay McDonald of the New York City Family Court put it when she directed the Legal Aid Society's juvenile division in Manhattan, a defense lawyer should be "a lawyer-plus"; in the formulation of Assistant Attorney General Barbara Babcock, a former director of the District of Columbia Public Defender Service, a lawyer should be "a learned friend and wise counselor." One of the most significant by-products of the Santa Clara experiment was that lawyers began to see themselves in this light. One lawyer, who in the past had spent no more than fifteen minutes discussing sentencing alternatives with a client, discovered that he was now spending two hours or so going over the social worker's recommendations with a client before the dispositional hearing.

Some lawyers balk at this sort of expansion of their role, protesting that they are lawyers, not social workers. As the American Bar Association Standards Relating to Sentencing Alternatives and Procedures pointed out with disapproval, "Many lawyers view their functions at sentencing to involve superficial incantations of mercy; others merely seek the lightest possible sentence without much concern for the real needs of the defendant. Few, in any event, undertake the type of preparation which the sentencing procedure calls for, and which is a commonly understood duty at preceding stages of the case."

What defense lawyers do about disposition usually is the most important service they render their clients, since the overwhelming majority of clients are convicted through a plea of guilty, rather than at trial. Good defense lawyers do not simply rely upon the expertise available through the public defender service; their own energy and imagination can play a significant role.

ITEM: Working with his client's probation officer as well as the defender service's own staff, a Seattle public defender managed to persuade the prosecutor that attending a Job Corps center in Montana was a more appropriate disposition than committing the youngster to state training school; the seventeen-year-old boy seemed eager to learn a trade and "straighten himself out." As a result, the prosecutor joined the defense lawyer and the P.O. in "selling" the idea to the judge.

When defense lawyers represent their clients in this way, they are doing no more than what corporate lawyers routinely do for their clients. There is something disingenuous, in fact, about defense lawyers protesting that they want to be lawyers, not social workers. Lawyers involved in litigation with the antitrust division, the Securities and Exchange Commission, or the Environmental Protection Agency do not limit their role because they lack expertise in economics, corporate finance, and engineering; they master the specialized knowledge they require in order to be effective advocates for their clients. It is perfectly reasonable to demand, as the Juvenile Justice Standards Commission put it, that "counsel must be familiar with the alternatives formally available to the court and, equally important, with the actual character of those dispositions."[51] And it is not surprising that in courts such as those of Seattle and the District of Columbia, where this approach is routine, judges told me that their sentencing decisions are based on far more—and far more *accurate*—information than they used to have, or than they currently receive in most cases where a defendant is represented by private counsel. (The public defender services make these forms of assistance available to court-appointed and privately retained attorneys, but such lawyers rarely take advantage of them.)

Having a wide range of sanctions at their disposal makes it possible for juvenile courts to overcome one of their most serious defects: the absence of any relationship between the punishment youngsters receive and the seriousness of the offenses they have committed. A revised juvenile code should lay down statutory maximum dispositions for each offense, or group of offenses, with the nature and severity of the maximum penalty being proportional to the seriousness of the offense. The most severe penalty should be incarceration in a secure facility for two or, at most, three years; juveniles who need to be incarcerated for a longer period of time are criminals so hardened that they probably should be waived to criminal court. Incarceration should be prohibited for petty offenses, such as vandalism and shoplifting, and there should be a strong presumption against incarceration of first or second offenders charged with any nonviolent crime. In general, maximum juvenile sentences should be scaled down substantially from those that prevail in the criminal code, perhaps along the lines suggested by the Juvenile Justice Standards Project.[52] But in no case should a judge be permitted to give a juvenile a sentence more severe than the maximum an adult could receive for the same offense.*

This approach would mean, at the least, that incarceration of status offenders would be prohibited. By implication, it means that most status offenses should be abolished altogether; in general, courts should have jurisdiction over juveniles only when they engage in behavior that would be criminal if committed by an adult. But it would be a mistake to abolish jurisdiction altogether, or to pretend that doing nothing will solve the real problems with which incorrigible and acting-out children are plagued. On the contrary, calling for abolition of status offenses is what Franklin Zimring

---

* The most notorious such instance involved Gerald Gault, whose appeal led to the Supreme Court's ruling in *In re Gault*. The fifteen-year-old Gault was committed to the Arizona state training school until his majority—a potential term of six years —for allegedly making an obscene phone call "of the irritatingly offensive, adolescent, sex variety," as Mr. Justice Fortas described it. Had he been an adult, Gault would have been subject to a maximum sentence of two months in jail. (One has to refer to Gault's offense as "alleged." The complainant was not present at the adjudicatory hearing, nor did the judge speak to her at any other time; no witnesses were sworn, and no transcript or record of the proceeding was made.)

calls "an empirically based choice of the least worst alternative policy"—a judgment not that nonintervention is desirable, but that too little intervention is likely to do less damage to children than too much intervention.[53]

There are times when intervention may be necessary; any revised code should provide for short-term intervention in clearly defined and sharply circumscribed crisis situations—holding a runaway for twenty-four hours until parents can be contacted, for example, or using the coercive power of the court to put a suicidal youngster in touch with a psychiatrist.[54] Provisions of this sort, along the lines proposed by the Juvenile Justice Standards Project, might be extended in another way, as Zimring suggests: juvenile court jurisdiction might be based on a presumption of nonintervention, but a revised code might make provision for parents or others to rebut that presumption in situations in which a child's mental state or capacity to make rational decisions indicate that a "hands off" policy would be damaging to the child.

In the approach to sentencing policy proposed here, the notion of proportionality, or "just deserts" (making the punishment fit the crime), would determine the maximum sentence for each offense. Judges would have discretion to give less than the maximum; it is even harder in the juvenile than in the adult system to define offenses with the precision needed to mandate sentences in advance. Juvenile offenses frequently are committed in groups, with culpability varying widely—from a leader who plans the crime to a younger child who goes along reluctantly, out of fear of being ostracized or ridiculed, or even beaten up. And, as I have pointed out, there are big differences in the seriousness of the crimes lumped under any one offense category.

Discretion is needed, too, if a judge is to give any

weight at all to the best interests of the child as well as of the state. Just as culpability varies from one participant in a given offense to another, so does the willingness to accept limits, the desire to change or to accept help of one form or another. Juveniles' malleability makes it inappropriate to require the same sentence for everyone. While some offenders may need a secure institution, others might only have their violent tendencies exacerbated, and some are almost certain candidates for victimization.[55]

Abuse of power can be reduced if judges publish, and periodically review, their own rules for intake and dispositional decisions, along the lines I suggested for criminal courts. (Intake decisions are an integral part of sentencing policy; in deciding which cases will be petitioned and which adjusted, intake officers are deciding who will be eligible for punishment.) Guidelines need not be limited to formal rules; they may be laid down in the form of hypothetical examples, drawn from real life, with alternative responses suggested for each situation. Guidelines may also define situations or circumstances in which discretion is desirable or required. What is crucial is that the people who actually make the decisions participate in drawing up the guidelines and in reviewing—and revising—them at regular intervals.

A major advantage of guidelines for intake and judicial discretion is that they can make punishment more predictable, thereby enhancing the deterrent power of the court. It makes good sense for a court to adopt the often used "three strikes and you're out" approach, with the definition of "out" varying according to the seriousness of the offense. For minor offenses, such as shoplifting and other forms of larceny, the first arrest might mean automatic adjustment of the Counsel, Warn, and Release variety; a second arrest would carry a presumption of adjustment, with informal probation; and the third arrest would mean automatic petition to the court, with formal probation as the likely sentence. For moderately serious crimes—burglary, say, or unarmed robbery with no injury or threat of injury—"strike one" might mean adjustment with informal probation or, in more serious cases, petition with a sentence of probation. Thus a second arrest would mean an automatic petition with restrictive probation or periodic detention, and a third would carry a rebuttable presumption of placement in a training school. The cost of each "strike" would be higher with serious crimes.

This is the approach that adults who work effectively with adolescents often adopt on intuitive grounds. Since adolescence involves a frequent testing of limits, one has to assume that adolescents will miscalculate where the limits are and where they will be imposed. If they are to learn from their miscalculations—if they are to develop their own controls as a result of such learning —they need time and psychological space in which to readjust their calculations.[56]

In deciding the balance between punishment and rehabilitation, another principle should be applicable as well. The principle is contained in a story about the great educator Horace Mann, who was invited to speak at the dedication of a juvenile reformatory; Mann's thesis was that all the money being spent for the reformatory would be justified if only one child were to be saved. When he had finished, a cynical listener asked Mann if he had not let his enthusiasm run away with him. Wasn't Mann exaggerating, the listener demanded, when he said that the whole expenditure would be worthwhile if it saved a single child? Horace Mann's reply was brief but eloquent: "Not if it were my child."

10

"To Reclimb the Slope": The Limits of Correctional Reform

> The descent to hell is easy
> The gates stand open day and night
> But to reclimb the slope
> And escape to the upper air
> This is labor . . .
>
> —VIRGIL, *The Aeneid*

> True sanction of political laws is to be found in the penal legislation; and if that sanction is wanting, the law will sooner or later lose its cogency. He who punishes the criminal is therefore the real master of society.
>
> —ALEXIS DE TOCQUEVILLE, *Democracy in America*

> When a sheriff or a marshal takes a man from a courthouse in a prison van and transports him to confinement for two or three or ten years, this is our act. We have tolled the bell for him. And whether we like it or not, we have made him our collective responsibility. We are free to do something about him; he is not.
>
> —CHIEF JUSTICE WARREN BURGER

I

"The American correctional system today appears to offer minimum protection to the public and maximum harm to the offender," the 1973 Standards and Goals

Commission declared in its summary report. "The system is plainly in need of substantial and rapid change."

It always has been. Except for a brief period of euphoria in the early nineteenth century, when penal reformers from around the world came to the United States to study that American invention the penitentiary, there never has been a time when the correctional system did not appear to be in need of rapid and substantial change. Since the Republic was founded, the historian David Rothman has written, each generation has produced "a dedicated coterie" of prison reformers. Yet each generation "discovers anew the scandals of incarceration, each sets out to correct them and each passes on a legacy of failure. The rallying cries of one period echo dismally into the next."[1]

For nearly two centuries, in fact, prison reformers have been trying to create an institution that could punish without brutalizing. The ball and chain and the rock pile are gone, along with enforced silence, lockstep marching, and other harsh disciplinary methods designed to keep prisoners docile and compliant. Yet prisons, especially the maximum-security institutions which contain the majority of the inmate population, remain brutal, and brutalizing, places. In the last few years, federal courts have held that living conditions in prisons in Alabama, Arkansas, Florida, Louisiana, Mississippi, and Rhode Island have violated the Eighth Amendment's prohibition against "cruel and unusual punishment."

Americans also have looked to prisons to reform the criminals confined within them. The Quakers of the early nineteenth century thought that if prisoners were kept in solitary confinement, they would have time to reflect on their sins; with nothing to do but read the Bible, penitence and prayer would stimulate inmates' consciences and produce a reformation of their character. Others had more modest goals. "I do not believe in a complete reform, except with young delinquents," Elam Lynds, the first warden of New York's Auburn and Sing Sing prisons, told Beaumont and Tocqueville in 1831. His aim was to change his inmates' behavior rather than their character—to make them, if not better, at least more obedient to the criminal law. In Lynds' view, this was "the only reform . . . which society has a right to expect."[2]

Rightful or not, the expectation has not been met. As instruments of punishment, prisons have been a resounding success; they never have achieved their goal of rehabilitation. Over the last half-century, one crime commission after another has criticized prisons for their failure to rehabilitate inmates and has called for new approaches to achieve success. "We cannot hope to make serious progress in our attempts to reduce the number of crimes committed or the proportion of criminals to the general population without discovering ways and means sharply to modify the organization and administration of our penal and correctional institutions," the 1931 Wickersham Commission declared. "For a great many offenders," the 1967 Crime Commission wrote, "corrections do not correct. Indeed, experts are increasingly coming to feel that the conditions under which many offenders are handled, particularly in institutions, are often a positive detriment to rehabilitation." Hence the Commission recommended greater use of community-based correctional programs, both residential and nonresidential, as a substitute for incarceration in traditional prisons.[3]

The Crime Commission's faith in the possibility of rehabilitation has given way to pessimism and doubt. The last ten years have seen a flood of scholarly literature documenting the failure of one approach after another. "With few and isolated exceptions, the rehabilitative efforts that have been reported so far have had no appreciable effect on recidivism," the criminologist Robert Martinson wrote in 1974, summing up the conclusion he and two colleagues had reached after evaluating some 231 research studies. Whether incarcerated or placed on probation, whether given psychotherapy, group counseling, job training, or no assistance at all, the proportion of offenders who return to crime seems to be about the same—roughly one in three.*[4] If recidivism is the same whether offenders are incarcerated or not, scholars and reformers argued, criminals could be kept in the community without endangering the public.

For a time, it looked as though the United States was moving away from the heavy reliance on incarceration that had characterized the past. When I began my research in 1972, "de-institutionalization" and "community-based corrections" had become popular terms; Massachusetts had just closed its juvenile training schools; and a number of states were reducing their adult prison populations. At the 1972 year-end, there were 11 percent fewer people in state and federal prisons than there had been in 1961, despite a nearly two-and-one-half-fold increase in the number of Index crimes. The decline in prison population represented

---

* Recidivism statistics are even less reliable than other crime statistics. What figure one gets depends heavily on the way recidivism is defined—whether it is measured by counting arrests, or convictions, or returns to prison (and, if the latter, whether it is returns to prison following new convictions or returns as a result of parole revocations). Recidivism rates vary, too, according to the length of time offenders are followed (as might be expected, recidivism rates tend to increase with time), the age of the offenders being studied (recidivism tends to decline as criminals age), and their prior records (the greater the number of prior offenses, the higher the recidivism rate). Recidivism rates also reflect variations in parole board policies and the attitudes of individual parole agents; some agents and/or parole boards return parolees to prison for behavior that other agents or boards ignore.[5]

a dramatic turnaround from the trend of the preceding fifteen years, when the number of prison inmates had grown twice as rapidly as the crime rate. Those interested in corrections debated the speed at which de-institutionalization should or could proceed; that the trend would continue did not appear to be in doubt.

Support for de-institutionalization came from a remarkably broad spectrum of informed and interested citizens. At the end of a three-day meeting in mid-December, 1972, the seventy participants in the Forty-Second American Assembly—correctional administrators, law enforcement officers, judges, government officials, law professors, bar association leaders, members of Congress, criminologists, and clergymen—adopted a report advocating "incarceration only as a last resort." States "should abandon large congregate institutions for sentenced offenders," the report continued, adding that "It must become firm public policy to avoid construction of adult prisons, jails, or juvenile training schools." A month later, the Standards and Goals Commission proposed a ten-year moratorium on the construction of new adult prisons "except when total system planning shows that the need for them is imperative." The "most hopeful move toward effective corrections," the Commission flatly stated, would be "to continue and strengthen the trend away from confining people in institutions and toward supervising them in the community."[6]

But the trend never was as strong as it appeared; the decline in prison population had run its course by 1968, when the number of inmates was down to 188,000—15 percent below the 1961 high. The number of defendants sentenced to prison turned up in 1969 and increased steadily thereafter; by 1971, new commitments had increased 35 percent, and by 1975 they were 80 percent higher than they had been in 1968. Neither critics nor proponents of incarceration noticed the reversal of trend because it was obscured, for a time, by a continued reduction in the average length of the sentences being served; the number of people leaving prison continued to grow, offsetting the rise in new commitments, so that the total number of prison inmates was relatively stable from the end of 1969 through the end of 1972. Since then, sentences have lengthened somewhat, and the number of inmates has increased at an accelerating annual rate; by December 31, 1976, the prison population was 42 percent above its 1968 low and 36.4 percent higher than it had been in 1972.

This upsurge in population has led to widespread overcrowding in state prisons and state and local jails, making already intolerable living conditions even worse. Overcrowding has been particularly severe in Southern states, which have always incarcerated a higher proportion of convicted felons than has the rest of the country.

• A 110-year-old cellblock in South Carolina's Central Correctional Institution, built in the 1860s to house 200 men, has contained 550 to 600 inmates in recent years, with two and even three men jammed into the tiny one-man cells. (The state's total prison population is 60 percent above capacity.)

• In Louisiana's Angola prison, four to five inmates have been housed in cells measuring six feet by six feet.

• On three occasions in 1974 and 1975, the Florida corrections department refused to accept any more inmates until space became available; although the department opened four new prisons in 1976, overcrowding has worsened, with inmates housed in warehouses, trailers, and tents as well as in cells.[7]

Overcrowding has generated a wave of litigation challenging the constitutionality of entire state prison systems; at least six states have been under court orders to reduce overcrowding and relieve other conditions described, in one judicial opinion, as "philosophically, psychologically, physically, racially, and morally intolerable."* Paradoxically, efforts to relieve overcrowding in state prisons have increased congestion in local jails, where living conditions are generally worse than in most prisons. The result has been still more litigation challenging the constitutionality of living conditions in jails; according to a survey taken in early 1977, some ninety-five jails had been ordered to stop accepting new inmates, and seven had been closed altogether.[8]

Interest in prison reform has been stimulated, too, by the long series of riots and disturbances that began in Salem, Oregon, in 1968 and spread rapidly across the country; the horrifying climax came at Attica, where forty-three people were killed, thirty-nine of them by gunfire during the fifteen minutes it took the State Police to recapture the prison on September 13, 1971. Since then, riots, strikes, and random violence have been endemic in American prisons.

Although public indifference to prison conditions has not ended, the riots of the late 1960s and '70s occurred in a more responsive environment than inmates had ever faced before. Many riots received broad (and often sympathetic) attention from the press; some, like the bloody encounter at Attica, were covered live on television and were followed by blue-ribbon investigating

---

* Several of the suits seem to have been welcomed by state correctional officials who were frustrated by their inability to get larger budgets. "Many of the things the judge ordered are things the department of corrections has wanted to do for fifty years and couldn't because it was hamstrung by a lack of funds," the attorney hired to defend the state of Alabama remarked after U.S. District Court Judge Frank M. Johnson, Jr., had issued the most sweeping order ever aimed at a state correctional system. (At the end of the seven-day trial, the attorney had conceded in open court that "the evidence conclusively established aggravated and existing violations of plaintiffs' Eighth Amendment rights.")

commissions and Congressional and state legislative hearings and inquiries. Moreover, the riots and other outbreaks of prison violence persuaded journalists to go beyond day-to-day coverage; the result has been TV documentaries, books, and investigative reporting in newspapers and magazines, most of it sympathetic to inmate grievances.

In retrospect, the riots were an understandable and perhaps predictable response to a profound change in the nature of American society—specifically, to the growing emphasis on individual dignity and rights and the growing acceptance of the legitimacy of dissent. In the 1950s and '60s, black Americans began asserting their right to equality through demonstrations and civil disobedience, as well as in the courtroom, and other disadvantaged or excluded groups—Latinos, women, gays, draft resisters—quickly followed suit. Members of the middle class, too, took to the streets to protest the war in Vietnam.

In a television age, the language of social and political protest rapidly became part of the vocabulary of those confined in prison, especially in large industrial states, where black offenders comprise a majority of the prison population. Following charismatic leaders and influenced by inmate or ex-inmate writers such as Malcolm X, Eldridge Cleaver, and the late George Jackson, incarcerated black felons have redefined themselves as "political prisoners." Inevitably, prison inmates have come to expect amenities and rights for which earlier generations never even thought to ask.[9]

In the process, "prisoners' rights" have become an eminently respectable cause. The politicalization of prison dissent and rebellion placed the question high on the agenda of the left and brought inmates into a loose and often uneasy coalition with civil libertarians, prison reform groups, and other liberal groups. Sympathy with legitimate inmate grievances, meanwhile, led church groups, charitable foundations, and so-called "establishment" organizations such as the American Bar Association to take up the cause of prison reform. At the same time, old-line civil rights and civil liberties organizations and new public-interest law firms began representing prison inmates in suits challenging the conditions of prison life and the near-total discretion that prison administrators have always enjoyed.

The new intellectual climate made it difficult for judges to cling to the "dogma of the independence of prison authorities," as it has been called. Through litigation, they learned about the sordid details of life in American maximum-security prisons: the "Tucker telephones" used by Arkansas prison guards to give electric shocks to inmates' genitals; the unheated, unventilated isolation cells, filthy with excrement and lacking even a mattress, in which inmates were kept for weeks or months at a time in California, North Carolina, and any number of other states; the refusal to permit Black Muslims to practice their religion; the rampant violence on the part of inmate guards and trusties in Louisiana, Arkansas, and other Southern states; the barbarous punishment inflicted on a New York inmate for filing a suit against the warden to secure his right to un-restricted correspondence with his attorney. As a result, a number of judges abandoned the "hands off" approach they previously had taken to suits challenging prison procedures and practices. "The record in this case documents a shocking display of barbarism which should not escape the remedial action of this court," the Supreme Court declared in a case involving a Florida prisoner. Practices in North Carolina's 100-year-old penitentiary are "so bizarre," the members of the Fourth U.S. Circuit Court of Appeals wrote in a unanimous 1976 opinion, "that it is difficult to believe that such a situation could exist in our society."[10]

To be sure, judicial intervention has had limited goals —to bring prison conditions up to the threshold of constitutional acceptability—and court orders have not been translated easily or automatically into substantive change. But judicial decrees nonetheless have ameliorated some of the harshest conditions of prison life and corrected some of the worst abuses of power. A number of jails and prisons have been ordered closed, and judges have forced significant changes in the operation of others that have remained open, e.g., more opportunities for recreation, better food, improved sanitation and medical care. They also have set limits on the discretion of prison officials, requiring the introduction of at least some (but not all) elements of due process before inmates can be put in solitary confinement or punished in other ways.

It would be a mistake, therefore, to underestimate the importance of the judicial revolution, as some radical critics have done. Its significance lies less in the specific changes that have occurred than in the principle that has been laid down: that the Constitution does not stop at the prison's walls—that inmates have at least some constitutional rights that prison officials are obliged to respect. "Let there be no mistake in the matter," Chief Judge W. Smith Henley of the U.S. District Court for the Eastern District of Arkansas declared in an opinion ordering sweeping changes in the Arkansas prison system. "If Arkansas is going to operate a Penitentiary System, it is going to have to be a system that is countenanced by the Constitution of the United States."[11] Precisely what the Constitution requires remains a matter of uncertainty and dispute. But acceptance of the principle that prisons must conform to the Constitution has ushered in a new era in prison organization and administration; prisons will never be the same again.

Whether they will be *better*—more humane, less violent, less brutal—is another question. Wrong as it is to underestimate the significance of the judicial revolution, it would be an even greater mistake to exaggerate the degree to which it can improve prison life. The wrongs that prison suits are designed to remedy—mistreatment, abuse of power, and neglect by wardens, guards, and other officials—are not the only reasons (perhaps not the most important reasons) prisons are such noxious places.

Much of the misery of prison life stems from the fact of incarceration itself—of being locked up in a social and psychological, as well as physical, sense. To use Erving Goffman's phrase, prison is a "total institution" —a human environment from which there is no escape and over which the inmate has no control. Indeed, the inmate is denied the most rudimentary choices of everyday life. Where he lives, what time he goes to bed and when he gets up, the food he eats, the people with whom he eats, works, plays, and sleeps, until recently the clothes he wears—all these are chosen for him. The deprivation of choice, as of liberty, tends to be felt as an attack on the inmate's manhood—an attack made all the more severe by the anxieties about one's masculinity that confinement in an all-male society tends to generate.[12]

Except in a handful of minimum-security prisons, maintaining custody and order—preventing riots and escapes—overshadows every other consideration. This leads to constant supervision and regimentation and to an incredibly elaborate system of rules and regulations that seem all the more onerous because of the societal condemnation and stigmatization that underly them.

Even in the most humane institution, life is a constant put-down—a daily challenge to inmates' dignity and sense of self. "It is not necessary to look for a venal warden, or even a merely inept one," Paul Keve, who has directed the prison systems of two states, has written. "It is not necessary to look for sadistic guards, political chicanery from the governor's office, inadequate food, or stingy budgets from an uncaring legislature. . . . When we look for such factors we are missing the real guts of the problem, which is that in the best of prisons with the nicest of custodians and the most generous of kitchens, the necessary minutiae of management tend to deny and even insult the basic needs of individuals."[13]

Not all the minutiae is necessary; much of it is vestigial—the result of rules adopted thirty or even fifty years ago, for reasons no one can remember. Litigation may be able to eliminate or modify regulations or procedures that are arbitrary and unrelated to questions of custody and security. It seems unlikely that inmates or public-interest law firms can mount a successful challenge to incarceration itself.

Nor is it likely that litigation can protect inmates from their fellow inmates, who constitute the major threat to their safety and well-being. Because official brutality and mistreatment are so abhorrent, and because the pain of incarceration is so overwhelming, prison critics and reformers have tended to overlook the fact that most of the violence and exploitation that occur in prison involve attacks by one inmate, or group of inmates, against another. Prison rights suits have served to protect inmates from their keepers; but in tandem with a host of other changes within and without prison walls, they have left inmates more vulnerable to intimidation and brutality on the part of other inmates. Intra-inmate violence has increased dramatically in recent years, although precise statistics are hard to come by. To avoid being disciplined, inmates try to cover up fights and other incidents of violence; and prison officials have reason to understate the number of violent crimes, since violence may reflect on their ability to maintain control. North Carolina inmates interviewed by Thomas Orsagh and Dan Fuller of the University of North Carolina reported eleven times as many assaults as were shown in official prison records.[14]

Even so, enough quantitative and qualitative information is available to document the trend. According to estimates for the country as a whole, intra-inmate homicides more than tripled in a decade, from an annual average of 40 in 1964–65 to 120–130 in 1974–75. The estimates may be on the low side: in San Quentin alone, twelve inmates were murdered in 1974. And murder is but the tip of the iceberg: for every inmate who is stabbed to death—homemade "shanks" are the principal weapon in prison—at least nine or ten others are stabbed and survive.[15]

Less comprehensive data confirm the picture of rampant intra-inmate violence.

• In California, 4 inmates in every 100 were seriously injured in 1974—a fourfold increase in just four years.

• From 1969 through the end of 1972, there were 211 reported stabbings, 11 of them fatal, in Louisiana's Angola prison. During the first eleven months of 1973, there were 137 stabbings, 9 of them fatal; in the eighteen months that followed, there were 213 stabbings and 20 deaths.

• From early 1972 until January, 1975, 15 inmates at Massachusetts' Walpole Prison were murdered, and hundreds were stabbed, assaulted with pipes, and beaten by a small group of prisoners who roamed the 500-inmate facility.

• In all four Alabama prisons, U.S. District Court Judge Frank M. Johnson, Jr., found in a January, 1976, ruling, "robbery, rape, extortion, theft and assault are everyday occurrences among the general inmate population. Rather than face this constant danger, some inmates voluntarily subject themselves to the inhuman condition of prison isolation cells."[16]

Perhaps the best measure of the increase in intimidation and violence is the exponential growth in the number of inmates in "protective custody." In the past, protective custody—segregation from the rest of the prison population, usually in cramped quarters with little or no chance for recreation or work—was used almost entirely to protect informers and "weaklings," i.e., inmates who were obvious candidates for homosexual rape and exploitation. Increasingly, however, inmates who just a few years ago would have scorned protective custody as unmanly now request it, often for their entire term; segregation units have come to be seen as refuges from the random violence that prevails in the regular cellblocks. In the Washington State Prison at Walla Walla, the number of men in protective custody shot up from 3 to 4 in 1974 to more than 100 in 1976. At New York's Green Haven prison, with an inmate population of about 1,700, 195 men were sent to segregation for disciplinary reasons in 1976, and another 115 were placed in protective segregation—74 of them at their own request. Of 60 representative state prisons surveyed by Robert Freeman, Simon Dinitz, and John Conrad, 8 had more than 100 inmates in protective custody.[17]

The increase in violence and disorder, in turn, has generated powerful pressures toward repression, offsetting (and often undoing) the liberal reforms of the 1950s and '60s. Not knowing what else to do to main-

tain and restore order, even the most liberal and humane wardens and state administrators have fallen back
on the traditional remedies: general lockup (keeping
all inmates locked in their cells for a few hours, days, or
weeks) and segregation of the troublemakers (putting
the more violent and aggressive inmates in solitary confinement or in secure cellblocks isolated from the rest
of the prison).

At Illinois' Stateville Penitentiary, 5.5 to 6 percent
of the inmates were kept in isolation and segregation in
1970–75—two to three times the proportion that prevailed during the twenty-five-year reign (1936–61) of
Warden Joseph Ragen, who boasted of running "the
world's toughest prison." And Stateville is not at all
exceptional; of the sixty prisons surveyed by Freeman,
Dinitz, and Conrad, nineteen reported that the number
of inmates in solitary confinement ranged from 250 to
600.[18]

Perhaps the largest irony is that the return to traditional methods of control has gained support from the
prisoner rights movement itself; the judicial response
to some recent suits has been to order the kinds of indignities that litigation was initially designed to remedy.
In his sweeping order to Alabama prison authorities,
Judge Johnson required a number of changes designed
to make Alabama prisons fit for human habitation, e.g.,
decent food, adequate medical care, enough toilets and
showers, and ordered administrative changes to provide
due process before inmates could be confined in isolation. But Judge Johnson also directed prison authorities
to adopt a number of measures to eliminate "the rampant violence and jungle atmosphere existing throughout Alabama's penal institutions"—measures that could
have been taken out of a prison rule book of the 1950s.
For example:

• Prison officials "shall make reasonable efforts, including classification and monitoring, to segregate inmates known to engage in violence and aggression."

• Prison officials "shall establish regular procedures, including frequent shakedowns and frisks of inmates returning to the institutions, to reduce the number of weapons held by inmates."

• Officials "shall enforce prison regulations designed to reduce violence, including rules against fighting, possession of weapons, gambling, or possession of currency within the institutions. Inmates, except those in prerelease and work-release type programs, shall not possess currency. . . ."

And these orders, it should be understood, are contained in a court decision generally regarded as one of the triumphs of the prisoner rights movement.

II

When one looks closely at what prisons are like, what is puzzling is not why there is so much violence and disorder now, but why there was so much less in the past. One would expect to find predatory and violent behavior in an institution inhabited by predatory and violent people. And tendencies toward violent or predatory behavior that may exist among the inmate population are exacerbated by the conditions of prison life. "If men had deliberately set themselves the task of designing an institution that would systematically maladjust men," wrote the late Hans Mattick, director of the University of Illinois Center for Research in Criminal Justice and a former deputy warden of the Cook County Jail, "they would have invented the large, walled, maximum security prison."[19] Certainly the forces that contribute to violence and lawlessness in urban slums and ghettos are present, in highly magnified form, in prison: extreme material deprivation;

the absence of any exit or opportunity for upward mobility; and the sense of being rejected and ignored by the rest of society.

The last is the most important; the central problem inmates face and with which they must come to terms is the moral condemnation and rejection by society that imprisonment represents. Malcolm Braly, a novelist who spent much of his life in prison, explains, "That single thing that grinds you down and finally begins to erode your confidence, your vitality, your most basic sense of yourself, is the moment-to-moment condemnation implicit in this situation."[20]

Wherever he turns in a maximum- or medium-security prison (and 85 to 90 percent of all inmates are held in such institutions), an inmate sees the symbols of his rejection quite literally cast in concrete and steel. For the most part, prison architecture follows the principle that a building's form should reflect its purpose. An early prison architect wrote that prisons should inspire "darkness" and "terror"—and they do. Moreover, prisons were built to last; of the 113 maximum-security state prisons in operation in 1971, 56 were built before the turn of the century, and 6 were constructed before 1830. (The 56 nineteenth-century prisons contained more than two-thirds of the inmates held in maximum-security institutions.) Nor are most newer prisons significantly better; in some ways, William Nagel found, new jails and prisons are even more dehumanizing than the old ones because surveillance is handled by closed-circuit television and electronically operated gates rather than by live guards.[21]

The basic routines of the prison also provide daily reminders of rejection and worthlessness.[22] The process begins with an inmate's arrival in prison; a new inmate, or "fish," is introduced to prison life through a series of "degradation ceremonies" designed to dramatize the moral condemnation being heaped on him and to create a sense of worthlessness and degradation. Brought to the "fish tank," the layers of the inmate's ego and sense of self are successively peeled away: his clothes and other personal possessions are taken from him; until recently, his head was shaved; he is stripped naked, forced to shower, deloused (in some jails and prisons, by a guard wielding a spray gun), and subjected to a humiliating search of every orifice in his body.

The psychological consequences are profound; they are not diminished by the fact that some of the measures may be justified on security grounds.* Stripping prisoners naked has long been a way of establishing dominance over them—of making them feel emotionally, as well as physically, vulnerable and exposed. Shaving their heads is an even more effective device: since Samson's time, at least, hair has been associated with virility and sexuality, and having one's hair cut off involuntarily has symbolized emasculation. (If the haircut did not represent power and control to one side and impotence and dependency to the other, hair length would not be such a bone of contention among parents and children, nor would the Afro hair style be viewed as a political statement.) Losing one's name is an even more powerful blow to the ego. In human societies, names always have been surrounded with magic and mystery; to lose one's name is to lose the essence of one's identity. And this is what happens—or used to happen—to the new inmate: his name was replaced by a number, with the number emblazoned on his newly issued (and usually ill-fitting) prison clothing, as well as on his file. (In

* Drugs and weapons may be hidden in an inmate's mouth or rectum, sewn into his clothing, or secreted in a compartment in his shoes. But the real reason for most of the measures is to put the inmate in his place; certainly, security cannot be the reason some prisons subject prisoners to a strip-search before they are released.

some prisons, it still is easier to ask for a prisoner by his number than by his name.)

The assault on the inmate's sense of self does not end when he leaves the fish tank; prison life is a continuous process of mortification. There is, first, the extreme sensory deprivation of prison life. Until one has experienced it, it is hard to imagine how oppressive is the overwhelming grayness of the prison environment; the unrelieved harshness of the metallic surfaces, which seem to amplify every sound; the absence of flowers, plants, and trees, indeed, of any direct contact with nature or the outside world.

Moreover, material deprivation takes on an added dimension in a prison setting. Possessions are important for the symbolism they represent, not just the material comfort they provide; we express our sense of self through the clothes we wear, the records we play, the colors we paint our walls and the pictures we hang on them, the furniture we buy and the way we arrange it, the games we play—in a word, the life style we develop. To be stripped of one's material possessions, then, is to be stripped of an integral part of the self— all the more so since contemporary society tends to equate material deprivation with personal inadequacy. Just how important possessions are as assertions of the self is demonstrated by the risks and expense to which inmates go in trying to give their clothes and their cells a touch of individuality: violating regulations by bribing inmate laundry workers or tailors to change the cut of their clothing or to use extra starch; draping a rag or piece of torn blanket over the toilet or dresser top; hanging pinups and other pictures on cell walls. Indeed, it is impossible to walk through a cellblock without being moved by the poignancy of inmates' attempts to invest something of themselves in their stark, interchangeable cells.

Inmates' feelings of inadequacy are heightened by the constant surveillance under which they are kept. "The prisoner is confronted daily with the fact that he has been stripped of his membership in society at large, and now stands condemned as an outcast, an outlaw so dangerous that he must be kept behind closely guarded walls and watched both day and night," Gresham Sykes and Sheldon Messinger write. "He has lost the privilege of being *trusted* and his every act is viewed with suspicion by the guards, the surrogates of the conforming social order."[23] The fact that distrust stems from criminal conduct does not lessen its psychic impact, especially since wardens and guards practice a kind of "overkill": because it is impossible to predict which inmates may try to escape, the safest course is to proceed on the assumption that every inmate is a custody risk. Hence inmates are constantly being counted: when they leave their cells for meals and when they return; when they begin work and when they finish; when they leave the cellblock for recreation and when they return; when they go to bed and when they arise. Even if they manage to forget the walls, the constant counting reminds them of their impotence.

So does the absence of women, of any opportunity for heterosexual relationships; as Sykes has written, the inmate is "figuratively castrated by his involuntary celibacy." At the very least, being confined in an all-male society generates intense anxieties about one's masculinity. When one is constantly being seduced by other inmates or threatened with homosexual rape, latent fears about one's own homosexual tendencies are brought much closer to the surface; if an inmate feels tempted, as many do, he is likely to develop a sense of guilt, even if he refrains from overt activity. And given the traditions of machismo from which most inmates come and to which they give vocal adherence, the lack of heterosexual relationships involves far more than physiological frustration alone; it threatens their sense of manhood.[24]

Faced with daily evidence of societal rejection and condemnation and with daily blows to their manhood and sense of self, inmates have no choice but to seek their own sources of dignity and pride, their own ways of investing their lives with meaning. This is not to suggest that the hardships of prison life are the only factors influencing behavior. The backgrounds that inmates bring with them directly affect the ways in which they respond to rejection and deprivation; there are profound differences between inmate culture in men's and women's prisons, and institutions populated by white-collar criminals and "light" thieves have a different atmosphere and tone from those inhabited mostly by "heavy" criminals. Inmate culture is affected, too, by the nature of the institution itself: its relationship with the surrounding community; the relative emphasis on custody and treatment; the relationships between guards and professional staff, and between staff and administration; and the overall style of prison government.[25]

Even so, there are similarities in inmate attitudes and behavior from one institution to another and one time period to another. All inmates confront the same problem: how to maintain their sense of self—how to prove (to themselves, as well as to others) that they are people of substance and worth—in an environment designed to destroy any sense of self. As Lloyd McCorkle and Richard Korn have written, the social system inmates create provides "a way of life which enables [them] to avoid the devastating psychological effects of internalizing and converting social rejection into self-rejection. In effect, it permits the inmate to reject his rejectors."[26]

He does so, in part, by persuading himself that he is

more victim than victimizer—that it is unjust and hypocritical to single him out for punishment in a society in which everyone is corrupt. Inmates may not be familiar with George Bernard Shaw, but they have absorbed his thesis that "the thief who is in prison is not necessarily more dishonest than his fellows at large."* They see themselves, in Malcolm Braly's description, as "up-front, natural men, who lived out the truth of our human condition."[27]

As in the slum and ghetto, the usual symbols of status (money, possessions, job, title) are absent. Indeed, status is in such short supply in prison that it can be gained only at someone else's expense—by putting him down verbally, physically, financially, or sexually. Since manhood cannot be demonstrated through heterosexual prowess, there is an exaggerated emphasis on toughness: the ability either to victimize others or to withstand victimization, especially by people who appear to be bigger and stronger. By the same token, every slight— every *presumed* slight—must be countered, lest the person being slighted be branded as a weakling or "punk," a characterization that will make him the target of anyone eager to improve his status by downing someone else. The most casual interactions (brushing against someone in line, using the "wrong" tone of voice) may erupt into lethal violence. All the more so because of the inverted morality that often prevails: in prison, as in the ghetto, "bad" is "good," and inmates compete to see who is the "baddest" of all.

Thus prison life is a crucible of intimidation and conflict. Because of its scarcity, status cannot simply be

* The prisoner "snatches a loaf of bread from the baker's counter and is promptly run into gaol," Shaw wrote in *The Crime of Imprisonment.* "Another man snatches bread from the tables of hundreds of widows and orphans and simple credulous souls who do not know the ways of company promoters; and, as like as not, he is run into Parliament."

achieved and then consolidated; it must be continually renewed. Lacking the devices that middle-class people can call upon to sustain or enhance their status—lacking even the devices available to members of the lower class— inmates must constantly reaffirm the credentials on which their fragile identity is based. Every challenge must be met; and the challenges are endless, because of the shifting composition of the inmate population. Each inmate who arrives represents an opportunity and a threat: an opportunity to victimized inmates, who may be able to improve their status by downing the newcomer; a threat to the victimizers, who may themselves be victimized if the newcomer is tough enough. The more frequently inmates come and go, therefore, the more volatile the atmosphere is likely to be—which is why jails are often more brutal than prisons.

It is the rare inmate who escapes victimization altogether, although many will be both victim and victimizer. In their study of the victimization process in a secure Ohio reformatory, Clemens Bartollas, Stuart Miller, and Simon Dinitz found that seven youngsters in ten were exploited in some fashion or at some time or other—a striking statistic in view of the fact that the institution contained the most violent and aggressive young men in Ohio's juvenile system. Nearly half of those who were exploited were exploiters themselves; this "give-and-take" group was the largest of the five categories into which the authors classified the boys. Only one inmate in ten was neither a victim nor a victimizer.[28]

Victimization takes a variety of forms, only some of them physical (although the threat of physical harm underlies everything else). The scarcity of goods gives an exaggerated value to cigarettes, food, clothing, and other possessions. Testing of a new inmate may begin when someone demands a cigarette, or walks over to him at lunch or dinner, picks up his dessert, and walks away, saying, "You don't want this, do you?" The newcomer has two options: to hand over the cigarette (or yield the dessert), or to stand firm, which means being ready and willing to fight. Which he chooses depends partly on his own toughness and bravado, vis-à-vis that of his challenger, and partly on the value of the item being demanded. In any institution, possessions tend to have a rank ordering of value only dimly related to their cost in the free world. In the training schools studied by Bartollas, Miller, and Dinitz, radios had the highest value of any possession—in part because of their cost and scarcity within the institution, but principally because a radio symbolized maternal love. (Anyone who had a radio usually had received it as a gift from home.) For the same reason, candy and soda brought or sent by parents were considered more valuable than the same items purchased in the canteen. This ranking of possessions made it easier for inmates to decide where to draw the line: a youngster might yield candy or cigarettes on demand but fight to hold on to personal clothing or a radio. Since inmates believed that anyone who gave up a radio would give up anything, failure to fight over a radio would make a physical beating and/or forced homosexual relations virtually inevitable.[29]

Victimization may also involve more intangible tokens of power: who chooses the programs to be watched on a ward's or a cell-block's TV set; who "owns" the sunniest or shadiest spot in the recreation yard; who sits in which row at the movies; who controls access to the ping-pong table; who has first rights to the shower; and so on. Almost any aspect of prison life can provide an opportunity for some inmates to "mess over" others, i.e., to demonstrate their domination and other inmates' submission.

After death, the ultimate form of victimization is

sexual—understandably so, given all the conscious and unconscious links between sexuality and power. In the macho world, manhood tends to be defined as aggressive heterosexual activity; homosexuality is sneered at, and a man is measured by the number of female conquests rather (or more) than by the quality of the relationships. In prison, the complete absence of women shifts the criterion to toughness and aggression alone. At the same time, inmate culture creates a new arena for demonstrating manhood by redefining homosexuality: only the passive partner in homosexual relations is considered homosexual or effeminate.

Thus the aggressive inmate—the "wolf" or "jocker" —can demonstrate his manhood by forcing another inmate to submit to buggery or oral sodomy. It is not simply that being the aggressor strips the homosexual act of the effeminacy inmates assign to it in the outside world; what is crucial is that the wolf has forced or seduced the "punk" or "fag" into submission, which in prison culture means playing a feminine role.* In the zero-sum games that inmates play, one man's defeat is another's triumph; the ultimate triumph is to destroy another man's manhood—to break his will, defile his body, and make him feel totally (and often permanently) degraded. Indeed, the triumph may be a double one: a wolf may convert a punk into a possession, to be offered to other inmates in exchange for favors of one sort or another. And when the wolf is black and

---

* Inmates generally draw a sharp distinction between a punk and a fag, or "queen"; as an inmate saying puts it, punks are made, whereas fags are born. A fag is a genuine homosexual who enjoys playing the female role; a punk is someone who is coerced or seduced—the two usually are indistinguishable— into playing the passive role. In the inmate world, the punk has turned himself into a woman by the act of submission itself; he is seen as a coward, hence as more effeminate and contemptible than the fag, who is simply following his own sexual preference.

the punk is white (the most frequent arrangement, by far), the wolf's demonstration of power is infinitely sweeter; sexual exploitation becomes a political statement—a symbolic reversal of racial roles.[30]

Sexual exploitation may proceed in a variety of ways. The simplest—and in some jails, with their transient populations, perhaps the most frequent—is homosexual rape. A young offender, particularly a white offender, is likely to be subjected to gang rape his first night in jail. In a number of large cities, jail officials automatically place young whites in protective custody for their own safety. Sometimes the move comes too late; young offenders are often raped in the van transporting men to jail. Nor are they safe in maximum- and medium-security prisons.

ITEM (from Judge Frank Johnson's Memorandum Opinion in *Pugh* v. *Locke*): One twenty-year-old inmate, after relating that he had been told by medical experts that he has the mind of a five-year-old, testified that he was raped by a group of inmates on the first night he spent in an Alabama prison. On the second night, he was almost strangled by two other inmates who decided that they could use him to make a profit by selling his body to other inmates.

ITEM (testimony of a nineteen-year-old Philadelphia inmate): On Tuesday morning, the first week of June at about 9:30 A.M., I was in my cell on "D" block and I had started to clean up. A tall heavy set fella came into the cell and asked for a mirror and shaving brush and a comb that my cell partner said he could borrow. He then said he had heard something about me concerning homosexual acts. I told him what he had heard was not true. He then started to threaten me if I didn't submit to him. Then I hit him with my fist in his face before he could hit me. Then about three more men came into the cell, and they started to beat me up too. I fought back the best I could and then I fell on the floor and I got kicked in the ribs. Three guys were holding me while the other one tore my pants off; I continued to fight until one of the guys knocked me out. One of the guys was holding me on the floor and had my arm pinned to the floor. And about 7 or 8 guys came into the cell and they took turns sticking their penis up my A—. When they finished, they left my cell, and I was still laying on the floor.

As a conservative estimate, the authors of the Philadelphia study concluded, at least 2,000 separate incidents of homosexual rape occurred among the 60,000 inmates passing through the Philadephia jails and prison system in the twenty-six-month period from June, 1966, to July, 1968.[31] And this was ten years ago—before the upsurge in prison violence had gotten under way.

Most of the time rape is unnecessary. Having witnessed one or more rapes in jail or having heard lurid stories from a relative or friend, some inmates may be intimidated by the spoken or unspoken threat and give in without a fight. Others may submit to a wolf who offers to protect them from other, more fearsome inmates. Wolves often "set up" a victim by having friends threaten him with rape; the wolf then comes along and "rescues" the victim, who may or may not know the price he will have to pay: servicing his protector's friends, as well as the protector himself. In either case, the alternative to submission is to fight—at the possible cost of one's life.

Still others, especially inmates in prison for the first time, may discover that they have inadvertently become someone's punk as a result of having accepted cigarettes, candy, or other gifts or favors. Under the inmate code, there is no such thing as a "free gift"; accepting gifts or other favors obligates the recipient to become the donor's female partner. Frightened, confused, and disoriented, newly arrived and naïve inmates may accept help, advice, or gifts in the spirit in which they seem to be offered, i.e., as a gesture of friendship; they learn their mistake too late. In the case of a more seasoned or sophisticated newcomer, a wolf may try to force him to accept a gift—for example, by placing it in his cell when he is absent. To escape bondage, the intended victim must insist that the donor take the gift back; if the donor refuses, the recipient must fight him then and there in order to escape submission later on.

For the new inmate, in short, danger lurks almost everywhere; Piri Thomas provides a particularly vivid portrait in his powerful autobiography, *Down These Mean Streets.* " 'Just handle yourself right, don't make fast friends, and act cool,' " he tells Tico, a friend's younger brother. " 'Don't play and joke too much, and baby, don't, just don't accept candy or smokes from stranger cons. You might end up paying for it with your ass.' " But Tico already has accepted cigarettes, food, candy, and advice from a "gorilla" named Rube, who was demanding that Tico become his "old lady." "My God, I thought, what can I tell him?" Thomas continues. "Tico had to show man or he was finished." Returning the gifts will not suffice; Rube has already made it clear that only one kind of repayment will be acceptable. Determining that Rube works in the same shop as Tico, Thomas gives him this advice:

> "Well, the first time he says something to you or looks wrong at you, have a piece of pipe or a good heavy piece of two-by-four. Don't say a damn thing to him, just get that heavy wasting material and walk right up to him and bash his face in and keep bash-

ing him till he's down and out, and yell loud and clear for all the other cons to hear you, 'Motherfucker, I'm a man. I came in here a motherfucking man and I'm going out a motherfucking man. Next time I'll kill you.' "

"And?" Tico said softly.

"And nuttin', baby. You'll be free, an accepted man —part of this jailhouse scene. All the weight will be off your back. The word will get around you ain't to be messed with 'cause you got heart and you ain't afraid to deal."

Thomas knows that Tico might be badly hurt himself—that Rube or his friends might be able to overpower him—but he also believes that physical injury is a lot better than losing one's manhood:

I figured that even if he didn't get a chance to hurt Rube, even if Rube took that washing stick from him and messed him up, everybody would know he had heart to stand up to muscle-bound Rube; and it was better to get hurt outside where it could be seen and attended to than inside, where it would stay all his life.*[32]

III

Clearly, prison life brings out the worst—the most brutal, violent, and sadistic—tendencies in human behavior. Inmates require protection against callousness, arbitrariness, and brutality on the part of their keepers; but they have at least as great a need for their keepers to protect them against their fellow inmates. Without

---

* Tico followed instructions and bashed Rube on the head with an iron bar, for which he was sentenced to a week in isolation—a small price to pay, as Thomas remarks, for keeping his manhood.

effective government to maintain peace and order, prisons tend to be a Hobbesian world "wherein men live without other security than what their own strength and their own invention shall furnish them."

But how govern a society of captives? Under ordinary circumstances, government depends on the consent of the governed; orders are issued and laws laid down on the assumption that they will be obeyed. The central dilemma faced by prison authorities is that they can neither expect cooperation from inmates nor govern without it. Force is a grossly inefficient way of getting people to behave in complex ways; yet the day-to-day operation of most prisons depends on convict labor. Instead of remaining in their cellblocks, inmates have to move from one part of the prison to another several times a day. The nature of their work also gives them access to materials that can be forged into weapons or used to produce contraband for sale in the black market that flourishes in every prison.

The problem of control is complicated still more by efforts to make prisons more humane, and more effective in rehabilitating inmates. Inmates move about the prison for a variety of reasons apart from work and meals: they go to and from the gymnasium, recreation yard, and movie theater; they have appointments with counselors for individual or group therapy; they visit the prison hospital or clinic to see a doctor or dentist; they go to school; and they attend meetings of the Jaycees (Junior Chamber of Commerce), Alcoholics Anonymous, or any of a number of other self-help, religious, or fraternal organizations.

There is no way to regulate this kind of movement through force alone. On the contrary, reliance on force may backfire: in the tinderbox atmosphere of a prison yard or cellblock, striking an inmate may invite retaliation, and the slightest scuffle may be the spark that sets off a riot or a massed assault on a single guard or group of guards. This is not to deny that brutality occurs; as a group, guards are no better (but also no worse) than the rest of the human species. And there are occasions —especially after a guard has been injured or killed —when ordinarily nonbrutal guards lose their self-control and lash out in a violent way.

In general, however, guards eschew the use of force, if only because their self-interest requires it. For one thing, guards are badly outnumbered; inmates can overpower them anytime they want. Hence guards who work inside the prison walls are not allowed to carry guns (although in maximum-security prisons the guards stationed in turrets on top of the prison walls usually are armed). Equally important, guards are well aware of the fact that they may be taken hostage if a riot should break out; a major inhibition on their use of excessive force is the knowledge that, if taken hostage, their lives may depend on whether they have a reputation for fairness or brutality.

Few people, outside the prison world itself, have any idea how badly outnumbered the guards really are. A few years ago, Stateville, the maximum-security prison outside Chicago, had 400 guards for an inmate population of 1,500, a ratio of one guard to every 3.75 prisoners. The ratio seems reasonable enough—until one realizes that prison is a total institution that operates twenty-four hours a day, seven days a week, fifty-two weeks a year. As a rough rule of thumb, it takes at least 4.5 full-time guards to keep one position manned around the clock.* If the guards were distributed evenly

* There is a minimum of three shifts a day, which means twenty-one shifts a week; since guards work a five-day week, or five shifts a week, slightly more than four employees are needed to fill all twenty-one shifts. Additional employees are needed

among the three shifts, there would be no more than eighty-nine guards on duty at any one time—a ratio of one guard to every seventeen prisoners.

Paul Keve provides an even clearer picture of the impotence of the guards. In 1968, when he was Minnesota's Corrections Commissioner, Keve had a staff of about 280 for a prison population of 900 to 1,000. Many of those employees worked in clerical or maintenance jobs or served as counselors. Under ordinary circumstances, only twenty-eight guards were on duty during the evening (4 P.M. to midnight) shift—when men were working out in the recreation yard or gym, watching television, playing cards, attending a meeting or class, or moving about the cellblocks. And these twenty-eight guards had to be distributed among the front gate, the wall towers, the power plant, the segregation unit, the main cellblocks, the recreation yard, the gym, the hospital, and the schoolrooms. (During the late-night shift, the complement dropped to eighteen.) It was unusual for there to be more than two guards on duty in the main cellblock, a unit of some 500 cells. As Keve writes, "The walls, the bars, the sally ports, and all the impressive clanging hardware are deceptive in their promise of security."[33]

If prisons are to be reasonably secure and orderly, most inmates must be willing to follow most rules most of the time; prison authorities must gain the consent of the governed. They do so in three general ways:

• Through fear, which is to say, by convincing inmates that resistance is futile, even suicidal;

• By persuading inmates that acquiescence is in their own best interest;

---

to cover when guards are out on vacation, sick leave, paid holidays, or unexcused absences, or on some special assignment, such as taking a prisoner to the hospital and guarding him there.

• By mutual accommodation, i.e., by a kind of trade-off, whereby prison authorities tacitly yield control over some aspects of prison life to particular inmate groups, in return for these inmates' cooperation in maintaining order.[34]

The three approaches are not mutually exclusive; elements of all three usually are present, with prisons differing mainly in the relative importance attached to each. In the past, in what might be called the "old prison," wardens relied on regimentation and fear. Their goal was to control inmate initiative—to make inmates believe that they had no chance to act and thereby to destroy their *will* to act. "Above all, a warden must be thoroughly convinced, as I have always been, that a dishonest man is ever a coward," Elam Lynds, the first warden of the New York State prisons at Auburn and at Sing Sing, told Beaumont and Tocqueville. "This conviction, which the prisoners will soon perceive, gives him an irresistible ascendancy, and will make a number of things very easy, which, at first glance, may appear hazardous." "During all this conversation, which lasted several hours," Beaumont and Tocqueville added, "Mr. Elam Lynds constantly returned to this point—that it was necessary to begin with curbing the spirit of the prisoner, convincing him of his weakness. This point attained, everything becomes easy, whatever may be the construction of the prison, or the place of his labor."[35]

To some degree, wardens such as Lynds and, more recently, Joseph Ragen were able to terrorize inmates—in Tocqueville's phrase, "to break the prisoner into a state of *passive obedience*"—through the sheer force of personality. Hearing that an inmate had threatened to kill Lynds at the first opportunity, the fearless warden is supposed to have sent for the man, brought him to his bedroom and ordered the inmate to shave him. As

Beaumont and Tocqueville tell the story, Lynds then dismissed the inmate, saying, "I knew you intended to kill me, but I despise you too much to believe that you would ever be bold enough to execute your design. Single and unarmed, I am always stronger than you are." More than a century later, Joseph Ragen created the same impression at Stateville. According to James Jacobs, Ragen's daily inspection of the prison—the warden always walked alone, accompanied only by his two dogs—helped generate "a mystique about his own invincibility and omniscience."*[36]

But mystique is not enough: "If you stress the small things," Ragen used to tell his staff, "you will never have to worry about the big ones." By "the small things," Ragen meant the myriad rules and daily rituals of degradation that provide constant reminders of inmates' subordination and their keepers' superiority. The prison haircut; the prison uniform, issued in a single size, regardless of an inmate's dimensions; the "silent system" at meals and when inmates marched in line and in step from one activity to another; the Prussian punctuality with which the prison functioned (Ragenites used to boast that they could set their watches by the movement of prisoners); the meaningless and backbreaking labor on the coal pile, to which all "fish" were assigned for their first six months (using shovels and wheelbarrows, inmates moved coal from one pile to another)—all these were ways of dramatizing inmates' impotence and dependency, of assuring unquestioned compliance by destroying the will to resist.

Authoritarian wardens were able to destroy inmates' initiative, too, by maintaining a near-total monopoly

---

* Ragen contributed to this impression of omniscience through heavy use of informers. "Any time you see three inmates together in the yard," he used to boast, "one of them is mine."

on information. In the days of judicial nonintervention,
inmates were largely cut off from the outside world.
(At Stateville they were permitted to write only one
letter a week; outgoing and incoming mail was cen-
sored.) They were cut off from communication with
one another as well. All chairs faced the same way in
prison dining halls, so that inmates saw only the backs
of the people at their table, and inmates usually were
not allowed to keep pencils or paper in their cells.
Guards were forbidden to have any conversation with
inmates beyond what was essential for purposes of control. (In old-time prisons, guards might be disciplined
or fired for "fraternizing" with inmates.) The result
was to make inmates feel completely isolated and alone,
and therefore helpless to rebel or even to complain.

Inmates were also kept off-balance by uncertainty—
over who would be punished, when, and for what reason. Inmates were not told who had accused them of a
disciplinary infraction, and they had no notice, hearing,
counsel, or appeal when they were accused; punishment
was summary and swift. Under Ragen, Stateville had
so many rules that no inmate could possibly comply
with every one—hence any inmate could be found
guilty of some offense at any time. And to be accused
of an infraction was to enter a *Catch-22* world: if an
inmate admitted his guilt, he would be punished; and
if he denied his guilt, he would be charged with calling
a guard a liar and punished for that offense, instead of
(or in addition to) the one with which he was originally
charged.

Even so, no warden—certainly none in the twentieth century—was able to govern a prison by fear
alone; in the most authoritarian prisons, inmates found
ways of resisting, of asserting their own will against
that of their keepers.[37] Since they could not forestall
resistance altogether, prison authorities had to supple-

ment terror by some other means of control. They could acknowledge the strength of the inmate social order and try to harness it to their own ends, or they could try to shape inmate behavior through the use of punishments and rewards. The difficulty with the latter is that prison authorities have such a narrow range of options at their disposal. Solitary confinement is physically and psychologically painful, to be sure, but the difference between being in "the hole" and in an ordinary cell is far smaller than the difference between freedom and incarceration.

The rewards available to prison authorities were equally meager. At Trenton, when Sykes studied it, inmates had the right to send and receive mail, to be visited by relatives, to have some opportunity for recreation, and so on. The result, Sykes wrote, was that inmates were "unable to win any significant gains by means of compliance, for there are no gains left to be won."[38]

At Stateville, on the other hand, there were a great many rewards for compliance—precisely because, under Ragen, inmates had no rights whatsoever. The Ragen approach made it possible to convert almost anything (recreation, visits from relatives, writing or receiving letters) into privileges that could then be used to reward good behavior.* On the day of his arrival at Stateville, an old-timer told James Jacobs, he and the other "fish" were taken to the isolation unit for an orientation lecture. "I was told, in effect, *these walls are our walls; you will stay off our walls . . . or we will most certainly blow you away.* And I was told, too, that everything in the universe was a privilege.

---

* The coal pile served the same function: after six months, inmates were eager for the "reward" of a less painful (and less degrading) job. They also tried to avoid being punished by a return to the coal pile.

Work was a privilege, communication with family and friends was a privilege, and even the spending of one's own money was a privilege. At Stateville prison, even the grass was sacred: *Stay off our grass or we will put your stinkin' self in the hole.*" [emphasis in original][39]

It is not surprising, therefore, that contemporary "liberal" wardens often use punishment more freely than did the "reactionary" officials whom they replaced. Nor is it surprising that prison reformers have had to invent new means of punishment as a way of bolstering their control—"bus therapy," for example, which involves transferring recalcitrant inmates from one institution to another. Large and liberal prison systems, such as those of California and the U.S. Bureau of Prisons, comprise a variety of institutions. Inmates in maximum security may be rewarded by transfer to a medium- or minimum-security institution—and inmates in the latter may be punished by transfer in the opposite direction. In minimum- and medium-security prisons, in fact, the threat of transfer to maximum (or maxi-maxi) security for the balance of one's term may loom considerably larger than the threat of a week or two in "the hole."[40] Prison officials have used "bus therapy" for another purpose: to keep inmates isolated from one another. Frequent transfer of inmates from one facility to another means that friendship ties are constantly being disrupted; inmates feel isolated and alone, which helps prevent the development of any coherent or sustained inmate organization.[41]

Most prison authorities have preferred to purchase order by sharing some of their power with inmates— with inmates as a whole, or with a particular group (or groups) of inmates. For one thing, inmates have far more potent sanctions at their disposal than do officials themselves. In any society, the threat of exclusion is a powerful means of persuading members to conform to group norms. Ostracism is a more dreaded punishment in prison than in the outside world. A West Point cadet who is ostracized may drop out of the academy altogether. A prison inmate does not have the option; thus failure to comply with inmate norms may make his life psychologically unbearable.*

Custodians yield some of their power to inmates for other reasons as well. Guards tend to be evaluated by the conduct of the men they control. A noisy, dirty, or quarrelsome cellblock reflects on the guard or guards in charge; so does a recreation yard in which fights break out with some frequency, or in which inmates refuse to return to their cells. As we have seen, guards cannot rely on force to control inmates in their day-to-day routine; nor can they rely too heavily on other sanctions. In theory, guards are supposed to write a charge slip, or "ticket," every time a rule is broken. But a guard who does so puts a heavy burden on the prison's disciplinary committee. More to the point, a guard who writes a great many tickets is perceived by his superiors as someone who is unable to exercise control over his men; the fewer the tickets a guard writes, the more competent he appears to be. To achieve a smoothly running tour, therefore, a guard has to gain acquiescence with the carrot rather than the stick. The best reward

---

* Inmate society tends to be even more authoritarian and coercive than is the government established by custodians. During the Attica rebellion, as a great many inmates told the members of the McKay Commission (the New York State Special Commission on Attica), the society that emerged in "D yard" "was arranged in the same way that the authorities against whom they were rebelling ran Attica." Restrictions were placed on inmates' movements: no one was permitted to leave D yard without a pass—and the pass that was used was the same form the prison had used to allow trusted inmates to move about the prison without an escort. Other behavior (fighting, the use of drugs, homosexual relations) was forbidden under the threat of death.[42]

a guard can offer is to ignore certain offenses when they are committed or to make sure that he is not around when a rule is being broken; one need not report what one has neither seen nor (formally) heard about.[43]

The analogy with policing is clear enough. As I pointed out in Chapter 7, patrolmen (and detectives as well) are concerned less with crime in general than with preventing those crimes that are "on them"— hence their distinction between "inside" and "outside" crimes. Similarly, guards are less concerned with preventing violations of prison rules as a whole than with preventing infractions that might come to the attention of their superiors. A tacit deal is struck: the guards will overlook some kinds of violations—black market traffic in food or other contraband, for example—so long as the inmates involved keep things "cool" overall.*

In making these trade-offs, guards have had the unspoken approval of their colleagues and superiors, who strike bargains of their own with privileged inmates. Inmate society has been shaped in good measure by the fact that prison officials have developed an employer-

* The more human desire to be liked creates still another incentive for guards to overlook minor infractions. "There are many pressures in American culture to 'be nice,' to be a 'good Joe,' and the guard in the maximum security prison is not immune," Sykes has written. "The guard is constantly exposed to a sort of moral blackmail in which the first signs of condemnation, estrangement, or rigid adherence to the rules is countered by the inmates with the threat of ridicule or hostility. And in this complex interplay, the guard does not always start from a position of determined opposition to 'being friendly.'"[44] On the contrary, guards are on the bottom of the official hierarchy, and they often resent the way they are treated by their superiors, who give arbitrary and often incomprehensible orders without explanation or consultation. Like the inmates, guards often see themselves as the victims of unreasoned (and unreasoning) authority. Inmates are quick to sense and exploit these chinks in their guards' psychic armor.

employee—at times, almost a patron-client—relationship with certain prisoners.[45] Until fairly recently, inmates filled most of the clerical jobs needed to keep a prison running, and they also provided a wide range of personal services to officials, especially those above the rank of guard. Indeed, prisons were feudal princedoms in which officers were paid in kind. Low salaries usually were offset by the fact that guard lieutenants and captains, maintenance supervisors, and deputy wardens and wardens lived in state-provided houses that were staffed by inmate cooks, gardeners, and "houseboys."

Given the range of services provided by inmates, prison officials used to compete with their colleagues for the ablest and most dependable inmates, dangling certain inducements and advantages before the "employees" they wanted to "hire." Well aware of the competition for their services, inmates ranked institutional jobs according to their desirability, defined as the economic opportunities the jobs provided. Some jobs rank high because of the "legitimate graft" that comes with them: inmates working in the kitchen or dining room are likely to be better fed than other inmates, and those working in the laundry, clothing factory, or storeroom are more likely to have clean and well-fitting clothes.

A surprising number of prison jobs offer opportunities for "illegitimate graft" as well. Kitchen employees are in a good position to steal food or manufacture home-brew liquor for sale in the inmate economy; those who work in the laundry or tailor shop can provide a particular sharp crease in other inmates' trousers, more starch in their shirts, or alterations of one sort or another. Clerks can sell stationery and office supplies; nurses' aides and doctors' helpers can sell drugs (or, if they are valued by the doctor, a more careful medical exam, a medical excuse from work, or perhaps a stay in the prison hospital); metal shop employees can sell knives and tools; electricians may be able to repair or even manufacture radios.

Even the most menial jobs can be turned to advantage. Before the rebellion at Attica, inmates could shower only once a week; they received two quarts of water a day with which to wash themselves, launder personal clothing (only state-issued clothing could be sent to the prison laundry for a once-a-week washing), shave, and clean their cells. Thus inmate water boys did a brisk business selling extra pails of hot water. As one inmate told the McKay Commission, with rhetorical excess, "it is very expensive to live in prison." The cost of living cannot be met through legitimate earnings; in New York prisons in 1977, inmate jobs paid from 35 cents to $1.15 a day. Some inmates improve their meager standard of living through packages sent from home, and some through gambling winnings; most are forced to "hustle" in order to make ends meet.[46]

The most valued commodities have been information and influence; hence the best jobs were those that provided (or seemed to provide) an inmate with access to the decision-making process. Working for the warden or deputy warden, the captain of the guards, or some other influential official gave an inmate access to prison files or other confidential information, as well as advance knowledge of decisions affecting other inmates, which he could use for sale or, more important, to enhance his status in inmate society. A bright inmate also gained a measure of influence by making himself indispensable to the official for whom he worked—relieving him of a mass of onerous detail, reminding him when reports were due, covering for him when he forgot something or came in drunk, and in general showing his devotion and trustworthiness. It was easy for an official to rationalize his dependence on an inmate-employee on therapeutic grounds (he was getting the inmate used to responsibility by displaying trust in him) and thus to close his eyes to the fact that the inmate was using (and exploiting) him more than he was using (and exploiting) the inmate.[47]

It is not surprising that, in the past, inmates who became an official's "key man" became the key men in inmate society as well. Knowledge is power in any organization, especially in prison—and above all in the old, authoritarian prison, in which officials maintained control through their monopoly on information. ("We don't have to make excuses to inmates.") The barriers to communication and the official refusal to explain what was happening made the possession of information particularly valuable. Therefore, new inmates had to turn to experienced prisoners to find out what they could and could not do.

This, in turn, made seniority a significant factor in the inmate status hierarchy. "Old inmates knew the limits of official tolerance in a system which, of necessity, prohibited more than it punished," Richard McCleery writes, "and they could share on their own terms the physical goods and adaptive myths which made prison life tolerable. This control over the rites and tests of initiation gave senior inmates the power to assign new men a subordinate status and hold them there until they accepted the norms of inmate culture."[48]

New inmates were not the only ones with a craving for information; because of their isolation and impotence, every inmate was psychologically dependent on those who could explain what was happening. "Knowledge of prison operations made for physical adjustment," McCleery observes, "but knowledge of explanations was required to make life psychologically tolerable." The requirement is part of the human condition. Inmates, no less than other people, find it difficult to live in a completely random universe; to give life meaning and purpose, they need ways of explaining (or rationalizing) the ebb and flow of events. (This is why street crime evokes so much fear; being victimized makes it impossible to take things at face value—to rely on subtle and largely unconscious cues to explain and predict how others will act.)

Understandably, power accrued to inmates who could explain and predict, and perhaps even control, the otherwise mysterious ways of prison officials. Since power is the supreme virtue in prison, other inmates attached themselves to these leaders, paying tribute in money, goods, sex, or simply respect, in return for protection. Their large followings, in turn, gave inmate leaders considerable influence over inmate behavior.

Custodial goals were well-served thereby. Like the police in lower-class neighborhoods, prison officials try to regulate what they cannot suppress; if illegal activity is inevitable in prison, officials are better off if the activity is in the hands of inmates capable of maintaining stability and order. Since a weak leader is useless, officials go out of their way to grant the kinds of favors that will enhance or reinforce a leader's position. And traditional inmate leaders generally shared their keepers' interest in stability and order. They tended to be professional criminals who were serving long terms; safe-crackers and armed robbers had more status in inmate society to begin with, and it took time to move up into a "key man" job. Because they had a considerable amount of time to serve, moreover, members of the inmate elite were eager to hold on to the privileges they had gained—and unless they could prevent or control disruptive behavior among the prisoner population, officials were likely to depose them and shift their favors to inmates who showed more promise of being able to maintain control.

The result was a prison society organized through a

steeply graduated hierarchy of power, status, and privilege, and an inmate culture whose norms and values emphasized accommodation to custodial values. The commandment "Never talk to a screw" helped maintain the inmate elite's control of information and communication. And as Richard McCleery points out, "Do your own time" and "Don't bring on the heat" are norms of adjustment to the prison world, not rebellion against it. Their internalization permitted inmate society to treasure a sense of independence and contempt for the custodian without anarchic consequences in behavior. In fact, by defining a "real man" as someone who "pulls his own time," inmate culture turned the notion of manhood away from rebellion; a real man became someone who was "cool"—someone who could take what the "screws" dished out without a show of emotion, i.e., without rebellion or subservience.

There always were a few men, to be sure, who defied the guards, rejecting their orders and attacking them without regard to consequences. These "ball-busters," or "outlaws," played much the same role in prison that the "bad nigger" played in black communities; McCleery notes that there was a certain Promethean quality to their continued defiance in the fact of certain defeat—to their refusal to accept their own impotence. But despite a certain admiration for the ball-buster's courage, inmate culture labeled him a dangerous fool —someone willing to sacrifice the well-being of the entire inmate population (by bringing closer surveillance and more restrictions) for the sake of a pointless, hence childish, outburst of anger. Aggression against other inmates was another question altogether: the "tough" —the man who exploded into violence against his peers —received the respect denied the ball-buster, thereby channeling aggression away from the custodians and toward other inmates. If inmate leaders were to be free to pursue and profit from their black market operations, defiance and rebellion had to be kept to an absolute minimum. Thus inmate culture, as Sykes puts it, "shifted the measure of the individual's worth from rebellion to adjustment."[49]

IV

It is no wonder, then, that order has broken down. The basic difference between the prisons of 1950 and those of today, Raymond Procunier, Director of the California Department of Corrections, told a reporter just before his retirement in 1975, was that in 1950 "the inmates were so much better in terms of buying all the bullshit we put out."[50] Contemporary prisoners—especially black prisoners, who comprise a majority of the prison population in a number of states and about 50 percent nationwide—are no longer "buying all the bullshit"; they are unwilling to accept the kinds of mutual accommodations and understandings between inmates and staff that, in the past, had kept the pressures toward anarchy and violence under some sort of control. In effect, inmates have withdrawn the consent on which prison government has always rested; they have shifted the measure of an individual's worth from adjustment back to rebellion.

There has been a loss of faith, meanwhile, on the part of their keepers—faith in the legitimacy of their own absolute power. Wardens of the Ragen school were not afflicted with self-mockery, let alone self-doubt; nor did they concern themselves with questions of due process or prisoners' rights. Procunier's first job was as a guard at the California Institution for Men at Chino, which in 1950, when he was hired, was considered the model of an open, progressive, minimum-security institution. Yet Chino was run almost as tightly as a maximum-security prison is run today. The warden "used to teach us in class that these guys, when they call you a son of a bitch, you can ignore them because they haven' got any rights," Procunier recalls. "If we had an inmate down there who sang too loud in church, we sent him to Folsom. No wonder Chino ran so good." As Procunier adds, "This is probably the biggest part of the revolution in prison reform in the last years—accepting that inmates have any rights."

It is hard to run an authoritarian institution without a firm belief in authoritarianism. That belief began to break down after World War II, with the emergence of a new breed of warden and state correctional administrator, ambivalent about, if not actually critical of, totalitarian methods of control. The "old" wardens generally came up through the ranks; any formal education they may have had was incidental to their sense of themselves or their conception of their role. The "new" wardens usually were college graduates with a background in social work, public administration, or some related field. In 1965, when Ragen retired as state commissioner, every warden in the state had come up through the ranks, and none had a college degree; by 1974, no warden had started as a guard, and six of the eight held master's degrees. At Stateville, in particular, as James Jacobs has described in his invaluable book, Ragen's totalitarian structure has been dismantled, but the reform wardens—four of them since 1970 —have been unable to erect an effective system of control in its stead. Faced with violence and disorder, they have reverted to disciplinary measures that are harsher, in many respects, than those that Ragen used.[51]

Even at Stateville, terror never had been a sufficient basis for control; officials there, as elsewhere, enlisted the help of the inmate elite, giving its members a variety of privileges in return for their help in maintaining order. The power of the old cons who comprised the inmate elite was based in part on their monopoly of information—their ability to interpret and explain (and occasionally to influence) the behavior of officials who refused to offer their own explanations. Reform wardens' willingness to give explanations—to meet with inmates face to face and to discuss a change in the rules over the prison radio—eliminated the old cons' control over information and explanations.

Reform wardens destroyed another source of inmate leaders' power as well: their monopoly over the black market sale of food, clothing, liquor, and drugs; bookmaking and numbers operations; and loan-sharking. Control over the rackets depended on the "key man" jobs the leaders held—jobs that gave them access to necessary materials or the chance to move about the prison with some degree of freedom—and on their ability to influence, or, in some prisons, to control) the jobs to which other inmates were assigned. In Oahu Prison, the old inmate elite was displaced when the new warden decided to change the basis on which jobs were assigned, tying the allocation of privileges to rehabilitative goals. Shorn of their privileges, inmate leaders lost their authority and, with it, their ability to resolve conflicts and settle disputes; the result was an immediate increase in violence and disorder. "As the authority of the old inmate leaders narrowed to their immediate circle of associates," McCleery writes, "the inmate body ceased to be a community in any meaningful sense of that term and became a set of conflicting factions confined by all-too-narrow walls."[52]

Much the same happened at Stateville in the early 1970s; there, reform administrators abolished a number of "key man" jobs altogether. As James Jacobs sardonically explains, "The reform ideology held that inmates should be clients, not servants"—clients, moreover, to whom the prison's professional staff delivered a variety of social services. But the reformers did not just abolish inmate jobs involving the provision of personal services to prison officials; they removed inmates from all clerical jobs, on the grounds that only professionals should have access to inmate records. (Some sixty-seven inmates had been assigned to jobs in the administration building alone, as clerks, porters, "runners," and the like.) In the name of professionalism, inmates were replaced by civilians in other desirable jobs, too—as teachers, vocational instructors, bookkeepers, and so on. The consequences were as serious as they were unintended. Inmate clerks and "runners" had served as intermediaries between officials and the inmate population, expressing inmate concerns and grievances to the staff and conveying staff concerns and explanations to the inmates. Removing inmates from clerical and "runner" jobs produced a near-total breakdown in communications, for rapid bureaucratization of the prison's administration had also destroyed most other informal channels.[53]

Eliminating inmate jobs weakened custodians as well as inmate leaders. Since patronage—the ability to reward cooperative inmates with good jobs—had been one of the few significant rewards, it was the means by which officials influenced the selection of inmate leaders. Filling "key man" jobs with civilians instead of prisoners eliminated a major incentive to good conduct, thereby destroying the mechanism through which inmate norms had been made to serve custodial ends.

Both custodial power and inmate norms have been weakened, too, by the fact that inmates serve shorter terms than they used to. Incentives, such as a good job, are less attractive to someone serving two or three years than to an inmate facing a ten- or fifteen-year term, especially if it takes a year or two of hard work to prove one's eligibility. Shorter sentences also weaken the authority of the old cons, whose outlook has been shaped, in part, by the fact that prison will be their home for a long time.

Given all these changes, prison officials would have found it difficult to maintain control even if there had been no prisoners' rights movement; the fact that there was enormously complicated their job. Prisons have been attacked for being "lawless agencies," as indeed they are.[54] It is that lawlessness that makes the idea of due process so threatening and so disruptive, for lawlessness and due process are incompatible with one another. To require that charges be proven before a prisoner can be punished, for example, is to introduce far more than a procedural change. Requiring a hearing implies that a guard can be wrong and an inmate right; it conveys an implicit promise that an inmate can refuse a guard's order or challenge his veracity and get away with it.*

It would be hard to imagine a more subversive idea. If inmates can challenge their keepers successfully, they are not entirely powerless; inmates who have "beaten" a guard in a disciplinary hearing are not likely to remain completely passive. Docility is even less likely for

---

* At Stateville, old-time guards and custodial officials specify just when the "trouble" began—in the summer of 1965, when Ross Randolph, who had just succeeded Ragen as State Commissioner, decreed that inmates could remove their gray caps if they wished during the summer heat. This easing of the inmate dress code was followed by an order permitting inmates to talk in the dining room and while marching in line from one activity to another. "Capitulation" in these matters, the Ragenites argued, would only lead to demands for additional "privileges," and to further capitulation by authorities. They were right; the changes were important because of the symbolism they conveyed. They implied, however fleetingly, that inmates had at least some meager rights that officials were bound to respect.

inmates who have beaten their warden or state commissioner in court. At Stateville, television and newspaper coverage of a 1965 Black Muslim suit against
Ragen, then the state commissioner, and Frank Pate,
his hand-picked successor as warden, was an electrify-
ing event for the inmate population. The picture of Pate
and Muslim leader Thomas Cooper testifying in court
as equal adversaries increased the Muslims' prestige
and greatly strengthened inmates' readiness to challenge their traditional status.[55]

Due process has altered the balance of power between keepers and kept in other ways. Even in the old
prison, as we have seen, guards felt compelled to make
deals with inmates, overlooking some infractions so
long as inmates kept things "cool" overall. The need
to get the approval of a superior officer and then of a
disciplinary board before an inmate can be punished
makes guards even more reluctant to enforce the rules.
When their judgments are questioned by their superiors,
guards feel that they, rather than the inmate, are on
trial; and when their disciplinary recommendations are
overturned, guards feel that they have been made fools
of in front of the inmates they are expected to control.
"Under such conditions," Leo Carroll writes, "to exercise custodial control is to place oneself on the line."[56]

All the more so when guards feel abandoned, or even
betrayed, by their superiors. Like patrolmen, guards
must decide how to handle an explosive situation in an
instant, often in situations of imminent danger to themselves; a wrong judgment, or even a moment's hesita-
tion in reaching the right judgment, may cost them their
lives. As a group, reform wardens and state commissioners have been insensitive to the fears and anxieties
of their guards, and have made little effort to persuade
them that new approaches are necessary, let alone
desirable. Paul Keve, one of the more thoughtful of

the new breed of reformers from within, provides a case in point. "The warden cannot run his prison without some degree of loyalty from his beleaguered staff," Keve explains, "and yet with his minimal staff and budget *he often finds it literally impossible to set up the kind of communication with them that would promote a mutual philosophy.*" [emphasis added][57] Why wardens cannot simply talk to the guards directly Keve does not say.

In many prisons, therefore, guards have abdicated their custodial responsibility. Because submitting a disciplinary report may mean that their own competence or integrity is questioned, some guards prefer to look the other way no matter what an inmate does, so long as no one is seriously injured. This, in turn, puts pressure on other guards to do the same, for to enforce a rule his colleagues ignore may subject a guard to vituperation or reprisal. In such a situation, guards go about their work so as to cause themselves the least amount of trouble. Feeling unable to enforce the rules, they try to gain some degree of control— more important, perhaps, some measure of safety for themselves—by becoming friendly with inmates, overlooking even serious infractions and providing advance warning of official actions that may affect their inmate friends. "It's gotten so that I cannot tell an officer things I should be telling him," a senior captain of the guards complained to Leo Carroll. "I can't tell them anything serious because he runs right to the inmates. . . . I can't figure it out. But one thing I do know, most of 'em ain't working for me, they're working for the inmates."[58] (Some guards work for the inmates in a more direct way, bringing narcotics or other contraband to inmate dealers or participating in other prison rackets for a set fee or a share in the profits.)

In other prisons, the entire custodial force—guards,

lieutenants, captains, possibly even the assistant or deputy warden in charge of discipline—may unite against their common enemy: an interventionist judge, a reform warden or state commissioner, or both. "They can do whatever they want in the courts or the state capital," custodians often remark; "but we still run the joint." Indeed they do; a united custodial force may simply sabotage the warden's, or court's, demand for due process—holding disciplinary hearings for example, but simply using them to validate decisions already made. A united custodial force may fight the warden in other ways, such as undermining the treatment program the warden has introduced by harassing inmates who participate. And when they are unionized, guards and officers may force a liberal warden to use repressive measures by threatening to walk off the job unless he agrees to a general lockup or more frequent use of "the hole." As their membership has mushroomed and their members' concerns have changed, guard unions have turned their attention away from bread-and-butter issues to questions of prison policy—for example, the kinds of security measures the prison adopts and the ways in which guards are assigned.[59]

To explain why guards feel beleaguered is not to approve their responses, any more than to explain why inmates turn to violence implies approval of their actions. People who feel victimized and threatened frequently behave in irrational, even self-destructive ways. This was clearly the case at Attica, where a guard union "victory" helped pave the way for the inmate rebellion that followed. Under a new contract that went into effect in New York State prisons in April, 1970, the union took the responsibility for assigning guards to their posts away from the P.K. (Principal Keeper), as the deputy warden was called; guards won the right to "bid" for assignments on the basis of seniority. Feeling threatened by the erosion of their own power and the growing deviance among the inmate population, the older, more experienced guards began to choose assignments involving the smallest amount of contact with inmates. In the past, manning a gun on the wall had been considered a "bad" assignment, especially during the night shift; such posts were reserved for new guards, who started on the wall and "worked their way inside," or for incompetent older guards. By the fall of 1970, the old arrangement had been reversed; the most experienced guards took over the wall posts and inside assignments on the night shift, when inmates were locked in their cells. After the riot, guards and officers agreed that the change had been disastrous, for it had left the day-to-day supervision of inmates to untrained and inexperienced young guards.*[60]

The failure to deal intelligently with the custodial force has exacerbated the breakdown in control in American prisons; the breakdown would have occurred in any case, as a result of changes among the inmate population. To be sure, each generation of keepers has been convinced that it was dealing with a new breed of inmate, and each generation has mourned the passing

---

* The problem was compounded by the Attica administration's decision to assign guards to the cellblocks as a whole, rather than to a particular section within a block. As the McKay Commission pointed out, the two changes together meant that "inmates not only faced inexperienced officers but might face new ones every day. The inmates could never learn what would be expected of them from one day to the next, and the officers could never learn whether an inmate's uncooperative behavior resulted from belligerence, indifference, illness, or some other medical or personal problem. Inmates no longer could adjust to one officer who commanded them, but had to readjust to a succession of officers who changed from day to day." And since officers were likely to work with a different group of inmates from day to day, they had no chance, and no real incentive, to establish rapport or mutual understanding.

of the good old days, when inmates knew their place.*
Each generation may well have been correct: a general
erosion of authority has been going on for more than a
century. But the process accelerated after World War I,
and again in the 1960s. In the United States, as we have
seen, a demographic revolution transformed relationships between the generations; a civil-rights revolution
shattered the caste system and altered the relationship
between the races; and the women's movement is now
challenging, and rapidly overturning, relations between
the sexes. Wherever one turns, one can see a weakening of tradition and of informal controls, and a growing
skepticism about (if not outright rejection of) authority.

There was no way the prisons could have been kept
immune from social and cultural changes as sweeping
as these. In a television age, ideas move rapidly, in both
directions, between prisons and the outside world; and
the accelerating growth in the number of inmates has
filled American prisons with aggressive young offenders
unfamiliar with, and unwilling to abide by, the norms
of the old inmate culture. "The joint ain't like it used
to be," an inmate in his thirties told me. During his
first term, he said, he rather enjoyed being in a dormi-

---

* In every generation, too, keepers have tended to attribute
the change to "outside agitators" of one sort or another. "In
spite of the fact that great advancement has been made in
methods of control, it is also undoubtedly true that in no corresponding length of time have there been more serious outbreaks and revolts in prison," a Wisconsin official told the members of the American Prison Association in 1913. The cause
was clear enough—"the agitation of so-called social workers,"
whose "misrepresentation of the conditions of prisons and
prison life have led prisoners living under admirable prison conditions to believe that they are treated worse than the worst,
and their condition is nothing more nor less than that of abject
slavery." In fact, social workers are "not only causing unrest
within prisons but are contributing a great deal to the development of lawlessness without."[61]

tory; the companionship made up for the lack of privacy, and since most inmates gave at least lip service to the "do your own time" norm, he felt free to develop his own "hustle" so long as he did not anger a guard. Now he would give anything for his own cell. "It's not the screws you have to worry about," he explained; "it's the other cons."

Irreverence for tradition affects inmate-guard relationships, as well as relationships among the inmates themselves. To use Procunier's phrase, prisoners no longer are "buying all the bullshit" their keepers put out; they no longer are accepting their keeper's view of them, nor are they acquiescing in their own subordination. Instead, inmates are protesting the conditions under which they live and are demanding a wide variety of changes; at times, they seem to be rejecting the legitimacy of prison government itself.

Although the entire inmate population has been affected, the change in outlook has been most dramatic among black prisoners, who always have had a double set of grievances. "We're third-class citizens in a second-class society," a black inmate told Leo Carroll. "It's as simple as that." Indeed it was: in addition to the normal pains of imprisonment, black inmates were forced to suffer the pain of racial discrimination. Blacks occupied the lowest positions within inmate society, and they were expected to conduct themselves with appropriate docility. Both Northern and Southern prisons assigned blacks to the dirtiest and most menial jobs; keeping them out of "key man" jobs as clerks, runners, and the like made it virtually impossible for black inmates to move into leadership roles in inmate society. At Stateville, the only blacks who worked in the administration building had jobs as janitors. It was not until 1969, when a court order forced a change, that Stateville officials stopped assigning black and white inmates to separate—and unequal—work crews, as well as to separate cells (until the court order, even the isolation cells were segregated).

For black inmates, as Eldridge Cleaver wrote, imprisonment was "a continuation of slavery on a higher plane." To understand the interracial violence which now afflicts our prisons, we must start with the fact that rebellious black inmates had to fight two sets of enemies: the white officials who assigned them to the bottom caste and the white inmates who cooperated in keeping them there. Until the 1960s, white inmates at Stateville automatically took the front line, with blacks falling into place in the rear, whenever inmates moved through the prison or lined up for meals. At Rhode Island, or "Eastern Correctional Institution," as Leo Carroll calls it, the white editors of the prison newspaper refused to publish articles submitted by black inmates in 1967-68, on the grounds that the paper should reflect only interests and problems shared by all inmates. (The articles were attempts to express black inmates' newly found racial identity.) And when a black vice president of the prison chapter of the "Jaycees" ((the Junior Chamber of Commerce) unexpectedly succeeded to the presidency after the president's unanticipated parole, white officers and committee chairmen moved to impeach him, using physical coercion to get the necessary votes. A few months later, a group of black inmates were placed in segregation for defying the warden's order to disband their Afro-American Society; their cells were set on fire, and the personal possessions they had left behind were totally destroyed.[62]

The last ten or fifteen years have seen a monumental reversal of roles. In their relations with authorities, blacks have become the most defiant, rather than the most compliant, inmate group. "It's a frightening ef-

fect," a Rhode Island guard told Leo Carroll. "Here
you are all alone surrounded by ten or fifteen blacks
and it's your problem, you know. Good luck! What are
they gonna do to me? Are they gonna drive me into
the ground? Or is one gonna come at me with a razor
blade and slash my throat? Or are they gonna beat the
shit outta me? Believe me, all this is possible." If he
can possibly avoid it, therefore, the guard avoids "book-
ing" a black inmate on a disciplinary charge: "Maybe I
should book him, but I can do without that kind of
aggravation." "Any man who says he wasn't afraid,
I'd have to call him a liar," a middle-aged Statesville
guard told James Jacobs after a 1974 riot.

Guards, especially white guards, have good reason to
be afraid. Physical attacks on guards have risen dramatically, and every guard lives with the knowledge
that he may be taken hostage in a riot or protest—or
that he may find a shiv in his back. Violence aside,
black inmates often refuse to obey guards' orders; when
guards or superior officers try to move in to "walk" a
black inmate to "the hole" or lock him in his cell, they
may find their way barred by ten or twenty-five other
inmates who have rallied to the support of their
"brother." Unless the incident is so serious that it cannot be ignored, the guards are likely to back off rather
than risk triggering a large-scale riot. Understandably,
the turnover rate among guards is high; of those who
voluntarily quit their jobs at Stateville in a one-year
period, 50 percent gave "lack of safety" as the reason.[63]

Black defiance is the result of the conjunction of a
number of changes. For one thing, many young black
offenders seem thoroughly unfrightened by the prospect
of a prison term, which they see—or claim to see—as
a continuation of their life in the streets. "I'm doing
time all my life, man," a black inmate told Leo Car-

roll. "Don't make much difference if I do it here or out there, it's still time." "We be used to time so we be immune to it," another black remarked. "Because we been slaves for 400 years."

For young offenders who have been affiliated with a gang, coming into prison may be almost like coming home. At Stateville, the chief of one Chicago gang counted about seventy-five of his members when he arrived; the gang issued a set of ten written rules to all its Stateville members. Although less formal, other gangs made certain that members felt at home, giving coffee, tea, cigarettes, deodorant, and soap to new members on their arrival. Most important of all, gang membership provides psychological support—a sense of "being somebody"—that cushions or even offsets the prison's general assault on inmates' self-image. (Kinship relations perform the same functions for Mexican-American and Puerto Rican prisoners, although gang membership also plays a role.[64])

In both prisons and ghettos, manhood tends to be defined as toughness. Indeed, the Stackolee role always has existed in inmate culture; but because inmate leaders were committed to stability and order, "ballbusters" and "outlaws" were looked down upon and effectively neutralized by inmate norms as well as by official action. Whenever the old system of control broke down, however, the Stackolee types tended to take over the leadership roles.[65]

What has happened, in part, is that prisons have been filled with young black offenders incarcerated precisely because they were playing Stackolee on the streets; they see no reason to surrender their "bad nigger" image just because they are behind walls. For three centuries, black Americans lived in fear of whites; it is hard to overestimate the liberating effect on blacks when they discover that the shoe is now on the other foot—that it is whites who fear them, and that they can inspire fear by their very presence.

In a world where "bad" is good, and "baddest" is best of all, the sanctions that guards have at their disposal often are ineffectual, if not actually counter-productive. In the old authoritarian prisons, officials were free to keep inmates in "the hole" for their entire term, and terms were long; inmates hesitated to defy authorities. But court orders have limited the length of time an inmate can be kept in "the hole"; at Stateville, the limit is fifteen days, and the Chicago gang members incarcerated there seem quite unconcerned about doing one or two such terms, especially when it means being thrown into a cell with a half-dozen colleagues. For young black inmates, in fact, showing that they are not afraid of being sent to "the hole" have become a way of demonstrating their manhood.

Officials have responded by finding ways of evading court orders and imposing tougher forms of punishment. At Stateville, the "solution" was to construct the Special Program Unit (SPU), a maximum-security unit designed to hold "a relatively small but highly visible and significant element which is extremely disruptive, difficult to control, and seriously threatening to the welfare of our institutions." SPU contained mesh grating over the cells (so that inmates could not throw things at guards), strip cells, and a mobile iron cage designed to protect guards from attack; by providing behavior modification and other intensive "treatment," Stateville officials hoped to satisfy liberal critics and bolster control at the same time. The idea backfired: for violent gang members, assignment to SPU became a status symbol—evidence that they were indeed the "baddest motherfuckers" of all. Lest anyone doubt their credentials, SPU residents tore down the wire mesh, then the heavier bars with which the mesh was replaced, and hurled porcelain and metal missiles, as well as urine and feces, at guards and other officials (including Dr. Karl Menninger, who served as special consultant to the unit). Black inmates' defiance of authority simply overwhelmed the prison's capacity for punishment and exposed reform administrations' inability to create a humane and effective approach to governance.[66]

Within inmate society, meanwhile, black prisoners have turned the old caste system upside down. They are the majority in most large prisons; even where they are in the minority, their solidarity, combined with a willingness to resort to violence, enables them to assume the dominant role. "They think they're superior and they push us around all the time," a white inmate in the Rhode Island prison, where more than three-quarters of the inmates are white, told Leo Carroll. "Like in the dining room. If I was late and tryin' to catch up with a buddy and cut in front of one of them, I'd probably get piped [hit over the head with a piece of pipe]. But they cut in front of white men all the time and nothin' happens."[67]

"Nothin' happens" because neither white inmates nor guards are willing to risk a confrontation. At Green Haven, one of New York State's five maximum-security prisons, nearly half the inmates avoid the prison mess halls altogether, preparing their own meals instead. "If one of the new element jumps in line ahead of me or makes a remark about honkies and he knows I've heard it, I'd have to hit him and that would get me into trouble," a middle-aged inmate who has spent thirty-six of his last thirty-nine years behind bars told Susan Sheehan of *The New Yorker.* "I don't need trouble," he added. "But I can't let such a remark go by. I'm not from a blue-blooded family, I don't have a million dollars. All I have is my image, how I'm regarded in

prison, how I carry myself." More than pride is involved; failure to respond to a calculated insult marks
an inmate as someone who can be pushed around at
any time. "They'll let a remark go by, and the next
thing you know they'll be standing in the yard in front
of the TV set and some guy standing behind them will
say, 'Hey, creep, get out of here,' and they'll have to
go."[68]

Black inmates are using their power of intimidation
to gain the status denied them in the free world. In
prison, they are the dominant caste, standing in the
front of the line, taking the front row at the movies, deciding which records will be played, taking over the
best "courts" in the prison yard, and controlling the use
of the gym and recreation room. Segregation is as rigid
as it ever was, but it is enforced by blacks rather than
whites. In prisons with Puerto Rican or Mexican-American as well as black and Anglo populations, the caste
line defines Hispanic inmates as "white"; they often see
themselves as allies against the common (black)
enemy.[69]

And prisons have become racial battlefields. Stackolee was no rebel, after all; he was more concerned with
demonstrating his "badness" than with achieving any
goal or accomplishing any purpose. His violence was
directed at anyone in his range, often in a self-destructive, almost suicidal way. Black prison violence has
little to do with political protest or rebellion. For the
most part, its purpose is expressive rather than instrumental—gaining revenge for three and a half centuries
of oppression and humiliation, rather than eliminating
the sources of oppression and humiliation. Hence politically sophisticated black inmates decry violence
against white inmates, with whom they would like to
form a political alliance.

There is no better form of revenge than homosexual rape, which offers black inmates a means of demonstrating their manhood and "getting back at Whitey" at the same time. "You guys been cuttin' our b——— off ever since we been in this country. Now we're just gettin' even," a black Rhode Island inmate told Leo Carroll. "It's a way for the black man to get back at the white man," another said. "It's one way he can assert his manhood. Anything white, even a defenseless punk, is part of what the black man hates. It's part of what he's had to fight all his life just to survive, just to have a hole to sleep in and some garbage to eat." Thus a black inmate "can show he's a man by making a white guy into a girl." "The black man's just waking up to what's been going on," a more sophisticated inmate told Carroll, by way of rationalizing the high rate of black-on-white rapes. "Now that he's awake, he's gonna be mean. He's been raped—politically, economically, morally raped. He sees this now, but his mind's still small so he's getting back this way. But it's just a beginning."

It is a large "beginning." After analyzing prison records and talking with inmates and guards, Leo Carroll estimated that there were forty to fifty sexual assaults a year in Rhode Island prison—an extraordinary number for an inmate population of less than 200; about 75 percent involve a black attacker and white victim. In his report on sexual assaults in the Philadelphia prisons in the late 1960s, Alan Davis found that 56 percent of the incidents involved black offenders and white victims. (Twenty-nine percent involved black offenders and black victims, and 15 percent involved white offenders and white victims; there were no instances in which the offender was white and the victim black.) Clemens Bartollas, Stuart Miller, and Simon Dinitz found the same

pattern of interracial victimization in the Ohio training
school they studied. "Exploit whites" was such a cardinal rule, Bartollas, Miller, and Dinitz report, that blacks
who did not conform to it were looked upon as deviant
and were subjected to considerable verbal harassment
from their black peers. In Rhode Island, Professor Carroll found, virtually every black prisoner played the
"ripper" (or "wolf," or "jocker," or "gorilla," depending on the argot) role at one time or another, usually
when they were new to the prison and trying to gain
their "brothers'" acceptance. Raping a white prisoner
serves as an initiation rite—a means by which new
black inmates demonstrate their manhood and their
blackness to their peers. And rape is only one of a number of ways in which black inmates exploit white inmates; the mere threat of rape is enough to persuade
many white inmates to pay tribute to blacks in money,
cigarettes, other merchandise, or "voluntary" sex. An
Ohio inmate sums up the situation in one sentence:
"The blacks want to bring slavery back to us now."[70]

V

There can be no hope of reform, no chance of making
prisons more decent and humane, unless order is restored. Conjugal visits, work release programs, home
furloughs, recreation fields, vocational training, psychological counseling—all are useless if inmates live in
constant fear of being raped or "piped." Court guarantees of due process are irrelevant if inmates ask to be
placed in segregation for their own protection. In short,
prison officials' ability or inability to maintain order
affects inmates' well-being more directly, and far more
profoundly, than does any other aspect of prison life.

But order cannot be restored by returning to the

totalitarian methods of the past.* The courts would forbid it. And as the experience of the Special Program Unit at Stateville suggests, inmate opposition would make the effort futile; not even a Joe Ragen could run a contemporary prison in the Ragen manner.

Judging by the experience of the Vienna Correctional center (VCC), a minimum-security institution in southern Illinois, it is possible to maintain order without repression.[71]

• VCC has not had a riot, strike, or any other disturbance in the twelve years it has been in operation; no correctional officer has been hurt, and there has been no serious violence among the inmate population. With 560 residents, as the inmates are called, in a congregate living situations, tension and problems do arise, but it is rare for residents to stray beyond the acceptable limits of behavior.

• Some 5,000 offenders have done time at VCC during those twelve years; despite a total absence of walls, fences, barbed wire, guard towers, or other perimeter security, there have been only seventeen escapes, involving a grand total of twenty-seven residents.

• Morale is so high among guards and other employees that staff turnover averages about 2 percent a year, compared to an annual turnover rate of about 110 percent at Stateville. In November, 1977, VCC had applications from about 2,000 job seekers on file.

This stability has not come about because VCC is filled with choirboys; the prison holds some of the most serious offenders in the Illinois penal system. (Most have been convicted of robbery, burglary, murder, or a major drug offense.) On the basis of offenses committed, the VCC population is no different from

---

* When those methods worked, they did so at a heavy cost; "going stir bugs"—the Stateville term for a paranoid breakdown—was an almost daily occurrence during Ragen's reign.

that of Stateville, Joliet, or Menard; in fact, almost every VCC resident was transferred from one of those maximum-security prisons. The disorder that has plagued most prisons could have developed easily at VCC if the facility had been managed differently.

Indeed, one might have expected a good deal of racial animosity and tension, given VCC's location and the wildly divergent backgrounds of residents and staff. Residents come mostly from Chicago, some 350 miles to the north; Rockford, which is even more distant; and East St. Louis, about 150 miles to the west. More than half the residents are black, constituting 53 to 57 percent of the prison population. Correctional officers are predominantly white and for the most part come from the conservative, rural areas of southern Illinois. (Until a few years ago, there rarely were more than a handful of black officers; as a result of some aggressive recruiting, blacks now comprise about 15 percent of the custodial force.) Vienna itself is a town of 1,300, about twenty miles from the Kentucky border; culturally, it is more Southern than Northern, as is true of most of southern Illinois.

The location was chosen for the same reason most prisons are built in rural areas: to provide patronage for powerful politicians. In this instance, two of the most influential members of the Illinois legislature came from Vienna; for some time, they had been lobbying for construction of a large state institution—a mental hospital would also have been satisfactory—as a way of reversing the area's long-term economic decline. The prison has done just that. It is the largest employer in the county; more than 60 percent of Vienna's 282 employees are long-time county residents, including the mayors of Vienna and another town, a former Vienna mayor, the presidents of the Vienna Kiwanis

Club and Chamber of Commerce, several local athletic heroes, and members of a number of influential families. The prison does much of its purchasing locally, and inmates and their families shop in town with some frequency; because of those expenditures, as well as the purchasing power generated by the prison's payroll, the county's three banks have increased their assets steadily since VCC opened in 1965. The county is the only one in southern Illinois that has grown in population since the 1960 census.

Economic dependency does not normally breed affection. Residents of company towns usually resent the company; when the "company" is a prison, resentment generally turns into suspicion and hostility, with local residents erecting an impenetrable social barrier between themselves and prison inmates and inmates' relatives and friends.* (When inmates are black and residents are white, the social barrier is even higher.) Initially, it appeared as though Vienna would follow the usual pattern; there was considerable fear and resistance among townspeople when the prison was first proposed.

Those fears have been overcome, thanks to the political and professional skill of Warden Vernon G. Housewright. Housewright's predecessor, together with

---

* I encountered that barrier early in my research, when my wife and I were driving through a largely rural area to visit a prison for youthful offenders (fifteen- to eighteen-year-olds). We stopped at a gas station a few miles from the prison; the owner chatted amiably with us until I asked for directions to the prison. Then his body stiffened, his amiability disappeared, and his conversation stopped. He watched us suspiciously, and with evident dislike, until we drove away. Since we were of an age to have a son in prison, it seemed apparent that he took us for parents on a visit; having made this assumption, he wanted to have as little to do with us as possible—and to get us out of his station as soon as he could.

local business and political leaders, had tried to "sell" the economic advanges that would flow from the construction of a prison. When Housewright took over in 1968, he redirected the public relations effort away from the value of a prison as such, and toward the desirability of making it an open, progressive institution. By using VCC to provide a wide variety of services, he has given citizens a stake in the continuation of its programs and open style of government.

When the county suddenly found itself with no ambulance service, for example (service had been provided by undertakers, who were barred from the business by a new state licensing law), Housewright rapidly obtained a government grant to buy ambulances and to train inmates as emergency medical technicians. The Emergency Medical Technician Program now provides round-the-clock emergency medical care, with radio-directed ambulances, to two other counties as well; inmate medical technicians have saved the lives of a number of people injured or stricken ill in remote areas of the three counties. As an added service, inmate-technicians now teach cardiac-pulmonary resuscitation to local citizens in a course given in the prison school, and VCC residents, trained in fire-fighting techniques, constitute the local fire department.

Prison labor and facilities also have been used to expand recreational facilities. VCC residents built and maintain, without charge, a Little League baseball field for Vienna; residents serve as umpires for Little League games, the boys' and girls' summer softball leagues, and elementary and high school games. (The prison band entertains at interscholastic games, as well as at free concerts.) The prison gym is the site of an annual invitational basketball tournament, sponsored by the prison, which is entered by teams from all over southern Illinois; the prison also provides fishing permits to local sportsmen who want to fish in its seventy-acre lake.

And this is not all, by any means. A series of federal grants has enabled faculty members from Southern Illinois University and Shawnee Community College to offer a wide range of vocational training programs and academic courses at the prison. By opening the courses to town and county citizens, Housewright avoided the resentment they might have felt over felons being offered opportunities denied them. In the process, the prison school has become the adult education center for the whole area; in the fall of 1977, some 300 citizens were attending day and night courses, sitting side by side with VCC residents. Now that adults have become accustomed to mingling with prisoners, Housewright has invited local high schools to use the prison's equipment and staff to provide vocational education programs which the schools themselves cannot offer. In the fall of 1977, when the program began, twenty-six high school students were in attendance, spending some two and a half hours a day in the prison shops. (After three or four months, the program was working so well that Housewright and high school officials were planning to expand it the following year.)

None of this would have been possible if the prisoners had behaved like prisoners, i.e., if they had been disorderly or violent, or if they had taken advantage of the opportunities to escape or to victimize townspeople. That they have not done so is a tribute to Warden Housewright's thoughtfulness and ability—confirmation of his belief that under the right conditions even serious felons can demonstrate a capacity for responsible behavior. "You don't accomplish much by the use of force," Housewright told me. "I think we've shown that it is more effective to treat men as men."

This was not the premise on which the institution

was originally planned. Vienna started out as a conventional prison—indeed, as Joe Ragen's vision, or nightmare, of what a minimum-security prison should be. The first building erected (there were to be eight more) was an X-shaped cellblock, with four cement block dormitories radiating out from a fortress-like control center; the bulletproof center was designed so that guards could bring unobstructed rifle fire to bear on the entire inmate population. The nine cellblocks, in turn, were to have been surrounded by a barbed-wire fence with guard towers; at night, the armed guards in the towers would have been supplemented by a roving dog patrol. But Ragen was forced out as state commissioner in 1965, the year the first building opened. The new state administration scrapped the plans and hired a different architect to design a prison more in keeping with its liberal, humane approach.

The new facility, which opened in 1971, looks more like a suburb, or college campus, than a prison. Instead of a prison yard, there is a "town square," surrounded by two chapels, a large school building, kitchen and dining room, library, gym, and small, detached buildings containing a commissary, barbershop, and other services. Paths lead from the town square to several "neighborhoods"—clusters of buildings, resembling row town houses or garden apartments, which house the 560 residents in individual rooms. Each room has a bed, desk, closet, and solid-wood locking doors, for which residents are issued their own keys.

The architecture and design are helpful, for they convey a set of positive expectations about the way in which VCC residents will act. The decision to give each prisoner a key to his own room extends those expectations; so does Warden Housewright's insistence that they be called "residents," rather than "prisoners," "inmates," or "cons." This is not just another of the euphemisms and circumlocutions with which the field of "corrections" is plagued; it is a means of changing the way correctional officers view the prisoners in their charge; and thus the way the two groups interact. (In the overall environment Housewright has created, calling guards "correctional officers" also alters the way the kept perceive their keepers.)

The fatal flaw in the traditional approach to prison government, Housewright believes, is that by expecting the worst, it succeeds in bringing out the worst in people's attitudes and behavior. Traditional prison rules are geared to the lowest common denominator. Because some inmates will try to escape, every inmate is kept behind bars and guard towers; because some inmates may attack guards or other inmates, every prisoner is kept under close and rigid surveillance. In fact, Housewright argues, only a minority of prisoners are unwilling to abide by prison rules; instead of gearing everything to that minority, it makes more sense to erect a prison government around the majority of conforming inmates, and then to zero in on those who refuse to conform.

It is a lot easier to do this at VCC than at Stateville or other maximum-security prisons. VCC decides which inmates it will accept, rejecting those who have been "troublemakers" elsewhere and taking only inmates who have "earned their way out" of a maxi-prison by demonstrating their willingness and ability to abide by institutional rules. (In making their decisions, members of the VCC screening committee place primary emphasis on "how quiet the man has been inside.") VCC residents, therefore, are less likely to rebel against authority than the average Stateville inmate; having served much or most of their term elsewhere, they are close to parole and thus have another incentive to conform.*

Even so, it is the nature of the relationship between inmates and staff that is mainly responsible for VCC's success. "You can talk to staff here," residents say; "they really listen, and they try to help." The help is substantial—first-rate job training and education, as well as counseling to deal with personal and familial problems. And the advantages of conforming to the rules far outweigh the disadvantages. The advantages are clear enough: VCC is an infinitely pleasanter place in which to do time than any maximum- or medium-security prison. ("We'd rather go home by Greyhound than by bloodhound" is a popular refrain among inmates.) The cost of not conforming is equally clear: return to Stateville, Joliet, or Menard. Precisely because VCC is so attractive, Housewright has a powerful sanction at his disposal.† Equally important, inmates recognize the fact that disorder could easily and rapidly undermine the community acceptance VCC has gained—hence they make sure that new residents are socialized into an inmate culture that emphasizes the value of cooperation.

If the Vienna Correctional Center offers a glimpse of what can be, it also reveals the different choices reformers must face and the magnitude of the changes

---

* In November, 1977, for example, there were sixty-seven residents whose crimes had been serious enough to draw fifty-year sentences; most of them were within approximately five years of being eligible for parole. (Inmates usually are eligible for parole after serving a third of the term to which they were sentenced.)

† The sanction is used; in 1976, about 5 percent of those transferred to Vienna were returned to a maximum-security prison. Before transferring a resident, authorities try other punishments; VCC has six jail cells to which residents who commit serious infractions may be sent. The cells are used mainly for new arrivals who feel the need to test the limits.

that are required. On the one hand, the prospect of being sent to VCC is a strong incentive for inmates in maximum-security prisons to avoid violence and to comply with institutional rules. Concentrating tractable prisoners in some institutions means that rebellious inmates are concentrated in the rest. Without the stabilizing influence of the first group, the whole burden of control is placed on the guards and administration.

To restructure our correctional system along VCC lines would be a monumental task. In Illinois alone, fourteen new prisons would have to be built; the construction bill might come to $350 million.[72] (The necessary talent might be in even shorter supply than money.) Moreover, there is a certain risk in building new prisons, for old ones rarely are shut down: Pennsylvania's Eastern State Penitentiary, which was opened in 1829, was not closed until 1969. Instead of replacing existing institutions, new prisons frequently are used to expand the capacity of the whole system—another example of reforms backfiring.

It makes more sense, therefore, to try to transform existing institutions, and VCC's Warden Housewright believes it can be done. Most prisons consist of a number of more or less separate (or separable) units; to reduce a huge institution to something approaching a human scale, each of these units could be run as if it were a separate prison. The way to reorganize, Housewright suggests, is to take a single unit, empty it completely, then start all over again as if it were a brand-new institution. This would mean training staff (before the new facility at Vienna opened in 1971, every correctional officer attended an intensive six-week training program at Southern Illinois University's School of Criminal Justice) and beginning with a relatively small number of inmates who have demonstrated a willingness to conform to reasonable rules. Once a new inmate

culture has evolved, the unit could expand by adding
a few inmates at a time; what is crucial is that growth be
slow enough for new inmates to be absorbed into the
existing social structure.

There is no guarantee that such an approach would
work; it would be fatuous to pretend otherwise. Nor
should we be under any illusions that making prisons
more humane will solve the problem of criminal violence. Reform is essential for our sake, not just for the
sake of the inmates and guards. As the Judaeo-Chris-
tian tradition teaches, the character of any society is
judged by the way that society treats the least of its
members.

11

Afterword: "Whatever Is, Is Possible"

If men define situations as real, they are real in their consequences.

—W. I. THOMAS

... what we call necessary institutions are often no more than institutions to which we have grown accustomed. ... in matters of social constitution the field of possibilities is much more extensive than men living in their various societies are ready to imagine.

—ALEXIS DE TOCQUEVILLE

More is learned from the single success than from the multiple failures. A single success proves it can be done. ... Whatever is, is possible.

—ROBERT K. MERTON

I

Ten minutes after the lights went out, the looting began; "they're coming across Bushwick Avenue like buffalo," a caller told the desk sergeant at Brooklyn's 81st Precinct at about 9:40 P.M. on the night of July 13, 1977. Armed with crowbars, sometimes formed by

This chapter is based in part on research by Arlene Silberman.

wrenching steel parking meters out of their concrete bases, the looters tore steel shutters and grilles off storefronts as though they were opening flip-top soda cans. They quickly shattered the plateglass windows and scooped up everything that could be carried, occasionally putting the buildings to the torch when they were done.

In some neighborhoods, the looters went about their work in a systematic way, starting with appliance, furniture, jewelry, and liquor stores—TV sets and stereos were in particular demand—and turning to food and clothing stores only when nothing else was left. Some individuals were even more selective. In one appliance store, a man was seen returning a black-and-white television set and taking a color set in exchange. In a furniture store, a woman wandered about, asking if anyone had seen end tables; when none could be found, she left in disgust, complaining, "I just can't use a thing up here." Elsewhere, looters were completely undiscriminating: one man was caught with 300 sink stoppers; another, with a case of clothespins. "Window shoppers finally got a chance to fulfill their desires and not just live with bare necessities," one observer told reporters for *The Village Voice*. "Everybody stepped into the television commercials for a few hours and took what they wanted."[1]

It was more complicated than that. Although many people were acquiring luxuries for their own use—children descended on shoe stores en masse, looking for "Pro-Keds" and other name-brand sneakers—others were stocking up with merchandise for resale. Entrepreneurial types drove up to furniture and appliance stores in stolen or rented trucks and loaded them with couches, tables, beds, refrigerators, stereos, TV sets, and whatever else they could find. Others arrived in their own cars and trucks, sometimes using their headlights to illuminate store interiors so that they could make a more discerning selection.

Explanations of the looting had a hollow ring. "When the lights went out, people just said, 'Here's our chance to get back at the mothers who have been ripping us off,'" Father Vincent Gallo, an activist Catholic priest, told a *Time* reporter. But the looting lacked the political content and racial anger that characterized the riots of the 1960s. Indeed, the "mothers" whom the looters were "getting back at" came in every color and nationality. Looters did not distinguish between businesses owned by whites and those owned by blacks or Hispanics, as they had during the riots of the 1960s; nor did they distinguish between locally owned stores and those owned by "outsiders." Eight of the sixteen stores of the Fedco supermarket chain, the largest black-owned retailing firm in the country, were broken into, and two stores were utterly wiped out. In the Fort Greene section of Brooklyn, a cooperative supermarket set up by local black residents after the 1968 riots suffered the same fate; the co-op had not protected its windows with metal grilles. "We thought we were part of the community," the store manager explained; "we were wrong." (A privately owned supermarket a block away went unscathed; looters found it too difficult to pry open the metal gates.)[2]

Black merchants found themselves the target of class animus. "Why us, man?" Kermith Morgan, co-owner of LeMans, a Manhattan men's clothing store that had become a national style-setter for the black middle class, asked one of the people looting his store. (Morgan and his partner had opened the store nine years earlier, with $3,000 in savings and a $25,000 loan from the Small Business Administration; they expanded the store five times, and by the night of the looting had an investment of $500,000 in inventory and fixtures.) "Your bourgie

customers drive up in their Mercedes and think we're
s—t because we ain't got nothing," the man replied.
"Well, we getting something."[3] (In some neighborhoods, "getting something" meant stealing it from other
looters, as well as from merchants.)

The contrast with what happened during the great
blackout of 1965 was striking. In 1965, New Yorkers
were gripped with a camaraderie that made the metropolis resemble Grover's Corners, the benign village of
Thornton Wilder's *Our Town*. The crime rate fell; only
96 arrests were made all night, compared to 3,076 arrests for looting during the 1977 blackout. To be sure,
the 1965 blackout occurred at 5:30 P.M. on a cool November afternoon, when people were indoors or on
their way home from work; since it was the first such
experience, New Yorkers had no way of knowing that
the lights would be out for a long time. Moreover, many
storeowners who had not yet locked up for the night
decided to stay in their stores, providing a deterrent to
looting. In 1977, by contrast, most stores were already
closed for the night when the lights went out, and many
poor people were in the streets, trying to escape the
heat that had built up indoors during a long heat wave.
And the number of unemployed black and Hispanic
youths was larger in 1977 than it was in 1965, in part
because of the explosive increase in the teenage population, and in part as a residue of the economic stagnation
of the early and mid-1970s.

Even so, the '65 blackout occurred at an inoppor-
tune time. Just three months earlier, thirty-four people
had been killed in the week-long riot in the Watts section of Los Angeles. There had been rioting the summer before in New York's Harlem and Bedford-Stuyvesant, as well as in other cities, but the number of
people killed, together with the scale and duration of
the Watts riot, made it a watershed in race relations.

The unleashing of black anger was fueled by the fact, widely noted in the black press, that for all the reports of "marauding mobs" that "pillaged, burned, and killed," the Watts rioters killed only one person, whereas the police and National Guardsmen killed twenty-six rioters and bystanders.* Against this backdrop, one might well have expected mass looting during the 1965 blackout; yet there was no looting or disorder of any kind.

The ingredients for mass looting were present on both occasions; they are *always* present in urban ghettos and slums, with their heavy concentrations of poor, angry, and alienated people. But, except on rare occasions, the overwhelming majority of people restrain their anger and their desire to "step into the television commercials and take what they want." On the night of July 13, 1977, poverty was just as severe and unemployment just as high at 9:29 P.M., when the lights were on, as they were at 9:31, when the city was plunged into darkness. And there were no more policemen on the streets at 9:29 than there were at 9:40, when the looting was well under way. In just ten minutes, an ordinary summer evening turned into a Hobbesian "war of every man against every man."

The only thing that changed during those ten minutes was black and Hispanic New Yorkers' willingness to obey the law voluntarily; when the lights went out, they extinguished the self-control that had held lawlessness in check. "It was just like *Lord of the Flies*," psychologist Ernest Dichter told a *Time* reporter. "People resort to savage behavior when the brakes of civilization fail." Why those brakes fail on one occasion and not on

---

* In addition, a store owner killed someone looting his store; one policeman was killed when another accidentally discharged his gun; a fireman was killed when a wall collapsed; and four deaths were unexplained.[4]

another is a question to which there is no answer; we know far too little about the psychology of mob behavior.

If I dwell on the blackout looting, it is because it gave such a vivid demonstration of how limited a role the institutions of the criminal justice system normally play in maintaining order. What seem to be failures of law enforcement, Roscoe Pound pointed out more than a half-century ago, when crime also was a major concern, in reality are manifestations of our tendency to ask more of the criminal justice system than it is able to deliver. For in contemporary society, Dean Pound wrote, the criminal justice system "is called on to do the whole work" of social control, "where once it shared the task with other agencies and was invoked, not for every occasion, but exceptionally."[5]

This is not to suggest that the criminal justice system is irrelevant; far from it. Law may appear to be "a tiny thing, an infinitesimal part of civilization," Karl Llewellyn wrote. "In a similar way, medicine may perhaps appear to be a tiny thing. Few of us are interested in the doctor while we are well, or until an epidemic threatens. But like medicine, law is needed desperately when it is needed at all. It operates upon the fringe. But that fringe is a fringe of high necessity."[6]

This is so for several reasons. In any society, some people will observe the law only under the threat of coercion and punishment. More important, as I have argued throughout the last five chapters, the law and the institutions through which it is administered and enforced are educating institutions. From them, there emanates what Johannes Andenaes calls "a flow of propaganda" that encourages or discourages respect for law. It is essential, therefore, that we develop more just, as well as more effective, law enforcement institutions. We will have to do more than that; the institutions of the criminal justice system cannot bear the entire burden of social control. In contemporary society, no less than in the past, the ultimate source of order is not coercion but custom and habit—the habit of voluntary and automatic (and often unconscious) compliance that keeps most people law-abiding most of the time, even in situations in which detection or punishment are unlikely. Without voluntary compliance, no government could maintain order without turning society into an armed camp.

Even then, the consent of the governed is essential; so long as the people being controlled outnumber their controllers, the latter depend on the acquiescence of the former. This is true in prison, as we saw in the last chapter, and it was true in New York on the night of the blackout. When the lights went out, fewer than 3,500 police officers were on patrol, the normal complement for that time of night; officials estimate that they would have needed at least ten times that number to prevent the looting or to stop it quickly. Had most looters been unwilling to leave voluntarily when the police, augmented by off-duty officers, made a show of force, the police would have been unable to restore order without the help of the armed forces. "If they'd wanted us, they could have had us any time that night," one patrolman observed. "There was nothing we could have done about it."[7]

Thus the development of more effective social controls in poor communities can provide a far larger payoff in reduced crime and improved order than can the development of more effective methods of policing, more efficient courts, or improved correctional programs. There is truth, besides rhetorical exaggeration, in E. H. Sutherland's dictum: "When the mores are adequate, laws are unnecessary; when the mores are inadequate, the laws are ineffective." It is not a question of either/or; both laws and mores are needed. The point is that they are complementary: the stronger the mores, the more effective the laws tend to be.

II

But are there grounds for believing that poor communities can develop more effective social controls—that "the mores" can be strengthened to the point where laws are effective?

The answer is yes. In the face of widespread gloom about the disintegration of social controls in poor black and Hispanic communities, and doubts about whether the process can be reversed, it is useful to recall the "law" of human society that Robert Merton laid down: "Whatever is, is possible."[8] I have looked at what is; from Puerto Rico to New York to California, I have seen evidence that it is possible to infuse poverty-stricken neighborhoods with a sense of community and purpose, and thus to develop the internal controls that help reduce (or prevent) crime. Not that nirvana has been achieved; in most instances, "success" means not that a community had been transformed, but that a serious effort is being made—that approaches are being tried that offer hope of significant change.

The central dilemma of any anti-poverty effort is that the cure may be worse than the disease. With rare exceptions, impoverished communities need massive infusions of help from the outside; almost everything in poor people's lives persuades them that they are victims, rather than masters, of their fate. But receiving help from the outside often perpetuates the sense of impotence and powerlessness that is a cause, as well as consequence, of poverty. Independence is difficult when one person is constantly in the position of magnanimous donor and the other in the position of perennial recipient; receiving help is a submission, one that erodes dignity and destroys the spirit.[9]

If a community development program is to have any chance of success, those in charge must understand that the controls that lead to reduced crime cannot be imposed from the outside; they must emerge from changes in the community itself, and in the people who compose it. Hence the emphasis must be on enabling poor people to take charge of their own lives—on helping them gain a sense of competence and worth, a sense of being somebody who matters.

Changes of this sort have been occurring in St. Louis, where tenant groups have taken over management of five deteriorating and crime-ridden housing projects. A series of Ford Foundation grants totaling $500,000 made it possible to teach the resident managers the technical and managerial skills needed for day-to-day operations; but the tenant management corporations, elected by project residents, have defined their goals in broader terms. In Carr Square, a 658-unit complex, residents have created an impressive degree of order in a community that had been bordering on complete chaos. ("The whole thing was a hellhole," the city housing director recalls.) The management corporation organized a daycare center for preschool children and hired teenage girls to deliver meals and perform other household chores for elderly shut-ins; the exteriors of the crumbling buildings have been repaired, and tiny gardens—a useful index of how people feel about the neighborhood they inhabit—seem to blossom everywhere. Carr Square is not Scarsdale; older people still fear going out at night. But there has been a significant change in behavior. Serious crimes have been cut by more than 50 percent since the program began in 1969, and as a result similar efforts are under way in a number of other cities.

In East Palo Alto, California, a poverty-stricken, predominantly black community of 18,000, the Community Youth Responsibility Program is trying to attack juvenile crime more directly. (In the now-classic manner, East Palo Alto is physically separated from the adjoining and prosperous all-white suburbs of Palo Alto and Menlo Park.) Technically, the Community Youth Responsibility Program (CYRP) is a juvenile court diversion program supported by state and federal funds; slightly more than half the youngsters it serves are referred by the police or courts, with the remainder being referred by schools, social-service agencies, churches, and parents.

What distinguishes CYRP is its attempt to integrate —or, perhaps more correctly, insinuate—its operations into community norms, and to create an indigenous leadership, cutting across age and generation lines, that can enforce those norms. This attempt takes several forms. Responsibility for the program's overall operation is vested in the twelve-member Board of Directors composed of seven adults and five youngsters below the age of nineteen, all of them community residents.

The unit around which the program revolves is the seven-member "Community Panel"—four adults and three youngsters—which meets regularly to hear cases referred to CYRP, make an adjudication, and recommend an appropriate "sentence." If the Community Panel finds the "defendant" guilty of vandalism, say, it may order the youngster to repair the window that was broken, replant trampled flower beds, or make restitution in some other appropriate way. To underscore the fact that shoplifting and other forms of theft are offenses against the whole community, not just the victim, guilty offenders may be ordered to perform a so-called "involvement task," i.e., working a specified number of hours a week, without pay, in some local

community agency. The panel may also direct youngsters to attend a weekly counseling session with one of
the social workers on CYRP's all-black staff. (More
often than not, the panel orders counseling plus either
restitution or an involvement task, or both.)

Like the Peace Corps, CYRP may have a greater impact on its volunteer workers than on the people it is
designed to serve. At the time of my visit, the program
had been remarkably successful in finding and nurturing leadership ability; although it had been in operation
for only two and a half years, adult members of the
Board of Directors and of the Community Panel had
gone on to membership in the East Palo Alto Municipal
Council and the county redevelopment commission,
and several younger members had become actively involved in student government at the colleges they attended. For the youngsters I met who were of high
school age, membership on the panel clearly had given
focus and purpose to their lives. But the Community
Panel had not yet developed the ability to enforce its
own edicts, an essential first step in the development of
effective community norms. Whether it can do so remains to be seen; in the meantime, several other cities
are experimenting with their own adaptations of the
CYRP approach.

Using more traditional methods of social work, the
Sisters of the Good Shepherd have had considerable
initial success in creating a sense of neighborhood and
community in the Park Slope section of Brooklyn. With
about 70,000 residents, Park Slope is full of contrasts:
it includes a newly fashionable section, in which young
professional couples are buying and renovating town
houses, and several deteriorating neighborhoods inhabited by poor Italian, Puerto Rican, and black families. Sister Mary Paul, the charismatic former director
of social services for the Order of the Good Shep-

herd, chose Park Slope as a place to test some of her
ideas because it was *not* the most deteriorated neighborhood around. Measures that would be insufficient or
ineffectual in a completely blighted neighborhood, she
reasoned, had some chance of success in Park Slope;
the neighborhood maintained enough stability to offer
hope that it could be revitalized.

Hence Sister Mary Paul and her young assistant,
Sister Mary Geraldine, created what they like to call
"a presence"—the Family Reception Center, a community facility that is open around the clock, seven
days a week, to anyone in need of help. The name reflects Sister Mary Paul's conviction that the problems
of troubled and delinquent youngsters can be solved
best by working with the entire family. "You cannot
posit all the solutions on the child," she insists; "you
have to help the entire family." Thus a staff of religious
and lay social workers, psychologists, and psychiatrists
provide individual and group therapy for children, parents, and whole families; the emphasis is on finding the
often hidden strengths in people and using them as
a lever for change. The Center also offers a wide range
of recreational programs—sometimes for children
alone, sometimes for parents alone, and sometimes for
family groups.* And social workers help local residents grapple with the welfare bureaucracy, arranging
for medical care and providing assistance to people

* Initially designed to provide an outlet for parents who cannot afford baby-sitters, the recreational programs came to serve
another function as well. A mother who is receiving counseling
at the Center often thinks that her neighbor's family also needs
help but is afraid the neighbor will take offense if she suggests
consultation with a social worker. What happened was that
people began bringing their friends to Parents' Night for an
ostensibly social outing; the visit provided a back door through
which the friends could seek help without feeling any onus.

having difficulty obtaining food stamps, welfare payments, or other benefits to which they are entitled.

Had the Family Reception Center stopped there, it would have been just one more center, albeit a superior one, for the dispensing of social services. Instead, it is a return to the activist, reformist tradition of Jane Addams' Hull-House. Sister Mary Paul's genius lies in her ability to combine rare empathy for children and parents with hard-headed realism about their problems and needs, along with the capacity to respond programmatically to those needs, whatever they may be and whether or not they were part of the original program design.

As originally conceived, one of the main features of the Family Reception Center was a "crash pad" that would provide a place where youngsters could stay for a night or two when things got out of hand at home. When Sisters Mary Paul and Mary Geraldine discovered that the youngsters' need for a crash pad was usually for much longer periods of time, the rules were changed so that they could stay weeks, or even months, while a social worker used intensive intervention to try to make it possible for them to go home. But it is not always possible to go home again; some youngsters come from homes so damaged, or so brutal, that "placement" cannot be avoided.* Since long stays limited the number of youngsters the crash pad could accommodate, the Sisters opened a group home in a town house next door to the Center.

---

* During one of my visits, the crash pad contained, among other children, four sisters who had been there for six months. The girls' mother was a seemingly hopeless alcoholic; after six months of working with the mother, Sister Mary Geraldine had concluded that there was no way to make the home viable and was trying to find an appropriate group or foster home that would enable the four sisters to stay together.

As time went on, moreover, the Sisters realized that children were not the only ones who needed a crash pad; adult women did, too. The result was the opening of several "Safe Homes" for battered wives, operated by clergymen in the neighborhood. It would have been easier for the Sisters to operate such a shelter themselves; persuading local clergymen to take on the responsibility was another way of knitting the community together in a common purpose.

The Center's educational programs evolved in the same organic manner. At the start, a social worker was assigned to work with the schools full-time, helping them develop programs to meet particular youngsters' needs, and when this could not be done, to find other schools for them to attend. As she walked the streets of Park Slope, however, Sister Mary Paul discovered large numbers of youngsters who never went to school. Children as young as eight or ten were permanent dropouts; some had never been enrolled at all. Her first response was to set up an alternative school designed in part to keep the youngsters off the streets, and in part to educate them—to teach them to read and write, and to give them enough sense of self to feel able to return to school. But Sister Mary Paul quickly realized that while the alternative school helped individual children, it did not help the public schools. On the contrary, it helped preserve the status quo by relieving the schools of their responsibility to teach hard-to-educate youngsters. With enormous tact and diligence, Sister Mary Paul and her staff set out to make the public schools part of the solution instead of part of the problem. Thus the Center now operates an alternative school inside each of the area's three elementary schools. Rather than competing with ordinary classroom teachers, the Center's staff works closely with them, educating teachers and guidance counselors in how to respond to youngsters they previously considered unteachable. These mini-schools, in turn, have spawned a variety of programs for parents of the children enrolled in them.

The cumulative impact of these and other programs —working with local businessmen to develop jobs for neighborhood youngsters, for example, and stationing someone at Park Slope's two precinct houses to work with the police and with troubled children and families—has been to give children and parents a sense of belonging to a community. Whether this sense of community will be translated into a reduction in criminal violence remains to be seen. The answer probably will depend on how well the Family Reception Center itself survives the departures of Sister Mary Paul (who resigned as Director of Social Services for her Order to take a position in state government) and Sister Mary Geraldine (who left to begin a similar program in an adjoining community); the Center may have been too dependent on their extraordinary energy and charismatic presence.

III

The best example of community regeneration I found anywhere in the United States is the Centro de Orientación y Servicios (Center for Orientation and Services, or C.O.S.), a "delinquency prevention" project in Puerto Rico. Situated in La Playa, the most impoverished section of Ponce, the island's second largest city, the Center is technically a Youth Service Bureau whose nominal function is to divert youngsters from juvenile court. That goal has been achieved; the number of adjudicated delinquents has been reduced by about 85 percent since 1970. But El Centro, as almost everyone in La Playa refers to it, is far more than a juvenile court diversion project. It has originated several programs

for adults as well as juveniles—programs that are re-
shaping the tone and fabric of the entire community;
in the process, the delinquency rate has been cut in half,
despite an exploding teenage population.

The premise of Sister Isolina Ferre, the Center's
founder and director, was that the most effective way
to change juvenile behavior is to change adult behavior
—and that the most effective way to change adult behavior is to create a structure that enables people to
assume roles that require responsibility in and to their
own community. For in the last analysis it is the dis-
organization of the community at large—the evidence
on all sides that their parents are unable to control their
own lives, unable to impose sanctions on people who
threaten their own or their community's well-being—
that persuades the young that the cards are hopelessly
stacked against them, that fate (or the omnipotent and
omnipresent "they") will not permit them to "make
it" in any legitimate form, thereby allowing crime to
seem a rewarding alternative.

When the project began, fatalism and disorganiza-
tion were the dominant characteristics of the area—the
kind of hopelessness and fatalism that springs from
generations of grinding poverty. La Playa residents saw
themselves as powerless victims, as indeed they were;
but the definition they gave to their situation helped
perpetuate it. Two-thirds to three-quarters of its 16,000
residents lived below the poverty line, many of them
in lean-to shacks made of castoff wood and metal; the
1970 Census found that 91 percent of all housing units
lacked some or all plumbing facilities. (A new public
housing project has increased the population to 20,-
000.) The unemployment rate was (and still is) cata-
strophic—on the order of 30 percent—with a significant proportion of those who are employed able to
find only casual or part-time work. Education is scanty;

according to the 1970 Census, only 13 percent of the adults had finished high school, and 7 percent had had no schooling at all. Children begin dropping out of school in the third grade, and school-leaving reaches a peak in seventh grade.

Hopelessness was compounded by the barriers that separate La Playa from the rest of Ponce. The area is physically cut off from the rest of the city by a six-lane highway on one side, a series of small rivers and canals on another, and the harbor on a third. The cultural and psychological barriers have been even harder to cross. When it was an active port, La Playa had a thriving red-light district to service the sailors passing through; its longshoremen had a reputation for violence, drunkenness, and gambling, and its women a reputation for promiscuity. This notoriety still lingers. To grow up in La Playa is to carry a life-long stigma; anyone from the area, even someone who has "made it" and moved away, is known as a Playero, in contradistinction to the Ponceñas who inhabit the rest of Ponce. In short, if any community could be said to contain a self-perpetuating "culture of poverty," it was La Playa.

No longer; the seeds of change have been laid. Not that La Playa has become a middle-class enclave; grinding poverty is still the norm—Puerto Rico is a depressed, as well as underdeveloped, area—and it is difficult to abandon cultural traits that help people adjust to poverty. But the area has a different tone and "feel" than it had ten years ago.

Although the Center was organized in 1968–69 and the Youth Service Bureau in 1970, the roots go back to the creation in 1950 of the Dispensario San Antonio, a small clinic operated by the Catholic Missionary Sisters of the Most Blessed Trinity. The gift of Don Antonio Ferre, Sister Isolina's father and the founder of Ferre Industries,* the Dispensario began as a classic act of noblesse oblige, with a doctor coming to visit two mornings a week. Even so, the Dispensario gradually became an important institution in La Playa. Living in the same building that housed the clinic, a building larger but no more grand than others in the area, the Sisters were present twenty-four hours a day, seven days a week. For all its limitations, the Dispensario developed into a place where local residents felt *en su casa* (at home), for it was virtually the only source of refuge, comfort, and help to troubled individuals.

In 1968, Sister Isolina Ferre returned to Ponce to become Director of the Dispensario; she brought a radically different perspective with her, and neither the Dispensario nor La Playa (nor Ponce itself) will be the same again. That perspective had been forged over the years of work in impoverished communities—in Appalachia, in the mountains of Puerto Rico, in Cape Cod (with migrant workers), and, for the preceding ten years, in a black and Puerto Rican section of Brooklyn, where she became deeply involved in community organization and urban politics while earning a master's degree in sociology at Fordham University. When Sister Isolina arrived in La Playa, she found that the Dispensario was providing health care to ten children a day. "That seemed a little silly," she says bluntly. "There were hundreds of kids in the streets, some of whom never went to school at all. And those who did go had only a half-day program, so they were on the streets the rest of the day." It seemed unlikely that

* The Ferre family is one of the most prominent in Puerto Rico; Sister Isolina's brother, Don Luis Ferre, was Governor of Puerto Rico when the project began. (Don Luis has donated a large art museum to the city of Ponce, and family members also have been major benefactors of Catholic University in Ponce.)

youngsters with nothing to do all day would stay out of trouble; with 10 percent of Ponce's population, La Playa accounted for nearly 20 percent of its juvenile crime.

Although it was the plight of the children that troubled her the most, Sister Isolina rejected a narrow concern with delinquency in favor of a focus on the community as a whole. The overall, long-range goal, she decided, should be to build individual and community competence, so that Playeros could begin to take control of their own lives. At the same time, Sister Isolina understood that she could accomplish little if she simply imposed a project of her own design on the community; she would have to engage adult Playeros in ways that had meaning for *them*. From the beginning, therefore, she walked the streets and alleys of the twenty barrios, getting to know Playeros on a personal level and listening to the ways in which they defined their problems and needs.

This is how any successful community organizer begins; but creating personal relationships with people and learning how they viewed their own reality was essential in La Playa because of the importance Puerto Ricans attach to a quality they call *personalismo*—a conception of the world as consisting primarily of a network of personal relationships. No community organization can succeed unless people conceive of it as belonging to them. In Puerto Rico, as in most Latin countries, "belonging" is thought of in terms of personal relationships, rather than power and control; whereas the mainlander asks, "Do I control the people who run the organization?" the Puerto Rican asks, "Do I *know* the people who run it, and do I have a personal relationship that ensures that my welfare will be served?" These are radically different world views, and they lead to profoundly different conceptions of the nature and source of power. To the Puerto Rican, power is derived from, and exercised through, personal relationships rather than through formal organization, and preserving those relationships takes precedence over achieving organizational goals. As a result, mainland Americans often see Puerto Ricans as inefficient, while Puerto Ricans regard mainlanders as cold and impersonal.[10]

Adapting mainland styles of community organization to Puerto Rican culture made it possible for Sister Isolina to convert what might have been a liability into a major asset. El Centro's programs could not have had such impact without her ability to use the Ferre family's network of relationships with governmental and business leaders to attract public and private resources for job training, compensatory education, recreation, medical care, social service, and court diversion programs. But that same ability might have destroyed everything Sister Isolina was trying to do. Had she played Lady Bountiful—had she merely brought outside funds and personnel into La Playa—she would have exacerbated the dependency that, after poverty itself, is the area's greatest curse.

She chose otherwise. What makes the Playa-Ponce project so significant, as well as so successful, is that it is providing help in ways that reduce dependency and enhance dignity and self-respect. The central mechanism has been the creation of a corps of ten full-time, paid "advocates"—local residents trained to look out for, protect, represent, and help youngsters in trouble with the law, other governmental agencies, or the community itself. Some of the advocates are ex-addicts or ex-offenders, and many never went beyond the seventh grade. They are selected for their knowledge of the community and their leadership potential, which is considerable; at the time of my first visit, the chief advocate was a man who had started as the Center's janitor —a job he had held while on parole as a drug offender.

Under the original project design, developed with the help of Sister Isolina's former teachers, Father Joseph Fitzpatrick and Dr. John Martin of the Fordham University Institute for Social Research, the advocates were to become aggressive champions of community youth. Their major role was to be to pressure public-service bureaucracies to become more responsive to the needs and interests of the juvenile delinquents they were representing, and, through them, to the needs of Playero youth as a whole.

That design was modified from the start; advocacy in the aggressive, mainland sense was not suited to the Puerto Rican temperament, which shrinks from confrontation. In addition to *cariño,* the care and concern that binds people together in a *personalismo* network, the cardinal virtues of Puerto Rican culture are *dignidad* (dignity) and *respeto* (respect). To be aggressive toward another is to show *falta de respeto,* a lack of respect which violates that person's *dignidad;* one is expected to settle disputes *a la buena* (in a nice way), in accordance with the axiom that "courtesy does not imply lack of valor."[*11]

The advocates (*intercesores*) were therefore temperamentally unable to play the assertive, adversarial role envisioned for them. Nor was a more limited, mediating role available; the professionals in the agencies with whom the advocates were expected to deal followed the traditional rule that professionals talk only

---

* When they try to capture the essence of the national character or temperament, Puerto Ricans use the term *la pelea monga* (literally, "the limp cock")—a term drawn from the popular national sport of cockfighting. *La pelea monga* is the cock who wins by constantly retreating until it exhausts the aggressor to such an extent that it can quickly come in for the kill.

to one another. Hence the project's own professionals took over most of the interagency relationships that the advocates had been expected to handle.

Instead of trying to achieve the original goals, the advocates accommodated their role to what could be done; the constraints on their activities pushed them in unexpected, and in some ways more productive, directions. Rejected by the professionals, who communicated their conviction that local residents could be chauffeurs and aides but nothing more, the advocates turned inward toward their own community. They began to bring children's medical problems to the attention of their parents and to put the whole family in touch with the clinic operated by the Dispensario; they helped organize and lead recreation programs and community outings, urged residents to attend meetings and participate in community programs, and in general became mediators between the Center and the community, linking people with problems to those able to provide help.

One important by-product was a redefinition of the advocates' clientele. Initially, the advocates worked only with youngsters referred by the juvenile court. But since they were doing relatively little advocacy, they began picking up "cases" on their own—youngsters who needed, or could benefit from, the services provided by El Centro or by the advocates themselves. Sister Isolina promptly recognized the enormous advantage of this ad hoc arrangement and turned it into formal policy. By including youngsters who have *not* been in trouble with the law—such youngsters often comprise a majority of the advocates' caseloads—the Center has avoided the stigmatization that otherwise would have been attached to involvement in the program. Thus the Youth Service Bureau is perceived as serving the entire community. (The Center's education and recreation programs have been open to all community youths from the start; during the summer, when children are out of school, virtually the entire juvenile population is involved in one or another C.O.S. program.)

As the advocates turned inward toward the community, they began to be assigned to a specific barrio or group of barrios, rather than to a caseload of individual youngsters who might live anywhere in La Playa. This made it easier for advocates to use their existing networks of personal relationships and encouraged them to broaden those networks—to increase their identification with the communities in which they worked, and vice versa.

At the same time, the advocates learned how to do things *with* people instead of *for* them. One of the turning points occurred when an advocate came to Sister Isolina to report that, in his barrio of La Boca, a water spigot—the only source of water for several families— had been shut off by municipal officials. A single phone call from Sister Isolina undoubtedly would have gotten the water turned back on, but it also would have perpetuated the residents' dependency. Instead of making the call, she asked the project's community organizer to work with the advocate in mobilizing La Boca residents; together, they organized a campaign to restore water service. After a mass meeting and a series of letters and petitions to the Public Works Department, the spigot was turned back on. It was a small matter to the department, but a major achievement for La Boca residents; acting for the first time in their own behalf, they discovered that they could affect change.

The lesson was applied (and learned) again. In making their rounds in Barrio Palmita, advocates heard adults complaining that teenagers were keeping them awake at night by engaging in raucous hooliganism.

The teenagers, on the other hand, complained that there was nothing else for them to do; from their perspective, they were not causing any real harm. The advocates organized a public meeting, at which the barrio elders acknowledged that the absence of recreational facilities contributed to the hooliganism; the teenagers suggested that a basketball court might channel their energies in a more constructive direction. Since the barrio contained a piece of vacant land that could be turned into a basketball court, the advocates turned to the community organizer for help.

"I knew that a few phone calls to the Kiwanis and Rotary Club might have produced the money for the court," Antonio Justiniano, the community organizer, later recalled, "but our real goal was to get the members of the barrio to realize that they had the means to help themselves." Whereas the Palmita residents saw the basketball court as an end in itself, Justiniano saw it as a means to a larger end; he suggested that the advocates help the residents raise the money themselves. It was considered an outlandish proposal, but Justiniano persuaded the advocates to give it a try. He helped them muster up a steel band, which, with a sound truck belonging to the Center, went from block to block, playing music and putting on improvised skits; teenagers circulated with coin boxes, collecting contributions of nickels and dimes. Huge posters were painted and placed all over Ponce to publicize the campaign, leading to a radio marathon that brought in additional contributions. Playero housewives organized "friendship lunches," inviting workers from nearby factories and charging $2 for the meals they cooked themselves. Over the course of the summer, residents raised some $700, a remarkable achievement for a poverty-stricken barrio that had never taken joint action of any sort.

Having created a formal organization to handle the

money, residents then appointed a committee to call upon executives of the National Packing Company, a tuna-packing plant located in the barrio, with a request for additional help. An engineer retained by El Centro had estimated the cost of materials at $1,500, and the company agreed to donate whatever was needed over and above what the community raised. Another committee approached the Parks and Recreation Department and secured a promise that the labor to build the court would be provided by the department.

Since then, the advocates have become increasingly involved in community organization, to the point where it is hard to know where their work ends and that of the community organizer begins. For the most part, projects have been modest; rapid and tangible results are needed to persuade poor people that they can change some of the circumstances of their lives.[12] However modest the accomplishments may seem from the outside, they have been significant in the lives of the people involved: installation of a pay telephone in a barrio with no phone service at all; a paved street in another barrio, so that garbage could be removed via city garbage trucks; swamp drainage; persuading a previously unresponsive bus company to change to a route more convenient for La Playa residents; getting the police to crack down on organized prostitution in one barrio where young girls were being actively recruited. Each victory chips away at the tradition of impotence and dependency and develops a sense of individual and community competence.

No one has changed as much as the advocates themselves. Several of the advocates told me in 1974 that none of them were the same people they had been three or four years before. They had lost their "shyness," they explained, and had gained the self-confidence needed to make decisions, as well as to represent the youngsters in their caseload and, indeed, the entire barrios to which they are assigned. The change was made possible by the compelling force of Sister Isolina's faith in their capacity to change, together with the support she and other members of the professional staff provided. Change was nurtured, too, by the continuous training the advocates have received. But the most important source of change has been the sense of competence that derives from solid achievement.

The growing self-confidence has enabled the advocates to assume the role initially envisioned for them; they now feel able to take the initiative in interceding with governmental agencies on behalf of youngsters with one or another problem, and they have become sophisticated in dealing with some of the same professionals who used to shun them. In one more or less representative incident, a recently returned Nuyorican (a Puerto Rican born and raised in New York) got into a fracas in a local school. In the breezy manner of a Nuyorican, he had simply walked into the school to visit his girl friend, not realizing that Puerto Rican schools are exceptionally formal institutions that refuse to permit any nonstudent or nonteacher to enter without prior arrangement. The volatile young man got into an argument with the policeman stationed in the school, who called for reinforcements. An advocate happened to be passing by when the police car arrived, and he stopped to investigate; upon learning what had happened, he persuaded the policeman, whom he knew, to release the Nuyorican in his custody, promising to bring the young man to the police station later, after he had cooled off. Since it was the principal who wanted to press charges (the policeman was willing to forget about the incident once he had calmed down), the advocate negotiated with the principal until he, too, agreed to forget the matter, thereby obviating the need to bring the boy to the police station.

But the advocate would not leave it at that. He persuaded the unemployed youth to enter one of the vocational training programs operated by the Center and referred him to a Center counselor, for help in learning to put some internal restraints on his temper; at last contact, the boy held a steady job. "I managed to convince the kid that we were willing to accept him, but that we could not accept his antisocial behavior," the advocate told me by way of explaining his success.

Experience of this sort have been commonplace. A significant by-product has been a widespread strengthening of family life. Parents who in the past had called the police or the juvenile court because they knew no other way of controlling their children began turning to the advocates instead. With the advocates' help, these parents have gained some understanding of their children's behavior and have learned more effective ways of responding to it; and the children, in turn, have had their energies directed in more productive channels.

After an initial period of suspicion mixed with hostility, the police also have come to rely more and more on the advocates. La Playa policemen now bring juveniles to the barrio advocate, instead of making an arrest, unless the youngster's offense is particularly serious; and when the police are called to settle a domestic dispute or put down some sort of disorder, they are likely to contact the barrio advocate and ask him to meet them at the location to which they have been called. As a result, several advocates now have police "hot lines" installed in their homes, so that they can be notified instantly of any after-hours trouble that may occur.

Much of the same has happened in juvenile court,

which was more sympathetic to the advocates from the start, perhaps because the judge sitting in juvenile court when the project began was himself a Playero. In any event, the judge and his successor discovered that the advocates knew far more about the juveniles brought to court, and provided far more (and far more accurate) information about their progress than the court's own probation officers. As time went on, the judges also discovered that the advocates were more effective than probation officers in changing juvenile behavior. As a result, the great majority of juveniles who get into trouble with the law are now diverted to the program before any formal proceedings begin; in 1976, delinquency proceedings were filed against only 20 youngsters, compared to 144 in the year the program began.

Thus the advocates now play an almost bewildering variety of roles. At times, they are friendly mediators between child and parents, or between child and other adults. On other occasions, they play the role of parent or older sibling, standing up on behalf of a child about whom they care deeply and intervening on his behalf with teachers, principals, doctors, policemen, judges, probation officers, and any other person or institution that impinges on the youngster's life. But advocates also represent the community to its juvenile population, and the juveniles to the community. With their intimate knowledge of the barrios to which they are assigned, advocates are able to gauge when a youngster, or group of youngsters, is overstepping the limits of acceptable behavior; depending on the behavior and the community, they may intervene to put firmer controls on juvenile behavior, or to expand the limits of the community's tolerance for deviant behavior. (The sense of community had been so fragile in some barrios that any deviance, no matter how trivial, seemed to threaten the community's survival; almost anything an advocate does to strengthen community ties tends to alter the way in which people respond to misbehavior.)

Whatever role they play, the advocates operate within a network of personal relationships that link them on one side to barrio residents and on the other to El Centro and its staff. Under the tradition of *personalismo,* this means that when an advocate takes action on behalf of an individual or a barrio, it appears (and feels) to residents as though the Center itself were acting—that the advocacy role is being exercised not by an individual, but by the project as a whole. More important, the close relationship Playeros have with Sister Isolina and the Center staff, as well as with the advocates, makes it feel as though the advocacy role is being exercised by the community as a whole—that things are being done by and with people, instead of for them.* And people's perception that they are acting on their own behalf in turn helps develop the sense of competence they need in order to act; as one of the basic axioms of sociology puts it, what people perceive as real is real in its consequences.

All elements of the program feed into this growing sense of competence. To bring educational, recreational, and social services closer to the people being served, four satellite centers have been created, each with its own governing board, in addition to the community board that oversees El Centro itself. The boards are beginning to raise money to contribute to each center's operating costs; to make their contributions appear more significant, the boards are raising money for a specific function—the center's phone bill, the cost of electricity used to illuminate the Palmita basketball

---

* Virtually all the members of the Center's staff are Playeros, with a strong effort to have every barrio represented. Only 10 percent of the staff are professionals; several began as advocates and moved up to positions as counselors or social workers.

court at night—rather than for the budget as a whole.

Sister Isolina has also used a new public health facility as a means of bringing the community together and expanding its capacity to manage its own affairs. When she learned that the Commonwealth government was planning to erect a building that, in her words, would have housed "a typical municipal clinic," she got in touch with officials of what was then the Office of Economic Opportunity. The result was a large federal grant that turned the clinic into a genuine community health facility—the Centro Diagnóstic y Tratamiento—with an annual budget of $1.4 million in federal and Commonwealth funds. The Health Center is an independent nonprofit corporation run by its own board of directors, consisting of fifteen elected Playeros (twelve represent individual barrios and three are chosen at large) and six people designated by various agencies in La Playa; each member has one vote. Elections are vigorous affairs that heighten people's sense that the health center is *their* organization.*

There is a limit to what the Center, or any program of community development, can do. Ultimately, La Playa's fate is tied to that of the Puerto Rican economy; unless it grows rapidly enough to supply jobs for anyone who wants to work, poverty and unemployment will continue to be the fate of all too many Playeros. And the disabilities growing out of past generations of poverty are such that massive help is needed if Playeros are to be able to take advantage of new opportunities

* When the Health Center came into being, board members were given a training course to provide them with the knowledge and skills they would need, and Sister Isolina served as president of the Board of Directors. "After a year or so," she recalls with delight, "they told me I didn't need to talk so much"—she had been feigning sore throats in order to encourage Playeros to talk at board meetings—and she stepped down as president.

as they arise. In the last analysis, El Centro's greatest
contribution has been its most subtle: it has given large
numbers of people the sense of dignity and worth that
enables them to accept help—to use help as a means
toward self-sufficiency rather than dependency. For
help now comes (or seems to come, which amounts to
the same thing) as a result of their own efforts, rather
than through charity. In the process, crime and delinquency have been reduced dramatically.

IV

It would be disingenuous of me to end on a euphoric
note. La Playa is a crime-ridden slum by traditional
Puerto Rican standards, but measured against mainland American cities it is almost benign. Although
burglary and theft are widespread, robbery and murder
are rare events; there is remarkably little criminal violence. I am not denigrating Sister Isolina's achievement, therefore, when I suggest that success would be
harder to come by in the harsher, more violent black
and Hispanic ghettos of Chicago, Philadelphia, New
York, and a hundred other cities.

It would be equally wrong to end on a note of un-
alloyed gloom. Important lessons can be learned from
El Centro, and from the Family Reception Center and
other efforts toward community change—lessons about
wasted talent and ability, and about the human capacity
for change. We have seen in our own time how rapidly
change can occur when the commitment is there.

In the end, we come back to a few simple and self-
evident truths; as George Orwell wrote forty years ago,
"We have now sunk to a depth at which the restatement
of the obvious is the first duty of intelligent men." It
has become fashionable to deny the obvious—to insist
that poverty and racial oppression have little or nothing

to do with criminal violence. I hope I have demonstrated that they do, and that we are not likely to enjoy the domestic tranquillity for which the Republic was founded until we become truly one society. The question is no longer what to do, but whether we have the will to do it.

Appendix:
Notes on Crime Statistics

Attacking the FBI's *Uniform Crime Reports* has long been a popular sport among criminologists. There has been a lot to attack. Until recently, the FBI statistics were the only source of data on national crime trends —and they offered only a rough approximation of the number of crimes committed each year. For one thing, the FBI measures crime by collecting data on just seven offenses, selected "because of their seriousness, frequency of occurrence, and likelihood of being reported to police." Originally called Part I crimes these offenses —murder, forcible rape, robbery, aggravated assault, burglary, larceny-theft, and auto theft—are now known as Crime Index offenses (or Index crimes, for short). Certainly they are serious offenses; but in measuring long-term trends the FBI makes an unstated (and untested) assumption that the ratio between Index crimes and other offenses is stable.[1]

A more important source of error derives from the fact that the FBI itself does not collect the data. Instead, it acts as a statistical clearing house for more than 13,000 cooperating law enforcement agencies. Each agency compiles its own statistics and submits them to the FBI, either directly or through a state agency; cooperating agencies serve jurisdictions comprising 96 percent of the nation's population. (Coverage is higher—98 percent—in the nation's Standard Metropolitan Statistical Areas and lower—89 percent —in rural areas.) Since law enforcement is a local responsibility, the same crime may be defined differently from one jurisdiction to another. The FBI has sought uniformity by providing standardized definitions of the seven Index crimes; but agencies vary in the precision with which they tailor their own categories to those of the FBI. It is not simply a matter of conscientiousness; professional—and often subjective—judgments also are involved. Whether a particular offense is classified as robbery or larceny, for example, depends on the amount of force, or threat of force, that is used; equally competent police officers may disagree over whether to classify a purse-snatching as robbery or larceny-theft. Similar problems arise with crimes such as aggravated assault and forcible rape.

The largest source of error comes from the fact that the *Uniform Crime Reports* include only those crimes that are reported to the police and that the police, in turn, record and pass on to the FBI. Error arises because many crimes are not reported to the police; until 1967, when the President's Crime Commission came up with the idea of using survey research methods to question a representative sample of Americans about their experience as crime victims, criminologists could only speculate about the nature and dimensions of this "dark figure" of unreported crime. It was impossible to know with any certainty, therefore, whether a reported increase in crime represented a real change or was merely the result of an increase in the proportion of crimes reported to the police.

It was equally impossible to know what proportion of the crimes reported to local police departments were recorded and transmitted to the FBI. Some departments record every citizen complaint; others record only those crimes that police officers decide are real, ignoring those that patrolmen report as "unfounded." (Such reports may reflect an officer's judgment that no crime occurred—as we saw in Chapter 7, people often try to use the police to settle a private grudge or to collect money from an insurance company—or a judgment that the offense was too trivial to bother with.)

More important, police departments may manipulate crime statistics for their own political purposes—inflating the figures in order to defeat a judge considered soft on crime or to persuade the city council to increase the department's budget, or understating the number of crimes to create an image of effective law enforcement. Understatement is particularly frequent in departments which assign responsibility for collecting crime statistics to precinct commanders, who may be judged by how low they keep the figures.* The magnitude of the distortion is often revealed when departments shift from a decentralized to a centralized system of recording complaints and crime statistics. New York City made such a shift in 1950, after the FBI refused to publish the city's crime statistics; the next year, reported robberies rose 400 percent and burglaries 1,300 percent. And when Chicago installed a centralized system in 1960, reported robbberies doubled.[2]

Thus during most of the 1960s (and in some instances well into the 1970s), criminologists tended to discount the significance of the sharp increase in reported crime. There was reason to think that minority-group members were reporting a larger proportion of

* In one such city, staff members of the President's Crime Commission were told of a precinct that maintained a separate "File 13" in which crime reports that were not forwarded to the central statistical office were kept so that the police could answer questions from insurance companies.

crimes to the police, in response to the fact that the police themselves were treating crimes against blacks more seriously than they had in the past. Police departments also seemed to be recording a larger proportion of the crimes reported to them—in part because of growing professionalism among police administrators, in part in response to pressure from the FBI, and in part as a by-product of the introduction of centralized police communications systems, whereby all complaints and calls for service are routed through a single number.*

Despite all these changes, there seems to be little doubt about the essential accuracy of the overall trends depicted in the *Uniform Crime Reports* during the last fifteen to twenty years. Intercity comparisons are another matter, since there still are a number of cities whose figures are suspect; and the margin of error in the aggregate statistics may well be larger than the year-to-year changes reported by the FBI. But the Bureau has been making a serious effort to adjust its data to correct for changes in reporting procedures and policies on the part of individual departments. The crime trends reported by each agency are scrutinized five times a year; if any significant increase or decrease shows up, the FBI asks the agency in question why the change has occurred. (In 1976, some 4,300 agencies were queried in this fashion.) If it appears that a change in reporting procedures is responsible for a significant proportion of the reported increase or decrease, the Bureau excludes that agency from its total for that year and the preceding year. When the Bureau determines the magnitude of the change stemming

* The recent spread of state Uniform Crime Reporting programs, in which state officials monitor local departments' crime reporting procedures, has further improved the quality of crime statistics; some forty-one states were operating such programs in 1976.

from new reporting procedures, it adjusts the agency's old statistics, using the new level as the base.

In any event, we now have a new source of crime statistics against which to check the *Uniform Crime Reports.* Since 1973, the Census Bureau, under contract with the Law Enforcement Assistance Administration (LEAA), has conducted semiannual surveys in which a scientifically chosen representative sample of the population is asked to report incidents in which they or the businesses they own or manage have been victims of robbery, rape, assault, burglary, or various forms of theft. Far from discrediting the *Uniform Crime Reports,* the data collected through these victim surveys have made it possible to use the FBI statistics with somewhat greater confidence.*

For one thing, we now know the approximate dimensions of the so-called "dark figure" of unreported crime. Victimization surveys show crime rates two to three times higher than those recorded in the *Uniform Crime Reports;* the difference between the two provides a rough measure of unreported crime, but only a rough measure: dependent as they are on people's memories, victimization surveys are not precise instruments, either. Errors arise in several ways. People may simply forget events that happened more than a short time before the interview; when individuals known to have been crime victims were interviewed in San Jose, California, 26 percent did not recall the crime. Forgetfulness (or "memory fade," as crime statisticians call it) is not a random phenomenon. In the San Jose interviews, only 22 percent of those who had been victimized by a relative recalled the incident; the recall rate

* Victim surveys do not collect information on the number of criminal homicides, but the FBI's murder statistics conform closely in level and trend to the data gathered independently by the National Center for Health Statistics' Division of Vital Statistics.

went up to 58 percent for crimes in which the offender had been an acquaintance, and 75 percent for crimes involving a total stranger.

Mistakes run in the other direction as well: the number of crimes may be inflated in victim surveys by a phenomenon called "telescoping," whereby people include crimes that were committed before the time period about which they are being questioned. Both telescoping and memory fade increase sharply after three months. As a compromise between the conflicting goals of maximizing accuracy and minimizing cost, the national surveys use a six-month reference period; i.e., respondents are asked about victimizations that occurred during the six months preceding the interview.* Occasional surveys of individual cities use a twelve-month reference period.[4]

Direct comparisons between the Victimization Survey data and the *Uniform Crime Reports* are difficult, moreover, because the two sets of figures measure slightly different phenomena. Police statistics report the number of criminal *incidents,* whereas victimization surveys report the number of criminal *victimizations.* The two are not the same; there are more victimizations than crimes, since some crimes, such as robbery or assault, may involve a number of victims. Further, the personal crimes covered in the surveys include those

---

* The Census Bureau reduces the error due to telescoping through a technique called "bounding." The people interviewed are divided into six groups, or rotations; the members of each rotation are interviewed once every six months for a period of three years. Thus the answers given during one interview can be used as a check on the answers given in the next. (A new rotation enters the sample every six months, replacing a group that is phased out.) Each rotation group, in turn, is divided into six subgroups; during each six-month period, the members of one subgroup are interviewed monthly, providing still more detail for purposes of bounding. (A modification of this approach is used in interviewing the sample of commercial establishments.)[3]

committed against people twelve years of age and older; the FBI statistics include crimes against victims of all ages.

What is remarkable, therefore, is how congruent the two sets of statistics have turned out to be. Although the aggregate levels differ, the victim surveys seem to confirm the *Uniform Crime Reports*' picture of the relative frequency of the major crimes and their distribution across geographic and urban-rural lines.[5] Additionally, the "dark figure" of unreported crime turns out to be less significant (and a good deal less mysterious) than criminologists had assumed. Besides asking people about their experience as crime victims, the victimization surveys ask them whether or not they reported the crime to the police, and if not, why. In general, unreported crimes are considerably less serious than those that are reported to the police. People report thefts only half as often as crimes of violence; within a single violent crime category, such as robbery, the percent of unreported crimes is also related to the seriousness of the offense. In 1975, 69 percent of attempted robberies without injury, but only 33 percent of completed robberies with serious injury to the victim, were not reported to the police. Except for rape, where the proportion of crimes reported to the police has increased steadily, there is no indication that the ratio between reported and total crime has changed significantly in recent years. (Contrary to what some had assumed, black victims report about the same proportion of crimes to the police as do whites.)[6]

I do not mean to sound like Pollyanna; the *Uniform Crime Reports* still leave much to be desired. The biggest weakness involves the paucity and inevitable crudity of information about criminal offenders. Knowledge that an offense has been committed does not, by itself, mean that anything is known about the nature of the offender or offenders; in crimes such as burglary and larceny-theft, the victim rarely sees the offender.

Of necessity, therefore, my analysis of offender characteristics has been based largely on arrest data supplied in the *Uniform Crime Reports.* (Although the FBI asks police departments to supply data on the total number of crimes committed only for the seven Index, or Part I, offenses, it collects arrest statistics for the twenty-two Part II offense categories as well.) As I explained in detail in Chapter 7, police officers arrest people for a variety of reasons, of which their presumed guilt is only one; making an arrest often is a way of restoring order—of "dealing with the situation." In situations involving a breach of the public order, whether or not an officer makes an arrest depends, in good measure, on his own skill and artistry in handling people. Arrest frequency also varies from department to department. Service-oriented forces such as Oakland's encourage patrolmen to resolve situations without resort to an arrest; in the legalistic Los Angeles department, on the other hand, failure to make an arrest may be viewed as weakness on the patrolman's part.

These objections to the use of arrest statistics are at a minimum where Index crimes are concerned. Although police are allowed great discretion in deciding whether or not to make an arrest, their decisions are more uniform when they have reason to suspect that someone has committed a serious offense. Even so, there are large disparities in police behavior, stemming from differences in individual officers' energy, ability, and ambition—witness the fact that in the District of Columbia fewer than 10 percent of the officers account for more than half of all felony arrests.

Arrest statistics are flawed in another way. Policemen are subject to the same prejudices of social class as the rest of us. They are also subject to political pressures. When they find a prominent citizen (or merely a well-dressed citizen) drunk and disturbing the peace, officers are less likely to make an arrest, and more likely to drive the offender home, than when they find an indigent drunk. But such class distinctions are not likely to play a significant role where Index crimes are concerned.

There are prejudices of age as well. To the police, juveniles spell trouble; where petty offenses are involved —but not crimes such as robbery or rape—officers may be more likely to arrest a troublesome juvenile than an adult. The offender's social class may also affect decisions; with youngsters found shoplifting, say, the police are less likely to arrest a youngster from an intact middle-class family than from a poor, single-parent family.* Again, these distinctions are less likely to play a role where Index crimes (especially violent Index crimes) are concerned.

A larger problem with arrest statistics grows out of the difference between juvenile and adult crime. Juveniles act in groups far more often than do adults; if arrested, juveniles are also more likely than adults to implicate their accomplices. Since the arrest statistics in the *Uniform Crime Reports* refer to the total number of arrests, rather than the number of offenses, they overstate the significance of juvenile crime. Arrest statistics can be used more confidently to analyze trends in juvenile crime, however, since there is no reason to assume that there has been any significant change in the relative importance of individual and group offenses.

The major criticism involves the role of race prejudice. If blacks are arrested more often than whites,

---

* From the cop's perspective, the decision not to arrest the first youngster is the result not of prejudice, but of a judgment that the intact family is more likely to keep the youngster on a tight rein than the single-parent family. The distinction cuts across race and class lines.

criminologists and others have argued, it could be because prejudiced policemen arrest blacks with less provocation than they arrest whites, rather than because blacks commit more crimes. Certainly race prejudice can affect police behavior; there is no reason why the police should be exempt from the prejudice that afflicts every other group in American society.

Whether police prejudice serves to elevate black arrest rates is another question. In the past, bigotry probably served to *reduce* the number of black arrests: police departments paid little attention to crimes that blacks committed against other blacks—and most black crime was intraracial. Although prejudice has hardly disappeared, it is far less overt than it used to be. The police may still view crimes against whites more seriously than crimes against blacks. But the frequency with which black city-dwellers now call the police for assistance, along with the high priority black civic and political leaders attach to demands for more police protection in black neighborhoods, suggests that whatever their private views, policemen now behave much the same way, whether the victim is white or black. Moreover, the ratio of black to white arrests does not seem to be different in cities with substantial numbers of black patrolmen than in cities with all-white or predominantly white departments.

What data are available from the victimization surveys support the view that current arrest statistics are a reasonably reliable, if rough, approximation of actual criminal behavior. Victims of crimes against the person are asked a number of questions about the offenders—their race, their estimated age, and whether they acted alone or in a group. In 1975, robbery victims identified the offender as black in 60 percent of the crimes; according to the *Uniform Crime Reports,* 58.8 percent of those arrested for robbery in 1975 were black. The "fit" between the two sources of information was almost as close for aggravated assault.

Objections to the use of arrest rates as an index of black criminal behavior can be met, in any case, by comparing arrest rates of blacks with those of Hispanic Americans, who also are the objects of prejudice and discrimination. It would be hard to convince a Puerto Rican New Yorker that the police treat Puerto Ricans or other Hispanic residents with more deference than they treat blacks; if arrest rates are distorted by discrimination, the distortion may very well run the other way, since there are proportionately fewer Puerto Rican than black policemen.* It would be even harder to persuade Mexican-Americans in the Southwest that they receive preferential treatment from the police; as a bitter joke among south Texas Chicanos has it, members of the feared and hated Texas Rangers all have Mexican blood—"on their boots." Comparing the rates at which black and Hispanic Americans are arrested (and where arrest rates are not available, the rates at which they are convicted or imprisoned for various crimes) thus offers a fair picture of the similarities and differences in criminal behavior from one group to another.

* Some distortion may creep into the New York statistics as a result of errors in racial and ethnic classifications. Policemen making arrests may list some dark-skinned Puerto Ricans, Dominicans, or other Hispanic Americans as "black" and some light-skinned Hispanics as "other," New York City's statistical euphemism for non-Hispanic whites. Given the clues provided by names, accents, and addresses, however, not to mention the "street sense" that New York City cops display, it seems unlikely that the error is large.

Notes

Part I
Criminal Violence

1. *Fear*

1. For Chicago, see Richard Block, "Homicide in Chicago: A Nine-Year Study (1965–1973)," *Journal of Crime and Criminology*, Vol. 66, No. 4 (December, 1976), pp. 496–510; Block and Franklin E. Zimring, "Homicide in Chicago, 1965–1970," *Journal of Research in Crime and Delinquency*, Vol. 10, No. 1 (January, 1973), pp. 1–112. On homicide trends generally, see Lynn A. Curtis, *Criminal Violence* (Lexington, Mass.: D. C. Heath & Co., 1974), esp. Ch. 3; A. Joan Klebba, *Mortality Trends for Homicide, by Age, Color, and Sex: United States, 1960–1972* (Rockville, Md.: National Center for Health Statistics, undated, mimeo). I have updated Curtis' analysis of trends in stranger homicide through use of the FBI's *Uniform Crime Reports*.

2. The discussion of crime trends is based on my own analysis of data contained in the following sources: Donald J. Mulvihill and Melvin M. Tumin, with Curtis, *Crimes of Violence*, A Staff Report to the National Commission on the Causes and Prevention of Violence, Vol. 11, Ch. 5 (Washington, D.C.: U.S. Government Printing Office, 1969); J. Edgar Hoover, *Crime in the United States: Uniform Crime Reports, 1967* (Washington, D.C.: U.S. Government Printing Office, 1968); Clarence M. Kelley, *Crime in the United States, 1975 (Uniform Crime Reports)*, and Kelley, *Crime in the United States, 1976 (Uniform Crime Reports)* (Washington, D.C.: U.S. Government Printing Office, 1976 and 1977); *Criminal Victimization in the United States, 1973*, A National Crime Panel Survey Re-

port (U.S. Government Printing Office, 1976); *Criminal Victimization in the United States: A Comparison of 1973 and 1974 Findings,* A National Crime Panel Survey Report (U.S. Government Printing Office, 1976); *Criminal Victimization in the United States: A Comparison of 1974 and 1975 Findings,* A National Crime Panel Survey Report (U.S. Government Printing Office, 1977). See also Curtis, *Criminal Violence,* Ch. 3.

3. Leon Radzinowicz and Joan King, *The Growth of Crime* (New York: Basic Books, Inc., 1977), p. 3. On the growth of crime throughout the world, see also Ted Robert Gurr, "Contemporary Crime in Historical Perspective: A Comparative Study of London, Stockholm, and Sydney," *Annals of the American Academy of Political and Social Science,* Vol. 434 (November, 1977), pp. 114–36; Gurr, *Rogues, Rebels, and Reformers: A Political History of Urban Crime and Conflict* (Beverly Hills, Calif.: Sage Publications, 1976); Marshall B. Clinard and Daniel J. Abbott, *Crime in Developing Countries* (New York: John Wiley & Sons, 1973).

4. Erving Goffman, *Relations in Public* (New York: Harper Colophon Books, 1971), p. 238.

5. Jane Jacobs, *The Death and Life of Great American Cities* (New York: Random House, Inc., 1961).

6. Jennie McIntyre, "Public Attitudes Toward Crime and Law Enforcement," *Annals of the American Academy of Political and Social Science,* Vol. 374 (November, 1967), pp. 38–39. See also *Crimes and Victims: A Report on the Dayton–San Jose Pilot Survey of Victimization* (Washington, D.C.: U.S. Department of Justice, Law Enforcement Assistance Administration, 1974), Table 13.

7. Robert Lejeune and Nicholas Alex, "On Being Mugged: The Event and Its Aftermath," *Urban Life and Culture,* Vol. 2, No. 3 (October, 1973), reprinted in *The Aldine Crime and Justice Annual, 1973* (Chicago, Ill.: Aldine Publishing Co., 1974), pp. 161–89.

8. Goffman, *Relations in Public,* pp. 11–12.

9. For a discussion of the complex rules governing eye contact in human society, see Michael Argyle, "The Laws of Looking," *Human Nature,* Vol. 1, No. 1 (January, 1978), pp. 32–40.

10. Sigmund Freud, "Thoughts on War and Death," in Freud, *On War, Sex, and Neurosis,* reprinted in Richard D. Don-

nelly et al., *Criminal Law* (New York: The Free Press, 1962), p. 347.

11. Lejeune and Alex, "On Being Mugged," p. 171.

12. Goffman, *Relations in Public,* pp. 265ff. On pickpockets, see David W. Maurer, *Whiz Mob* (Gainesville, Fla.: American Dialect Society, November, 1955), esp. Ch. 5.

13. Lejeune and Alex, "On Being Mugged," pp. 167–69.

14. Kai T. Erikson, *Everything in Its Path* (New York: Simon & Schuster, 1976), p. 234.

15. John Saar, "Attack at Bus Stop Wrecks Man's Life, Denies Ambition," Washington *Post* (March 9, 1975).

16. Ron Shaffer, "Tormented Gun Victim Asks Why," Washington *Post* (November 29, 1975).

17. Shaffer and Alfred E. Lewis, "You Go Out . . . and Might Not Get Back," Washington *Post* (August 23, 1975).

18. Maggie Scarf, "The Anatomy of Fear," *New York Times Magazine* (June 16, 1974), pp. 18–20.

19. John Saar, "Rape Victim's Memories Haunt Her," Washington *Post* (April 20, 1975).

20. Barry Cunningham, "Murder Victim's Family: One Year Later," New York *Post* (September 12, 1974), p. 54.

2. *As American as Jesse James*

1. In writing this section, I have placed particular reliance on the following sources: Hugh Davis Graham and Ted Robert Gurr, *Violence in America: Historical and Comparative Perspective,* Vols. 1 and 2, A Report to the National Commission on the Causes and Prevention of Violence (Washington, D.C.: U.S. Government Printing Office, 1969); *To Establish Justice, To Insure Domestic Tranquility,* Final Report of the National Commission on the Causes and Prevention of Violence (Washington, D.C.: U.S. Government Printing Office, 1969), Ch. 1; Richard Hofstadter and Michael Wallace, eds., *American Violence: A Documentary History* (New York: Vintage Books, 1971).

2. Richard Maxwell Brown, "The American Vigilante Tradition" and "Historical Patterns of Violence in America," in Graham and Gurr, *Violence in America,* Vol. 1.

3. Cf. Richard Hofstadter, "Reflections on Violence in the United States," in Hofstadter and Wallace, eds., *American Violence.*

4. Joe B. Frantz, "The Frontier Tradition: An Invitation to

Violence," in Graham and Gurr, *Violence in America,* Vol. 1. Cf. also Robert Sherrill, *The Saturday Night Special* (New York, Charterhouse, 1973).

5. Thomas Byrnes, *Professional Criminals of America, 1886* (New York: Chelsea House, 1969).

6. Cf. A. Joan Klebba, *Homicide Trends in the United States, 1900–1974* (National Center for Health Statistics, Division of Vital Statistics, Washington, D.C.: U.S. Government Printing Office, 1975); Klebba, *Mortality Trends for Homicide, by Age, Color, and Sex: United States, 1960–1972,* undated, mimeo.

7. Brown, "Historical Patterns of Violence," and Philip Taft and Philip Ross, "American Labor Violence: Its Causes, Character, and Outcome," in Graham and Gurr, eds., *Violence in America,* Vol. 1, Chs. 2, 8.

8. Arthur I. Waskow, *From Race Riot to Sit-In: 1919 and the 1960s* (Garden City, N.Y.: Doubleday & Co., Inc., 1966), esp. Chs. 1, 2, 7. See also Charles E. Silberman, *Crisis in Black and White* (New York: Random House, Inc., 1964), pp. 25–29.

9. Mark H. Haller, "Bootlegging in Chicago: The Structure of an Illegal Enterprise," unpublished paper prepared for the American Historical Association Convention, Chicago, December 29, 1974. See also Haller, "Organized Crime in Urban Society: Chicago in the Twentieth Century," *Journal of Social History* (Winter, 1971–72), pp. 210–34; John Landesco, *Organized Crime in Chicago,* in the Illinois Association for Criminal Justice, *The Illinois Crime Survey* (Montclair, N.J.: Patterson Smith Reprint Series in Criminology, Law Enforcement, and Social Problems, 1968), esp. pp. 923–31; Andrew Sinclair, *Prohibition: The Era of Excess* (Boston: Little, Brown & Co., 1962).

10. Klebba, *Homicide Trends;* Donald J. Mulvihill and Melvin M. Tumin, with Curtis, *Crimes of Violence,* Vol. 11, A Staff Report to the National Commission on the Causes and Prevention of Violence (Washington, D.C.: U.S. Government Printing Office, 1969), Ch. 3.

11. Norman Ryder, "The Demography of Youth," in *Youth: Transition to Adulthood,* Report of the Panel on Youth of the President's Science Advisory Committee (Washington, D.C.: U.S. Government Printing Office, June, 1973), p. 45.

12. *Report on the Causes of Crime,* Vol. 1 (Wickersham Reports), National Commission on Law Observance and En-

forcement (Montclair, N.J.: Patterson Smith Reprint Series, 1968), p. 73.

13. Leon Gibson Hunt and Carl D. Chambers, *The Heroin Epidemics* (New York: S.P. Books, Division of Spectrum Publications, Inc., 1976), Introduction and Ch. 4.

14. James S. Coleman, "Youth Culture," in *Youth: Transition to Adulthood,* p. 115.

15. Lee Kennett and James LaVerne Anderson, *The Gun in America* (Westport, Conn.: Greenwood Press, 1975), pp. 108, 120. Cf. also Sherrill, *The Saturday Night Special.*

16. Frantz, "The Frontier Tradition," in Graham and Gurr, *Violence in America,* Vol. 1.

17. See Robert K. Merton, "Social Structure and Anomie," in Merton, *Social Theory and Social Structure,* enlarged ed. (New York: The Free Press, 1968), Chs. 6, 7. (First published in 1938, Merton's essay is one of the seminal works of modern sociology.)

18. Carl B. Klockars, *The Professional Fence* (New York: The Free Press, 1974), p. 149, note 10.

19. Ronald Christensen, "Projected Percentage of U.S. Population with Criminal Arrest and Conviction Records," *Task Force Report: Science and Technology,* A Report to the President's Commission on Law Enforcement and the Administration of Justice (Washington, D.C.: U.S. Government Printing Office, 1967), App. J, esp. p. 221; Jacob Belkin et al., "Recidivism as a Feedback Process: An Analytical Model and Empirical Validation," *Journal of Criminal Justice,* Vol. 1, No. 1 (March, 1973), p. 13.

20. Marvin E. Wolfgang et al., *Delinquency in a Birth Cohort* (Chicago: University of Chicago Press, 1972), Ch. 1; Wolfgang, "Crime in a Birth Cohort," *Proceedings of the American Philosophical Society,* Vol. 117, No. 5 (October, 1973); personal communication with Prof. Wolfgang.

21. Kenneth Polk, "Special Report: Rural Delinquency and Maturational Reform," mimeo; *Teenage Delinquency in Small Town America,* National Institute of Mental Health Center for Studies of Crime and Delinquency Research Report 5; plus special tabulation by Dr. F. Lynn Richard.

22. Cf. James F. Short, Jr., and F. Ivan Nye, "Extent of Unrecorded Delinquency: Tentative Conclusions," *Journal of Criminal Law and Criminology,* Vol. 49, No. 4 (1958); Jay R. Williams and Martin Gold, "From Delinquent Behavior to Juvenile Delinquency," *Social Problems,* Vol. 20,

No. 2 (1972), pp. 209–29; Gold, "Undetected Delinquent Behavior," *Journal of Research in Crime and Delinquency*, Vol. 3, No. 1 (January, 1966); Nils Christie et al., "A Study of Self-Reported Crime," *Scandinavian Studies in Criminology*, Vol. 1 (London: Tavistock Publications, 1965). For thoughtful surveys of the literature on self-reported crime and delinquency, cf. Don C. Gibbons, *Society, Crime, and Criminal Careers* (Englewood Cliffs, N.J.: Prentice-Hall, Inc., 1968), pp. 107–12; Gibbons, *Delinquent Behavior* (Prentice-Hall, Inc., 1970), pp. 20–32, 142–71; Travis Hirschi and Hanan C. Selvin, *Delinquency Research* (New York: The Free Press, 1967), Chs. 7, 11. Cf. also Eugene Doleschal and Nora Klapmuts, "Toward a New Criminology," *Crime and Delinquency Literature*, Vol. 5, No. 4 (December, 1973), pp. 607–26.

23. Michael S. Lasky, "One in Three Hotel Guests Is a Towel Thief, Bible Pincher or Worse," *New York Times Travel Section* (January 27, 1974).

24. Mark Lipman, with Robert Daley, *Stealing* (New York: Harper's Magazine Press, 1973), pp. x–xii.

25. The President's Commission on Law Enforcement and the Administration of Justice, *Task Force Report: Crime and Its Impact—An Assessment* (Washington, D.C.: U.S. Government Printing Office, 1967), p. 103.

26. Christopher D. Stone, *Where the Law Ends* (New York: Harper & Row, 1975), pp. 54–55, 201–02.

27. Kenneth H. Bacon, "SEC Testimony Tells How Gulf Oil Gave $300,000 a Year to Politicians in the U.S.," *The Wall Street Journal* (November 17, 1975), p. 30.

28. William M. Carley, "Lockheed's Payoffs to Indonesians Were Difficult to Arrange," *The Wall Street Journal* (November 17, 1975), pp. 1, 23.

29. Ralph Nader, Foreword, in J. Esposito, *Vanishing Air*, quoted in Gilbert Geis and Herbert Edelhertz, "Criminal Law and Consumer Fraud: A Sociolegal View," *American Criminal Law Review*, Vol. 11, No. 4 (Summer, 1973), p. 1001.

30. John Brooks, *Once in Golconda* (New York: Harper Colophon Books, 1970), quoted by Gilbert Geis, "Avocational Crime," in Daniel Glaser, ed., *Handbook of Criminology* (Chicago: Rand McNally, 1974), p. 274.

31. Cf. Wyndham Robertson, "Those Daring Young Con Men of Equity Funding," *Fortune* (August, 1973). Cf. also

William E. Blundell, "Many People's Dreams Came Crashing Down with Equity Funding," *The Wall Street Journal* (March 29, 1974).

32. National Advisory Commission on Criminal Justice Standards and Goals, *Community Crime Prevention* (Washington, D.C.: U.S. Government Printing Office, 1973), p. 207.

3. *Robbers, Hustlers, and Other Dudes*

1. Marvin E. Wolfgang et al., *Delinquency in a Birth Cohort* (Chicago: University of Chicago Press, 1972), Chs. 2, 4–8.
2. See Andre Normandeau, *Trends and Patterns in Crimes of Robbery*, 1968 Ph.D. dissertation, University of Pennsylvania (Ann Arbor, Mich.: University Microfilms, 1974), Tables 98, 99; Julian B. Roebuck, *Criminal Typology* (Springfield, Ill.: Charles C. Thomas, 1967), p. 110; Adrianne Weir, "The Robbery Offender," in Floyd Feeney and Weir, eds., *The Prevention and Control of Robbery*, Vol. 1 (Davis: University of California—Davis, 1973, mimeo).
3. John E. Conklin, *Robbery and the Criminal Justice System* (Philadelphia: J. B. Lippincott Co., 1972), Ch. 4; Feeney and Weir, eds., *Prevention and Control of Robbery*, Vol. 1; William West, *Serious Thieves: Lower-Class Adolescent Males in a Short-Term Deviant Occupation*, Ph.D. dissertation, Northeastern University (Ann Arbor, Mich.: University Microfilms, 1974).

There are almost as many criminal typologies as there are criminologists. For a lucid summary of the literature, see Don C. Gibbons, *Society, Crime, and Criminal Careers* (Englewood Cliffs, N.J.: Prentice-Hall, Inc., 1968), Chs. 9–16. (What I call opportunistic robbers and semiprofessional robbers are lumped together in Gibbons' category of "semi-professional property criminal.") See also James A. Inciardi, "Vocational Crime," in Daniel Glaser, ed., *Handbook of Criminology* (Rand McNally, 1974); Andrew Walker, "Sociology and Professional Crime," in Abraham S. Blumberg, ed., *Current Perspectives on Criminal Behavior* (New York: Alfred A. Knopf, 1974); John Irwin, *The Felon* (Englewood Cliffs, N.J.: Prentice-Hall, Inc., 1970); Edwin H. Sutherland, *The Professional Thief* (Chicago: University of Chicago Press, 1937); David W. Maurer, *Whiz Mob* (Gainesville, Fla.: American Dialect Society, 1955).

4. John Allen, *Assault with a Deadly Weapon: The Auto-biography of a Street Criminal*, Dianne Hall Kelly and Philip Heymann, eds. (New York: Pantheon Books, 1977), pp. 53–54.

5. Bruce Jackson, *A Thief's Primer* (New York: Macmillan Co., 1969), p. 31.

6. Jackson, *In the Life* (New York: Macmillan Co., 1972), pp. 41–42.

7. Maurer, *Whiz Mob*, pp. 56, 9–10.

8. For analyses of professional robbers' operating techniques, see Werner Einstadter, "The Social Organization of Armed Robbery," *Social Problems*, Vol. 17 (Summer, 1969); Einstadter, *Armed Robbery: A Career Study in Perspective*, 1966 Ph.D. dissertation, University of California, Berkeley (Ann Arbor, Mich.: University Microfilms, 1976); Roebuck, *Criminal Typology*, Ch. 6.

9. Feeney and Weir, eds., *Prevention and Control of Robbery*, esp. Vol. 1. The description of opportunist and semiprofessional robbers that follows relies heavily on the Feeney-Weir and Conklin monographs, as well as on field research by Richard Van Wagenen, Arlene Silberman, and the author.

10. See Marvin E. Wolfgang and Franco Ferracuti, *The Sub-culture of Violence* (London: Social Science Paperbacks, 1967); Lynn A. Curtis, *Criminal Violence* (Lexington, Mass.: D. C. Heath & Co., 1974); Curtis, *Violence, Race, and Culture* (Lexington, Mass.: D. C. Heath & Co., 1975).

11. Leon G. Hunt and Norman E. Zinberg, *Heroin Use: A New Look* (Washington, D.C.: The Drug Abuse Council, Inc., 1976). See also Leroy C. Gould et al., *Connections: Notes from the Heroin World* (New Haven: Yale University Press, 1974), pp. 22–36; Leon Gibson Hunt and Carl D. Chambers, *The Heroin Epidemics*.

12. Allen, *Assault with a Deadly Weapon*, p. 52.

13. Inciardi, "Vocational Crime," pp. 336–37. See also Einstadter, "Social Organization of Armed Robbery," p. 80.

14. Tony Parker and Robert Allerton, *The Courage of His Convictions* (London: Hutchinson Publishing Group, 1962), quoted in John M. MacDonald, *Armed Robbery* (Springfield, Ill.: Charles C. Thomas, 1975), p. 143.

15. New York *Post* (July 22, 1975).

16. Quoted in The Fortune Society, *Fortune News* (December, 1975), p. 4.

17. See especially Walter B. Miller, *Violence by Youth Gangs and Youth Groups as a Crime Problem in Major American Cities* (Washington, D.C.: U.S. Government Printing Office, 1975), pp. 41–42.

18. George D. Newton and Franklin E. Zimring, *Firearms and Violence in American Life,* A Staff Report to the National Commission on the Causes and Prevention of Violence (Washington, D.C.: U.S. Government Printing Office, 1969), Vol. 7, Ch. 4; Joseph D. Alviani and William R. Drake, *Handgun Control . . . Issues and Alternatives* (Washington, D.C.: United States Conference of Mayors, 1975), pp. 27–28; Michael Pousner, "Triggers Ready to Be Pulled," New York *Daily News* (December 15, 1975); Timothy S. Robinson, "D.C. Criminals Seen Favoring Sawed-Off Guns," Washington *Post* (July 19, 1975); Franklin E. Zimring, "Street Crimes and New Guns: Some Implications for Firearms Control," *Journal of Criminal Justice,* Vol. 4, No. 2 (Summer, 1976), pp. 95–107.

19. Charles E. Silberman, *The Myths of Automation* (New York: Harper & Row, 1966), Ch. 6.

20. MacDonald, *Armed Robbery,* p. 141.

21. Normandeau, *Trends and Patterns in Crimes of Robbery,* pp. 301–11. Analysis of arrest data in New York, New Jersey, and California showed similar results. See Feeney and Weir, *Prevention and Control of Robbery,* Vol. I, pp. 123–27, 142–43.

22. Wolfgang, "Crime in a Birth Cohort," *Proceedings of the American Philosophical Society,* Vol. 117, No. 5 (October, 1973), pp. 407–08, and Wolfgang et al., *Delinquency in a Birth Cohort,* Chs. 10, 11. Although the delinquents in the cohort show some tendency to repeat the same offense, especially if the offense is robbery, the tendency is statistically insignificant.

23. Barry Krisberg, *Urban Leadership Training: An Ethnographic Study of 22 Gang Leaders,* 1971 Ph.D. dissertation, University of Pennsylvania (Ann Arbor, Mich.: University Microfilms, 1976), pp. 94–95.

24. David Matza, *Delinquency and Drift* (New York: John Wiley & Sons, Inc., 1964), pp. 55–56.

25. Harry King, as told to and edited by Bill Chambliss, *Box Man* (New York: Harper & Row, 1972), p. 76; Jackson, *In the Life,* p. 7.

26. Irwin, *The Felon,* p. 24.

27. Roebuck, *Criminal Typology*, pp. 175–76.

28. Ned Polsky, *Hustlers, Beats, and Others* (Chicago: Aldine Publishing Co., 1967), p. 132; Einstadter, "Social Organization of Armed Robbery," p. 81.

29. Malcolm Braly, *On the Yard* (Greenwich, Conn.: Fawcett Publications, Inc., 1967), p. 197; Jackson, *A Thief's Primer*, p. 180; John Bartlow Martin, *My Life in Crime* (Westport, Conn.: Greenwood Press, 1952, 1970 reprint), pp. 54–55; King (Chambliss), *Box Man*, p. 28.

30. Leroy Gould et al., *Crime as a Profession*, Final Report to the Office of Law Enforcement Assistance and President's Commission on Law Enforcement and Administration of Justice, 1967, mimeo, pp. 25–26.

31. Gould et al., *Crime as a Profession*, pp. 27–28. Neil Shover, *Burglary as an Occupation* (Ann Arbor, Mich.: University Microfilms, 1971), pp. 41–44; Martin, *My Life in Crime*, pp. 54–55. See also West, *Serious Thieves*, pp. 132–34.

32. James F. Haran and John M. Martin, "The Imprisonment of Bank Robbers: The Issue of Deterrence," *Federal Probation*, Vol. 41, No. 3 (September, 1977), pp. 27–30.

33. Francis A. J. Ianni, *Black Mafia* (New York: Simon & Schuster, 1974), pp. 234–35; see also Gould et al., *Crime as a Profession*, pp. 30–31.

34. Inciardi, "Vocational Crime," p. 326; Julian B. Roebuck and Wolfgang Frese, *The Rendezvous* (New York: The Free Press, 1976), p. 186.

35. Jackson, *In the Life*, pp. 40, 34–35.

36. Allen, *Assault with a Deadly Weapon*, pp. 142, 229–30; King (Chambliss), *Box Man*, p. x.

37. Edward Bunker, *No Beast So Fierce* (New York: W. W. Norton & Co., 1973), p. 83; Daniel Glaser, *Strategic Criminal Justice Planning* (Rockville, Md.: National Institute of Mental Health Center for Studies in Crime and Delinquency, 1975), pp. 79–80.

38. West, *Serious Thieves*, p. 17.

39. MacDonald, *Armed Robbery*, p. 163.

40. James Willwerth, *Jones* (New York: M. Evans and Co., Inc., 1975), p. 24.

41. See Erving Goffman, *Interaction Ritual* (Garden City, N.Y.: Anchor Books, 1967), pp. 174–81; Einstadter, *Armed Robbery*, pp. 74–76; Matza, *Delinquency and Drift*, pp. 85–90.

42. Peter Letkemann, *Crime as Work* (Englewood Cliffs, N.J.:

Prentice-Hall, Inc., 1973), p. 112; Einstadter, *Armed Robbery*, p. 100.

43. Malcolm Braly, *False Starts* (Boston: Little, Brown & Co., 1976), p. 213.

44. John MacIsaac, *Half the Fun Was Getting There* (Englewood Cliffs, N.J.: Prentice-Hall, Inc., 1968), p. 20, quoted in Shover, *Burglary as an Occupation*, p. 72.

45. Sutherland, *Professional Thief*, p. 183.

46. Letkemann, *Crime as Work*, pp. 44–45.

47. Irwin, *The Felon*, p. 25.

48. Bunker, *No Beast So Fierce*.

4. Poverty and Crime

1. Robert Coles, "The Children of Affluence," *The Atlantic Monthly*, Vol. 240, No. 3 (September, 1977), pp. 52–66.

2. Robert K. Merton, "Social Structure and Anomie," in Merton, *Social Theory and Social Structure*, enlarged ed. (New York: The Free Press, 1968), pp. 192–93.

3. John Allen, *Assault with a Deadly Weapon: The Autobiography of a Street Criminal*, Dianne Hall Kelly and Philip Heymann, eds. (New York: Pantheon Books, 1977), p. 1.

4. Allen, *Assault with a Deadly Weapon*, pp. 37, 5; Francis A. J. Ianni, *Black Mafia* (New York: Simon & Schuster, 1974), p. 285.

5. Frank Tannenbaum, *Crime and the Community* (New York: Columbia University Press, 1938), pp. 51–52.

6. Marilyn Walsh and Duncan Chappell, "Operational Parameters in the Stolen Property System," Hearings before the Select Committee on Small Business, U.S. Senate, on *Criminal Redistribution (Fencing) of Goods Stolen from Legitimate Business Activities and Their Effect on Commerce*, Part 3 (April 30 and May 2, 1974), pp. 765–66. A briefer version of the paper appears in *Journal of Criminal Justice*, Vol. 2, No. 2 (1974), pp. 113–29.

   The discussion that follows relies also on the following sources, as well as on research by Richard D. Van Wagenen: Carl B. Klockars, *The Professional Fence* (New York: The Free Press, 1974); Marilyn Walsh, *The Fence* (Westport, Conn.: Greenwood Press, 1977); Duncan Chappell and Marilyn Walsh, "Receiving Stolen Property,"

Criminology, Vol. 11, No. 4 (February, 1974), pp. 484–97; Chappell and Walsh, " 'No Questions Asked': A Consideration of the History of Criminal Receiving," *An Analysis of Criminal Redistribution Systems and Their Economic Impact on Small Business*, A Staff Report prepared for the Select Committee on Small Business, U.S. Senate (Washington, D.C.: U.S. Government Printing Office, 1972); Ianni, *Black Mafia*, pp. 37–47, 230–39, 246–75; Daniel Jack Chasan, "Good Fences Make Bad Neighbors," *New York Times Magazine* (December 29, 1974); Desmond Cartey, "How Black Enterprisers Do Their Thing: An Odyssey Through Ghetto Capitalism," in Glenn Jacobs, ed., *The Participant Observer* (New York: George Braziller, 1970), Ch. 1; William Gordon West, *Serious Thieves: Lower-Class Adolescent Males in a Short-Term Deviant Occupation*, Ph.D. dissertation, Northeastern University (Ann Arbor, Mich.: University Microfilms, 1974), pp. 156–66; Julian B. Roebuck and Wolfgang Frese, *The Rendezvous* (New York: The Free Press, 1972), pp. 181–201; Leroy C. Gould et al., *Crime as a Profession*, Final Report to the Office of Law Enforcement Assistance and President's Commission of Law Enforcement and Administration of Justice, 1967, mimeo.

7. Klockars, *Professional Fence*, p. 50, note 8, and pp. 62, 77–79.

8. Joseph T. Howell, *Hard Living on Clay Street* (Garden City, N.Y.: Anchor Books, 1973), p. 322.

9. Gould et al., *Crime as a Profession*, p. 42, note 1.

10. For an analysis of fences' other occupations, see Walsh, *The Fence*, Chs. 2–4.

11. Walsh, *The Fence*, pp. 43–47. For an analysis of the different ways in which fences use their "front," see Walsh, *The Fence*, Ch. 4, and Klockars, *The Professional Fence*, Chs. 4, 5.

12. For arguments that there is a national syndicate, see Donald R. Cressey, *Theft of the Nation: The Structure and Operations of Organized Crime in America* (New York: Harper & Row, 1969); Ralph Salerno and John S. Tompkins, *The Crime Confederation: Cosa Nostra and Allied Operations in Organized Crime* (Garden City, N.Y.: Doubleday & Co., 1969); The President's Commission on Law Enforcement and the Administration of Justice, *Task Force Report: Organized Crime* (Washington, D.C.: U.S.

Government Printing Office, 1967); Peter Maas, *The Valachi Papers* (New York: G. P. Putnam's Sons, 1968); among others.

For arguments on the other side, see Dwight C. Smith, Jr., *The Mafia Mystique* (New York: Basic Books, Inc., 1975); Joseph Albini, *The American Mafia* (New York: Appleton-Century-Crofts, 1971); Frederick D. Homer, *Guns and Garlic* (West Lafayette, Ind.: Purdue University Press, 1974); Gordon Hawkins, "God and the Mafia," *The Public Interest*, reprinted in John E. Conklin, ed., *The Crime Establishment* (Englewood Cliffs, N.J.: Prentice-Hall, Inc., 1973); among others.

13. The discussion also leans heavily on the following published sources: John Landesco, "Organized Crime in Chicago," *The Illinois Crime Survey*, Illinois Association for Criminal Justice (Montclair, N.J.: Patterson Smith Reprint Series in Criminology, Law Enforcement, and Social Problems, 1968), Chs. 3–8; Harold D. Lasswell and Jeremiah B. McKenna, *The Impact of Organized Crime on an Inner-City Community* (New York: The Policy Sciences Center, Inc., mimeo); Mark H. Haller, "Organized Crime in Urban Society: Chicago in the Twentieth Century," *Journal of Social History* (Winter, 1971–72), pp. 210–34; Haller, "Bootlegging in Chicago: The Structure of an Illegal Enterprise," unpublished paper prepared for the American Historical Association Convention, Chicago, December 29, 1974; Haller, "Urban Crime and Criminal Justice: The Chicago Case," *Journal of American History*, Vol. LVII, No. 3 (December, 1970), pp. 619–35; William J. Chambliss, "Vice, Corruption, Bureaucracy and Power," *Wisconsin Law Review*, Vol. 1971, No. 4, pp. 1150–73; Francis A. J. Ianni, with Elizabeth Reuss-Ianni, *A Family Business* (New York: Russell Sage Foundation, 1972); Ianni, *Black Mafia*; John A. Gardiner, *The Politics of Corruption: Organized Crime in an American City* (New York: Russell Sage Foundation, 1970); The President's Commission on Law Enforcement and the Administration of Justice, *Task Force Report: Organized Crime*; IIT Research Institute and the Chicago Crime Commission, *A Study of Organized Crime in Illinois*, 1971; St. Clair Drake and Horace R. Cayton, *Black Metropolis* (New York: Harper & Row, 1962), Chs. 17, 21; William Foote Whyte, *Street Corner Society*, 2nd ed. (Chicago: University of Chicago Press,

1951); Paul Bullock, *Aspiration vs. Opportunity: "Careers" in the Inner City* (Ann Arbor, Mich.: Institute of Labor and Industrial Relations, University of Michigan–Wayne State University, 1973); Mary Manoni, *Bedford-Stuyvesant* (New York: Quadrangle/New York Times Book Co., 1973).

14. Lasswell and McKenna, *Impact of Organized Crime*. See also Ivan H. Light, "Numbers Gambling: A Financial Institution of the Ghetto," Paper presented at 1st Annual Conference on Gambling, Sahara Hotel, Las Vegas, Nev., June 11, 1973, mimeo; Manoni, *Bedford-Stuyvesant*, Chs. 7–8; Jess Marcum and Henry Rowen, "How Many Games in Town?—The Pros and Cons of Legalized Gambling," *The Public Interest*, No. 36 (Summer, 1974); Ianni, *Black Mafia*; Fred J. Cook, "The Black Mafia Moves into the Numbers Racket," *New York Times Magazine* (April 4, 1971).

15. City of New York Criminal Justice Coordinating Council, *A Community Self-Study of Organized Crime* (New York: Institute for Social Analysis, 1974, mimeo), p. 60; Louise Meriwether, *Daddy Was a Number Runner* (New York: Pyramid Books, 1971), p. 15.

16. Light, "Numbers Gambling," pp. 15–17, 25–26.

17. Personal letter; I am indebted to Prof. Jackson for pointing out the rationality of numbers betting to me.

18. Whyte, *Street Corner Society*, p. 145.

19. Ianni, *Black Mafia*, pp. 109–20.

20. Gardiner, *Politics of Corruption*, pp. 79–82; Whyte, *Street Corner Society*, p. 142. See also Haller, "Organized Crime in Urban Society," esp. pp. 226–29, and Drake and Cayton, *Black Metropolis*, Vol. II, pp. 484–87.

21. Mark Harrison Moore, *Buy and Bust* (Lexington, Mass.: Lexington Books, 1977), pp. 92–111.

22. On changing patterns of drug use, see Edward Preble and Thomas Miller, "Methadone, Wine, and Welfare," in Robert S. Weppner, ed., *Street Ethnography* (Beverly Hills, Calif.: Sage Publications, 1977), Ch. 10; Edward Jay Epstein, *Agency of Fear* (New York: G. P. Putnam's Sons, 1977), Ch. 33; Leon Gibson Hunt and Carl D. Chambers, *The Heroin Epidemics* (New York: S.P. Books, Division of Spectrum Publications, Inc., 1976); Hunt and Norman E. Zinberg, *Heroin Use: A New Look* (Washington, D.C.: The Drug Abuse Council, Inc., 1976).

23. Ianni, *Black Mafia*, p. 284.

24. Ianni, with Reuss-Ianni, *A Family Business*, p. 133.

25. Howard Blum, "New York Gang Reported to Sell Death and Drugs," New York *Times* (December 16, 1977). For a detailed description of organized crime operations in the Pleasant Avenue neighborhood in East Harlem, see David Durk and Ira Silverman, *The Pleasant Avenue Connection* (New York: Harper & Row, 1976).

26. Albert K. Cohen, *Delinquent Boys* (New York: The Free Press, 1955), pp. 135–36. See also David Matza, *Delinquency and Drift* (New York: John Wiley & Sons, Inc., 1964), esp. Chs. 4, 6.

27. Walter B. Miller, "Lower Class Culture as a Generating Milieu of Gang Delinquency," *Journal of Social Issues*, Vol. 14, No. 3 (1958), pp. 5–19. See also Miller, "The Elimination of the American Lower Class as National Policy: A Critique of the Ideology of the Poverty Movement of the 1960s," in Daniel P. Moynihan, ed., *On Understanding Poverty* (New York: Basic Books, 1969), Ch. 10; Miller, "Violent Crimes in City Gangs," *Annals of the American Academy of Political and Social Science* (March, 1966), reprinted in Marvin E. Wolfgang, Leonard Savitz, and Norman Johnston, eds., *The Sociology of Crime and Delinquency*, 2nd ed. (New York: John Wiley & Sons, Inc., 1970), Ch. 36.

28. Edward C. Banfield, *The Unheavenly City* (Boston: Little, Brown & Co., 1970), pp. 211, 62–63.

29. Hylan Lewis, "Culture of Poverty? What Does It Matter?" in Eleanor Burke Leacock, ed., *The Culture of Poverty: A Critique* (New York: Simon & Schuster, 1971). See also Lewis, "Child Rearing Among Low-Income Families" (Washington, D.C.: The Washington Center for Metropolitan Studies, 1961), reprinted in Louis A. Ferman, Joyce L. Kornbluh, and Alan Haber, eds., *Poverty in America* (Ann Arbor, Mich.: University of Michigan Press, 1965); Leonard Goodwin, *Do the Poor Want to Work?* (Washington, D.C.: The Brookings Institution, 1972).

30. For an exploration of the way in which what Erik Erikson calls "identity foreclosure" or "negative identity" develops among black Americans, see Stuart L. Hauser, *Black and White Identity Formation* (New York: Wiley-Interscience, 1971).

31. For a fascinating analysis of the varied aims and forms of

action, see Erving Goffman's long essay "Where the Action Is," in Goffman, *Interaction Ritual* (Garden City, N.Y.: Anchor Books, 1967), pp. 149–270.

32. Malcolm Braly, *False Starts* (Boston: Little, Brown & Co., 1976), pp. 26–27.

33. Allen, *Assault with a Deadly Weapon*, pp. 102, xix.

34. Herbert J. Gans, *The Urban Villagers* (New York: The Free Press, 1962), p. 65.

35. Cohen, *Delinquent Boys*, p. 134.

36. Clifford R. Shaw and Henry D. McKay, "Social Factors in Juvenile Delinquency," *Report on the Causes of Crime* (Wickersham Commission), Vol. II, 1931, National Commission on Law Observance and Enforcement (Montclair, N.J.: Patterson Smith Reprint Series, 1968), pp. 122–23. See also Frederic M. Thrasher, *The Gang*, abridged ed. (Chicago: University of Chicago Press, 1963), esp. Ch. V.

37. Banfield, *The Unheavenly City*, p. 211.

38. Elliot Liebow, *Tally's Corner: A Study of Street Corner Men* (Boston: Little, Brown & Co., 1967), pp. 64–66. See also Lee Rainwater, *Behind Ghetto Walls* (Chicago: Aldine Publishing Co., 1970), pp. 220–30.

39. Hyman Rodman, "The Lower-Class Value Stretch," *Social Forces* (December, 1963), reprinted in Ferman et al., eds., *Poverty in America*.

40. Liebow, *Tally's Corner*, p. 222.

41. Hylan Lewis, Foreword, in Allen, *Assault with a Deadly Weapon*, p. xxi.

5. *"Beware the Day They Change Their Minds":* Race, Culture, and Crime

1. See *A Socio-Economic Profile of Puerto Rican New Yorkers* (New York: U.S. Department of Labor, Bureau of Labor Statistics, Middle Atlantic Regional Office Report 46, 1975), pp. 106–13.

2. David Burnham, "3 of 5 Slain by Police Here Are Black, Same as Arrest Rate," *New York Times* (August 25, 1973), p. 1; New York State Senate Standing Committee on Crime and Correction and Select Committee on Crime, mimeo. (Prison records are likely to record offenders' ethnic background accurately, since black, Puerto Rican, and non-Hispanic white inmates segregate themselves almost com-

pletely. There is no reason to believe that New York State judges are more likely to send black offenders to prison for any given offense than they are Puerto Rican offenders.)

3. National Commission on Law Observance and Enforcement, *Crime and the Foreign Born* (Wickersham Commission Reports, No. 10) (Montclair, N.J.: Patterson Smith Reprint Series, 1968), esp. Parts II, III, IV. (Originally published in 1931.)

4. Paul Bohannan, "Patterns of Murder and Suicide," in Bohannan, ed., *African Homicide and Suicide* (Princeton, N.J.: Princeton University Press, 1960), Ch. 9, esp. pp. 236–38.

5. Raymond Fosdick, *American Police Systems* (Montclair, N.J.: Patterson Smith Reprint Series, 1972), p. 45. (Fosdick's book was originally published in 1920.) Gunnar Myrdal, *An American Dilemma* (New York: Harper & Row, 1944), p. 559.

6. Lawrence W. Levine, *Black Culture and Black Consciousness* (New York: Oxford University Press, 1977), p. 251; Theodore Rosengarten, *All God's Dangers: The Life of Nate Shaw* (New York: Alfred A. Knopf, 1974), pp. 308, 302.

7. See for example Stanford M. Lyman, *Chinese Americans* (New York: Random House, Inc., 1974); Victor G. and Brett deBary Nee, *Longtime Californ': A Documentary Study of an American Chinatown* (New York: Pantheon Books, 1973); William Petersen, *Japanese Americans* (New York: Random House, Inc., 1971); Vine Deloria, *Custer Died for Your Sins* (New York: Macmillan Co., 1969); Wilcomb E. Washburn, ed., *The Indian and the White Man* (Garden City, N.Y.: Anchor Books, 1964); John R. Howard, ed., *Awakening Minorities* (New Brunswick, N.J.: Transaction Books, 1970); Stan Steiner, *La Raza* (New York: Harper & Row, 1970); Matt S. Meier and Feliciano Rivera, *The Chicanos* (New York: Hill & Wang, 1972); Julian Samora and Patricia Vandel Simon, *A History of the Mexican-American People* (Notre Dame, Ind.: University of Notre Dame Press, 1977); Ellwyn R. Stoddard, *Mexican Americans* (New York: Random House, Inc., 1973); Robert Coles, *Eskimos, Chicanos, Indians,* Vol. IV, *Children of Crisis* (Boston: Atlantic–Little, Brown, 1977), Parts II, IV.

8. The most recent (and, in some ways, most thoughtful)

statement of this view is in Thomas Sowell, *Race and Economics* (New York: David McKay Co., Inc., 1975). See also Oscar Handlin, *The Newcomers: Negroes and Puerto Ricans in a Changing Metropolis* (Cambridge, Mass.: Harvard University Press, 1969); Philip M. Hauser, "Demographic Factors in the Integration of the Negro," *Daedalus*, Vol. 94, No. 4 (Fall, 1965), pp. 847–77, and Hauser, *Rapid Growth: Key to Understanding Metropolitan Problems* (Washington, D.C.: Washington Center for Metropolitan Studies, 1961); Irving Kristol, "The Negro Today Is like the Immigrant of Yesterday," *New York Times Magazine* (September 11, 1966).

9. For an analysis of the roots of anti-black prejudice in English language and thought, see Winthrop D. Jordan, *White over Black* (Baltimore: Penguin Books, Inc., 1968), Preface and Part I, Ch. 1. A briefer and more popular analysis is contained in Jordan, *The White Man's Burden* (New York: Oxford University Press, 1974), Ch. 1.

10. For a thoughtful analysis of American attitudes toward poverty and the poor, see David Matza, "The Disreputable Poor," in Neil J. Smelser and S. M. Lipset, eds., *Social Structure and Mobility in Economic Development* (Chicago: Aldine Publishing Co., 1966), reprinted in F. James Davis and Richard Stivers, eds., *The Collective Definition of Deviance* (New York: The Free Press, 1975).

11. Stephan Thernstrom, *The Other Bostonians* (Cambridge, Mass.: Harvard University Press, 1973). See also Thernstrom, "Poverty in Historical Perspective," in Daniel P. Moynihan, ed., *On Understanding Poverty* (New York: Basic Books, Inc., 1969), Ch. 6.

12. See for example Joseph J. Barton, *Peasants and Strangers* (Cambridge, Mass.: Harvard University Press, 1975), esp. Ch. 5; Peter M. Blau and Otis Dudley Duncan, *The American Occupational Structure* (New York: John Wiley & Sons, Inc., 1967).

13. Thernstrom, *The Other Bostonians*, Ch. 8.

14. Thernstrom, *The Other Bostonians*, pp. 212–13; Herbert G. Gutman, *The Black Family in Slavery and Freedom, 1750–1925* (New York: Pantheon Books, 1976).

15. Myrdal, *An American Dilemma*, Appendix 6, esp. pp. 1087–89, 1099–107. See also St. Clair Drake and Horace Cayton, *Black Metropolis* (New York: Harcourt Brace Jovanovich, 1945), Ch. 9; Charles E. Silberman, *Crisis in*

Black and White (New York: Random House, Inc., 1964), pp. 102–08.

16. C. Vann Woodward, *The Strange Career of Jim Crow*, 3rd rev. ed. (New York: Oxford University Press, 1974).

17. See Ozzie G. Simmons, "The Mutual Images and Expectations of Anglo-Americans and Mexican-Americans," *Daedalus*, Vol. 90, No. 2 (Spring, 1961), pp. 186–299.

18. Coles, *Eskimos, Chicanos, Indians,* Ch. 6. See also Coles, *The Old Ones of New Mexico* (Garden City, N.Y.: Anchor Books, 1975), and Celia S. Heller, *Mexican American Youth: Forgotten Youth at the Crossroads* (New York: Random House, Inc., 1966), Ch. 2.

19. Ralph Ellison, *Invisible Man* (New York: New American Library, 1952), pp. 7–8.

20. W. E. B. DuBois, *Dusk of Dawn* (New York: Harcourt Brace Jovanovich, 1940), pp. 130–31, quoted in Silberman, *Crisis in Black and White,* p. 110.

21. Nathan Glazer and Daniel P. Moynihan, *Beyond the Melting Pot* (Cambridge, Mass.: M.I.T. Press and Harvard University Press, 1963), p. 53.

22. Robert R. Moton, *What the Negro Thinks* (Garden City, N.Y.: Doubleday & Co., 1929), p. 1.

23. Levine, *Black Culture and Black Consciousness.*

24. " 'A Very Stern Discipline': An Interview with Ralph Ellison," *Harper's* (March, 1967), pp. 76–95.

25. Claude McKay, *Home to Harlem* (New York: Pocket Books, Inc., 1965), p. 141.

26. Quoted in Albert Murray, *The Omni-Americans* (New York: Outerbridge & Dienstfrey, 1970), p. 162. See also Charles Keil, *Urban Blues* (Chicago: University of Chicago Press, 1966); Alan Lomax, "I Got the Blues," *Common Ground,* Vol. 8 (Summer, 1948), reprinted in Alan Dundes, ed., *Mother Wit from the Laughing Barrel* (Englewood Cliffs, N.J.: Prentice-Hall, 1973); Ben Sidran, *Black Talk* (New York: Holt, Rinehart & Winston, 1971).

27. Roger D. Abrahams, *Positively Black* (Englewood Cliffs, N.J.: Prentice-Hall, Inc., 1970), p. 61.

28. Bernard Wolfe, "Uncle Remus and the Malevolent Rabbit," *Commentary* (July, 1949), reprinted in Dundes, ed., *Mother Wit from the Laughing Barrel,* pp. 524–40.

29. Levine, *Black Culture and Black Consciousness,* pp. 118–20.

30. For an analysis of the John tales and some contemporary versions of them, see Abrahams, *Positively Black,* pp. 63–

69. See also Zora Neale Hurston, "High John de Con-
quer," and Harry Oster, "Negro Humor: John & Old
Marster," in Dundes, ed., *Mother Wit from the Laughing
Barrel*; Harold Courlander, ed., *A Treasury of Afro-American Folklore* (New York: Crown Publishers, Inc., 1976),
pp. 419–42; Levine, *Black Culture and Black Consciousness*, pp. 121–33.

31. Bruce Jackson, *"Get Your Ass in the Water and Swim Like
Me"* (Cambridge, Mass.: Harvard University Press, 1974).

32. Roger D. Abrahams, *Deep Down in the Jungle*, 1st rev. ed.
(Chicago: Aldine Publishing Co., 1970), p. 45.

33. Christina and Richard Milner, *Black Players* (Boston:
Little, Brown & Co., 1972), pp. 49–50. See also Thomas
Kochman, ed., *Rappin' and Stylin' Out* (Urbana: Uni-
versity of Illinois Press, 1972); Ulf Hannerz, *Soulside*
(New York: Columbia University Press, 1969), esp. Ch. 5.

34. Levine, *Black Culture and Black Consciousness*, pp. 344–
58. See also Peter Farb, *Word Play* (New York: Alfred A.
Knopf, 1974), pp. 110–11.

35. Jackson, *"Get Your Ass in the Water and Swim like Me,"*
p. 13. While Jackson's book contains the largest body of
toasts, Roger D. Abrahams was the first folklorist to analyze the role of toasts in lower-class black life and to provide complete versions of the most characteristic and popular toasts; see Abrahams, *Deep Down in the Jungle* and
Positively Black. The account that follows draws heavily
from both Jackson's and Abrahams' published work and the
author's correspondence with Jackson, as well as from the
following: Keil, *Urban Blues*; Hannerz, *Soulside*; Milner,
Black Players; Lee Rainwater, *Behind Ghetto Walls* (Chicago: Aldine Publishing Co., 1970); Elliot Liebow, *Tally's
Corner: A Study of Street Corner Men* (Boston: Little,
Brown & Co., 1967); Paul Carter Harrison, *The Great
MacDaddy*; Ron Milner, *What the Wine-Sellers Buy*; and
Al-Tony Gilmore, *Bad Nigger!* (Port Washington, N.Y.:
Kennikat Press, 1975).

36. William H. Grier and Price M. Cobbs, *Black Rage* (New
York: Bantam Books, 1969), p. 95. See also Abrahams,
Deep Down in the Jungle, pp. 34–38.

37. Jackson, *"Get Your Ass in the Water and Swim like Me,"*
p. 6. (Jackson's texts were recorded in prisons, bars, pool
halls, migrant labor camps, and street corners in the South,
East, and Midwest.)

38. Abrahams, *Deep Down in the Jungle*, pp. 66–68; a version with a different ending is presented on pp. 113–14. (Jackson offers six other versions in *"Get Your Ass in the Water and Swim like Me,"* pp. 161–72.)

39. Jackson, *"Get Your Ass in the Water and Swim like Me,"* pp. 46–47. For other versions, as well as other badman toasts, see Jackson, pp. 48–65; Abrahams, *Deep Down in the Jungle*, pp. 76–79, 129–42, 160–64, and *Positively Black*, pp. 45–47, 79–80.

40. Abrahams, *Deep Down in the Jungle*, p. 106.

41. Milner, *Black Players*, pp. 170–71.

42. Grier and Cobbs, *Black Rage*, pp. 54–55.

43. Gilmore, *Bad Nigger!*, esp. Ch. 1.

44. Ralph Bunche, "Conceptions and Ideologies of the Negro Problem," quoted in Myrdal, *An American Dilemma*, p. 763.

45. For a fascinating picture of the vitality of the Harlem of the 1910s and 1920s, see Jervis Anderson, *A. Philip Randolph* (New York: Harcourt Brace Jovanovich, 1973), esp. Chs. 4, 9, 10.

46. Quoted in Hollie I. West, "A Gentleman Scholar: The Last of the Great Schoolmasters," Washington *Post* (January 30, 1978).

47. Jackson, *"Get Your Ass in the Water and Swim like Me,"* pp. 3–4, 39–40.

48. Abrahams, *Positively Black*, pp. 52–53.

49. *Journal of the National Medical Association* (January, 1975), quoted in Therman E. Evans, "Media, Violence and Black People," Washington *Post* (August 4, 1976).

50. Claude Brown, *Manchild in the Promised Land* (New York: New American Library, 1965), pp. 126–27.

51. Quoted in Eldridge Cleaver, *Soul on Ice* (New York: McGraw-Hill Book Co., 1968), p. 14.

52. Imamu Amiri Baraka, "Black People!," in Richard Barksdale and Kenneth Kinnamon, eds., *Black Writers of America* (New York: Macmillan Co., 1972), pp. 750–51.

53. Richard Block, "Homicide in Chicago: A Nine-Year Study (1965–1973)," *Journal of Criminal Law and Criminology*, Vol. 6, No. 4 (December, 1975), pp. 496–510. See also Block and Franklin E. Zimring, "Homicide in Chicago, 1965–1970," *Journal of Research in Crime and Delinquency*, Vol. 10, No. 4 (January, 1973), pp. 1–12.

54. Levine, *Black Culture and Black Consciousness*, pp. 417–18.

55. A. Joan Klebba, *Homicide Trends in the United States, 1900–1974* (Washington: U.S. Government Printing Office, 1975); *Criminal Victimization in the United States: A Comparison of 1973 and 1974 Findings*, A National Crime Panel Survey Report (U.S. Government Printing Office, 1976).

56. Gloria Emerson, "In Mean Streets of His Own Past, Father Lives for His Son's Future," New York *Times* (November 5, 1973), p. 55.

57. Joseph D. Whitaker, "Fear Stalks Tyler House Hallways," Washington *Post* (February 16, 1976), pp. A1, A3.

58. William Raspberry, "Victimism," Washington *Post* (July 7, 1976).

59. See Sar A. Levitan, William B. Johnston, and Robert Taggart, *Still a Dream* (Cambridge, Mass.: Harvard University Press, 1975), Ch. 2.

60. James Q. Wilson, *Thinking About Crime* (New York: Basic Books, Inc., 1975), Ch. 1, esp. p. 4, and Ch. 3.

61. See Marvin E. Wolfgang, Robert M. Figlio, and Thorsten Sellin, *Delinquency in a Birth Cohort* (Chicago: University of Chicago Press, 1972), Ch. 4; Lynn A. Curtis, *Criminal Violence* (Lexington, Mass.: Lexington Books, 1974), pp. 148–51.

Part II
Criminal Justice

6. *"The Insufficiency of Human Institutions": An Introduction to the Criminal Justice System*

1. From a lecture given at the University of Naples, April 24, 1901, reprinted in Stanley E. Grupp, ed., *Theories of Punishment* (Bloomington, Ind.: University of Indiana Press, 1971), pp. 231–33.

2. Henry W. Anderson, "Separate Report of Henry W. Anderson," *Report on the Causes of Crime*, Vol. 1 (Wickersham Commission Reports, No. 13), National Commission on Law Observance and Enforcement (Montclair, N.J.: Patterson Smith Reprint Series, 1968), pp. LXVIII, LXVI.

3. See James Q. Wilson, *Thinking About Crime* (New York:

Basic Books, Inc., 1975); Ernest van den Haag, *Punishing Criminals* (New York: Basic Books, Inc., 1975). See also Macklin Fleming, *The Price of Perfect Justice* (New York: Basic Books, Inc., 1974).

4. Quoted in Raymond B. Fosdick, *American Police Systems* (Montclair, N.J.: Patterson Smith Reprint Series, 1972), p. 28. (Fosdick's book was first published in 1920.)

5. Mark H. Haller, "Historical Roots of Police Behavior: Chicago, 1890–1925," *Law and Society Review,* Vol. 10, No. 2 (Winter, 1976), pp. 317–21. See also Yale Kamisar, "When the Cops Were Not 'Handcuffed,'" *New York Times Magazine* (November 7, 1965), reprinted in Arthur Neiderhoffer and Abraham S. Blumberg, eds., *The Ambivalent Force: Perspectives on the Police* (San Francisco: Rhinehart Press, 1973), pp. 312–17. On the nature and extent of police brutality in the 1920s and early '30s, see Zechariah Chaffee, Jr., Walter H. Pollok, and Carl S. Stern, "The Third Degree," *Report on Lawlessness in Law Enforcement* (Wickersham Commission Reports, No. 11), National Commission on Law Observance and Enforcement (Montclair, N.J.: Patterson Smith Reprint Series, 1968), pp. 13–261.

6. Wilson, *Thinking About Crime,* pp. xv–xvi.

7. Edward Jay Epstein, *Agency of Fear* (New York: G. P. Putnam's Sons, 1977), pp. 109, 173–77.

8. Epstein, *Agency of Fear,* Ch. 8.

9. Epstein, *Agency of Fear,* p. 88. See also Epstein, "The Incredible War Against the Poppies," *Washington Post* (December 22, 1974); John F. Holahan, with the assistance of Paul A. Henningsen, "The Economics of Heroin," *Dealing with Drug Abuse,* The Drug Abuse Survey Project (New York: Praeger Publishers, 1972), Ch. 4. On the geographic and temporal patterns of heroin use, see Leon Gibson Hunt and Carl D. Chambers, *The Heroin Epidemics* (New York: S.P. Books, Division of Spectrum Publications, Inc., 1976), Part I; Hunt, *Recent Spread of Heroin Use in the United States: Unanswered Questions* (Washington, D.C.: The Drug Abuse Council, Inc., 1974); Mark H. Greene, Nicholas J. Kozel, Leon G. Hunt, and Roy L. Appletree, *An Assessment of the Diffusion of Heroin Abuse to Medium Sized American Cities* (Washington, D.C.: U.S. Government Printing Office, 1974); Hunt and Norman E. Zin-

berg, *Heroin Use: A New Look* (Washington, D.C.: The Drug Abuse Council, Inc., 1976).

10. Leon Dash, "Heroin Trail: From Mexico to Streets of D.C.," Washington *Post* (April 18, 1976), and Dash, "Tracing D.C. Drug Route," Washington *Post* (May 24, 1976); Howard Blum, "A Heroin War Is Coming to Harlem," *The Village Voice* (November 3, 1975); Nicholas Gage, "Latins Now Leaders of Hard-Drug Trade," New York *Times* (April 21, 1975); Selwyn Raab, "Illegal Narcotics Is Worst Here in 5 Years," New York *Times* (December 8, 1975); Martin Gottlieb, "The White Mob Gets Back into Heroin," New York *Daily News* (November 11, 1975); H. D. S. Greenway, "Misty Opium Land: Poppy-Fueled War," Washington *Post* (April 11, 1976); Michael Knight, "Influx of High-Quality, Bargain-Priced Heroin Is Reported in Eastern Cities," New York *Times* (December 15, 1974); *White Paper on Drug Abuse,* A Report to the President from the Domestic Council Drug Abuse Task Force (Washington, D.C.: U.S. Government Printing Office, September, 1975).

11. Hunt and Chambers, *The Heroin Epidemics.* I am indebted to Dr. Hunt for giving me the benefit of his expertise, as well as providing me with unpublished data from his own research.

12. Hunt and Zinberg, *Heroin Use.* See also Hunt and Chambers, *The Heroin Epidemics*; Fred Goldman, "Drug Markets and Addict Consumption Behavior," *Drug Use and Crime,* Report of the Panel on Drug Use and Criminal Behavior (Washington, D.C.: The National Institute on Drug Abuse, assisted by Research Triangle Institute, 1976); Leroy C. Gould et al., *Connections: Notes from the Heroin World* (New Haven: Yale University Press, 1974), pp. 22–36.

13. Lee N. Robins, *A Follow-Up of Vietnam Drug Users* (Washington, D.C.: Executive Office of the President, Special Action Office for Drug Abuse Prevention, Interim Final Report, 1973), p. 13. See also Epstein, *Agency of Fear,* p. 188.

14. See *Drug Use and Crime* and references therein. See also Marsh B. Ray, "The Cycle of Abstinence and Relapse Among Heroin Addicts," in Howard S. Becker, ed., *The Other Side* (New York: The Free Press, 1964); Horace Freeland Judson, *Heroin Addiction in Britain* (New York:

Harcourt Brace Jovanovich, 1974); Philip G. Baridon, *Opiate Addiction and Crime,* Ph.D. dissertation, State University of New York at Albany (Ann Arbor, Mich.: University Microfilms, 1975), pp. 94, 117, 144; Gould et al., *Connections,* pp. 22–36.

15. For a summary of the early experience with methadone, see Epstein, "Methadone: The Forlorn Hope," *The Public Interest,* No. 36 (Summer, 1974), pp. 3–24.

16. On the patterns of methadone use, see Edward Preble and Thomas Miller, "Methadone, Wine, and Welfare," in Robert S. Weppner, ed., *Street Ethnography* (Beverly Hills: Sage Publications, 1977), Ch. 10. I am indebted to Dr. Preble for giving me access to additional unpublished data, as well as for sharing his expertise with me.

17. Epstein, "Methadone: The Forlorn Hope," pp. 9–13.

18. See Gila J. Hayim, "Charges in the Criminal Behavior of Heroin Addicts Under Treatment in the Addiction Research and Treatment Corporation: Interim Report of the First Year of Treatment" (Cambridge, Mass.: The Center for Criminal Justice, Harvard Law School, February, 1973, mimeo); Dale K. Sechrest, James Vorenberg, and Irving Lukoff, *The Criminal Behavior of Drug Program Patients,* A Final Report of the Impact on Crime of the Methadone Maintenance Program of the Addiction Research and Treatment Corporation (Cambridge, Mass.: The Center for Criminal Justice, Harvard Law School, September, 1975, mimeo); *Drug Use in America: Problem in Perspective,* 2nd Report of the National Commission on Marijuana and Drug Abuse (Washington, D.C.: U.S. Government Printing Office, March, 1973), pp. 176–77; Stephanie Greenberg and Freda Adler, "Crime and Addiction: An Empirical Analysis of the Literature, 1920–1973," *Contemporary Drug Problems* (Summer, 1974), pp. 221–70; *Drug Use and Crime.* The report by the Drug Enforcement Agency's statistical division was uncovered by Edward Jay Epstein and is quoted in *Agency of Fear,* pp. 248–49.

19. Frank Tannenbaum, *Crime and the Community* (New York: Columbia University Press, 1938), pp. 19–20, 476–77. For contemporary formulations of Tannenbaum's position, see Edwin M. Lemert, *Human Deviance, Social Problems, and Social Control,* 2nd ed. (Englewood Cliffs, N.J.: Prentice-Hall, Inc., 1972), esp. Chs. 1–3; Howard S. Becker, *Outsiders* (New York: The Free Press, 1973);

Kai T. Erikson, *Wayward Puritans* (New York: John Wiley & Sons, Inc., 1969), esp. Ch. 1; Edwin M. Schur, *Labeling Deviant Behavior* (New York: Harper & Row, 1971); Schur, *Radical Non-Intervention* (Englewood Cliffs, N.J.: Prentice-Hall, Inc., 1973); Erving Goffman, *Stigma* (Englewood Cliffs, N.J.: Prentice-Hall, Inc., 1963).

20. Karl Menninger, *The Crime of Punishment* (New York: Viking Press, 1968), excerpted in Rudolph J. Gerber and Patrick D. McAnany, eds., *Contemporary Punishment: Views, Explanations, and Justifications* (Notre Dame, Ind.: University of Notre Dame Press, 1972), p. 179.

21. For a discussion of the evidence, see Ch. 10, p. 373 and note 4.

22. Herbert Wechsler, "Law, Morals, and Psychiatry," *Columbia Law School News*, Vol. 18 (1959), p. 4, quoted in Francis A. Allen, *The Borderland of Criminal Justice* (Chicago: University of Chicago Press, 1964) p. 34, note 13. See also Allen, "Legal Values and the Rehabilitative Ideal," in Allen, *The Borderland of Criminal Justice*, pp. 25–41.

23. John T. Noonan, Jr, *Persons and Masks of the Law* (New York: Farrar, Straus & Giroux, 1976). See also Bruce Jackson, *A Thief's Primer* (New York: Macmillan Co., 1969), pp. 237–43; Lawrence M. Friedman, *The Legal System* (New York: Russell Sage Foundation, 1975), Ch. 1.

24. Henry M. Hart, Jr., "The Aims of the Criminal Law," *Law and Contemporary Problems*, Vol. 23, No. 3 (Summer, 1958), pp. 404–05.

25. Emile Durkheim, *Rules of Sociological Method*, 8th ed., trans. by Sarah A. Solvay and John H. Mueller, edited by George E. G. Gatlin (New York: The Free Press, 1950).

26. See Hugo Adam Bedau, "Are There Really 'Crimes Without Victims?'" in Schur and Bedau, *Victimless Crimes*; John M. Junker, "Criminalization and Criminogenesis," in Jackwell Susman, ed., *Crime and Justice 1971–1972* (New York: AMS Press, 1974), pp. 303–17.

27. Joseph R. Gusfield, *Symbolic Crusade* (Urbana, Ill.: University of Illinois Press, 1972), pp. 4–5. See also Gusfield, "Moral Passage: The Symbolic Process in Public Designation of Deviance," *Social Problems*, Vol. 15, No. II (Fall, 1967), reprinted in F. James Davis and Richard Stivers, eds., *The Collective Definition of Deviance* (New York: The Free Press, 1975).

28. David L. Bazelon, "The Urge to Punish," *The Atlantic Monthly*, Vol. 206 (July, 1960), p. 46.

29. For particularly lucid statements of this Kantian view of punishment, see Herbert Morris, "Persons and Punishment," *The Monist*, Vol. 54, No. 4 (October, 1968), reprinted in Grupp, ed., *Theories of Punishment*, pp. 76–101, and Andrew von Hirsch, *Doing Justice*, Report of the Committee for the Study of Incarceration (New York: Hill & Wang, 1976), Chs. 6, 8, and 17. See also Joel Feinberg, "The Expressive Function of Punishment," in Feinberg, *Doing and Deserving* (Princeton: Princeton University Press, 1970); Johannes Andenaes, *Punishment and Deterrence* (Ann Arbor: University of Michigan Press, 1974); H. L. A. Hart, *Punishment and Responsibility* (New York: Oxford University Press, 1968), esp. Ch. 1.

30. von Hirsch, *Doing Justice*, p. 46 and Ch. 8.

31. Andenaes, *Punishment and Deterrence*, pp. 16–17; Franklin E. Zimring and Gordon J. Hawkins, *Deterrence* (Chicago: University of Chicago Press, 1973), pp. 167–69.

32. Andenaes, *Punishment and Deterrence*, p. 123.

33. Zimring and Hawkins, *Deterrence*, pp. 194–209; Charles R. Tittle and Charles H. Logan, "Sanctions and Deviance: Evidence and Remaining Questions," *Law and Society Review*, Vol. 7, No. 3 (Spring, 1973), esp. pp. 376–81.

34. For the results of recent research on deterrence, see Zimring and Hawkins, *Deterrence*; Tittle and Logan, "Sanctions and Deviance"; Andenaes, *Punishment and Deterrence*; Daniel Nagin, "General Deterrence: A Review of the Empirical Evidence," in Alfred Blumstein, Jacqueline Cohen, and Daniel Nagin, eds., *Deterrence and Incapacitation: Estimating the Effects of Criminal Sanctions on Crime Rates* (Washington, D.C.: National Academy of Sciences, 1978); Report of the Panel on Research on Deterrent and Incapacitative Effects, in Blumstein, Cohen, and Nagin, eds., *Deterrence and Incapacitation*, pp. 3–63.

See also Jack P. Gibbs, *Crime, Punishment, and Deterrence* (New York: Elsevier Publishing Co., 1975); Gordon Tullock, "Does Punishment Deter Crime?" *The Public Interest*, No. 36 (Summer, 1974); William J. Chambliss, "Types of Deviance and the Effectiveness of Legal Sanctions," *Wisconsin Law Review*, Vol. 1967, No. 3 (Summer, 1967), pp. 703–19; Llad Phillips, "Crime Control: The Case of Deterrence," and Charles R. Tittle, "Punishment and Deterrence of Deviance," in Simon Rottenberg, ed., *The Economics of Crime and Punishment* (Washington, D.C.: American Enterprise Institute for Public Policy Research, 1973); Gary S. Becker, "Crime and Punishment: An Economic Approach," and Isaac Ehrlich, "Participation in Illegitimate Activities: An Economic Analysis," in Gary S. Becker and William M. Landes, eds., *Essays in the Economics of Crime and Punishment* (New York: National Bureau of Economic Research, 1974).

For a contrary view, see William G. Nagel, "Some Very Hesitant and Tentative Thoughts About the Future of Corrections," paper presented at Annual Meeting, American Society of Criminology, November 5, 1976, mimeo, and Nagel, "A Statement on Behalf of a Moratorium on Prison Construction," paper presented to American Correctional Association, 1976, mimeo; Jack P. Nagel, *Crime and Incarceration* (Philadelphia: The Fels Center of Government, University of Pennsylvania (Fels Discussion Paper #112, 1977).

35. Blumstein et al., eds., *Deterrence and Incapacitation*, pp. 62–63.

The principal argument for the deterrent power of the death penalty is Isaac Ehrlich, "The Deterrent Effect of Capital Punishment: A Question of Life and Death," *The American Economic Review*, Vol. 65, No. 3 (June, 1975), pp. 397–417. See also van den Haag, "In Defense of the Death Penalty: A Legal-Practical-Moral Analysis," *Criminal Law Bulletin*, Vol. 4, No. 1 (January/February, 1978), pp. 51–68; van den Haag, *Punishing Criminals*, Ch. XVIII.

For critiques of Ehrlich and/or arguments against the deterrent power of the death penalty, see Lawrence R. Klein et al., "The Deterrent Effect of Capital Punishment: An Assessment of the Estimates," in Blumstein et al., eds., *Deterrence and Incapacitation*, pp. 336–60; Welsh S. White, "The Role of the Social Sciences in Determining the Constitutionality of the Death Penalty," and William C. Bailey, "Murder and Capital Punishment: Some Further Evidence," *American Journal of Orthopsychiatry*, Vol. 45, No. 4 (July, 1975), pp. 581–96, 669–88; "Analysis of Ehrlich Argument," Appendix C to Reply Brief for Petitioner in the case of Jesse Thurman Fowler v. North Carolina in the Supreme Court of the United States, October Term, 1974.

36. See Blumstein et al., eds., *Deterrence and Incapacitation,* pp. 60–101, and Klein et al., "The Deterrent Effect of Capital Punishment," pp. 336–60.

37. van den Haag, "In Defense of the Death Penalty," pp. 51–68.

38. Charles L. Black, Jr., *Capital Punishment: The Inevitability of Caprice and Mistake* (New York: W. W. Norton & Co., Inc., 1974), p. 96; Noonan, *Persons and Masks of the Law,* p. 6.

39. Blumstein, Cohen, and Nagin, eds., *Deterrence and Incapacitation,* pp. 5–6; Gibbs, *Crime, Punishment, and Deterrence,* p. 3.

40. See David F. Greenberg, "The Incapacitative Effect of Imprisonment: Some Estimates," *Law and Society Review,* Vol. 9, No. 4 (Summer, 1975), pp. 541–80; Stephan Van Dine, Simon Dinitz, and John Conrad, "The Incapacitation of the Dangerous Offender: A Statistical Experiment," *Journal of Research in Crime and Delinquency,* Vol. 14, No. 1 (January, 1977), pp. 22–34; Shlomo Shinnar and Reuel Shinnar, "The Effects of the Criminal Justice System on the Control of Crime: A Quantitative Approach," *Law and Society Review,* Vol. 9, No. 4 (Summer, 1975), pp. 581–611.

For a critical review of the entire literature on incapacitation, see Jacqueline Cohen, "The Incapacitative Effect of Imprisonment: A Critical Review of the Literature," in Blumstein, Cohen, and Nagin, eds., *Deterrence and Incapacitation,* pp. 187–243.

41. Andenaes, *Punishment and Deterrence,* pp. 112, 8, 36. See also Andenaes, "General Prevention Revisited: Research and Policy Implications," *Journal of Criminal Law and Criminology,* Vol. 66, No. 3 (September, 1975).

42. Quoted in John A. Robertson, *Rough Justice: Perspectives on Lower Criminal Courts* (Boston: Little, Brown & Co., 1974), pp. vii–viii.

7. *The Wisdom of Solomon, the Patience of Job: What the Police Do—and Don't Do*

1. Robert J. diGrazia, "Police Leadership: Challenging Old Assumptions," Washington *Post* (November 10, 1976). (The article was excerpted from a speech diGrazia gave to

the Police Foundation's Executive Forum on Upgrading the Police.)

2. Egon Bittner, *The Functions of the Police in Modern Society* (Rockville, Md.: National Institute of Mental Health Center for Studies of Crime and Delinquency, 1970), pp. 6–7.

3. See William Ruehlman, *Saint with a Gun* (New York: New York University Press, 1974), Chs. 1, 2; Arthur M. Schlesinger, Jr., "The Business of Crime," Introduction, in Thomas Byrnes, *Professional Criminals of America, 1886* (New York: Chelsea House Publishers, 1969).

4. Bittner, "Florence Nightingale in Pursuit of Willie Sutton: A Theory of the Police," in Herbert Jacob, ed., *The Potential for Reform of Criminal Justice* (Beverly Hills: Sage Publications, 1974), p. 30.

5. Bittner, *The Functions of the Police in Modern Society*, Ch. 6. See also Bittner, "Florence Nightingale in Pursuit of Willie Sutton"; William Ker Muir, Jr., *Police Streetcorner Politicians* (Chicago: University of Chicago Press, 1977); Jonathan Rubinstein, *City Police* (New York: Farrar, Straus & Giroux, 1973); James Q. Wilson, *Varieties of Police Behavior* (New York: Atheneum, 1971).

6. Theodore H. Schell et al., *Traditional Preventive Patrol* (Washington, D.C.: Law Enforcement Assistance Administration, National Institute of Law Enforcement and Criminal Justice, 1976), p. 1. See also William G. Gay et al., *Improving Patrol Productivity*, Vol. 1, *Routine Patrol* (Washington, D.C.: National Institute of Law Enforcement and Criminal Justice, Office of Technology Transfer, 1977), p. 1.

7. George L. Kelling et al., *The Kansas City Preventive Patrol Experiment: A Summary Report* (Washington, D.C.: Police Foundation, 1974), pp. 40–43, and Kelling and Tony Pate, "Response to the Davis-Knowles Critique of the Kansas City Preventive Patrol Experiment," *The Police Chief*, Vol. 42, No. 6 (June, 1975), pp. 33–34. See also Kelling et al., *The Kansas City Patrol Experiment: A Technical Report* (Washington, D.C.: Police Foundation, 1974), Ch. 11.

8. Rubinstein, *City Police*, Ch. 8.

9. See Schell et al., *Traditional Preventive Patrol*, p. 7.

10. Albert J. Reiss, Jr., *The Police and the Public* (New Haven: Yale University Press, 1971), pp. 95–96; "Police Operations—The Apprehension Process," *Task Force Report:*

Science and Technology, A Report to the President's Commission on Law Enforcement and Administration of Justice (Washington, D.C.: U.S. Government Printing Office, 1967), p. 12; Patrick V. Murphy and Thomas Plate, *Commissioner* (New York: Simon & Schuster, 1977), p. 234.

11. John Van Maanen, "Working the Street: A Developmental View of Police Behavior," in Herbert Jacob, ed., *The Potential for Reform in Criminal Justice* (Beverly Hills: Sage Publications, 1974).

12. Murphy and Plate, *Commissioner*, p. 225.

13. See Robert L. Bogomolny, "Street Patrol: The Decision to Stop a Citizen," *Criminal Law Bulletin*, Vol. 12, No. 5 (September/October, 1976), pp. 544–82.

14. For subtle and insightful descriptions of those techniques, see Rubinstein, *City Police*, esp. Ch. 6, and Muir, *Police*.

15. Joseph Wambaugh, *The New Centurions* (New York: Dell Publishing Co., 1970), p. 76.

16. Van Maanen, "Working the Street," pp. 92–93.

17. My account is taken from Muir, *Police*, pp. 154–60.

18. For an analysis of the three main styles of policing—what he calls the "watchman," "legalistic," and "service" orientations—see Wilson, *Varieties of Police Behavior*, Chs. 5–8. For a brilliant exploration of individual differences within a single department, see Muir, *Police*.

19. Joseph D. McNamara, "Preface," in Kelling et al., *The Kansas City Preventive Patrol Experiment*, pp. vi, 16. See also Kelling et al., Chs. 5, 6, 7, 14.

For criticisms of the experiment, and the researchers' response, see Richard C. Larson, "What Happened to Patrol Operations in Kansas City? A Review of the Kansas City Preventive Patrol Experiment," and Tony Pate et al., "A Response to 'What Happened to Patrol Operations in Kansas City?'" *Journal of Criminal Justice*, Vol. 3, No. 4 (Winter, 1975); Edward M. Davis and Lyle Knowles, "A Critique of the Report: An Evaluation of the Kansas City Preventive Patrol Experiment," and Kelling and Pate, "Response to the Davis-Knowles Critique of the Kansas City Preventive Patrol Experiment."

20. Malcolm Braly, *False Starts* (Boston: Little, Brown & Co., 1976), p. 213.

21. My analysis of the ways in which the police investigate crimes and apprehend suspects is based on the following sources, supplemented by my own field observations and

those of my research staff: *Task Force Report: Science and Technology*, A Report to the President's Commission on Law Enforcement and Administration of Justice (Washington, D.C.: U.S. Government Printing Office, 1967), Ch. 2 and Appendix B; Peter W. Greenwood, *An Analysis of the Apprehension Activities of the New York City Police Department* (New York: New York City Rand Institute, 1970); Greenwood et al., *The Criminal Investigation Process*, esp. Vol. III, *Observations and Analysis* (Santa Monica, Calif.: Rand Corp., 1975); *The Criminal Investigation Process: A Dialogue on Research Findings* (Washington, D.C.: National Institute of Law Enforcement and Criminal Justice, 1977); Floyd Feeney and Adrianne Weir, *The Prevention and Control of Robbery*, Vol. IV (Davis, Calif.: University of California—Davis, 1973, mimeo); John Conklin, *Robbery and the Criminal Justice System* (Philadelphia: J. B. Lippincott & Co., 1972); Reiss, *The Police and the Public*; Rubinstein, *City Police*; Pate et al., *Three Approaches to Criminal Apprehension in Kansas City: An Evaluation Report* (Washington, D.C.: Police Foundation, 1976); Pate et al., *Police Response Time: Its Determinants and Effects* (Washington: The Police Foundation, 1976); Muir, *Police*; Murphy and Plate, *Commissioner*; Herman Goldstein, *Policing a Free Society* (Cambridge, Mass.: Ballinger Publishing Co., 1977), Chs. 2, 3; Peter K. Manning, *Police Work: The Social Organization of Policing* (Cambridge, Mass.: The M.I.T. Press, 1977), esp. Ch. 8. For a summary of the literature, including other references, see Greenwood et al., *The Criminal Investigation Process*, Vol. III, Ch. 4.

22. For an analysis of victim-offender relationships, see Donald J. Mulvihill and Melvin M. Tumin, with Lynn A. Curtis, *Crimes of Violence*, A Staff Report to the National Commission on the Causes and Prevention of Violence, Vol. 11 (Washington, D.C.: U.S. Government Printing Office, 1969), Ch. 5; Lynn A. Curtis, *Criminal Violence* (Lexington, Mass.: Lexington Books, 1974), Chs. 3–5; *Felony Arrests: Their Prosecution and Disposition in New York City's Courts* (New York: The Vera Institute of Justice, 1977).

23. Vincent Bugliosi, with Curt Gentry, *Helter Skelter* (New York: W. W. Norton & Co., Inc., 1974).

24. See Greenwood et al., *The Criminal Investigation Process*,

Chs. 4, 6; *Task Force Report: Science and Technology*, Ch. 2 and Appendix B. See also William Smith, "How Cops Catch Robbers," in Feeney and Weir, *Prevention and Control*, Vol. IV, and Greenwood, *An Analysis of the Apprehension Activities of the New York City Police Department*.

25. See *Felony Arrests*, p. 19; Brian E. Forst et al., *What Happens After Arrest?* (Washington, D.C.: Institute for Law and Social Research, 1977), p. 24. The INSLAW figure is taken from police records and includes arrests in which the police recorded no relationship at all. Based on police experiences in other cities, the police were unaware of the existence of a relationship between victim and offender in a significant number of the arrests recorded as stranger-to-stranger crimes; victims often conceal the fact that they know the offender at the time the arrest is made. It seems reasonable to assume that the two sets of errors offset one another. (Statistics on the total number of robberies committed by non-strangers are taken from the National Crime Panel Surveys of victims in New York and Washington, D.C.)

26. Greenwood et al., *The Criminal Investigation Process*, pp. 79, 72.

27. Smith, "How Cops Catch Robbers," p. 59.

28. Smith, "How Cops Catch Robbers," pp. 47–63.

29. See John Kaplan, *Criminal Justice: Introductory Cases and Materials* (Mineola, N.Y.: The Foundation Press, Inc., 1973), Ch. 4; Kaplan, "The Limits of the Exclusionary Rule," *Stanford Law Review*, Vol. 26, No. 5 (May, 1974), pp. 1027–55.

30. William P. Brown, "Criminal Informants" (Albany: State University of New York at Albany, School of Criminal Justice, undated, mimeo). (Brown is a former New York City Police Department Inspector now teaching criminal justice at SUNY—Albany.)

31. See Murphy and Plate, *Commissioner*, pp. 240–45; Edward Jay Epstein, *Agency of Fear* (New York: G. P. Putnam's Sons, 1977), Ch. 11, esp. pp. 104–06.

32. Reiss, *The Police and the Public*, p. 133. See also Reiss, "Discretionary Justice in the United States," *International Journal of Criminology and Penology*, Vol. 2 (1974), pp. 181–205.

33. Roger Lane, *Policing the City* (Cambridge, Mass.: Harvard

University Press, 1967), pp. 10–11. See also Clarence
Schrag, *Crime and Justice: American Style* (Rockville,
Md.: National Institute of Mental Health Center for Studies
in Crime and Delinquency, 1971); Allan Silver, "The De-
mand for Order in Civil Society: A Review of Some
Themes in the History of Urban Crime, Police and Riot,"
in David J. Bordua, ed., *The Police: Six Sociological Essays*
(New York: John Wiley & Sons, Inc., 1967), pp. 1–24;
Rubinstein, *City Police*, Ch. 1.

34. Goldstein, *Policing a Free Society*, p. 24.

35. Muir, *Police*, p. 44.

36. Rubinstein, *City Police*, p. 199.

37. Muir, *Police*, pp. 178–83.

38. Muir, *Police*, pp. 129–37.

39. Kelling et al., *The Kansas City Preventive Patrol Experiment*, p. 533.

40. David G. Monroe and Earle W. Garret, under the direction
of August Vollmer, *Police Conditions in the United States*,
A Report to the National Commission on Law Observance
and Enforcement (Montclair, N.J.: Patterson Smith Reprint Series, 1968), pp. 97–98.

41. Gerald Caplan, "Studying the Police," unpublished remarks
to the Executive Forum on Upgrading the Police, April 13,
1976. See also James F. Elliott, *Interception Patrol* (Springfield, Ill.: Charles C. Thomas, 1973); Deborah K. Berman
and Alexander Vargo, "Response Time Analysis Study:
Preliminary Findings on Robbery in Kansas City," *The
Police Chief*, Vol. 43, No. 5 (May, 1976), pp. 74–77.

42. On frequency of crossover, see John E. Boydstun and
Michael E. Sherry, *San Diego Community Profile: Final
Report* (Washington, D.C.: The Police Foundation, 1975),
p. 61; Richard C. Larson, *Urban Police Patrol Analysis*
(Cambridge, Mass.: The M.I.T. Press, 1972), Ch. 8, esp.
p. 242; William G. Gay et al., *Improving Patrol Productivity*, Vol. I, *Routine Patrol* (Washington, D.C.: National
Institute of Law Enforcement and Criminal Justice, Office
of Technology Transfer, 1977), pp. 49–53. On patrolmen's
knowledge of boundaries, see Theodore H. Schell et al.,
Traditional Preventive Patrol (Washington, D.C.: National
Institute of Law Enforcement and Criminal Justice, 1976),
p. 35.

43. See Wilson, "Do the Police Prevent Crime?" *New York
Times Magazine* (October 6, 1974), pp. 96–97.

44. For a largely uncritical description of these experiments, see Peter B. Bloch and David Specht, *Neighborhood Team Policing* (Washington, D.C.: National Institute of Law Enforcement and Criminal Justice, 1973).

45. See Alfred I. Schwartz and Sumner N. Clarren, *The Cincinnati Team Policing Experiment: Summary Report* (Washington, D.C.: The Police Foundation, undated, mimeo). For details of the Cincinnati experience, I am indebted to Richard D. Van Wagenen and Joseph H. Lewis.

8. *Perry Mason in Wonderland: What Happens in Criminal Court*

1. Ernest van den Haag, *Punishing Criminals* (New York: Basic Books, Inc., 1975), pp. 158–66; *Fair and Certain Punishment,* Report of the Twentieth Century Fund Task Force on Criminal Sentencing (New York: McGraw-Hill Book Co., 1976), p. 3.

2. The President's Commission on Law Enforcement and the Administration of Justice, *Task Force Report: Science and Technology* (Washington, D.C.: U.S. Government Printing Office, 1967), p. 61.

3. Quoted in Ronald L. Goldfarb, *Jails: The Ultimate Ghetto* (Garden City, N.Y.: Anchor Press/Doubleday, 1975), pp. 6, 21. See also Hans Mattick, "The Contemporary Jails of the United States: An Unknown and Neglected Area of Justice," in Daniel Glaser, ed., *Handbook of Criminology* (New York: Rand McNally, 1974); Edith Elizabeth Flynn, "Jails and Criminal Justice," in Lloyd E. Ohlin, ed., *Prisoners in America* (Englewood Cliffs, N.J.: Prentice-Hall, Inc., 1973), Ch. 2.

4. Carl E. Pope, *Offender-Based Transaction Statistics: New Directions in Data Collection and Reporting* (Washington, D.C.: Law Enforcement Assistance Administration National Criminal Justice Information and Statistics Service, 1975), pp. 20–21. See also Pope, *The Judicial Processing of Assault and Burglary Offenders in Selected California Counties* (Washington, D.C.: National Criminal Justice Information and Statistics Service, 1975), p. 17.

5. *Felony Arrests: Their Prosecution and Disposition in New York City's Courts,* A Vera Institute of Justice Monograph (New York: The Vera Institute of Justice, 1977), pp. 1–22. (I am indebted to Herbert Sturz, former president of the

Institute, for giving me access to the monograph before publication.)

6. See *Expanding the Perspective of Crime Data: Performance Implications for Policymakers* (Washington, D.C.: Institute for Law and Social Research, 1977, mimeo).

7. C. E. Gehlke, "Recorded Felonies: An Analysis and General Survey," Illinois Association for Criminal Justice, *Illinois Crime Survey* (Montclair, N.J.: Patterson Smith Reprint Series, 1968), Ch. 1; Gehlke, "A Statistical Interpretation of the Criminal Process," *Missouri Crime Survey* (Montclair, N.J.: Patterson Smith Reprint Series, 1968), Part VII.

8. Alan Carlson and Floyd Feeney, "Handling Robbery Arrestees: Some Issues of Fact and Policy," in Floyd Feeney and Adrianne Weir, eds., *The Prevention and Control of Robbery*, Vol. II (Davis, Calif.: The Center on Administration of Criminal Justice, University of California—Davis, 1973), Ch. 8, esp. p. 133.

9. *PROMIS Research Project: Highlights of Interim Findings and Implications* (Washington, D.C.: Institute for Law and Social Research, 1977, mimeo), pp. 59–60.

10. Peter W. Greenwood et al., *Prosecution of Adult Felony Defendants in Los Angeles County: A Policy Perspective* (Washington, D.C.: Law Enforcement Assistance Administration, 1973), Table 46; *Felony Arrests*, pp. 81–114; David W. Neubauer, *Criminal Justice in Middle America* (Morristown, N.J.: General Learning Press, 1976), pp. 166–67.

11. *Felony Arrests*, pp. 166–67.

12. My own calculations from data presented in Greenwood et al., *Prosecution of Adult Felony Defendants in Los Angeles County*, Tables 41, 42, 44.

13. *Felony Arrests*, p. xv.

14. *Felony Arrests*, p. 20, Table E. See also *PROMIS Research Project*. I am indebted to Brian E. Forst, senior research analyst at INSLAW, for sharing the PROMIS findings with me before publication.

15. See particularly *Felony Arrests*, pp. 23–114; Carlson and Feeney, "Handling Robbery Arrestees," Vol. II, Chs. 1, 5, 6.

16. *Felony Arrests*, p. xii.

17. Francis X. Clines, "About New York: Battered Wives and the Police," New York *Times* (March 5, 1977).

18. Lief H. Carter, *The Limits of Order* (Lexington, Mass.: D. C. Heath & Co., 1974), p. 174.

    The discussion of prosecutorial decision-making is based on the following sources, in addition to field research by Richard D. Van Wagenen: Arthur Rosett and Donald R. Cressey, *Justice by Consent* (Philadelphia: J. B. Lippincott Co., 1976), esp. Chs. 1, 5; Raymond T. Nimmer, "Judicial Reform: Informal Processes and Competing Effects," in Herbert Jacob, ed., *The Potential for Reform of Criminal Justice* (Beverly Hills, Calif.: Sage Publications, 1974), and Nimmer, *Criminal Justice Reform Impact: Models of Behavior and a Case Study* (mimeo); Frank W. Miller, *Prosecution: The Decision to Charge a Suspect with a Crime* (Boston: Little, Brown, and Co., 1969); Neubauer, *Criminal Justice in Middle America*, esp. Chs. 3, 6, 9; Maureen Mileski, "Courtroom Encounters: An Observation Study of a Lower Criminal Court," in John A. Robertson, *Rough Justice: Perspectives on Lower Criminal Courts* (Boston: Little, Brown & Co., 1974); Jerome H. Skolnick, "Social Control in the Adversary System," *Journal of Conflict Resolution*, Vol. XI, No. 1 (March, 1967), and Skolnick, *Justice Without Trial: Law Enforcement in a Democratic Society* (New York: John Wiley & Sons, Inc., 1966); Carlson and Feeney, "Handling Robbery Arrestees"; Philip Bourdette, "The Prosecution of Robbery," in Feeney and Weir, eds., *The Prevention and Control of Robbery*, Vol. IV; Brian E. Forst and Kathleen B. Brosi, "A Theoretical and Empirical Analysis of the Prosecutor," *Journal of Legal Studies* (January, 1977); Donald M. McIntyre and David Lippmann, "Prosecutors and Early Disposition of Felony Cases," *American Bar Association Journal*, Vol. 56 (December, 1976).

19. On the development of court subcultures, see Rosett and Cressy, *Justice by Consent*, pp. 90–91. For examples of the differences in norms in two cities of comparable size, see Nimmer, *Diversion: The Search for Alternative Forms of Prosecution* (Chicago: American Bar Foundation, 1974), p. 15. For an analysis of the differences in norms among the eight offices of the Los Angeles County prosecutor's office, see Greenwood et al., *Prosecution of Adult Felony Defendants in Los Angeles County*, Chs. VI, VII. (Because of their size and geographical dispersion, the central office

and seven branch offices act as autonomous, or semiauton-
omous, units.)

20. See Feeney and Weir, *Prevention and Control of Robbery,*
Vol. II, pp. 92–93, and Vol. IV, p. 144.

21. Justice Jackson, quoted in Kenneth Culp Davis, *Discretionary Justice* (Baton Rouge: Louisiana State University
Press, 1969), p. 190. On prosecutorial discretion in general,
see Davis, *Discretionary Justice,* esp. Ch. 7; Miller, *Prosecution,* Chs. 1, 8–20; Davis, ed., *Discretionary Justice in
Europe and America* (Urbana: University of Illinois Press,
1976), Chs. 1, 2, 10; Rosett and Cressey, *Justice by Consent,* esp. Ch. 5; Raymond Moley, *Politics and Criminal
Prosecution* (New York: Minton, Balch & Co.), 1929.

22. See especially Skolnick, "Social Control in the Adversary
System," pp. 55–58, and Watergate Special Prosecution
Force, *Report* (Washington, D.C.: U.S. Government Printing Office, 1975), pp. 36–38. On the dual responsibility of
prosecutors as law enforcement officials and guardians of
the rights of defendants, see *The Prosecution Function and
the Defense Function,* American Bar Association's Project
on Minimum Standards for Criminal Justice (New York:
Institute for Judicial Administration, 1970).

23. Carlson and Feeney, "Handling Robbery Arrestees," Vol.
II, Ch. 6; Greenwood et al., *The Criminal Investigation
Process,* Vol. III, *Observations and Analysis* (Santa Monica,
Calif.: Rand Corp., 1975), Ch. 8.

24. Brian E. Forst, Judith Lucianovic, and Sarah J. Cox, *What
Happens After Arrest?* (Washington, D.C.: Institute for
Law and Social Research, 1977), Ch. 4.

25. McIntyre, "Impediments to Effective Police-Prosecutor Relationships," *American Criminal Law Review,* Vol. 13
(1975), p. 209.

26. See *PROMIS: Highlights,* p. 9; *Curbing the Repeat Offender: A Strategy for Prosecutors* (Washington: Institute
for Law and Social Research, 1977); Eduard Ziegenhagen,
"Toward a Theory of Victim-Criminal Justice System Interactions," in William F. McDonald, ed., *Criminal Justice
and the Victim* (Beverly Hills, Calif.: Sage Publications,
1976), pp. 268–71; Carlson and Feeney, "Handling Robbery Arrestees," pp. 114–15. See also W. D. Falcon, ed.,
Witness Cooperation (Lexington, Mass.: D. C. Health &
Co., 1976); Kristen M. Williams, "The Effects of Victim
Characteristics on the Disposition of Violent Crimes," and

Richard P. Lynch, "Improving the Treatment of Victims: Some Guides for Action," in McDonald, *Criminal Justice and the Victim*, Chs. 8 and 7.

27. Moley, *Politics and Criminal Prosecution*, Ch. 7. See also Rosett and Cressey, *Justice by Consent*, esp. pp. 53–54; Neubauer, *Criminal Justice in Middle America*, esp. Ch. 9; Jay Wishingrad, "The Plea Bargain in Historical Perspective," *Buffalo Law Review*, Vol. 23, No. 2 (Winter, 1974), pp. 499–527; Donald J. Newman, *Conviction: The Determination of Guilt or Innocence Without Trial* (Boston: Little, Brown & Co., 1966).

28. See James Eisenstein and Herbert Jacob, *Felony Justice* (Boston: Little, Brown & Co., 1977).

29. Thomas W. Church, Jr., "Plea Bargains, Concessions and the Courts: Analysis of a Quasi-Experiment," *Law and Society Review*, Vol. 10, No. 3 (Spring, 1976), pp. 377–401.

30. See Arnold Enker, "Perspectives on Plea Bargaining," *Task Force Report: The Courts*, President's Commission on Law Enforcement and Administration of Justice (Washington, D.C.: U.S. Government Printing Office, 1967), Appendix A; Rosett and Cressey, *Justice by Consent*, esp. Ch. 5; Malcolm M. Feeley, "Two Models of the Criminal Justice System: An Organizational Perspective," *Law and Society Review*, Vol. 7, No. 3 (Spring, 1973), esp. pp. 420–21; Lynn M. Mather, "The Outsider in the Courtroom: An Alternative Role for Defense," and Nimmer, "Judicial Reform," in Jacob, ed., *The Potential for Reform*, Chs. 7, 9; Neubauer, *Criminal Justice in Middle America*, Ch. 9; Watergate Special Prosecution Force, *Report*, pp. 34–49; Skolnick, "Social Control in the Adversary System," pp. 52–70.

31. See Harry Kalven, Jr., and Hans Zeisel, *The American Jury* (Chicago: University of Chicago Press, 1966), Ch. 2.

32. Kalven and Zeisel, *The American Jury*, pp. 31–32.

33. Kalven and Zeisel, *The American Jury*. See also Rita James Simon, ed., *The Jury System in America: A Critical Overview* (Beverly Hills, Calif.: Sage Publications, 1975).

34. See, for example, National Advisory Committee on Criminal Justice Standards and Goals, *Courts* (Washington, D.C., U.S. Government Printing Office, 1973), pp. 42–45; Albert W. Alschuler, "The Defense Attorney's Role in Plea Bargaining," *Yale Law Journal*, Vol. 84, No. 6 (May, 1975), pp. 1179–314; Abraham S. Blumberg, *Criminal Justice*

(Chicago: Quadrangle Books, 1970); Alschuler, "The Trial
Judge's Role in Plea Bargaining, Part I," *Columbia Law
Review*, Vol. 76, No. 7 (November, 1976), pp. 1059–154;
Alschuler, "The Prosecutor's Role in Plea Bargaining,"
University of Chicago Law Review, Vol. 36 (1968), pp.
50–112.

35. Bordenkircher v. Hayes (76–1334, January 18, 1978). See
    also Warren Weaver, Jr., "High Court Widens Prosecutors'
    Power in Plea Bargaining," New York *Times* (January 19,
    1978).

36. *Fair and Certain Punishment*, pp. 3–4.

37. Marvin E. Frankel, *Criminal Sentences* (New York: Hill &
    Wang, 1973), p. 21. See also Willard Gaylin, *Partial Jus-
    tice* (New York: Alfred A. Knopf, 1974); Andrew von
    Hirsch, *Doing Justice*, Report of the Committee for the
    Study of Incarceration (New York: Hill & Wang, 1976).

38. Nimmer, *Diversion*, p. 15.

39. Nimmer, *Criminal Justice Reform Impact*, pp. 72–79. I am
    indebted to Prof. Nimmer for sharing his manuscript with
    me.

40. Gaylin, *Partial Justice*, p. 77.

41. See Gottfredson et al., "Making Paroling Policy Explicit,"
    Crime and Delinquency, Vol. 21, No. 1 (January, 1975),
    Appendix A.

42. See Gottfredson et al., "Making Paroling Policy Explicit,"
    pp. 34–44; "Parole Release Decisionmaking and the Sen-
    tencing Process," *Yale Law Journal*, Vol. 84, No. 4
    (March, 1975), pp. 810–902; Gottfredson et al., *Parole
    Decision Making* (Washington, D.C.: National Institute
    of Law Enforcement and Criminal Justice, 1973); Leslie T.
    Wilkins et al., *Sentencing Guidelines: Structuring Judicial
    Discretion*, Final Report of the Feasibility Study (Albany,
    N.Y.: Criminal Justice Research Center, October, 1976,
    mimeo), pp. 13–19.

43. Wilkins et al., *Sentencing Guidelines*, pp. xi–xxiv, 20–108.

44. Wilkins et al., *Sentencing Guidelines*, p. 74; *Felony Arrests*,
    p. 136.

45. Wilkins et al., *Sentencing Guidelines*, pp. 24, 88–90.

46. Eisenstein and Jacob, *Felony Justice*. (The book came to
    my attention too late in my writing for me to incorporate
    Eisenstein and Jacob's interesting perspectives into my own
    analysis.)

47. Alschuler, "Sentencing Reform and Prosecutorial Power: A

Critique of Recent Proposals for 'Fixed' and 'Presumptive' Sentencing," *University of Pennsylvania Law Review*, Vol. 126, pp. 559–60, 554, 570–72.

48. *Fair and Certain Punishment*, pp. 19–25, 37–48; see also von Hirsch, *Doing Justice*, pp. 98–106.

49. See Franklin E. Zimring, "Making the Punishment Fit the Crime," *Hastings Center Report*, Vol. 6, No. 6 (December, 1976), pp. 13–17.

50. *Fair and Certain Punishment*, pp. 37–61.

51. See Alschuler, "Sentencing Reform and Prosecutorial Power," p. 550.

52. See for example *Report on New York Parole* (New York: Citizens Inquiry on Parole and Criminal Justice, Inc., 1974, mimeo); David T. Stanley, *Prisoners Among Us* (Washington, D.C.: The Brookings Institution, 1976); David Fogel, ". . . *We Are the Living Proof* . . ." (Cincinnati: W. H. Anderson Co., 1974), pp. 196–99; Robert M. Carter and Leslie Wilkins, eds., *Probation and Parole* (New York: John Wiley & Sons, Inc., 1970), Sections II, IV; John Irwin, *The Felon* (Englewood Cliffs, N.J.: Prentice-Hall, Inc., 1970), esp. Chs. 2, 5, 6, 7.

53. See Andrew von Hirsch and Kathleen J. Hanrahan, *Abolish Parole?* Report Submitted to the National Institute of Law Enforcement and Criminal Justice (December 1, 1977, mimeo), pp. 150–51.

54. Zimring, "Making the Punishment Fit the Crime," p. 15.

55. Roscoe Pound, "Criminal Justice in the American City—A Summary," *Criminal Justice in Cleveland*, Report of the Cleveland Foundation Survey of the Administration of Criminal Justice in Cleveland, Ohio (Montclair, N.J.: Patterson Smith Reprint Series, 1968), p. 576; Robert H. Jackson, "Criminal Justice: The Vital Problem of the Future," *American Bar Association Journal*, Vol. 39 (1953), p. 743; Herbert L. Packer, *The Limits of the Criminal Sanction* (Stanford, Calif.: Stanford University Press, 1968), Chs. 8–12.

56. See for example Mirjan Damaška, "Evidentiary Barriers to Conviction and Two Models of Criminal Procedure," *University of Pennsylvania Law Review*, Vol. 121, No. 3 (January, 1973), esp. pp. 575–76; Abraham S. Goldstein, "Reflections on Two Models: Inquisitorial Themes in American Criminal Procedure," *Stanford Law Review*, Vol. 26, No. 5 (May, 1974), esp. pp. 1015–19.

57. *Felony Arrests*, p. 134.
58. Jonathan D. Casper, *American Criminal Justice: The Defendant's Perspective* (Englewood Cliffs, N.J.: Prentice-Hall, Inc., 1972), p. 18.
59. See Chief Judge Bazelon's majority opinion in U.S. v. De-Coster, No. 72–1283, decided October 4, 1973.
60. Alschuler, "The Defense Attorney's Role in Plea Bargaining," p. 1185. See also Sheldon Krantz et al., *Right to Counsel in Criminal Cases: The Mandate of Argersinger v. Hamlin* (Cambridge, Mass.: Ballinger Publishing Co., 1976); Stephen R. Bing and S. Stephen Rosenfeld, *The Quality of Justice in the Lower Criminal Courts of Metropolitan Boston*, A Report by the Lawyers' Committee for Civil Rights Under Law to the Governor's Committee on Law Enforcement and the Administration of Justice, September, 1970; Richard Harris, "Annals of Law: In Criminal Court," *The New Yorker* (April 14, 1973); Casper, *American Criminal Justice*; Barlow F. Christiansen, "Delivery of Legal Services to Persons of Low and Modest Income: 'In the Shade of the Old Atrophy,'" American Bar Association, *Quest for Justice: A Report of the Commission on a National Institute of Justice*, 1973; Hon. Marvin E. Frankel, opinion in United States ex rel. Thomas v. Zekler, 332 F. Supp. 595 (S.D.N.Y. 1971); David L. Bazelon, "The Defective Assistance of Counsel," *University of Cincinnati Law Review*, Vol. 42, No. 1 (1973), pp. 1ff.
61. Alschuler, "The Defense Attorney's Role in Plea Bargaining," pp. 1181–206.
62. Casper, *Criminal Justice*, p. 36.
63. Gideon v. Wainright, 372 U.S. 335 (1963); Argersinger v. Hamlin, 407 U.S. 25 (1972). On the extent of noncompliance with the Argersinger decision, see Krantz et al., *Right to Counsel in Criminal Cases*.

9. *Juvenile Justice: "How Could It Happen When We Were So Sincere?"*

1. Julian B. Mack, "The Juvenile Court," *Harvard Law Review*, Vol. 23 (1909), pp. 104, 107. On the origins of the juvenile court, see J. Lawrence Schultz, "The Cycle of Juvenile Court History," *Crime and Delinquency*, Vol. 19, No. 4 (October, 1973); Robert M. Mennel, *Thorns & Thistles* (Hanover, N.H.: University Press of New England,

1973), Ch. 5; Mark H. Haller, "Urban Crime and Criminal Justice: The Chicago Case," *Journal of American History*, Vol. LVII, No. 3 (December, 1970); Steven L. Schlossman, *Love and the American Delinquent: Theory and Practice of "Progressive" Juvenile Justice, 1825–1920* (Chicago: University of Chicago Press, 1977), Ch. 4; The President's Commission on Law Enforcement and Administration of Justice, *Task Force Report: Juvenile Delinquency and Youth Crime* (Washington, D.C., U.S. Government Printing Office, 1967), Ch. 1; Anthony M. Platt, *The Child Savers* (Chicago: University of Chicago Press, 1969), esp. Chs. 5, 6; Sanford J. Fox, "Juvenile Justice Reform: An Historical Perspective," *Stanford Law Review*, Vol. 22, No. 6 (June, 1970), pp. 1187–239.

2. See Edwin M. Lemert, "The Juvenile Court—Quest and Realities," The President's Commission on Law Enforcement and Administration of Justice, *Task Force Report: Juvenile Delinquency and Youth Crime*, p. 91; Jane Addams, *My Friend, Julia Lathrop* (New York: Macmillan Co., 1935), p. 137, quoted in Mennel, *Thorns & Thistles*, p. 133; Platt, *The Child Savers*, p. 146.

3. "The Youth Crime Plague," *Time* (July 11, 1977), pp. 18–19. For other examples of this genre, see Nicholas Pileggi, "Inside the Juvenile Justice System: How Fifteen-Year-Olds Get Away with Murder," *New York* (June 13, 1977); Ted Morgan, "They Think, 'I Can Kill Because I'm 14,'" *New York Times Magazine* (January 19, 1975); Winston Groom, "Juvenile Justice System," *Washington Star* (June 7, 1975).

4. In re Gault, 387 U.S. 1 (1967); Kent v. United States, 383 U.S. 541 (1966). For examples of the ways in which judges and other juvenile court personnel violate the spirit of *Gault*, see "Juvenile Justice in Arizona," *Arizona Law Review*, Vol. 16, No. 2 (1974), esp. pp. 247–63, and Richard A. Chused, "The Juvenile Court Process: A Study of Three New Jersey Counties," *Rutgers Law Review*, Vol. 26, No. 3 (Spring, 1973).

5. Morales v. Turman, 383 F. Supp. 53 (1974), esp. pp. 70–121. See also Kenneth Wooden, *Weeping in the Playtime of Others* (New York: McGraw-Hill Book Co., 1976), Ch. 1; Howard Ohmart, *State Juvenile Incarceration in Texas: An Assessment* (Sacramento, Calif.: American Justice Institute, undated). For a probing description and

analysis of victimization in an Ohio juvenile institution, see
Clemens Bartollas et al., *Juvenile Victimization* (New York:
Sage Publications aand Halsted Press, 1976).

6. William O. Douglas, Foreword, in Edward Wakin, *Children Without Justice: A Report by the National Council
of Jewish Women* (New York: National Council of Jewish
Women, Inc., 1975), p. v.

7. Quoted in Platt, *The Child Savers*, p. 145.

8. Edward F. Waite, "How Far Can Court Procedure Be
Socialized Without Impairing Individual Rights?" *Journal
of Criminal Law, Criminology, and Police Science*, Vol. 12
(1922), p. 340.

9. Francis A. Allen, *The Borderland of Criminal Justice*
(Chicago: University of Chicago Press, 1964), p. 40;
Walter G. Whitlatch, "The Juvenile Court—A Court of
Law," *Western Reserve Law Review*, Vol. 18, No. 4 (May,
1967), pp. 1241–43. (This remains Judge Whitlatch's view;
as of 1974–75, he gave reprints of the paper to visitors.)

10. For a history of the *parens patriae* doctrine in this country,
see Fox, "Juvenile Justice Reform." For a much broader
view, relating the evolution of the *parens patriae* doctrine
in the United States to broader intellectual and social forces,
see Schlossman, *Love and the American Delinquent*, Chs.
1, 4, 9.

11. For a lucid discussion of juvenile court jurisdiction, see
Monrad G. Paulsen and Charles H. Whitebread, *Juvenile
Law and Procedure* (Reno, Nev.: National Council of
Juvenile Court Judges, 1974), Ch. IV.

12. See *Children Without Homes: An Examination of Public
Responsibility to Children in and out of Home Care*, A
Report by the Children's Defense Fund (Washington, D.C.:
Children's Defense Fund, 1977, mimeo); Patrick T. Murphy, *Our Kindly Parent—The State* (New York: Viking
Press, 1974); Alvin L. Schorr, ed., *Children and Decent
People* (New York: Basic Books, Inc., 1974); Joseph Goldstein et al., *Beyond the Best Interests of the Child* (New
York: The Free Press, 1973).

13. See *The Ellery C. Decision: A Case Study of Judicial
Regulation of Juvenile Status Offenders* (New York: Institute of Judicial Administration, Inc., 1975); *Standards
Relating to Noncriminal Misbehavior*, pp. 1–21; David
Gilman, "How to Retain Jurisdiction over Status Offenses:

Change Without Reform in Florida," *Crime & Delinquency*, Vol. 22, No. 1 (January, 1976), pp. 48–51.

14. See Rosemary C. Sarri, *Under Lock and Key: Juveniles in Jails and Detention* (Ann Arbor: National Assessment of Juvenile Corrections, University of Michigan, 1974); *Children in Adult Jails* (Washington: Children's Defense Fund, Inc., 1976); *Children in Custody: A Report on the Juvenile Detention and Correctional Facility Census of 1971* (Washington, D.C.: National Criminal Justice Information and Statistics Service, 1974); Jacqueline Corbett and Thomas S. Vereb, *Juvenile Court Statistics, 1974* (Washington, D.C.: National Institute for Juvenile Justice and Delinquency Prevention, undated); *Survey of Inmates of Local Jails, 1972* (Washington, D.C.: National Criminal Justice Information and Statistics Service, 1976).

The major analyses of the data are contained in Paul Lerman, *Community Treatment and Social Control* (Chicago: University of Chicago Press, 1975), esp. Ch. 10; Sarri, *Under Lock and Key*; Sarri and Robert D. Vintner, "Justice for Whom? Varieties of Juvenile Correctional Approaches," in Malcolm W. Klein, ed., *The Juvenile Justice System* (Beverly Hills, Calif.: Sage Publications, 1976), Ch. 7; and the following monographs, all published by the National Assessment of Juvenile Corrections (University of Michigan, Ann Arbor): Robert D. Vintner et al., *Juvenile Corrections in the States: Residential Programs and Deinstitutionalization*, 1975; Vintner, ed., *Time Out: A National Study of Juvenile Correctional Programs*, 1976; and Sarri and Yeheskel Hasenfeld, eds., *Brought to Justice? Juveniles, the Courts, and the Law*, 1976.

15. See "Juvenile Justice in Arizona," p. 286, note 172.

16. See Sarri, "Service Technologies: Diversion, Probation, and Detention," in Sarri and Hasenfeld, eds., *Brought to Justice?*, p. 173, and Michael Sosin and Sarri, "Due Process— Reality or Myth?" in *Brought to Justice?*, p. 189. On state laws governing detention, see Sarri, *Under Lock and Key*, pp. 31–32.

17. See Meda Chesney-Lind, "Judicial Paternalism and the Female Status Offender," and Allan Conway and Carol Bogdan, "Sexual Delinquency—The Persistence of a Double Standard," *Crime & Delinquency*, Vol. 23, No. 2 (April, 1977); Note, "Ungovernability: The Unjustifiable Jurisdiction," *Yale Law Journal*, Vol. 83 (1974), pp. 1383–

409; Institute of Judicial Administration/American Bar Association Juvenile Justice Standards Project, *Standards Relating to Noncriminal Behavior* (Cambridge, Mass.: Ballinger Publishing Co., 1977, tentative draft), pp. 1–21.

18. The description of the Los Angeles and Jefferson County detention centers come from an unpublished memorandum in the files of the Juvenile Justice Standards Project.

19. Sarri, *Under Lock and Key*, pp. 49–59.

20. On the changes, see Institute of Judicial Administration/American Bar Association Juvenile Justice Standards Project, *Standards Relating to Prosecution* (Cambridge, Mass.: Ballinger Publishing Co., 1977, tentative draft); M. Marvin Finkelstein et al., *Prosecution in the Juvenile Court: Guidelines for the Future* (Washington, D.C.: National Institute of Law Enforcement and Criminal Justice, 1973); Lynn M. Hufnagel and John P. Davidson, "Children in Need: Observations of Practices of the Denver Juvenile Court," *Denver Law Journal*, Vol. 51, No. 3 (1974); see also "Juvenile Justice in Arizona."

21. Corbett and Vereb, *Juvenile Court Statistics*, 1974, Table 3.

22. Hufnagel and Davidson, "Children in Need," p. 391, note 115.

23. Quoted in Jay Olson and George H. Shepard, *Intake Screening Guides: Improving Justice for Juveniles* (Washington, D.C.: Office of Youth Development, Department of Health, Education and Welfare, 1975), p. 19.

24. See for example Donald R. Cressey and Robert A. McDermott, *Diversion from the Juvenile Justice System* (Washington, D.C.: National Institute of Law Enforcement and Criminal Justice, 1974), and Andrew Rutherford and McDermott, *Juvenile Diversion*, National Evaluation Program Phase I Summary Report (Washington, D.C.: National Institute of Law Enforcement and Criminal Justice, 1976).

25. Roger Baron and Floyd Feeney, *An Exemplary Project: Juvenile Diversion Through Family Counseling* (Washington, D.C.: National Institute of Law Enforcement and Criminal Justice, 1976), pp. xix, 5.

26. Sarri, "Service Technologies," in Sarri and Hasenfeld, eds., *Brought to Justice?*, p. 159; Mark Creedmore, "Case Processing: Intake, Adjudication, and Disposition," in *Brought to Justice?*, pp. 148–49.

27. For a more recent version of the speech, see Lindsay G.

Arthur, "Status Offenders Need Help, Too," *Juvenile Justice,* Vol. 26, No. 1 (February, 1975).

28. Sarri, "Service Technologies," p. 167.

29. See Sarri, "Service Technologies," pp. 173–74; Sarri, *Under Lock and Key,* pp. 18–20; *Children in Adult Jails,* pp. 3, 4, 18; Chused, "The Juvenile Court Process," pp. 507–25, 530–31; Hufnagel and Davidson, "Children in Need," p. 530; Patricia M. Wald, "Pretrial Detention for Juveniles," in Rosenheim, ed., *Pursuing Justice for the Child,* Ch. 6; "Juvenile Justice in Arizona," pp. 269–77; Lawrence E. Cohen, *Pre-Adjudicatory Detention in Three Juvenile Courts,* Law Enforcement Assistance Administration, National Criminal Justice Information and Statistics Service, 1975 (Utilization of Criminal Justice Statistics Project Analytic Report 8).

30. Jackson Toby, "An Evaluation of Early Identification and Intensive Treatment Programs for Predelinquents," *Social Problems,* Vol. 13, No. 2 (Fall, 1965), pp. 160–75, esp. pp. 164–65, 169; Robert R. Stanfield and Brendan Maher, "Clinical and Actuarial Predictions of Juvenile Delinquency," in Stanton Wheeler, ed., *Controlling Delinquents* (New York: John Wiley & Sons, Inc., 1968), pp. 252–59; Joan and William McCord, "A Follow-Up Report on the Cambridge-Somerville Youth Study," *Annals of the American Academy of Political and Social Science,* Vol. 322 (March, 1959), pp. 89–96. See also Travis Hirschi and Hanan C. Selvin, *Delinquency Research* (New York: The Free Press, 1967), Ch. 14.

31. Stevens H. Clarke, "Some Implications for North Carolina of Recent Research in Juvenile Delinquency," *Journal of Research in Crime and Delinquency,* Vol. 12, No. 1 (January, 1975), pp. 54–55; Marvin E. Wolfgang et al., *Delinquency in a Birth Cohort* (Chicago: University of Chicago Press, 1972), pp. 70–75, 165.

One study does purport to prove the reverse. In an analysis of the records of some 2,092 juvenile offenders in Portsmouth and Virginia Beach, Va., over a five-year period, Charles W. Thomas of Bowling Green State University found that youngsters whose first court encounter involved a status offense had a slightly higher recidivism rate—38 percent—than those whose first offenses were felonies (32 percent) or misdemeanors (22 percent). But the recidivism rates were low, and the differences are easily explained by

Thomas' failure to control for age. In any juvenile court, status offenders tend to be considerably younger than delinquents—and the younger juveniles are at their first court appearance, the more likely they are to commit additional offenses. In any event, Thomas' data indicate that juveniles whose first offense was a felony were more than twice as likely to commit another felony than those whose first offense was a status offense. Charles W. Thomas, "Are Status Offenders Really So Different?" *Crime & Delinquency*, Vol. 22, No. 4 (October, 1976), pp. 438–55.

32. Goldstein et al., *Beyond the Best Interests*, p. 8. See also *Standards Relating to Noncriminal Misbehavior*, pp. 1–21; Rosenheim, "Notes on Helping Juvenile Nuisances," and National Task Force to Develop Standards and Goals for Juvenile Justice and Delinquency Prevention, *Jurisdiction—Status Offenses* (Washington, D.C.: National Institute for Juvenile Justice and Delinquency Prevention, 1977), pp. 4–18.

33. Note, "Ungovernability," esp. pp. 1393–94 and 1402–05. See also *Standards Relating to Noncriminal Misbehavior*, pp. 1–21.

34. Institute of Judicial Administration/American Bar Association Juvenile Justice Standards Project, *Standards Relating to Counsel for Private Parties* (Cambridge, Mass.: Ballinger Publishing Co., 1977, tentative draft), esp. Introduction and Parts I, II.

35. See for example "Juvenile Justice in Arizona," pp. 251–52.

36. George F. Will, in Washington *Post* (December 10, 1974).

37. For the arguments pro and con, see *Juvenile Delinquency and Youth Crime*, pp. 38–40; IJA/ABA Juvenile Justice Standards Project, *Standards Relating to Adjudication* (Cambridge, Mass.: Ballinger Publishing Co., 1977, tentative draft), pp. 70–72, and *Dissenting View*, pp. 77–78.

38. Paulsen and Whitebread, *Juvenile Law and Procedure*, p. 190; Murphy, *Our Kindly Parent*, p. 12. See also Paulsen and Whitebread, *Juvenile Law and Procedure*, pp. 183–84; IJA/ABA Juvenile Justice Standards Project, *Standards Relating to Appeals and Collateral Review* (Cambridge, Mass.: Ballinger Publishing Co., 1977, tentative draft), pp. 10–13, 32–34; Sosin and Sarri, "Due Process," pp. 183–84.

39. See Cohen, *Delinquency Dispositions*; Chused, "The Juvenile Court Process," pp. 527–29 and Table 152; Sarri and

Vintner, "Justice for Whom?" p. 181. See also *Standards Relating to Noncriminal Misbehavior,* p. 5.

40. See Michael D. Tate et al., *Cost and Service Impacts of Status Offenders in Ten States: "Responses to Angry Youth,"* Washington, D.C., Office of Juvenile Justice and Delinquency Prevention, 1978, quoted in *Criminal Justice Newsletter,* Vol. 9, No. 6 (March 13, 1978), pp. 1–3. See also "Senate Hearings Show Problems and Progress in Status Offender Deinstitutionalization," *Criminal Justice Newsletter,* Vol. 8, No. 20 (October 10, 1977), p. 1–4, and Elizabeth W. Vorenberg, "How Massachusetts Has Shifted Care of Status Offenders to Social Service Unit," *Criminal Justice Newsletter,* Vol. 9, No. 2 (January 16, 1978), pp. 1–2.

41. *Juvenile Violence: A Study of the Handling of Juveniles Arrested for Crimes Against Persons in New York City, July 1, 1973–June 30, 1974* (New York: Office of Children's Services, Division of Criminal Justices Services, 1976). I am indebted to Sheridan Faber of the Office of Children's Services for giving me access to additional unpublished data.

42. National Advisory Commission on Criminal Justice Standards and Goals, *A National Strategy to Reduce Crime* (Washington, D.C.: U.S. Government Printing Office, 1973), pp. 23, 109. See also Edwin M. Schur, *Radical Nonintervention* (Englewood Cliffs, N.J.: Prentice-Hall, Inc., 1973), and Michael H. Tonry, "Justice for the Child: Other Times, Other Places," in Margaret K. Rosenheim, ed., *Pursuing Justice for the Child.*

43. I am indebted to Prof. Franklin Zimring of the University of Chicago Law School for his analysis of the way age affects conviction and incarceration rates.

44. Sarri, *Under Lock and Key,* pp. 25, 75–76.

45. Matza, *Delinquency and Drift,* p. 186.

46. IJA/ABA Juvenile Justice Standards Project, *Standards Relating to Transfer Between Courts* (Cambridge, Mass.: Ballinger Publishing Co., 1977, tentative draft), pp. 15–16, 34, 37.

47. Shireman, "Perspectives on Juvenile Probation," in Rosenheim, ed., *Pursuing Justice for the Child,* pp. 140–41; "Scaring Juveniles," *Youth Forum,* Vol. 1, No. 1 (June, 1977), p. 3.

48. Robert Coles, "Race and Crime Control," *Kentucky Law*

Journal, Vol. 51 (1965), pp. 451ff, reprinted in Charles E. Reasons and Jack L. Kuykendall, eds., *Race, Crime, and Justice* (Pacific Palisades, Calif.: Goodyear Publishing Co., Inc., 1972), pp. 137–38.

49. See Shireman, "Perspectives on Juvenile Probation," p. 142.

50. I am indebted to Prof. Jackson Toby of Rutgers University for the description of periodic detention.

51. For a cogent analysis of the defense counsel's role in dispositions, see IJA/ABA Juvenile Justice Standards Project, *Standards Relating to Counsel for Private Parties,* pp. 168–87.

52. IJA/ABA Juvenile Justice Standards Project, *Standards Relating to Juvenile Delinquency and Sanctions,* pp. 43–48.

53. Franklin E. Zimring, "Background Paper," in *Confronting Youth Crime: Report of the Twentieth Century Fund Task Force on Sentencing Policy Toward Young Offenders* (New York: Holmes & Meier, Inc., 1978).

54. IJA/ABA Juvenile Justice Standards Project, *Standards Relating to Noncriminal Misbehavior,* esp. pp. 41–45.

55. See for example Bartollas et al., *Juvenile Victimization,* esp. Chs. 6–9, 12.

56. William Ker Muir, Jr., *Police: Streetcorner Politicians* (Chicago: University of Chicago Press, 1977), pp. 126–34.

10. *"To Reclimb the Slope": The Limits of Correctional Reform*

1. David J. Rothman, "Decarcerating Prisoners and Patients," *Civil Liberties Review,* Vol. 1 No. 1 (Fall, 1973), pp. 8–9.

2. Gustave de Beaumont and Alexis de Tocqueville, *On the Penitentiary System in the United States and Its Application to France* (Carbondale and Edwardsville: Southern Illinois University Press, 1964), pp. 163–64. On the early history of American prisons, see also David J. Rothman, *The Discovery of the Asylum* (Boston: Little, Brown & Co., 1971); William G. Nagel, *The New Red Barn: A Critical Look at the Modern American Prison* (New York: Walker & Co., 1973), pp. 1–15; Norman Johnston, *The Human Cage: A Brief History of Prison Architecture* (New York: Walker & Co., 1973).

3. National Commission on Law Observance and Enforcement, *Report on Penal Institutions, Probation and Parole* (U.S. Government Printing Office, 1931; Montclair, N.J.:

Patterson Smith Reprint Series, 1968), p. 6; The President's Commission on Law Enforcement and the Administration of Justice, *The Challenge of Crime in a Free Society* (Washington, D.C.: U.S. Government Printing Office, 1967), p. 159.

4. Robert Martinson, "What Works?—Questions and Answers About Prison Reform," *The Public Interest,* No. 35 (Spring, 1974), p. 25; Douglas Lipton et al., *The Effectiveness of Correctional Treatment: A Survey of Treatment Evaluation Studies* (New York: Praeger Publishers, 1975).

   See also Gene Kassebaum et al., *Prison Treatment and Parole Survival: An Empirical Assessment* (New York: John Wiley & Sons, Inc., 1971); David A. Ward, "Evaluative Research for Corrections," in Lloyd E. Ohlin, ed., *Prisoners in America* (Englewood Cliffs, N.J.: Prentice-Hall, Inc., 1973), Ch. 6; James O. Robison and Gerald Smith, "The Effectiveness of Correctional Programs," *Crime and Delinquency,* Vol. 17, No. 1 (January, 1971), pp. 67–80; Paul Lerman, *Community Treatment and Social Control* (Chicago: University of Chicago Press, 1975); David F. Greenberg, "The Correctional Effects of Corrections: A Survey of Evaluations," in Greenberg, ed., *Corrections and Punishment* (Beverly Hills, Calif.: Sage Publications, 1977), Ch. 6; Daniel Glaser, *The Effectiveness of a Prison and Parole System,* abridged ed. (Indianapolis: Bobbs-Merrill Co., Inc., 1969), esp. Chs. 2, 3.

5. Robert Martinson and Judith Wilks, with the assistance of Alita Buzel, Henrietta Carpentier, and Paul Honig, "Knowledge in Criminal Justice Planning: A Preliminary Report" (New York: The Center for Knowledge in Criminal Justice Planning, 1976, mimeo). See also Glaser, *The Effectiveness of a Prison and Parole System.* (Glaser's landmark study of recidivism during the 1960s indicated a recidivism rate of about one-third.)

6. *Prisoners in America* (Harriman, N.Y.: Report of the 42nd American Assembly, 1972), p. 6; National Advisory Commission on Criminal Justice Standards and Goals, *A National Strategy to Reduce Crime* (Washington, D.C.: U.S. Government Printing Office, 1973), p. 121.

7. See for example Rob Wilson, "U.S. Prison Population Sets Another Record," *Corrections Magazine,* Vol. III, No. 1 (March, 1977); Steve Gettinger, "U.S. Prison Population

Hits All-Time High," *Corrections Magazine,* Vol. II, No. 3 (March, 1976).

8. Wilson, "U.S. Prison Population Sets Another Record"; Norman A. Carlson, "The Jail Crisis: Concern Shown—But Problem Goes Unsolved," *American Journal of Correction* (July/August, 1977), p. 28.

9. James B. Jacobs, *Stateville: The Penitentiary in Mass Society* (Chicago: University of Chicago Press, 1977), esp. Introduction and Ch. 8. Jacobs' book is the best analysis I have seen of the relationship between changes in prison life and changes in the larger society. See also Leo Carroll, *Hacks, Blacks, and Cons: Race Relations in a Maximum Security Prison* (Lexington, Mass.: Lexington Books, 1974).

   For an analysis of the way in which these changes in American society—particularly the "civilization of authority"—were foreshadowed in the prison riots of the 1950s, see Richard H. McCleery, *Policy Change in Prison Management* (East Lansing: Michigan State University Bureau of Social and Political Research, 1957); McCleery, "Communications Patterns as Bases of Systems of Authority and Power," in Richard A. Cloward et al., *Theoretical Studies in Social Organization of the Prison* (New York: Social Science Research Council, 1960); McCleery, "Correctional Administration and Political Change," in Lawrence E. Hazelrigg, ed., *Prison Within Society* (Garden City, N.Y.: Anchor Books, 1969), Ch. 6.

10. On the growth of litigation and the changing judicial response, see Ronald L. Goldfarb and Linda R. Singer, *After Conviction* (New York: Simon & Schuster, 1973), Ch. VII; Rothman, "Decarcerating Prisoners and Patients"; Leonard Orland, *Prisons: Houses of Darkness* (New York: The Free Press, 1975), Chs. 1, 6, 8; Gordon Hawkins, *The Prison* (Chicago: University of Chicago Press, 1976), Ch. 6; David Fogel, ". . . *We Are the Living Proof* . . ." (Cincinnati: W. H. Anderson Co., 1975), Ch. 3; M. Kay Harris and Dudley P. Spiller, Jr., *After Decision: Implementation of Judicial Decrees in Correctional Settings* (Washington, D.C., American Bar Association Commission on Correctional Facilities and Services, Resource Center on Correctional Law and Legal Services, 1976); Fred Cohen, "The Discovery of Prison Reform," and Herman Schwartz, "A Note on Sostre v. McGinnis," *Buffalo Law Review,* Vol. 21, No. 3 (Spring, 1972); Schwartz, "Pris-

oners' Rights: Some Hopes and Realities," The Roscoe Pound–American Trial Lawyers Foundation, *A Program for Prison Reform*, 1972; "Tentative Draft of Standards Relating to the Legal Status of Prisoners," *American Criminal Law Review*, Vol. 14, No. 3 (Winter, 1977), Special Issue.

11. Holt v. Sarver, 309 F. Supp. 385 (affirmed).

12. Erving Goffman, *Asylums* (Garden City, N.Y.: Anchor Books, 1961), pp. 1–125; Gresham M. Sykes, *The Society of Captives* (Princeton: Princeton University Press, 1958), esp. Chs. 1, 4; Richard R. Korn and Lloyd W. McCorkle, *Criminology and Penology* (New York: Holt, Rinehart & Winston, 1959), Ch. 22.

13. Paul W. Keve, *Prison Life and Human Worth* (Minneapolis: University of Minnesota Press, 1974), pp. 41–42.

14. Dan Fuller and Thomas Orsagh, "Violence and Victimization Within a State Prison System," *Criminal Justice Review*, Vol. 2 (Fall, 1977), pp. 37–38.

15. Hans Toch, *Police, Prisons, and the Problem of Violence* (Rockville, Md.: National Institute of Mental Health Center for Studies of Crime and Delinquency, 1977), p. 52.

16. Toch, *Police, Prisons, and the Problem of Violence*, p. 52; Anthony Astrachan, "Profile/Louisiana," *Corrections Magazine*, Vol. 2, No. 1 (September/October, 1975), p. 19; Michael S. Serrill, "Walpole Prison: After the Storm," *Corrections Magazine*, Vol. II, No. 2 (November/December, 1975), pp. 49–50; Hon. Frank M. Johnson, Jr., Memorandum Opinion in Pugh v. Locke, January 13, 1976.

For a detailed description of the changes in maximum-security prisons in Illinois and Rhode Island, see Jacobs, *Stateville*, esp. Chs. 4, 5, 6, 8, and Carroll, *Hacks, Blacks, and Cons*, esp. Ch. 8.

17. Robert A. Freeman et al., "A Look at the Dangerous Offender and Society's Effort to Control Him," *American Journal of Corrections* (January/February, 1977), pp. 30–31. See also Susan Sheehan, "Annals of Crime: A Prison and a Prisoner," Part I, *The New Yorker* (October 24, 1977), p. 117; Sheehan, *A Prison and a Prisoner* (Boston: Houghton Mifflin Co., 1978).

18. Jacobs, *Stateville*, pp. 205–06, 109–10, and Table 10; Freeman et al., "A Look at the Dangerous Offender," p. 30.

19. Sykes, *The Society of Captives*, pp. 21–22, 77. Hans Mattick, as quoted in Hawkins, *The Prison*, p. 45.

20. Malcolm Braly, *False Starts* (Boston: Little, Brown & Co., 1976), p. 251.

21. Norman Johnston, *The Human Cage*, pp. 15–16; Nagel, *The New Red Barn*, p. 29; McCleery, "Authoritarianism and the Belief System of Incorrigibles," in Donald R. Cressey, ed., *The Prison: Studies in Institutional Organization and Change* (New York: Holt, Rinehart & Winston, Inc., 1961), p. 263.

22. In addition to McCleery's work (*Policy Change in Prison Management*, "Communications Patterns as Bases of Systems of Authority and Power," and "Correctional Administration and Political Change"), I have relied heavily on the following sources for the analysis of the impact of imprisonment that follows: Sykes, *The Society of Captives*, esp. Ch. 4; Goffman, *Asylums*, pp. 1–124; Lloyd W. McCorkle and Richard Korn, "Resocialization Within Walls," *Annals of the American Academy of Political and Social Science* (May, 1954), pp. 88–98; Korn and McCorkle, *Criminology and Penology*, Chs. 20–22, 25–27; Sykes and Sheldon L. Messinger, "The Inmate Social System," in Cloward et al., *Theoretical Studies in Social Organization of the Prison*, Ch. I; John Irwin, *The Felon* (Englewood Cliffs, N.J.: Prentice-Hall, Inc., 1970), Chs. 2–4; Anthony J. Manocchio and Jimmy Dunn, with Lamar T. Empey, *The Time Game* (New York: Delta Books, 1970), esp. Chs. 1–2; Hawkins, *The Prison*, Chs. 2–3; Donald Clemmer, *The Prison Community* (New York: Holt, Rinehart & Winston, 1958), Chs. 4, 5, 12; Braly, *False Starts* and *On the Yard* (Greenwich, Conn.: Fawcett Publications, Inc., 1967); Clemens Bartollas, Stuart J. Miller, and Simon Dinitz, *Juvenile Victimization* (New York: Sage Publications and Halsted Press, 1976).

23. Sykes and Messinger, "The Inmate Social System," p. 14.

24. Sykes, *Society of Captives*, p. 72.

25. See for example Irwin, *The Felon*, Ch. 3; David Ward and Gene Kassebaum, *Women's Prison* (Chicago: Aldine Publishing Co., 1965); Rose Giallombardo, *Society of Women* (New York: John Wiley & Sons, Inc., 1966); James B. Jacobs, "The Politics of Corrections: Town/Prison Relations as a Determinant of Reform," *Social Service Review*, Vol. 50, No. 4 (December, 1976); Eric H. Steele and Jacobs, "Untangling Minimum Security: Concepts, Realities and Implications for Correctional Systems," *Journal of*

Research in Crime and Delinquency, Vol. 14, No. 1 (January, 1977); Steele and Jacobs, "A Theory of Prison Systems," *Crime and Delinquency,* Vol. 21, No. 2 (April, 1975); Kassebaum et al., *Prison Treatment and Parole Survival,* Chs. I, 2, 6; David Street et al., *Organization for Treatment: A Comparative Study on Institutions for Delinquents* (New York: The Free Press, 1966); Hawkins, *The Prison,* Ch. 3.

26. McCorkle and Korn, "Resocialization Within Walls."
27. Braly, *False Starts,* p. 251.
28. Bartollas et al., *Juvenile Victimization,* pp. 133–36.
29. Bartollas et al., *Juvenile Victimization,* pp. 75–76.
30. See especially Sykes, *The Society of Captives,* pp. 95–99; Bartollas et al., *Juvenile Victimization,* Chs. 4, 8, 15; "Report on Sexual Assaults in a Prison System and Sheriff's Van," in Leon Radzinowicz and Marvin E. Wolfgang, eds., *The Criminal in Confinement,* Vol. III, *Crime and Justice* (New York: Basic Books, Inc., 1971), pp. 141–46; Anthony M. Scacco, Jr., *Rape in Prison* (Springfield, Ill.: Charles C. Thomas, 1975); Vergil L. Williams and Mary Fish, *Convicts, Codes, and Contraband: The Prison Life of Men and Women* (Cambridge, Mass.: Ballinger Publishing Co., 1974), pp. 58–71; Carl Weiss and David James Friar, *Terror in the Prisons* (Indianapolis: Bobbs-Merrill Co., Inc., 1974); Carroll, *Hacks, Blacks, and Cons,* pp. 178–87.
31. "Report on Sexual Assaults in a Prison System and Sheriff's Van," pp. 141–46. See also Alan J. Davis, "Sexual Assaults in the Philadelphia Prison System and Sheriff's Vans," *Transaction,* Vol. 6, No. 2 (December, 1968), pp. 8–16.
32. Piri Thomas, *Down These Mean Streets* (New York: New American Library, 1967), pp. 254–56.
33. On Stateville, see Jacobs, *Stateville,* p. 21; on Minnesota (and on staffing patterns generally), see Keve, *Prison Life and Prison Worth,* pp. 17, 56, 67.
34. In the analysis of prison government that follows, I rely particularly heavily on the works of James B. Jacobs, Richard H. McCleery, Gresham Sykes, and Hans W. Mattick. See especially Jacobs, *Stateville;* Steele and Jacobs, "A Theory of Prison Systems" and "Untangling Minimum Security"; McCleery, "The Governmental Process and Informal Social Control" and "Authoritarianism and the Belief System of Incorrigibles," in Cressey, ed., *The Prison,*

Chs. 4, 7; McCleery, *Policy Change in Prison Management*; McCleery, "Correctional Administration and Political Change," Ch. 6; Sykes, *The Society of Captives*; Hans M. Mattick, *The Prosaic Sources of Prison Violence* (Chicago: Occasional Papers from the Law School, University of Chicago, 1972). See also Sykes and Messinger, "The Inmate Social System"; McCleery, "Communication Patterns as Bases of Systems of Authority and Power"; Cloward, "Social Control in the Prison," in Cloward et al., *Theoretical Studies in Social Organization of the Prison*, Chs. 1–3.

35. Gustave de Beaumont and Alexis de Tocqueville, *On the Penitentiary System in the United States and Its Application to France*, p. 165.

36. Jacobs, *Stateville*, Ch. 2.

37. Frank Tannenbaum, *Wall Shadows* (New York: G. P. Putnam's Sons, 1922), p. 15.

38. Sykes, *The Society of Captives*, p. 55.

39. Jacobs, *Stateville*, p. 41.

40. Braly, *False Starts*, p. 152. On the use of "bus therapy" for purposes of control, see Kassebaum et al., *Prison Treatment and Parole Survival*, pp. 298–304; Irwin, *The Felon*, pp. 64–67; Steele and Jacobs, "Theory of Prison Systems" and "Untangling Minimum Security."

41. Kassebaum et al., *Prison Treatment and Parole Survival*, pp. 300–01; Irwin, *The Felon*, p. 66.

42. *Attica*, Official Report of the New York State Commission on Attica (New York: Bantam Books, 1972), p. 197.

43. Sykes, *The Society of Captives*, pp. 54–58; Korn and McCorkle, *Criminology and Penology*, pp. 490–92.

44. Sykes, *The Society of Captives*, p. 55.

45. Korn and McCorkle, *Criminology and Penology*, p. 493.

46. For a vivid picture of an inmate economy in operation, see Braly, *On the Yard*, and Sheehan, "Annals of Crime," esp. pp. 46–74. For a more systematic analysis, see Williams and Fish, *Convicts, Codes, and Contraband*, Ch. 3; Francis A. J. Ianni, *Black Mafia* (New York: Simon & Schuster, 1974), pp. 157–98; R. Theodore Davidson, *Chicano Prisoners: The Key to San Quentin* (New York: Holt, Rinehart & Winston, 1974), Ch. 6.

47. See Korn and McCorkle, *Criminology and Penology*, pp. 493–94.

48. McCleery, "The Governmental Process and Informal Social Control," p. 165.

49. Sykes, *The Society of Captives*, p. 102.

50. Michael Serrill, "Procunier: A Candid Conversation," *Corrections Magazine*, Vol. 1, No. 4 (March/April, 1975), p. 4.

51. See McCleery, *Policy Change in Prison Management*, Carroll, *Hacks, Blacks, and Cons*, and Jacobs, *Stateville*. My analysis of the breakdown of control relies heavily on these three sources.

52. McCleery, "Governmental Process and Informal Social Control," pp. 176–77.

53. Jacobs, *Stateville*, pp. 57–58, 91–93.

54. See for example David F. Greenberg and Fay Stender, "The Prison as a Lawless Agency," *Buffalo Law Review*, Vol. 21, No. 3 (Spring, 1972), pp. 799–838.

55. Jacobs, *Stateville*, p. 64.

56. Carroll, *Hacks, Blacks, and Cons*, pp. 54–59.

57. Keve, *Prison Life*, pp. 74–75.

58. Carroll, *Hacks, Blacks, and Cons*, pp. 58–59.

59. See for example Jacobs, *Stateville*, Ch. 7; McCleery, *Policy Change in Prison Management*, pp. 28–34; Robert E. Doran, "Organizational Stereotyping: The Case of the Adjustment Center Classification Committee," in Greenberg, ed., *Corrections and Punishment*, Ch. 2; *Attica*, Ch. 3.

60. *Attica*, pp. 126–27.

61. Quoted in Jessica Mitford, *Kind and Usual Punishment* (New York: Alfred A. Knopf, 1973), pp. 230–31.

62. Eldridge Cleaver, *Soul on Ice* (New York: McGraw-Hill Book Co., 1968), p. 4; Jacobs, *Stateville*, pp. 59–60; Carroll, *Hacks, Blacks, and Cons*, pp. 39–42.

63. For accounts of such incidents, see Carroll, *Hacks, Blacks, and Cons*, pp. 132–36; Jacobs, *Stateville*, pp. 161–63, 177; Toch, *Police, Prisons, and the Problem of Violence*, pp. 62–65.

64. Carroll, *Hacks, Blacks, and Cons*, pp. 104–08; Jacobs, *Stateville*, Ch. 6. See also Davidson, *Chicano Prisoners*, Ch. 2; Ianni, *Black Mafia*, pp. 157–98.

65. See for example McCleery, *Policy Change in Prison Management*, pp. 32–34.

66. Jacobs, *Stateville*, pp. 109–10, 161–64.

67. Carroll, *Hacks, Blacks, and Cons*, p. 147.

68. Sheehan, "Annals of Crime," p. 140.

69. See Carroll, *Hacks, Blacks, and Cons,* Ch. 7; Edward Bunker, "War Behind Walls," *Harper's,* Vol. 244, No. 1461 (February, 1972), p. 39; John Irwin, "The Changing Social Structure of the Men's Prison," in Greenberg, ed., *Corrections and Punishment,* Ch. 1; Jacobs, *Stateville,* Ch. 6 and Appendix 1; Ianni, *Black Mafia,* pp. 157–98; Sheehan, "Annals of Crime," p. 120; Bartollas et al., *Juvenile Victimization,* Ch. 4.

70. Carroll, *Hacks, Blacks, and Cons,* pp. 182–86; Davis, "Sexual Assaults in the Philadelphia Prison System and Sheriff's Van," p. 15; Bartollas et al., *Juvenile Victimization,* Ch. 4; Scacco, *Rape in Prison,* Ch. 4.

71. See Jacobs, "The Politics of Corrections," pp. 623–31; Steele and Jacobs, "Untangling Minimum Security," pp. 68–83; Fogel, ". . . *We Are the Living Proof* . . ." pp. 105–07; Nagel, *The New Red Barn,* pp. 43–45, 69; National Advisory Commission on Criminal Justice Standards and Goals, *Report on Corrections,* pp. 345–46 (Washington, D.C.: Government Printing Office, 1973).

    In addition to the published sources cited above, I am indebted to Warden Vernon G. Housewright, Prof. James B. Jacobs, and Prof. Hans M. Mattick for sharing their knowledge and time with me.

72. On the costs of two new minimum-security prisons planned for Illinois, see Andrew Rutherford et al., *Prison Population and Policy Choices,* Vol. I (Washington, D.C.: National Institute of Law Enforcement and Criminal Justice, 1977), pp. 55–57.

11. *Afterword: "Whatever Is, Is Possible"*

1. Michael Daly and Denis Hamill, "Here Comes the Neighborhood," *The Village Voice,* Vol. XXII, No. 30 (July 25, 1977). My account relies, in addition, on the cover stories in *Time* and *Newsweek* for July 25, 1977, on newspaper and television accounts, and on Robert Curvin and Bruce Porter, *A Report on the Blackout Looting,* unpublished report to the Ford Foundation, 1978.

2. Curvin and Porter, *A Report on the Blackout Looting.*

3. Orde Coombs, "The Trashing of LeMans: The New Civil War Begins," *New York* (August 8, 1977), p. 43.

4. Charles E. Silberman, " 'Beware the Day They Change Their Minds,' " *Fortune* (November, 1965).

5. Roscoe Pound, *Criminal Justice in America* (New York: Da Capo Press, 1972), pp. 14–15.

6. Karl N. Llewellyn, *The Bramble Bush* (Dobbs Ferry, N.Y.: Oceana Publications, 1960).

7. Curvin and Porter, *A Report on the Blackout Looting.*

8. Robert K. Merton, "The Self-Fulfilling Prophecy," in Merton, *Social Theory and Social Structure*, enlarged ed. (New York: The Free Press, 1968), p. 490.

9. Silberman, *Crisis in Black and White* (New York: Random House, Inc., 1964), Chs. 7, 10. See also Saul D. Alinsky, *Reveille for Radicals* (New York: Vintage Books, 1969), and Alinsky, *Rules for Radicals* (New York: Random House, Inc., 1971).

10. Sister Isolina Ferre and Father Joseph P. Fitzpatrick, "Community Development and Delinquency Prevention: Puerto Rican and Mainland Models," paper presented at the Annual Meeting of the American Society of Criminology, November 5, 1971, mimeo.

11. Ferre and Fitzpatrick, "Community Development and Delinquency Prevention," and Charles F. Grosser et al., "Advocacy Puerto Rican Style," in *Delinquency Prevention: The Convergence of Theory Building, Political Influence, and New Modes of Advocacy* (New York: The Institute for Social Research, Fordham University, 1971). See also Kal Wagenheim, *Puerto Rico: A Profile* (New York: Praeger Publishers, 1970), Ch. 10, and Fitzpatrick, *Puerto Rican Americans* (Englewood Cliffs, N.J.: Prentice-Hall, Inc., 1971), esp. Chs. 3, 6. For an angrily critical view of the Puerto Rican temperament by the island's leading contemporary writer, see René Marqués, *The Docile Puerto Rican* (Philadelphia: Temple University Press, 1976).

12. See Alinsky, *Rules for Radicals,* and Silberman, *Crisis in Black and White,* Ch. 10.

Appendix: Notes on Crime Statistics

1. My analysis of the strengths and weaknesses of the *Uniform Crime Reports* and *National Crime Survey Reports* is based largely on the following sources: Wesley G. Skogan, "Measurement Problems in Official and Survey Crime Rates," *Journal of Criminal Justice*, Vol. 3, No. 1 (Spring, 1975), pp. 17–31; Michael J. Hindelang, "The

Uniform Crime Reports Revisited," *Journal of Criminal Justice*, Vol. 2, No. 1 (Spring, 1974), pp. 1–17; Donald J. Mulvihill and Melvin M. Tumin, with Lynn A. Curtis, *Crimes of Violence*, A Staff Report to the National Commission on the Causes and Prevention of Violence, Vol. 11 (Washington, D.C.: U.S. Government Printing Office, 1969), esp. Chs. 2, 3, 5, and Appendices 1–9; The President's Commission on Law Enforcement and Administration of Justice, *Task Force Report: Crime and Its Impact—An Assessment* (Washington, D.C.: U.S. Government Printing Office, 1967), esp. Chs. 2, 5, 6, 10, and Appendix E; Lynn A. Curtis, *Criminal Violence* (Lexington, Mass.: Lexington Books, 1974); Daniel Glaser, *Strategic Criminal Justice Planning* (Rockville, Md.: National Institute of Mental Health Center for Studies of Crime and Delinquency, 1975), Ch. 9; Albert D. Biderman and Albert J. Reiss, Jr., "On Exploring the 'Dark Figure' of Crime," *Annals of the American Academy of Political and Social Science*, Vol. 374 (November, 1967), pp. 1–16; *Crimes and Victims: A Report on the Dayton–San Jose Pilot Survey of Victimization* (Washington, D.C.: National Criminal Justice Information and Statistics Service, 1974); James Garofalo, *Local Victim Surveys: A Review of the Issues* (Washington, D.C.: National Criminal Justice Information and Statistics Service, 1977). See also the annual volumes of *Crime in the United States* (*Uniform Crime Reports*), issued by the FBI, and the annual volumes of *Criminal Victimization in the United States*, published since 1973 by the National Criminal Justice Information and Statistics Service.

2. The President's Commission on Law Enforcement and Administration of Justice, *Task Force Report: Crime and Its Impact—An Assessment*, esp. pp. 22–24.

3. *Criminal Victimization in the United States: A Comparison of 1974 and 1975 Findings*, pp. 37–38, 47–48.

4. For analyses of the strengths and weaknesses of victimization surveys, see Skogan, "Measurement Problems in Official and Survey Crime Rates," pp. 17–31; Garofalo, *Local Victim Surveys*, pp. 9–14; Hindelang, "The Uniform Crime Reports Revisited," pp. 1–17; *Criminal Victimization in the United States: A Comparison of 1974 and 1975 Findings* (Washington, D.C.: National Criminal Justice Information and Statistics Service, 1977); *Crimes and Victims*;

National Research Council Panel for the Evaluation of Crime Surveys, *Surveying Crime* (Washington, D.C.: National Academy of Sciences, 1976).

5. Hindelang, "The Uniform Crime Reports Revisited," pp. 5–10.
6. Michael R. Gottfredson et al., *Sourcebook of Criminal Justice Statistics—1977* (Washington, D.C.: National Criminal Justice Information and Statistics Service, 1978), pp. 302–13, Tables 3.1 through 3.7.

Bibliography

Books and Reports

Abrahams, Roger D., *Deep Down in the Jungle*, 1st rev. ed. Chicago: Aldine Publishing Co., 1970.

———, *Positively Black*. Englewood Cliffs, N.J.: Prentice-Hall, Inc., 1970.

Addams, Jane, *My Friend, Julia Lathrop*. New York: Macmillan Co., 1935.

Albini, Joseph, *The American Mafia*. New York: Appleton-Century-Crofts, 1971.

Alinsky, Saul D., *Reveille for Radicals*. New York: Vintage Books, 1969.

———, *Rules for Radicals*. New York: Random House, Inc., 1971.

Allen, Francis A., *The Borderland of Criminal Justice*. Chicago: University of Chicago Press, 1974.

Allen, John, *Assault with a Deadly Weapon: The Autobiography of a Street Criminal*, Dianne Hall Kelly and Philip Heymann, eds. New York: Pantheon Books, 1977.

Andenaes, Johannes, *Punishment and Deterrence*. Ann Arbor: University of Michigan Press, 1974.

Anderson, Jervis, *A. Philip Randolph*. New York: Harcourt Brace Jovanovich, 1973.

Attica. Official Report of the New York State Commission on Attica. New York: Bantam Books, 1972.

Banfield, Edward C., *The Unheavenly City*. Boston: Little, Brown & Co., 1970.

Baridon, Philip C., *Opiate Addiction and Crime*. Ph.D. dissertation, State University of New York at Albany. Ann Arbor, Mich.: University Microfilms.

Barksdale, Richard, and Kinnamon, Kenneth, eds., *Black Writers of America*. New York: Macmillan Co., 1972.

Baron, Roger, and Feeney, Floyd, *An Exemplary Project: Juve-*

nile Diversion Through Family Counseling. Washington, D.C.: National Institute of Law Enforcement and Criminal Justice, 1976.

Bartollas, Clemens, Miller, Stuart J., and Dinitz, Simon, *Juvenile Victimization.* New York: Sage Publications and Halsted Press, 1976.

Barton, Joseph J., *Peasants and Strangers.* Cambridge: Harvard University Press, 1975.

Becker, Gary S., and Landes, William M., eds., *Essays in the Economics of Crime and Punishment.* New York: National Bureau of Economic Research, 1974.

Becker, Howard S., ed., *The Other Side.* New York: The Free Press, 1964.

———, *Outsiders.* New York: The Free Press, 1973.

Bing, Stephen R., and Rosenfeld, S. Stephen, *The Quality of Justice in the Lower Criminal Courts of Metropolitan Boston.* A Report by the Lawyers' Committee for Civil Rights Under Law to the Governor's Committee on Law Enforcement and the Administration of Justice, September, 1970.

Bittner, Egon, *The Functions of the Police in Modern Society.* Rockville, Md.: National Institute of Mental Health Center for Studies of Crime and Delinquency, 1970.

Black, Charles L., Jr., *Capital Punishment: The Inevitability of Caprice and Mistake.* New York: W. W. Norton & Co., Inc., 1974.

Blau, Peter M., and Duncan, Otis Dudley, *The American Occupational Structure.* New York: John Wiley & Sons, Inc., 1967.

Bloch, Peter M., and Specht, David, *Neighborhood Team Policing.* Washington, D.C.: National Institute of Law Enforcement and Criminal Justice, 1973.

Blumberg, Abraham S., *Criminal Justice.* Chicago: Quadrangle Books, 1970.

———, ed., *Current Perspectives on Criminal Behavior.* New York: Alfred A. Knopf, 1974.

Blumstein, Alfred, Cohen, Jacqueline, and Nagin, Daniel, eds., *Deterrence and Incapacitation: Estimating the Effects of Criminal Sanctions on Crime Rates.* Washington, D.C.: National Academy of Sciences, 1978.

Bordua, David J., ed., *The Police: Six Sociological Essays.* New York: John Wiley & Sons, Inc., 1967.

Boydstun, John F., and Sherry, Michael E., *San Diego Com-*

munity Profile: Final Report. Washington, D.C.: The Police Foundation, 1975.

Braly, Malcolm, *False Starts.* Boston: Little, Brown & Co., 1976.

————, *On the Yard.* Greenwich, Conn.: Fawcett Publications, Inc., 1967.

Brooks, John, *Once in Golconda.* New York: Harper Colophon, 1970.

Brown, Claude, *Manchild in the Promised Land.* New York: New American Library (A Signet Book), 1965.

Buehlman, William, *Saint with a Gun.* New York: New York University Press, 1974.

Bugliosi, Vincent, with Gentry, Curt, *Helter Skelter.* New York: W. W. Norton & Co., Inc., 1974.

Bullock, Paul, *Aspiration vs. Opportunity: "Careers" in the Inner City.* Ann Arbor: Institute of Labor and Industrial Relations, University of Michigan—Wayne State University, 1973.

Bunker, Edward, *No Beast So Fierce.* New York: W. W. Norton & Co., Inc., 1973.

Byrnes, Thomas, *Professional Criminals of America, 1886.* New York: Chelsea House, 1969.

Carroll, Leo, *Hacks, Blacks, and Cons: Race Relations in a Maximum Security Prison.* Lexington, Mass.: Lexington Books, 1974.

Carter, Lief F., *The Limits of Order.* Lexington, Mass.: D. C. Heath & Co. (A Lexington Book), 1974.

Carter, Robert M., and Wilkins, Leslie, eds., *Probation and Parole.* New York: John Wiley & Sons, Inc., 1970.

Casper, Jonathan D., *American Criminal Justice: The Defendant's Perspective.* Englewood Cliffs, N.J.: Prentice-Hall, Inc. (A Spectrum Book), 1972.

————, *Criminal Justice: The Consumer's Perspective.* Washington, D.C.: National Institute of Law Enforcement and Criminal Justice, 1972.

Children in Adult Jails. Washington, D.C.: Children's Defense Fund, 1976.

Children in Custody: A Report on the Juvenile Detention and Correctional Facility Census of 1971. Washington, D.C.: National Criminal Justice Information and Statistics Service, 1974.

Children Without Homes: An Examination of Public Responsibility to Children in and out of Home Care. A Report by the Children's Defense Fund. Washington, D.C.: Children's Defense Fund, 1977. (mimeo)

City of New York Criminal Justice Coordinating Council, *A Community Self-Study of Organized Crime.* New York: Institute for Social Analysis, 1974. (mimeo)

Cleaver, Eldridge, *Soul on Ice.* New York: McGraw-Hill Book Co. (A Ramparts Book), 1968.

Clemmer, Donald, *The Prison Community.* New York: Holt, Rinehart & Winston, 1958.

Clinard, Marshall B., and Abbott, Daniel J., *Crime in Developing Countries.* New York: John Wiley & Sons, 1973.

Cloward, Richard A., et al., *Theoretical Studies in Social Organization of the Prison.* New York: Social Science Research Council, 1960.

Cohen, Albert K., *Delinquent Boys.* New York: The Free Press, 1955.

Cohen, Lawrence E., *Pre-Adjudicatory Detention in Three Juvenile Courts.* Law Enforcement Assistance Administration, National Criminal Justice Information and Statistics Service, 1974 (Utilization of Criminal Justice Statistics Project Analytic Report 8).

Coles, Robert, *Eskimos, Chicanos, Indians,* Vol. IV, *Children of Crisis.* Boston: Atlantic–Little, Brown & Co., 1977.

———, *The Old Ones of New Mexico.* Garden City, N.Y.: Anchor Books, 1975.

Conklin, John E., *Robbery and the Criminal Justice System.* Philadelphia: J. B. Lippincott Co., 1972.

———, ed., *The Crime Establishment.* Englewood Cliffs, N.J.: Prentice-Hall, Inc., 1973.

Corbett, Jacqueline, and Vereb, Thomas S., *Juvenile Court Statistics, 1974.* Washington, D.C.: National Institute for Juvenile Justice and Delinquency Prevention, undated.

Courlander, Harold, ed., *A Treasury of Afro-American Folklore.* New York: Crown Publishers, Inc., 1976.

Cressey, Donald R., *Theft of the Nation: The Structure and Operations of Organized Crime in America.* New York: Harper & Row, 1969.

———, ed., *The Prison: Studies in Institutional Organization and Change.* New York: Holt, Rinehart & Winston, Inc., 1961.

———, and McDermott, Robert A., *Diversion from the Juvenile Justice System.* Washington, D.C.: National Institute of Law Enforcement and Criminal Justice, 1974.

Crime in the United States (Uniform Crime Reports). Issued by the FBI, annual volumes.

Crimes and Victims: A Report on the Dayton–San Jose Pilot Survey of Victimization. Washington, D.C.: National Criminal Justice Information and Statistics Service, 1974.

The Criminal Investigation Process: A Dialogue on Research Findings. Washington, D.C.: National Institute of Law Enforcement and Criminal Justice, 1977.

Criminal Victimization in the United States. National Criminal Justice Information and Statistics Service, annual volumes since 1973.

Criminal Victimization in the United States, 1973. A National Crime Survey Report. U.S. Department of Justice, Law Enforcement Assistance Administration. Washington, D.C.: U.S. Government Printing Office, 1976.

Criminal Victimization in the United States: A Comparison of 1973 and 1974 Findings. A National Crime Panel Survey Report. Washington, D.C.: U.S. Government Printing Office, 1976.

Criminal Victimization in the United States: A Comparison of 1974 and 1975 Findings. A National Crime Panel Survey Report. Washington, D.C.: U.S. Government Printing Office, 1977.

Curbing the Repeat Offender: A Strategy for Prosecutors. Washington, D.C.: Institute for Law and Social Research (PROMIS Research Project Publication 3), 1977.

Curtis, Lynn A., *Criminal Violence*. Lexington, Mass.: D. C. Heath & Co. (Lexington Books), 1974.

——, *Violence, Race, and Culture*. Lexington, Mass.: D. C. Heath & Co. (Lexington Books), 1975.

Curvin, Robert, and Porter, Bruce, *A Report on the Blackout Looting*. Unpublished report to The Ford Foundation, 1978.

Davidson, R. Theodore, *Chicano Prisoners: The Key to San Quentin*. New York: Holt, Rinehart & Winston, 1974.

Davis, F. James, and Stivers, Richard, eds., *The Collective Definition of Deviance*. New York: The Free Press, 1975.

Davis, Kenneth Culp, *Discretionary Justice*. Baton Rouge: Louisiana State University Press, 1969.

——, ed., *Discretionary Justice in Europe and America*. Urbana: University of Illinois Press, 1976.

de Beaumont, Gustave, and Tocqueville, Alexis de, *On the Penitentiary System in the United States and Its Application to France.* Carbondale and Edwardsville, Ill.: Southern Illinois University Press, 1964.

Deloria, Vine, *Custer Died for Your Sins.* New York: Macmillan Co., 1969.

Donnelly, Richard C., Goldstein, Joseph, and Schwartz, Richard D., *Criminal Law.* New York: The Free Press, 1962.

Drake, St. Clair, and Cayton, Horace R., *Black Metropolis.* New York: Harper & Row (Harper Torch Books), 1962.

Drug Use and Crime. Report of the Panel on Drug Use and Criminal Behavior. Washington, D.C.: The National Institute on Drug Abuse, assisted by Research Triangle Institute, 1976.

Drug Use in America: Problem in Perspective. 2nd Report of the National Commission on Marijuana and Drug Abuse. Washington, D.C.: U.S. Government Printing Office, March, 1973.

DuBois, W. E. B., *Dusk of Dawn.* New York: Harcourt Brace Jovanovich, 1940.

Dundes, Alan, ed., *Mother Wit from the Laughing Barrel.* Englewood Cliffs, N.J.: Prentice-Hall, Inc., 1973.

Durk, David, and Silverman, Ira, *The Pleasant Avenue Connection.* New York: Harper & Row, 1976.

Durkheim, Emile, *Rules of Sociological Method,* 8th ed.; trans. by Sarah A. Solvay and John H. Mueller; George E. G. Gatlin, ed. New York: The Free Press, 1950.

Einstadter, Werner J., *Armed Robbery: A Career Study in Perspective.* 1966 Ph.D. dissertation, University of California, Berkeley. Ann Arbor, Mich.: University Microfilms, 1976.

Eisenstein, James, and Jacob, Herbert, *Felony Justice.* Boston: Little, Brown & Co., 1977.

The Ellery C. Decision: A Case Study of Judicial Regulation of Juvenile Status Offenders. New York: Institute of Judicial Administration, Inc., 1975.

Elliott, James F., *Interception Patrol.* Springfield, Ill.: Charles C. Thomas, 1973.

Ellison, Ralph, *Invisible Man.* New York: New American Library (A Signet Book), 1952.

Epstein, Edward Jay, *Agency of Fear.* New York: G. P. Putnam's Sons, 1977.

Erikson, Kai T., *Everything in Its Path.* New York: Simon & Schuster, 1976.

————, *Wayward Puritans.* New York: John Wiley & Sons, Inc., 1966.

Expanding the Perspective of Crime Data: Performance Implications for Policymakers. Washington, D.C.: Institute for Law and Social Research (PROMIS Research Project Publication 2), 1977. (mimeo)

Fair and Certain Punishment. Report of the Twentieth Century Fund Task Force on Criminal Sentencing. New York: McGraw-Hill Book Co., 1976.

Falcon, W. D., ed., *Witness Cooperation.* Lexington, Mass.: D. C. Heath & Co. (A Lexington Book), 1976.

Farb, Peter, *Word Play.* New York: Alfred A. Knopf, 1974.

Feeney, Floyd, and Weir, Adrianne, eds., *The Prevention and Control of Robbery.* Davis, Calif.: The Center on Administration of Criminal Justice, University of California—Davis, 1973. (mimeo)

Feinberg, Joel, *Doing and Deserving.* Princeton, N.J.: Princeton University Press, 1970.

Felony Arrests: Their Prosecution and Disposition in New York City's Courts. A Vera Institute of Justice Monograph. New York: The Vera Institute of Justice, 1977.

Ferman, Louis A., Kornbluh, Joyce L., and Haber, Alan, eds., *Poverty in America.* Ann Arbor: University of Michigan Press, 1965.

Finkelstein, M. Marvin, Weiss, Ellyn, Cohen, Stuart, and Fisher, Stanley Z., *Prosecution in the Juvenile Court: Guidelines for the Future.* Washington, D.C.: National Institute of Law Enforcement and Criminal Justice, 1973.

Fitzpatrick, Joseph P., *Puerto Rican Americans.* Englewood Cliffs, N.J.: Prentice-Hall, Inc., 1971.

Fleming, Macklin, *The Price of Perfect Justice.* New York: Basic Books, Inc., 1974.

Fogel, David, ". . . *We Are the Living Proof . . .*" Cincinnati: W. H. Anderson Co., 1975.

Forst, Brian E., Lucianovic, Judith, and Cox, Sarah J., *What Happens After Arrest?* Washington, D.C.: Institute for Law and Social Research (PROMIS Research Project Publication 4), 1977.

Fosdick, Raymond B., *American Police Systems.* Montclair, N.J.: Patterson Smith Reprint Series, 1972.

Frankel, Marvin E., *Criminal Sentences.* New York: Hill & Wang, 1973.

Friedman, Lawrence M., *The Legal System.* New York: Russell Sage Foundation, 1975.

Gans, Herbert J., *The Urban Villagers.* New York: The Free Press, 1962.

Gardiner, John A., *The Politics of Corruption: Organized Crime in an American City.* New York: Russell Sage Foundation, 1970.

Garofalo, James, *Local Victim Surveys: A Review of the Issues.* Washington, D.C.: National Criminal Justice Information and Statistics Service, 1977.

Gay, William G., Schell, Theodore H., and Schack, Stephen, *Improving Patrol Productivity,* Vol. I, *Routine Patrol.* Washington, D.C.: National Institute of Law Enforcement and Criminal Justice, Office of Technology Transfer, 1977.

Gaylin, Willard, *Partial Justice.* New York: Alfred A. Knopf, 1974.

Gerber, Rudolph J., and McAnany, Patrick D., eds., *Contemporary Punishment: Views, Explanations, and Justifications.* Notre Dame, Ind.: University of Notre Dame Press, 1972.

Giallombardo, Rose, *Society of Women.* New York: John Wiley & Sons, Inc., 1966.

Gibbons, Don C., *Delinquent Behavior.* Englewood Cliffs, N.J.: Prentice-Hall, Inc., 1970.

————, *Society, Crime and Criminal Careers.* Englewood Cliffs, N.J.: Prentice-Hall, Inc., 1968.

Gibbs, Jack P., *Crime, Punishment, and Deterrence.* New York: Elsevier Publishing Co., 1975.

Gilmore, Al-Tony, *Bad Nigger!* Port Washington, N.Y.: Kennikat Press, 1975.

Glaser, Daniel, *The Effectiveness of a Prison and Parole System,* abridged ed. Indianapolis: Bobbs-Merrill Co., Inc., 1969.

————, *Strategic Criminal Justice Planning.* Rockville, Md.: National Institute of Mental Health Center for Studies of Crime and Delinquency, 1975.

————, ed., *Handbook of Criminology.* Chicago: Rand McNally, 1974.

Glazer, Nathan, and Moynihan, Daniel P., *Beyond the Melting Pot.* Cambridge: M.I.T. Press and Harvard University Press, 1963.

Goffman, Erving, *Asylums.* Garden City, N.Y.: Anchor Books, 1961.

————, *Interaction Ritual.* Garden City, N.Y.: Anchor Books, 1967.

————, *Relations in Public.* New York: Harper Colophon Books, 1971.

————, *Stigma.* Englewood Cliffs, N.J.: Prentice-Hall, Inc., 1963.

Goldfarb, Ronald L., *Jails: The Ultimate Ghetto.* Garden City, N.Y.: Anchor Press/Doubleday, 1975.

————, and Singer, Linda R., *After Conviction.* New York: Simon & Schuster, 1973.

Goldstein, Herman, *Policing a Free Society.* Cambridge, Mass.: Ballinger Publishing Co., 1977.

Goldstein, Joseph, Freud, Anna, and Solnit, Albert J., *Beyond the Best Interest of the Child.* New York: The Free Press, 1973.

Goodwin, Leonard, *Do the Poor Want to Work?* Washington, D.C.: The Brookings Institution, 1972.

Gottfredson, Don M., Wilkins, Leslie T., Hoffman, Peter B., and Singer, Susan M., *Parole Decision Making.* Washington, D.C.: National Institute of Law Enforcement and Criminal Justice, 1973.

Gottfredson, Michael R., Hindelang, Michael J., and Parisi, Nicolette, *Sourcebook of Criminal Justice Statistics—1977.* Washington, D.C.: National Criminal Justice Information and Statistics Service, 1978.

Gould, Leroy C., Walker, Andrew L., Crane, Lansing E., and Lidy, Charles W., *Connections: Notes from the Heroin World.* New Haven, Conn.: Yale University Press, 1974.

————, et al., *Crime as a Profession.* Final Report to the Office of Law Enforcement Assistance and President's Commission on Law Enforcement and Administration of Justice, 1967. (mimeo)

Graham, Hugh Davis, and Gurr, Ted Robert, *Violence in America: Historical and Comparative Perspective.* A Report to the National Commission on the Causes and Prevention of Violence. Washington, D.C.: U.S. Government Printing Office, 1969.

Greenberg, David F., ed., *Corrections and Punishment.* Beverly Hills, Calif.: Sage Publications (Sage Criminal Justice System Annuals, Vol. 8), 1977.

Greene, Mark H., Kozel, Nicholas J., Hunt, Leon G., and Appletree, Roy L., *An Assessment of the Diffusion of Heroin*

Abuse to Medium Sized American Cities. Washington, D.C.:
U.S. Government Printing Office, 1974.

Greenwood, Peter W., *An Analysis of the Apprehension Activities of the New York City Police Department.* New York:
New York City Rand Institute, 1970.

————, Chaiken, Jan M., Petersilla, Joan, and Prusoff, Linda,
The Criminal Investigation Process, Vol. III, *Observations
and Analysis.* Santa Monica: Rand Corp., 1975.

————, Wildhorn, Sorrel, Poggio, Eugene C., Strumwasser,
Michael J., and De Leon, Peter, *Prosecution of Adult Felony
Defendants in Los Angeles County: A Policy Perspective.*
Washington, D.C.: Law Enforcement Assistance Admin-
istration, 1973.

Grier, William H., and Cobbs, Price M., *Black Rage.* New
York: Bantam Books, 1969.

Grupp, Stanley E., ed., *Theories of Punishment.* Bloomington,
Ind.: University of Illinois Press, 1972.

Gurr, Ted R., *Rogues, Rebels, and Reformers: A Political History of Urban Crime and Conflict.* Beverly Hills, Calif.: Sage
Publications, 1976.

Gusfield, Joseph R., *Symbolic Crusade.* Urbana: University of
Illinois Press, 1972.

Gutman, Herbert C., *The Black Family in Slavery and Freedom, 1750–1925.* New York: Pantheon Books, 1976.

Handlin, Oscar, *The Newcomers: Negroes and Puerto Ricans
in a Changing Metropolis.* Cambridge, Mass.: Harvard University Press, 1969.

Hannerz, Ulf, *Soulside.* New York: Columbia University Press,
1969.

Harris, M. Kay, and Spiller, Dudley P., Jr., *After Decision: Implementation of Judicial Decrees in Correctional Settings.*
Washington, D.C.: American Bar Association Commission
on Correctional Facilities and Services, Resource Center on
Correctional Law and Legal Services, 1976.

Harrison, Paul Carter, *The Great MacDaddy.* (a play)

Hart, H. L. A., *Punishment and Responsibility.* New York:
Oxford University Press, 1968.

Hauser, Philip H., *Rapid Growth: Key to Understanding
Metropolitan Problems.* Washington, D.C.: Washington Center for Metropolitan Studies, 1961.

Hauser, Stuart L., *Black and White Identity Formation.* New
York: Wiley-Interscience, 1971.

Hawkins, Gordon, *The Prison*. Chicago: University of Chicago Press, 1976.

Hayim, Gila J., *Changes in the Criminal Behavior of Heroin Addicts Under Treatment in the Addiction Research and Treatment Corporation: Interim Report of the First Year of Treatment*. Cambridge, Mass.: The Center for Criminal Justice, Harvard Law School, February, 1973. (mimeo)

Hazelrigg, Lawrence E., ed., *Prison Within Society*. Garden City, N.Y.: Anchor Books, 1969.

Hindelang, Michael J., Gottfredson, Michael R., Dunn, Christopher S., and Parisi, Nicolette, *Sourcebook of Criminal Justice Statistics—1976*. Washington, D.C.: National Criminal Justice Information and Statistics Service, 1977.

Hirschi, Travis, and Selvin, Hanan C., *Delinquency Research*. New York: The Free Press, 1967.

Hofstadter, Richard, and Wallace, Michael, eds., *American Violence: A Documentary History*. New York: Vintage Books, 1971.

Homer, Frederick D., *Guns and Garlic*. West Lafayette, Ind.: Purdue University Press, 1974.

Hoover, J. Edgar, *Crime in the United States: Uniform Crime Reports, 1967*. Washington, D.C.: U.S. Government Printing Office, 1968.

Howard, John R., ed., *Awakening Minorities*. New Brunswick, N.J.: Transaction Books, 1970.

Howell, Joseph T., *Hard Living on Clay Street*. Garden City, N.Y.: Anchor Books, 1973.

Hunt, Leon Gibson, *Recent Spread of Heroin Use in the United States: Unanswered Questions*. Washington, D.C.: The Drug Abuse Council, Inc., 1974.

———, and Chambers, Carl D., *The Heroin Epidemics*. New York: S.P. Books, Division of Spectrum Publications, Inc., 1976.

———, and Zinberg, Norman E., *Heroin Use: A New Look*. Washington, D.C.: The Drug Abuse Council, Inc., 1976.

Ianni, Francis A. J., *Black Mafia*. New York: Simon & Schuster, 1974.

———, with Elizabeth Reuss-Ianni, *A Family Business*. New York: Russell Sage Foundation, 1972.

Inciardi, James A., *The History and Sociology of Professional Crime*. 1973 Ph.D. dissertation. Ann Arbor, Mich.: University Microfilms, 1974.

Institute of Judicial Administration/American Bar Association

Juvenile Justice Standards Project, *Standards Relating to Appeals and Collateral Review*. Cambridge, Mass.: Ballinger Publishing Co., 1977. (tentative draft)

———, *Standards Relating to Counsel for Private Parties*. Cambridge, Mass.: Ballinger Publishing Co., 1977. (tentative draft)

———, *Standards Relating to Juvenile Delinquency and Sanctions*. Cambridge, Mass.: Ballinger Publishing Co., 1977. (tentative draft)

———, *Standards Relating to Non-Criminal Misbehavior*. Cambridge, Mass.: Ballinger Publishing Co., 1977. (tentative draft)

———, *Standards Relating to Prosecution*. Cambridge, Mass.: Ballinger Publishing Co., 1977. (tentative draft)

Irwin, John, *The Felon*. Englewood Cliffs, N.J.: Prentice-Hall, Inc. (A Spectrum Book), 1970.

Jackson, Bruce, *"Get Your Ass in the Water and Swim like Me."* Cambridge, Mass.: Harvard University Press, 1974.

———, *In the Life*. New York: Macmillan Co., 1972.

———, *A Thief's Primer*. New York: Macmillan Co., 1969.

Jacob, Herbert, ed., *The Potential for Reform of Criminal Justice*. Beverly Hills: Sage Publications (Sage Criminal Justice Systems Annuals, Vol. III), 1974.

Jacobs, Glenn, ed., *The Participant Observer*. New York: George Braziller, 1970.

Jacobs, James B., *Stateville: The Penitentiary in Mass Society*. Chicago: University of Chicago Press, 1977.

Jacobs, Jane, *The Death and Life of Great American Cities*. New York: Random House, Inc., 1961.

Johnston, Norman, *The Human Cage: A Brief History of Prison Architecture*. New York: Walker & Co., 1973.

Jordan, Winthrop D., *White Over Black*. Baltimore, Md.: Penguin Books, Inc., 1968.

———, *The White Man's Burden*. New York: Oxford University Press, 1974.

Judson, Horace Freeland, *Heroin Addiction in Britain*. New York: Harcourt Brace Jovanovich, 1974.

Juvenile Violence: A Study of the Handling of Juveniles Arrested for Crimes Against Persons in New York City, July 1, 1973–June 30, 1974. New York: Office of Children's Services, Division of Criminal Justice Services, 1976.

Kalven, Harry, Jr., and Zeisel, Hans, *The American Jury*. Chicago: University of Chicago Press, 1966.

Kaplan, John, *Criminal Justice: Introductory Cases and Materials*. Mineola, N.Y.: The Foundation Press, Inc., 1973.

Kassebaum, Gene, Ward, David A., and Wilner, Daniel M., *Prison Treatment and Parole Survival: An Empirical Assessment*. New York: John Wiley & Sons, Inc., 1971.

Keil, Charles, *Urban Blues*. Chicago: University of Chicago Press, 1966.

Kelley, Clarence M., *Crime in the United States, 1975 (Uniform Crime Reports)*. Washington, D.C.: U.S. Government Printing Office, 1976.

———, *Crime in the United States, 1976 (Uniform Crime Reports)*. Washington, D.C.: U.S. Government Printing Office, 1977.

Kelling, George L., Pate, Tony, Dieckman, Duane, and Brown, Charles E., *The Kansas City Patrol Experiments: A Technical Report*. Washington, D.C.: Police Foundation, 1974.

———, Pate, Tony, Dieckman, Duane, and Brown, Charles E., *The Kansas City Preventive Patrol Experiment: A Summary Report*. Washington, D.C.: Police Foundation, 1974.

Kennett, Lee, and Anderson, James LaVerne, *The Gun in America*. Westport, Conn.: Greenwood Press, 1975.

Keve, Paul W., *Prison Life and Human Worth*. Minneapolis: University of Minnesota Press, 1974.

King, Harry, as told to and edited by Bill Chambliss, *Box Man*. New York: Harper & Row, 1972.

Klebba, A. Joan, *Homicide Trends in the United States, 1900–1974*. National Center for Health Statistics, Division of Vital Statistics. Washington, D.C.: U.S. Government Printing Office, 1975.

———, *Mortality Trends for Homicide by Age, Color, and Sex: United States, 1960–1972*. Rockville, Md.: National Center for Health Statistics, undated. (mimeo)

Klein, Malcolm W., ed., *The Juvenile Justice System*. Beverly Hills, Calif.: Sage Publications (Sage Criminal Justice System Annuals, Vol. V), 1976.

Klockars, Carl B., *The Professional Fence*. New York: The Free Press, 1974.

Kochman, Thomas, ed., *Rappin' and Stylin' Out*. Urbana: University of Illinois Press, 1972.

Korn, Richard R., and McCorkle, Lloyd W., *Criminology and Penology*. New York: Holt, Rinehart & Co., 1959.

Krantz, Sheldon, Smith, Charles, Rossman, David, Froyd, Paul, and Hoffman, Janis, *Right to Counsel in Criminal Cases: The*

Mandate of Argersinger v. Hamlin. Cambridge, Mass.: Ballinger Publishing Co., 1976.

Krisberg, Barry, *Urban Leadership Training: An Ethnographic Study of 22 Gang Leaders.* 1971 Ph.D. dissertation, University of Pennsylvania. Ann Arbor, Mich.: University Microfilms, 1976.

Lane, Roger, *Policing the City.* Cambridge: Harvard University Press, 1967.

Larson, Richard C., *Urban Police Patrol Analysis.* Cambridge, Mass.: The M.I.T. Press, 1972.

Lasswell, Harold D., and McKenna, Jeremiah B., *The Impact of Organized Crime on an Inner-City Community.* New York: Policy Sciences Center, Inc., undated. (mimeo)

Leacock, Eleanor Burke, ed., *The Culture of Poverty: A Critique.* New York: Simon & Schuster (A Clarion Book), 1971.

Lemert, Edwin M., *Human Deviance, Social Problems, and Social Control,* 2nd ed. Englewood Cliffs, N.J.: Prentice-Hall, Inc., 1972.

Lerman, Paul, *Community Treatment and Social Control.* Chicago: University of Chicago Press, 1975.

Letkemann, Peter, *Crime as Work.* Englewood Cliffs, N.J.: Prentice-Hall, Inc. (A Spectrum Book), 1973.

Levine, Lawrence W., *Black Culture and Black Consciousness.* New York: Oxford University Press, 1977.

Levitan, Sar A., Johnston, William B., and Taggart, Robert, *Still a Dream.* Cambridge: Harvard University Press, 1974.

Liebow, Elliot, *Tally's Corner: A Study of Street Corner Men.* Boston: Little, Brown & Co., 1967.

Lipman, Mark, with Daley, Robert, *Stealing.* New York: Harper's Magazine Press, 1973.

Lipton, Douglas, Martinson, Robert, and Wilks, Judith, *The Effectiveness of Correctional Treatment: A Survey of Treatment Evaluation Studies.* New York: Praeger Publishers, 1975.

Llewellyn, Karl N., *The Bramble Bush.* Dobbs Ferry, N.Y.: Oceana Publications, 1960.

Lyman, Stanford M., *Chinese Americans.* New York: Random House, Inc., 1974.

Maas, Peter, *The Valachi Papers.* New York: G. P. Putnam's Sons, 1968.

McCleery, Richard H., *Policy Change in Prison Management.*

East Lansing: Michigan State University Bureau of Social and Political Research, 1957.

MacDonald, John M., *Armed Robbery.* Springfield, Ill.: Charles C. Thomas, 1975.

McDonald, William F., ed., *Criminal Justice and the Victim.* Beverly Hills, Calif.: Sage Publications (Sage Criminal Justice System Annuals, Vol. VI), 1976.

MacIsaac, John, *Half the Fun Was Getting There.* Englewood Cliffs, N.J.: Prentice-Hall, Inc., 1968.

McKay, Claude, *Home to Harlem.* New York: Pocket Books, Inc., 1965.

Manning, Peter K., *Police Work: The Social Organization of Policing.* Cambridge, Mass.: The M.I.T. Press, 1977.

Manocchio, Anthony J., and Dunn, Jimmy, with Lamar T. Empey, *The Time Game.* New York: Delta Books, 1970.

Manoni, Mary, *Bedford-Stuyvesant.* New York: Quadrangle/New York Times Book Co., 1973.

Marqués, René, *The Docile Puerto Rican.* Philadelphia: Temple University Press, 1976.

Martin, John Bartlow, *My Life in Crime.* Westport, Conn.: Greenwood Press Publishers, 1952, 1970 reprint.

Martinson, Robert, and Wilks, Judith, with the assistance of Alita Buzel, Henrietta Carpentier, and Paul Honig, *Knowledge in Criminal Justice Planning: A Preliminary Report.* New York: The Center for Knowledge in Criminal Justice Planning, 1976. (mimeo)

Mattick, Hans W., *The Prosaic Sources of Prison Violence.* Chicago: Occasional Papers from the Law School, University of Chicago, 1972.

Matza, David, *Delinquency and Drift.* New York: John Wiley & Sons, Inc., 1964.

Maurer, David W., *Whiz Mob.* Gainesville, Fla.: American Dialect Society, November, 1955.

Meier, Matt S., and Rivera, Feliciano, *The Chicānos.* New York: Hill & Wang, 1972.

Mennei, Robert M., *Thorns and Thistles.* Hanover, N.H.: The University Press of New England, 1973.

Menninger, Karl, *The Crime of Punishment.* New York: Viking Press, 1968.

Meriwether, Louise, *Daddy Was a Number Runner.* New York: Pyramid Books, 1971.

Merton, Robert K., *Social Theory and Social Structure*, enlarged ed. New York: The Free Press, 1968.

Miller, Frank W., *Prosecution: The Decision to Charge a Suspect with a Crime*. Boston: Little, Brown & Co., 1969.

Miller, Walter B., *Violence by Youth Gangs and Youth Groups as a Crime Problem in Major American Cities*. Washington, D.C.: U.S. Government Printing Office, 1975.

Milner, Christina, and Milner, Richard, *Black Players*. Boston: Little, Brown & Co., 1972.

Milner, Ron, *What the Wine-Sellers Buy*. (a play)

Mitford, Jessica, *Kind and Usual Punishment*. New York: Alfred A. Knopf, 1973.

Moley, Raymond, *Politics and Criminal Prosecution*. New York: Minton, Balch & Co., 1929.

Monroe, David G., and Garret, Earle W., under the direction of August Vollmer, *Police Conditions in the United States*. A Report to the National Commission on Law Observance and Enforcement. Montclair, N.J.: Patterson Smith Reprint Series, 1968.

Moore, Mark Harrison, *Buy and Bust*. Lexington, Mass.: Lexington Books, 1977.

Moton, Robert R., *What the Negro Thinks*. Garden City, N.Y.: Doubleday & Co., 1929.

Moynihan, Daniel P., ed., *On Understanding Poverty*. New York: Basic Books, Inc., 1969.

Muir, William Ker, Jr., *Police: Streetcorner Politicians*. Chicago: University of Chicago Press, 1977.

Mulvihill, Donald J., and Tumin, Melvin M., with Lynn A. Curtis, *Crimes of Violence*. A Staff Report to the National Commission on the Causes and Prevention of Violence, Vol. 11. Washington, D.C.: U.S. Government Printing Office, 1969.

Murphy, Patrick T., *Our Kindly Parent—The State*. New York: Viking Press, 1974.

Murphy, Patrick V., and Plate, Thomas, *Commissioner*. New York: Simon & Schuster, 1977.

Murray, Albert, *The Omni-Americans*. New York: Outerbridge & Dienstfrey, 1970.

Myrdal, Gunnar, *An American Dilemma*. New York: Harper & Row, 1944.

Nagel, Jack P., *Crime and Incarceration*. Philadelphia: The Fels Center of Government, University of Pennsylvania (Fels Discussion Paper #112), 1977.

Nagel, William G., *The New Red Barn: A Critical Look at the Modern American Prison*. New York: Walker & Co., 1973.

National Advisory Commission on Criminal Justice Standards and Goals, *Community Crime Prevention.* Washington, D.C.: U.S. Government Printing Office, 1973.

———, *A National Strategy to Reduce Crime.* Washington, D.C.: U.S. Government Printing Office, 1973.

National Commission on Law Observance and Enforcement, *Crime and the Foreign Born* (Wickersham Commission Reports, No. 10). Montclair, N.J.: Patterson Smith Reprint Series, 1968. (Originally published in 1931.)

———, *Report on Penal Institutions, Probation and Parole.* U.S. Government Printing Office, 1931. Montclair, N.J.: Patterson Smith Reprint Series, 1968.

National Task Force to Develop Standards and Goals for Juvenile Justice and Delinquency Prevention, *Jurisdiction—Status Offenses.* Washington, D.C.: National Institute for Juvenile Justice and Delinquency Prevention, 1977.

Nee, Victor G., and Brett, deBary, *Longtime Californ': A Documentary Study of an American Chinatown.* New York: Pantheon Books, 1973.

Neiderhoffer, Arthur, and Blumberg, Abraham S., eds., *The Ambivalent Force: Perspectives on the Police.* San Francisco: Rinehart Press, 1973.

Neubauer, David W., *Criminal Justice in Middle America.* Morristown, N.J.: General Learning Press, 1974.

Newman, Donald J., *Conviction: The Determination of Guilt or Innocence Without Trial.* Boston: Little, Brown & Co., 1966.

Newton, George D., and Zimring, Franklin E., *Firearms and Violence in American Life,* Vol. 7. A Staff Report to the National Commission on the Causes and Prevention of Violence. Washington, D.C.: U.S. Government Printing Office, 1969.

Nimmer, Raymond T., *Criminal Justice Reform Impact: Models of Behavior and a Case Study.* Unpublished. (mimeo)

———, *Diversion: The Search for Alternative Forms of Prosecution.* Chicago: American Bar Foundation, 1974.

Noonan, John T., Jr., *Persons and Masks of the Law.* New York: Farrar, Straus & Giroux, 1976.

Normandeau, Andre, *Trends and Patterns in Crimes of Robbery.* 1968 Ph.D. dissertation, University of Pennsylvania. Ann Arbor, Mich.: University Microfilms, 1974.

Ohlin, Lloyd E., ed., *Prisoners in America*. Englewood Cliffs, N.J.: Prentice-Hall, Inc., 1973.

Ohmart, Howard, *State Juvenile Incarceration in Texas: An Assessment*. Sacramento, Calif.: American Justice Institute, undated.

Olson, Jay, and Shepard, George H., *Intake Screening Guides: Improving Justice for Juveniles*. Washington, D.C.: Office of Youth Development, Department of Health, Education and Welfare, 1975.

Orland, Leonard, *Prisons: Houses of Darkness*. New York: The Free Press, 1975.

Owen, Henry, and Schultze, Charles L., eds., *Setting National Priorities: The Next Ten Years*. Washington, D.C.: The Brookings Institution, 1976.

Packer, Herbert L., *The Limits of the Criminal Sanction*. Stanford, Calif.: Stanford University Press, 1968.

Parker, Tony, and Allerton, Robert, *The Courage of His Convictions*. London: Hutchinson Publishing Group, 1962.

Pate, Tony, Bowers, Robert A., and Parks, Ron, *Three Approaches to Criminal Apprehension in Kansas City: An Evaluation Report*. Washington, D.C.: The Police Foundation, 1976.

―――, Ferrara, Amy, Bowers, Robert A., and Lorence, Jon, *Police Response Time: Its Determinants and Effects*. Washington, D.C.: The Police Foundation, 1976.

Paulsen, Monrad G., and Whitebread, Charles H., *Juvenile Law and Procedure*. Reno, Nev.: National Council of Juvenile Court Judges, 1974.

Petersen, William, *Japanese Americans*. New York: Random House, Inc., 1971.

Platt, Anthony M., *The Child Savers*. Chicago: University of Chicago Press, 1969.

Polsky, Ned, *Hustlers, Beats, and Others*. Chicago: Aldine Publishing Co., 1967.

Pope, Carl E., *The Judicial Processing of Assault and Burglary Offenders in Selected California Counties*. Washington, D.C.: National Criminal Justice Information and Statistics Service (Utilization of Criminal Justice Statistics Project Analytic Report 7).

―――, *Offender-Based Transaction Statistics: New Directions in Data Collection and Reporting*. Washington, D.C.: Law Enforcement Assistance Administration, National Criminal Justice Information and Statistics Service (Utilization of

Criminal Justice Statistics Project Analytic Report 5), 1975.

Pound, Roscoe, *Criminal Justice in America.* New York: Da Capo Press, 1972.

The President's Commission on Law Enforcement and the Administration of Justice, *The Challenge of Crime in a Free Society.* Washington, D.C.: U.S. Government Printing Office, 1967.

————, *Task Force Report: Crime and Its Impact—An Assessment.* Washington, D.C.: U.S. Government Printing Office, 1967.

————, *Task Force Report: Juvenile Delinquency and Youth Crime.* Washington, D.C.: U.S. Government Printing Office, 1967.

————, *Task Force Report: Organized Crime.* Washington, D.C.: U.S. Government Printing Office, 1967.

————, *Task Force Report: Science and Technology.* Washington, D.C.: U.S. Government Printing Office, 1967.

Prisoners in America. Harriman, N.Y.: Report of the 42nd American Assembly, 1972.

PROMIS Research Project: Highlights of Interim Findings and Implications. Washington, D.C.: Institute for Law and Social Research (PROMIS Research Project Publication 1), 1977. (mimeo)

The Prosecution Function and the Defense Function. American Bar Association's Project on Minimum Standards for Criminal Justice. New York: Institute for Judicial Administration, 1970.

Radzinowicz, Leon, and King, Joan, *The Growth of Crime.* New York: Basic Books, Inc., 1977.

————, and Wolfgang, Marvin E., eds., *The Criminal in Confinement,* Vol. III, *Crime and Justice.* New York: Basic Books, Inc., 1971.

Rainwater, Lee, *Behind Ghetto Walls.* Chicago: Aldine Publishing Co., 1970.

Reasons, Charles E., and Kuykendall, Jack L., eds., *Race, Crime and Justice.* Pacific Palisades, Calif.: Goodyear Publishing Co., Inc., 1972.

Reiss, Albert J., Jr., *The Police and the Public.* New Haven: Yale University Press, 1971.

Report on the Causes of Crime, Vol. 1 (Wickersham Reports). National Commission on Law Observance and Enforcement. Montclair, N.J.: Patterson Smith Reprint Series, 1968.

Report on New York Parole. New York: Citizens Inquiry on Parole and Criminal Justice, Inc., 1974. (mimeo)

Robertson, John A., *Rough Justice: Perspectives on Lower Criminal Courts.* Boston: Little, Brown & Co., 1974.

Robins, Lee N., *A Follow-Up of Vietnam Drug Users.* Washington, D.C.: Executive Office of the President, Special Action Office for Drug Abuse Prevention, Interim Final Report, 1973.

Roebuck, Julian B., *Criminal Typology.* Springfield, Ill.: Charles C. Thomas, 1967.

———, and Frese, Wolfgang, *The Rendezvous.* New York: The Free Press, 1976.

Rosengarten, Theodore, *All God's Dangers: The Life of Nate Shaw.* New York: Alfred A. Knopf, 1974.

Rosenheim, Margaret K., ed., *Pursuing Justice for the Child.* Chicago: University of Chicago Press, 1976.

Rosett, Arthur, and Cressey, Donald R., *Justice by Consent.* Philadelphia: J. B. Lippincott Co., 1976.

Rothman, David J., *The Discovery of the Asylum.* Boston: Little, Brown & Co., 1971.

Rottenberg, Simon, ed., *The Economics of Crime and Punishment.* Washington, D.C.: American Enterprise Institute for Public Policy Research, 1973.

Rubinstein, Jonathan, *City Police.* New York: Farrar, Straus & Giroux, 1973.

Rutherford, Andrew, and McDermott, Robert, *Juvenile Diversion.* National Evaluation Program Phase I Summary Report. Washington, D.C.: National Institute of Law Enforcement and Criminal Justice, 1976.

———, et al., *Prison Population and Policy Choices,* Vols. I, II. Washington, D.C.: National Institute of Law Enforcement and Criminal Justice, 1977.

Salerno, Ralph, and Tompkins, John S., *The Crime Confederation: Cosa Nostra and Allied Operations in Organized Crime.* Garden City, N.Y.: Doubleday & Co., Inc., 1969.

Samora, Julian, and Simon, Patricia Vandel, *A History of the Mexican-American People.* Notre Dame, Ind.: University of Notre Dame Press, 1977.

Sarri, Rosemary C., *Under Lock and Key: Juveniles in Jails and Detention.* Ann Arbor, Mich.: National Assessment of Juvenile Corrections, University of Michigan, 1974.

———, and Hasenfeld, Yeheskel, eds., *Brought to Justice? Juveniles, the Courts, and the Law.* Ann Arbor: National

Assessment of Juvenile Corrections, University of Michigan, 1976.

Scacco, Anthony M., Jr., *Rape in Prison,* Springfield, Ill.: Charles C. Thomas, 1975.

Schell, Theodore H., Overly, Don H., Schack, Stephen, and Stabile, Linda L., *Traditional Preventive Patrol.* Washington, D.C.: Law Enforcement Assistance Administration, National Institute of Law Enforcement and Criminal Justice, 1976.

Schlossman, Steven L., *Love and the American Delinquent: Theory and Practice of "Progressive" Juvenile Justice, 1825–1920.* Chicago: University of Chicago Press, 1977.

Schorr, Alvin L., ed., *Children and Decent People.* New York: Basic Books, Inc., 1974.

Schrag, Clarence, *Crime and Justice: American Style.* Rockville, Md.: National Institute of Mental Health Center for Studies in Crime and Delinquency, 1971.

Schur, Edwin M., *Labeling Deviant Behavior.* New York: Harper & Row, 1971.

———, *Radical Non-Intervention.* Englewood Cliffs, N.J.: Prentice-Hall, Inc., 1973.

———, and Bedau, Hugo Adam, *Victimless Crimes.* Englewood Cliffs, N.J.: Prentice-Hall, Inc. (A Spectrum Book), 1974.

Schwartz, Alfred I., and Clarren, Sumner N., *The Cincinnati Team Policing Experiment.* Summary Report. Washington, D.C.: The Police Foundation, undated. (mimeo)

Sechrest, Dale K., Vorenberg, James, and Lukoff, Irving, *The Criminal Behavior of Drug Program Patients.* A Final Report of the Impact on Crime of the Methadone Maintenance Program of the Addiction Research and Treatment Corporation. Cambridge, Mass.: The Center for Criminal Justice, Harvard Law School, September, 1975. (mimeo)

Sheehan, Susan, *A Prison and a Prisoner.* Boston: Houghton Mifflin Co., 1978.

Sherrill, Robert, *The Saturday Night Special.* New York: Charterhouse, 1973.

Sidran, Ben, *Black Talk.* New York: Holt, Rinehart & Winston, 1971.

Silberman, Charles E., *Crisis in Black and White.* New York: Random House, Inc., 1964.

———, *The Myths of Automation.* New York: Harper & Row, 1966.

Simon, Rita James, ed., *The Jury System in America: A Critical*

Overview. Beverly Hills, Calif.: Sage Publications (Sage Criminal Justice System Annuals, Vol. IV), 1975.

Sinclair, Andrew, *Prohibition: The Era of Excess.* Boston: Little, Brown & Co., 1962.

Skolnick, Jerome H., *Justice Without Trial: Law Enforcement in a Democratic Society.* New York: John Wiley & Sons, Inc., 1966.

Smelser, Neil J., and Lipset, S. M., eds., *Social Structure and Mobility in Economics Development.* Chicago: Aldine Publishing Co., 1966. (reprinted)

Smith, Dwight C., Jr., *The Mafia Mystique.* New York: Basic Books, Inc., 1975.

A Socio-Economic Profile of Puerto Rican New Yorkers. New York: U.S. Department of Labor, Bureau of Labor Statistics, Middle Atlantic Regional Office Regional Report 46, July, 1975.

Sowell, Thomas, *Race and Economics.* New York: David McKay Co., Inc., 1975.

Stanley, David T., *Prisoners Among Us.* Washington, D.C.: The Brookings Institution, 1976.

Steiner, Stan, *La Raza.* New York: Harper & Row, 1970.

Stoddard, Ellwyn R., *Mexican Americans.* New York: Random House, Inc., 1973.

Stone, Christopher D., *Where the Law Ends.* New York: Harper & Row, 1975.

Street, David, Vintner, Robert D., and Perrow, Charles, *Organization for Treatment: A Comparative Study on Institutions for Delinquents.* New York: The Free Press, 1966.

Survey of Inmates of Local Jails, 1972. Washington, D.C.: National Criminal Justice Information and Statistics Service, 1976.

Susman, Jackwell, ed., *Crime and Justice. 1971–1972.* New York: AMS Press, 1974.

Sutherland, Edwin, *The Professional Thief.* Chicago: University of Chicago Press, 1937.

Sykes, Gresham M., *The Society of Captives.* Princeton, N.J.: Princeton University Press, 1958.

Tannenbaum, Frank, *Crime and the Community.* New York: Columbia University Press, 1938.

———, *Wall Shadows.* New York: G. P. Putnam's Sons, 1922.

Tate, Michael D., et al., *Cost and Service Impacts of Status Offenders in Ten States: "Responses to Angry Youth."* Administration Office of Juvenile Justice and Delinquency Prevention, 1978.

Thernstrom, Stephan, *The Other Bostonians: Poverty and Progress in the American Metropolis, 1880-1970.* Cambridge: Harvard University Press, 1973.

Thomas, Piri, *Down These Mean Streets.* New York: New American Library, 1967.

Thrasher, Frederic M., *The Gang,* abridged ed. Chicago: University of Chicago Press, 1963.

To Establish Justice, To Insure Domestic Tranquility. Final Report of the National Commission on the Causes and Prevention of Violence. Washington, D.C.: U.S. Government Printing Office, 1969.

Toch, Hans, *Police, Prisons, and the Problem of Violence.* Rockville, Md.: National Institute of Mental Health Center for Studies of Crime and Delinquency, 1977.

van den Haag, Ernest, *Punishing Criminals.* New York: Basic Books, Inc., 1975.

Vintner, Robert D., ed., *Time Out: A National Study of Juvenile Correctional Programs.* Ann Arbor: National Assessment of Juvenile Corrections, University of Michigan, 1976.

———, Downs, George, and Hall, John, *Juvenile Corrections in the States: Residential Programs and Deinstitutionalization.* Ann Arbor: National Assessment of Juvenile Corrections, University of Michigan, 1975.

von Hirsch, Andrew, *Doing Justice.* Report of the Committee for the Study of Incarceration. New York: Hill & Wang, 1976.

———, and Hanrahan, Kathleen J., *Abolish Parole?* Report submitted to the National Institute of Law Enforcement and Criminal Justice, December 1, 1977. (mimeo)

Wagenheim, Kal, *Puerto Rico: A Profile.* New York: Praeger Publishers (Praeger Paperbacks), 1970.

Wakin, Edward, *Children Without Justice: A Report by the National Council of Jewish Women.* New York: National Council of Jewish Women, Inc., 1975.

Walsh, Marilyn, *The Fence.* Westport, Conn.: Greenwood Press, 1977.

Wambaugh, Joseph, *The New Centurions.* New York: Dell Publishing Co., 1970.

Ward, David, and Kassebaum, Gene, *Women's Prison.* Chicago: Aldine Publishing Co., 1965.

Washburn, Wilcomb E., ed., *The Indian and the White Man.* Garden City, N.Y.: Anchor Books, 1964.

Waskow, Arthur I., *From Race Riot to Sit-In: 1919 and the 1960s.* Garden City, N.Y.: Doubleday & Co., Inc., 1966.

Watergate Special Prosecution Force, *Report.* Washington, D.C.: U.S. Government Printing Office, 1975.

Weiss, Carl, and Friar, David James, *Terror in the Prisons.* Indianapolis: Bobbs-Merrill Co., Inc., 1974.

Weppner, Robert S., ed., *Street Ethnography.* Beverly Hills, Calif.: Sage Publications (Sage Annual Reviews of Drug and Alcohol Abuse, Vol. 1), 1977.

West, William Gordon, *Serious Thieves: Lower-Class Adolescent Males in a Short-Term Deviant Occupation.* 1974 Ph.D. dissertation, Northeastern University. Ann Arbor, Mich.: University Microfilms, 1974.

Wheeler, Stanton, ed., *Controlling Delinquents.* New York: John Wiley & Sons, Inc., 1968.

White Paper on Drug Abuse. A Report to the President from the Domestic Council Drug Abuse Task Force. Washington, D.C.: U.S. Government Printing Office, September, 1975.

Whyte, William Foote, *Street Corner Society,* 2nd ed. Chicago: University of Chicago Press, 1955.

Wilkins, Leslie T., Kress, Jack M., Gottfredson, Don M., Calpin, Joseph C., and Gelman, Arthur M., *Sentencing Guidelines: Structuring Judicial Discretion.* Albany, N.Y.: Criminal Justice Research Center (Final Report of the Feasibility Study), October, 1976. (mimeo)

Williams, Vergil L., and Fish, Mary, *Convicts, Codes, and Contraband: The Prison Life of Men and Women.* Cambridge, Mass.: Ballinger Publishing Co., 1974.

Willwerth, James, *Jones.* New York: M. Evans & Co., Inc., 1975.

Wilson, James Q., *Thinking About Crime.* New York: Basic Books, Inc., 1975.

———, *Varieties of Police Behavior.* New York: Atheneum, 1971.

Wolfgang, Marvin E., and Ferracuti, Franco, *The Subculture of Violence.* London: Social Science Paperbacks, 1967.

———, Figlio, Robert M., and Sellin, Thorsten, *Delinquency in a Birth Cohort.* Chicago: University of Chicago Press, 1972.

———, Savitz, Leonard, and Johnston, Norman, eds., *The*

Sociology of Crime and Delinquency, 2nd ed. New York: John Wiley & Sons, Inc., 1970.

Wooden, Kenneth, *Weeping in the Playtime of Others.* New York: McGraw-Hill Book Co., 1976.

Woodward, C. Vann, *The Strange Career of Jim Crow,* 3rd ed. New York: Oxford University Press, 1974.

Youth: Transition to Adulthood. Report of the Panel on Youth of the President's Science Advisory Committee. Washington, D.C.: U.S. Government Printing Office, June, 1973.

Zimring, Franklin E., and Hawkins, Gordon J., *Deterrence.* Chicago: University of Chicago Press, 1973.

ARTICLES

Alschuler, Albert W., "The Defense Attorney's Role in Plea Bargaining," *Yale Law Journal,* Vol. 84, No. 6 (May, 1975).

———, "The Prosecutor's Role in Plea Bargaining," *University of Chicago Law Review,* Vol. 36 (1968).

———, "Sentencing Reform and Prosecutorial Power: A Critique of Recent Proposals for 'Fixed' and 'Presumptive' Sentencing," *University of Pennsylvania Law Review,* Vol. 126.

———, "The Trial Judge's Role in Plea Bargaining, Part I," *Columbia Law Review,* Vol. 76, No. 7 (November, 1976).

Alviani, Joseph D., and Drake, William R., "Handgun Control . . . Issues and Alternatives." Washington, D.C.: United States Conference of Mayors, 1975.

"Analysis of Ehrlich Argument," Appendix C to Reply Brief for Petitioner in the case of Jesse Thurman Fowler v. North Carolina in the Supreme Court of the United States, October Term, 1974.

Andenaes, Johannes, "General Prevention Revisited: Research and Policy Implications," *The Journal of Criminal Law and Criminology,* Vol. 66, No. 3 (September, 1975).

Argyle, Michael, "The Laws of Looking," *Human Nature,* Vol. 1, No. 1 (January, 1978).

Arthur, Lindsay G., "Status Offenders Need Help, Too," *Juvenile Justice,* Vol. 26, No. 1 (February, 1975).

Astrachan, Anthony, "Profile/Louisiana," *Corrections Magazine,* Vol. 2, No. 1 (September/October, 1975).

Bacon, Kenneth H., "SEC Testimony Tells How Gulf Oil Gave

$300,000 a Year to Politicians in the U.S." *The Wall Street Journal* (November 17, 1975).

Bailey, William C., "Murder and Capital Punishment: Some Further Evidence," *American Journal of Orthopsychiatry*, Vol. 45, No. 4 (July, 1975).

Bazelon, David L., "The Defective Assistance of Counsel," *University of Cincinnati Law Review*, Vol. 42, No. 1 (1973).

————, "The Urge to Punish," *The Atlantic Monthly*, Vol. 206 (July, 1960).

Belkin, Jacob, Blumstein, Alfred, and Glass, William, "Recidivism as a Feedback Process: An Analytical Model and Emperical Validation," *Journal of Criminal Justice*, Vol. 1, No. 1 (March, 1973).

Berman, Deborah K., and Vargo, Alexander, "Response Time Analysis Study: Preliminary Findings on Robbery in Kansas City," *The Police Chief*, Vol. 43, No. 5 (May, 1976).

Biderman, Albert D., and Reiss, Albert J., Jr., "On Exploring the 'Dark Figure' of Crime," *Annals of the American Academy of Political and Social Science* (November, 1967).

Bittner, Egon, "Preliminary Concept Paper: Police and Juveniles" (Unpublished paper prepared for Juvenile Justice Standards Project, undated).

Block, Richard, "Homicide in Chicago: A Nine-Year Study (1965–1973)," *Journal of Criminal Law and Criminology*, Vol. 66, No. 4 (December, 1976).

————, and Zimring, Franklin E., "Homicide in Chicago, 1965–1970," *Journal of Research in Crime and Delinquency*, Vol. 10, No. 1 (January, 1973).

Blum, Howard, "A Heroin War Is Coming to Harlem," *The Village Voice* (November 3, 1975).

————, "New York Gang Reported to Sell Death and Drugs," *New York Times* (December 16, 1977).

Blundell, William E., "Many People's Dreams Came Crashing Down with Equity Funding," *The Wall Street Journal* (March 29, 1974).

Bogomolny, Robert L., "Street Patrol: The Decision to Stop a Citizen," *Criminal Law Bulletin*, Vol. 12, No. 5 (September/October, 1976).

Bohannan, Paul, "Patterns of Murder and Suicide," *African Homicide and Suicide*. Princeton, N.J.: Princeton University Press, 1960.

Brown, William P., "Criminal Informants." Albany: State University of New York at Albany, School of Criminal Justice, undated, mimeo.

Bunker, Edward, "War Behind Walls," *Harper's,* Vol. 244, No. 1461 (February, 1972).

Burnham, David, "3 of 5 Slain by Police Here Are Black, Same as Arrest Rate," *New York Times* (August 25, 1973).

Caplan, Gerald, "Studying the Police" (Unpublished remarks to the Executive Forum on Upgrading the Police, April 13, 1976).

Carley, William M., "Lockheed's Payoffs to Indonesians Were Difficult to Arrange," *The Wall Street Journal* (November 17, 1975).

Carlson, Norman A., "The Jail Crisis: Concern Shown—But Problem Goes Unsolved," *American Journal of Correction* (July/August, 1977).

Chaffee, Zechariah, Jr., Pollok, Walter H., and Stern, Carl S., "The Third Degree," *Report on Lawlessness in Law Enforcement* (Wickersham Commission Reports, No. 11), National Commission on Law Observance and Enforcement. Montclair, N.J.: Patterson Smith Reprint Series, 1968.

Chambliss, William J., "Types of Deviance and the Effectiveness of Legal Sanctions," *Wisconsin Law Review,* Vol. 1967, No. 3 (Summer, 1967).

———, "Vice, Corruption, Bureaucracy and Power," *Wisconsin Law Review,* Vol. 1971, No. 4 (1971).

Chappell, Duncan, and Walsh, Marilyn, " 'No Questions Asked': A Consideration of the History of Criminal Receiving," *An Analysis of Criminal Redistribution Systems and Their Economic Impact on Small Business,* A Staff Report prepared for the Select Committee on Small Business, J.S. Senate. Washington, D.C.: U.S. Government Printing Office, 1972.

———, and Walsh, Marilyn, "Receiving Stolen Property," *Criminology,* Vol. 11, No. 4 (February, 1974).

Chasan, Daniel Jack, "Good Fences Make Bad Neighbors," *New York Times Magazine* (December 19, 1974).

Chesney-Lind, Meda, "Judicial Paternalism and the Female Status Offender," *Crime and Delinquency,* Vol. 23, No. 2 (April, 1977).

"Children and the Law," *Newsweek* (September 8, 1975).

Christensen, Ronald, "Projected Percentage of U.S. Population with Criminal Arrest and Conviction Records," *Task Force Report: Science and Technology,* A Report to the President's

Commission on Law Enforcement and the Administration of Justice. Washington, D.C.: U.S. Government Printing Office, 1967.

Christiansen, Barlow F., "Delivery of Legal Services to Persons of Low and Modest Income: 'In the Shade of the Old Atrophy,'" *Quest for Justice: A Report of the Commission on a National Institute of Justice,* American Bar Association, 1973.

Christie, Nils, Andenaes, Johannes, and Skirbekk, Sigurd, "A Study of Self-Reported Crime," *Scandinavian Studies in Criminology,* Vol. I. London: Tavistock Publication, 1965.

Church, Thomas W., Jr., "Plea Bargains, Concessions and the Courts: Analysis of a Quasi-Experiment," *Law and Society Review,* Vol. 1, No. 3 (Spring, 1976).

Chused, Richard A., "The Juvenile Court Process: A Study of Three New Jersey Counties," *Rutgers Law Review,* Vol. 26, No. 3 (Spring, 1973).

Clarke, Stevens H., "Some Implications for North Carolina of Recent Research in Juvenile Delinquency," *Journal of Research in Crime and Delinquency,* Vol. 12, No. 1 (January, 1975).

Clines, Francis X., "About New York: Battered Wives and the Police," *New York Times* (March 5, 1977).

Cohen, Fred, "The Discovery of Prison Reform," *Buffalo Law Review,* Vol. 21, No. 3 (Spring, 1972).

Coles, Robert, "The Children of Affluence," *The Atlantic Monthly,* Vol. 240, No. 3 (September, 1977).

Conway, Allan, and Bogdan, Carol, "Sexual Delinquency—The Persistence of a Double Standard," *Crime and Delinquency,* Vol. 23, No. 2 (April, 1977).

Cook, Fred J., "The Black Mafia Moves into the Numbers Racket," *New York Times Magazine* (April 4, 1971).

Coombs, Orde, "The Trashing of LeMans: The New Civil War Begins," *New York* (August 8, 1977).

Cunningham, Barry, "Murder Victim's Family: One Year Later," *New York Post* (September 12, 1974).

Daly, Michael, and Hamill, Denis, "Here Comes the Neighborhood," *The Village Voice,* Vol. XXII, No. 30 (July 25, 1977).

Damaška, Mirjan, "Evidentiary Barriers to Convention and Two Models of Criminal Procedure," *University of Pennsylvania Law Review,* Vol. 121, No. 3 (January, 1973).

Dash, Leon, "Heroin Trail: From Mexico to Streets of D.C.," Washington *Post* (April 18, 1976).

———, "Tracing D.C. Drug Route," Washington *Post* (May 24, 1976).

Davis, Alan J., "Sexual Assaults in the Philadelphia Prison System and Sheriff's Van," *Transaction*, Vol. 6, No. 2 (December, 1968).

diGrazia, Robert J. "Police Leadership: Challenging Old Assumptions," Washington *Post* (November 10, 1976).

Doleschal, Eugene, and Klapmuts, Nora, "Toward a New Criminology," *Crime and Delinquency Literature*, Vol. 5, No. 4 (December, 1973).

Ehrlich, Isaac, "The Deterrent Effect of Capital Punishment: A Question of Life and Death," *American Economic Review*, Vol. 65, No. 3 (June, 1975).

Einstadter, Werner J., "The Social Organization of Armed Robbery," *Social Problems*, Vol. 17 (Summer, 1969).

Emerson, Gloria, "In Mean Streets of His Own Past, Father Lives for His Son's Future," *New York Times* (November 5, 1973).

Enker, Arnold, "Perspectives on Plea Bargaining," *Task Force Report: The Courts*, The President's Commission on Law Enforcement and Administration of Justice. Washington, D.C.: U.S. Government Printing Office, 1967.

Epstein, Edward Jay, "The Incredible War Against the Poppies," Washington *Post* (December 22, 1974).

———, "Methadone: The Forlorn Hope," *The Public Interest*, No. 36 (Summer, 1974).

Evans, Therman E., "Media, Violence and Black People," Washington *Post* (August 4, 1976).

Feeley, Malcolm M., "Two Models of the Criminal Justice System: An Organizational Perspective," *Law and Society Review*, Vol. 7, No. 3 (Spring, 1973).

Ferre, Sister Isolina, and Fitzpatrick, Father Joseph P., "Community Development and Delinquency Prevention: Puerto Rican and Mainland Models." (Paper presented at the Annual Meeting of the American Society of Criminology, November 5, 1971, mimeo).

Forst, Brian S., and Brosi, Kathleen B., "A Theoretical and Empirical Analysis of the Prosecutor," *Journal of Legal Studies* (January, 1977).

The Fortune Society, *Fortune News* (December, 1975).

Fox, Sanford J., "Juvenile Justice Reform: An Historical Perspective," *Stanford Law Review*, Vol. 22, No. 6 (June, 1970).

Freeman, Robert A., Dinitz, Simon, and Conrad, John P., "A Look at the Dangerous Offender and Society's Effort to Control Him," *American Journal of Corrections* (January/February, 1977).

Fuller, Dan, and Orsagh, Thomas, "Violence and Victimization Within a State Prison System," *Criminal Justice Review*, Vol. 2, No. 2 (Fall, 1977).

Gage, Nicholas, "Latins Now Leaders of Hard-Drug Trade," *New York Times* (April 21, 1975).

Gehlke, C. E., "Recorded Felonies: An Analysis and General Survey," *The Illinois Crime Survey*, Illinois Association for Criminal Justice. Montclair, N.J.: Patterson Smith Reprint Series, 1968.

————, "A Statistical Interpretation of the Criminal Process," *The Missouri Crime Survey*. Montclair, N.J.: Patterson Smith Reprint Series, 1968.

Geis, Gilbert, and Edelhertz, Herbert, "Criminal Law and Consumer Fraud: A Sociolegal View," *American Criminal Law Review*, Vol. 11, No. 4 (Summer, 1973).

Gettinger, Steve, "U.S. Prison Population Hits All-Time High," *Corrections Magazine*, Vol. III, No. 3 (March, 1976).

Gilman, David, "How to Retain Jurisdiction over Status Offenses: Change Without Reform in Florida," *Crime and Delinquency*, Vol. 22, No. 1 (January, 1976).

Gold, Martin, "Undetected Delinquent Behavior," *Journal of Research in Crime and Delinquency*, Vol. 3, No. 1 (January, 1966).

Goldstein, Abraham S., "Reflections on Two Models: Inquisitorial Themes in American Criminal Procedure," *Stanford Law Review*, Vol. 26, No. 5 (May, 1974).

Gottfredson, Don M., Hoffman, Peter B., Sigler, Maurice H., and Wilkins, Leslie T., "Making Paroling Policy Explicit," *Crime and Delinquency*, Vol. 21, No. 1 (January, 1975).

Gottlieb, Martin, "The White Mob Gets Back into Heroin," New York *Daily News* (November 11, 1975).

Greenberg, David F., "The Incapacitative Effect of Imprisonment: Some Estimates," *Law and Society Review*, Vol. 9, No. 5 (Summer, 1975).

————, and Stender, Fay, "The Prison as a Lawless Agency," *Buffalo Law Review*, Vol. 21, No. 3 (Spring, 1972).

Greenberg, Stephanie, and Adler, Freda, "Crime and Addic-

tion: An Empirical Analysis of the Literature, 1920–1973,"
Contemporary Drug Problems (Summer, 1974).

Greenway, H. D. S., "Misty Opium Land: Poppy-Fueled War,"
Washington *Post* (April 11, 1976).

Groom, Winston, "Juvenile Justice System," Washington *Star*
(June 7, 1975).

Grosser, Charles F., Martin, John M., and Fitzpatrick, Joseph
P., "Advocacy Puerto Rican Style," *Delinquency Prevention:
The Convergence of Theory Building, Political Influence, and
New Modes of Advocacy*. New York: The Institute for Social
Research, Fordham University, 1971.

Gurr, Ted Robert, "Contemporary Crime in Historical Perspective: A Comparative Study of London, Stockholm, and Sydney," *Annals of the American Academy of Political and
Social Science*, Vol. 434 (November, 1977).

Haller, Mark H., "Bootlegging in Chicago: The Structure of an
Illegal Enterprise." (Unpublished paper prepared for the
American Historical Association Convention, Chicago, De-
cember 29, 1974.)

————, "Historical Roots of Police Behavior: Chicago, 1890–
1925," *Law and Society Review*, Vol. 10, No. 2 (Winter,
1976).

————, "Organized Crime in Urban Society: Chicago in the
Twentieth Century," *Journal of Social History* (Winter,
1971–72).

————, "Urban Crime and Criminal Justice: The Chicago
Case," *Journal of American History*, Vol. LVII, No. 3
(December, 1970).

Haran, James F., and Martin, John M., "The Imprisonment of
Bank Robbers: The Issue of Deterrence," *Federal Probation*, Vol. 41, No. 3 (September, 1977).

Harris, Richard, "Annals of Law: In Criminal Court," *The
New Yorker* (April 14, 1973).

Hart, Henry M., Jr., "The Aims of the Criminal Law," *Law
and Contemporary Problems*, Vol. 23, No. 3 (Summer,
1958).

Hauser, Philip M., "Demographic Factors in the Integration
of the Negro," *Daedalus*, Vol. 94, No. 4 (Fall, 1965).

Hindelang, Michael J., "The Uniform Crime Reports Revisited," *Journal of Criminal Justice*, Vol. 2, No. 1 (Spring,
1974).

Holahan, John F., with the assistance of Paul A. Henningsen,
"The Economics of Heroin," *Dealing with Drug Abuse*, The

Drug Abuse Survey Project. New York: Praeger Publishers, 1972.

Hufnagel, Lynne M., and Davidson, John P., "Children in Need: Observations of Practices of the Denver Juvenile Court," *Denver Law Journal*, Vol. 51, No. 3 (1974).

Jackson, Robert H., "Criminal Justice: The Vital Problem of the Future," *American Bar Association Journal*, Vol. 39 (1953).

Jacobs, James B., "The Politics of Corrections: Town/Prison Relations as a Determinant of Reform," *Social Service Review*, Vol. 50, No. 4 (December, 1976).

Journal of the National Medical Association (January, 1975), quoted in Evans, Therman E., "Media, Violence and Black People," Washington *Post* (August 4, 1976).

"Juvenile Justice in Arizona," *Arizona Law Review*, Vol. 16, Nos. 2, 4 (1974).

Kamisar, Yale, "When the Cops Were Not 'Handcuffed,'" *New York Times Magazine* (November 7, 1965).

Kaplan, John, "The Limits of the Exclusionary Rule," *Stanford Law Review*, Vol. 26, No. 5 (May, 1974).

Kelling, George L., and Pate, Tony, "Response to the Davis-Knowles Critique of the Kansas City Preventive Patrol Experiment," *The Police Chief*, Vol. XLII, No. 6 (June, 1975).

Knight, Michael, "Influx of High-Quality, Bargain-Priced Heroin Is Reported in Eastern Cities," *New York Times* (December 15, 1974).

———, "U.S. Crime Force Enters Con. Jai Alai Case," *New York Times* (October 18, 1975).

Kristol, Irving, "The Negro Today Is like the Immigrant of Yesterday," *New York Times Magazine* (September 11, 1966).

Larson, Richard C., "What Happened to Patrol Operations in Kansas City? A Review of the Kansas City Preventive Patrol Experiment," *Journal of Criminal Justice*, Vol. 3, No. 4 (Winter, 1975).

Lasky, Michael S., "One in Three Hotel Guests Is a Towel Thief, Bible Pincher, or Worse," *New York Times Travel Section* (January 27, 1974).

Lejeune, Robert, and Alex, Nicholas, "On Being Mugged: The Event and Its Aftermath," *Urban Life and Culture*, Vol. 2, No. 3 (October, 1973).

Light, Ivan H., "Numbers Gambling: A Financial Institution of the Ghetto." (Paper presented at 1st Annual Conference on

Gambling, Sahara Hotel, Las Vegas, Nev., June 11, 1973, mimeo.)

McCord, Joan and William, "A Follow-Up Report on the Cambridge-Somerville Youth Study," *Annals of the American Academy of Political and Social Science,* Vol. 322 (March, 1959).

McCorkle, Lloyd W., and Korn, Richard, "Resocialization Within Walls," *Annals of the American Academy of Political and Social Science* (May, 1954).

McIntyre, Donald M., "Impediments to Effective Police-Prosecutor Relationships," *American Criminal Law Review,* Vol. 13 (1975).

————, and Lippmann, David, "Prosecutors and Early Disposition of Felony Cases," *American Bar Association Journal,* Vol. 56 (December, 1970).

McIntyre, Jennie, "Public Attitudes Toward Crime and Law Enforcement," *Annals of the American Academy of Political and Social Science,* Vol. 374 (November, 1967).

Mack, Julian B., "The Juvenile Court," *Harvard Law Review,* Vol. 23 (1909).

Marcum, Jess, and Rowen, Henry, "How Many Games in Town?—The Pros and Cons of Legalized Gambling," *The Public Interest,* No. 36 (Summer, 1974).

Martinson, Robert, "What Works?—Questions and Answers About Prison Reform," *The Public Interest,* No. 35 (Spring, 1974).

Merton, Robert K., "The Self-Fulfilling Prophecy," in Merton, *Social Theory and Social Structure,* enlarged ed. (New York: The Free Press, 1968).

Miller, Walter B., "Lower Class Culture as a Generating Milieu of Gang Delinquency," *Journal of Social Issues,* Vol. 14, No. 3 (1958).

Morgan, Ted, "They Think, 'I Can Kill Because I'm 14,'" *New York Times Magazine* (January 19, 1975).

Nagel, William G., "Some Very Hesitant and Tentative Thoughts About the Future of Corrections." (Paper presented at Annual Meeting, American Society of Criminology, November 5, 1976, mimeo.)

————, "A Statement on Behalf of a Moratorium on Prison Construction." (Paper presented to American Correctional Association, 1976, mimeo.)

New York State and Senate Standing Committee on Crime and Correction and Select Committee on Crime, mimeo.

"Parole Release Decisionmaking and the Sentencing Process," *Yale Law Journal*, Vol. 84, No. 4 (March, 1975).

Pate, Tony, Kelling, George L., and Brown, Charles, "A Response to 'What Happened to Patrol Operations in Kansas City?'" *Journal of Criminal Justice*, Vol. 3, No. 4 (Winter, 1975).

Pileggi, Nicholas, "Inside the Juvenile Justice System: How Fifteen-Year-Olds Get Away with Murder," *New York* (June 13, 1977).

Polk, Kenneth, "Special Report: Rural Delinquency and Maturational Reform." (mimeo)

————, *Teenage Delinquency in Small Town America*, National Institute of Mental Health Center for Studies of Crime and Delinquency Research Report No. 5.

Pound, Roscoe, "Criminal Justice in the American City—A Summary," *Criminal Justice in Cleveland*, Report of the Cleveland Foundation Survey of the Administration of Criminal Justice in Cleveland, Ohio. Montclair, N.J.: Patterson Smith Reprint Series, 1968.

Pousner, Michael, "Triggers Ready to Be Pulled," New York *Daily News* (December 15, 1975).

Raab, Selwyn, "Illegal Narcotics Is Worst Here in 5 Years," *New York Times* (December 8, 1975).

Raspberry, William, "Victimism," Washington *Post* (July 7, 1976).

Reiss, Albert J., Jr., "Discretionary Justice in the United States," *International Journal of Criminology and Penology*, Vol. 2 (1974).

Robertson, Wyndham, "Those Daring Young Con Men of Equity Funding," *Fortune* (August, 1973).

Robison, James O., and Smith, Gerald, "The Effectiveness of Correctional Programs," *Crime and Delinquency*, Vol. 17, No. 1 (January, 1971).

Robinson, Timothy S., "D.C. Criminals Seen Favoring Sawed-Off Guns," Washington *Post* (July 19, 1975).

Rothman, David., "Decarcerating Prisoners and Patients," *Civil Liberties Review*, Vol. 1, No. 2 (Fall, 1973).

Saar, John, "Attack at Bus Stop Wrecks Man's Life, Denies Ambition," Washington *Post* (March 9, 1975).

————, "Rape Victim's Memories Haunt Her," Washington *Post* (April 20, 1975).

Scarf, Maggie, "The Anatomy of Fear," *New York Times Magazine* (June 16, 1974).

"Scaring Juveniles," *Youth Forum,* Vol. 1, No. 1 (June, 1977).

Schultz, J. Lawrence, "The Cycle of Juvenile Court History," *Crime and Delinquency,* Vol. 19, No. 4 (October, 1973).

Schwartz, Herman, "A Note on Sostre v. McGinnis," *Buffalo Law Review,* Vol. 21, No. 3 (Spring, 1972).

————, "Prisoners' Rights: Some Hopes and Realities," *A Program for Prison Reform,* The Roscoe Pound–American Trial Lawyers Foundation, 1972.

"Senate Hearings Show Problems and Progress in Status Offender Deinstitutionalization," *Criminal Justice Newsletter,* Vol. 8, No. 20 (October 10, 1977).

Serrill, Michael S., "Procunier: A Candid Conversation," *Corrections Magazine,* Vol. 1, No. 4 (March/April, 1975).

————, "Walpole Prison: After the Storm," *Corrections Magazine,* Vol. II, No. 2 (November/December, 1975).

Shaffer, Ron, "Tormented Gun Victim Asks Why," Washington *Post* (November 29, 1975).

————, and Lewis, Alfred E., "You Go Out . . . and Might Not Get Back," Washington *Post* (August 23, 1975).

Shaw, Clifford R., and McKay, Henry D., "Social Factors in Juvenile Delinquency," *Report on the Causes of Crime* (Wickersham Commission), Vol. II, National Commission on Law Observance and Enforcement, 1931. Montclair, N.J.: Patterson Smith Reprint Series, 1968.

Sheehan, Susan, "Annals of Crime: A Prison and a Prisoner," *The New Yorker* (October 24, 1977). Cf. *A Prison and a Prisoner.* Boston: Houghton Mifflin Co., 1978.

Shinnar, Shlomo, and Shinnar, Reuel, "The Effects of the Criminal Justice System on the Control of Crime: A Quantitative Approach," *Law and Society Review,* Vol. 9, No. 4 (Summer, 1975).

Short, James F., Jr., and Nye, F. Ivan, "Extent of Unrecorded Delinquency: Tentative Conclusions," *Journal of Criminal Law and Criminology,* Vol. 49, No. 4 (1958).

Silberman, Charles E., " 'Beware the Day They Change Their Minds,' " *Fortune* (November, 1965).

Simmons, Ozzie G., "The Mutual Images and Expectations of Anglo-Americans and Mexican-Americans," *Daedalus,* Vol. 90, No. 2 (Spring, 1961).

Skogan, Wesley G., "Measurement Problems in Official and Survey Crime Rates," *Journal of Criminal Justice,* Vol. 3, No. 1 (Spring, 1975).

Skolnick, Jerome H., "Social Control in the Adversary System,"

Journal of Conflict Resolution, Vol. XI, No. 1 (March, 1967).

"Special Project: Juvenile Justice in Arizona," *Arizona Law Review,* Vol. 16, No. 12 (1974).

Steele, Eric H., and Jacobs, James B., "A Theory of Prison Systems," *Crime and Delinquency,* Vol. 21, No. 2 (April, 1975).

————, and Jacobs, James B., "Untangling Minimum Security: Concepts, Realities and Implications for Correctional Systems," *Journal of Research in Crime and Delinquency,* Vol. 14, No. 1 (January, 1977).

"Tentative Draft of Standards Relating to the Legal Status of Prisoners," *American Criminal Law Review,* Vol. 14, No. 3 (Winter, 1977), Special Issue.

Thomas, Charles W., "Are Status Offenders Really So Different?" *Crime and Delinquency,* Vol. 22, No. 4 (October, 1976).

Tittle, Charles R., and Logan, Charles H., "Sanctions and Deviance: Evidence and Remaining Questions," *Law and Society Review,* Vol. 7, No. 3 (Spring, 1973).

Toby, Jackson, "An Evaluation of Early Identification and Intensive Treatment Programs for Pre-Delinquents," *Social Problems,* Vol. 13, No. 2 (Fall, 1965).

Tullock, Gordon, "Does Punishment Deter Crime?" *The Public Interest,* No. 36 (Summer, 1974).

"Ungovernability: The Unjustifiable Jurisdiction," *Yale Law Journal,* Vol. 83 (1974).

van den Haag, Ernest, "In Defense of the Death Penalty: A Legal-Practical-Moral Analysis," *Criminal Law Bulletin,* Vol. 4, No. 1 (January/February, 1978).

Van Dine, Stephan, Dinitz, Simon, and Conrad, John, "The Incapacitation of the Dangerous Offender: A Statistical Experiment," *Journal of Research in Crime and Delinquency,* Vol. 14, No. 1 (January, 1977).

"'A Very Stern Discipline': An Interview with Ralph Ellison," *Harper's* (March, 1967).

Vorenberg, Elizabeth W., "How Massachusetts Has Shifted Care of Status Offenders to Social Service Unit," *Criminal Justice Newsletter,* Vol. 9, No. 2 (January 16, 1978).

Waite, Edward F., "How Far Can Court Procedure Be Socialized Without Impairing Individual Rights?" *Journal of Criminal Law, Criminology, and Police Science,* Vol. 12 (1922).

Weaver, Warren, Jr., "High Court Widens Prosecutors' Power

in Plea Bargaining," *New York Times* (January 19, 1978).

Wechsler, Herbert, "Law, Morals, and Psychiatry," *Columbia Law School News*, Vol. 18 (1959). Quoted in Francis A. Allen, *The Borderland of Criminal Justice*. Chicago: University of Chicago Press, 1974.

West, Hollie I., "A Gentleman Scholar: The Last of the Great Schoolmasters," Washington *Post* (January 30, 1978).

Whitaker, Joseph D., "Fear Stalks Tyler House Hallways," Washington *Post* (February 16, 1976).

White, Welsh S., "The Role of the Social Sciences in Determining the Constitutionality of the Death Penalty," *American Journal of Orthopsychiatry*, Vol. 45, No. 4 (July, 1975).

Whitlatch, Walter G., "The Juvenile Court—A Court of Law," *Western Reserve Law Review*, Vol. 18, No. 4 (May, 1967).

Will, George F., Washington *Post* (December 10, 1974).

Williams, Jay R., and Gold, Martin, "From Delinquent Behavior to Juvenile Delinquency," *Social Problems*, Vol. 20, No. 2 (1972).

Wilson, James Q., "Do the Police Prevent Crime?" *New York Times Magazine* (October 6, 1974).

Wilson, Rob, "U.S. Prison Population Sets Another Record," *Corrections Magazine*, Vol. III, No. 1 (March, 1977).

Wishingrad, Jay, "The Plea Bargain in Historical Perspective," *Buffalo Law Review*, Vol. 23, No. 2 (Winter, 1974).

Wolfgang, Marvin E., "Crime in a Birth Cohort," *Proceedings of the American Philosophical Society*, Vol. 117, No. 5 (October, 1973).

"The Youth Crime Plague," *Time* (July 11, 1977).

Zimring, Franklin E., "Background Paper," *Confronting Youth Crime: Report of the Twentieth Century Fund Task Force on Sentencing Policy Toward Young Offenders*. New York: Holmes & Meier, Inc., 1978.

———, "Making the Punishment Fit the Crime," *Hastings Center Report*, Vol. 6, No. 6 (December, 1976).

———, "Street Crimes and New Guns: Some Implications for Firearms Control," *Journal of Criminal Justice*, Vol. 4, No. 2 (Summer, 1976).

COURT DECISIONS

Argersinger vs. Hamlin, 407 U.S. 25 (1972).

Bazelon, David, Chief Judge majority opinion in U.S. v. De-Coster, No. 72-1283, decided October 4, 1973.

Bordenkircher v. Hayes, 76-1334, January 18, 1978.

Frankel, Marvin E., opinion in United States ex rel. Thomas v. Zekler, 332 F. Supp. 591 (S.D.N.Y. 1971).

In re Gault, 387 U.S. 1 (1967).

Gideon v. Wainright, 372 U.S. 335 (1963).

Holt v. Sarver, 309 F. Supp. 385.

Johnson, Hon. Frank M., Jr., Memorandum Opinion in Pugh v. Locke, January 13, 1976.

Kent v. United States, 383 U.S. 541 (1966).

Morales v. Turman, 383 F. Supp. 53 (1974).

Index

About the Author

CHARLES E. SILBERMAN is well known for two of the most provocative and influential books in recent memory, *Crisis in Black and White* and *Crisis in the Classroom.* A former senior editor of *Fortune,* he is director of the Study of Law and Justice, a Ford Foundation research project. Married and the father of four sons, Silberman lives in New York City.